Xuhua Li

xuhua @ cco. caltech.edu

COMPILER DESIGN

INTERNATIONAL COMPUTER SCIENCE SERIES

Consulting Editor **A D McGettrick** University of Strathclyde

SELECTED TITLES IN THE SERIES

Software Development with Z   *J B Wordsworth*

Program Verification   *N Francez*

Performance Modelling of Communication Networks   *P G Harrison and N M Patel*

Concurrent Systems: An Integrated Approach to Operating Systems, Database, and Distributed Systems   *J Bacon*

Introduction to Parallel Processing   *B Codenotti and M Leoncini*

Concurrent Programming   *A Burns and G Davies*

Comparative Programming Languages (2nd Edn)   *L B Wilson and R G Clark*

Functional Programming and Parallel Graph Rewriting   *R Plasmeijer and M van Eekelen*

Object-Oriented Database Systems: Concepts and Architectures   *E Bertino and L D Martino*

Programming in Ada (4th Edn)   *J G P Barnes*

Software Design   *D Budgen*

Ada from the Beginning (2nd Edn)   *J Skansholm*

Programming Language Essentials   *H E Bal and D Grune*

Human-Computer Interaction   *J Preece et al.*

Distributed Systems: Concepts and Design (2nd Edn)   *G Coulouris, J Dollimore and T Kindberg*

Fortran 90 Programming   *T M R Ellis, I R Philips and T M Lahey*

Parallel Processing: The Transputer and its Applications   *M E C Hull, D Crookes and P J Sweeney*

Foundations of Computing: System Development with Set Theory and Logic   *T Scheurer*

Principles of Object Oriented Engineering   *A Eliëns*

COMPILER DESIGN

Reinhard Wilhelm

University of the Saarland, Saarbrücken

Dieter Maurer

Saarbrücken Zeitung

Translated by Stephen S. Wilson

ADDISON-WESLEY PUBLISHING COMPANY

HARLOW, ENGLAND •READING, MASSACHUSETTS •MENLO PARK, CALIFORNIA •NEW YORK
DON MILLS, ONTARIO •AMSTERDAM •BONN •SYDNEY •SINGAPORE
TOKYO •MADRID •SAN JUAN •MILAN •MEXICO CITY •SEOUL •TAIPEI

Addison Wesley Longman Limited
Edinburgh Gate
Harlow
Essex CM20 2JE

Cover designed by Designers & Partners of Oxford
and printed by Oxted Press Ltd, Oxted, Surrey.
Printed in Great Britain by T. J. Press (Padstow) Ltd, Cornwall.

First printed 1995. Reprinted 1996.

ISBN 0-201-42290-5

British Library Cataloguing in Publication Data
A catalogue record for this book is available from the British Library.

Library of Congress Cataloging in Publication Data applied for.

For Margret, Hannah, Eva, Barbara
R.W.

Preface

Compilers for high-level programming languages are large, complex software systems. However, they have a number of special characteristics which distinguish them from most other software systems.

Their functionality is (almost) well defined. Ideally, there exist formal, or at least precise descriptions of the source language and the target language. Frequently, there also exist descriptions of the interfaces to the operating system, to the programming environment, to other compilers and to program libraries.

The decomposition of the compilation tasks into subtasks with well-defined interfaces is well understood. This results in a natural modular structure, which, incidentally, is also reflected in the usual structure of books on compiler design.

Some of the various subtasks of compilation have been very extensively studied. The corresponding theories were developed specifically or taken over from the theory of formal languages and automata. They provide a good basis for the implementation of modules for compiler subtasks. For some of the subtasks, there even exist mechanisms for their formal description and generation procedures that generate parts of compilers automatically from such formal descriptions. Many such generators are available and in use.

This book is not a cook book. You will not find recipes of the form 'to construct a compiler from source language X into machine language Y, take ...'. The presentation reflects the special characteristics of compiler design listed above, including, in particular, the existence of the theory and the automatic generation methods.

This book is intended for advanced undergraduate and graduate students specializing in computer science. A knowledge of imperative programming languages is a prerequisite. While the chapters on the compilation of functional, logic and object-oriented programming languages each contain a long introduction to the concepts of these language classes, it is advisable to learn a modern functional language, Prolog and Smalltalk, Eiffel or C++, for a better understanding of the corresponding chapters. In addition, the reader will profit from a good grounding in the theory of formal languages and automata, although the theory needed is always presented in full.

Structure of the book

Chapters 2 to 5 describe *what* a compiler *does*, in other words, the correspondence that it generates between a source program and an object program. For this, we introduce an appropriate abstract machine for an imperative, a functional and a logic programming language and give a precise description of the compilation of programs in each source language into the language of the associated abstract machine. Object-oriented languages developed from imperative languages by extending them by a number of new concepts which essentially relate to the type system. Thus, only the compilation of these extensions is described in Chapter 5.

In each case, the starting point is an analysed source program, which we shall later refer to as associated decorated abstract syntax.

In Chapters 6 to 12 we describe the *how* of compilation, namely how the compilation process is divided into individual phases, the tasks performed by these phases, the techniques used in them, how what they do can be formally described and how a compiler module can be generated (even automatically) from such a description.

Material for a two- or three-term lecture course can be selected from this book, depending on the time available. Chapter 2 and material from Chapters 6–9, 11 and 12 would suffice for a conventional one-term lecture course on the compilation of imperative programming languages. A two-term lecture course would cover the compilation of functional, logic and object-oriented programming languages together with areas of current research such as abstract interpretation and code generation for parallel target architectures.

Acknowledgements

The book developed from a number of lecture courses given by both authors at the University of the Saarland in Saarbrücken, Germany. The (then) three-term course was first given in 1987/1988.

The number of those who have actively cooperated in this work and/or provided constructive criticism of it is so large that we are unable to thank them all personally here. We are particularly grateful to Martin Alt, Ingrid Biehl, Christian Fecht, Christian Ferdinand, Reinhold Heckmann, Andreas Hense, Stefan Kahrs, Peter Lipps, Gudula Rünger, Georg Sander and Helmut Seidl. The TEXnicians Christine Wentz and Patrik Zeimetz have patiently processed several revisions.

Reinhard Wilhelm, Dieter Maurer
April 1992

Preface to the English edition

The major change from the German edition is that a chapter on the compilation of object-oriented languages has been added, in which we discuss the implementation of simple and multiple inheritance.

Since the German edition is apparently extensively used, we have received numerous suggestions for improvements, for which we are especially grateful to Reinhold Heckmann, Helmut Seidl and, in particular, Helmut Partsch.

Material related to this book, for example, a specification of an accompanying compiler laboratory project, can be obtained by anonymous ftp from `ftp.cs.uni-sb.de` in `/pub/compiler`.

Reinhard Wilhelm, Dieter Maurer
Saarbrücken, St. Ingbert, April 1995

For reasons of simplicity, the pronoun 'he' is used to relate to both male and female throughout the book.

Contents

Preface   **vii**

1   Introduction   **1**

   1.1   High-level programming languages   2

   1.2   The implementation of programming languages   3

2   Compilation of imperative programming languages   **7**

   2.1   Language constructs and their compilation   8

   2.2   The architecture of the P machine   9

   2.3   Assignments and expressions   10

   2.4   Conditional and iterative statements, sequences of statements   13

   2.5   Memory allocation for variables of simple type   18

   2.6   Memory allocation for arrays   19

   2.7   Memory allocation for records   27

   2.8   Pointers and dynamic memory allocation   28

   2.9   Procedures   32

   2.10 Main program   56

   2.11 Exercises   57

   2.12 Literature   61

3   Compilation of functional programming languages   **63**

   3.1   Language type and introductory example   64

   3.2   LaMa, a simple functional programming language   72

   3.3   Introduction to the compilation of LaMa   77

   3.4   Environments and bindings   81

   3.5   The MaMa architecture   83

3.6	Stack management and addressing	87
3.7	Instruction set and compilation	90
3.8	Implementation of lists	104
3.9	Exercises	109
3.10	Literature	111

4   Compilation of logic programming languages   113

4.1	Logic programming languages	114
4.2	Logical foundations	118
4.3	Unification	120
4.4	Execution of logic programs	124
4.5	Prolog	132
4.6	Abstract Prolog machine	138
4.7	Compilation of Prolog	142
4.8	Efficiency improvements	161
4.9	Exercises	167
4.10	Literature	169

5   Compilation of object-oriented languages   171

5.1	Concepts of object-oriented languages	172
5.2	The compilation of methods	180
5.3	Schemes for compilation of inheritance	182
5.4	Genericity	207
5.5	Exercises	214
5.6	Literature	219

6   The structure of compilers   221

6.1	Compiler subtasks	222
6.2	Lexical analysis	223
6.3	Screening	225
6.4	Syntax analysis	225
6.5	Semantic analysis	226

6.6   Machine-independent optimization   228

6.7   Address assignment   229

6.8   Generation of the target program   230

6.9   Machine-dependent code improvement   231

6.10   Real compiler structures   231

6.11   Formal specification and generation of compiler modules   232

6.12   Literature   233

7   **Lexical analysis**   **235**

7.1   The task of lexical analysis   236

7.2   Theoretical foundations   236

7.3   A language for specifying the lexical analysis   248

7.4   The generation of a scanner   251

7.5   The screener   256

7.6   Flex, a scanner generator under UNIX   259

7.7   Exercises   261

7.8   Literature   263

8   **Syntax analysis**   **265**

8.1   The task of syntax analysis   266

8.2   Theoretical foundations   269

8.3   Top-down syntax analysis   300

8.4   Bottom-up syntax analysis   339

8.5   Bison, an LALR(1)-parser generator   375

8.6   Exercises   377

8.7   Literature   382

9   **Semantic analysis**   **385**

9.1   Task of the semantic analysis   386

9.2   Attribute grammars   405

9.3   Examples of attribute grammars   410

9.4   The generation of attribute evaluators   417

	9.5	Exercises	453
	9.6	Literature	456
10		**Abstract interpretation**	**457**
	10.1	Introduction	458
	10.2	Abstract interpretation based on denotational semantics	462
	10.3	Abstract interpretation based on operational semantics	484
	10.4	Exercises	506
	10.5	Literature	510
11		**Trees: pattern matching and parsing**	**513**
	11.1	Program transformations	514
	11.2	Code selection	519
	11.3	The pattern-matching problem	523
	11.4	The tree-parsing problem	526
	11.5	Finite tree automata	529
	11.6	Generation of pattern matchers	531
	11.7	Generation of tree parsers	535
	11.8	Tree automata with costs	537
	11.9	Implementation	542
	11.10	Exercises	544
	11.11	Literature	545
12		**Code generation**	**547**
	12.1	Abstract and real machines	548
	12.2	Classification of architectures	554
	12.3	Program representations	558
	12.4	Code generation, integrated methods	561
	12.5	Register allocation by graph colouring	568
	12.6	Instruction scheduling	570
	12.7	Exercises	588
	12.8	Literature	590

Bibliography   591

Index   599

1

Introduction

- High-level programming languages

- The implementation of programming languages

1.1 High-level programming languages

Nowadays, programs are mainly written in so-called problem-oriented, high-level programming languages. These programming languages are removed (to a varying degree) from the structure and the details of the computers on which the programs written in them are executed. The four most important classes of universal programming languages are:

- The class of **imperative languages** such as Algol 60, Algol 68, Fortran, COBOL, Pascal, Ada, Modula 2 and C. These are closely oriented towards the structure of so-called von Neumann computers which include almost all commercially available computers. These machines consist of an (active) central processing unit (CPU), a (passive) memory and a bus for the traffic between the CPU and the memory.

- The class of **functional languages** such as LISP, HOPE, Miranda, Haskell and FP. This class is characterized by the following properties:
  - There is no distinction between statements and expressions.
  - Names are only used to identify expressions and functions; they are not used to identify memory locations.
  - Functions may occur as the arguments and the results of functions.

  The execution principle for functional languages is **reduction**; in other words, a functional program is evaluated by successively replacing expressions (subexpressions) by equivalent simpler expressions (subexpressions) until the normal form is obtained, when the process ends.

- The class of **logic programming languages** such as Prolog and its various dialects. These languages are based on an operational view of predicate calculus. The execution mechanism is **resolution**, a procedure that was developed for proving implications in first-order predicate calculus.

- **Object-oriented programming languages** are essentially imperative, have type systems that support data abstraction and permit an 'evolutionary' form of software development. This form of software development, the refinement and adaptation of existing software components, is usually supported by an appropriate development environment.

In addition to these four classes, there are many other languages, for particular applications, which have a number of things in common with programming languages:

- Hardware description languages. These are used to specify computers and computer components. Such specifications may describe the functional behaviour, hierarchical structure and geometrical arrangement of components.

- Operating system command languages. These include primitive constructs, for example for activating system functions and user programs, together with facilities that provide for the coordinated interworking of a number of such programs and system functions, the creation and termination of processes and the detection and handling of abnormal situations.

- Text and graphics specification languages. These may be used to describe text or graphics objects. In the case of graphics, the object is usually complete, in other words, specified by the entry of geometrical coordinates, or the like. For text objects, which are usually called documents, only page layout restrictions for a text formatter are normally specified.

1.2 The implementation of programming languages

In order that programs in a certain programming language L may be executed on a computer, that language must be made available, or **implemented**, on the particular type of computer. This may be achieved in various ways. Implementations are divided into interpreters and compilers.

1.2.1 Interpreters

Let us consider a programming language L. The input to an interpreter I_L consists of a program p_L in L and an input sequence e, from which I_L computes an output sequence a. The interpretation of p_L may lead to an error. Thus, I_L has the functionality

$$I_L : L \times D^* \to D^* \cup \{error\}$$

when the input and output data belong to the same domain D. The execution of the program p_L with input sequence e and result sequence a is then described by the equation

$$I_L(p_L, e) = a$$

What are the characteristics of an interpreter? It processes program p_L and input e simultaneously. Each construct is new to it, even in the case of repeated execution. It does not use any information independent from the input data, which it could obtain by inspecting the program text (for example, the number of declared variables in a block, a function or a clause). It could use this information to allocate the memory for efficient access to the variable values.

1.2.2 Compilers

The aim is to avoid the inefficiency associated with interpretation. This involves the use of a principle commonly applied in computer science, which is usually referred to as **precomputation** or sometimes **partial evaluation** or **mixed computation**.

Whereas the interpreter I receives and processes both its arguments, the program p_L and the input sequence e, at the same time, the program and the input sequence are now processed at two different times. First, the program p_L is 'preprocessed'; in other words, it is analysed independently of all input data and converted into another form which provides for the efficient execution of the program with arbitrary input sequences. The additional cost of preprocessing the program is assumed to be offset by executing it with one or more input sequences.

What does preprocessing programs involve? Usually, it comprises the translation (compilation) of the program p_L, written in the language L, now called the **source language**, into the machine or assembly language M of a specific or abstract computer. The time at which this translation takes place is called **compile time** and the resulting program p_M, corresponding to p_L, is called the **object program**.

In particular, compiling source programs into object programs avoids the two sources of inefficiency associated with interpretation. Each program is analysed once at compile time; the analysis of the corresponding object program (let us suppose that this is a program in the machine code of a real computer) only involves the decoding of the instruction code by the computer's command unit. Efficient, and sometimes direct, access to variable values and locations is provided for by a memory management scheme which assigns fixed (relative) addresses to all the program variables. These addresses are then used in the corresponding object program.

The corresponding object progam p_M is executed with the input sequence e at some time after compile time, known as **run time**. Naturally, one requirement on compilation is that when object program p_M is executed with input e it should produce the result sequence a, where $I_L(p_L, e) = a$. The following is a minimum requirement on compilation. Suppose that p_L is a program which is syntactically correct and satisfies the context conditions of L; in other words, suppose that p_L is correctly typed. Suppose that the compiler generates the object program p_M corresponding to p_L. If I_L does not encounter any errors when p_L is executed with e and produces the output a, then no errors should occur when p_M is executed with input sequence e and both the interpretation of p_L and the execution of p_M with e should provide the same result.

Let us suppose that machine M is an interpreter I_M for its machine language, then the following must hold for such combinations (p_L, e):

If $I_L(p_L, e) = a$ then $I_M(p_M, e) = a$, where p_M is the object program corresponding to p_L.

There are also a number of error situations. For example, p_L may contain syntax errors or violations of the context conditions in parts of the program that do not affect the interpreter in the case of execution with e. Thus, interpretation could be successful, although the compiler, which analyses the whole program, would fail to produce the object program, as a result of detecting errors. On the other hand, although p_L is syntactically correct and satisfies the context conditions, I_L may encounter a (runtime) error when executing with input e. Since I_L is considered to be the definition of the semantics of L, the corresponding object program p_M must also encounter errors when executed with e.

1.2.3   Real and abstract machines

Usually, the programmer will have a so-called **real** computer at his or her disposition. A large variety of real computers is available on the market, with different hardware, that is, the motherboards with their various processors, memory chips and whatever else is required. In this case, the compiler's target language is defined by the type of processor used. As we shall see, real computers are largely oriented towards imperative programming languages; in other words, the operations and structures of real computers, such as pointers, branches, linear storage, indexed access, and so on, are to some extent mirrored in the concepts of imperative programming languages, while the other concepts of imperative languages are relatively easy to translate into the structures and instruction sequences of real computers.

There is no similar correspondence between functional or logic programming languages and present-day computers. This is one reason for the introduction of so-called **abstract** machines which are better adapted to these language types. These computers support the concepts of these languages better than real machines and thus simplify their implementation. They also facilitate the porting of a compiler from one machine to another, because they are realized in software rather than hardware.

Furthermore, an abstract machine may also be designed and used for teaching purposes. For those wishing to consider the principles of programming language compilation, suitably designed abstract machines enable the fundamental problems to be isolated from those facing the compiler designer as a result of the latest advances in computer architectures.

Compilation of imperative programming languages

- Language constructs and their compilation

- The architecture of the P machine

- Assignments and expressions

- Conditional and iterative statements, sequences of statements

- Memory allocation for variables of simple type

- Memory allocation for arrays

- Memory allocation for records

- Pointers and dynamic memory allocation

- Procedures

- Main program

- Exercises

- Literature

In this chapter, we shall give an intuitive description of **what** a compiler of imperative programming languages does; we shall only consider **how** it does this later. For this, we give a precise but intuitive definition of the correspondence between programs in an imperative source language and programs on a target computer obtained by compilation.

For the source language, we choose a slightly thinned down version of Pascal. For the target computer, we choose an abstract machine, the P machine, whose architecture was designed to make compiling Pascal into its machine language as simple as possible.

The correspondence is defined using compilation functions, which are given one by one for the individual Pascal constructs.

2.1   Language constructs and their compilation

Imperative programming languages possess the following constructs and concepts which must be mapped onto the constructs, concepts and instruction sequences of abstract or real computers:

- **Variables** are containers for data objects whose contents (values) may be changed during the execution of the program. The values are changed by the execution of **statements** such as assignments. A number of variables may be combined into aggregates, arrays and records. The current values of the variables at any given time form part of the **state** of the program at that time. Variables in programs are identified by **names**. Since constants, procedures and so on are also identified by names, we speak of variable identifiers, constant identifiers, and so on, when we wish to distinguish between these special types of names. Variable identifiers must be assigned machine memory locations containing the current values. If the programming language contains recursive procedures with local names, the calling of a procedure gives rise to new **incarnations** of the local variable identifiers, to which new storage space must be assigned. When the procedure is exited the memory locations for these incarnations are released. Thus, these languages are implemented using a stack-like memory management.

- **Expressions** are terms formed from constants, names and operators which are **evaluated** during execution. Their value is generally state dependent, since on each evaluation the current values of the variables in the expression are used.

- **Explicit specification of the control flow**. The branch instruction **goto**, which exists in most imperative programming languages, can be directly compiled into the unconditional branch instruction of the target machine. Higher-level control constructs such as conditional (if) or iterative (while, repeat, for) statements are compiled using conditional branches. A conditional branch follows an instruction sequence to evaluate a condition. For some source languages, the distinction of case conditions can be efficiently implemented on some target machines using indexed branches, in which the branch address in the instruction is modified by a previously computed value. Procedures provide a means of activating a sequence of statements from a point in a program to which control is returned after their execution. For this, the machine must have a branch instruction that does not forget its origin. The body of the procedure can be supplied with actual parameters whenever it is called. This, together with the creation of incarnations of local names, requires a complex memory organization, which is often supported by special machine instructions.

2.2   The architecture of the P machine

The (abstract) P machine was developed to make the Zurich implementation of Pascal portable. Anyone wishing to implement Pascal on a real computer had only to write an interpreter for the instructions of this abstract machine. The Pascal compiler, written in Pascal and compiled into P-code, could then be run on the real computer. The architecture and the instructions of the P machine will be introduced gradually as they are needed to compile the individual concepts in the source code. For now, we shall introduce only the memory, some registers and the main machine cycle of the P machine. The P machine has a data memory *STORE* of length *maxstr+1* and a program memory *CODE* of length *codemax+1*. At the lower end of the data memory (from address 0) is a variable stack. A register *SP* (stack pointer) points to the highest occupied location. Note that later, for clarity in figures in which stacks are represented vertically, the 'highest' stack location is always at the bottom, while the lower addresses of memory locations are shown at the top of the diagram. Some instructions store the contents of explicitly addressed locations on top of the stack and thus extend the stack; conversely, other instructions store the contents of the highest stack location in an explicitly addressed location and thus shorten the stack, see Table 2.2. The instructions are partially parameterized according to type: *N* stands for numerical type (integer), *T* stands for arbitrary simple types (numerical,

Figure 2.1   The memory of the P machine and some registers.

logical, character and enumeration type) and for addresses, i is for integer, r is for real, b is for Boolean and a is for addresses. The arithmetic operations on addresses are the same as those on integer operands, but the value ranges are generally different. Operators indexed by a type denote the corresponding operations on the underlying value ranges, for example $<_i$ denotes the comparison of two integers to determine the smaller.

Other instructions use the contents of *SP* implicitly, in that they operate on the contents of one or more of the **highest occupied stack locations**; they may also alter the contents of *SP* and store the result of the operation in the (new) highest stack location, see Table 2.1.

Of course, the P machine also has a program counter, the *PC* register, which contains the address of the next instruction to be executed. All instructions in the P machine occupy a single location in the program memory, so that, except in the case of branches, the PC register is incremented in steps of 1. Thus, the main cycle of the P machine has the following form:

> **do**
> > $PC := PC+1$;
> > execute the instruction in location $CODE[PC-1]$
> **od**

Initially, the *PC* register is initialized with the program start, in other words, it is set to 0, since the program begins at *CODE*[0].

2.3 Assignments and expressions

Tables 2.1 and 2.2 list all the instructions we need to compile assignments and expressions into P machine code. The instruction sequences that are generated for an assignment or an expression are specified using *code* functions. The argument of a code function is an assignment or a bracketed expression. The code function decomposes this argument recursively and assembles the instruction sequences generated for each component into the overall instruction sequence.

When compiling assignments, we note that a variable identifier on the left of an assignment is compiled differently from a variable identifier on the right. For the variable identifier on the left, the address of the location assigned to it is required so that its contents may be overwritten; the value of the variable identifier on the right is needed to compute the value of the expression. Therefore, we talk about the **left values** (L values) and **right values** (R values) of variables, when we wish to indicate that we are interested in the address of the variable or its current value, respectively.

Thus, we index the *code* functions with *L* or *R*, where $code_L$ generates instructions to compute the L value and $code_R$ generates instructions to compute the R value. The function *code* (without a subscript) is used to compile statements for which we expect neither addresses nor values.

Table 2.1 P-instructions for expressions. The 'Condition' column gives the necessary condition at the top of the stack, the 'Result' column gives the resulting situation. Here, (N, N) in the condition column means that there must be two numerical values of the same type at the top of the stack. All occurrences of N or T in the description of an instruction always refer to the same type. If the 'Condition' column contains more type characters than the 'Result' column, this means that the stack is shortened when this instruction is executed.

Instr.	Meaning	Cond.	Result
add N	$STORE[SP-1] := STORE[SP-1] +_N STORE[SP];$ $SP := SP-1$	(N, N)	(N)
sub N	$STORE[SP-1] := STORE[SP-1] -_N STORE[SP];$ $SP := SP-1$	(N, N)	(N)
mul N	$STORE[SP-1] := STORE[SP-1] *_N STORE[SP];$ $SP := SP-1$	(N, N)	(N)
div N	$STORE[SP-1] := STORE[SP-1] /_N STORE[SP];$ $SP := SP-1$	(N, N)	(N)
neg N	$STORE[SP] := -_N STORE[SP]$	(N)	(N)
and	$STORE[SP-1] := STORE[SP-1] \ and \ STORE[SP];$ $SP := SP-1$	(b, b)	(b)
or	$STORE[SP-1] := STORE[SP-1] \ or \ STORE[SP];$ $SP := SP-1$	(b, b)	(b)
not	$STORE[SP] := not \ STORE[SP]$	(b)	(b)
equ T	$STORE[SP-1] := STORE[SP-1] =_T STORE[SP];$ $SP := SP-1$	(T, T)	(b)
geq T	$STORE[SP-1] := STORE[SP-1] \geq_T STORE[SP];$ $SP := SP-1$	(T, T)	(b)
leq T	$STORE[SP-1] := STORE[SP-1] \leq_T STORE[SP];$ $SP := SP-1$	(T, T)	(b)
les T	$STORE[SP-1] := STORE[SP-1] <_T STORE[SP];$ $SP := SP-1$	(T, T)	(b)
grt T	$STORE[SP-1] := STORE[SP-1] >_T STORE[SP];$ $SP := SP-1$	(T, T)	(b)
neq T	$STORE[SP-1] := STORE[SP-1] \neq_T STORE[SP];$ $SP := SP-1$	(T, T)	(b)

Table 2.2   Store and load instructions. **ldo** loads from a location given by an absolute address, **ldc** loads a constant given in the instruction, **ind** loads indirectly using the highest stack location, **sro** stores in a location given by an absolute address, and **sto** stores in a location addressed by the second-highest location on the stack.

Instr.	Meaning	Cond.	Result
ldo $T\,q$	$SP := SP+1;$ $STORE[SP] := STORE[q]$	$q \in [0,maxstr]$	(T)
ldc $T\,q$	$SP := SP+1;$ $STORE[SP] := q$	$\text{Type}(q) = T$	(T)
ind T	$STORE[SP] := STORE[STORE[SP]]$	(a)	(T)
sro $T\,q$	$STORE[q] := STORE[SP];$ $SP := SP-1$	(T) $q \in [0,maxstr]$	
sto T	$STORE[STORE[SP-1]] := STORE[SP];$ $SP := SP-2$	(a, T)	

Thus, the compilation of an assignment $x := y$ for integer variables x and y is given by the following instruction sequence

Compute L value of x
Compute R value of y
sto i

Here, we are not concerned with the problem of how a Pascal program is analysed syntactically, but how its syntactic structure is determined. This is discussed in Chapter 8 on syntax analysis. Similarly, we also assume that the input program has already been checked for 'type correctness'. Chapter 9 on semantic analysis explains how this is done. The conditions in *code* definitions are only used to determine the correct type of the parameters for the instructions to be generated.

As a second parameter, the *code* functions use a function ρ which assigns an address in *STORE* to all declared variables. As we shall see later, this address is a **relative address**; that is, it is a constant difference between two absolute addresses in *STORE*, namely the actual address of the location of this variable and the start address of the memory area for all the variables and parameters of the procedure in which the variable is declared. For the moment, we may suppose that $\rho(x)$ is the address of x relative to the start of *STORE*.

Remark   Of course, we could compile the occurrence of a variable identifier x in an expression with a single instruction, namely **ldo** $T\,\rho(x)$. We have refrained from doing this in order to achieve consistency with the subsequently extended *code* scheme for variables.

Table 2.3   The compilation of assignments.

Function		Condition
$code_R(e_1 = e_2)\,\rho$	$= code_R\ e_1\ \rho;\ code_R\ e_2\ \rho;$ **equ** T	$\text{Type}(e_1) = \text{Type}(e_2) = T$
$code_R(e_1 \neq e_2)\,\rho$	$= code_R\ e_1\ \rho;\ code_R\ e_2\ \rho;$ **neq** T	$\text{Type}(e_1) = \text{Type}(e_2) = T$
$\vdots$		
$code_R(e_1 + e_2)\,\rho$	$= code_R\ e_1\ \rho;\ code_R\ e_2\ \rho;$ **add** N	$\text{Type}(e_1) = \text{Type}(e_2) = N$
$code_R(e_1 - e_2)\,\rho$	$= code_R\ e_1\ \rho;\ code_R\ e_2\ \rho;$ **sub** N	$\text{Type}(e_1) = \text{Type}(e_2) = N$
$code_R(e_1 * e_2)\,\rho$	$= code_R\ e_1\ \rho;\ code_R\ e_2\ \rho;$ **mul** N	$\text{Type}(e_1) = \text{Type}(e_2) = N$
$code_R(e_1/e_2)\,\rho$	$= code_R\ e_1\ \rho;\ code_R\ e_2\ \rho;$ **div** N	$\text{Type}(e_1) = \text{Type}(e_2) = N$
$code_R(-e)\,\rho$	$= code_R\ e\ \rho;$ **neg** N	$\text{Type}(e) = N$
$code_R\ x\ \rho$	$= code_L\ x\ \rho;$ **ind** T	x variable identifier of type T
$code_R\ c\ \rho$	$=$ **ldc** $T\ c$	c constant of type T
$code(x := e)\,\rho$	$= code_L\ x\ \rho;\ code_R\ e\ \rho;$ **sto** T	x variable identifier
$code_L\ x\ \rho$	$=$ **ldc a** $\rho(x)$	x variable identifier

Example 2.1   Suppose we are given a program with three integer variables, a, b, c. The memory allocation function ρ maps a, b, c onto the addresses 5, 6 and 7. Then the assignment $a := (b + (b * c))$ is compiled as follows:

$code(a := (b + (b * c)))\,\rho$
 $= code_L\ a\ \rho;\ code_R(b + (b * c))\ \rho;$ **sto** i
 $=$ **ldc a** 5; $code_R(b + (b * c))\ \rho;$ **sto** i
 $=$ **ldc a** 5; $code_R(b)\ \rho;\ code_R(b * c)\ \rho;$ **add** i; **sto** i
 $=$ **ldc a** 5; **ldc a** 6; **ind** i; $code_R(b * c)\ \rho;$ **add** i; **sto** i
 $=$ **ldc a** 5; **ldc a** 6; **ind** i; $code_R(b)\ \rho;\ code_R(c)\ \rho;$ **mul** i; **add** i; **sto** i
 $=$ **ldc a** 5; **ldc a** 6; **ind** i; **ldc a** 6; **ind** i; $code_R(c)\ \rho;$ **mul** i; **add** i; **sto** i
 $=$ **ldc a** 5; **ldc a** 6; **ind** i; **ldc a** 6; **ind** i; **ldc a** 7; **ind** i; **mul** i; **add** i; **sto** i

$\qquad\qquad\qquad\qquad\qquad\qquad\qquad\qquad\qquad\qquad\qquad\qquad\qquad\qquad$ □

2.4   Conditional and iterative statements, sequences of statements

We now turn to the compilation of conditional and iterative statements. We give compilation schemes for the bidirectional and unidirectional if statements, **if** e **then** st_1 **else** st_2 **fi** and **if** e **then** st **fi**, and for the while and repeat loops, **while** e **do** st **od** and **repeat** st **until** e.

Table 2.4 Conditional and unconditional branch.

Instr.	Meaning	Comments	Cond.	Result
ujp q	$PC := q$	Unconditional branch	$q \in [0,codemax]$	
fjp q	**if** $STORE[SP] = false$	Conditional branch	(b)	
	then $PC := q$		$q \in [0,codemax]$	
	fi			
	$SP := SP - 1$			

The syntax is slightly modified from Pascal to achieve unambiguous parsing of the if statement and to eliminate the **begin–end** bracketing.

We use a new tool in the compilation scheme for the *code* function defined here. We label instructions and the end of the scheme with names which we use in branch instructions. This insertion of a label as the object of a branch instruction may be explained as follows: we insert the address that the instruction with this label receives or has received. Of course, a code scheme can be applied several times or even recursively when compiling a Pascal program. However, it is clear how the definition of a label and its use in a branch instruction correspond on each occasion. So that the control flow described in the statements discussed here can be implemented on the P machine, the latter has conditional and unconditional branches. These are described in Table 2.4.

We can now describe the *code* function for conditional statements and loops.

$code($**if** e **then** st_1 **else** st_2 **fi**$) \rho =$
$\quad code_R \ e \ \rho;$ **fjp** $l_1; code \ st_1 \ \rho;$ **ujp** $l_2; l_1: code \ st_2 \ \rho; l_2:$

After evaluation of the condition e, the code for st_1 is executed if the value is *true*; otherwise, a branch to the code for st_2 takes place, skipping the code for st_1 and the unconditional branch.

The unidirectional conditional statement is compiled as follows:

$code($**if** e **then** st **fi**$) \rho = code_R \ e \ \rho;$ **fjp** $l; code \ st \ \rho; l:$

The instruction sequences for both types of conditional statement may be illustrated graphically as shown in Figure 2.2.

The two iterative statements are compiled as follows:

$code \ ($**while** e **do** st **od**$) \rho = l_1: code_R \ e \ \rho;$ **fjp** $l_2; code \ st \ \rho;$ **ujp** $l_1; l_2:$
$code \ ($**repeat** st **until** $e$$) \rho = l: code \ st \ \rho; code_R \ e \ \rho;$ **fjp** l

The generation schemes for these two types of loop are illustrated in Figure 2.3.

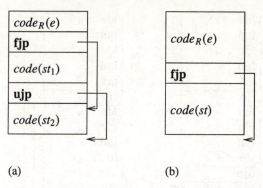

(a)   (b)

Figure 2.2   Instruction sequences for conditional statements. (a) Bidirectional, (b) unidirectional.

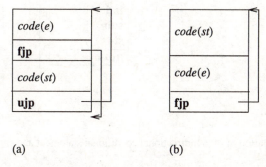

(a)   (b)

Figure 2.3   Code generation for loops, (a) **while** e **do** st **do** and (b) **repeat** st **until** e.

Example 2.2   Suppose once again that $\rho(a) = 5$, $\rho(b) = 6$ and $\rho(c) = 7$. Compile the statement

> **if** $a > b$ **then** $c := a$ **else** $c := b$ **fi**

as in Figure 2.4(a) and the loop

> **while** $a > b$ **do** $c := c + 1; a := a - b$ **od**

as in Figure 2.4(b).   □

The compilation scheme for a sequence of consecutive statements is very simple:

> $code\ (st_1;st_2)\ \rho = code\ st_1\ \rho;\ code\ st_2\ \rho$

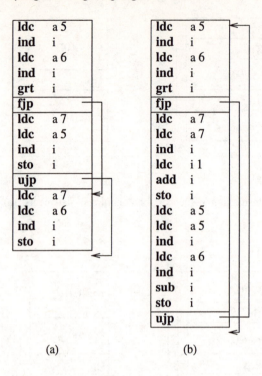

(a)   (b)

Figure 2.4 Compilation of (a) a bidirectional conditional statement and (b) a **while** loop.

Let us consider a *case* statement which is simplified in comparison with Pascal. Only selectors between 0 and a constant k which is obvious from the program are allowed. Components for all selectors 0, 1, ..., k are present and these are arranged in increasing order. Thus, *case* statements have the following form:

> **case** e **of**
>   0: st_0 ;
>   1: st_1 ;
> $\vdots$
> k: st_k ;
> **end**

One method of compiling *case* statements uses an **indexed branch**, in other words, a branch in which the given target address is increased by a value defined immediately beforehand. The **ixj** instruction in the P machine (see Table 2.5) adds the value in the highest stack location to the target address.

Table 2.5   Indexed branch.

Instr.	Meaning	Cond.	Result
ixj q	$PC := STORE[SP] + q$; $SP := SP - 1$	(i)	

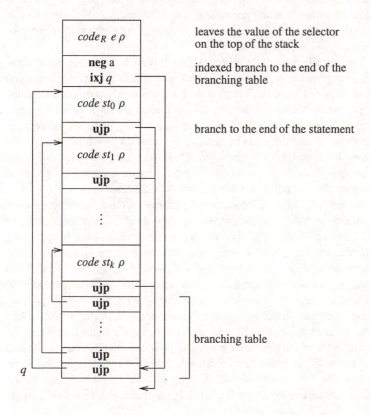

$code_R\ e\ \rho$ — leaves the value of the selector on the top of the stack

neg a
ixj q — indexed branch to the end of the branching table

$code\ st_0\ \rho$

ujp — branch to the end of the statement

$code\ st_1\ \rho$

ujp

$\vdots$

$code\ st_k\ \rho$

ujp
ujp

$\vdots$

ujp
q **ujp**

branching table

Figure 2.5   Code generation for a case statement.

Figure 2.5 illustrates the instruction sequences generated for *case* statements. Note that in this scheme the value of the selector expression is negated. In the **ixj** instruction this negative value is added to the address q of the last unconditional branch in the branch table. Thus, the branches in the branch table are arranged in the reverse order to the components. The last branch leads to the address of the instruction sequence for st_0, the first to that for st_k. This permits a recursive specification of the compilation (see Exercise 5).

2.5 Memory allocation for variables of simple type

In this section we introduce a number of very important concepts in compiler design, namely the concepts of **compile time** and **run time**, and **static** and **dynamic** information. At **compile time** a given Pascal program is compiled into a P program. At **run time** this P program is executed with input data. All information about a Pascal program that is available from this program alone or can be computed or generated from available information at compile time is said to be **static**. All information that only becomes available at run time when the corresponding P program is executed with input data is said to be **dynamic**.

We have already met a number of examples of static and dynamic information about Pascal programs. For example, the target addresses of conditional and unconditional branches are static because they are ultimately computed from the source program using the *code* function. This is true as a whole for a P program generated from a Pascal program; thus, the latter is also static. Dynamic information includes the values of variables and of expressions in which variables occur. These variables generally depend on program input values, which are only available at run time. Because the values of the conditions in statements are dynamic, the nature of control flow after the evaluation of the condition is also dynamic.

Before we can assign variables declared in the source program to memory locations, we need to make a number of assumptions about the number of memory locations and our generosity with memory. To each variable of the simple types integer, real, character and bool and of the enumeration or set type and to each pointer variable we shall assign one memory location to hold its value. Thus, unlike in real compilers, we make no attempt to pack more than one 'small value' (for example, Boolean values or characters) into a single word. We also temporarily ignore the fact that mathematicians, physicists and engineers often wish to carry out highly accurate calculations with real numbers with long mantissas. Thus, for the time being, we can only compile programs in which the accuracy is limited by the word length of the P machine. However, this word length is not specified. As a minimum, the word length should be such that a single word may contain Boolean values, characters from a sufficiently large alphabet and, above all, a single instruction.

We then have a very simple memory allocation scheme. The variables in the declaration part of the program (we are currently still considering programs without blocks or procedures) are assigned consecutive addresses from the start of the stack memory, according to the order in which they occur. For reasons which will become clear later, the first address assigned is not 0 but 5. For reasons which will also become clear when we consider procedures and blocks, we shall call the addresses assigned **relative addresses**. The (actual) absolute address 5 is therefore defined to be the address 5 relative to the base 0.

The function that records the assignment of variables to relative addresses is $\rho : Var \to \mathbb{N}_0$.

Let us consider the variable declaration part of a Pascal program, where the types that occur are all simple; that is,

var $n_1 : t_1; \ldots; n_k : t_k;$

The memory allocation strategy outlined above would then define the function ρ as follows:

$$\rho(n_i) = i + 4 \text{ for } 1 \le i \le k$$

It is easy to see that the relative addresses assigned are static quantities, since they are derived (in a very simple way) from the source program, namely from the positions of the variables in the variable declaration part.

Of course, these addresses lie within the range of the memory we have reserved for the P machine stack. When procedures and functions are involved, it becomes clear that we are talking about two nested stacks, namely a 'large' stack consisting of the data areas of all currently active procedures, which grows when a procedure is entered and shrinks when a procedure is exited, and a 'small' stack for every active procedure which holds interim results determined during the processing of statements in the body. Up to now, we have only met the latter, for example in the processing of assignments. The assignment of memory locations and/or addresses to declared variables defines the structure of the data area.

2.6   Memory allocation for arrays

First, we consider the case of static arrays, as in the original Pascal; we shall then consider dynamic arrays as in Algol 60 and ISO Pascal.

2.6.1   Static arrays

How many memory locations will an array a occupy if it is declared as follows?

var a: **array**$[-5..5, 1..9]$ **of integer**

According to our previous assumptions, every component of the array occupies one location. Clearly, there are 99 components

$$a[-5,1], a[-5,2], \ldots, a[-5,9],$$
$$a[-4,1], a[-4,2], \ldots, a[-4,9],$$
$$\vdots$$
$$a[5,1], a[5,2], \ldots, a[5,9],$$

which we shall store consecutively in the memory in this order.

This allocation scheme is known as **row-major ordering**. It is intuitively described by the principle that 'the order of the array components in the memory is such that the last index varies most quickly'. Here is a precise definition. Suppose that a k-dimensional array is defined by the declaration:

$$\text{var } b: \textbf{array}[u_1..o_1, \ldots, u_k..o_k] \textbf{ of integer } (u_i, o_i \text{ integer constants})$$

Then the array components

$$b[i_1, \ldots, i_j, o_{j+1}, \ldots, o_k] \text{ and } b[i_1, \ldots, i_{j+1}, u_{j+1}, \ldots, u_k]$$

are immediately adjacent in memory if $u_j \leq i_j < o_j$.

In the above declaration of the array b, the array components occupy $\prod_{i=1}^{k}(o_i - u_i + 1)$ locations in the order

$$b[u_1, \ldots, u_k], \qquad b[u_1, \ldots, u_{k-1}, u_k + 1], \qquad \ldots b[u_1, \ldots, u_{k-1}, o_k],$$
$$b[u_1, \ldots, u_{k-1} + 1, u_k], \quad b[u_1, \ldots, u_{k-1} + 1, u_k + 1], \ldots b[u_1, \ldots, u_{k-1} + 1, o_k],$$

$$\vdots$$

$$b[o_1, \ldots, o_{k-1}, u_k], \qquad b[o_1, \ldots, o_{k-1}, u_k + 1], \qquad \ldots b[o_1, \ldots, o_{k-1}, o_k]$$

We again record the first memory location occupied by the array using the function ρ. Of course, we now have a somewhat more complicated allocation strategy. We introduce a function $size : Type \rightarrow \mathbb{N}$, which specifies the size of an object of the given type, in other words, the number of memory locations occupied by the variables of this type. According to the above, we have

$$size(t) = 1 \qquad\qquad \text{for types integer, real, char, bool}$$
pointer, and enumeration and set types.

$$size(t) = \prod_{i=1}^{k}(o_i - u_i + 1) \quad \text{for the type of the array } b \text{ declared above.}$$

Then, for a variable declaration part

$$\textbf{var } n_1 : t_1; n_2 : t_2; \ldots; n_m \, t_m;$$

the function ρ is given by

$$\rho(n_i) = 5 + \sum_{j=1}^{i-1} size(t_j) \quad \text{for } 1 \leq i \leq m$$

At this point, it should be clear to the reader that in the previous case of static arrays discussed above, the quantities $k, u_1, u_2, \ldots, u_k, o_1, o_2, \ldots, o_k$, and therefore also the functions $size$ and ρ which depend on these, are known at compile time; in other words, they are read or computed from a given Pascal program. Correspondingly, in order to store, for example, the value 0 in the first location of the above array a we could generate the instruction sequence

ldc a $\rho(a)$;
ldc i 0;
sto i;

where $\rho(a)$ is an address which is known at compile time.

However, it becomes interesting when, for example, we have to compile the assignment $a[i, j] := 0$ in which i and j are integer variables that only acquire their values at the time the compiled program is executed. In this case we have to generate instructions that load the current values $\bar{i}$ and $\bar{j}$ of i and j using the addresses $\rho(i)$ and $\rho(j)$ and then compute the following expression:

$$(\bar{i} - (-5)) * (9 - 1 + 1) + \bar{j} - 1 = (\bar{i} + 5) * 9 + \bar{j} - 1$$

When added to the initial address $\rho(a)$, this value gives the address of the location $a[\bar{i}, \bar{j}]$. Thus, in this process we encounter the compile-time quantities -5, 1 and 9, the bounds of the array a, and its start address, $\rho(a)$, together with the execution-time quantities $\bar{i}$ and $\bar{j}$, the values of i and j at the time the instruction sequence for the Pascal statement $a[i, j] := 0$ is executed.

Let us consider our general array declaration

var b: **array** $[u_1..o_1, u_2..o_2, \ldots, u_k..o_k]$ **of integer**

Let $d_i = o_i - u_i + 1$ for $1 \leq i \leq k$ denote the **ranges** of the array b in the individual **dimensions**. How do we determine the relative address of the component of b denoted by $b[i_1, i_2, \ldots, i_k]$ relative to the start address of b?

We again let $\bar{i}_1, \ldots, \bar{i}_k$ denote the current values of $i_1, \ldots, i_k$ at execution time for the corresponding statement. According to our arrangement of the array components in memory, the value of

$$(\bar{i}_1 - u_1) * size(\textbf{array}[u_2..o_2, \ldots, u_k..o_k] \textbf{ of integer})$$

brings us to the start of the $(k - 1)$-dimensional subarray in which the addressed component lies. Adding

$$(\bar{i}_2 - u_2) * size(\textbf{array}[u_3..o_3, \ldots, u_k..o_k] \textbf{ of integer})$$

leads us to the start of the correct $(k - 2)$-dimensional subarray, and so on. Thus, the expression

$$
\begin{aligned}
r = \ &(\bar{i}_1 - u_1) * size(\textbf{array}[u_2..o_2, \ldots, u_k..o_k] \textbf{ of integer}) + \\
&(\bar{i}_2 - u_2) * size(\textbf{array}[u_3..o_3, \ldots, u_k..o_k] \textbf{ of integer}) + \\
&\vdots \\
&(\bar{i}_{k-1} - u_{k-1}) * size(\textbf{array}[u_k..o_k] \textbf{ of integer}) + \\
&(\bar{i}_k - u_k)
\end{aligned}
$$

computes the desired address relative to the start of the array. If we substitute the values of the *size* expressions (known at compile time), we obtain:

$$
\begin{aligned}
r = \ &(\bar{i}_1 - u_1) * d_2 * d_3 * \ldots * d_k + (\bar{i}_2 - u_2) * d_3 * d_4 * \ldots * d_k \\
&+ \ldots + (\bar{i}_{k-1} - u_{k-1}) * d_k + (\bar{i}_k - u_k)
\end{aligned}
$$

Table 2.6 Computation of indexed address. $STORE[SP-1]$ contains a 'start address'. $STORE[SP]$ contains the index of the selected subarray and q contains the size of the subarray.

Instr.	Meaning	Cond.	Results
ixa q	$STORE[SP-1] := STORE[SP-1] +$ $STORE[SP] *q$ $SP := SP - 1$	(a,i)	(a)

Multiplying this out and splitting it into $\overline{i}_j$ and u_j expressions, we have

$$
\begin{aligned}
r \; = \; & (\overline{i_1} * d_2 * d_3 \ldots * d_k + \overline{i_2} * d_3 * d_4 * \ldots * d_k \\
& + \ldots + \overline{i_{k-1}} * d_k + \overline{i_k}) \\
& - (u_1 * d_2 * d_3 * \ldots * d_k + u_2 * d_3 * d_4 * \ldots * d_k \\
& + \ldots + u_{k-1} * d_k + u_k)
\end{aligned}
\tag{2.1}
$$

We see that the second part of this expression contains only quantities that are known at compile time. Thus, the compiler can evaluate this expression to a constant d. We can also simplify the first part of the expression. Because the ranges are known in the case of static arrays, we can evaluate all the products of ranges at compile time. This only leaves a sum of the form $h = \sum_{j=1}^{k} \overline{i}_j \cdot d^{(j)}$, where

$$
d^{(j)} = \prod_{l=j+1}^{k} d_l
$$

We now generalize the address computation one last time before giving the compilation scheme for addressing the components of arrays. Our declaration for the array b specified the component type as integer. Thus, the storage requirement was one memory location per component. Let us now consider arbitrary component types (including non-simple components) t with a known storage requirement of $size(t)$ locations; in this case, the array c with the declaration

var c: **array** $[u_1..o_1, u_2..o_2, \ldots, u_k..o_k]$ **of** t

requires $d_1 * d_2 \ldots d_k * g$ storage locations where g stands for $size(t)$. The relative address of the array component $c[i_1, \ldots, i_k]$, again relative to the start of the array, is then $h * g - d * g$ where, in our case of static arrays, the term $d * g$ can again be computed by the compiler.

Table 2.6 gives a P machine instruction which can be used to move gradually through increasingly lower-dimensional subarrays. Here, the parameter q can be used for the factors $g \cdot d^{(j)}$.

Table 2.7   Incrementing and decrementing are defined in Pascal for all types that have a *succ* function.

Instr.	Meaning	Cond.	Result
inc $T\,q$	$STORE[SP] := STORE[SP] + q$	(T) and type $(q) = i$	(T)
dec $T\,q$	$STORE[SP] := STORE[SP] - q$	(T) and type $(q) = i$	(T)

In addition, we require other instructions for arithmetic on addresses. These include increment and decrement instructions (see Table 2.7). To compile the index sequence, we use a function $code_I$, whose second parameter is the component size. The compilation scheme for computing the address of the array component $c[i_1, \ldots, i_k]$ with component size g and start address $\rho(c)$ is

$$
\begin{aligned}
code_L\, c[i_1, \ldots i_k]\, \rho \;&=\; \textbf{ldc a}\ \rho(c);\ code_I\, [i_1, \ldots, i_k]\, g\, \rho \\
code_I\, [i_1, \ldots, i_k]\, g\, \rho \;&=\; code_R\, i_1\, \rho;\ \textbf{ixa}\ g \cdot d^{(1)}; \\
&\qquad code_R\, i_2\, \rho;\ \textbf{ixa}\ g \cdot d^{(2)}; \\
&\qquad \vdots \\
&\qquad code_R\, i_k\, \rho;\ \textbf{ixa}\ g \cdot d^{(k)}; \\
&\qquad \textbf{dec a}\ g \cdot d;
\end{aligned}
$$

However, this compilation scheme has the same disadvantage as the scheme described earlier for the *case* statement; namely, there is no check to verify that the values of the index expressions $i_1, \ldots, i_k$ lie within the allowed bounds. We shall now change this. The **chk** instruction given in Table 2.8 checks whether the computed index value lies within the bounds.

The improved compilation scheme is then

$$
\begin{aligned}
code_I\, [i_1, \ldots, i_k]\, arr\, \rho \;&=\; code_R\, i_1\, \rho;\ \textbf{chk}\ u_1\, o_1;\ \textbf{ixa}\ g \cdot d^{(1)}; \\
&\qquad code_R\, i_2\, \rho;\ \textbf{chk}\ u_2\, o_2;\ \textbf{ixa}\ g \cdot d^{(2)}; \\
&\qquad \vdots \\
&\qquad code_R\, i_k\, \rho;\ \textbf{chk}\ u_k\, o_k;\ \textbf{ixa}\ g \cdot d^{(k)}; \\
&\qquad \textbf{dec a}\ g \cdot d;
\end{aligned}
$$

where $arr = (g; u_1, o_1, \ldots, u_n, o_n)$.

Table 2.8   Check whether the highest stack value lies between p and q, inclusive. Halt with error message if not.

Instr.	Meaning	Cond.	Result
chk $p\,q$	**if** $(STORE[SP] < p)$ **or** $(STORE[SP] > q)$ **then** $error(\text{'value out of range'})$ **fi**	(i)	(i)

Example 2.3 Suppose we have the declarations

> **var** i, j: **integer**;
> a: **array**$[-5..5, 1..9]$ **of integer**

then $\rho(i) = 5$, $\rho(j) = 6$ and $\rho(a) = 7$ and for the array a, we have the ranges $d_1 = 11$, $d_2 = 9$, the component size $g = 1$ and $d = -44$. The compilation of $a[i+1, j] := 0$ is then given by:

$$code(a[i+1, j] := 0)\ \rho =$$

ldc	a 7	**ldc** a 6	
ldc	a 5	**ind** i	
ind	i	**chk** 1 9	
ldc	i 1	**ixa** 1	
add	i	**dec** a -44	
chk	-5 5	**ldc** i 0	
ixa	9	**sto** i	

□

In this section, we have shown how static arrays may be implemented. Here is a summary of the features. The bounds, the ranges, the component sizes and the relative address of each array are known at compile time. All expressions (for example, in indexing) that consist of these alone can be evaluated by the compiler. The results become operands of the instructions generated. Each array is stored together with the other declared variables. The relative address assigned to an array is the relative address of its first location.

2.6.2 Dynamic arrays

The ISO standard for Pascal eliminates some of the design faults in the original language, in that it allows arrays as formal parameters which adjust their size to that of the actual parameter. For a given procedure declaration **procedure** p (**value** a: **array**$[u_1..o_1, \ldots, u_k..o_k]$ **of** *type*) the bounds for a are only determined when the procedure p is called. A similar thing holds for a declaration **var** a: **array**$[u_1..o_1, \ldots, u_k..o_k]$ **of** *type*, when not all the u_i and o_i are constant, but are global variables or formal parameters of the procedure. In both cases, a is a **dynamic array**; its bounds, the ranges in the individual dimensions, and thus its size, are dynamic. Only the dimension itself remains static. Thus, neither the previous allocation scheme nor the component addressing can be used. We shall therefore treat these aspects afresh for the case of dynamic arrays.

The storage of dynamic arrays in memory causes problems, because as soon as there are two such arrays a static assignment of start addresses is no longer possible. Because the storage space required by an array is only known when the procedure is entered, memory reservation can only take place at that time. As we shall see later in our discussion of procedures, dynamic arrays are stored in the dynamic part of the procedure space, after the static part.

How can we generate instruction sequences for component addressing or at least to determine the start address? Even if we do not know the start address, we can still determine statically where it will be stored at run time. For this we use an **array descriptor** to which we assign a static start address and a size. Its size depends only on the dimensions of the array. Its first location is used for the start address of the array, which is stored there when the array is created, in other words, when the procedure is entered and the array declaration is processed. The remaining structure will become apparent.

Let us again turn to the problem of generating instruction sequences to address the array component $b[i_1, \ldots, i_k]$, but now in a dynamic array b: **array**$[u_1..o_1, \ldots, u_k..o_k]$ **of integer**. The variables $u_1, \ldots, u_k, o_1, \ldots, o_k$ only acquire their values at run time. Let us again consider the formula for computing the relative address of $b[i_1, \ldots, i_k]$ in Equation (2.1) on page 22. Except for k, the dimension of the array, all the quantities in (2.1) are now dynamic. Thus, we have to compute their values at run time and statically provide space for them. However, there is a difference between $i_1, \ldots, i_k$ and $u_1, \ldots, u_k, d_2, \ldots, d_k$. The values of $i_1, \ldots, i_k$ depend on the particular indexing of the array, while the values of $u_1, \ldots, u_k$ and $d_2, \ldots, d_k$ are defined once for the whole lifetime of the array. In the case of a formal dynamic array parameter the values of $u_1, \ldots, u_k, d_2, \ldots, d_k$ are retrieved from the actual parameter when the parameters are passed. In the case of a declared dynamic array, the values of the bounds and of $d_2, \ldots, d_k$ are computed once when the array is created. The whole of the second part of Equation (2.1), namely $(u_1 * d_2 * d_3 * \ldots * d_k + \ldots)$, gives the same value d however the array is indexed, and this is therefore passed with the parameters or computed once when the array is created. For each form of indexing, to save ourselves from having to subtract $d \cdot g$ every time, we subtract $d \cdot g$ immediately from the start address of the array and store the result, the **adjusted** start address, in the array descriptor instead of the actual start address.

Now, in order to address the component $b[i_1, \ldots, i_k]$, we need only add the value of $h \cdot g$, where $h = \overline{i_1} * d_2 * d_3 * \ldots * d_k + \overline{i_2} * d_3 * d_4 * \ldots * d_k + \ldots + \overline{i_{k-1}} * d_k + \overline{i_k}$, to this adjusted start address. To save multiplications we compute this expression using a Horner scheme

$$h = (\ldots ((\overline{i_1} * d_2 + \overline{i_2}) * d_3 + \overline{i_3}) * d_4 + \ldots) * d_k + \overline{i_k}$$

For the evaluation, we must be able to access the values of d_i. Thus, we provide room for these in the array descriptor, which now has the structure shown in Figure 2.6.

The second and third locations are needed for copying arrays. The contents of the third location are used to compute the adjusted start address of the copy. The values of the upper and lower bounds are required for the test to ensure that the range bounds are not violated.

For indexing in dynamic arrays we use two new code functions $code_{Ld}$ and $code_{ld}$. Here, $code_{Ld}$ only generates an **ldc** instruction which loads the address of the array descriptor at the top of the stack. The code generated by $code_{ld}$ duplicates this address, uses the upper duplicate to load the adjusted start address (with an

Address

Address	
0	Adjusted start address: a
1	Array size: i
2	Subtract for adjusted start address: i
3	u_1:i
4	o_1:i
$\vdots$	$\vdots$
$2k+1$	u_k:i
$2k+2$	o_k:i
$2k+3$	d_2:i
$\vdots$	$\vdots$
$3k+1$	d_k:i

Figure 2.6 Array descriptor for the k-dimensional array b. The address in the left column is given relative to the start.

indirection) and accesses the remainder of the array descriptor indirectly using the lower duplicate. The lower duplicate is no longer required once the address has been computed and is therefore removed from the stack and replaced by the resulting address. We could still address the individual locations of the array descriptor of an array b statically using $\rho(b) + j$; however, later, we would have to give another coding scheme for when this is no longer the case.

$code_{Ld}\ b[i_1, \ldots, i_k]\ \rho =$
  ldc a $\rho(b)$;   descriptor address
  $code_{Id}\ [i_1, \ldots, i_k]\ g\ \rho$ (static) component size g
$code_{Id}\ [i_1, \ldots, i_k]\ g\ \rho =$
  dpl a;   duplicate highest stack entry
  ind a;   adjusted start address
  ldc i 0;
  $code_R\ i_1\ \rho$; **add** i; **ldd** $2k+3$; **mul** i;
  $code_R\ i_2\ \rho$; **add** i; **ldd** $2k+4$; **mul** i;
  $\vdots$
  $code_R\ i_{k-1}\ \rho$; **add** i; **ldd** $3k+1$; **mul** i;
  $code_R\ i_k\ \rho$; **add** i;
  ixa g
  sli a

Table 2.9 Instructions for dynamic arrays.

Instr.	Meaning	Cond.	Result
dpl T	$SP := SP + 1;$ $STORE[SP] := STORE[SP - 1]$	(T)	(T, T)
ldd q	$SP := SP + 1;$ $STORE[SP] := STORE[STORE][SP - 3] + q]$	(a, T_1, T_2)	(a, T_1, T_2, i)
sli T_2	$STORE[SP - 1] := STORE[SP];$ $SP := SP - 1$	(T_1, T_2)	(T_2)

The new instructions **dpl**, **ldd** and **sli** are defined in Table 2.9. **dpl** copies the highest stack entry, **ldd** accesses descriptor arrays indirectly and **sli** moves the highest stack entry to the second highest position.

The general case of dynamic arrays of an arbitrary (including dynamic) type will be handled in an exercise, as will the necessary introduction of the range check.

2.7 Memory allocation for records

We shall now discuss the problem of memory allocation and addressing for records. Our records are simplified in comparison with Pascal records, in that we do not allow variants and also require that the names of record components should not be multiply declared, for instance outside the record type. This means that we can also use our function ρ for names of records and their components. Suppose, for example, that the record variable v is declared as

var v: **record** a: **integer**; b : **bool end**

Then we assign the address of the first free memory location to the variable v according to the previous strategy and relative addresses within the record (0 and 1, here) to the component names (for reasons which will become clear in the next section). Thus, if the above declaration follows the declarations **var** i, j: **integer**, we have $\rho(i) = 5$, $\rho(j) = 6$, $\rho(v) = 7$, $\rho(a) = 0$ and $\rho(b) = 1$.

The computation of the relative addresses of record components uses the *size* function in a similar way to the computation of relative addresses in declaration parts. In general, for a record declaration **var** v: **record** $c_1 : t_1; c_2 : t_2; \ldots; c_k : t_k$ **end**, we have

$$\rho(c_i) = \sum_{j=1}^{i-1} size(t_j)$$

The size of the record variable v is determined inductively from the sizes of the components

$$size(v) = \sum_{i=1}^{k} size(t_i)$$

Note that these sizes are static in Pascal; that is, they are known at compile time. Thus, using what we learnt in the last section, we can now handle an array of records and generate instruction sequences to compute the start address of a component in such an array.

Conversely, let us suppose that a record component is a dynamic array. Here too, we wish to keep the static addressing of all record components. We again achieve this by storing only the array descriptor in the record, rather than the array itself.

The addressing of record components involves the following steps:

- loading the start address of the record;
- increasing the address by the relative address of the component.

Thus, we obtain the address, which is a usable L value. If we require the value of the (simple) component, we must load it (indirectly) using the address. If the component addressed is itself a record or an array, another record component or array component can be selected based on the computed address.

To increase an address by a relative address we use the **inc** instruction given in Table 2.7. The following P instruction sequence is generated to address the component c_i in the record v:

ldc a $\rho(v)$; **inc** a $\rho(c_i)$

2.8 Pointers and dynamic memory allocation

Pointers and the dynamic memory occupancy of anonymous objects are two closely related concepts in imperative programming languages. So far, we have only considered memory allocation for objects introduced by a declaration. A name for the object is given in the declaration and a static (relative) address is assigned to this name. If a programming language includes pointers, these may be used to access nameless objects; pointers may be used to implement dynamically growing and shrinking chained structures, where the individual objects are not defined by a declaration but created by executing a suitable statement, such as the Pascal **new** statement. The semantics of both Pascal and C are not very precise as far as the lifetime of dynamically created objects is concerned. Of course, the implementation of a programming language may release the memory occupied by such an object before the end of its lifetime without violating the semantics, provided it is certain that the running program can no longer access the object. The process of releasing memory occupied by unreachable objects is called **garbage collection**.

As previously mentioned, when a procedure is entered, a data area for all its local storage requirements (and for organizational purposes) is created in the lower part of the data memory; this area is released when the procedure is exited. This stack-like memory allocation and release is not matched to the lifetime of dynamically created objects; garbage collection will generally not release memory in a stack-like manner or synchronously with exits from procedures.

Thus, dynamically created objects are allocated space in a storage area called a **heap** at the higher end of the memory. The heap grows downwards towards the stack as objects are dynamically created. A new register in the P machine, *NP* (new pointer), points to the lowest occupied location in the heap. Thus, the memory of the P machine has the following form:

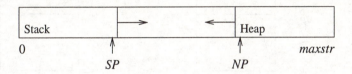

A new object is created in the heap using the P instruction **new** (see Table 2.10 and Figure 2.7).

This expects the size of the object to be created to be at the top of the stack, with the address of the pointer to the future object below it. The start address of the new object is stored indirectly in the pointer using this address. When the new lower end of the heap is computed, a check is made to determine whether the stack and the heap would collide. This uses the *EP* (extreme stack pointer) register. As we shall see in the next section, this register points to

Table 2.10   The **new** instruction.

Instr.	Meaning	Cond.	Result
new	**if** $NP - STORE[SP] \leq EP$	(a,i)	
	then *error*('store overflow')		
	else $NP := NP - STORE[SP]$;		
	$\quad STORE[STORE[SP - 1]] := NP$;		
	$\quad SP := SP - 2$		
	fi;		

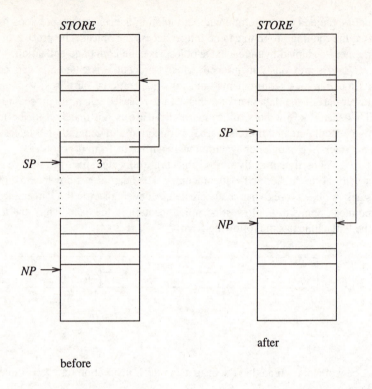

Figure 2.7 The effect of the **new** instruction in the P machine.

the highest stack location to which *SP* can point when evaluating expressions in the statement part. As Exercise 3 is intended to show, the maximum number of stack locations needed to evaluate any given expression can be precomputed at compile time. Thus, *EP* can be increased by this static quantity whenever a procedure is entered, after the necessary dynamic arrays have been created.

The check to determine whether the stack extension would collide with the heap should only take place on entry to a procedure; otherwise, this test would have to be repeated whenever *SP* was increased. Using the *EP* register in this way is clearly more efficient.

We can now describe the compilation of a Pascal new statement into P machine code, essentially into a P **new** instruction.

$code(\textbf{new}(x)) =$
    ldc a $\rho(x)$; **ldc** i $size(\text{t})$; **new**   if x is a variable of type $\uparrow t$

The **ind** instruction is again used for **dereferencing**, in other words, to address an object via a pointer to it.

To conclude the last three sections, we consider the problem of address computation for variable denotations with an arbitrarily complicated structure; in other words, variable denotations containing an arbitrary number of indexes, selections and dereferences in an arbitrary order. Thus, this involves the compilation of words such as $x \uparrow [i + 1, j].a \uparrow [i] \uparrow$ and $y.a.b.c \uparrow [i, j + 1].d$. For this, we introduce a number of new cases of the recursive $code$ function, which compile address modifications, in other words, indexes, selections and dereferences. We note that the function $code_{Id}$ has two arguments; in addition to the list of index expressions it also includes the (static) array-component size.

The compilation scheme given below decomposes composite variable denotations from left to right; it picks the variable name first, followed by any subsequent selections, dereferences and indexes.

$$code_L(xr)\ \rho = \textbf{ldc a } \rho(x);$$
$$code_M(r)\ \rho \qquad\qquad \text{for name } x$$
$$code_M(.xr)\ \rho = \textbf{inc a } \rho(x); \qquad\qquad \text{for name } x$$
$$code_M(r)\ \rho$$
$$code_M(\uparrow r)\ \rho = \textbf{ind a};$$
$$code_M(r)\ \rho$$
$$code_M([i]r)\ \rho = code_{Id}\ [i]\ g\ \rho; \qquad\quad \text{where } g \text{ is the component size}$$
$$code_M(r)\ \rho \qquad\qquad\qquad \text{of the indexed array}$$
$$code_M(\varepsilon) = \varepsilon$$

The following assertion holds for this $code$ function. Let us assume that the prefix u of a composite term uv is compiled into an instruction sequence b; $code_L(uv)\rho = h$; $code_M v\rho$. The execution of b then computes:

- the address of an array descriptor into the highest stack location, if v begins with an index, or
- the start address of the variables denoted by u into the highest stack location, otherwise.

Example 2.4   Suppose we have the following declaration.

$$\textbf{type}\quad t =\quad \textbf{record}$$
$$a: \textbf{array}[-5.. + 5, 1..9]\ \textbf{of integer}$$
$$b: \uparrow t$$
$$\textbf{end};$$
$$\textbf{var}\quad i, j\ : \textbf{integer};$$
$$pt\quad : \uparrow t;$$

Assuming that $\rho(i) = 5$, $\rho(j) = 6$ and $\rho(pt) = 7$, the variable denotation $pt \uparrow .b \uparrow .a[i + 1, j]$ is compiled as follows:

ldc a 7;	Load address of *pt*
ind a;	Load start address of record
inc a 99;	Compute start address of record component *b*
ind a;	Dereference pointer
inc a 0;	Start address of component *a*
$code_{ld}[i+1, j]\, 1\ \rho$;	As in Example 2.3

$\square$

This completes our discussion of memory allocation for records and the addressing of record components. Note that the compilation scheme given here only yields correct instruction sequences for correctly composed variable denotations. It does not include the verification of context conditions, for example that x in $x \uparrow$ is also a pointer variable, that x in $x[i_1, \ldots, i_k]$ is a k-dimensional array, or that x in $x.a$ is a record variable with a component with name a.

2.9   Procedures

In preparation for the compilation of procedures, we shall now briefly discuss the associated concepts, terms and problems.

A **procedure declaration** consists of

- a name under which it may be called,
- the specification of the formal parameters which form the input/output interface,
- a sequence of (local) declarations, and
- a statement part, the **body**.

If it is a function procedure, the result type must also be given.

Procedures are **called** (that is to say, activated) when an occurrence of their name in the statement part of the main program or a procedure is processed. A called procedure can in turn call another procedure or even itself. When the statement part of a procedure has been processed in full, the procedure is exited and its caller (in other words, the procedure that activated it) continues the execution following the call.

The chains of procedure calls that arise during the execution of a program form an ordered tree, the **calling tree** for the program execution. The root of the calling tree is labelled with the name of the main program. Every internal node of the calling tree is labelled with a procedure name p (more precisely, with one of possibly several defining occurrences of p), its immediate predecessor is labelled with the name of the procedure that executed this call to p, and its immediate successors form a list of procedures ordered in the sequence in which they are called by p. The

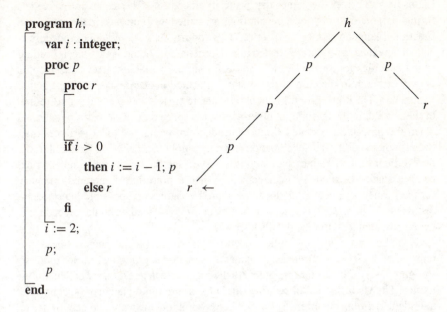

program h;

    var i : **integer**;

    proc p

        proc r

        if $i > 0$

            then $i := i - 1$; p

            else r

        fi

    $i := 2$;

    p;

    p

end.

Figure 2.8   A program and its calling tree. The brackets mark the declaration part and the statement part of the procedure.

label p may occur several times in the calling tree; more precisely, it occurs exactly as often as p is called during the processing of the program. Every occurrence of p is called an **incarnation** of p. It is characterized by the path from the root of the tree (which corresponds to the main program) to the particular node. This path is called the **incarnation path** for this incarnation of p.

    Let us consider the state of the program execution when a particular incarnation of p is active. According to the above, all ancestors of this incarnation, in other words, all nodes on the incarnation path, have already been called but not yet exited, or, in the case of the main program, started but not yet ended. All these incarnations are said to be **live** at this point in time.

Example 2.5   Figure 2.8 shows a program and its calling tree. The arrow points to an incarnation of r, which is reached after the first three recursive calls to p. At this time, the main program h, three incarnations of p and one incarnation of r are live.

    It should be stressed here that:

- a program may have more than one calling tree
- there may be infinitely many calling trees.   ☐

Let us now consider the names that occur in procedures. The names introduced as formal parameters or by local declarations are called **local names** (in the section on functional languages, they are referred to as **bound** names). When a procedure is called, new **incarnations** are created for all local names. At the same time, according to the specification or declaration, space for simple variables, arrays and records is reserved and, in the case of parameters, allocated in accordance with the actual parameters. The **lifetime** of the incarnations created in this way is equal to the lifetime of the procedure incarnation; in other words, the space they occupy can be released when the procedure is exited (in this introduction, we ignore local variables that, because of an additional specification (**own** in Algol 60, STATIC in PL/I and in C), outlive their procedure incarnations). It is easy to see that this can be implemented using a stack-like memory management. When a procedure is entered, memory for the formal parameters, the locally declared variables and possible intermediate results (see Figure 2.10) is reserved; this memory is released when the procedure is exited. We shall discuss the details later.

The treatment of applied occurrences of non-local names (these are referred to as **free** occurrences of names in functional programs) is not quite so straightforward. Names that are global to the procedure in question are called **global names**. The **visibility** and/or **scoping** rules of a programming language specify how to find the defining occurrence of a name corresponding to an applied occurrence of that name. The converse, but equivalent, approach begins with a defining occurrence of a name and specifies the program segment in which all occurrences of the name relate to this defining occurrence.

The following scoping rule is familiar from Algol-like languages. A defining occurrence of a name is valid throughout the program unit whose declaration or specification part includes the definition, except in any program units properly contained in this program unit that contain a new definition of the name. Here, a 'program unit' means a procedure and/or a block.

Based on this scoping rule, we shall discuss these two approaches in further detail. If we search for the defining occurrence corresponding to an applied occurrence, we clearly find it if we begin our search in the declaration part of the program unit in which the applied occurrence occurs. A declaration or specification there is the object of our search. If there is no such declaration or specification, we continue our search in the immediately surrounding program unit, and so on. If there is no defining occurrence in all the surrounding program units, including the main program, there is a programming error.

The alternative approach, beginning with a defining occurrence, sweeps over the containing program unit and associates this defining occurrence with all applied occurrences of the name found. The sweeping process is blocked on the boundaries of all program units containing a new definition of the same name. These concepts are considered in more detail in Chapter 9 on semantic analysis.

Example 2.6   Figure 2.9 shows a program with several nested procedures together with the relationship between applied and defining occurrences of variables.   □

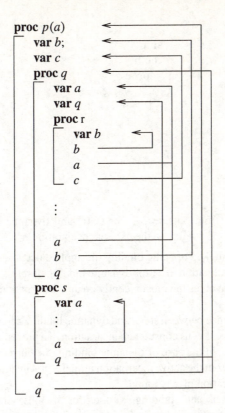

Figure 2.9   The arrows point from applied occurrences to the associated defining occurrences.

This scoping rule is used to derive the so-called **static binding**, in which global names in a procedure are associated with defining occurrences in the surrounding (textual) procedures. This association is static, since it relates only to the program text and not to a (dynamic) execution of the program. Whenever the global name is used, an **incarnation of the statically associated defining occurrence** is accessed at execution time.

This contrasts with **dynamic binding** (static binding is principally used in Algol-like languages; some LISP dialects have a static binding, others a dynamic binding) in which an access to a global name accesses the most recently created incarnation of this name, irrespective of the procedure in which its defining occurrence occurred.

Example 2.7

```
var x
proc p
    ⎡   proc q
    ⎢       ⎡   var x
    ⎢       ⎢       p
    ⎢       ⎣   x
    ⎣   q
    p
```

(1) Call to p (from outside p). For static and dynamic binding the applied occurrence of x refers to the external declaration.

(2) Call to p (in q). For static binding the applied occurrence of x refers to the external declaration of x; for dynamic binding, it refers to the declaration of x in q. It involves the most recently created incarnation of x.   □

The difference between static and dynamic binding can be clearly illustrated using the calling tree. Let us consider an incarnation of a procedure p which accesses a global variable x. In the case of dynamic binding, the current incarnation path is traced backwards from the active incarnation until the first incarnation of a procedure containing a declaration of x is found.

In the case of static binding, we look for the most recent incarnation of a procedure containing the innermost p that contains a definition of x. Any earlier incarnations of x on the incarnation path must be skipped over. It is easy to see that while the calling tree reflects the calling relationship between procedures, it is not well suited to efficient searches for the right incarnation of a global variable. A more detailed consideration shows that, as far as access to global variables is concerned, the following unique tree, called the tree of *static predecessors*, may be assigned to each incarnation path. The immediate predecessor of a node (a procedure incarnation) in this tree is the last incarnation of the immediately surrounding procedure created before this. Let us consider a path from an incarnation of p to the root in this tree of static predecessors. The right incarnations of global variables for this p all lie in an incarnation on this path.

Example 2.8　The incarnation path in Figure 2.8 h–p–p–p–r has the static predecessor tree:

All accesses to global variables in all incarnations of *p* lead to the main program. Only accesses from *r* lead to the corresponding incarnation of *p*. □

2.9.1 Memory organization for procedures

Let us again be clear that:

- all incarnations of procedures (and the main program) that are live at a given time form the current incarnation path,

- when a procedure is exited, a step is taken from the current incarnation to its parent in the calling tree, and

- all variables reachable from the current incarnation lie in ancestors of the current incarnation in the tree of static predecessors for the current incarnation path.

At any given time, the memory organization described below, the so-called **runtime stack**, contains a sequence of storage areas for the set of living incarnations, in the same order in which these occur on the incarnation path. So that the procedures can be exited efficiently, the dynamic predecessors are linked together. So that global variables can be accessed efficiently, the static predecessors are linked together from the inside out. Thus, the runtime stack contains both the current incarnation path and the current tree of static predecessors. As a minimum, this supports exiting from procedures and access to global variables. In addition to these two pointer locations, there are also other organizational cells.

A stack frame is therefore created in the memory of the P machine for a calling procedure (or an incarnation); the structure of this stack frame is shown in Figure 2.10.

The components of a stack frame and their use are described below.

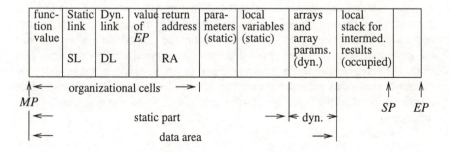

Figure 2.10 The highest stack frame.

- A location for the result, in the case of a function procedure. Here, we assume that, as in Pascal, the results of function procedures can only be of simple type.

- A location, SL, for a pointer to the stack frame of the static predecessor, in other words, the immediate predecessor in the tree of static predecessors. This is the start of the chain via which we can access the right incarnations of all global variables. In what follows we shall refer to this pointer as the static link.

- A location, DL, for a pointer to the stack frame of the dynamic predecessor, namely, the program unit that activated the current program unit. This is the start of the current incarnation path on which all living incarnations lie. This pointer is now called the dynamic link. Looked at in another way, this location contains the current state of the *MP* register, so that the latter can be restored later.

- A location to record the state of *EP* so that this can be restored later on return from a called procedure to the current procedure.

- The return address, RA, for the calling program unit, in other words, the address of the next instruction in the code memory, at which execution will be continued when the called procedure is exited.

We refer to these five locations as the **organizational cells**, because they ensure that the procedure entry and exit code and global accesses run correctly.

These organizational cells form the start of the **data area** for the incarnation. This also contains:

- Space for the values, addresses and descriptors of the actual parameters;
- Space for the local variables of the procedure, and
- Space for dynamic arrays.

It is clear from what was said in Sections 2.5 to 2.7 that, in addition to dynamic arrays, all local variables and parameters of Pascal procedures have static sizes. Together with the organizational cells, they form the static part of the data area for the procedure. From Section 2.6, we also know that in the case of dynamic arrays and array parameters passed by value, a copy must be created in the data area, and the space requirement of the copy is determined dynamically. Thus, the static part of the data area is followed by a dynamic part in which dynamic arrays and array parameters passed by value are stored. Their size is determined when the procedure is entered or when the actual parameters are passed. The static area contains the descriptors of these arrays.

Finally, we have

- The local stack, which is the stack we met in Section 2.3 when evaluating expressions. As can be seen, its maximum length can also be determined statically (see Exercise 3).

We already know something about the registers *MP*, *SP* and *EP*.

- *MP* (mark pointer) points to the start of the stack frame of the current incarnation. The organizational cells, the locations for the parameters and the local variables are addressed relative to *MP*.

- *SP* points to the highest occupied location in the local stack. In the case of an empty local stack, *SP* points to the last location of the data area.

- *EP* points to the highest location occupied throughout the execution of the procedure as a whole. *EP* is used to determine possible collisions between the stack and the heap. Thus, the test for collisions between the stack and the heap does not have to be carried out every time *SP* is increased.

Let us suppose that the stack of the P machine is occupied by such stack frames during the execution of a program and that the pointer chains are set as described above. Then the dynamic chain links the stack frames of the incarnations on the current incarnation path. The static links form the tree of static predecessors belonging to the incarnation path.

Example 2.9   Let us consider the program in Figure 2.11(a) after the second (recursive) call of *s*. At that point the stack has the form shown in Figure 2.11(b). DL pointers are shown to the left of the stack frames and SL pointers to the right. The tree of static predecessors is shown in Figure 2.11(c).   □

2.9.2   Addressing of variables

In languages that, like Pascal, have nested scopes and permit the dynamic creation of new incarnations of names local to procedures, variable names can no longer be assigned static absolute storage addresses. In general, different incarnations of a name will occupy different memory locations. As described in the previous section, a stack frame is established for each procedure incarnation. All quantities stored in the static part of the stack frame are assigned a static relative address relative to the start of the stack frame. Thus, all incarnations of these quantities have the same relative addresses within the stack frames, but not necessarily the same absolute addresses in *STORE*. The relative addresses are assigned as described in the preceding section. Thus, access to a local variable can be implemented if there exist instructions that fetch the start address of the current stack frame from the *MP* register and add it to the static relative address of the variable. These are the instructions **lod**, **lda** and **str**, to be introduced later.

We shall now discuss the addressing of global variables. For this, we define the concept of the **nesting depth** (nd) of a program construct.

The nesting depth of the main program is 0. The nesting depth of a defining (applied) occurrence of a name in the declaration or specification (statement) part of a program unit with nesting depth n is $n + 1$.

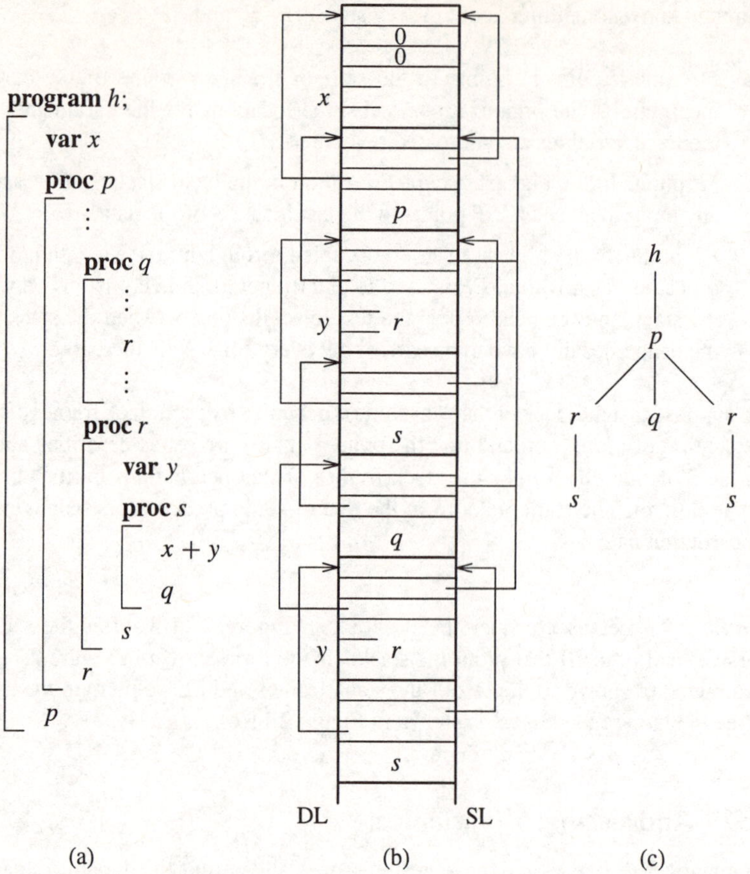

Figure 2.11   (a) A program, (b) a stack configuration and (c) the associated tree of static predecessors.

Example 2.10   The nesting depths in Figure 2.11 are:

Defining occurrence		Applied occurrence	
p	1	p	1
q	2	q	4
r	2	r (in p)	2
s	3	r (in q)	3
		s	3

Non-local variables are addressed from a procedure incarnation using the pointer to the static predecessor of the incarnation. We assume the following assertion holds (ISL):

ISL In every frame created in the stack for the incarnation of a procedure p, the static link points to the stack frame of the correct incarnation of the program unit immediately surrounding p. In programs without formal procedures, in other words, with procedures as parameters, this is the youngest living incarnation of the program unit immediately surrounding p. This is not necessarily the case in programs with procedures.   □

Let us now consider two different classes of non-local names, variable names and procedure names. To access non-local variables, in other words, to calculate their address, we use the assertion (ISL); to call a procedure (including a non-local procedure), we also use (ISL) to generate the condition of assertion (ISL) for the stack frame to be created.

Let us consider access to the non-local names x and y from the procedure s in Figure 2.11. Let us suppose that the defining occurrence of x in the main program is visible there. According to the above definition, its nesting depth is 1. The nesting depth of the applied occurrences of x and y in s is 4. In Figure 2.11, it is clear that the stack frame of the main program which contains x is reached by following the static links three times. The correct incarnation of y from procedure r is reached by following this pointer once; the difference between the nesting depths of the applied and defining occurrences is 1. In fact, if we can guarantee (ISL), then it follows by induction that:

An access from a nesting depth n to a defining occurrence at nesting depth m, where $m \leq n$, involves following the static links $(n - m)$ times to reach the stack frame containing the correct incarnation of the name. The (static) relative address must then be added to its start address to obtain the address of the global variable. Read and write access and address computation for global variables are implemented using new P instructions which are defined in Table 2.11. Accesses to local variables are also covered, by the special case $p = 0$.

Let us now consider how we may guarantee the condition of the assertion (ISL) when executing a procedure call.

If a procedure q is declared at nesting depth n, it can be called:

(1) in the statement part of the program unit p immediately surrounding it; this would be at nesting depth n;

(2) in procedures whose declarations (arbitrarily deeply nested) are surrounded by p if p is not hidden by a declaration. These calls are at a nesting depth greater than or equal to n.

Figure 2.12 shows examples of these situations. In each case, p is the calling procedure and q the called procedure. Let d be the difference between the nesting

Table 2.11 Loading and storing for a given difference in nesting depths p and a given relative address q. **lod** loads values, **lda** loads addresses.
$base(p,a) = \textbf{if } p = 0 \textbf{ then } a \textbf{ else } base(p - 1, STORE[a + 1])$.

Instr.	Meaning
lod $T\ p\ q$	$SP := SP + 1;$
	$STORE[SP] := STORE[base(p, MP) + q]$
lda $p\ q$	$SP := SP + 1;$
	$STORE[SP] := base(p, MP) + q$
str $T\ p\ q$	$STORE[base(p, MP) + q] := STORE[SP];$
	$SP := SP - 1$

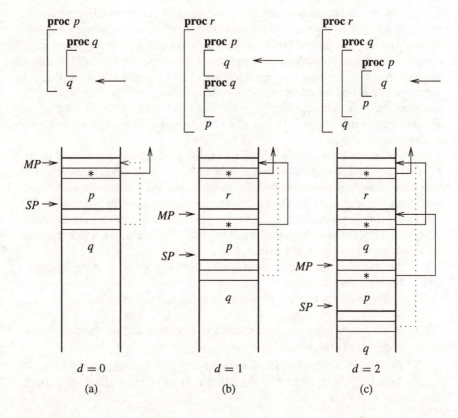

Figure 2.12 Three different call and stack situations. In each case, the current call is marked by the arrow. The dotted line shows the new static link to be set. $* = $ static link.

depths of the call and the declaration of the procedure.

Let us consider the situation in which procedure q is called in procedure p so that the difference in the nesting depths d is greater than or equal to 1 (in other words, we temporarily exclude case (a) of Figure 2.12). The desired static predecessor of q is of course a direct or indirect static predecessor of p and is therefore reachable via the chain of static links. How far do we have to go along this chain, beginning with the pointer in the stack frame of q? It is easy to see that we have to follow the pointers d times.

In case (a) of Figure 2.12, we have $d = 0$. In fact, in this case, we do not need to follow the static link in p, since the static link in the stack frame of q must point to the stack frame of p.

In particular, this last case ensures that the condition of the assertion (ISL) can be satisfied when procedures are called in the statement part of the main program. These calls can only involve procedures declared in the main program. For these, the static link must point to the stack frame of the main program. The *MP* register points to this. The difference between the nesting depths of call and declaration is 0. Thus, there is no need to follow a static link. In fact no such pointer exists.

Thus, it should be intuitively clear how access to global names, whether procedure or variable names, is implemented. Access to global variables is formally described in Section 2.9.6, and the setting of the pointer to the static predecessor on procedure entry in Section 2.9.4.

2.9.3   Computation of the address environments

In Section 2.5, we described how the names defined in a declaration part can be assigned to memory locations and addresses. Since at that point we were only considering programs with one declaration part and one statement part (that is, without procedures), the problem of global variables did not arise. The address environment ρ computed in a declaration part assigned names to (relative) addresses. We shall now extend ρ and its computation in two directions:

For each defining occurrence of a **variable name**, in addition to a relative address, ρ must also contain its nesting depth, for, as we saw in the previous section, the addressing of global variables requires precisely these two pieces of information.

What should ρ bind a procedure name to? Naturally, procedure names should be bound to everything we need to compile procedure calls. As in the case of variable names, this includes the nesting depth of the procedure declaration. In addition, the compiler has to generate the branch to the start of the compilation of the procedure; therefore, ρ binds each procedure name to a symbolic label, whose value will be the start address of the procedure code.

Thus, for **address environments** such as ρ we introduce the domain

$$Addr\_Env = Name \rightarrow Addr \times ST \text{ where } Addr = \mathbb{N} \text{ and } ST = \mathbb{N}$$

Here, variable names are bound to relative addresses in the stack frame and procedure names are bound to *CODE* addresses.

The nature of the computation of ρ must ensure that at every application point ρ has a precise knowledge of the names visible there. We can achieve this when processing the declaration part of a procedure by overwriting those entries in the external ρ that are hidden by a new declaration. However, outside the procedure, we must continue with the external ρ.

The functions *elab_specs*, *elab_vdecls* and *elab_pdecls* which are now defined recursively decompose specification lists of formal parameters and variable and procedure declaration parts. Thus, based on an external address environment ρ, they construct the local address environment for the statement part of the procedure. If they encounter a new declaration of a known name, they overwrite its entry in the address environment by the new entry. Thus, the external name is hidden. The function $f' : A \to B$, which takes the value $b \in B$ at $a \in A$ and otherwise agrees with the function $f : A \to B$, is denoted by $f[b/a]$.

elab_specs takes a list of parameter specifications, an address environment, a relative address which is the next to be assigned and a nesting depth and produces a new address environment and the relative address of the next free location after the space for the formal parameters. Thus, the functionality of *elab_specs* is given by:

$$elab\_specs : Spec^* \times Addr\_Env \times Addr \times ST \to Addr\_Env \times Addr$$

$elab\_specs$ (**var** x: t; $specs$) ρ n_a $st =$
  $elab\_specs$ $specs$ $\rho[(n\_a, st)/x](n\_a + 1)$ st
$elab\_specs$ (**value** x: **array**$[u_1..o_1, \ldots, u_k..o_k]$ **of** t'; $specs$) ρ n_a $st =$
  $elab\_specs$ $specs$ $\rho'(n\_a + 3k + 2)$ st where
    $\rho' = \rho[(n\_a, st)/x][(n\_a+2i+1, st)/u_i]_{i=1}^k[(n\_a+2i+2, st)/o_i]_{i=1}^k$
$elab\_specs$ (**value** x: t; $specs$) ρ n_a $st =$
  $elab\_specs$ $specs$ $\rho[(n\_a, st)/x](n\_a + size(t))$ st for static types t
$elab\_specs$ () ρ n_a $st = (\rho, n\_a)$

For var parameters (reference parameters) a location is reserved in which the caller stores the pointer to the current parameter. For k-dimensional value array parameters, a descriptor consisting of $3k+2$ locations is provided. This contains the start address, the array size, the subtrahend for calculating the adjusted start address, the lower and upper limits (for range checking) and the ranges. We note how the formal bounds $u_1, \ldots, u_k, o_1, \ldots, o_k$ of the formal value array parameter are bound to their corresponding positions in the descriptor. The second case of the static value parameters covers the other cases. The last case concerns exhausted specification lists.

The definition of the function *elab_vdecls* follows. This looks after memory allocation for variable declarations. Here, we must distinguish between static and dynamic objects. The first three cases handle the declaration of static variables. The addressing of record components will be taken from Section 2.7.

The functionality of *elab_vdecls* is given by:

$$elab\_vdecls : Vdecl^* \times Addr\_Env \times Addr \times ST \to Addr\_Env \times Addr$$

$elab\_vdecls$ (**var** $x : t$; $vdecls$) ρ n_a $st =$ for non-array types t
  $elab\_vdecls$ $vdecls$ $\rho[\,(n\_a, st)/x\,]$ $(n\_a + size(t))$ st

$elab\_vdecls$ (**var** $x : $ **array**$[u_1..o_1, \ldots, u_k..o_k]$ **of** t; $vdecls$) ρ n_a $st =$
  $elab\_vdecls$ $vdecls$ $\rho[(n\_a, st)/x]$

$$\times \underbrace{\left(n\_a + 3k + 2\right.}_{} + \underbrace{\left.\prod_{i=1}^{k} (o_i - u_i + 1) \cdot size(t)\right)}_{} st$$

Space for the descriptor   Space for the array components

if x is a static array.

$elab\_vdecls$ ( ) ρ n_a $st = (\rho, n\_a)$

This is the memory allocation for local variables previously described in Section 2.9.2. Only the storage of arrays has changed. A descriptor is created for each array, because it could occur as the actual parameter of a procedure. In this case, we require the information contained in the descriptor. For static arrays, the descriptor and the array are stored consecutively. The start address of the array and the limits and ranges are entered in the descriptor using an instruction sequence. The generation of this instruction sequence is left as an exercise. In the case of dynamic arrays, only the descriptor has a static length. It is stored in the static part of the stack frame. The array name is bound to the start address of the descriptor. When the procedure is entered an instruction sequence is executed which stores the array itself in the dynamic part of the stack frame and sets up the entries in the descriptor.

The function $elab\_pdecls$ processes procedure declaration parts.

$elab\_pdecls : Pdecl^* \times Addr\_Env \times ST \rightarrow Addr\_Env \times Code$

$elab\_pdecls$ (**proc** $p_1(\ldots)$; $\ldots$;
       $\vdots$

       proc $p_k(\ldots)$; $\ldots$;) ρ $st =$
  $(\rho',$ $l_1 : code$ (**proc** $p_1(\ldots)$; $\ldots$) ρ' $st + 1$;
       $\vdots$

       $l_k : code$ (**proc** $p_k(\ldots)$; $\ldots$) ρ' $st + 1$)
where $\rho' = \rho[(l_1, st)/p_1, \ldots, (l_k, st)/p_k]$

The function $elab\_pdecls$ has a functionality we have not yet encountered; it generates both an address environment and the code of the procedure declaration part. The latter may contain simultaneously recursive procedures, provided that forward declarations as in Pascal are not required; in that case the compiler encounters procedure names it does not yet know and has to generate subprogram branches to addresses that are not yet specified. We help ourselves again by introducing symbolic labels for the compilation of procedures, binding the procedure names to these and compiling the procedures in this environment (the same 'circular-environment' technique is also used in functional languages to implement simultaneous recursion, see Chapter 3). Note that all the procedures are compiled in the same address environment. The address environments computed inside the procedures are not used outside the procedures.

2.9.4   Entering and exiting procedures

Let us now consider some important actions in the implementation of procedures, namely the call and thus the entry to the procedure and the exit from the procedure after its body has been executed.

Let us first consider the procedure call. Suppose that p is the currently active procedure. Its stack frame is the highest in the stack. Suppose that the pointers in the stack frame are correctly set, in other words, the static link points to the correct incarnation of the procedure immediately surrounding p, and the dynamic link points to the incarnation from which p was called. Now suppose that p calls a procedure q.

What actions must be executed in order that the processing of q may begin?

(1)   The static link must be set to point to the frame of the correct incarnation of the procedure immediately surrounding q.

(2)   The dynamic link must be set to point to the start of the frame for p.

(3)   The current state of the *EP* register must be saved.

(4)   The values and addresses of the actual parameters must be determined and stored. In particular, descriptors must be stored for formal value array descriptors. The copies of the associated actual parameters are created later (we delay our discussion of the passing of parameters slightly).

(5)   The *MP* register must be increased so that it points to the start of the new stack frame.

(6)   The return address must be stored.

(7)   A branch to the first instruction in the code of q must be executed.

(8)   *SP* must point to the upper end of the area occupied by the static parameters and local variables.

(9)   The copies of the actual value array parameters must be created. Here, the size of each such parameter is computed using its descriptor and the *SP* register is increased by this quantity.

(10) *EP* must be set to take into account the space requirement for the local stack. A check for collision of the stack and heap is made here.

Actions (1) to (3) are usually executed using the **mst** instruction. Of course, parameter evaluation is carried out by the caller, because the actual parameters must be evaluated in the environment of the call. Actions (5) to (7) are carried out using

Table 2.12   Instructions for calling and entering procedures, **mst** (mark stack), **cup** (call user procedure), **ssp** (set stack pointer) and **sep** (set extreme stack pointer). $base(p, a) =$ **if** $p = 0$ **then** a **else** $base(p - 1, STORE[a + 1])$ **fi**.

Instr.	Meaning	Comments
mst p	$STORE[SP +2] := base(p,MP);$	Static link
	$STORE[SP +3] := MP;$	Dynamic link
	$STORE[SP +4] := EP;$	Save EP
	$SP := SP +5$	The parameters can now be evaluated starting from $STORE[SP +1]$
cup $p\ q$	$MP:= SP -(p + 4);$	p is the storage requirement for the parameters
	$STORE[MP +4] := PC;$	Save return address
	$PC := q$	Branch to procedure start address q
ssp p	$SP:= MP +p - 1$	p size of static part of data area
sep p	$EP := SP +p;$	p max. depth of local stack
	if $EP \geq NP$ **then** $error($'store overflow'$)$	Check for collision of stack and heap
	fi	

the **cup** instruction, which is also executed by the caller. Then the called procedure begins its work. It executes action (8) using the **ssp** (set stack pointer) instruction, executes action (9) using an initialization sequence which we shall discuss later, and executes action (10) (to increase EP) using the instruction **sep** (set extreme stack pointer). The instructions used are listed in Table 2.12.

Remark: In the original P machine, which only supported static arrays, actions (8) and (10) were executed together using the **ent** instruction. The copying of static value array parameters was executed later.

ent $p\ q$	$SP := MP +q - 1$	q data-area size
	$EP := SP +p$	p max. depth of local stack
	if $EP \geq NP$	Collision of stack
	then $error($'*store overflow*'$)$	and heap
	fi	

Table 2.13 Return from function procedures and proper procedures.

Instr.	Meaning	Comments
retf	$SP := MP$;	Function result in the local stack
	$PC := STORE[MP+4]$;	Return branch
	$EP := STORE[MP+3]$;	Restore EP
	if $EP \geq NP$	
	then error('store overflow')	
	fi	
	$MP : STORE[MP+2]$	Dynamic link
retp	$SP := MP-1$;	Proper procedure with no results
	$PC := STORE[MP+4]$;	Return branch
	$EP := STORE[MP+3]$;	Restore EP
	if $EP \geq NP$	
	then error('store overflow')	
	fi	
	$MP := STORE[MP+2]$	Dynamic link

When the body of a procedure or function has been executed in full, the corresponding stack frame must be released and the return jump to the caller executed. This is carried out by the P instruction **retf** for function procedures and **retp** for actual procedures (see Table 2.13).

Thus, we are now able to compile both procedure declarations and procedure calls, except for the passing of parameters.

The compilation scheme for a procedure declaration is:

$$
\begin{array}{ll}
code\ (\textbf{procedure } p\ (specs);\ vdecls;\ pdecls;\ body)\ \rho\ st = & \\
\quad \textbf{ssp } n\_a''; & \text{Storage requirement of static part} \\
\quad code_P\ specs\ \rho'\ st; & \text{Storage requirement of dynamic part} \\
\quad code_P\ vdecls\ \rho''\ st; & \text{Create and initialize} \\
\quad \textbf{sep } k; & k\ \text{max. depth of the local stack} \\
\quad \textbf{ujp } l; & \\
\quad proc\_code; & \text{Code for the local procedures} \\
l:\ code\ body\ \rho'''\ st; & \text{Code for procedure body} \\
\quad \textbf{retp} & \\
\textbf{where} \quad (\rho', n\_a') = & elab\_specs\ specs\ \rho\ 5\ st \\
\quad\quad\quad\quad (\rho'', n\_a'') = & elab\_vdecls\ vdecls\ \rho'\ n\_a'\ st \\
\quad\quad\quad\quad (\rho''', proc\_code) = & elab\_pdecls\ pdecls\ \rho''\ st
\end{array}
$$

The use of the *code_P* function on the specification part covers the possible specification of a value array parameter. In this case, code to copy the array has to be generated (cf. page 52). Instruction sequences must also be generated for the arrays declared in the variable declaration part to fill the descriptors and reserve space for dynamic arrays by increasing the *SP* register (see Exercise 13).

Compilation of the declaration of a function procedure is carried out using the **retf** instruction rather than the **retp** instruction. This leaves the result of the function procedure on the top of the stack.

The compilation scheme for a procedure call $p(e_1, \ldots, e_k)$ is:

$$code\ p(e_1, \ldots, e_k)\ \rho\ st = \textbf{mst}\ st - st';$$
$$code_A\ e_1\ \rho\ st;$$
$$\vdots$$
$$code_A\ e_k\ \rho\ st;$$
$$\textbf{cup}\ s\ l$$

where $\rho(p) = (l, st')$ and s is the space requirement for the actual parameters.

2.9.5 Parameter passing

Pascal, like a number of other imperative languages, has two different parameter types: value and var parameters (reference parameters). In addition, procedures, known as **formal procedures**, may also occur as parameters.

The compilation of an actual parameter requires information about the associated formal parameters. This information is provided by the semantic analysis which is executed prior to code generation. The instruction sequences generated for an actual parameter are executed in the following context. The calling procedure has already executed the **mst** instruction and the *SP* register points to the last location below the parameter area.

If the formal parameter x of a procedure is specified as a var parameter, the actual parameter corresponding to x must be a variable or a formal var parameter. In this case, the passing of parameters involves calculating the address, whence the L value, of the actual parameter and storing it at the relative address assigned to x. For an array parameter the L value is the address of its descriptor. Every access to the formal parameter in the body of the procedure then requires indirect access using its relative address (see Section 2.9.6).

$$code_A\ x\ \rho\ st = \qquad \text{if the formal parameter corresponding to } x$$
$$code_L\ x\ \rho\ st \qquad \text{is a var parameter}$$

The *code_L* and the *code_R* functions are redefined in the next section.

If the formal parameter x of a procedure p is specified as a value parameter of scalar type, an expression e of this type may occur as an actual parameter corresponding to x in a call to p. This call then involves the following. The expression e is evaluated and its value is stored in the parameter area of the called procedure at the

Table 2.14 The block copy instructions. **movs**, for the case in which the area to be copied has static size, copies the contents of q memory locations starting at the address $STORE[SP]$ to the area pointed to by SP. The copying is carried out backwards, so that $Store[SP]$ is last to be overwritten. **movd**, in the dynamic case, expects an array descriptor in the highest stack frame starting at relative address q. It copies this field, whose size is given in the descriptor, to the area above the location pointed to by SP. Then, the adjusted address in the descriptor is set to that of the copy of the array, so that the descriptor no longer refers to the original array but to the copy.

Instr.	Meaning	Cond.	Result
movs q	**for** $i := q - 1$ **down to** 0 **do** $\quad STORE[SP+1] := STORE[STORE[SP]+i]$ **od**; $SP := SP + q - 1$	(a)	
movd q	**for** $i = 1$ **to** $STORE[MP+q+1]$ **do** $\quad STORE[SP+i] :=$ $\quad\quad STORE[STORE[MP+q]$ $\quad\quad + STORE[MP+q+2]+i-1]$ **od**; $STORE[MP+q] := SP+1- STORE[MP+q+2]$ $SP := SP + STORE[MP+q+1]$		

relative address specified for x. During the processing of the procedure x functions as a local variable which is initialized with the value of the actual parameter.

$$
\begin{aligned}
code_A \; e \; \rho \; st = & \quad \text{if the formal parameter corresponding to } e \\
code_R \; e \; \rho \; st & \quad \text{is a value parameter}
\end{aligned}
$$

Actual value parameters of record type are handled by reserving space for their corresponding formal parameters and their value; in other words, the structured object consisting of the component values is copied to the reserved storage space. This involves the use of the static variant of the move instruction, see Table 2.14 (the original P machine only needed one move instruction for the case of storage areas with static length; it was called **mov** and its effect was the same as that of **movs**).

$$
\begin{aligned}
code_A \; x \; \rho \; st = & \quad \text{if the formal value parameter corresponding to } x \\
code_L \; x \; \rho \; st & \quad \text{is of structured type } t \text{ with static size } size(t) = g \\
. \; \textbf{movs} \; g &
\end{aligned}
$$

This last scheme copies, for example, record or array descriptors. Here, g is the storage space for the record or descriptor. The target address is derived from the contents of the highest stack location.

For dynamic value parameters, as we have seen, the treatment divides into several parts:

- The creation of a descriptor, where all entries, including the start address, are taken from the descriptor of the actual parameter; this requires the existence of such a descriptor (also for static arrays).
- The copying of the contents of the array.
- The entry of the adjusted start address in the descriptor.

We shall discuss these steps in more detail and finally give a compilation scheme for storing value array parameters. The first step, copying the descriptor of the actual array parameter into the parameter area of the called procedure, is carried out by the caller. This requires that such a descriptor must exist, even in the case of a static array. We recall that, in the treatment of static arrays in Section 2.6, the descriptor information for the compilation of array indexing was introduced into instruction sequences in the form of constants. Now that our source language has dynamic arrays, a descriptor must be stored (or an equivalent provision made) for every static field that occurs as an actual array parameter. The structure of the descriptor is shown in Figure 2.13.

Address

0	Adjusted start address: a
1	Array size: i
2	Subtract for adjusted start address: i
3	u_1: i
4	o_1: i
$\vdots$	$\vdots$
$2k+1$	u_k: i
$2k+2$	o_k: i
$2k+3$	d_2: i
$\vdots$	$\vdots$
$3k+1$	d_k: i

Figure 2.13 Array descriptor for a k-dimensional array. The left column gives the address relative to the start.

The array descriptor is copied using the same code sequence used to copy structured actual parameters with static size. Thus, the descriptor is copied using the static move instruction **movs**. In particular, the adjusted start address of the actual array parameter is copied with it. This is used by the called procedure to copy the array itself, using the dynamic move instruction **movd**, which is passed the relative address of the descriptor. The **movd** instruction uses the array size and the fictitious source address from the descriptor and $SP + 1$ as the target address.

After the actual array has been copied, the adjusted start address of the copy is calculated and entered in the descriptor.

The following code scheme compiles the specification of a formal value array parameter x. The instruction sequence is executed when a procedure is entered in order to create the dynamic array locally. The given code sequence assumes that the caller has already copied the descriptor of the actual array parameter. Thus, this is found from the relative address ra in the frame of the procedure, where $\rho(x) = (ra, st)$. Another instruction sequence, which creates the descriptor and the storage area for a local dynamic array, is left as an exercise.

$$code_P \ (\textbf{value } x: \textbf{array}[u_1..o_1, \ldots, u_k..o_k] \textbf{ of } t) \ \rho \ st =$$
$$\textbf{movd } ra; \qquad \text{copy the array}$$

Note that both the evaluation of value parameters and the address calculation for actual var parameters are carried out by the calling procedure. This knows the correct static predecessor of the call position so that it can access global variables correctly.

2.9.6   Access to variables and formal parameters

Finally, we redefine the compilation function $code_L$, which provides for the addressing of variables, in such a way that it can compile access to local and global variables and also to formal parameters.

As previously explained in detail, the following cases arise:

- local variables and formal value parameters are addressed using their known relative addresses relative to the MP register;

- formal var parameters are addressed indirectly via their location, which is also addressed relative to MP;

- global variables are addressed by first calculating the base address of the correct stack frame using the static link chain and then adding this to their relative address.

We may combine the addressing of local and global variables and formal value parameters, since for the case $d = 0$ (access to a local quantity) **lda** uses MP as base address.

The compilation scheme $code_L$ is now redefined for the case of the applied occurrence of names.

$$code_L(x\ r)\ \rho\ st = \quad \textbf{lda a}\ d\ ra;$$

$$code_M\ r\ \rho\ st,$$

where $\rho(x) = (ra, st')$ and $d = st - st'$, if x is a
variable or a formal value parameter,

$$code_L(x\ r)\ \rho\ st = \quad \textbf{lod a}\ d\ ra;$$

$$code_M\ r\ \rho\ st$$

where $\rho(x) = (ra, st')$ and $d = st - st'$, if x is a
formal var parameter

In all cases, r is a word (possibly empty) which describes indexing, selection or
dereferencing.

2.9.7   Procedures as parameters

In Pascal, as in Algol 60, procedures may be passed as parameters. The corresponding
formal parameters are called **formal procedures**. We shall now discuss the
compilation of these parameters and the calling of formal procedures. Let us consider
the example in Figure 2.14.

If a formal procedure, h in the example, is called, this has the same effect as
the call to the corresponding actual procedure f or g. For this, the start address for
the code of the actual procedure must be known to the caller of the formal procedure
p. This must therefore be passed to p at the time of the call.

But, how should the pointer to the static predecessor be set when creating the
stack frame for the actual procedures? Static binding means that when $p(f)$ is called
the global variables of f are sought firstly in q and then in the main program; when
$p(g)$ is called, the global variables of g are sought directly in the main program.
The actual procedure must be visible to each caller of p. As usual, the caller can
then determine the start address of the stack frame of the correct incarnation of the
program unit in which the actual procedure was declared or specified by following
the chain of static predecessors. Thus, this start address is supplied as additional
information about the actual procedure at the time of the call.

Hence, we know that for passing an actual procedure, the start address of its
code and the start address of the stack frame of its static predecessor are stored in
the parameter area of the called procedure. However, we must distinguish between
two cases, when the actual procedure is declared and when it is in turn specified as
a formal procedure.

$$code_A\ f\ \rho\ st = \quad \text{if } f \text{ is a declared procedure with } \rho(f) = (addr, st')$$

$$\text{and } d = st - st'$$

ldc p *addr;*	start address of the code
lda a d 0;	static link for later call

$code_A\,f\,\rho\,st =$ if f is a formal procedure with $\rho(f) = (ra, st')$
                           and $d = st - st'$

lda a d ra;   load descriptor address (ra is relative address of
                       descriptor)

movs 2;   copy descriptor

In the first case, a procedure descriptor is created. For this the start address of the code of the procedure must be loaded. The P machine does not have a 'program-storage address' type. Thus, p is introduced as a type. In the last case, the contents of the descriptor are copied to the formal procedure f.

Finally, it remains to discuss the call to a formal procedure. In comparison with the scheme for calling a declared procedure, only the following change:

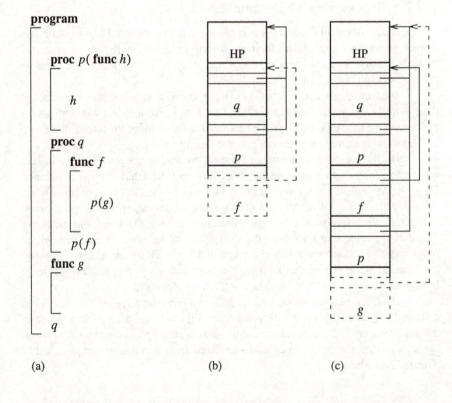

(a)   (b)   (c)

Figure 2.14   Example of formal procedures. (a) Program with formal procedures. (b) Stack situation after the call to $p(f)$ and (dashed) after the call to h. (c) Stack situation after the call to $p(g)$ and (dashed) after the call to h.

Table 2.15   The instructions **smp** (set *MP*), **cupi** (call user procedure indirectly) and **mstf** (mark stack for formal procedure).

Instr.	Meaning	Comments
smp p	$MP := SP - (p + 4);$	
cupi p q	$STORE[MP + 4] := PC;$	Return address
	$PC := STORE[base(p, STORE[MP + 2]) + q]$	
mstf p q	$STORE[SP + 2] := STORE[base(p, MP) + q + 1];$	
	$STORE[SP + 3] := MP;$	
	$STORE[SP + 4] := EP$	
	$SP := SP + 5;$	

- The pointer to the static predecessor is loaded from the second location of the formal procedure. A modified **mst** instruction is used for this, see Table 2.15.
- The subprogram branch takes place indirectly using the first location of the formal procedure. A new instruction **cupi** (call user procedure indirectly) is used for this; **cupi** is defined in Table 2.15.

Thus, the functions of the old **cup** instruction are split across two instructions, since otherwise there would be too many parameters.

The code for calling a formal procedure f is given by the following scheme:

$$
\begin{aligned}
code \; f(e_1, \ldots, e_k) \; \rho \; st = \quad & \textbf{mstf} \; (st - st') \; ra \\
& \textbf{code}_A \; e_1 \; \rho \; st \\
& \vdots \\
& code_A \; e_k \; \rho \; st \\
& \textbf{smp} \; s \\
& \textbf{cupi} \; (st - st') \; ra
\end{aligned}
$$

where $\rho(f) = (ra, st')$ and s is the space requirement for the actual parameter. At this point the declarative information for the formal parameter is available to the procedure f. However, it is first used in the $code_A$ scheme. The management of the declarative information is described in Chapter 3.

Lastly, we must extend the definition of *elab_specs* to include the cases of formal procedures and formal functions. In this process, the names of these are bound to the relative addresses of the (two) storage locations for their descriptors.

2.10 Main program

Finally, we describe how a main program is compiled. Here, we assume that all the registers of the P machine except for SP are initialized to 0. The SP register is initialized to -1. In particular, this means that the execution of the P program begins with the instruction in $CODE[0]$.

$$
\begin{aligned}
&code\ (\textbf{program}\ vdecls;\ pdecls;\ stats)\ 0\ = \\
&\quad \textbf{ssp}\ n\_a; \\
&\quad code_P\ vdecls\ \rho\ 1; \quad \text{generates code to fill} \\
&\qquad\qquad\qquad\qquad\qquad\quad \text{array descriptors} \\
&\quad \textbf{sep}\ k; \qquad\qquad\qquad \text{max. depth of local stack} \\
&\quad \textbf{ujp}\ l; \\
&\quad proc\_code; \\
&l:\ code\ stats\ \rho'\ 1; \\
&\quad \textbf{stp} \\
&\quad \text{where} \quad (\rho, n\_a) = elab\_vdecls\ vdecls\ 0\ 5\ 1 \quad \text{and} \\
&\qquad\qquad\quad (\rho', proc\_code) = elab\_pdecls\ pdecls\ \rho\ 1
\end{aligned}
$$

The instruction **stp** which ends the compilation has the effect of stopping the machine. The instructions **ssp** and **sep** are described in Table 2.12.

Warnings

In this chapter, which is now coming to a close, we have greatly simplified matters, for the sake of clarity. A number of harsh realities have been ignored. In particular, the restriction to a fixed word length yet to be specified conceals difficult problems and forces modifications to the architecture and the instructions of the P machine.

Let us single out the problem of the treatment of constants. We have always used constants as operands in P instructions; in the **chk** instruction, we have even used two at once. At the same time, it is clear that, however large the word length is chosen to be, eventually the operands of a **chk** instruction will include two constants which cannot fit into a single word together with the instruction code. Thus, the actual P machine distinguishes between the cases in which the constant operands fit into the instruction and those in which they do not. Therefore, there are differing instructions for an operation, according to whether the instructions expect their operands to be in the instruction or in a table of constants. In the latter case, the instruction contains the address of the constant required. For this purpose, a table of constants is created at the upper end of the stack, above the heap, to store the large constants that occur in the program. The compiler, or, in the case of the Zurich P4 compiler, an attached assembler, then generates different instructions independently of the size of the constants and stores the constants either in the instructions or in the table of constants.

Open questions and pointers to what is to come

In this chapter, we have provided an intuitive explanation of **what** the compilation of a Pascal-like language into the language of a suitably abstract machine is. Curious readers should now wonder **how** the given compilation schemes are implemented.

- The schemes are defined using the syntactic structure of programs. They assume that this syntactic structure is known *a priori*. In principle, the schemes can be interpreted as recursive functions that recognize the structure of programs which they then compile. However, this would not be efficient, since, locally, the templates for expressions or the two conditional statements would not always know which was the right scheme to use next. Thus, they would have to try schemes out and make good a wrong choice later. Therefore, we describe efficient methods for recognizing program structures in Chapters 7 and 8 on lexical and syntax analysis, respectively.

- The types of variables and expressions are used when compiling assignments and expressions. We do not describe how they are computed. This is a subtask of semantic analysis, which is discussed in Chapter 9.

- In the examples, it is easy to see that the use of the given compilation schemes does not always lead to the best possible or the shortest P-code instruction sequences. In Chapter 12, as part of the code generation problem, we discuss the question of the definition of better, or even optimal, instruction sequences. If non-local information about dynamic (that is, runtime) characteristics of programs is used for this, this information must be computed by abstract interpretation. The foundations, algorithms and applications of abstract interpretation are described in Chapter 10.

- The use of abstract machines has to some extent taken the edge off the compilation problem. Major new problems arise when object programs are generated for real machines and it is desired to make the best possible use of their architecture. The problems involve making optimal use of the registers of the target machines and selecting the best of the many possible instruction sequences for source program blocks. These problems are also dealt with under 'code generation' in Chapter 3.

2.11   Exercises

1:   Let $\rho(a) = 5$, $\rho(b) = 6$ and $\rho(c) = 7$. Determine:

(a) $code\ (a := ((a + b) = c))\rho$

(b) $code_R\ (a + (a + (a + b)))\rho$

(c) $code_R\ ((a + a) + a) + b)\rho$

(d) How many stack locations are occupied during the execution of the instruction sequences generated in case (b) and in case (c)?

2:   It is immediately apparent that, in special cases, there exist 'better' instruction sequences for compiling an assignment. Modify the corresponding scheme.

3:   How does the maximum number of stack locations needed to evaluate an expression depend on the structure of the expression?

Hint: consider the two 'extreme cases' $a + (a + (a + \ldots) \ldots)$ and $(\ldots ((a + a) + a) + \ldots)$!

4:   Compile the following sequence of statements:

```
a := 1; b := 0;
repeat
    b := b + c;
    a := a + 1
until a = 10
```

with the assumption that $\rho(a) = 5$, $\rho(b) = 6$ and $\rho(c) = 7$.

5:

(a) Give a recursive compilation scheme for the simplified case statement.

(b) The given compilation scheme for the case statement contains a small slip. Think about what could go wrong during the execution of the code generated. Correct this mistake.

(c) Think about what realistic case statements would look like, in other words, allow for the fact that the case components may occur in arbitrary order, that different selectors may select the same sequence of statements and that not all selectors from the interval $[0, k]$ need be present.

6:

(a) Define what is meant by column-major ordering of arrays.

(b) Develop a code generation scheme to access array components when column-major storage is used.

7:   Outline the compilation of access to dynamic arrays with component types of dynamic size. Give a compilation scheme for array indexing and the necessary extensions to the array descriptors.

8:   Define a new **chk** instruction, called **chd**, to check the ranges for dynamic arrays.

9: Suppose the declaration part of Example 2.4 is given. Compile the assignment

$$pt \uparrow .a[i, i] := pt \uparrow .b \uparrow .b \uparrow .a[j, j] + 1$$

10: Suppose the following type and variable declarations are given:

> **type** $t = $ **record**
> $\qquad\qquad a := $ **array** $[-5..5, 1..9]$ **of integer**;
> $\qquad\qquad b :\uparrow t$
> $\qquad$ **end**;
> **var** i, j; **integer**
> $\qquad box: t$;
> $\qquad pt: \uparrow t$;

The first relative address to be assigned is 5, in other words, $\rho(i) = 5$. Using this assumption, compile the assignment:

$$pt \uparrow .a[i, j] := pt \uparrow .b \uparrow .b \uparrow .a[i, j] + box.a[0, 0];$$

11: Suppose that a dynamic array is declared in the declaration part of a procedure.

> **proc** p;
> **var** b: **array**$[u1..o1, u2..o2]$ **of integer**;
> $\qquad i, j$: **integer**;
> **begin**
> $\qquad b[i, j] := b[i - 1, j + 1] + 1$;
> **end**;

(a) When the procedure is entered, the global variables $u1, o1, u2$ and $o2$ have the following values: $u1 = -4, o1 = 5, u2 = 1$ and $o2 = 10$. Suppose that the relative address of b is $\rho(b) = 5$. Give the array descriptor for b.

(b) Compile the assignment in the statement part of the procedure.

12: Consider the accompanying program fragment (where b is a Boolean variable):

(a) Give two calling trees for the program p.

(b) The structure of a program may be represented by its nesting tree. The nodes of this tree are procedures and the main program. The root is the main program. The children of a node are the procedures directly contained by it in the sequence of the program text. Give the nesting tree for the program p.

(c) Think about how the tree of static predecessors for a given incarnation path can be determined from the calling tree and the nesting tree. Consider two different incarnation paths in the recursive trees of (a) and give their trees of static predecessors.

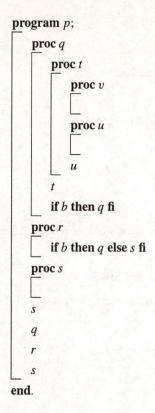

13:

(a) Give the compilation schemes for the construction of the array descriptors for static and dynamic arrays when a procedure is entered or in the main program.

(b) Generate an instruction sequence for the construction of the descriptor for the (static) array

$$\textbf{var } a \,:\, \textbf{array}\,[1..7, -5.. +5]\textbf{ of integer}$$

where $\rho(a) = 5$.

(c) Generate an instruction sequence for the construction of the descriptor for the dynamic array

$$\textbf{var } b \,:\, \textbf{array}\,[1..x, y..z]\textbf{ of integer}$$

where x and y are formal parameters of the current procedure with $\rho(x) = 5$ and $\rho(y) = 6$ and z is a global variable declared in the surrounding procedure, with $\rho(z) = 7$.

14: The compiler needs the maximum depth of the local stack in order to set *EP*. How is this (static) value calculated?

Hint: note what happens when an actual parameter is evaluated and use the results of Exercise 3.

15: Compile the following program:

```
program test;
var i, factor, sum: integer;
proc q(x: integer; var y: integer);
begin
  y := factor * x + y
end;
begin
  i := 1; sum := 0; factor := 2;
  while i ≤ 10
  do q(i + 1, sum);
     i = i + 1
  od
end.
```

16: In this exercise, we consider a number of simple extensions to our Pascal-like language. Think about how these might be implemented on the P machine.

(a) In addition to changing the contents of v, an assignment $v := e$ should denote a value, namely that of e. Thus, for example, expressions of the form $(x := a+b) > 0$ are possible.

(b) Previously, functions could only return a result of scalar type. Now, we assume that their result may be of any static type, including record type.

(c) A variable local to a procedure is called an 'own variable' (static variable in C) if it outlives procedure calls. In other words, when the procedure is called again it has the same value as when the procedure was last exited following the previous call.

2.12 Literature

Language-oriented abstract machines have been available for quite some time. They have been used to simplify compilation and to facilitate porting to other machines. An abstract machine for Algol 60, the Algol Object Code (AOC), was described in Randell and Russel (1964).

The P machine described in the present chapter was used for the Zurich P4 Pascal compiler, which is in use throughout the world. It is described in Ammann (1981) and Pemberton and Daniels (1982), which contain the sources of the P4 compiler, the assembler and the P machine interpreter.

Both the AOC and the P machine are designed for particular source languages. In the 1950s, attempts were made to solve the problem that $m \cdot n$ compilers are required for m source languages and n target machines, by searching for a universal intermediate language called UNCOL (UNiversal Communication Oriented Language). This would then have required only m compilers into UNCOL and n compilers from UNCOL into machine languages. The search resulted in certain proposals, such as Steel (1961). However, it turns out that universality cannot be achieved at the same time as the other design objectives. Searches for an UNCOL are still continuing.

3

Compilation of functional programming languages

- Language type and introductory example

- LaMa, a simple functional programming language

- Introduction to the compilation of LaMa

- Environments and bindings

- The MaMa architecture

- Stack management and addressing

- Instruction set and compilation

- Implementation of lists

- Exercises

- Literature

3.1 Language type and introductory example

Functional programming languages originated with LISP, and thus date back to the beginning of the 1960s. However, this class of languages was only freed from the dominance of LISP at the end of the 1970s, when, with the development of new concepts and implementation methods, it developed into the language type (represented by Miranda) to be discussed here.

Imperative languages have (at least) two worlds, the world of expressions and the world of statements. Expressions provide values; statements alter the state of variables or determine the flow of control. With appropriate programming, the state of variables may be altered, as a side-effect, when evaluating expressions. Functional languages only contain expressions and the execution of a functional program involves the evaluation of the associated program expression which defines the program result. Its evaluation may also involve the evaluation of many other expressions, if an expression calls other expressions via a function application; however, there is no explicit statement-defined control flow. A variable in a functional program identifies an expression; unlike in imperative languages, it does not identify one or more storage locations. Its value cannot change as a result of the execution of the program; the only possibility is the 'reduction' of the expression it identifies to its value.

A modern functional programming language includes most of the following concepts:

Function definitions

This involves either λ-**abstraction** or **recursive equations**. An expression $\lambda x_1 \ldots x_n.E$ defines an expression in the n arguments $x_1 \ldots x_n$ with the defining expression E. Thus, this defines an anonymous (nameless) function which can be applied to arguments by inserting $\lambda x_1 \ldots x_n.E$ before the argument expressions. However, that is not attractive to program. It would be desirable to give functions names which could then be combined with arguments into function applications. In addition, the introduction of names makes it easier to define recursive functions by using them in the defining expressions. This leads to *recursive equations*, which are used in modern functional programming languages to define functions. A sequence

$$f_1 \quad x_1 \ldots x_{n_1} = E_1$$
$$\vdots$$
$$f_k \quad x_1 \ldots x_{n_k} = E_k$$

defines k (possibly) simultaneously recursive functions. Thus, in addition to $x_{i_1}, \ldots, x_{i_n}$, the names $f_1, \ldots, f_k$ may also be used in the expression E_i. It should also be possible to define functions over a number of cases, that is, if the definition of the function naturally divides into various cases which can be characterized by properties of the argument tuple, the programming language should permit such a definition over cases. The classification of cases via patterns, when the arguments are structured objects, lists or user-defined types (see below), is particularly attractive.

Higher-order functions

We shall introduce two higher-order functions which are predefined in Miranda and one user-defined higher-order function, which occur in the following example. The first is the *map* function. Its first argument is a function f and its second a list l; the list elements have a type corresponding to the type of the arguments of f. *map f l* applies f to all list elements and returns the list of results (see Figure 3.1).

map is defined as follows:

```
map f [ ]      =   [ ]
map f (x:xs)   =   f x : map f xs
```

It must handle two cases. In the first case, application to the empty list, it returns the empty list as the result. For a non-empty list, it applies f to the head of the list, x, and concatenates the result with the list formed by applying *map* to f and the remainder of the list xs.

The higher-order function *foldr* takes a binary operator, for example +, and an element in the value domain (often the neutral element for the operator) and recursively folds the second argument, a list, with the operator. If the operator is '+', it sums the elements of the argument list. In general,

$$foldr\ op\ r[e_1, e_2, \ldots, e_n] = e_1\ \$op(e_2\$op(\ldots(e_n\$opr)\ldots))$$

where $\$op$ is the infix version of the operator op. *foldr* is defined as follows:

```
foldr op r  =  f   where   f [ ]    = r
                           f (a:x)  = op a (f x)
```

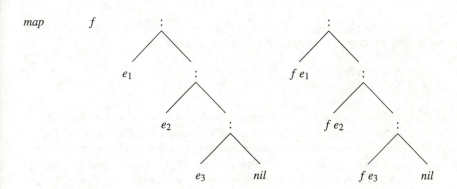

Figure 3.1 An application of the higher-order function *map* to a function f and a list. ':' denotes list concatenation.

For the third higher-order function with a function argument and a function result, we define the function *modify*. This takes a function f, an element x from its argument domain and an element y from the value domain and returns the function that agrees with f except that it takes the value y at x. In the previous chapter, we denoted such modifications of functions by $f[y/x]$:

```
modify f x y  =  g   where  g z = y   , z = x
                                = f z , otherwise
```

Polymorphism

The type of a function may be given by a type scheme containing type variables. This type scheme may be defined by a declaration or derived from the points of application of the function using a **type inference algorithm**. In any case, a type inference algorithm derives the most general type scheme for all quantities not fully typed by the programmer and checks that all expressions are constructed according to the typing rules. This subtask of the semantic analysis of functional programs is discussed in more detail in Chapter 9.

The functions described above have the following polymorphic types:

$$
\begin{aligned}
map\ &::\ (* \to **) \to [*] \to [**] \\
foldr\ &::\ (* \to ** \to **) \to ** \to [*] \to ** \\
modify\ &::\ (* \to **) \to * \to ** \to (* \to **)
\end{aligned}
$$

The '$*$' and '$**$' denote arbitrary types. *map* may be applied to an integer function and an integer list or a Boolean function and a Boolean list, for example to *sign* $:: num \to bool$ and a list of type $[num]$, where *sign* is defined by

```
sign n  =  True,  n >= 0
        =  False, otherwise
```

map sign $[5, 4, -1, 0, -1]$ would then be [*True, True, False, True, False*]. Similarly, we may apply *map* to a function *cbn* $:: bool \to num$ where

```
cbn True  =  1
cbn False =  0
```

and a list of Boolean values, for example [*True, False, True*], to give $[1, 0, 1]$. The type of *map* only requires that the type of the first, functional argument should agree with the type of the elements of the second argument, a list. The result then has a list type, where the list elements have the type of the result of the functional argument.

foldr is somewhat more general than described above. Instead of the binary operator, any function of type $(* \to ** \to **)$ is allowed as the first argument, where $*$ is at the same time the element type of the third argument, a list. This list is folded together by *foldr* into a result of type '$**$'. The call *foldr* $(+)$ $0\ l$ for a list of numbers l forms the sum of the list elements. *foldr* $(\&)$ *True l* for a list l of

Boolean values computes the value of the conjunction of all list elements. For a list of numbers l and *noneg n b = (sign n) & b, foldr (noneg) True l* has value *True* if and only if all elements of l are non-negative.

modify takes a function f of type $* \rightarrow **$, an object x of type $*$ and an object y of type $**$ and changes the function f in the argument x, by specifying the value y. We use *modify* later in the long example of a program with type

$$(ident \rightarrow addr) \rightarrow ident \rightarrow addr \rightarrow (ident \rightarrow addr)$$

One more word about defining the functionality of functions. In the case of *modify*, we would in general expect the functionality $((* \rightarrow **) \times * \times **) \rightarrow (* \rightarrow **)$, and in general for an n-place function f something like $(t_1 \times t_2 \times \ldots \times t_n) \rightarrow t$, where the tuple-forming constructor $\times$ denotes the Cartesian product. However, some functional programming languages assume that such an n-place function f is represented by n single-place functions $f_1, \ldots, f_n$, with the following functionalities $f_i :: t_i \rightarrow (t_{i+1} \rightarrow (t_{i+2} \rightarrow \ldots (t_n \rightarrow t) \ldots))$, where $f_1 x_1$ is a function f_2 which when applied to an argument x_2 yields a function f_3, which $\ldots$, yields a function f_n with the property that $f_n x_n = f x_1 \ldots x_n$. This conversion of n-argument functions into unary functions is called **currying** (after the logician H.B. Curry). One example close to home is the binary operation addition. Let *add* denote the corresponding binary function symbol; then *inc2 = add 2* is the unary function that adds 2 to its argument.

User-defined data types

The programmer may introduce problem-related data types by listing a set of constructors with a specific number of arguments and given operand types for each type. The objects of such a declared type are then the terms that can be constructed using the constructors, subject to the arity and operand-type conditions. Certain constructors, such as list, tuple and function constructors, are generally built-in. When we wish to define and work with the (abstract) syntax of Pascal, we define a new data type

```
ident ==  num    || Identifier identified by number
                 || ident is a synonym of the type num
var ::= Id ident | Sel var ident | Deref var | Ind var [expr]
```

This type definition says that the objects of type *var* consist of the constructor *Id* applied to the number of an identifier, or the selector *Sel* applied to an object of type *var* and one of type *ident*, or the constructor *Deref* applied to an object of type *var*, or the constructor *Ind* applied to a *var*-object and a sequence of objects of type *expr*.

The following Miranda program is part of a compiler in the style of the compilation scheme of Chapter 2. A prerequisite is that there should already exist a source program in 'abstract syntax', in other words, in a form representing the essential syntactic structure. Identifiers are represented by uniquely assigned numbers; as far as constants are concerned, in this section, only numerical constants are representable by their values. We also only admit integers as an elementary variable type, since otherwise we would have to amass and carry forward too much type information. However, we shall see how the compiler can be extended to achieve this. The numbers in brackets refer to comments which follow this example program.

```
|| Part of a compiler, programmed in Miranda
||
|| the abstract syntax in the form of data types
ident   ==   num                                        || (1)
cons    ==   num
var     ::=  Id ident | Sel var ident | Deref var
             | Ind var [expr]
expr    ::=  Exp var | Cons cons | Plus expr expr
             | Minus expr expr | Times expr expr
             | Div expr expr
sts     ==   [st]
st      ::=  Ass var expr | While expr sts
             | If1 expr sts | If2 expr sts sts
decls   ==   [decl]
decl    ::=  Decl ident type
type    ::=  Int | Rec decls | Poin type
             | Arr [(cons,cons)] type
prog    ::=  Prog decls sts

|| The target language

p_prog  ==   [ p_ins ]
p_ins   ==   [ char ]

|| Auxiliary functions and definitions

addr        ==   num            || Relative address
n_i         ==   num            || Addr. of next instr. gen.
n_a         ==   num            || Next rel. addr. to be alloc.
addr_env    ==   ident -> addr

modify           :: (* -> **) -> * -> ** -> (* -> **)
modify r x n =  p
                where p y = n, y=x
                        = r y, otherwise
size             :: type -> num
size Int       = 1
size (Poin t)  = 1
size (Rec d)   = foldr (+) 0 (map size
                          [ t | (Decl x t) <- d ])     || (2)

|| Program compilation

code_P (Prog d s) = code_STS s 0 rho'
                where (rho',c) = elab_decs d undef 5   || (3)
```

```
|| Processing of declaration sequences
elab_decs :: decls -> addr_env -> n_a -> (addr_env, n_a)
elab_decs [ ] rho n_a = (rho,n_a)
elab_decs (d:ds) rho n_a
          = elab_decs ds new_rho new_n_a
              where (new_rho, new_n_a) = elab_dec d rho n_a
elab_dec (Decl x t) rho n_a
          = (modify rho x n_a , n_a+(size t))

|| Compilation of statements
code_STS :: [st] -> n_i -> addr_env -> (p_prog , n_i)

code_STS [ ] n rho = ([ ],n)
code_STS (s:rest) n rho = (cs ++ cr, nr)
              where (cs,ns) = code_ST s n rho
                    (cr,nr) = code_STS rest ns rho

code_ST :: st -> n_i -> addr_env -> (p_prog , n_i)        || (4)

code_ST (Ass (Id x) ((Exp (Id x)) $Plus (Cons c))) n rho
          = (["ldo i", show (rho x),
             "inc i", show c,
             "sro i", show (rho x)], n+3)                 || (5)

code_ST (Ass x e) n rho = ( cv ++ ce ++ ["sto i"] , ne+1)
          where (cv,nv) = code_V x n rho
                (ce,ne) = code_E e nv rho                 || (6)

code_ST (While e b) n rho
          = (ce   ++   ["fjp",show  (n2+1)]   ++   cb   ++
                ["ujp",show n],n2+1)
                  where (ce,n1) = code_E e n rho
                        (cb,n2) = code_STS b (n1+1) rho

code_ST (If2 e s1 s2) n rho
          = (ce ++ ["fjp", show (n1+1)] ++ cs1 ++
             ["ujp", show n2] ++ cs2 , n2)
                where (ce,ne) = code_E e n rho
                      (cs1,n1) = code_STS s1 (ne+1) rho
                      (cs2,n2) = code_STS s2 (n1+1) rho

|| Compilation of expressions
code_E  :: expr -> n_i -> addr_env -> (p_prog , n_i)

code_E (e1 $Plus e2) n rho = (ce1 ++ ce2 ++ ["add i"] , n2+1)
          where (ce1,n1) = code_E e1 n rho
                (ce2,n2) = code_E e2 n1 rho

code_E (Exp x) n rho = (cv ++ ["ind i"] , nv+1)
          where (cv,nv) = code_V x n rho

code_V  :: var -> n_i -> addr_env -> (p_prog , n_i)

code_V (Id x) n rho = ( ["ldc a", show (rho x)], n+1)
code_V (Deref x) n rho = (cv ++ ["ind i"] , nv+1)
          where (cv,nv) = code_V x n rho
```

```
|| Example                                            (7)
z = code_P (Prog
              [ Decl 1 Int,  Decl 2 Int]
              [( Ass (Id 1) ((Exp (Id 1)) $Plus (Cons 1)) ),
              ((Id 2) $Ass Exp (Id 1) $Plus
              Exp( Id 2 ) $Plus Exp(Id 2) )])
```

The value of z after the execution of the program is:

```
(["ldo i","5","inc i","1","sro i","5",
"ldc a","6","ldc i","5","ind i","ldc a","6","ind i",
"ldc a","6","ind i","add i","add i","sto i"],13)
```

Here are the comments on the interesting points of the program.

(1) This is the definition of a **type synonym**, in other words, a new name for an existing type or a type that can be defined with type constructors. We shall use a number of synonyms for the type *num*, for example n_i for the address of the next instruction to be generated, n_a for the next relative address to be occupied. The introduction of new type names increases the legibility and clarity of programs, since it makes it easier to see what a function is used for.

(2) This powerful expression contains the two higher-order functions *map* and *foldr* which we met above. Here, the construction $[t|(Declxt) \leftarrow d]$ is an example of a so-called ZF (Zermelo–Fraenkel) list abstraction. It forms the list of all t which occur as types in the declaration list d. Here, the pattern $(Decl\ x\ t)$ runs over the list d; every occurrence of the pattern, that is, every occurrence of a term with the structure '*Decl* constructor with two operands o_1 and o_2' leads to the binding of x to o_1 and t to o_2. The term o_2 bound to t is entered in the result list. The whole expression has the following meaning. The ZF abstraction provides the list l of all types occurring in the list of declarations d. *map size l* uses this to form the list of the sizes of these types. *foldr* $(+)$ 0, applied to this, calculates the sum.

(3) This is an example of a *local definition*. Functional programming languages distinguish between top-level and local definitions. The scope of a name introduced in a top-level definition is the whole program; however, local definitions may hide such a name. The scope of a name x, introduced by a local definition E_1 *where* $x = E_2$, is the expression E_1.

(4) This is an example of a function (*code_ST*), defined for different cases. The various cases are distinguished by patterns for the first argument. In the case of the compilation of statements, all the cases that occur in the definition of

the type *st* must be covered by at least one pattern. Otherwise, statements that did not match any pattern could not be compiled and the program would stop with an error message. However, it is possible to specify several 'competing' patterns that simultaneously match at least one statement. Thus, for example, special cases may be handled in special ways. This happens, for example, for points 5 and 6 in the compilation of the assignment statement.

(5)   This case handles assignment statements of the form $x := x + c$ more efficiently than the general case. Out of several matching cases, Miranda always selects the first that occurs in the order in which they are listed.

(6)   This is the general case of assignment statements.

(7)   Here, for legibility, we have used the Miranda infix notation for constructors. *$Plus* is the infix version of the constructor *Plus*. Since such infix constructors bind more strongly than anything except function applications, we can also dispense with brackets.

We complete our discussion of the Miranda program with a few thoughts about the 'open ends' of this compiler. This is only a fragment of a compiler and its limitations, for example in the form of undefined cases for the *code_ST* function, are apparent. Where did we cheat to keep the example simple? The answer is, essentially, everywhere where additional information, which is not available locally, was used. When compiling applied occurrences of names, we have always assumed that these refer to integer variables. Otherwise, we would have had to use type information from the point of declaration. For the same reasons, the addressing of array components was not compiled, since there too, information from the declaration, namely the bounds and the array-component type, would have to have been available.

In principle, it would of course be possible to provide the required information at the points of application. This is done in real compilers using so-called symbol tables (see Chapter 9, 'Semantic Analysis'). We shall briefly indicate how a modified function *rho* could achieve this.

For this, we consider what must be known about a program variable in order that its applied occurrences may be correctly compiled.

- For a variable of simple type it is only necessary to know the type and relative address.

- For a record variable we need to know the names, types and relative addresses of the components and the relative address of the record variables. In the case of records kept in the heap, the latter is not necessary because it is produced dynamically.

- For an array variable we need to know the list of the pairs of bounds, the component type and the relative address.

- For pointer variables, the type 'pointed to' and the relative address must be recorded.

The following data type would be capable of representing this information:

```
decl_info ::= Simpl type addr | Re (Ident -> decl_info) addr
            | Ar [(cons,cons)] addr | Poin type addr
```

Functions of the type Ident → decl_info would transport this information from the declaration to the statement part.

3.2 LaMa, a simple functional programming language

We now introduce a simple functional programming language LaMa, which we use to explain the principles of compiling functional programming languages. Here, as in Chapter 2, we are more interested in an appropriate abstract machine and code generation for this than in other compilation tasks such as type checking. Thus, we assume that a luxury such as polymorphism is present, but that it is supported by a different part of the compiler. Neither shall we deal with function definitions involving cases and patterns.

We shall now describe the language constructs of LaMa. For this, we assume that LaMa possesses certain domains of basic values and operations on these. What these are is of no further importance, except that they should include Boolean values and that values in these domains should fit into one storage location in the abstract machine. LaMa expressions can be constructed inductively from (representations of) basic values and variables using built-in operators with functional abstraction and application. The abstract syntax of LaMa is summarized in Table 3.1.

For each of the domains shown in the table, we give a 'typed' name, which, in what follows, will denote elements of such a set.

The meaning of most LaMa constructs is clear. However, functional abstraction, functional application and simultaneously recursive definitions require explanation.

The construction $\lambda v.e$ defines a unary function with defining expression e. An application of the function $\lambda v.e$ to an expression e' is written as $(\lambda v.e)e'$. Depending on the semantics and the implementation of the language, its effect is to replace all (free) occurrences of the formal parameter v with the expression e' (or its value) or to bind v to e' (or to the value of e').

The LaMa syntax permits nesting of both function definitions and function applications. n-ary functions can be defined using $f == \lambda v_1.\lambda v_2.\cdots.\lambda v_n.e$ and a function may be applied to several arguments using $f\ e_1 \ldots e_m$. For efficiency of writing and execution, it is actually advisable to represent $\lambda v_1.\lambda v_2.\cdots.\lambda v_n.e$ as an n-ary function, writing it as $\lambda v_1 \cdots v_n.e$, and to represent and implement $f\ e_1 \ldots e_m$ as a *single* application.

To ensure that the semantics of the function application are quite clear, two further specifications must be made. The first concerns the mechanism for parameter

Table 3.1   The syntax of LaMa.

Element name	Domain	
b	B	Set of basic values, e.g. Boolean values, integer, character,...
op_{bin}	Op_{bin}	Set of binary operators on basic values, e.g. $+, -, =, \neq,$ **and, or,**...
op_{un}	Op_{un}	Set of unary operators on basic values, e.g. $-,$ **not,**...
v	V	Set of variables
e	E	Set of expressions

$$e = b \mid v \mid (op_{un}e) \mid (e_1 op_{bin} e_2)$$

$\qquad \mid (\textbf{if } e_1 \textbf{ then } e_2 \textbf{ else } e_3)$

$\qquad \mid (e_1 e_2)$ Function application

$\qquad \mid (\lambda v.e)$ Functional abstraction

$\qquad \mid (\textbf{letrec} \quad v_1 == e_1;$ Simultaneously recursive definitions

$\qquad\qquad\qquad\quad v_2 == e_2;$

$\qquad\qquad\qquad\quad \vdots$

$\qquad\qquad\qquad\quad v_n == e_n$

$\qquad \textbf{in } e_0)$

To save brackets, the following precedences are used: function applications have the highest precedence and are bracketed towards the left; arithmetic and logical operators have the usual precedence. λ-abstraction chooses the greatest possible syntactic expression for the body of $\lambda v.e$.

passing, namely what is passed to e_1 for a function application $e_1 e_2$. The second specifies whether static or dynamic binding is used in the interpretation of free variables, in other words, whether a free variable obtains its value from the innermost surrounding definition in the text or from the most recently generated binding.

The parameter-passing mechanism of the programming language determines whether the expression e_2 or its value is passed in an application $e_1 e_2$. Algol 60 and later Pascal have the *call-by-value* mechanism. In addition Algol 60 has the *call-by-name* and Pascal the *call-by-reference* mechanism. The latter loses its meaning in functional programming languages, since these use names and values, but not addresses. Let us discuss the various possibilities. It is a matter of whether in a function application $(\lambda v.e_1)e_2$ the argument e_2 is passed in evaluated or unevaluated form. Thus, we can also characterize the parameter-passing mechanism as an order of evaluation; what is evaluated first, e_2 or e_1, until it uses the value of e_2?

In functional languages, we distinguish the following three cases:

(A) **call-by-value/applicative order evaluation:** e_2 is evaluated and its value passed to e_1.

Advantage: e_2 is only evaluated once; no additional expense other than evaluation.

Disadvantage: e_2 is evaluated, even if e_1 does not use the value of e_2. This is critical if the evaluation of e_2 does not terminate. (The program in Example 3.2 does not terminate in the case of *call-by-value*, since the application *one*(*fac* (-2)) requires the evaluation of *fac* (-2), which does not terminate.)

(B) **call-by-name/normal order evaluation:**

This begins with the evaluation of e_1; the value of e_2 is evaluated whenever it is required. Thus, e_2 is passed unevaluated to all points in e_1 where the corresponding formal parameter occurs.

Advantage: e_2 is only evaluated when its value is actually required. (The program in Example 3.2 terminates, giving the result 3.) In general, *call-by-name* has better termination properties than *call-by-value*.

Disadvantage: e_2 may be evaluated several times, each time to the same value.

(C) **call-by-need/lazy evaluation:** e_2 is only evaluated when its value is required, and then only once. Thus, the first access causes the evaluation of e_2, and all others access the value obtained. *Call-by-need* combines the advantages of *call-by-value* and *call-by-name*.

LaMa uses *call-by-need* for user-defined functions.

In the discussion of the parameter-passing mechanisms, we left the decision between static and dynamic binding temporarily open, although these two specifications are not mutually independent. In **static binding** (static scoping) an applied occurrence of a name always refers to the innermost surrounding construct in the text that defines this name. In **dynamic binding** (dynamic scoping) the last binding dynamically generated for this name specifies the value.

Example 3.1

$$\textbf{letrec}\ x == 2$$
$$f == \lambda y.x + y$$
$$F == \lambda g\ x.g\ 2$$
$$\textbf{in}\ F\ f\ 1$$

For static binding the free variable x in the body of f refers to the definition $x == 2$; correspondingly, the value of $F\ f\ 1$ is 4. For dynamic binding, the binding of x to 1 is generated before the access to the value of x in the body of f (by the call $F\ f\ 1$); thus, the result is now 3. □

One consequence of static binding is the highly praised **referential transparency** of many functional programming languages. This is the property of expressions: for a fixed binding of their free variables, the result of their evaluation is always the same. Thus, we choose static binding for LaMa.

This has a number of consequences as far as the implementation of function applications is concerned. Let us consider the evaluation of the above application $F f 1$ with *call-by-name* or *call-by-need* parameter passing. Static binding requires that all free variables on the right-hand side $\lambda y.x + y$ of f (the variable x, here) obtain their values according to the bindings specified by the textually surrounding construct (letrec, here) whenever this right-hand side is evaluated in evaluating F. These are the bindings for x, f and F, and, in particular, the binding of x to 2. Such lists of bindings are generally called environments. To make the right environment for a free variable of an argument available on every occurrence of this variable, the relevant environment u is passed with the argument e. The pair (e, u) formed in this way is called a **closure**. The environment u in a closure (e, u) is always used to ensure that the free variables of e are correctly interpreted (however, closures must sometimes also be formed for *call-by-value*, namely when functions with free variables are passed as arguments (see Example 3.1)).

A letrec expression **letrec** $v_1 == e_1; \ldots; v_n == e_n$ **in** e_0 enters n new names $v_1, \ldots, v_n$ and their scope $G = e_0 e_1 \ldots e_n$. The sense of this can be explained intuitively as follows. The right-hand side of the equation defining a name is used whenever one of these names is encountered within its scope and its value is required.

LaMa may be simple; however, it is possible to program in it.

Example 3.2

> **letrec** *fac* $== \lambda n.$**if** $n = 0$ **then** 1 **else** $n * fac(n - 1)$;
> *fib* $== \lambda n.$**if** $n = 0$ **or** $n = 1$ **then** 1 **else** $fib(n - 1) + fib(n - 2)$;
> *one* $== \lambda n.1$
> **in** $fib((fac\ 2) + one(fac\ -2))$

$\square$

LaMa exhibits one important feature of functional languages, namely higher-order functions. Functions may occur as the arguments and as the results of functions.

Example 3.3

> **letrec** $F\quad == \lambda x\ y.x\ y$;   Functional argument
> $inc\quad == \lambda x.x + 1$
> **in** $F\ inc\ 5$ Value is 6
>
> **letrec** $comp == \lambda f.\lambda g.\lambda x.f\ (g\ x)$;   Functional argument and result
> $F\quad == \lambda y. \cdots$
> $G\quad == \lambda z. \cdots$
> $h\quad == comp\ F\ G$
> **in** $h(\ldots) + F(\ldots) + G(\ldots)$

$\square$

Every n-ary function can be used as a higher-order function, when it is applied to $m < n$ arguments, it is under-supplied, so to speak. The result of such an application is an $(n - m)$-place function.

In imperative programming languages, declarations of variables, types, and so on and specifications of formal parameters introduce new names. In LaMa names are defined on the left-hand side of letrec equations and in the λ-list $\lambda v_1 \ldots v_n$ of a function definition $\lambda v_1 \ldots v_n.e$. In what follows, we shall refer to the former as *equation defined*, and the latter as λ-*defined*. As far as the semantics of a functional program and thus its compilation are concerned, the defining occurrence to which a free applied occurrence of a (global) variable in an expression relates is important. To this end, we inductively define the set *freevar* of the free variables of an expression. Then, we define those variables of a subexpression that are bound by its syntactic context.

Definition 3.1 (variables occurring freely)

$freevar(b) = \emptyset$ An expression consisting of a basic value contains no free variables.

$freevar(v) = \{v\}$ A variable as an expression contains itself as the only free variable.

$freevar(op_{un}\ e) = freevar(e)$

$freevar(e_1 op_{bin}\ e_2) = freevar(e_1) \cup freevar(e_2)$

$freevar(\textbf{if}\ e_1\ \textbf{then}\ e_2\ \textbf{else}\ e_3) = freevar(e_1) \cup freevar(e_2) \cup freevar(e_3)$

$freevar(e_1 e_2) = freevar(e_1) \cup freevar(e_2)$

$freevar(\lambda v_1 \ldots v_n.e) = freevar(e) - \{v_1, \ldots, v_n\}$

the free variables among the $v_1, \ldots, v_n$ occurring in e are bound.

$freevar(\textbf{letrec}\ v_1 == e_1; \ldots; v_n == e_n\ \textbf{in}\ e_0)$
$$= \bigcup_{i=0}^{n} freevar(e_i) - \{v_1, \ldots, v_n\} \qquad \text{(as above)}$$

If $x \in freevar(e)$, we say that x **occurs freely in** e. $\qquad\qquad\square$

Analogously, we define the set of variables with bound occurrences.

Definition 3.2 (variables with bound occurrences)

$bdvar(b) = \emptyset$

$bdvar(v) = \emptyset$

$bdvar(op_{un}e) = bdvar(e)$

$bdvar(e_1 op_{bin}\ e_2) = bdvar(e_1) \cup bdvar(e_2)$

$bdvar(\textbf{if}\ e_1\ \textbf{then}\ e_2\ \textbf{else}\ e_3) = bdvar(e_1) \cup bdvar(e_2) \cup bdvar(e_3)$

$bdvar(e_1 e_2) = bdvar(e_1) \cup bdvar(e_2)$

$bdvar(\lambda v_1 \ldots v_n.e) = bdvar(e) \cup (\{v_1, \ldots, v_n\} \cap freevar(e))$

$bdvar(\textbf{letrec } v_1 == e_1; \ldots; v_n == e_n \textbf{ in } e_0) = \bigcup_{i=0}^{n} bdvar(e_i) \cup \{v_1, \ldots, v_n\}$

If $x \in bdvar(e)$, we say, that x **has a bound occurrence in** e.   □

Example 3.4

$$e = (\lambda x \; y.(\lambda z.x + z)(y + z)) \, x$$

$$freevar(e) = \{x, z\}$$
$$bdvar(e) = \{x, y, z\}$$ □

Thus, variables may have both free and bound occurrences in an expression. However, an individual occurrence of a variable is always either free or bound.

Definition 3.3 (free, bound occurrence)   The *occurrence* of a variable x is said to be *free*, if this occurrence is not a subterm of a term e in $\lambda \cdots x \cdots .e$ or in **letrec** $v_1 == e_1; \ldots; v_n == e_n$ **in** e_0 with $x = v_j$ and $e = e_i$ $(0 \leq i \leq n, 1 \leq j \leq n)$. Otherwise, the occurrence of x is said to be bound.   □

Example 3.5 (continuation of Example 3.4)   The occurrence of z in $x + z$ is bound, that in $y + z$ is free.   □

Static binding is stipulated in LaMa; in other words, a free occurrence of a variable in a (sub)expression relates to the first surrounding **letrec** definition or λ-abstraction of this variable.

3.3   Introduction to the compilation of LaMa

Later, we shall introduce an abstract machine MaMa, which was designed in such a way that LaMa programs and, more generally, functional programming languages with *call-by-need* semantics and static binding compile well into its machine language. This machine has a stack in which all quantities whose lifetime permits are managed, together with a heap in which all other quantities are stored.

In this section, we shall use a series of examples to motivate the subsequently described compilation of LaMa programs into MaMa programs. We begin with simple examples and progress to increasingly complicated ones.

In what follows, we define the *program expression* as the 'outermost' expression of a LaMa program, in other words, the expression whose evaluation gives the result of the program.

Example 3.6   LaMa program expression $e = 1 + 2$. What do we expect of the instruction sequence representing the compilation of e? When it is executed, it should leave the value of e accessible to MaMa in storage (stack or heap). Since our compiler is not so clever (in the sense of optimization: 'constant propagation'), to compute the value of e at compile time it will generate an addition instruction operating on the stack. Of course, the result could stay on the stack. However, we would like to compile all program expressions in the same way, independently of the nature of the expected result. If this result were a function, it could not be stored on the stack. Thus, the results of LaMa program expressions will always be stored in the heap with a pointer to them at the top of the stack.   □

Example 3.7   **letrec** $x == 1/y;\ y == 0;\ z == x$ **in** $1 + 2$ □

This program expression should be compiled in such a way that the result 3 is again stored in the heap with a pointer to it at the top of the stack. This example includes variables. In functional languages, variables stand for values. Fast access to such values is important as far as the efficiency of an implementation is concerned. In a compiler (rather than an interpreter) implementation, memory locations that can be accessed as directly as possible will be assigned to the variables. In our LaMa implementation, variables introduced by letrec or functional abstraction will be assigned locations in the MaMa stack.

How should the equations for x, y and z be compiled? This should always be done in such a way that the instruction sequences generated do not evaluate the right-hand sides of the equations. On the other hand, the bindings of x, y and z must be available for possible future use. Thus, the instruction sequences generated must construct closures for x, y and z and leave pointers to the addresses of x, y and z there. Since the expression $1 + 2$ can be evaluated without accessing the values of x, y and z, the three closures are never evaluated.

We now introduce two clear improvements. The equation for y does not require a closure, since the right-hand side contains no free variables. In such cases, we do not construct a closure but set a pointer to an object, consisting of the basic value 0 and a tag identifying the object as a base object. The variable z would be associated with a closure, containing the expression x and the environment for x. For access to the value of z this would act as an indirect access. Thus, we can also bind z directly to the closure to which x is bound.

It is already apparent that the context clearly determines how an expression is compiled. The expression $1 + 2$ in the above letrec must be compiled in such a way that the generated code produces its value, while the code for the expression $1/y$ must produce a closure for it.

Example 3.8   **if (if** $1 \neq 2$ **then true else false) then** 1 **else** 2   □

If we again expect the result in the heap, expressions 1 and 2 must be compiled in such a way that their values are stored there. What is the position in the case of the conditional expression (**if** $1 \neq 2$ **then true else false**)? Exactly as in the P machine, the MaMa instruction **jfalse** (to be introduced later) expects the truth value to be tested at the top of the stack. Thus, this conditional expression must be compiled in such a way that, loosely speaking, its code, the instruction sequence generated for it, leaves its value on the stack. Then, of course, the expressions **true** and **false** must themselves be compiled in such a way that at run time their values are stored at the top of the stack.

Example 3.9

> **letrec** $f == \lambda y\ z.\textbf{if } z = 0 \textbf{ then } 1 \textbf{ else } 1/y;$
> $\qquad x == 5$
> **in** $f\ 1\ (x+1)$

$\square$

This example may be used to study two problems: the construction of closures for the arguments of functions and for function-valued expressions. Let us begin with the latter. As could be seen in Example 3.7, the code generated for a letrec equation must form a closure for the right-hand side and store a pointer to it at the address for the left-hand side. We have already met an optimization for equations such as $x == 5$. Now we shall also deal with function definitions separately. When a closure for $\lambda y\ z.\textbf{if } z = 0 \textbf{ then } 1 \textbf{ else } 1/y$ is constructed, the code for the application of f must firstly ensure that f is made 'applicable', by making the closure into a *FUNVAL* object. This *FUNVAL* object only differs from the closure in that it contains space for pointers to arguments. We combine these two steps, the creation of a closure and the conversion into a *FUNVAL* object (still without arguments), and leave them to be performed directly by the code for this equation.

How do we compile the arguments 1 and $x + 1$ of f? LaMa's *call-by-need* semantics specify that arguments must be passed in the form of closures, which must only be evaluated when their value is required. Thus a closure is generated for the argument $x+1$ of f. This consists of an instruction sequence, whose execution gives the value of the argument, and a vector, which contains pointers to the (representation of) the values of the free variables occurring in the argument. This vector contains a pointer to the closure for x. The instruction sequences for the equations for f and x are executed beforehand and result in a *FUNVAL* object for f and a corresponding base object for x and pointers to these heap objects in stack locations assigned to f and x. When the closure for $x + 1$ is constructed, the pointer to the closure for x can be copied from the stack into the binding vector of the closure. In the case of the argument 1 of f, the creation of a closure as described above is unnecessary since it does not contain any free variables.

Example 3.10

> **letrec** $x == 2 + 1;$
> $\qquad f == \lambda a\ b.g\ a + h\ b;$
> $\qquad g == \lambda x.\cdots$
> $\qquad h == \lambda y.\cdots$
> **in** $f\ x\ x$

$\square$

This example shows that an expression in a LaMa program (in the form of a closure or its value) can be transported to any number of points as a function argument, the value of a global variable, and so on. Thus, in the implementation of LaMa, pointers to values and pointers to closures, rather than values and closures, are always passed and stored in bindings and stack frames. Since we copy a pointer to an expression rather than the expression itself (or, more precisely, its closure), only one instance of the expression exists and all occurrences have only one pointer to it. The first occurrence of the expression to be executed forces the evaluation of the closure for all occurrences. Later occurrences can then access the value immediately, without re-evaluation.

Example 3.11

> **letrec** f == **letrec** x == 2;
>   **in** $\lambda y.x + y$
> **in** f 5

□

The example illustrates a crucial difference between imperative and functional languages concerning the lifetime of local variables. In Pascal, all objects created by a procedure incarnation, except those created in the heap by *new*, have the same lifetime as the procedure incarnation and may be destroyed when the latter is exited.

This is no longer the case for LaMa functions. In the above example, in order to apply f to 5, we require the functional value which is constructed by evaluating the innermost letrec. However, this involves the variable x local to this letrec. This innermost letrec has already been evaluated. A memory-efficient, stack-like management would like to 'forget' everything belonging to this letrec, including, in particular, its local variables. This example shows that higher-order functions may extend the lifetime of local variables, which means that local variables must live on in the heap, being packed into a *FUNVAL* object in the above example.

3.3.1 The compilation functions

These examples have shown clearly that the same expression has to be compiled into different instruction sequences, depending on the context. The context is essentially characterized by the nature of the result required from the execution of the instruction sequence. In the examples we met four such contexts, which we denote by the letters P (program), B (basic), V (value) and C (closure).

    P Compilation of a complete program expression. The result is expected in the heap, with a pointer to it on the stack. This is always the outermost context in which the compilation begins.

    B The result must be a basic value and be stored on the stack. This context occurs, for example, for the condition in conditional expressions.

V   The result is expected in the heap with a pointer to it at the top of the stack. This is the 'normal case' for an evaluation except when the resulting basic value needs to be on the stack.

C   The result must be a closure for the expression to be compiled. This always occurs for function arguments and the right-hand sides of recursive equations.

The four contexts correspond to four compilation functions P_code, B_code, V_code and C_code, which generate instruction sequences for the associated context.

3.4   Environments and bindings

LaMa has two types of name definitions: λ-defined, that is, in the name list of a λ-abstraction; and equation-defined, that is, on the left-hand side of an equation in a letrec expression. As in Examples 3.6 to 3.11, defining occurrences of names are always associated with closures: a name on the left-hand side of an equation is associated with the closure for the right-hand side of the equation when the equation is compiled, and a bound name in a λ-abstraction is associated with a closure for the argument for a function application. This is illustrated in Table 3.2.

Applied occurrences of names must be compiled in such a way that they acquire the value of the associated defining occurrence. A correct implementation of the LaMa *call-by-need* semantics results if the closure assigned to the defining occurrence is evaluated and overwritten by the value obtained whenever an applied occurrence of a name is accessed for the first time. From then on, the value is always accessed directly (the MaMa instruction **eval** handles both cases).

As we saw in the previous chapter, it is a standard task of compilers to provide for the communication that takes place at run time between defining and applied occurrences of names by means of a memory allocation and addressing scheme; for example, actual parameters of a function application should be stored so that the translation of applied occurrences of the formal parameters accesses the

Table 3.2   Association of closures with defining occurrences of names. Note the following difference between the two cases: the argument for a λ-defined name arises dynamically; the right-hand side of an equation for an equation-defined name is statically fixed.

	Association with	Time
λ-defined name	Closure for argument	Function application
Equation-defined name	Closure for right-hand side of the equation	Processing of the equation

Table 3.3 Primary and derived static information for functions. In the first two cases, the information determines the addressing in stack frames created for the applications of the function. In the last case, the information permits static relative addressing in a 'binding vector'.

Primary	Derived
Number of arguments	Addresses of the formal parameters relative to the address of the first formal parameter
Set of equation-defined local names visible at each point of the body	Addresses of the equation-defined local names relative to the first equation-defined local name
Set of the global names in the body	Addresses of the global names

correct arguments. The compiler provides for this communication between defining and applied occurrences of variables using environments, which assign names to addresses.

The LaMa → MaMa compiler follows the conventional philosophy, in that it uses the statically available information at compile time to handle the dynamic objects arising at run time more efficiently.

Let us investigate which information in LaMa programs is static and therefore already available to the compiler. For this, we consider a function defined in a LaMa program. Table 3.3 lists the static information readable from the program, the so-called primary static information, and the information that may be derived from this.

Thus, it is clear that for every applied occurrence of a variable in a LaMa program, the compiler knows whether this is local (bound) or global (free) to the letrec or function definition immediately surrounding it, respectively, and which index in a corresponding vector or which relative address is assigned to it. This static information is contained in the corresponding **environment** (see Table 3.4).

Address environments in Pascal compilers assign variable identifiers their addresses and nesting depths. Thus, the environments for LaMa compilers contain, for each variable, its address and information about whether it is free or bound at the point in question.

Table 3.4 Positions and environments.

Name	Domain	Comment
p	$P = \{LOC, GLOB\} \times$ integer	Positions
β	$B = (V \to P)$	Environments

When does the environment change when a LaMa program is compiled? Naturally, when the compilation of a **letrec** expression or a functional abstraction begins. Then the newly introduced local variables must be admitted into the environment. Global variables must be admitted into the current environment when code for constructing closures or *FUNVAL* objects is generated.

Local variables are assigned memory locations and thus also relative addresses in MaMa stack frames. Locations in a so-called binding vector are assigned to the global variables of an expression. Their relative addresses indicate where the pointers to their values will lie in the binding vector at run time.

Care must be taken to distinguish between the two newly introduced concepts of environment and binding. The environment is a compile-time object in which the compiler records positions of variables. This corresponds to the address environment of the previous chapter and the symbol tables in real compilers. At run time, the binding contains (in a sequence specified by a corresponding environment) pointers to the values of the global variables for an expression.

In the following sections we shall describe, step by step, the architecture and the instruction set of the abstract machine MaMa and the compilation scheme for compiling LaMa into MaMa. After reviewing the architecture we shall consider the compilation of expressions as in Section 2.3. Here, except for the case of variables, there will be few differences from the compilation of Pascal into P machine code. Then we shall discuss the concepts of LaMa that necessitate radical changes from the Pascal memory management, namely lazy evaluation and higher-order functions.

3.5   The MaMa architecture

The MaMa memory includes an array *PS* (program store) in which the compiled LaMa program is held in the form of a MaMa program. Each location contains a MaMa instruction. Some MaMa instructions have an operand. The *PC* register (program counter) always contains the address of the current instruction. In the normal mode MaMa repeatedly executes the following three-phase cycle of instructions:

- The current instruction is loaded.
- *PC* is increased by 1.
- The current instruction is interpreted.

Interpretation of the **stop** instruction or an error ends the normal mode. MaMa then stops.

In addition, the memory contains two potentially infinite arrays *ST*, the stack, and *HP*, the heap. Here, we remain rather more abstract than in the P machine; of course, the two must ultimately be implemented in the same memory of a specific machine. Our only requirement of the machine is that it should have a heap memory management, which, on execution of a *new* instruction, reserves a memory area of the appropriate size in the heap and returns a pointer to that area. We also assume that memory that is no longer required is automatically released.

3.5.1 The MaMa stack

The MaMa stack *ST* is very similar to that of the P machine. It grows upwards (ascending addresses). The address of the highest occupied location is always found in the MaMa register *SP* (stack pointer). One of the following objects may be stored in each location on the stack:

- A basic value, for example an integer, a truth value, and so on.
- A stack address.
- A heap address.
- A program-store address.

Just as in the P machine, the occupied part of the stack is subdivided into stack frames. Stack frames are created for the application of functions and the evaluation of closures. The former corresponds to the creation of stack frames for the execution of called procedures in the P machine. The second has no analogue there and follows from the fact that LaMa's *call-by-need* semantics prescribe the delayed evaluation of arguments. We shall discuss this in more detail in the next section. Figure 3.2 shows the structure of the stack frames for the two cases.

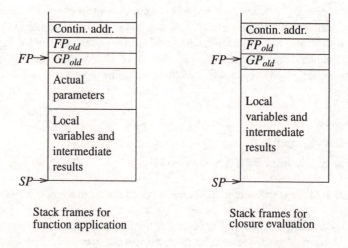

Stack frames for function application

Stack frames for closure evaluation

Figure 3.2 The structure of stack frames.

Except for locations for (pointers to) actual parameters, which are not present in the case of the evaluation of a closure, the stack frames have the same structure. The *FP* (frame pointer) register addresses the highest of the three organizational locations. The first contains the instruction address from which execution should continue when the current activity (application of a function or evaluation of a closure) ends. Above this is the stack address to which the *FP* register should be reset when this frame is released. The last location contains the value of the *GP* register (global pointer) to be restored. As we shall see later, the *GP* register always contains the pointer to the vector of the values of all global variables.

The storage of the register state FP_{old} serves the same purpose and is implemented in the same way as the storage of the pointer to the dynamic predecessor in the Pascal implementation of Chapter 2. The storage of GP_{old} serves the same purpose as the pointer to the static predecessor in Chapter 2. However, the pointer there is the beginning of a chain via which all global variables may be reached. Here, as we shall see, *GP* points to a vector containing the pointers to the values of the free (global) variables of a function or expression. These pointers are, as it were, 'copied up'.

Here we include a warning and a hint of what is to come. By analogy with Pascal compilation, an attempt might have been made to propose a similarly simple assignment of relative addresses for all objects stored in a stack frame. A complication stands in the way of this in the case of the function application, namely the previously mentioned possibility of applying n-place functions to fewer or more than n arguments. Since the relative addresses are assigned when the function definition is compiled, the function application is generally compiled without a knowledge of the number of places (higher-order functions), and the starting section of the stack frame in which the arguments are found cannot have a statically known length. However, we shall see that, rather cleverly, our LaMa → MaMa compiler is able to assign relative addresses to local variables.

The stack-frame structure suggests a fixed sequence of instructions for creating and releasing stack frames (see Figure 3.3).

Variants of this can be found in the MaMa **mark** and **eval** or **return** instructions.

$$ST[SP+1] := \text{Continuation address}; \quad PC := ST[FP-2];$$
$$ST[SP+2] := FP; \quad\quad\quad\quad\quad\quad\quad GP := ST[FP];$$
$$ST[SP+3] := GP; \quad\quad\quad\quad\quad\quad\quad ST[FP-2] := ST[SP];$$
$$SP := SP+3; \quad\quad\quad\quad\quad\quad\quad\quad SP := FP-2;$$
$$FP := SP; \quad\quad\quad\quad\quad\quad\quad\quad\quad FP := ST[FP-1];$$

(a)   (b)

Figure 3.3 Instruction sequences for creating and releasing stack frames. (a) Creation of a stack frame. (b) Release of a stack frame (new highest stack location contains a pointer to the result).

3.5.2 The MaMa heap

The MaMa heap (as in the Pascal implementation) stores objects whose lifetime is incompatible with a stack-like management. The objects in the heap have a tag which indicates their nature. The heap objects may be viewed as variants of a Pascal record type. The four tags *BASIC, FUNVAL, CLOSURE* and *VECTOR* characterize the following objects:

- *BASIC*   A location *b* for a basic value.

- *FUNVAL*   The object represents a functional result. It is a triplet (*cf, fap, fgp*) consisting of a pointer *cf* to the program memory (where the compilation of the function body is), a pointer *fap* to a vector of existing arguments for the function and a pointer *fgp* to a vector of values for the global variables of the function. These two vectors are also stored in the heap. *FUNVAL* objects are constructed when the translation of a function definition is processed. A function definition is an expression and therefore has a value, in our case a *FUNVAL* object. Here, the vector of the arguments is of course empty, since there are as yet no arguments. *FUNVAL* objects with non-empty argument vectors arise when functions are under-supplied in function applications. As previously stated, the result of an under-supplied application is again a function. It is represented by a *FUNVAL* object, namely that obtained when the arguments are packed into the *FUNVAL* object of the function applied.

- *CLOSURE*   The object is a closure and represents a suspended computation. Because of the *call-by-need* parameter passing the code for arguments is packed into a closure together with the values for the global variables and only executed when the value is required. The object contains two components, *cp*, a pointer to the code for the computation, and *gp*, a pointer to a vector of pointers to the values for the global variables of the computation. As we shall see in the next section, all defining occurrences of variables are assigned closures.

- *VECTOR*   The object is a vector of pointers to heap objects. Vectors store links to the existing arguments of a function and to values of global variables in *FUNVAL* and *CLOSURE* objects.

The selector '.*tag*' may be used to address the tag of a heap object, as the component names are used to address other components. A function *size* for *VECTOR* objects gives the size of the vector.

Some MaMa instructions sample the tag of heap objects and interpret the contents depending on the tag, or report errors when they cannot be applied to an object of the given type. Other instructions construct such objects from the components of the highest stack locations and leave a pointer to the newly created heap object at the top of the stack. These instructions are listed in Table 3.5.

Table 3.5   Instructions for creating heap objects.

Instruction	Meaning	Comments
mkbasic	$ST\,[SP] := \text{new}(BASIC{:}\ ST\,[SP])$	create basic heap object
mkfunval	$ST\,[SP-2] := \text{new}(FUNVAL{:}\ ST\,[SP],$ $ST\,[SP-1], ST\,[SP-2]);$ $SP := SP - 2$	create functional heap object
mkclos	$ST\,[SP-1] :=$ $\text{new}(CLOSURE{:}\ ST\,[SP], ST\,[SP-1]);$ $SP := SP - 1$	create closure
mkvec n	$ST\,[SP-n+1] :=$ $\text{new}(VECTOR{:}\ ST\,[SP-n+1],$ $ST\,[SP-n+2], \ldots, ST\,[SP]);$ $SP := SP - n + 1$	create vector with n components
alloc	$SP := SP + 1;$ $ST\,[SP] := \text{new}(CLOSURE{:}\ \text{NIL, NIL})$	create empty closure locations

3.6   Stack management and addressing

In the P-machine implementation of Pascal a stack frame for organizational information, formal parameters and local variables was created for each procedure call. The lifetime of these quantities matched the lifetime of the procedure, so that when the procedure was exited the stack frame created could then be released. The storage requirement for these quantities was static, that is, known at compile time; thus, relative addresses relative to the start of the stack frame could be assigned for the individual quantities.

The example of Pascal compilation clearly shows the following. When compiling a procedure declaration the compiler assigns relative addresses relative to the start of the stack frame for all statically addressable local quantities, including, in particular, the formal parameters of the procedure. When a call to the procedure is compiled it uses this address assignment and generates instruction sequences that store the addresses or values of the actual parameters at these addresses. The compiler has perfect information at both points; at a procedure declaration with n parameters, it is clear that every call to the procedure with fewer or more parameters will be rejected as incorrect. At the call, the procedure and the number of formal parameters involved are clear (from the semantic analysis).

This is completely different in LaMa! The compilation of a function definition must take into account the fact that applications may be under- or over-supplied but still remain legal. When compiling an application $e\ e_1 \ldots e_m$ the compiler does not always know the number of arguments of the function to be applied; for example, e may be a formal parameter of a surrounding (higher-order) function.

3.6.1 Addressing of names in MaMa

What form can an assignment of static relative addresses to formal parameters and local variables take under these circumstances? Let us consider the possible ways in which an application $e\ e_1 \ldots e_m$ may be compiled. It is clear that the instruction sequence generated for the application must generate m closures and one *FUNVAL* object. Pointers to these must be contained in the stack frame appropriate to the particular application. These pointers may be arranged in either of two sensible ways in the stack frame (see Figure 3.4).

Let us discuss these two alternatives. Storage of the arguments according to Figure 3.4(a) permits addressing of the arguments and the formal parameters corresponding to them relative to the contents of *FP*, as we are used to in Pascal. However, since the value of m is not known when compiling the function definition, we cannot address the local variables of the function, which should be stored in the stack frame next to the formal parameters, relative to *FP*. In addition, an expensive reorganization of the stack frame would be necessary if an over-supplied n-place function had consumed its n arguments $e_1 \ldots e_n$, so that the functional result would encounter the correct situation on the stack.

Storage of the arguments according to Figure 3.4(b) does not permit addressing of the formal parameters relative to the contents of *FP*. However, the formal parameters and the local variables can be addressed relative to the contents of *SP*. This may be surprising at first sight since, unlike *FP*, whose value is constant

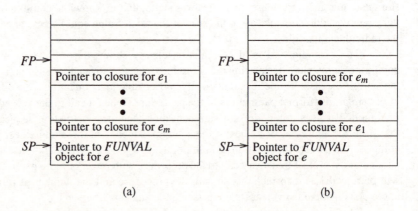

(a)   (b)

Figure 3.4 Possible arrangement of arguments in stack frames.

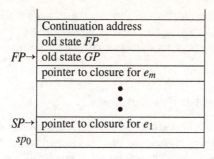

| Continuation address |
| old state *FP* |
| old state *GP* |
| pointer to closure for e_m |
| |
| pointer to closure for e_1 |

Figure 3.5   Stack situation prior to processing a function body.

during the processing of a function application, *SP* changes throughout with the creation of new local variables and intermediate results. If it is desired to address local variables with static addresses relative to *SP*, these changes in *SP*, which occur at run time, must be foreseen at compile time and the resulting information used accordingly.

We therefore select memory allocation according to Figure 3.4(b) and choose a certain dynamic address to act as a base for relative addressing of formal parameters and local variables. For our purposes, the address (let us call it sp_0) of the location above the pointer to the closure for e_1 is appropriate. Consequently, for the formal parameters $v_1, \ldots, v_n$ of a function $\lambda\, v_1 \ldots v_n.e$ we must assign the relative addresses $-1, -2, \ldots, -n$ and address local variables in increasing order from 0 upwards.

The following situation occurs at the beginning of the processing of a function body (produced by the **apply** instruction to be described later). The *PC* register is set to the start of the translation of the body; the pointer *GP* is set to the correct global binding. The stack contains three organizational locations containing (in this order) the continuation address and the saved frame and binding pointers, a pointer to the closure for $e_m, \ldots$, and a pointer to the closure for e_1. *SP* points to this last link. The address above the closure for e_1 is sp_0, see Figure 3.5.

If the body is processed, other local variables, for which room in the stack must be created, may be introduced using letrec expressions. Thus, *SP* increases correspondingly. However, the distance between the current value of *SP* and the value of sp_0 is static for every point in the function body, since the numbers of new local variables introduced and intermediate results arising are known. This difference, which is known at compile time, is held in a parameter *sl* to the compilation functions. In other words, if we consider a point *a* in the body of the function to be compiled and the value sl_a of *sl* at compile time together with the value sp_a of *SP* before the execution of the instruction sequence generated, the following addressing assertion holds

$$sp_a = sp_0 + sl_a - 1 \qquad\qquad\text{(AA)}$$

Thus, we can generate instructions that use the compile-time quantity sl_a and the runtime quantity sp_a to compute the runtime value sp_0. The formal parameters will be addressed with negative addresses and the local variables with non-negative addresses relative to sp_0.

3.6.2 Construction of bindings

As discussed earlier, for every function definition and indeed every other expression, the set of free variables is statically known. Thus, this set can be ordered in an arbitrary fixed way, assigning every free variable its position in this list as its relative address.

The relative addresses assigned in this way are used at run time to access the values of these free (global) variables. Pointers to these values are stored in a vector which is contained in the heap as part of a *FUNVAL* or *CLOSURE* object or can be addressed via the binding pointer *GP*. The latter is the case when a closure is evaluated or a function is applied. It is still unclear how the pointers to the values of the global variables are entered in such a vector. It is clear that there exist an empty set of free variables and a corresponding empty vector of values, when the whole program expression is compiled and the compiled program is started (see the definition of the *P_code* function).

Let us now suppose that either a functional object or a closure is to be constructed. In both cases, the vector of pointers to the values of all global variables must be packed in with it. Because of the static binding prescribed for LaMa, the formal parameters and local and global variables of the surrounding function definition just processed should be considered as global variables of the function definition or the expression. In the previous sections, we showed that formal parameters and local variables can be correctly addressed directly at run time. If we assume, inductively, that we have access to the current global variables via *GP* then we may copy all the pointers to the values of all new global variables to the stack, form a vector and include it as part of a heap object or point to it using *GP*.

3.7 Instruction set and compilation

After our analysis of the problem and intuitive introduction, there now follows the step-by-step description of the compilation and all the necessary MaMa instructions. The compilation functions are assigned to the contexts introduced above; thus, there are four functions *P_code, B_code, V_code* and *C_code*, corresponding to the nature of the result expected from the execution of the code generated. The *code* functions have three parameters: the expression to be compiled e, the environment for the valid variables β and a stack level sl. As previously described, sl defines the difference between the state of the *SP* register before the code to be generated is executed and the address sp_0, relative to which formal parameters and local variables are addressed.

Table 3.6   The *stop* instruction.

Instruction	Meaning
stop	Stop the machine

3.7.1   Program expressions

The compilation of a LaMa program expression e always begins with an application of the P_code function.

$$P\_code\ e = V\_code\ e\ [\ ]\ 0;$$
$$\mathbf{stop}$$

Since e cannot contain any free variables, the environment is empty; since the stack is not filled, the stack level sl is 0. The **stop** instruction stops the machine.

3.7.2   Simple expressions

We shall now compile 'simple expressions', that is, those constructed solely from basic values, operators and **if**s. In what follows, we shall compile these in a context that requires a basic value as a result of the execution of the code generated. The compilation function B_code is appropriate for this.

The instructions generated by B_code are listed in Table 3.7. Note that for each LaMa unary operator op_{un} and binary operator op_{bin} we have a corresponding machine instruction $\mathbf{op}_{un}$ or $\mathbf{op}_{bin}$ in MaMa.

$B\_code\ b\ \beta\ sl = \mathbf{ldb}\ b$
$B\_code\ (e_1 op_{bin} e_2)\ \beta\ sl =$
    $B\_code\ e_1\ \beta\ sl;$
    $B\_code\ e_2\ \beta\ sl+1;$
    $\mathbf{op}_{bin}$
$B\_code\ (op_{un}\ e)\ \beta\ sl = B\_code\ e\ \beta\ sl;\ \mathbf{op}_{un}$
$B\_code\ (\mathbf{if}\ e_1\ \mathbf{then}\ e_2\ \mathbf{else}\ e_3)\ \beta\ sl =$
    $B\_code\ e_1\ \beta\ sl;$
    $\mathbf{false}\ l_1;$
    $B\_code\ e_2\ \beta\ sl;$
    $\mathbf{ujmp}\ l_2;$
$l_1:\ \ B\_code\ e_3\ \beta\ sl;$
$l_2:$
$B\_code\ e\ \beta\ sl = V\_code\ e\ \beta\ sl;\ \mathbf{getbasic}$

In the scheme for B_code we use local label names as in Chapter 2. These are defined exactly once before an instruction or after the last instruction of the scheme. Their value is the address of the location in the program store PS in which the instruction they label is stored.

Table 3.7 Instructions for basic values, labels and branches.

Instruction	Meaning	Remarks
ldb b	$SP := SP + 1;$ $ST[SP] := b$	loads basic value
getbasic	**if** $HP[ST[SP]].tag \neq BASIC$ **then** *error* **fi**; $ST[SP] := HP[ST[SP]].b$	loads basic value from the heap to the stack
op$_{bin}$	$ST[SP-1] := ST[SP-1]op_{bin}ST[SP];$ $SP := SP - 1$	binary operation
op$_{un}$	$ST[SP] := op_{un} ST[SP];$	unary operation
false l	**if** $ST[SP] = false$ **then** $PC := l$ **fi**; $SP := SP - 1$	conditional branch
ujmp l	$PC := l$	unconditional branch
ldl l	$SP := SP + 1;$ $ST[SP] := l$	push label onto stack

The corresponding cases for the V_code function have a completely analogous form, except that after the execution of the instruction sequence generated the resulting basic value is in the heap with a pointer to it at the top of the stack.

$V\_code\ b\ \beta\ sl = B\_code\ b\ \beta\ sl;$ **mkbasic**
$V\_code\ (e_1 op_{bin} e_2)\ \beta\ sl = B\_code\ (e_1\ op_{bin}\ e_2)\ \beta\ sl;$ **mkbasic**
$V\_code\ (op_{un}\ e)\ \beta\ sl = B\_code\ (op_{un}\ e)\ \beta\ sl;$ **mkbasic**
$V\_code\ (\textbf{if}\ e_1\ \textbf{then}\ e_2\ \textbf{else}\ e_3)\ \beta\ sl =$
    $B\_code\ e_1\ \beta\ sl;$
    false l_1;
    $V\_code\ e_2\ \beta\ sl;$
    ujmp l_2;
l_1: $V\_code\ e_3\ \beta\ sl;$
l_2:

In the last case the meaning of the context for the code generated is clearly recognizable. The conditional expression **if** e_1 **then** e_2 **else** e_3 is compiled in the V context; that is, the execution of the code generated must return its result in the heap. Thus, the two expressions e_2 and e_3, from one of which this result is computed, are also compiled in the V context. However, the condition e_1 must be compiled in the B context, since the **j** = **false** instruction expects its result at the top of the stack.

3.7.3 Applied occurrences of variables

Applied occurrences must be compiled into an access to the value when the context requires this (V), and into an access to a closure when the context is C. In the former case, the value must first be computed from a closure, if this has not already been done.

$$V\_code \ v \ \beta \ sl = getvar \ v \ \beta \ sl;$$
$$\textbf{eval}$$
$$C\_code \ v \ \beta \ sl = getvar \ v \ \beta \ sl$$

We must consider the code-generating function $getvar$ in more detail:

$$getvar \ v \ \beta \ sl = \textbf{let} \ (p, i) = \beta(v)$$
$$\textbf{in if} \ p = LOC \quad \textbf{then pushloc} \ sl - i$$
$$\textbf{else} \quad \textbf{pushglob} \ i$$
$$\textbf{fi}$$

It generates a *pushloc* instruction for formal parameters and local variables, in other words, for quantities that are stored in the current stack frame, and a *pushglob* instruction for global variables, which are addressed by the binding pointer to the heap. The definitions of the instructions are given in Table 3.8.

Let us consider a call $getvar \ v \ \beta \ sl_a$ for a variable v, which is a formal parameter or local variable in the context of the function application in question. The environment β will have bound it to a pair (LOC, i), where i may be a non-negative number (for local variables) or a negative number (for formal parameters). Thus, $getvar$ generates a **pushloc** $sl_a - i$.

We assume the addressing assertion (AA) holds for the parameter sl_a and the state sp_a of the SP before the execution of the **pushloc** instruction, that is: $sp_a = sp_0 + sl_a - 1$. The effect of executing **pushloc** $sl_a - i$ is:

$$ST \ [sp] := \ ST \ [sp - (sl_a - i)] \text{ where } sp \ = \ sp_a + 1$$

for SP is increased by 1 before the memory access. But we also have $sp - (sl_a - i) = sp_a + 1 - sl_a + i = (sp_0 + sl_a - 1) + 1 - sl_a + i = sp_0 + i$. Thus, a formal parameter

Table 3.8 Stacking of variable values.

Instruction	Meaning	Comments
pushloc j	$SP := SP + 1$; $ST \ [SP] := ST \ [SP - j]$	push pointer to value of formal parameter or local variable
pushglob j	$SP := SP + 1$; $ST \ [SP] := HP \ [GP].v[j]$	push pointer to value of global variable

is correctly loaded with the (negative) relative address i and a local variable with the non-negative relative address i.

As far as access to global variables is concerned, we assume that (at compile time) the environment β defines an index for all global variables in a vector, and that (at run time) the *GP* register points to a vector filled with the pointers to the global variables, according to this allocation. The *pushglob* instruction then has the effect of loading the pointer from the vector onto the stack.

3.7.4 Function definitions

Function definitions may be compiled in two contexts, namely the value context V and the closure context C. As already described in the introduction to compilation, the generated code should construct closures. However, for efficiency, subsequent applications of the functions are prepared in advance, in that a *FUNVAL* object is created immediately. We recall the contents of such an object: a program-store address at which the code begins, a pointer to a vector (initially empty) for (pointers to) arguments, and a pointer to a binding vector, that is, a vector with pointers to the values of the global variables. These pointers must now be set at the point of definition, using the same address assignment as that used for the global variables in the compilation of the function body. These, together with the relative addresses of the formal parameters, are incorporated into the environment with which the compilation of the body begins:

$$V\_code \ (\lambda v_1 \ldots v_n.e) \ \beta \ sl = C\_code \ (\lambda v_1 \ldots v_n.e) \ \beta \ sl$$

$$C\_code \ (\lambda v_1 \ldots v_n.e) \ \beta \ sl =$$

	pushfree fr β *sl*;	copies the pointers to the values	
	mkvec	g;	of the global variables;
	mkvec	0;	empty argument vector
	ldl	l_1;	address of the function code
	mkfunval;		
	ujmp	l_2;	
l_1 :	**targ**	n;	test for satisfactory arguments
	$V\_code \ e \ ([v_i \mapsto (LOC, -i)]_{i=1}^{n} \ [v_j' \mapsto (GLOB, j)]_{j=1}^{g}) \ 0$		
	return	n	
l_2 :			

where $fr = [v_1', \ldots, v_g'] = list(freevar(\lambda v_1 \ldots v_n.e))$

$$pushfree \ [v_1', \ldots, v_g'] \ \beta \ sl = getvar \ v_1' \ \beta \ sl;$$
$$getvar \ v_2' \ \beta \ (sl+1);$$
$$\vdots$$
$$getvar \ v_g' \ \beta \ (sl+g-1)$$

A number of explanations of the above are required. It should be clear that the instruction sequence generated by the *C_code* function is responsible for the construction of a *FUNVAL* object. At the same time, however, the *C_code* function also has to compile the function definition. This second task occurs as the l_1 : ... **return** n part of the overall scheme. The remainder provides for the generation of the *FUNVAL* object, and involves the incorporation of the start address of the translation of the function (value of l_1) into the *FUNVAL* object. The **ujmp** instruction is used to jump over the translation of the function.

The treatment of the global variables of the function should be noted. They are statically known, and the set of these variables is constructed using the function *freevar*. The application of *list* creates from this set a list of its elements without repeats. The ordering of the global variables also determines the ordering of (the pointers to) their values in bindings for this function. The call *pushfree fr β sl* generates the instruction sequence to create this vector. *pushfree* $[v_1, \ldots, v_g]$ *β sl* uses *getvar* to load the pointers to the variable values $v_1, \ldots, v_g$ consecutively onto the stack. *getvar* uses the information from the environment *β* for addressing. The static expression $sl - i$ is used to address local variables. (Negative) relative addresses in stack frames are assigned according to the addressing scheme described above. The compilation of the body *e* begins with the value 0 for the parameter *sl*. Before the code for the body is executed, the situation in the stack is as shown in Figure 3.5. Thus, the addressing assertion (AA) holds before the processing of the body begins, since we have

$$sp_a = sp_0 + 0 - 1$$

Since every *getvar* generates an instruction whose execution increases *SP* by 1, increasing the *getvar sl* parameter by 1 simulates this increase correctly at compile time and ensures that the addressing assertion (AA) holds and that local variables and formal parameters are correctly addressed.

3.7.5   Function applications

The instruction sequence generated for a function application must ensure that when the function is entered the situation in the stack holds, which is assumed during the compilation of the function definition. This was illustrated in Figure 3.5 (stack situation before entry).

$$
\begin{aligned}
V\_code\ (ee_1 \ldots e_m)\ \beta\ sl = \ &\mathbf{mark}\ l; \\
e \neq e'e'' \qquad\qquad\quad &C\_code\ e_m\ \beta\ (sl+3); \\
&\qquad\vdots \\
&C\_code\ e_1\ \beta\ (sl+m+2); \\
&V\_code\ e\ \beta\ (sl+m+3); \\
&\mathbf{apply}; \\
l :\qquad\qquad\quad &
\end{aligned}
$$

mark l creates a new stack frame for this application; the continuation address l and the current values of *FP* and *GP* are saved. Then the instruction

Table 3.9 Creation of a stack frame with given continuation address.

Instruction	Meaning	Comments
mark l	$ST\,[SP+1] := l;$	create stack frame
	$ST\,[SP+2] := FP;$	reserve organizational
	$ST\,[SP+3] := GP;$	locations
	$SP := SP+3;$	
	$FP := SP$	

sequence generated creates the closures for the arguments in the heap and the pointers to these on the stack. Note that execution of **mark** increases SP by 3. If the addressing assertion (AA) holds at the start of compilation and at execution, respectively, it also holds before the compilation of e_m and the execution of the corresponding code. Since each link to a closure requires one memory location, increasing the parameter sl by 1 in each case ensures that the addressing assertion (AA) holds throughout the scheme. Table 3.9 contains the definition of the **mark** instruction. The effect of **mark** l on the stack is illustrated in Figure 3.6.

Table 3.10 contains the definition of the **apply** instruction. It jumps to the translation of the function body after the arguments have been loaded from the *FUNVAL* object onto the stack and the binding pointer has been set. After its execution, the situation is as shown in Figure 3.7.

As far as the overall task of implementing functions is concerned, we have now dealt with the following subtasks: the generation of *FUNVAL* objects from function definitions, and within this the compilation of the body with the correct environment; the creation of a stack frame for the function application using the **mark** instruction and the subsequent storage of pointers to closures for the arguments; and, finally, the activation of the code for the function after the establishment of the correct binding for a *FUNVAL* object using the **apply** instruction.

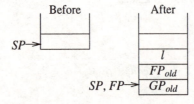

Figure 3.6 The **mark** instruction creates a stack frame and reserves the organizational locations.

Table 3.10　Application of a function.

Instruction	Meaning	Comments
apply	**if** $HP\,[ST\,[SP]].tag \neq$ FUNVAL **then** *error* **fi**;	apply function
	let (FUNVAL: *cf, fap, fgp*) $= HP\,[ST\,[SP]]$	
	in $PC := cf$;	
	$GP := fgp$;	pointer to
	$SP := SP - 1$;	binding
	for $i := 1$ **to** $size(HP\,[fap].v)$ **do**	load arguments
	$SP := SP + 1$;	from *FUNVAL*
	$ST\,[SP] := HP\,[fap].v[i]$	object onto
	od	the stack
	tel	

There still remains the 'framework' surrounding the compilation of the function body, namely the **targ** and **return** instructions. **targ**, which is defined in Table 3.11 and illustrated in Figure 3.8, carries out the necessary dynamic test for under-supply of the function. In the case of under-supply it packs the existing arguments into a *FUNVAL* object and releases the stack frame.

The **return** instruction is responsible for the treatment of the end of function appplications and closure evaluations. Its parameter defines the number of arguments consumed by the completed processing. It deals with two cases. In the first case, the stack frame contains as many pointers to arguments as were required by the applied function; the result can then be copied to the appropriate place and the current stack

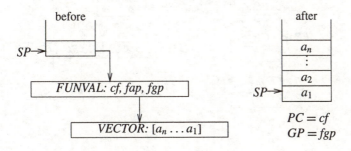

Figure 3.7　The **apply** instruction begins the application of a function; it loads the pointers to the existing arguments onto the stack, loads the pointer to the binding vector and jumps to the code for the function.

Table 3.11   Test the number of arguments; in case of under-supply, form a *FUNVAL* object and release the stack frame.

Instruction	Meaning
targ n	**if** $SP - FP < n$
	then % under-supply
	$h := ST\,[FP - 2]$;
	$ST\,[FP - 2] := \text{new}(FUNVAL: PC - 1,$
	$\qquad \text{new}(VECTOR: [ST\,[FP + 1], ST\,[FP + 2], \dots, ST\,[SP]]), GP)$;
	$GP := ST\,[FP]$;
	$SP := FP - 2$;
	$FP := ST\,[FP - 1]$;
	$PC := h$
	fi

frame released. In the second case, a functional result is present for which pointers to further arguments are stored in the stack frame. This may occur if a function is over-supplied. The **return** instruction is defined in Table 3.12, and its effect illustrated in Figure 3.9.

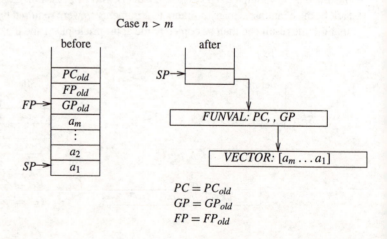

Figure 3.8   The instruction **targ** detects under-supply and creates a *FUNVAL* object with the existing arguments.

Table 3.12   Treatment of the end of function applications and closure evaluations.

Instruction	Meaning	Comments
return n	**if** $SP = FP + 1 + n$	
	then	finished
	$PC := ST[FP - 2]$;	continuation
	$GP := ST[FP]$;	address
	$ST[FP - 2] := ST[SP]$;	result
	$SP := FP - 2$;	
	$FP := ST[FP - 1]$	
	else	more arguments
	if $HP[ST[SP]].tag \neq FUNVAL$ **then** $error$ **fi**;	present, function
	let $(FUNVAL: cf, fap, fgp) = HP[ST[SP]]$	result applied
	in $PC := cf$;	to remaining
	$GP := fgp$;	arguments;
	$SP := SP - n - 1$;	n arguments
	for $i := 1$ **to** $size(HP[fap].v)$ **do**	consumed
	$SP := SP + 1$;	
	$ST[SP] := HP[fap].v[i]$	
	od	
	tel	

3.7.6   Construction and evaluation of closures

The *C_code* function compiles expressions so that the execution of the generated code results in the creation of a closure for the given expression. The closure, a *CLOSURE* object in the heap, consists of a pointer to the translation of the expression and a pointer vector for the values of global variables. Since these values are present, a closure is an object that requires nothing else of its surroundings. In analogy with the treatment of functions, we can begin the compilation of an expression in the C context with a new environment, which knows only the global variables, and the value 0 for the parameter *sl*. The evaluation of a closure, like the function application, requires the creation of a stack frame in which the local variables can be addressed according to the known scheme.

Like the compilation of function definitions, the scheme involves an outer block (for the creation of the closure) and an inner block (for the compilation of the expression).

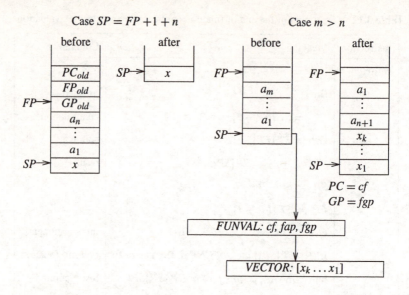

Figure 3.9 The two cases for the **return** instruction. Left: the case where the function had the right number of arguments; the stack frame is released. Right: the case of an over-supplied function with a functional result.

$$
\begin{array}{lll}
C\_code\ e\ \beta\ sl = & pushfree\ fr\ \beta\ sl; & \text{stacks the values of the global variables} \\
e \neq v & \textbf{mkvec}\quad g; & \text{puts them in a vector} \\
& \textbf{ldl}\qquad l_1; \\
& \textbf{mkclos}; \\
& \textbf{ujmp}\quad l_2; \\
l_1 : & V\_code\ e\ [v_i \mapsto (GLOB,i)]_{i=1}^{g}\ 0 \\
& \textbf{update} \\
l_2 :
\end{array}
$$

where $fr = [v_1, \ldots, v_g] = list(freevar(e))$.

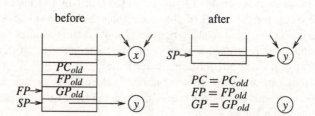

Figure 3.10 The effect of the **update** instruction on the stack.

Table 3.13   The **update** instruction.

Instruction	Meaning	Comments
update	$HP[ST[SP-4]] := HP[ST[SP]];$ $PC := ST[FP-2];$ $GP := ST[FP];$ $SP := FP-3;$ $FP := ST[FP-1]$	Communicate result (overwrite!)

By way of an easy optimization, basic expressions may be handled more efficiently. The explicit construction of a closure is unnecessary in this case.

$$C\_code\ b\ \beta\ sl = V\_code\ b\ \beta\ sl$$

The code generated for e is then executed when the value of the generated closure is required. This is provided for by the **eval** instruction which we now describe. If it finds a pointer to a closure at the top of the stack it creates a stack frame to evaluate it and evaluates it there. As prescribed by context V, the evaluation leaves the result in the heap with a pointer to it above the closure pointer in the stack. **update** (Figure 3.10 and Table 3.13) then overwrites the closure object with the result. This represents the *call-by-need* semantics of LaMa. The first access to an element finds a closure, which it evaluates and overwrites with the result.

Figure 3.11 illustrates the effect of **eval** on the stack. It is defined in Table 3.14.

Table 3.14   Creation of stack frames by **eval** during the evaluation of closures.

Instruction	Meaning	Comments
eval	**if** $HP[ST[SP]].tag = CLOSURE$ **then** $\quad ST[SP+1] := PC;$ $\quad ST[SP+2] := FP;$ $\quad ST[SP+3] := GP;$ $\quad GP := HP[ST[SP]].gp;$ $\quad PC := HP[ST[SP]].cp;$ $\quad SP := SP+3;$ $\quad FP := SP$ **fi**	evaluate closure pointer to the binding start of the compilation

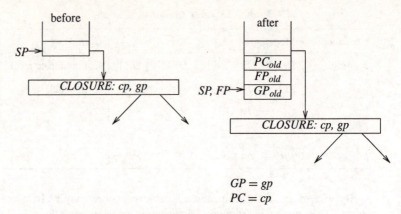

Figure 3.11 The effect of the **eval** instruction.

3.7.7 Letrec expressions and local variables

Suppose we are given a letrec expression **letrec** $v_1 == e_1; \ldots; v_n == e_n$ **in** e_0. When we compile it in the V context, the following must apply:

(1) An instruction sequence must be generated to create the closures for the n expressions $e_1, \ldots, e_n$.

(2) An instruction sequence must be generated to evaluate e_0.

(3) An identical environment for $e_0, e_1, \ldots, e_n$ must be constructed, with a knowledge of the global variables and also of $v_1, \ldots, v_n$.

This is provided by the following scheme:

V_code (**letrec** $v_1 == e_1; \ldots; v_n == e_n$ **in** e_0) β $sl =$
  repeat n **alloc**;
  $C\_code\ e_1\ \beta'\ sl'$;
  rewrite n;
  $C\_code\ e_2\ \beta'\ sl'$;
  rewrite $n - 1$;
  $\vdots$
  $C\_code\ e_n\ \beta'\ sl'$;
  rewrite 1;
  $V\_code\ e_0\ \beta'\ sl'$;
  slide n

where $\beta' = \beta[v_i \mapsto (LOC, sl+i-1)]_{i=1}^{n}$; $sl' = sl + n$;
   repeat $n\ c =$ **if** $n = 0$ **then** *nocode*
          else c; *repeat* $(n - 1)\ c$ **fi**

Table 3.15   **rewrite** and **slide**.

Instruction	Meaning	Comments
rewrite m	$HP[ST[SP - m]] := HP[ST[SP]];$	overwrite
	$SP := SP - 1$	heap object
slide m	$ST[SP - m] := ST[SP];$	copy
	$SP := SP - m$	result

Let us examine the scheme step by step. First, n **alloc** instructions are generated, which at run time create n empty closure objects in the heap with pointers to them on the stack. Then instruction sequences are generated by each 'block',

$$C\_code\ e_j\ (\beta[v_i \mapsto (LOC, sl + i - 1)]_{i=1}^n)\ (sl + n);$$
$$\textbf{rewrite}\ (n - j + 1)$$

which actually produce the individual closures for the e_j and thus overwrite the corresponding empty closure objects. For this, the empty closure objects must already exist, for the code that creates a closure may use pointers to such objects. However, it may not access components of the closure.

Here, we have to make an assumption about the order of the definitions. The C_code scheme for variables was improved in such a way that the binding of the variables is returned instead of the creation of a closure. This would be fatal in the case of Example 3.12. In fact, here the still empty closure for b would be bound to a. To avoid this, we sort the definitions so that variable renaming such as $a == b$ is always preceded by a definition of b. Cyclic renaming does not make sense and can therefore be rejected by the compiler.

Example 3.12   letrec $a == b;\ b == 0$ **in** a ;   □

It remains to determine whether the addressing assertion (AA) still holds in this case if it holds before the compilation of a letrec and before the execution of the code generated, respectively. Let the corresponding starting value of sl be sl_0. The n-fold *alloc* increases SP by the (static) value n. Consequently, e_1 is compiled with parameter $sl_0 + n$. The *rewrite* releases the uppermost stack location. Thus, the other expressions $e_2, \ldots, e_n, e_0$ are also compiled with the correct sl parameter.

The individual local variables v_i are given the address $sl_0 + i - 1$; thus, v_1 gets the address sl_0, v_2 the address $sl_0 + 1$, and so on. If the compiled letrec is the first in a function body, v_1 gets the relative address 0, v_2 the relative address 1, and so on. Thus, the addressing of local variables in the function *getvar* using the **pushloc** instruction would also be correct.

3.8 Implementation of lists

Up to this point, LaMa only permits computations on flat values, such as logical values, numbers, and so on, and on functions. However, every usable functional programming language has objects of recursive type, such as lists. Thus, LaMa will now be extended to include lists.

The syntax of LaMa expressions will be extended to include list expressions $[e_1, \ldots, e_n]$. There are also four new operators:

- ':' inserts its first argument before the second argument, a list, and thus is of polymorphic type: $* \rightarrow [*] \rightarrow [*]$. It is used as infix operator.
- **head** (Type $[*] \rightarrow *$) returns the head of a (non-empty) argument list;.
- **tail** (Type $[*] \rightarrow [*]$) returns the rest (that is, headless list) of a (non-empty) argument list.
- [ ] (Type $[*]$) generates the empty list.

Example 3.13 The expression

> **letrec** *append* $== \lambda x y.$ **if** $x = [\ ]$ **then** y
>
> **else**   ((**head** x): (*append* (**tail** x) y))
> **in head** (**tail** (**tail** (*append* [1,2] [3,4])))

gives the value 3. □

By analogy with the call-by-need semantics of functions in LaMa, we consider the : operator to be lazy; that is, $h : t$ leads to the creation of a list object which contains only closures for h and t and not the values of h and t. Thus, : does not evaluate its arguments.

Example 3.14 Let us consider the expression:

> **letrec**
>   *nats* $== from$ 1;
>   *from*$== \lambda n.n$**:** *from* $(n + 1)$
> **in head** (**tail** *nats*)

from 1 constructs a list, consisting of a closure for 1 (may be replaced by the heap object (BASIC: 1) for increased efficiency) as the head and a closure for *from* $(1 + 1)$ as the tail. The binding vector contains pointers to the *FUNVAL* object for *from* or 1, respectively. In the evaluation of **head** (**tail** *nats*) the closure for *from* $(n + 1)$ is first evaluated into a new list with a closure for 2 as the head and a closure for *from* $(n + 1)$ as the tail, then 2 is returned. In the binding vector, in this case, n is bound to 2. □

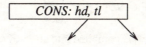

Figure 3.12   List node as MaMa heap object.

Table 3.16   Instructions for constructing and decomposing lists.

cons	**if**	*HP* [*ST* [*SP* −1]].*tag* = *CONS* **or**
		HP [*ST* [*SP* −1]].*tag* = *NIL* **or**
		HP [*ST* [*SP* −1]].*tag* = *CLOSURE*
	then	*ST* [*SP* −1] := *new*(*CONS*: *ST* [*SP*],*ST* [*SP* −1]);
		SP := *SP* −1
	else	*error* **fi**
hd	**if**	*HP* [*ST* [*SP*]].*tag* = *CONS*
	then	*ST* [*SP*] := *HP*[*ST* [*SP*]].*hd*
	else	*error* **fi**
tl	**if**	*HP* [*ST* [*SP*]].*tag* = *CONS*
	then	*ST* [*SP*] := *HP* [*ST* [*SP*]].*tl*
	else	*error* **fi**
nil	*SP* := *SP* + 1;	
	ST [*SP*] := *new*(*NIL*:)	

List values do not in general fit into one stack location; thus, they are stored in the heap. Two new sorts of heap object are introduced for this. One consists of the two pointers and the tag CONS, see Figure 3.12. These heap objects represent non-empty lists. There is also another heap object, representing the empty list, which simply consists of the tag NIL. Corresponding to the four new operations on lists, there are four new MaMa instructions which construct lists, see Table 3.16.

Compilation of list expressions

First, we shall see how list expressions that occur explicitly in LaMa expressions (programs) are compiled. In all contexts, the empty list is compiled into a single instruction which generates the empty list object (NIL:) in the heap and loads a pointer to it onto the stack.

$$C\_code\ [\ ]\ \beta\ sl = V\_Code\ [\ ]\ \beta\ sl = \textbf{nil}$$

A non-empty list $[e_1, \ldots, e_n]$ is compiled into an instruction sequence that generates n CONS heap objects with closures for the heads.

$$C\_code\ [e_1, \ldots, e_n]\ \beta\ sl = V\_code\ [e_1, \ldots, e_n]\ \beta\ sl$$

$$
\begin{aligned}
V\_code\ [e_1, \ldots, e_n]\ \beta\ sl = &\ \textbf{nil}; \\
&\ C\_code\ e_n\ \beta\ (sl+1); \\
&\ \textbf{cons}; \\
&\ C\_code\ e_{n-1}\ \beta\ (sl+1); \\
&\ \textbf{cons}; \\
&\ \vdots \\
&\ C\_code\ e_1\ \beta\ (sl+1); \\
&\ \textbf{cons}
\end{aligned}
$$

Compilation of operations on lists

When generating code for operations on lists, one should take into account the fact that the operator ':' is lazy. Thus, the V_code for $e_1 : e_2$ must create a CONS location, containing links to the closures of the operands.

$$
\begin{aligned}
V\_code\ (e_1 : e_2)\ \beta\ sl = &\ C\_code\ e_2\ \beta\ sl; \\
&\ C\_code\ e_1\ \beta\ (sl+1); \\
&\ \textbf{cons}
\end{aligned}
$$

The (optimized) cases of the C_code function for variables and constants, given in Sections 3.7.6 and 3.7.3, prevent the creation of closures in a harmless manner.

The compilation of **head** and **tail** operations in the V context generates instruction sequences that evaluate the operands up to the first CONS, then select the head or tail and evaluate a closure, if it exists.

$$
\begin{aligned}
V\_code\ (\textbf{head}\ e)\ \beta\ sl = &\ V\_code\ e\ \beta\ sl; \\
&\ \textbf{hd}; \\
&\ \textbf{eval} \\
V\_code\ (\textbf{tail}\ e)\ \beta\ sl = &\ V\_code\ e\ \beta\ sl; \\
&\ \textbf{tl}; \\
&\ \textbf{eval}
\end{aligned}
$$

The compilation of list expressions in the C context need not be specified. It follows the scheme of Section 3.7.6. This uses the V_code function, as just defined.

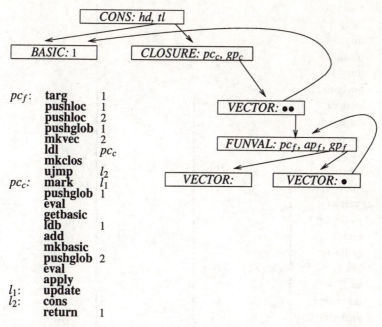

Figure 3.13   Heap object constructed for *from*1 in the evaluation of the function body of *from* in Example 3.14.

Example 3.15   Here now is the MaMa code for Example 3.14.

```
    alloc;
    alloc;
    pushloc 1;
    mkvec 1;
    ldl l₂;
    mkclos;
    ujmp l₄;
l₂: mark l₁;
    ldb 1;
    mkbasic;
    pushglob 1;
    eval;
    apply;
l₁: update;
```

V_code
(*from* 1)
β₄
2

C_code
(*from* 1)
β₁
2

l_4: **rewrite** 2;
   pushloc 1;
   mkvec 1;
   mkvec 0;
   ldl l_8;
   mkfunval;
   ujmp l_9;
l_8: **targ** 1;
   pushloc 1;
   pushloc 2;
   pushglob 1;
   mkvec 2;
   ldl l_6;
   mkclos;
   ujmp l_7;
l_6: **mark** l_5;
   pushglob 1;
   eval;
   getbasic;
   ldb 1;
   add;
   mkbasic;
   pushglob 2;
   eval;
   apply;

l_5: **update**;

l_7: **cons**;
   return 1;
l_9: **rewrite** 1;
   pushloc 2;
   eval;
   tl;
   eval;
   hd;
   eval
   slide 2

V_code
$(from\ (n+1))$
β_3
0

C_code
$(from\ (n+1))$
β_2
1

C_code
$(\lambda\, n.\, n : from\ (n+1))$
β_1
2

V_code
(head (tail $nats$))
β_1
2

$$
\begin{aligned}
\beta_1 &= \{nats \mapsto (LOC,0), from \mapsto (LOC,1)\} \\
\beta_2 &= \{n \mapsto (LOC,-1), from \mapsto (GLOB,1)\} \\
\beta_3 &= \{n \mapsto (GLOB,1), from \mapsto (GLOB,2)\} \\
\beta_4 &= \{from \mapsto (GLOB,1)\}
\end{aligned}
$$

$\square$

3.9   Exercises

1:   To gain confidence with LaMa, write down LaMa expressions for the following functions:

(a) A function *gcd* to determine the greatest common divisor of two numbers *a* and *b*.

(b) *isperfect* checks whether a natural number is perfect. A number is said to be perfect if it is equal to the sum of its proper divisors. For example, 6 is a perfect number, since $6 = 1 + 2 + 3$.

(c) A function to generate the list of all perfect numbers.

2:   Following Miranda we introduce certain abbreviated notation for lists.

$$[a..b]$$ List of all numbers between a and b inclusive

$$[a, b..c]$$ List of all numbers between a and c in steps of $b - a$

$$[a..]$$ List of all numbers starting with a

together with simple ZF expressions of the form:

$$[e|v < -L; B]$$

Here, the variable v runs over the list L; B is a Boolean expression which is applied to the individual list elements, filtering out undesired elements.

Example: $[1..5]$ $\Rightarrow [1, 2, 3, 4, 5]$
         $[1, 3..7]$ $\Rightarrow [1, 3, 5, 7]$
         $[1..]$ $\Rightarrow [1, 2, 3, 4, ...]$
         $[square\ x|x < -[1, 2, 3, 4, 5]; odd\ x]$ $\Rightarrow [1, 9, 25]$

Compile these abbreviated list expressions into normal LaMa expressions.

3:   Determine the sets of free and bound variables in the following LaMa expressions:

$$(\lambda x.xy)(\lambda y.y)$$
$$\lambda xy.z(\lambda z.z(\lambda x.y))$$
$$(\lambda xy.xz(yz))(\lambda x.y(\lambda y.y))$$
$$\lambda x.x + \quad \textbf{letrec} \quad a == x;$$
$$x == f\ y;$$
$$y == z$$
$$\textbf{in}\ x + y + z$$

4:   Compile the following LaMa expressions into instruction sequences for the MaMa abstract machine.

(a) $(\lambda x.x + 1)\ 3$

(b) **letrec** $F == \lambda x\ y.x\ y;$

   $inc == \lambda x.x + 1$

   in $F\ inc\ 5$

Show how the stack and heap change during the stepwise processing of the MaMa instructions generated.

5: Compile the following LaMa expression into MaMa code.

letrec

   $fac\ \ == \lambda n.$ **if** $n = 0$ **then** 1 **else** $n * fac(dec\ n);$

   $dec\ == \lambda n.n - 1$

in $fac\ 4$

6: Consider LaMa programs of the following form (the uppermost expression is a **letrec**):

letrec

   $v_1 == e_1;$

   $\vdots$

   $v_n == e_n$

in e

Check that the variables v_i can be addressed by their absolute addresses at the start of the stack. Introduce a new class of so-called ABS variables and modify the compilation scheme accordingly. Which optimizations are possible?

7: When variables are compiled in the C context, the given scheme generates code that creates closures for them. However, an optimization is possible.

(a) Suppose the following LaMa expression is compiled so that closures are created for variables in the C context.

letrec

   $a == 1;$

   $f == \lambda x\ y.$ **if** $x = 0$ **then** y **else** $f(x - 1)\ y$

in $f\ 100\ a$

What happens when the limit of the recursion is reached at run time and the value of y in the 'then' part is accessed?

(b) A simple optimization is possible. Instead of generating closures for variables, we use $C\_code\ v\ \beta\ sl = getvar\ v\ \beta\ sl$ to generate a *pushloc* or *pushglob* instruction, which loads a pointer to the 'value' of the variable in the runtime environment onto the stack. This pointer points either to a closure or to the actual value of the variable. In any case, no expressions are evaluated before their values are needed. Unfortunately, this optimization leads to errors in a number of pathological cases. Compile the following LaMa expression with this optimization and execute the code generated.

letrec
$$a == b;$$
$$b == 3$$
in a

What do you find? Try to alter the compilation scheme for **letrec**s so that this error no longer occurs.

8: In this exercise, we optimize recursive functions of the following form:

$$f == \lambda \, v_1 \cdots v_n. \cdots (f \; e_1 \cdots e_n) \cdots$$
$$\textbf{in} \cdots$$

The recursive call $(f \; e_1 \cdots e_n)$ is said to be **tail recursive**, if it is neither an operand of an operator nor a function argument. In this case, the function value is computed by another function call, to the same function. What does this mean at run time? The function body is evaluated in the current frame. If the tail-recursive call $(f \; e_1 \cdots e_n)$ is reached, a new stack frame has to be created for it. However, the local stack in the current frame is either empty or will no longer be used after the return from the recursive call (letrec). Thus, instead of creating a new frame, we can evaluate the recursive call in the current frame. In this case, the pointers to the old arguments are simply replaced by those to the new arguments.

Define corresponding instructions and modify the compilation scheme so that it recognizes tail-recursive calls and handles them more efficiently. (Hint: extend the code functions by extra parameters, which contain information about the context of the expression to be compiled.)

9: Modify the structure of the *FUNVAL* objects and the code schemes for function definitions and applications, so that unpacking and repacking of arguments is avoided for under-supplied functions.

3.10 Literature

One of the first abstract machines to explain the compilation of functional programming languages was Landin's SECD machine (Landin, 1964). It was developed to define the semantics of LISP programs with static binding and call-by-value parameter passing. The G machine was the first machine with compiled graph reduction. It was introduced by Th. Johnsson (Johnsson, 1984). This machine, together with the Tim (Three Instruction Machine) (Fairbairn and Wray, 1987), influenced the design of the MaMa machine. A survey of the implementation of functional programming languages is given in Peyton Jones (1987).

4

Compilation of logic programming languages

- Logic programming languages

- Logical foundations

- Unification

- Execution of logic programs

- Prolog

- Abstract Prolog machine

- Compilation of Prolog

- Efficiency improvements

- Exercises

- Literature

4.1 Logic programming languages

The history of logic programming dates from the beginning of the 1970s when R. Kowalski and A. Colmerauer discovered that an operational interpretation could be given to sentences of predicate logic. The computational model used for this is the resolution method for mechanical theorem-proving procedures proposed by J.A. Robinson in 1965. A logic formula α is a logical consequence of a set of formulae S if and only if $S \cup \{\neg\alpha\}$ is inconsistent. The resolution method mechanizes proofs of inconsistency.

Three different terminologies are used in discussions of logic programs. When programming is involved, we speak of procedures, alternatives of procedures, calls, variables, and so on. When explaining the logical foundations, we use words such as variable, function and predicate symbols, terms, atomic formulae, and so on. Finally, terms such as literal, Horn clause, unification and resolution come from the mechanization of predicate logic in automated theorem-proving procedures.

Structure of this chapter

After an intuitive description of logic programs from a procedural viewpoint, Section 4.2 presents the predicate-logic foundations of logic programming. Section 4.3 describes the most important operation in the execution of logic programs, the unification of terms. Section 4.4 gives the operational semantics for logic programs, using SLD resolution. A first, non-deterministic interpreter is described. It traverses a tree, the search tree for a program and a query. Prolog uses fixed search and computation rules for this traversal. These are described in Section 4.5, in which a deterministic interpreter for Prolog is also presented. In Sections 4.6 and 4.7, a first abstract machine for Prolog is defined, together with the recursive compilation schemes. This is designed to be as similar as possible to the P machine of Chapter 2 and the MaMa of Chapter 3. More efficient versions of this Prolog machine (which improve efficiency in terms of time and space) are described in a series of steps in Section 4.8.

Logic programs

Logic programs compute using relations between terms. Let us consider an example.

Example 4.1

$$append \,([\,], ys, ys) \leftarrow$$
$$append \,(.(x, xs), ys, .(x, zs)) \leftarrow append \,(xs, ys, zs)$$

The *append* predicate defines a ternary relation between list terms. Lists are formed from the empty list, [ ], and elements of unspecified type using the list constructor '.' which concatenates the first and second operands by placing the first operand, an element, in front of the second operand, a list. *append* (a, b, c) says that the list c is formed by concatenating the two lists a and b. The first line in the

Table 4.1   Examples of *append*.

Query	Solution
← *append* ([ ], .(2, [ ]), .(2, [ ]))	yes
← *append* (.(1, [ ]), .(2, [ ]), .(1, .(2, [ ])))	yes
← *append* (.(1, .(2, [ ])), .(3, .(4, [ ])), w)	$w = .(1, .(2, .(3, .(4, [ ]))))$
← *append* (.(1, x), y, .(1, .(2, .(3, .(4, [ ])))))	$x = [ ], y = .(2, .(3, .(4, [ ])))$
	$x = .(2, [ ]), y = .(3, .(4, [ ]))$
	$x = .(2, .(3, [ ])), y = .(4, [ ])$
	$x = .(2, .(3, .(4, [ ]))), y = [ ]$
← *append* (x, .(3, .(4, [ ])), .(1, z))	infinitely many solutions, e.g.
	$x = .(1, [ ]), z = .(3, .(4, [ ]))$
	$x = .(1, .(2, [ ])), z = .(2, .(3, .(4, [ ])))$
← *append* (.(1, x), y, .(2, z))	no solution

definition of *append* says that the list *ys* is formed when *ys* is appended to the empty list. The second line defines an implication. If *zs* is formed by concatenating the lists *xs* and *ys*, then the list .(*x*, *zs*) is formed by concatenating the lists .(*x*, *xs*) and *ys*.

So far, this explanation gives the impression that *append* is just a function that links together two list terms. However, since *append* is a relation, *append* (*a*, *b*, *c*) can also be read as follows:

- The lists *a* and *b* form a possible decomposition of the given list *c*.
- Suppose the lists *b* and *c* are given. Then *a* is the list to which *b* is appended to give *c*.
- Suppose the lists *a* and *c* are given. Then *b* is the list which is appended to *a* to give *c*.

Table 4.1 contains various 'queries', or calls to the predicate *append* with various combinations of parameters, including both list terms and variables *x*, *y* and *z*. The second column gives values of the variables for which the predicate is valid.

In general, a logic program consists of a set of **rules** of the form:

$$p_0(s_1^0, \ldots, s_{k_0}^0) \leftarrow p_1(s_1^1, \ldots, s_{k_1}^1), \ldots, p_n(s_1^n, \ldots, s_{k_n}^n) \qquad (4.1)$$

The p_i are predicate symbols, and the s_i^j are terms, that is, they consist solely of function symbols, variables and constants. One such rule might be: 'for all assignments to variables occurring in the rule, the predicate p_0 is valid for the tuple of terms $(s_1^0, \ldots, s_{k_0}^0)$, if all predicates p_i are valid for the tuples of terms $(s_1^i, \ldots, s_{k_i}^i)$, for $(1 \leq i \leq n)$'. $p_0(s_1^0, \ldots, s_{k_0}^0)$ is called the **head** of the rule, and the finite sequence $p_1(s_1^1, \ldots, s_{k_1}^1), \ldots, p_n(s_1^n, \ldots, s_{k_n}^n)$ is called the **body**. If $n = 0$, the body is empty, and the rule is called a **fact**. The above rule (4.1) is one of several possible **alternatives** for p_0. All alternatives for p_0 together form the definition of the **procedure** p_0. In this approach, the $p_i(s_1^i, \ldots, s_{k_i}^i)$ in the body of the rule may be referred to as **calls**. However, the term **goal**, which we shall use in the implementation part, is more customary. A **query** is a sequence of calls (goals):

$$\leftarrow q_1(t_1^1, \ldots, t_{k_1}^1), \ldots, q_m(t_1^m, \ldots, t_{k_m}^m) \tag{4.2}$$

Such a query can be interpreted as meaning: 'is there a variable assignment for which the validity of the predicate q_i for the terms $(t_1^i, \ldots, t_{k_i}^i)$ follows from the program?'

Let us return to our example and the above table. The query follows from the program for each of the variable assignments given in the second column of the table. If the query contains no variables, as in the first two lines, the answer is just yes or no; in other words, the query follows from the program, or it does not. The first query follows by virtue of the first rule, if we set $ys = .(2, [\,])$. If we then accept *append* $([\,], .(2, [\,]), .(2, [\,]))$ as proven, it is easy to see that *append* $(.(1, [\,]), .(2, [\,]), .(1, .(2, [\,])))$ follows from the program by virtue of the second rule. There is no assignment for which the query $\leftarrow$ *append* $(.(1, v), y, .(2, z))$ follows from the program. Neither rule applies, the first because the first operand in the query is not the empty list, the second, because both occurrences of x in the head of the rule must be bound to the same list element. However, in the query, these are two different elements, namely 1 and 2. In general, the proof of an implication together with a corresponding variable assignment is determined by a logical computation. $\square$

The query consists of a sequence of calls. This forms the **initial call list**. The execution of the logic program begins with the processing of one of these calls. Except for the nature of 'parameter passing' and its consequences, procedures in logic programs behave like procedures in imperative programming languages or functions in functional programming languages. The processing of a procedure call begins with the choice of an appropriate 'alternative' for the procedure. The current call is then replaced in the call list by the sequence of calls that forms the right-hand side of this alternative. The selection of facts eliminates calls from the call list. The execution terminates successfully when the call list is empty. On the other hand, an execution is deemed to have failed when, for a non-empty call list, it is unable to find a suitable alternative for a call.

Both the head and the calls on the right-hand side of a rule consist of a predicate symbol and a tuple of terms. These terms may be variables or may contain variables. If a call $p(t_1, \ldots, t_k)$ is chosen from the current call list together with the alternative $p(s_1, \ldots, s_k) \leftarrow B_1, \ldots, B_n$ for the procedure p, the lists of terms $(t_1, \ldots, t_k)$ and $(s_1, \ldots, s_k)$ must be 'made to fit' one another. If this is possible, the process used, the **unification** of the two lists, produces a **substitution**, an assignment of terms to variables occurring in $s_1, \ldots, s_k, t_1, \ldots, t_k$. If this substitution is applied to both lists, that is, the bindings for the variables are inserted, the pairs of terms s_i and t_i will become the same. This substitution is then in turn applied to the whole of the new call list. Finally, the next call is selected.

Example 4.2   We again consider the query

$$\leftarrow append\,(.(1, .(2, [\,])), .(3, .(4, [\,])), w)$$

How do we obtain the given solution $w = .(1, .(2, .(3, .(4, [\,]))))$? We use the above informal description and bear in mind the given interpretations of rules and queries.

In other words, 'we look for an assignment of the query variables such that *append* is valid with this assignment for the triple $(.(1, .(2, [\,])), .(3, .(4, [\,])), w)$'. The first rule cannot provide this assignment; it does not fit it because it requires the first argument to be the empty list.

The second rule fits if we set:

$$x = 1, \quad xs = .(2, [\,]), \quad ys = .(3, .(4, [\,])), \quad w = .(1, zs)$$

Thus, we have reduced the problem of finding a suitable assignment for w to the search for a suitable assignment for zs. The new query is:

$$\leftarrow append(.(2, [\,]), .(3, .(4, [\,])), zs)$$

Further application of the second rule (with 'fresh' variables x', xs', ys', zs') gives:

$$x' = 2, \quad xs' = [\,], \quad ys' = .(3, .(4, [\,])), \quad zs = .(2, zs')$$

The new call (the new inquiry) is:

$$\leftarrow append([\,], .(3, .(4, [\,])), zs')$$

Now only the first rule is applicable. This gives (with a fresh variable ys''):

$$ys'' = .(3, .(4, [\,])), \quad zs' = ys''$$

If we combine the equations found for w and the variables occurring in them, we obtain:

$$w = .(1, zs) = .(1, .(2, zs')) = .(1, .(2, ys'')) = .(1, .(2, .(3, .(4, [\,]))))$$

$\square$

4.2   Logical foundations

We now present the most important concepts and the foundations from first-order predicate logic. This brief introduction is not intended as a replacement for appropriate introductory literature, but is designed to facilitate understanding of the operational semantics of logic programs, described later.

Table 4.2 lists the alphabet of a first-order language. Table 4.3 defines the structure of formulae of a first-order predicate logic. The formulae that can be constructed in this way form a **first-order language**.

Terms without variables are called **ground terms**, those with variables **non-ground terms**. The logic operators have the usual meaning. We shall also permit ourselves to write $G \leftarrow F$ instead of $F \rightarrow G$. Within quantifications such as $\forall x\ (F)$ or $\exists x\ (F)$, the two **quantifiers**, the existential quantifier $\exists$ and the universal quantifier $\forall$, bind free occurrences of the quantified variables x within their **scope** F, analogously to the λ-abstraction, $\lambda x.e$, in the previous chapter. Unbound occurrences of variables in a formula are **free**; a formula with no free occurrences of variables is said to be **closed**.

In logic programming, clauses, that is, formulae with a restricted structure, are of interest. Their structure is given in Table 4.4.

Table 4.2   The alphabet of a first-order language.

	Generic names	List
Constants	$a, b, c, \ldots$	
Variables	$u, v, w, x, y, z, \ldots$	
Function symbols	$f, g, h, \ldots$	
Predicate symbols	$p, q, r, \ldots$	
Logic operators		$\wedge, \vee, \neg, \rightarrow, \leftrightarrow$
Quantifiers		$\forall, \exists$

Table 4.3   The structure of formulae of a first-order language.

	Generic names	Structure
Term	t	$u \mid a \mid f(t_1, \ldots, t_n)$ (where f is n-ary)
Atomic formula	A	$p(t_1, \ldots, t_n)$ (where p is n-ary)
Formulae	$F, G, \ldots$	$A \mid (F \wedge G) \mid (F \vee G) \mid (\neg F) \mid (F \rightarrow G) \mid$ $(F \leftrightarrow G) \mid \forall x\ (F) \mid \exists x\ (F)$

Table 4.4   The structure of clauses.

		Structure	Comments/condition
Literal	L	$A \mid \neg A$	Positive literal | Negative literal
Clause		$\forall x_1 \ldots \forall x_s (L_1 \vee \ldots \vee L_m)$	$x_1, \ldots, x_s$ are all variables occurring in $L_1, \ldots, L_m$

If $x_1, \ldots, x_s$ are the free variables of a formula F, then, from now on, $\forall F$ will stand for $\forall x_1 \ldots \forall x_s (F)$ and $\exists F$ for $\exists x_1 \ldots \exists x_s (F)$. $\forall F$ is called the **universal closure** of F; $\exists F$ is the **existential closure** of F.

If we now separate the positive and negative occurrences of literals in a clause, we obtain

$$\forall x_1 \ldots \forall x_s (A_1 \vee \ldots \vee A_k \vee \neg B_1 \vee \ldots \vee \neg B_n)$$

Noting that **all variables in clauses are universally quantified** and using the fact that $\neg B_1 \vee \ldots \vee \neg B_n$ is equivalent to $\neg(B_1 \wedge \ldots \wedge B_n)$ and $(A \vee \neg B)$ is equivalent to $(A \leftarrow B)$, we obtain the **clause notation** for the above clause:

$$A_1, \ldots, A_k \leftarrow B_1, \ldots, B_n$$

Here, the comma stands for the logical OR on the left-hand side and for the logical AND on the right-hand side.

The logic programming languages considered here impose further restrictions on the structure of clauses, see Table 4.5.

Thus, program clauses contain precisely one literal, which is not negated, namely their **head**, and a possibly empty set of negative literals, their **body**. All program clauses with the same head predicate are **definitions** of (alternatives for) this predicate. A finite set of program clauses forms a **program**. **Query clauses**, being headless, are not program clauses. Program clauses and query clauses are called **Horn clauses**. Thus, they contain at most one positive literal. The set of all Horn clauses over an alphabet is called a Horn-logic language. All languages that

Table 4.5   Program clauses, query clauses and the empty clause.

Terminology from theorem proving	Programming language terminology	Structure
Definite clause	Program clause, rule	$A \leftarrow B_1, \ldots, B_n \quad (n \geq 0)$
Unit clause	Fact	$A \leftarrow$
Query clause	Query	$\leftarrow B_1, \ldots, B_n \quad (n \geq 1)$
Empty clause		$\leftarrow$

occur in what follows are first-order Horn-logic languages. The empty clause is an empty disjunction. It cannot be satisfied and stands for a contradiction.

Up to here everything is syntax. Syntax also includes a calculus which can be used to **derive** formulae. The derivability relation is often denoted by the symbol $\vdash$. As far as semantics are concerned, questions concerning the truth of a formula and the **implication** are of interest. Here, variable, function and predicate symbols are interpreted over suitable domains, the variable symbols as elements of an underlying universe of (say) atoms, the function symbols as functions and the predicates as relations. Then, a check is made to determine whether the formulae interpreted in this way translate into valid statements. If there exists an interpretation that translates a formula into a valid statement, this interpretation is called a **model** for this formula. Finally, a formula G **is a logical consequence** of a formula F (written $F \models G$), if every model for F, whence every interpretation in which F is valid, is also a model for G. In logic programming the variables are interpreted over a domain of terms, the so-called Herbrand universe. The function symbols are interpreted as constructors for terms.

Let us return to Example 4.1. The program defines a ternary predicate symbol *append* on list terms. The nullary function symbol [ ], and the binary function symbol '.', are interpreted as constructors on (list) terms, and *append* is interpreted as a ternary relation. The universe of atoms is not specified. Variables are interpreted over the universe of terms that can be constructed from atoms and [ ] using '.'. The solutions in the right-hand column of Table 4.1 are models for the associated queries in the left-hand column.

It is an unfortunate fact that the implication '$\models$' is in general undecidable. This means that logical computations whose goal is the proof of an implication cannot always terminate with a 'yes' or 'no' decision. Sometimes, they will not even terminate.

Let us now rewrite the query clause $\leftarrow B_1, \ldots, B_n$ in explicitly universally quantified and disjunctive form $\forall(\neg B_1 \vee \ldots \vee \neg B_n)$, which is equivalent to $\neg\exists(B_1 \wedge \ldots \wedge B_n)$. If it can be shown that a program P together with the query clause $\leftarrow B_1, \ldots, B_n$ is inconsistent, then the formula $\exists(B_1 \wedge \ldots \wedge B_n)$ follows logically from P.

4.3 Unification

If program clauses are considered as procedures which are activated by calls, then unification corresponds to parameter passing in imperative and functional programming languages. However, in imperative languages, only objects or object addresses can be passed to a called procedure. Functional languages permit the definition of functions over various cases, characterized by patterns for the arguments. In the application of a function, the patterns are compared with the arguments, and if the patterns match the arguments, the pattern variables are bound to the corresponding parts of the arguments. However, terms with variables are only allowed in the function definition and not as arguments. Thus, arguments in function applications are always ground terms. Therefore, only the variables in the patterns must be bound.

Unification in logic languages allows patterns, that is, terms with variables, in both the definition and the call. Thus, a successful unification will bind variables both in the call and in the chosen rule.

The result of a successful unification, **the set of variable bindings generated**, is a substitution.

Definition 4.1 (substitution) A **substitution** Θ is a finite set of pairs $\{v_1/t_1, \ldots, v_n/t_n\}$, such that the variables v_i and v_j are pairwise distinct for $i \neq j$, and no v_i is equal to the corresponding term t_i. Each pair v_i/t_i is called a **binding** of v_i. Θ is called a **ground substitution**, if all the t_i are ground terms (with no variables). Θ is called a **renaming substitution**, if all the t_i are variables, pairwise distinct and different from all the v_j. □

Example 4.3 $\Theta_1 = \{x/u, y/v, z/w\}$ with the variables u, v, w, x, y, z is a renaming substitution, $\Theta_2 = \{x/[\,], y/.(1, [\,])\}$ is a ground substitution. □

Thus, a substitution may be viewed as a total function from an (infinite) set of variables to a set of terms, which is represented finitely and in minimal form, that is, restricted to the set of variables on which it does not act as the identity.

We shall discuss the unification both of terms and of atomic formulae. These are constructed in a similar way, except that they are of a different 'type'. Thus, we introduce the term 'structure' for this. Substitutions will be applied to various kinds of formulae. Thus, we introduce the term 'expression'.

Definition 4.2 (structure, expression) A **structure** is a term or an atomic formula. An **expression** is a term, a literal, a disjunction or a conjunction of literals. □

Application of a substitution to an expression yields an instance of the expression. Thus, the substitution may be viewed as an extension to a homomorphism on expressions.

Definition 4.3 (instance) Suppose that $\Theta = \{v_1/t_1, \ldots, v_n/t_n\}$ is a substitution and E is an expression. $E\Theta$, the **instance** of E with respect to Θ, is obtained from E by replacing each occurrence of v_i in E by the corresponding term t_i. If $E\Theta$ is a ground expression, then $E\Theta$ is called a **ground instance** of E. If Θ is a renaming substitution, then $E\Theta$ is called a **variant** of E. □

If $S = \{S_1, \ldots, S_n\}$ is a set of expressions and Θ is a substitution, then we set $S\Theta = \{S_1\Theta, \ldots, S_n\Theta\}$.

If substitutions are viewed as (finitely represented) homomorphisms on expressions, it is possible to define the composition of substitutions.

Definition 4.4 (composition of substitutions)
Take Θ and Ψ as in the book and define the result of composing Ψ after Θ as:
$$(\{u_1/s_1\Psi, \ldots, u_m/s_m\Psi\} - \{u_1/u_1, \ldots, u_m/u_m\})u$$
$$(\{v_1/t_1, \ldots, v_k/t_k\} - \{v/t | v \in \{u_1, \ldots, u_m\}\}).$$

If the composition of substitutions is viewed as the composition of functions, then the bindings to v_i are generated by composing the 'identical portions' v_i/v_i, of Θ with Ψ. The deletions ensure that the result of the composition again gives the minimal representation of a function.

Example 4.4 Let $\Theta = \{x/f(y), y/z\}$, $\Psi = \{x/a, y/b, z/y\}$. Then $\Theta\Psi = \{x/f(b), z/y\}$. $\square$

In particular, substitutions occur as the result of unifications.

Definition 4.5 (unifier)   A substitution Θ is a **unifier** for two terms s and t, if $s\Theta = t\Theta$. More generally, let S be a finite non-empty set of structures (terms or atomic formulae). A substitution Θ is a **unifier** for S, if $S\Theta$ consists of a single element. A unifier Θ for S is said to be a **most general unifier** (mgu) for S, if for every unifier Ψ for S there exists a substitution Φ such that $\Psi = \Theta\Phi$. $\square$

Example 4.5   Let $S = \{f(x, a), f(g(u), y), z\}$. A most general unifier for S is found to be $\Theta = \{x/g(u), y/a, z/f(g(u), a)\}$. Then $S\Theta = \{f(g(u), a)\}$ has one element and for every other unifier Ψ for S there exists a substitution Φ with $\Psi = \Theta\Phi$. $\Theta' = \{x/g(h(b)), u/h(b), y/a, z/f(g(h(b)), a)\}$ is a unifier, but not a most general unifier for S, since $\Theta' = \Theta\Phi$ where $\Phi = \{u/h(b)\}$. $\square$

Most general unifiers are unique up to the consistent renaming of variables.

We now come to a unification algorithm. It is described in Table 4.6 by two functions *unify* and *unifylist*. When the function *unify* is applied to two unifiable structures t_1 and t_2, it computes a most general unifier. If t_1 and t_2 are not unifiable, the outcome is *fail*.

The function *unify* is defined by a table giving all combinations of cases. *unifylist* is defined in the customary way for the two cases of an empty or a non-empty list. It processes its two (equally long) list arguments from left to right. Thus, it unifies the current heads of the two lists, and, if this works, applies the unifier found to the two residual lists and forms the composition of this new unifier with the substitutions collected so far in an accumulating parameter. If any of the pairs cannot be unified, the outcome is *fail*.

When the unification involves a variable and a term, the 'occur check' is executed, to test whether a variable x is bound to a structure in which it itself occurs. The last case in Example 4.7 is a unification that fails because of this test. It is easy to check that if Y were to be bound to $h(Y)$, the resulting substitution would not be a unifier. This 'occur check' is usually omitted in implementations of Prolog, since it is expensive.

Table 4.6   Result of $unify(t_1, t_2)$ for the various combinations of cases. The function *unify* shown in the table has type *structure* $\times$ *structure* $\rightarrow$ $\{fail\} \cup subs$, where *var* is the set of variables, *structure* is the set of structures and $subs \subseteq \mathcal{P}_{fin}(var \times structure)$ is the set of all substitutions for the given language.

$t_2 =$ $t_1 =$	Constant c_2	Variable x_2	Structure $g(r_1, \ldots, r_k)$
Constant c_1	$\emptyset$ if $c_1 = c_2$, else *fail*	$\{x_2/c_1\}$	*fail*
Variable x_1	$\{x_1/c_2\}$	$\{x_1/x_2\}$ if $x_1 \neq x_2$ else $\emptyset$	$\{x_1/g(r_1, \ldots, r_k)\}$ if x_1 does not occur in $g(r_1, \ldots, r_k)$, else *fail*
Structure $f(s_1, \ldots, s_n)$	*fail*	$\{x_2/f(s_1, \ldots, s_n)\}$, if x_2 does not occur in $f(s_1, \ldots, s_n)$ else *fail*	*unifylist* $(s_1, \ldots, s_n)(r_1, \ldots, r_k)\emptyset$, if $f = g$ and $n = k$, else *fail*

$$unifylist\; [\,]\; [\,]\; \Theta = \Theta$$
$$unifylist\; t_1 : rest_1\; s_1 : rest_2\; \Theta =$$
$$\begin{cases} unifylist\; rest_1\Theta'\; rest_2\Theta'\; \Theta\Theta', & if\; \Theta' = unify\; t_1\; s_1 \neq fail \\ fail & otherwise \end{cases}$$

Example 4.6   The application of *unifylist* to the two lists $(g(x_1, y_1), f(x_1, b))$ and $(g(f(y_2), x_2), f(z_1, y_2))$ is shown in Table 4.7. $\square$

Table 4.7   An application of *unifylist*.

Mgu	Residual list	Composition of the unification
	$(g(x_1, y_1), f(x_1, b))$ $(g(f(y_2), x_2), f(z_1, y_2))$	
$\{x_1/f(y_2), y_1/x_2\}$	$(f(x_1, b))$ $(f(z_1, y_2))$	$\{x_1/f(y_2), y_1/x_2\}$
$\{z_1/x_1, y_2/b\}$	$(\,)$	$\{x_1/f(b), y_1/x_2, z_1/f(b)\}$

Example 4.7 The following table lists pairs of terms, together with the resulting bindings if the terms are unifiable.

t_1	t_2	Result/binding
a	b	*fail*
a	a	$\emptyset$
x	a	$\{x/a\}$
a	x	$\{x/a\}$
x	y	$\{x/y\}$
$f(a,x)$	$f(y,b)$	$\{y/a, x/b\}$
$f(g(a,b),y)$	$f(c,x)$	*fail*
$f(g(a,x),h(c))$	$f(g(a,b),y)$	$\{x/b, y/h(c)\}$
$p(y,f(g(a)),y)$	$p(x,f(x),g(a))$	$\{x/g(a), y/g(a)\}$
$f(g(a,x)),h(y))$	$f(g(a,b),y)$	*fail*

$\square$

4.4 Execution of logic programs

Suppose we are given a logic program P and the query $A \equiv\leftarrow B_1, \ldots, B_n$. The goal of the execution of P with A is a refutation of A from P, that is, a proof that $\neg A$ follows from P. $\leftarrow B_1, \ldots, B_n$ stands for $\forall(\neg B_1 \vee \ldots \vee \neg B_n)$, which is equivalent to $\forall(\neg(B_1 \wedge \ldots \wedge B_n))$ and $\neg\exists(B_1 \wedge \ldots \wedge B_n)$. Thus, $\neg A$ means $\exists(B_1 \wedge \ldots \wedge B_n)$.

The execution of P with A may produce three results:

- Success. Proof of the implication $P \models \exists(B_1 \wedge \ldots \wedge B_n)$ using an answer substitution Θ. Here $P \models \forall(B_1 \wedge \ldots \wedge B_n)\,\Theta$.

- Failure. The implication does not hold.

- Non-termination.

Definition 4.6 (answer, correct answer) Suppose P is a logic program and A a query (note that A should be a negated formula). An **answer** for $P \cup \{A\}$ is a substitution for the variables of A. If A is the query $\leftarrow A_1, \ldots, A_n$, then an **answer** Θ for $P \cup \{A\}$ is **correct**, if $\forall(A_1 \wedge \ldots \wedge A_n)\Theta$ follows from P. In addition, 'no' is a correct answer, if $P \cup \{A\}$ is satisfied. $\square$

This definition specifies which answers are accepted by the declarative semantics (those based on logic). We now consider how these correct answers are computed.

The computation mechanism is **resolution**, in this case SLD resolution (selective linear resolution for definite clauses). It is used in proofs of the form 'a formula A follows from a set of formulae P' in which one shows that $P \cup \{\neg A\}$ is inconsistent. This is shown by deriving the empty clause from $P \cup \{\neg A\}$.

Following popular terminology, we shall now speak of **goals** rather than atoms or calls. Thus, a query represents an initial **goal list**. The 'derivation' or resolution step described below derives a new goal list from a given one.

Definition 4.7 (derivation)   Let GL be a goal list and G a goal in GL, defined to be the **selected goal**, that is, $GL \equiv \leftarrow \alpha.(G).\beta$, where α and β are goal lists and '.' represents list concatenation. Let C be a clause $B \leftarrow B_1, \ldots, B_n$, which is made name-disjoint with GL by a renaming substitution. Then the goal list GL' is **derived directly** from GL using C and a substitution Θ, if Θ is a most general unifier of G and B, and $GL' \equiv \leftarrow (\alpha.(B_1, \ldots, B_n).\beta)\Theta$. GL' is also called the **resolvent** of GL and C. If P is a program and A a query, then a **derivation** of $P \cup \{A\}$ is a (possibly infinite) sequence of triples (GL_i, C_i, Θ_i) $(0 \leq i)$, where each GL_i is a goal list, each C_i is a clause, obtained from P by renaming variables, and each Θ_i is a most general unifier, such that GL_{i+1} is derived from GL_i using C_{i+1} and Θ_{i+1}. In addition, we set $GL_0 \equiv A$. $\square$

Definition 4.8 (refutation)   A **refutation** of $P \cup \{A\}$ is a finite derivation which ends in a triple with the empty goal list $[\,]$, that is, in the empty clause $\square$. Such a derivation is also said to be **successful**. An **unsuccessful** derivation is one that ends in a goal list in which the selected goal cannot be unified with any of its alternatives. $\square$

Definition 4.9 (computed answer)   Let P be a logic program and A a query. A **computed answer** for $P \cup \{A\}$ is the composition $\Theta_1 \ldots \Theta_n$ of the most general unifiers of a successful derivation of $P \cup \{A\}$, restricted to the variables of A. If there is no successful derivation for $P \cup \{A\}$, the answer 'no' should be given. $\square$

Let us be clear that a successful computation gives a correct answer. To see this, we consider a logic program P and the derivation step from GL to GL' described above. In what follows, we use $\bigwedge GL$ to denote the conjunction of the goals in a goal list GL. For the empty goal list $[]$, $\bigwedge[]$ stands for true.

Every clause $B \leftarrow B_1, \ldots, B_n$ follows naturally from the program containing it, that is, $P \models \forall (B_1 \wedge \ldots \wedge B_n \rightarrow B)$. Since in the derivation step considered, B can be unified with the selected goal using the most general unifier Θ, $P \models \forall (B_1 \wedge \ldots \wedge B_n \rightarrow Z)\Theta$ also holds.

Substitution in GL gives:

$$P \models \forall (\bigwedge \alpha \wedge B_1 \wedge \ldots \wedge B_n \wedge \bigwedge \beta)\Theta \rightarrow (\bigwedge \alpha \wedge G \wedge \bigwedge \beta)\Theta$$

However, this means that $P \models \forall (\bigwedge GL' \rightarrow (\bigwedge GL)\Theta)$. For a successful computation $(GL_0, C_0, \Theta_0), \ldots, (GL_k, C_k, \Theta_k)$ with $\Theta_0 = \{\}$ we then have:

$$P \models \forall (\bigwedge[] \rightarrow \bigwedge GL_0 \Theta_0 \Theta_1 \ldots \Theta_k)$$

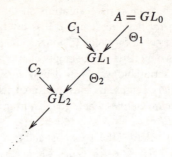

Figure 4.1   Graphical representation of a derivation.

Since $\bigwedge[]$ stands for true, we obtain $P \models \forall((A_1 \wedge \ldots \wedge A_n)\Theta_0\Theta_1 \ldots \Theta_k)$. In other words, the composition of the substitutions is a correct answer.

In order to understand that the clauses to be used in a step and the current goal list must be name-disjoint, one must remember that the scope of a variable is precisely the clauses in which it occurs. If name disjointedness were not ensured, unifications would fail as a result of the occur check, because two variables with the same name occurred in the selected goal and the clause head.

A derivation $\{GL_i, C_i, \Theta_i\}_{0 \leq i}$ for P and $A \equiv GL_0$ can be illustrated graphically as in Figure 4.1.

Example 4.8   Let us again consider the appending of lists, as in Examples 4.1 and 4.2. We describe it using the predicate *append* with the rules:

$$C_1 \equiv append\,([\,], ys, ys) \leftarrow$$
$$C_2 \equiv append\,(.(x, xs), ys, .(x, zs)) \leftarrow append\,(xs, ys, zs)$$

Figure 4.2 shows a derivation for the query *append* $(.(a, .(b, [\,])), .(c, [\,]), us)$.
The composition $\Theta_1\Theta_2\Theta_3$ gives the binding $us/.(a, .(b, .(c, [\,])))$ for us. □

It is unclear how the goal for the next step is chosen in each derivation step. Comfortingly, the selection of the next goal does not affect the success or failure of a computation, that is, for a given program P, the following holds for any goal list GL and any goal G:

If there exists a successful computation, beginning with another goal G' in GL, then there also exists a successful computation beginning with G. If the next goal is not selected arbitrarily at each stage but systematically, that is, in the same way for the same goal lists, we speak of a computation rule.

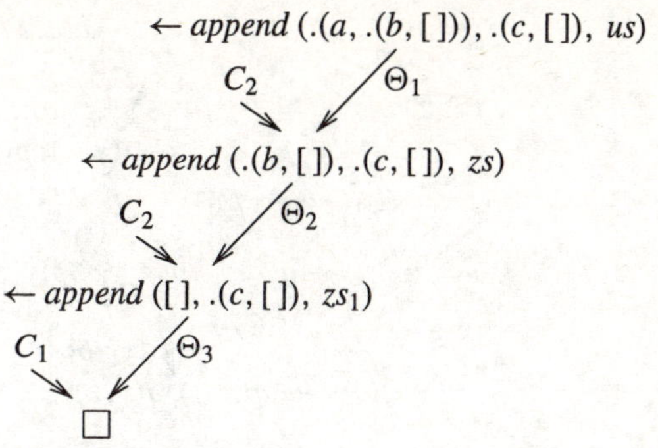

$$\leftarrow append\ (.(a, .(b, [\,])), .(c, [\,]),\ us)$$

$$\leftarrow append\ (.(b, [\,]), .(c, [\,]),\ zs)$$

$$\leftarrow append\ ([\,], .(c, [\,]),\ zs_1)$$

$$\square$$

$$\Theta_1 = \{x/a,\ xs/.(b, [\,]),\ ys/.(c, [\,]),\ us/.(a,\ zs)\}$$
$$\Theta_2 = \{x/b,\ xs/[\,],\ ys/.(c, [\,]),\ zs/.(b,\ zs_1)\}$$
$$\Theta_3 = \{ys/.(c, [\,]),\ zs_1/.(c, [\,])\}$$

Figure 4.2 A derivation.

Definition 4.10 (computation rule) A function that maps a goal list onto one of its goals is called a **computation rule**. $\square$

Example 4.9 The program

$$C_1 \equiv p(x, z) \leftarrow q(x, y),\ p(y, z)$$
$$C_2 \equiv p(x, x) \leftarrow$$
$$C_3 \equiv q(a, b) \leftarrow$$

with the query $\leftarrow p(u, b)$ has the derivations shown in Figure 4.3.

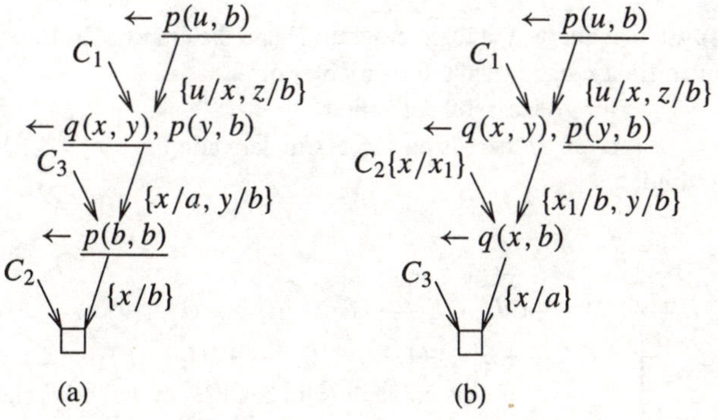

(a)

(b)

Figure 4.3 Two successful derivations for the query $\leftarrow p(u, b)$. (a) uses the computation rule 'select the first goal', (b) the rule 'select the last goal'.

$$\leftarrow p(u, b)$$

$$C_1 \searrow \quad \downarrow \{u/x, z/b\}$$

$$\leftarrow q(x, y), \underline{p(y, b)}$$

$$C_1\{x/x_1, y/y_1\} \searrow \quad \downarrow \{x_1/x, z/b\}$$

$$\leftarrow q(x, y), p(y, y_1), \underline{p(y_1, b)}$$

$$C_2 \searrow \quad \downarrow \{y_1/b\}$$

$$\leftarrow q(x, y), \underline{q(y, b)}$$

$$C_3 \searrow \quad \downarrow \{y/a\}$$

$$\leftarrow q(x, a)$$

Figure 4.4 An unsuccessful derivation for the query $\leftarrow p(u, b)$.

There also exist unsuccessful derivations for the same query (see Figure 4.4) together with non-terminating derivations. One such arises if the computation rule 'select last goal' is used, with variants of the clause C_1 throughout. $\qquad \square$

In particular, the above statement says that the success of a derivation for a program P and a query A does not depend on the computation rule used.

We are now in a position to give a first (non-deterministic) interpreter for logic programs (see Figure 4.5).

Input: a query A, a logic program P and the empty substitution.

Output: a substitution Φ for variables of A,

for a successful derivation,

or *no*, if there is no successful derivation.

Method:

$([\,], P, \Phi)$ ready, output $\Phi|_{Var(A)}$

$(GL + +[G] + +GL', CL + +(H \leftarrow B) + +CL', \Phi) \Rightarrow$

$$\begin{cases} ((GL + +B' + +GL')\Theta, CL + +(H \leftarrow B) + +CL', \Phi\Theta) \\ \qquad \text{if } G \text{ is unifiable with head } H' \text{ of the 'new' clause } H' \leftarrow B' \\ \qquad \text{with most general unifier } \Theta \\ no \qquad \text{otherwise} \end{cases}$$

Figure 4.5 An interpreter for logic programs.

The interpreter works with a goal list to be derived. Initially, this is the list of the query goals. If it reduces the goal list to the 'empty' list the computation was successful. The solution found is then given by the composition of the substitutions of the derivation, restricted to the variables of the query.

The interpreter configurations consist of three components: the current goal list, the program and the composition of the unifications found so far. The interpreter begins with the query as the current goal list and with the empty substitution.

The interpreter decomposes the goal list non-deterministically into three parts, the initial piece GL, the current goal G and the final piece GL'. The program, the second component which never changes, is also decomposed (non-deterministically) in order to determine the next clause to be used, $H \leftarrow B$. This is converted by renaming into a 'fresh' clause, $H' \leftarrow B'$, which is name-disjoint with the current list. H' is unified with the current goal G, yielding the most general unifier Θ. The right-hand side of the (renamed) clause B' is substituted for G and Θ is applied to the newly generated goal list. In addition, Θ is composed with the substitutions found so far. Since the interpreter is non-deterministic, we assume that it is capable of successful guessing. In other words, if it does not manage to choose a goal and a clause that form a step in the computation of an existing successful computation, there will be no further steps in the computation. Finally, if the current goal list is empty the computation was successful. The substitution computed is restricted to the variables of the query. This is the result of the computation.

The interpreter acts non-deterministically, because neither the goal to be chosen from the goal list nor the corresponding clause to be used is specified. As we have seen above, the first decision is unimportant. If there exists a successful computation departing from the chosen goal, there also exist other successful computations departing from any other goal. The second choice is also made non-deterministically. However, the choice of a wrong clause can lead to a dead end or to non-termination, even though a successful computation exists.

If this interpreter were made deterministic, specifications would be given for taking these two decisions, the choice of a goal and the choice of a corresponding clause. The first question, namely the choice of a computation rule, is essentially unimportant, and thus may be determined by technical aspects of the implementation or on efficiency grounds.

We first consider a representation of the search space to be traversed. Since the choice of computation rule is (theoretically) of no interest, we specify an arbitrary computation rule. The search space is then represented by a search tree.

Definition 4.11 (search tree)   A **search tree** for a program P and a query A is the following tree:

- Its nodes are labelled by goal lists; for non-empty goal lists the goal selected by the computation rule is designated.
- The root is labelled by A.
- A node with a non-empty goal list GL and designated goal G has as

successors all the different goal lists that can be derived directly from GL by means of some clause C and a most general unifier Θ.

• Empty goal lists have no successors. □

The successors of a node in the search tree represent all the possible ways in which the designated goal of the node can be successfully unified with the head of program clauses to generate a new goal list with these clauses. Every path in the search tree represents a derivation for the program P and the query A. The finite paths belonging to successful computations are called **successful paths**; the finite paths that lead to unsuccessful computations are called **unsuccessful paths**.

Thus, the search tree represents the whole search space, in which solutions for a program P and a query A can be found. If one is only interested in an arbitrary single solution, it is sufficient to find a successful path; if one wishes to see all solutions, the whole search tree must be traversed.

Example 4.10 Let us again consider the *append* predicate, this time with the query $\leftarrow append\,(xs, ys, .(a, .(b, [\,])))$. There are three successful paths (see Figure 4.6). □

Example 4.11 Figure 4.7 shows the search trees corresponding to the computation rules 'select the first goal' (a) and 'select the last goal' (b) of Example 4.9. Both trees have the same number of successful paths. However, the tree in Figure 4.7(b) also has infinitely long paths. □

The following two strategies for traversing the search tree are of interest. The **breadth-first search** traverses the search tree layer-wise, beginning with the root and passing to all the children of the root, then all the grandchildren, and so on. It is evident that this strategy finds a successful path when there is one, and all successful

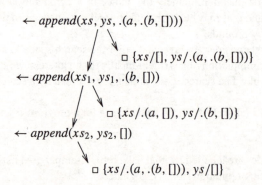

Figure 4.6 A search tree for the query $\rightarrow append(xs, ys, .(a, .(b, [\,])))$.

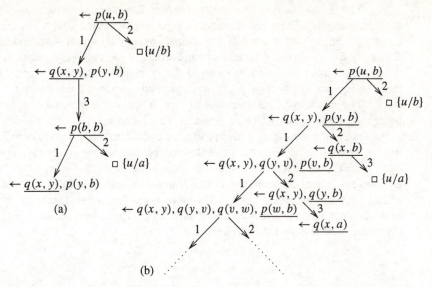

Figure 4.7   Two search trees. The selected goal is underlined in each case. The edges are labelled with the clause number.

paths when this is required. Thus, this strategy is said to be **complete**. However, it is very expensive because it is always necessary to remember the current layer or an equivalent structure.

The other strategy, which is used in Prolog, is the **depth-first search**. This investigates the various possibilities consecutively, rather than simultaneously, until some possibility leads to success (that is, the empty goal list) or failure (that is, impossible to proceed, for non-empty goal lists). Since it can also lead to non-terminating computations, although successful terminating computations are possible, it is said to be **incomplete**.

The depth-first search is only uniquely defined when the sequence in which the children of each node are to be processed is specified. This specification involves the choice of a **search rule**.

Definition 4.12 (search rule)   Suppose we are given a logic program P. A total ordering on the alternatives for a predicate is called a **search rule**. $\square$

The specification of a search rule enables one to turn a search tree into an ordered tree. The children of a node are ordered according to the given ordering on the alternatives for the goal predicate.

For Prolog, this amounts to the following:

Computation rule: select the first goal of the goal list.
Search rule: select the alternatives for a predicate in the order in which they occur in the program text.

The search tree is only a concept for explaining the search for solutions in logic programming. Every search tree for a logic program P and a query A contains a (possibly empty) set of successful computations, in the form of paths ending in the empty list. The set of solutions obtained from the successful computations for the various search trees found are identical. This is again a manifestation of the fact that the sequence in which the goals are substituted in a goal list is irrelevant.

The search tree for a query and a program does not exist as a data structure in the computer memory. Rather, the search for a solution is a process in which paths in the search tree are dynamically constructed and dismantled. A node in the tree (that is, a goal list) is said to be **active** after its creation, as long as not all the paths that can be constructed from it have been fully constructed (and dismantled); that is, if there is at least one path from this node that does not end in an empty goal list or in a goal list that cannot be derived further. For a depth-first search, this is the case when not all the alternatives for the selected goal have been traced to the end. Otherwise, a node is said to be **inactive**.

4.5   Prolog

From now on, we shall adhere more closely to the normal Prolog notation. Variables in Prolog always begin with capital letters, predicates and function symbols with small letters. There is an abbreviated notation for list terms: instead of the binary function symbol '.', in prefix notation it is customary to use the character '|' in infix notation. Thus, $[Hd|Tl]$ stands for $.(Hd, Tl)$, $[a|[\,]]$ for $.(a, [\,])$. In addition, the list elements may be listed separated by commas; $[a, b, c]$ stands for $[a|[b|[c|[\,]]]]$. Standard Prolog systems use the computation rule 'the goal to be selected is the leftmost in the goal list' and the search rule 'try the clauses for the current goal predicate in the order in which they are listed'.

A **Prolog computation** for a given logic program P and a query A then constitutes a depth-first traverse of the search tree which is uniquely determined by the computation rule. A Prolog computation finds all solutions if no infinite paths exist. Otherwise, the Prolog computation does not terminate and may not find all the solutions.

The DFLR algorithm in Figure 4.8 finds all solutions for a Prolog program P and a query A with a left–right depth-first search, provided it does not get into a non-terminating computation before it has found them all. For this, it uses the following types and functions: the configurations of the DLFR interpreter each comprise a sequence of started computations, the first of which is the current computation.

*Conf = Computation**

Every started computation comprises a sequence of frames and the composition of the substitutions that have previously occurred in that computation.

Input: Prolog program P, query A.
Output: On termination, all solutions to P and A.
Method: Apply the following transition rules to the initial configuration
$[([(A, P)], \emptyset)]$:

Transition rules:

$[\,]$		End configuration	(1)
$([([\,], \_)], \Theta) : BBL \Rightarrow$	BBL	Solution found,	(2)
	Output: $\Theta\vert_{Vars(A)}$	one computation ends	
$\left((G : GL, [\,]) : FL, \Theta\right) : BBL \Rightarrow$	BBL	Backtrack, remaining	(3)
		goals not unifiable	

$((G : GL, (H \leftarrow B) : CL) : FL, \Theta) : BBL \Rightarrow$ $\qquad\qquad\qquad\qquad$ (4)

$$\begin{cases} ((B', P) : (GL, P) : FL, \Theta\Phi) : ((G : GL, CL) : FL, \Theta) : BBL, & (4.1) \\ \quad \text{if } G\Theta \text{ unifiable with head } H' \text{ of the 'new' clause} \\ \quad H' \leftarrow B' \text{ with most general unifier } \Phi \\ \\ ((G : GL, CL) : FL, \Theta) : BBL \qquad \text{otherwise} & (4.2) \end{cases}$$

Figure 4.8   DFLR algorithm.

$$Computation = Frame^* \times Subst$$

Each frame consists of a goal list and a sequence of clauses.

$$Frame = Goal^* \times Clause^*$$

The goals in the goal list are processed from left to right, according to the Prolog computation rule; the goals on the right-hand side of a given clause are entered at the beginning of the list (transition 4). Thus, the whole program P is always included in the frame. According to the Prolog search rule, the clauses are investigated in the order in which they occur in the program.

Some of the DFLR transitions are defined for multiple cases relating to the list of computations started (transitions 1 and 2); others are defined via the current computation (transitions 3 and 4). Case 1 describes the end configuration, in which no more started computations remain. In case 2, the interpreter ends a started computation successfully and issues a solution. Case 3 calls for backtracking, since all the clauses of the program have been tried and it has not been possible to prove all the goals. Finally, case 4 describes a resolution step; the goal G is unified with the head of the (renamed) clause $H \leftarrow B$.

The following generic names are used in the computation:

G Goal
GL Goal list
H Head
B Body (right-hand side)
CL List of clauses
FL List of frames
P Program
BBL List of started computations
Θ, Φ Substitutions

To distinguish the list of started computations (outer parentheses) from the list of frames (inner parentheses), larger parentheses are used for the outer list.

4.5.1   Proof tree

Every path in a search tree is associated with a sequence of **proof trees**. A proof tree for a node in the search tree has the query as the root label and the goal list of the node in the search tree as the leaf word, that is, the word of the leaf labels. With the possible exception of the root, all nodes are labelled by individual goals. The children of the root node are labelled by the individual goals of the query. The construction of the proof tree for a path in the search tree is defined as follows.

Suppose BB_1 is the proof tree for a node n_1 with goal list GL_1 in the search tree. The leaf word of BB_1 is thus GL_1. Suppose that a child node n_2 of n_1 is labelled by the goal list GL_2 which is obtained by:

- Unification of the goal G in GL_1, selected according to the computation rule, with the head of a clause $A \leftarrow A_1, \ldots, A_k$ (previously made name-disjoint with all earlier goals by renaming) (Result: most general unifier Θ),

- Replacement of G in GL_1 by $A_1, \ldots, A_k$, and

- Application of Θ to the goal list thus obtained.

The proof tree BB_2 for n_2 is then obtained from the proof tree BB_1 as follows :

(1)   If $k > 0$, that is, if the body of the given clause is non-empty, the leaf node of BB_1 labelled by G is then assigned the new children $A_1, \ldots, A_k$ in that order, and the substitution Θ is applied to the whole proof tree.

(2)   If $k = 0$, that is, a fact is used, the leaf node of BB_1 labelled by G is assigned a child labelled *true*. The unifier Θ is then applied to the proof tree thus obtained.

Thus, the leaf word of a proof tree for a node n in a search tree is equal to the goal list labelled by n. Here, the leaves of the proof tree labelled *true* are omitted; since the goal lists are conjunctions of goals, omission is a legal simplification.

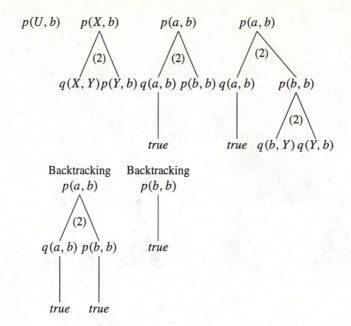

Figure 4.9 The sequence of proof trees for the search tree in Figure 4.7(a). The next alternative to use, if there is one, is shown in brackets.

In every node of a proof tree a record of the as yet untested alternatives for the associated goal is kept. If such an alternative still exists, the node is called a **backtrack point**. The nodes that are generated after a backtrack point is established form its **segment**. Backtracking, either because all alternatives to a goal have failed or because another solution is desired, involves a return to the last backtrack point created and the removal of its segment from the proof tree. The bindings of variables generated by unification since the establishment of the backtrack point are undone, which requires a list of these variables. The next alternative for the backtrack point is chosen.

Thus, the proof tree becomes larger when a clause is applied and smaller on backtracking. Its leaves are labelled by the goals of the current goal list that remain to be proved. The inner nodes are labelled by fully or partially proved goals. Assuming the Prolog computation rule, that is, selection of the leftmost goal, we are able to make a more precise statement. All clauses whose processing has started but not ended have a rightmost goal that is either the current goal or an inner node.

This points to a possible further compaction. Let us assume that given any goal A_i on the right-hand side of a clause $A_0 \leftarrow A_1, \ldots, A_k$ one always finds the goal A_{i+1}; this is easy to realize for interpreting or compiling implementations. Then there is no need to store any leaf nodes except the current goal. They can all

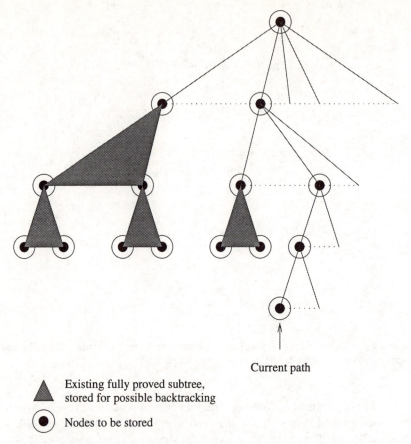

Current path

▲ Existing fully proved subtree,
   stored for possible backtracking

(●) Nodes to be stored

Figure 4.10   A proof tree with a compact representation.

be reached from the current goal or from an inner node. Figure 4.10 shows a proof tree with such a compact representation.

As in the case of the search tree, the discussion of the proof tree also shows that a stack discipline is an obvious candidate for the management of the proof tree. The stack is initialized with a frame for the query. A frame is created in the stack for every clause applied. When backtracking occurs, all frames belonging to clauses in its segment are removed from the stack.

4.5.2   Environments

Let us again describe an expansion step in the proof tree. The process seeks the next clause whose head can be unified with the current goal, the label of the leftmost unprocessed leaf. Renaming is carried out before unification to ensure that the variables in the clause do not occur in any of the previous goals. Successful unification yields the most general unifier Θ for the current goal and the clause head. The sequence of goals on the right-hand side is appended beneath the current goal (we have already indicated that it is sufficient to label the first goal on the right-hand side if the storage representation is suitably organized). Finally, the substitution Θ is applied to the whole of the proof tree. This procedure has a number of unpleasant features as far as the implementation is concerned. The renaming of the clause variables, in other words, the generation of a new copy of the clause with newly introduced names, is an expense one would like to eliminate. The application of the most general unifier to the whole of the proof tree at the end of every step is also much too expensive. In particular, this makes it impossible to undo efficiently the application of a clause that has not led to success.

Therefore, we introduce the concept of an **environment**. An environment represents the (combined) effect of the application of one or more substitutions to an applied clause. Instead of applying the most general unifier to the whole proof tree in every clause application, the bindings of the local variables of each clause applied in the proof tree are stored in an environment associated with this clause application (in the implementation of functional languages, this corresponds to delaying the β-reduction, which is also implemented by the generation of environments). An environment is created when a clause is applied; it is initialized with the bindings for the local variables which are obtained from the unification of the current goal and the clause head. Later unifications may introduce more bindings.

Our aim is to manage environments for the variables of clauses in a stack-like manner. The representation of an environment is then part of a stack frame for an applied clause. The stack frames are established when the clause is applied and removed when all the goals on the right-hand side have been proved and this environment is no longer needed for backtracking. Backtracking may release one or more frames.

At this point, it is appropriate to investigate the similarities to and differences from the implementations of imperative and functional languages. In all three cases, incarnations of program units are managed in a stack-like manner. This includes:

- in imperative languages: the incarnations of proper and function procedures;
- in functional languages: the applications of functions and, in the case of languages with call-by-need semantics, the evaluation of closures;
- in logic languages: the evaluation of clauses.

A frame in the stack is assigned to each such incarnation. Among other things, these frames contain memory locations for the incarnations of the variables of the program units, that is, the procedures, functions and clauses. As far as the release of stack frames is concerned, logic programming languages fall out of line as a result of backtracking; whether a clause application is complete after its goal has been processed and its frame can be released becomes apparent only at run time.

4.6   Abstract Prolog machine

4.6.1   Development of the Prolog implementation

We began with the operational semantics of logic programs in the form of a non-deterministic interpreter. The next goal to be derived and the clauses to be applied were chosen non-deterministically. We noted that the first of the two choices is not critical. Thus, it can be made using a computation rule, where selection is based on implementation-related aspects.

For a given computation rule, for every logic program and every query, there exists precisely one search tree describing the search space to be scanned for solutions. This search tree can be scanned by a breadth-first search as a complete search strategy. Since this is expensive to implement, a (recursive) depth-first search is chosen for Prolog. The search tree is ordered according to the sequence of the alternatives in the program and the depth-first search progresses from left to right.

It is known how to convert recursive programs into iterative programs. Iterative programs must manage the stack themselves; recursive programs use it implicitly. The iterative variant of the deterministic Prolog interpreter is the DFLR algorithm in Figure 4.8. Its stack entries are triplets consisting of the current goal list, the next alternative for the current goal and the substitution applied.

In the next step, each such stack entry was represented by a proof tree; more precisely, the goal list was represented by a proof tree and, for each goal, the number of the next alternative to be applied. The push and pop operations of the DFLR algorithm were implemented by adding clause applications to and removing them from the proof tree. Case 3 in DFLR corresponds to the removal of the segment for the current backtrack point in the proof tree.

The cancellation of variable bindings cannot be efficiently implemented with the previous organization. Proof trees with environments have to be introduced for this. These arise by delaying the substitutions. Each clause application is assigned an environment, that is, a binding of variables in the clause. For each goal, a backtracking list records the variables that are bound by the unification of this goal with a clause head, to permit the variable bindings to be reset. On backtracking, the variables in the backtracking list are 'unbound'.

Backtracking involves the removal of a subtree from the proof tree, namely the segment that was created after the associated backtrack point was established. Thus, the last segments created are removed first. This again calls for a stack implementation. A frame is created on the stack for every clause application. This contains the environment for the clause application, locations required for stack management and the list of variables whose binding was generated by unification with the clause head. On backtracking, stack frames belonging to the segment of the current backtrack point are removed, bindings generated since it was created are deleted and the procedure continues by using the next alternative for the backtrack point.

We now make the step from an interpreter to a compiler. A suitable abstract machine, the WiM, is introduced for this. Here are some important characteristics of the execution of Prolog programs on the WiM:

- direct addressing of clause variables via statically assigned relative addresses;
- release of stack storage space as soon as possible;
- efficient unification by compiling head terms into 'unification code'.

4.6.2 The architecture of the WiM

The first design of an abstract Prolog machine, the WiM, strives for simplicity and the greatest possible similarity to the previous machines, the P machine and the MaMa. Efficiency is not a design goal. A number of improvements, to be described later, will make the WiM (almost) usable. Other efficiency-increasing measures, such as those realized in Prolog implementations on the Warren abstract machine, are too complicated to be treated here. Details can be found in the relevant books.

The WiM has

- a **program store** *PS*; the program counter *PC* always points to the current instruction;
- a **stack** *ST*, containing frames with *SP* and *FP* registers; in addition, a register *BTP*, which points to the current backtrack point in the stack, is used for backtracking;
- a **heap** *H* with a heap pointer *HP*; the heap actually behaves like a stack which is always shortened by backtracking;
- a **trail** *TR* which is pointed to by a register *TP*;
- a variable *mode* used for the unification.

The following invariant holds before and after the execution of WiM instructions: *SP* and *TP* point to the last occupied location in *ST* and *TR*, respectively. *HP* points to the next free location in *H*.

The main cycle of the WiM looks like that of the P machine or the MaMa:

- Load the instruction in *PS*[PC];
- Increase *PC* by 1;
- Execute the instruction loaded.

The WiM heap

Atoms, variables and structures are stored, as in the MaMa, in tagged objects, in the WiM heap, see Figure 4.11. Atoms are represented by the tag ATOM and a unique code for the atom. Bound variables are represented by the tag REF and a pointer to the object bound to them. Objects of unbound variables can be recognized from the

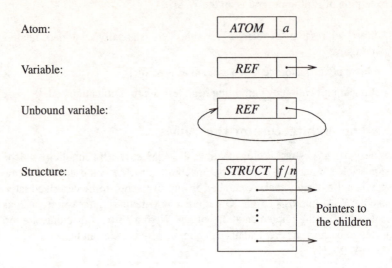

Figure 4.11 The WiM heap objects.

fact that their pointers point to themselves. Structures tagged STRUCT contain names and the arity of the functor, together with pointers to representations of the children. In this representation, a term is used to communicate between calls and procedures and for unification.

The heap pointer *HP* always points to the next free heap location. The heap management provides an operation *new* which creates the desired tagged object in the heap and returns a pointer to it.

Stack frames

When a clause is applied a stack frame is established on the WiM stack. As shown in Figure 4.12, it contains organizational cells, pointers to the arguments and an environment for the clause variables. The entries in the environment are empty to begin with. When the first occurrence of a variable is encountered a pointer to a heap object (frequently to an unbound variable) is entered in its environment location. Another local stack at the end of the stack space is used for the unification of the head of the clause and the associated call and for the construction of argument terms. Of the total of six organizational cells, only two are initially required. These two also occur in implementations of imperative and functional languages. Returning to the dynamic predecessor that created the current incarnation requires the corresponding value of the frame pointer *FP*. In addition, the address in the code from which execution will continue after successful processing of the clause is stored.

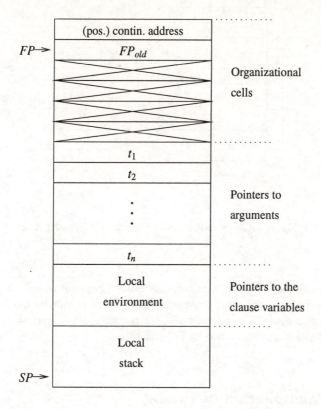

Figure 4.12   The structure of WiM stack frames.

We shall call this the **positive continuation address**. We shall meet the negative continuation address later; it is used for continuation when backtracking is required, for example if a unification fails. Other locations are used to handle backtracking; these will be discussed later.

Storage representation of terms

Unstructured objects are (as we have seen) represented by an appropriate heap object. Structures have a standard representation in the heap and are transferred between the callers and the procedures called.

Example 4.11   The term $f(g(X, Y), a, Z)$ with bound variable X and unbound variables Y and Z is represented in the heap as shown in Figure 4.13. □

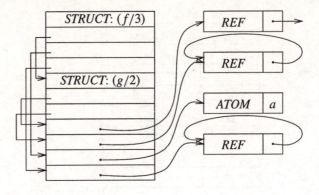

Figure 4.13   Representation of the term $f(g(X, Y), a, Z)$.

The protocol, that is, the rule for communication between call and procedure, has the following form: the caller constructs a heap representation for the ith argument term according to the above rules and sets a pointer to it in a frame location whose relative address is given by adding a constant to i.

4.7   Compilation of Prolog

4.7.1   Goals

A stack frame is established for a goal; the arguments are passed and finally the corresponding procedure is called.

Passing of arguments

The first code function we shall meet is *code_A* which compiles a term t into a sequence of instructions, the execution of which constructs an instance of t in the heap.

  code_A uses an address environment ρ to address clause variables relative to the contents of the *FP* register. The stack location with the address $FP + \rho(X)$ is reserved for a pointer to the heap object for the variable X. We assume that first and non-first occurrences of clause variables are denoted differently for the purposes of compilation, for example, by X and $\tilde{X}$, respectively. At run time, the first occurrence of a variable does not yet have a heap object and the corresponding stack-frame location does not contain a pointer. Thus, a heap object, an unbound variable, must first be created and pointers to it stored both in the environment and

Table 4.8   Instructions for creating term instances in the heap.

Instruction	Meaning	Comments
putatom a	$SP := SP + 1;$ $ST[SP] := new\,(ATOM\ :\ a)$	Atom
putvar i	$SP := SP + 1;$ $ST[FP + i] := new\,(REF\ :\ HP)$ $ST[SP] := ST[FP + i]$	Unbound variable
putref i	$SP := SP + 1;$ $ST[SP] := ST[FP + i]$	Bound variable
putstruct f/n	$SP := SP - n + 1;$ $ST[SP] := new\,(STRUCT\ :\ f/n,$ $ST[SP], \ldots, ST[SP + n - 1])$	

in the argument location. An occurrence which is not the first occurrence already has a pointer to a heap object. Thus, it is only necessary to copy the pointer into the argument location.

code_A compiles a term in a post-order pass, that is, the instruction for an internal node is only generated after its subterms have been compiled. Here the following assertion holds:

(AI)   Let $t_1, \ldots, t_k$ be the maximal subterms which have already been compiled, for example, into the instruction sequence B_{1k}. Then the execution of B_{1k} leaves the pointers to the instances for $t_1, \ldots, t_k$ in the stack locations $ST[SP - k + 1], \ldots, ST[SP]$.

In particular, it follows from this assertion that the compilation of an argument t generates an instruction sequence that leaves a pointer to the instance for t at the top of the stack.

Table 4.8 defines the instructions for constructing arguments. The definition of *code_A* follows:

$$
\begin{aligned}
code\_A\ a\ \rho &= \textbf{putatom } a \\
code\_A\ n\ \rho &= \textbf{putint } n \\
code\_A\ X\ \rho &= \textbf{putvar } \rho(X) \qquad \text{first occurrence of } X \\
code\_A\ \tilde{X}\ \rho &= \textbf{putref } \rho(X) \qquad \text{non-first occurrence of } X \\
code\_A\ f(t_1, \ldots, t_n)\ \rho &= code\_A\ t_1\ \rho; \\
&\qquad \vdots \\
&\quad\ code\_A\ t_n\ \rho; \\
&\quad\ \textbf{putstruct } f/n
\end{aligned}
$$

Table 4.9 The **enter** and **call** instructions.

Instruction	Meaning	Comments
enter	$SP := SP + 6$; $ST[SP - 4] := FP$	Space for organizational cells Pointer to the frame of the call
call p/n	$FP := SP - (n + 4)$; $ST[FP - 1] := PC$; $PC := Addr\,(Code\,(p/n))$	FP now points to new frame Continuation address

Example 4.12 The compilation of the term $f(g(X, a), \tilde{Y})$ in the environment ρ is:

> **putvar** $\rho(X)$;
> **putatom** a;
> **putstruct** $g/2$;
> **putref** $\rho(Y)$;
> **putstruct** $f/2$ □

Compilation of a goal

It is now quite clear how a goal is compiled. A frame for the called clause is created, the arguments are constructed in the heap and pointers to them are passed on the stack. The procedure is then called. *code_G* compiles the goals:

$$code\_G \; p(t_1, \ldots, t_n) \; \rho \quad = \quad \begin{array}{l} \textbf{enter}; \\ code\_A \; t_1 \; \rho; \\ \vdots \\ code\_A \; t_n \; \rho; \\ \textbf{call} \; p/n \end{array}$$

The **enter** instruction (see Table 4.9) creates a stack frame, reserves space for the organizational cells and saves the current state of the *FP* register. After incrementing the *FP* register and setting the continuation address, **call** jumps to the code for the procedure.

4.7.2 Head terms

Let us consider a goal $p(t_1)$ and a head $p(t_2)$ of an alternative to p. We have seen that t_1 is compiled into an instruction sequence that constructs an instance of t_1 in the heap, leaving a pointer to it on the stack. We shall now deal with the compilation of t_2. t_2 is compiled into an instruction sequence that executes the unification of t_2 with corresponding goal terms, in this case, t_1. The code for t_2 passes through

t_1 recursively, compares functors and atoms and binds unbound variables in t_2 to corresponding subterms in t_1. This last action involves the setting of pointers to the heap representation of the subterms. But what happens when an unbound variable is encountered in t_1? It has to be bound to the corresponding subterm in t_2, which does not exist and therefore has to be created.

Thus, the unification instructions operate in one of two modes: **read mode** and **write mode**. They begin in read mode when they compare functors and atoms and bind head variables to goal terms as indicated above. When an unbound variable X is encountered in the goal they switch to write mode and construct the necessary head terms in the heap, setting a pointer to them in the heap object for X. When the subterm has been traversed, they switch back to read mode. Hence, for every subterm, a record of the mode in which it is processed must be made.

Once again, a local stack is used to traverse the representation of the goal term in the heap (read mode) or to construct it (write mode). This is done using the instructions **down**, **brother** i and **up**.

$$
\begin{array}{lcll}
code\_U\ a\ \rho & = & \textbf{uatom}\ a & \text{Unify with atom} \\
code\_U\ X\ \rho & = & \textbf{uvar}\ \rho(X) & \text{Unify with unbound variable} \\
code\_U\ \tilde{X}\ \rho & = & \textbf{uref}\ \rho(X) & \text{Unify with bound variable} \\
code\_U\ f(t_1, \ldots, t_n)\ \rho & = & \textbf{ustruct}\ f/n; & \text{Unify with structure} \\
 & & \textbf{down}; & \\
 & & code\_U\ t_1\ \rho; & \\
 & & \textbf{brother}\ 2; & \\
 & & code\_U\ t_2\ \rho; & \\
 & & \vdots & \\
 & & \textbf{brother}\ n; & \\
 & & code\_U\ t_n\ \rho; & \\
 & & \textbf{up} & \\
\end{array}
$$

We begin with the definition of the walk instructions. These are given in Table 4.10. In read mode, these can be used to walk the tree in an obvious way with the aid of the local stack. In this case, pointers to the roots of subterms are stored on the local stack (**down** and **brother**) and removed when the subterm has been fully traversed (**up**). In write mode the subterms do not yet exist. In this case, a location is reserved on the local stack, in which the pointer to the subterm created will be entered.

We now come to the unification instructions. Their execution assumes the following situation: $ST[SP]$ contains a pointer to the representation of the (sub)term which is involved in the unification.

Let us consider the occurrence of an atom a in a head term. This is compiled into the instruction **uatom** a (see Table 4.11). What should this instruction mean? For this, we consider the two modes and the possible cases for the corresponding argument term. In write mode, an $(ATOM : a)$ object has to be created in the heap. In read mode, there are two possibilities for successful unification:

Table 4.10.   The walk instructions.

Instruction	Meaning	Comments

down	**case** *mode* **of**
	   read: $ST[SP + 1] := H[ST[SP] + 1]$;
	
	   write: $ST[SP + 1] := ST[SP] + 1$;
	endcase;
	$SP := SP + 1$
		First pointer location
		   for functor
		Reserve pointer location

brother *i*	**case** *mode* **of**
	   read: $ST[SP + 1] := H[ST[SP] + i]$;
	
	   write: $ST[SP + 1] := ST[SP] + i$;
	endcase;
	$SP := SP + 1$
		First pointer location
		   for functor
		Reserve pointer location

up	$SP := SP - 1$; **if** *mode* = *write* **then** *mode* := $ST[SP]$; $SP := SP - 1$ **fi**	Restore the mode

- The argument term is the same argument a. There is nothing more to do.
- The argument term is an unbound variable. It will be bound to an object $(ATOM : a)$, to be created. This is done using the statement $H[v] := (REF : new(ATOM : a))$. A more efficient possibility would be to overwrite the object $(REF : -)$ by an object $(ATOM : a)$.

Atoms and functors different from a cause the unification to fail. We must consider the case of bound variables in more detail. If unification instructions meet a bound variable X, the latter may point to another bound variable Y, and so on. Before unification can be applied to the term to which X is bound, the whole chain of such pointers must be traversed. This is done using the function *deref*, which is part of the runtime system.

```
function deref (a : heapaddr) : heapaddr;
    case H[a] of
        (REF : b):    if a = b
                      then return a    (*Unbound variable*)
```

else *deref* (*b*)   (∗Bound variable∗)

fi;

otherwise: **return** *a*;

endcase;

The definitions of the unification instructions involve an auxiliary function *trail*, which is described later. It is responsible for logging bindings which must subsequently be cancelled during backtracking.

The global label *backtrack* is jumped to if the unification fails.

Table 4.11.   The **uatom** instruction.

Instruction	Meaning	Comments

uatom *a*	**case** *mode* **of**
	read:
	 begin
	  $v := deref (ST[SP])$;
	  $SP := SP - 1$;
	  case $H[v]$ **of**
	   $(ATOM : a)$: ;
	   $(REF : -)$:
	   begin
	    $H[v] := (REF : new(ATOM : a))$;
	    trail (v);
	   end
	   otherwise: **goto** *backtrack*
	  endcase;
	 end
	write:
	 begin
	  $H[ST[SP]] := new (ATOM : a)$;
	  $SP := SP - 1$;
	 end
	endcase
		Unification with atom
		
		Unbound variable
		is bound

Table 4.12   Unification with unbound variable.

Instruction	Meaning	Comments
uvar i	**case** *mode* **of** *read*: $ST[FP + i] := deref\ (ST[SP])$; *write*: $H[ST[SP]] := ST[FP + i] :=$ $new(REF: HP)$; **endcase**; $SP := SP - 1$	Set variable link

Table 4.13   Unification with bound variable.

Instruction	Meaning	Comments
uref i	**case** *mode* **of** *read*: $unify\ (ST[SP], ST[FP + i])$; *write*: $H[ST[SP]] := ST[FP + i]$; **endcase**; $SP := SP - 1$	The dynamic case

For the first occurrence of a variable X in the head **uvar** $\rho(X)$ is generated. What is the situation before the execution of this instruction? The environment location for X does not yet contain a pointer to a heap object. On the top of the local stack there is a pointer to the heap representation of the corresponding goal term. In read mode, this pointer is dereferenced and the resulting pointer copied into the environment location. In write mode, an object for an unbound variable must be created in the heap and pointers to it must be copied into the environment location and the 'parent location' in the heap.

Let us consider the compilation of an occurrence $\tilde{X}$ of a variable X, which is not the first occurrence. At execution time, X will be bound. $\tilde{X}$ is compiled into a **uref** instruction. In write mode, a pointer to the heap object bound to X must be entered. The unification, to be performed in read mode, of a bound variable in the head and an argument term gives the 'dynamic' case. The two terms involved are unknown at compile time. Then, the *unify* function introduced earlier is called, albeit modified in such a way that it generates bindings to the associated variable objects in the heap.

Let us now consider the instruction **ustruct**. In write mode, an object $(STRUCT : f/n)$ with n *NIL* pointers is created in the heap. The current mode is saved so that it can be restored later. The interesting case is the occurrence of an

Table 4.14   Unification with a structure.

Instruction	Meaning

ustruct f/n	**case** *mode* **of**
	read:
	  begin
	   $v := deref\ (ST[SP])$;
	   case $H[v]$ **of**
	    $(STRUCT\ :\ f/n)$: $ST[SP] := v$;
	    $(REF\ :\ -)$:
	     begin
	      $ST[SP] := mode$;
	      $SP := SP + 1$;
	      $h := new\ ((STRUCT\ :\ f/n), NIL, \ldots, NIL)$;
	      $ST[SP] := h$;
	      $H[v] := (REF\ :\ h)$;
	      $mode := write$;
	      $trail\ (v)$;
	     end
	    otherwise: **goto** *backtrack*
	   endcase
	  end;
	write:
	  begin
	   $H[ST[SP]] := ST[SP + 1]$
	    $:= new\ ((STRUCT\ :\ f/n), NIL, \ldots, NIL)$;
	   $ST[SP] := mode$;
	   $SP := SP + 1$
	  end
	endcase

unbound variable in read mode. Here, a (*STRUCT*: f/n) heap object is created. The mode is switched from read to write. The old mode is stored, so that a mode switch can be made upon return to this point.

Example 4.13   The head term $f(U, a, g(b, V))$ is compiled into the following instruction sequence:

ustruct $f/3$;	f
down;	(
uvar $\rho(h)$;	U
brother 2;	,
uatom a;	a
brother 3;	,
ustruct $g/2$;	g
down;	(
uatom b;	b
brother 2;	,
uvar $\rho(V)$;	V
up;	)
up	)

Note that it is assumed that the pointer to the corresponding argument term is in $ST[SP]$. □

4.7.3   Compilation of clauses

We now know almost all we need to know to compile clauses. We shall delay our treatment of backtracking a little. The compiler function *btinit* will be introduced later. It suffices to note here that it generates instructions to create, modify or abandon backtrack points. Similarly, *fin* generates different instructions for finalizing the stack frame for the clause for different values of *btparam*.

$code\_C$ ($C : p(t_1, \ldots, t_n) \leftarrow g_1, \ldots, g_m$) *btparam btcont* =

pushenv $n + r + 4$;	} Space for arguments and clause variables
btinit btparam btcont;	} Provision for backtracking
pusharg 1;	
code_U $t_1\ \rho$;	
pusharg 2;	
code_U $t_2\ \rho$;	Unification with
$\vdots$	argument terms
pusharg n;	
code_U $t_n\ \rho$;	

Table 4.15   **pushenv** and **pusharg**.

Instruction	Meaning
pushenv k	$SP := FP + k$
pusharg i	$SP := SP + 1;$ $ST[SP] := ST[FP + 4 + i]$

$code\_G\ g_1\ \rho;$
$code\_G\ g_2\ \rho;$ ⎫ Process goals
$\vdots$ ⎬ of the body
$code\_G\ g_m\ \rho;$ ⎭
fin btparam;   } Abandon the stack frame
where $\rho = [X_i \mapsto n + i + 4]_{i=1}^r$ **and** $\{X_1, X_2, \ldots, X_r\} = vars\,(C)$

Table 4.15 introduces the instructions **pushenv** and **pusharg**. Let us consider the set $\{X_1, X_2, \ldots, X_r\}$ of variables of the clause C. Suppose they are temporarily arranged in an arbitrary order and assigned the frame addresses $n + 5, n + 6, \ldots, n + r + 4$ by the address environment ρ.

When the code generated for the clause C is executed, the caller has previously created a stack frame using the **enter** instruction, constructed the argument terms, generated pointers to these on the stack and set the FP register to point to the second organizational cell. **pushenv** then reserves space for the n arguments and the r clause variables; **pusharg** i copies the pointer to the ith argument to the local stack, as the unification instructions expect. The overall interworking between call and clause is as follows:

Goal   Reserve space for organizational cells; construct argument terms in the heap; stack pointers; call.

Clause   Reserve space for arguments and clause variables; create/modify/delete backtrack point; execute unification with argument terms; process right-hand side calls; abandon frame; release storage if possible; jump to continuation address.

4.7.4   Backtracking

Backtracking occurs when unification with a clause head is unsuccessful or a further solution is desired after a first has been found. This involves restoring the state that was current the last time one of several alternatives for a procedure was chosen. There were then several possible ways to proceed. Thus, the computation returns to the parent goal of the youngest ongoing clause application for which there exists at least one other alternative. Such a clause application is called a **backtrack point** or **choice point**. In the search tree, this involves a return to the predecessor of the longest

Pos. contin. addr.
FP_{old}
BTP_{old}
TP_{old}
HP_{old}
Neg. contin. addr.

On successful execution of the clause

Chaining of backtrack points
On creation of the last backtrack point
On creation of the last backtrack point

On backtracking

Figure 4.14   Organizational cells in the stack frame.

right-hand backbone, ending in the current goal list. In the proof tree, it corresponds to the removal of the corresponding clause applications.

Clauses that are the last or the only alternatives of their procedure are called **deterministic clauses**. Other clauses are called **non-deterministic clauses**. In the same way, a procedure with several alternatives is called a **non-deterministic procedure**. For every clause, it is (statically) known whether it is the first alternative, last alternative or one of the other alternatives for a procedure. Thus, these three types of clause can be compiled into different instruction sequences. The application of a first clause creates a backtrack point. Later alternatives modify it. The last clause abandons the backtrack point. Of course, no backtrack points are created for procedures with just one alternative. Since backtrack points are tried in the inverse order to which they are created, the youngest first, their stack frames are chained in such a way that each backtrack point points to the one created immediately before it. The *BTP* register points to the last backtrack point created. The creation of a backtrack point involves saving the current state of the computation, since this state must be restored if backtracking is required.

What does the state of the computation consist of? First, it includes the address of the next alternative for the current goal, the so-called **negative continuation address**. Then it includes the contents of a number of machine registers and the state of the trail and the heap at the time the previous failed alternative for the new current goal was tried. Thus, we now know the purpose of all the organizational cells in the stack frame, see Figure 4.14. Backtracking involves not only removing frames from the stack, but also cancelling bindings in variable objects in the heap generated since the last backtrack point. The variables (more precisely, their addresses) bound during that period are recorded in another stack, the trail *TR*. For each backtrack point there is a pointer to the start of this list. On backtracking, the trail is emptied from the top to the position given in the stack frame and the variables removed are set to be unbound.

The **setbtp** instruction stores state information in the current stack frame. **nextalt** changes the negative continuation address at the current backtrack point to a new value, and **delbtp** deletes the current backtrack point (see Table 4.16).

Table 4.16   Creation and modification of backtrack points.

Instruction	Meaning	Comments
setbtp l	$ST[FP + 1] := BTP;$	Create new backtrack point
	$ST[FP + 2] := TP;$	
	$ST[FP + 3] := HP;$	
	$ST[FP + 4] := l;$	Negative continuation address
	$BTP := FP$	New current backtrack point
nextalt l	$ST[FP + 4] := l$	Continuation address for next alternative
delbtp	$BTP := ST[FP + 1]$	Delete backtrack point

It is now clear what the possible values of the parameter *btparam* of *code_C* are and what the code segment *btinit* must look like. The first of several alternatives generates a new backtrack point using the **setbp** instruction, the last of several alternatives deletes that point, and other alternatives alter it. Thus, the set of possible values of *btparam* is given by {*first*, *last*, *middle*, *single*}. The code segment for *btinit* is:

> *btinit btparam btcont =*
>> **case** *btparam* **of**
>>> *first*: **setbtp** *btcont*;
>>> *middle*: **nextalt** *btcont*;
>>> *last*: **delbtp**;
>>> *single*: ;
>> **endcase**

Backtracking leads to the stack frame of a clause of a procedure with several alternatives. In what configuration should the processing of the next alternative be started? It is clear that these alternatives must be given the same arguments, since this is determined by the call being executed. The local environment of the next alternative is re-initialized (that is, without the variable pointers). The negative continuation address is updated to the next alternative, if there is one. The other organizational cells retain their values. Overall, as much as possible is transferred from one alternative to the next. The instruction sequence at the global label *backtrack* executes the backtracking as follows:

> *backtrack*: $FP := BTP;$
>> $HP := ST[FP + 3];$
>> $reset(ST[FP + 2], TP);$
>> $TP := ST[FP + 2];$
>> $PC := ST[FP + 4]$

Table 4.17 Clause processing.

Instruction	Meaning	Comments
popenv	**if** $FP > BTP$ **then** $SP := FP - 2$ **fi**; $PC := ST[FP - 1]$; $FP := ST[FP]$	Complete clause application? Release clause frame
restore	$PC := ST[FP - 1]$; $FP := ST[FP]$	Incomplete clause application

End processing of clauses

We still have to add what the last instruction of a clause is and what it does. A first hypothesis might be that it terminates the processing of a clause and releases its stack frame. However, that would be fatal if we could return to the clause because of backtracking.

A stack frame for a clause application can be released if the application is 'complete', that is, if the applied clause is the last alternative for its procedure and if the clause applications for all the goals on its right-hand side are also complete. Thus, a clause application is complete precisely when there exist no younger backtrack points. There is an efficient test for this, namely $FP > BTP$.

Thus, we can give the code for *fin*. It differentiates between the cases of last, single and other alternatives. In the first two cases the **popenv** instruction is generated with the above test.

$$fin = \textbf{case } btparam \textbf{ of}$$
$$last, single: \textbf{popenv};$$
$$first, middle: \textbf{restore}$$
$$\textbf{endcase}$$

The two instructions **popenv** and **restore** are defined in Table 4.17.

Trail

In backtracking the heap is emptied down to the level it had reached when the last backtrack point was established. All variable objects created in the heap since then are released. Of course, older variables may also have been bound since then. These are not 'unbound' by the resetting of the heap level and thus require further attention. The *trail* procedure used in the unification instructions records these bindings in the heap.

```
proc trail (a : address);
    if a < ST[BTP + 3]
    then TP := TP + 1;  (*Variable created before curr. backtr. point*)
        TR[TP] := a
    fi
```

On backtracking, the *reset* procedure scans the list of addresses of old variables bound since the last backtrack point and deletes the bindings.

```
proc reset (tpu , tpo : address);
    for i := tpu upto tpo do
        H[i] := i    (*Unbinding a variable object*)
    od
```

If the binding was generated by overwriting the unbound variable, unbinding must involve the creation of an unbound variable object, that is, $H[i] := (REF : i)$.

4.7.5 Procedures, programs and queries

After what has been said above, it is now clear how a procedure is compiled. We distinguish between the two cases of one or more than one alternative.

$$code\_PR\ C_1, \ldots, C_n =$$
$$code\_C\ C_1\ first\ l_2;$$
$$l_2:\quad code\_C\ C_2\ middle\ l_3;$$
$$l_3:$$
$$\vdots$$
$$l_{n-1}:\ code\_C\ C_{n-1}\ middle\ l_n;$$
$$l_n:\quad code\_C\ C_n\ last\ 0$$

if $C_1, \ldots, C_n$ is the list of all alternatives for a predicate, in the order in which they are listed in the program.

$$code\_PR\ C = code\_C\ C\ single\ 0$$

if C is the only alternative for a predicate.

The procedure definitions in a Prolog program are compiled by the *code_P* function.

$$code\_P\ p_1, \ldots, p_n =$$
$$code\_PR\ p_1;$$
$$code\_PR\ p_2;$$
$$\vdots$$
$$code\_PR\ p_n$$

The query is compiled together with the program.

Table 4.18 Initialization.

Instruction	Meaning
init	$TP := 0;$
	$HP := 0;$
	$BTP := 1;$
	$SP := 5;$
	$ST[5] :=$ Address of fail code
	$ST[3] := -1;$
	$ST[4] := -1$

$$code\,(p, q) =$$
$$\quad code\_Q\;q;$$
$$\quad code\_P\;p$$

where p is a Prolog program and q is the associated query.

The execution begins with the code for the query; thus, this includes an initialization sequence. In addition, the query creates the first stack frame.

$$code\_Q\;G_1, \ldots, G_n =$$
$$\quad \textbf{init};$$
$$\quad \textbf{pushenv}\;r + 4;$$
$$\quad code\_G\;G_1\;\rho;$$
$$\quad code\_G\;G_2\;\rho;$$
$$\quad \vdots$$
$$\quad code\_G\;G_n\;\rho;$$
$$\quad \textbf{halt}$$
$$\rho = [X_i \mapsto i + 4]_{i=1}^r \text{ and } \{X_1, \ldots, X_r\} = vars\,(G_1, \ldots, G_n)$$

4.7.6 An example

Suppose we are given the Prolog program

$$p \leftarrow q(X), r(X)$$
$$q(X) \leftarrow s(X)$$
$$r(a) \leftarrow$$
$$s(X) \leftarrow t(X)$$
$$s(X) \leftarrow u(X)$$
$$t(b) \leftarrow$$
$$u(a) \leftarrow$$

with the query $\leftarrow p$. It has the following translation:

	q_1:	s_1:	t_1:
init	pushenv 6	pushenv 6	pushenv 5
pushenv 4	pusharg 1	setbtp l	pusharg 1
enter	uvar 6	pusharg 1	uatom b
call p_0	enter	uvar 6	popenv
halt	putref 6	enter	
	call s_1	putref 6	u_1: pushenv 5
p_0: pushenv 5	popenv	call t_1	pusharg 1
enter		restore	uatom a
putvar 5	r_1: pushenv 5	l: pushenv 6	popenv
call q_1	pusharg 1	delbtp	
enter	uatom a	pusharg 1	
putref 5	popenv	uvar 6	
call r_1		enter	
popenv		putref 6	
		call u_1	
		popenv	

In what follows, we describe and graphically illustrate a number of important steps in its execution. We use the following notation: $[p \leftarrow q_1, \ldots, \cdot q_i, \ldots, q_n]$ stands for the address of the translation $code\_G\ q_i$ in the context of the translation of this clause; $[\cdot p \leftarrow q_1, \ldots, q_n]$ denotes the start address of the code for this clause.

Each time the content of the stack ST is represented, that of the trail TR and that of the heap H. The stack frames are annotated on the left by the heads of the applied clauses; in the case of s, $s_1 \leftarrow$ denotes the first and $s_2 \leftarrow$ the second alternative for s.

The first situation shown in Figure 4.15(a) is that before the application of $t(b) \leftarrow$. TR is still empty; the heap contains only one object for the unbound variable X of the clause $p \leftarrow q(X), r(X)$. The stack contains frames for the query $\leftarrow p$ and for the application of the clauses for p, q and s_1. The positive and negative continuation addresses are given: FP_{old} is omitted, for clarity of the figure. The first of the two stack locations for X is for X as an argument of the head, the second for X as a clause variable.

Figure 4.15(b) shows the situation after the application of $t(b) \leftarrow$. By virtue of the unification of the atom b with X, the previously unbound variable X is bound to a heap object $(ATOM : b)$ in all relevant clause applications.

This object is created by the execution of an instruction **uatom** b. Since clause variables which are older than the current backtrack point are bound, a pointer to the corresponding heap object must be stored in the trail TR.

The application of the fact $t(b) \leftarrow$ is complete; thus, **popenv** can remove its stack frame. This results in the situation of Figure 4.16(a) the FP register set to the state FP_1.

Then the stack frame for the application of $s_1 \leftarrow$ is logically released with the FP register reset to the state FP_2. However, its space cannot be released, since this application has created a backtrack point and another alternative exists. The

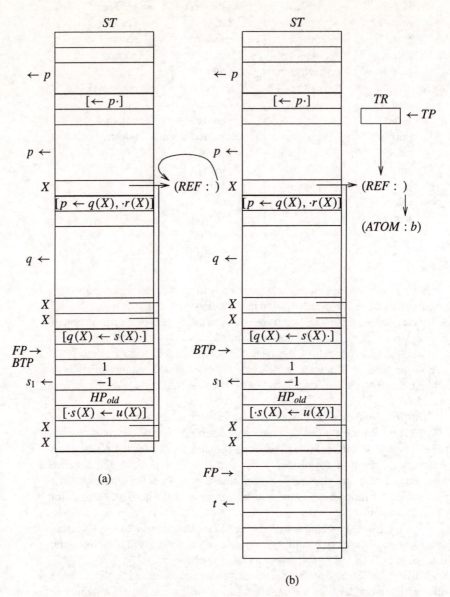

Figure 4.15 Situation (a) before and (b) after the application of $t(b) \leftarrow$.

same is true for the application of $q \leftarrow$. It is exited with the FP register reset to the state FP_3 and the positive continuation address $[p \leftarrow q(X), \cdot r(X)]$ is jumped to. A stack frame for the fact $r(a) \leftarrow$ is created as shown in Figure 4.16(b).

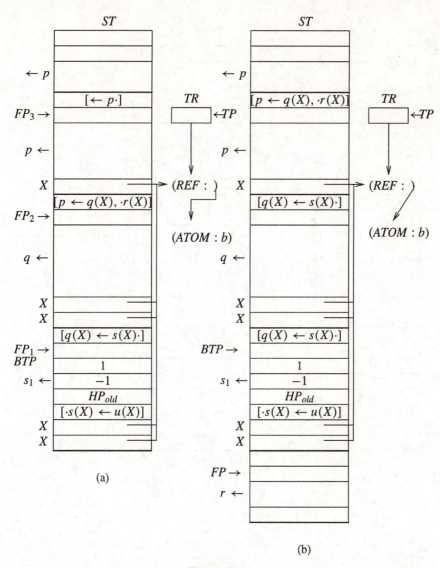

Figure 4.16.

The unification of the atoms a and b fails. The *backtrack* label is jumped to. The frame for $r(a) \leftarrow$ is released, the last backtrack point is returned to, and this is now removed by resetting the *BTP* register. The section of the trail containing the addresses of the variables to be unbound is identified using the stored state of the *TP* register. These variables are again set to be unbound. Thus, *TR* is again empty. The negative continuation address $[\cdot s(X) \leftarrow u(X)]$ is jumped to. This results in the situation of Figure 4.17(a).

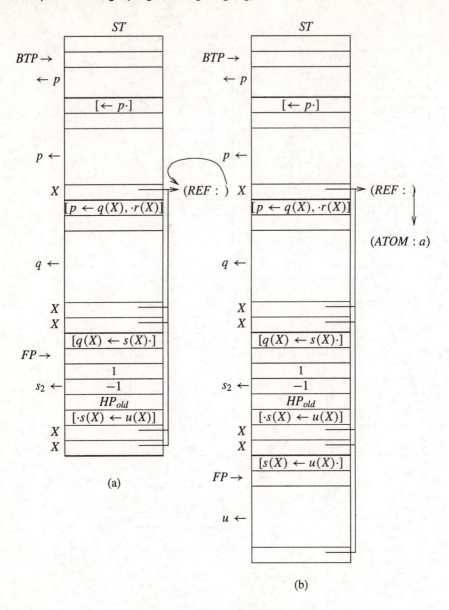

Figure 4.17.

Now the second alternative for s is tried. A stack frame for s_2 is created, the binding for X is passed and u is called. X is now bound to a by the unification. This results in the situation of Figure 4.17(b).

Now the applications of $u \leftarrow$, $s_2 \leftarrow$ and $q \leftarrow$ are all successful. Their frames are released. The unification with $r(a)$ is successful; thus, the last frames are removed and the execution of the program is complete.

4.8   Efficiency improvements

In the previous sections, we described an abstract machine on which compiled Prolog programs can be executed. This machine was designed to be as close to the P machine and the MaMa as possible. It is not as efficient in terms of time and space as one might wish. Thus, we now describe a number of efficiency improvements which make the WiM faster and, in particular, more efficient in terms of space.

4.8.1   Argument registers

We consider a deterministic clause, thus, a clause which is the only or the last alternative of a procedure. The pointers to the argument terms are clearly no longer required after unification with the head terms. Their space in the stack frame could be released. This is difficult with the previous organization because the local environment for the clause variables lies above these locations.

On the other hand, let us consider a non-deterministic clause. This can be returned to by backtracking to the next alternative for the procedure. Of course, this is supplied with the same arguments. Thus, the pointers to the arguments should be preserved.

In short, until now, we have always retained the pointers to the arguments, although this is superfluous in the case of deterministic clauses. Let us now follow the reverse path. We shall only save the argument pointers in exceptional cases, namely when backtrack points are created. We introduce the argument registers $A_1, \ldots, A_k$ for this. When a call $p(t_1, \ldots, t_n)$ is processed, the first n of these are used to pass pointers to the heap representations of $t_1, \ldots, t_n$. If the clause application does not create a backtrack point, the argument registers can be released after unification. At a backtrack point the pointers to the argument terms in the argument registers must be saved. The organization for this will be described in the next section, in which we shall also describe the new stack organization, the necessary instructions and the modified compilation scheme. It is already clear that the pointers to the arguments are now written into the argument registers and that they must be pushed onto the local stack from the argument registers before unification. The *code_G* function and the **pusharg** instruction must be changed for this.

4.8.2   Backtrack frames

Each stack frame so far contains four organizational cells which (like the stored pointers to the arguments) are only relevant for backtrack points. To save storage space, we shall now use different stack frames for deterministic and

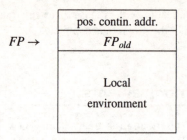

Figure 4.18   Stack frame for deterministic clauses.

non-deterministic clause applications. The frames for non-deterministic clauses, which we shall call ND frames, have the same form as before; those for deterministic clauses, which we shall call D frames, contain only two organizational cells and the local environment, see Figure 4.18.

Thus, the clause variables in the two different types of frame are addressed in different ways. In D frames, the r clause variables are addressed using $FP + 1, \ldots, FP+r$; in ND frames, the variables are addressed using $FP+n+5, \ldots, FP+ n + 4 + r$, where n denotes the arity of the predicate.

Other changes to the compilation scheme *code_C* are needed. Since the argument pointers are no longer passed in the stack frame but in the argument registers, we have $SP = FP$ when the code for the clause is entered. The four organizational cells are or are not created and the argument registers are not saved, depending on whether a D or an ND frame is created. After backtracking, the argument registers must be reloaded from the stack frame.

> *code_C* $(C : p(t_1, \ldots, t_n) \leftarrow g_1, \ldots, g_m)$ *btparam btcont* $=$
> *btinit btparam btcont n*;
> **pushenv** $r + l$;
> **pusharg** 1;
> *code_U* $t_1\ \rho$;
>
> $\vdots$
>
> **pusharg** n;
> *code_U* $t_n\ \rho$;
> *code_G* $g_1\ \rho$;
>
> $\vdots$
>
> *code_G* $g_m\ \rho$;
> *fin btparam*;
> **where** $\rho = [X_i \mapsto l + i]_{i=1}^{r}$ **and**
> $vars\,(C) = \{X_1, \ldots, X_r\}$ **and**
> $l = \begin{cases} n + 4, & \text{If } C \text{ creates ND frame} \\ 0, & \text{otherwise} \end{cases}$

btinit btparam btcont args =
    case *btparam* **of**;
       single :
       first :   **begin**
                setbtp *btcont*;
                saveargs *args*
              end;
       middle :   **begin**
                nextalt *btcont*;
                restoreargs *args*
              end;
       last :   **delbtp**
              restoreargs *args*
    endcase

The code for a call will now execute a modified **enter** instruction reserving only two locations. The other cells in ND frames are reserved and allocated by the **setbtp** and **saveargs** instructions. The precise modifications are left as an exercise for the reader, see Exercise 10.

A further change is necessary. The unification code should exploit the fact that the pointers to the roots of the arguments are stored in the argument registers. It would be a waste of time and space to copy them into the local stack. Therefore, instructions for unification with the root of an argument term are now introduced. These are called **getatom**, **getvar**, **getref** and **getstruct**. They each have the index of an argument register as an additional parameter. The definition of these instructions and the modification of the code scheme are also left to the reader (see Exercise 11).

4.8.3 Trimming the local environment

With clever use of the argument registers, the creation of a local environment can sometimes be suppressed. In addition, it is also possible to analyse the lifetime of a clause variable and exploit this to release storage early.

Let us consider a clause $p(t_1, \ldots, t_n)$ $\leftarrow$. Pointers to the arguments are contained in the n argument registers $A_1, \ldots, A_n$. For all t_i which are the first occurrences of variables X_i, the binding of the variables resulting from unification is in register A_i. Sometimes it is possible to avoid storing the content of the register in a frame location.

Example 4.14 $p(X, X) \leftarrow$
As a result of unification with the first argument, register A_1 contains the binding for the variable X. The content of register A_2 has to be unified with the atom a. The unification of the third argument with the bound variable X is effected by unification of the contents of A_1 and A_3. In fact, no locations have to be created for X.   □

Neither is there any need to create a binding environment for facts, because all variables in facts can be held in registers.

Example 15 $p(X, Y, Z) \leftarrow q(Y, Z), r(Z, W, W)$
For this clause we see that:

- X is not used again after its first occurrence, in which it is bound; storage of its binding is superfluous.

- Y is only used once after its definition in the head; this use occurs in the first goal on the right-hand side; the binding of Y can be reloaded from register A_2 into register A_1 to avoid storing it.

- The definition and the sole use of W occur in the last goal on the right-hand side.

- A location on the stack must be created for Z to store the content of A_3, for there is no guarantee that on return from q the register A_3 will contain the binding for Z.

Thus, in this case, it is only necessary to create one location for Z on the stack. With the previous organization, a location on the stack and a variable object in the heap are provided for each variable of a clause application. We have now seen that it is not necessary to create a location on the stack for all variables. This is only the case if the variable has to outlive the call. This leads to a classification of clause variables. □

Definition 4.13 (temporary, permanent variables)   A clause variable is a *temporary variable* if

- it occurs in at most one goal in the body, and
- it does not occur both in the head and in a goal other than the first goal.   □

Variables that are not temporary are said to be *permanent*.
Space on the stack need only be reserved for permanent variables. The bindings of temporary variables can be held in registers. This reduces the size of the clause's stack frame.
Permanent variables can be ordered so that those with the longest lifetimes are at the bottom. Those whose last occurrence lies furthest to the left in the body are at the top. The relative addresses are then assigned to the variables in this order. When a goal has been supplied with its arguments, the stack frame can be 'clipped', that is, shortened by the amount of storage space for the variables whose last occurrence was in this goal. This is advantageous in terms of storage space provided the frame does not lie below a frame of a backtrack point.
According to the above definition of temporary variables, facts and clauses with just one goal in the body have no permanent variables. Thus, it is never necessary to create a binding environment for them, since all variable bindings can be held in registers.

4.8.4 Last call optimization and tail recursion

A clause is said to be *tail recursive* if it has the form $p(\ldots) \leftarrow \ldots p(\ldots)$; in other words, if its last call is a recursive call. Tail recursive clauses in logic programming languages, like tail recursive functions in functional programming languages, are the typical replacement for the loops of imperative languages. In comparison with tail-recursive clauses, loops in imperative languages have a crucial advantage as far as efficiency is concerned. Excluding dynamically created (with **new**) objects, the space requirement is independent of the number of passes through a loop, while the space needed to apply recursive functions or recursive clauses is linearly dependent on the depth of the recursion. The optimization which now follows is a generalization of the elimination of tail recursion. It eliminates the space-efficiency problem and also leads to a constant space requirement for tail recursive clauses.

We shall consider the last call in a clause $p(\ldots) \leftarrow g_1, \ldots, g_m$. The code for g_m generates a new stack frame (**enter**), constructs the argument terms, leaves their heap addresses in the argument registers and executes the call to g_m (**call**). It is clear that the local environment can be abandoned immediately before the call, since all the required pointers to clause variables are stored in the argument terms.

Thus, in this case the **popenv** or **restore** instruction and the following **call** instruction could be transposed. For a tail recursive clause, which is the last alternative, this would have the effect that **popenv** would release the frame and that the next frame would be created at the same place on the stack. This would achieve the constant (stack) space requirement for tail-recursive predicates.

Let us consider the following example program:

(1) $p \leftarrow q, r$

(2) $r \leftarrow \ldots$

with the query $\leftarrow p, s$.

Previously, we would only have returned from (2) to (1) to release the stack for (1) and jump to the positive continuation address. The return to (1) is now avoided.

The stack frame for (1) is (logically) released before the call of r in (1), that is, FP is reset and storage space may possibly be released; then, for (2), the address of the code for s is set as the positive continuation address and (2) is jumped to, instead of being called.

However, things may go slightly wrong when **popenv/restore** and **call** are transposed. To this end, we shall consider the sequence of actions arising in the execution of **call** and **restore**:

> **call**   set FP to new frame;
> set continuation address;
> jump to the procedure code;
> **restore** set PC to continuation address;
> reset FP.

The necessary sequence of actions is now:

passing of continuation address;

reset *FP*;

jump to the procedure code.

In order to pass the continuation address to the called procedure, it can be stored, for example, in a dedicated register. That would lead to modified **restore** and **popenv** instructions. Instead of the **call** instruction a new instruction, **execute**, would be used which executes a jump to the beginning of the procedure code. The definition of the instructions and the modification of the code scheme are left to the reader, see Exercise 12.

4.8.5   Indexing of clauses

The semantics of Prolog specify that when a procedure *p* is called the alternatives for *p* are tried in the order in which they are listed. On backtracking to this call of *p* the alternatives that have not yet been tried are tried in the order in which they are listed. When, for example, an atom *a* occurs in a call argument position, in general only a small number of alternatives for successful unification have to be considered, namely those that contain an *a* or a variable in the corresponding position in the head. An expensive sequential scan of this small number of alternatives is often replaced in Prolog implementations by an indexed access to clause subsets. For example, in our example, the atom *a* was used as an index (key) to access the subset of alternatives that are unifiable with *a* in the corresponding argument.

The precise procedure is as follows. The implementor (pragmatically) chooses an argument position on which to base the indexing. This is usually the first position. Then the compiler computes a hash function which, for atoms and functors, selects the sublist of the unifiable alternatives. These alternatives must be ordered in the list in the sequence in which they are listed in the program, since the semantics of the program should not be changed by this implementation mechanism.

When a variable occurs in the first argument position in the head of a clause this alternative must, of course, be contained in every indexed sublist, for none of these alternatives can be excluded as being impossible.

In addition, precautions have to be taken against the case in which a free variable occurs in the first argument position of a goal. Then, unification of the first argument with all clause heads is in principle possible. Thus, there must be a list of all alternatives which is selected by the hash function when the first argument of the goal is a free variable.

The various sublists are clearly not disjoint. To avoid creating copies of the code for alternatives the sublists are interleaved.

When a procedure is called, this technique may often be used to choose a small subset of the alternatives as candidates for a successful unification. The number of alternatives may even be reduced to one so that there is no need to create a backtrack point. Thus, early release of completed clause applications is possible in this case. This would also save time and space.

4.9 Exercises

1: In this exercise, we investigate a number of properties of substitutions.
(a) Show that for arbitrary expressions E and substitutions Θ and Φ we have $(E\Theta)\Phi = E(\Theta\Phi)$.
(b) Show that the composition of substitutions is associative, that is, that for arbitrary substitutions Θ, Φ and T, we have $(\Theta\Phi)T = \Theta(\Phi T)$.
(c) Show that two substitutions Θ and Φ are equal if and only if for all expressions E we have $E\Theta = E\Phi$.

2: A substitution Θ is said to be idempotent if $\Theta\Theta = \Theta$. Suppose that $\Theta = \{x_1/t_1, \ldots, x_n/t_n\}$ and that V is the set of variables occurring in the terms $t_1, \ldots, t_n$.
(a) Show that Θ is idempotent if and only if $\{x_1, \ldots, x_n\} \cap V = \emptyset$.
(b) Show that every most general unifier computed by the *unify* function is idempotent.

3: Apply the *unify* function to the following pairs of expressions:

$$p(f(y), w, g(z)) \qquad p(u, u, v)$$
$$p(f(y), w, g(z)) \qquad p(v, u, v)$$
$$p(a, x, f(g(y))) \qquad p(z, h(z, w), f(w))$$

4: Unify

$$t_1 = p(x_1, \ldots, x_n)$$
$$t_1 = p(f(x_0, x_0), f(x_1, x_1), \ldots, f(x_n - 1, x_n - 1))$$

using the *unify* function. Compare the cost of the unification with and without the occur check.

5: On efficiency grounds, the occur check is omitted in unification in most Prolog systems. This can sometimes lead to incorrect or unexpected answers, or even to no answers at all. Consider the following Prolog program and query. What answers are obtained when the occur check is omitted?
(a)
```
smaller(X,succ(X)).
?- smaller(succ(X),X).
```
(b)
```
smaller(X,succ(X)).
test :- smaller(succ(X),X).
?- test.
```

(c)
```
test :- p(X,X).
p(X,f(X)) :- p(X,X).
?- test.
```

6: Give search trees for the following programs and queries. Assume that the leftmost goal is selected in each goal list.

(a)
```
male(jan).
male(hugo).
male(thomas).
male(martin).
female(bertha).
female(else).
parents(jan,hugo,bertha).
parents(hugo,martin,else).
parents(bertha,thomas,else).
grandfather(X,Y) :-
        parents(Y,F,M),parents(F,X,GM),male(X).
grandfather(X,Y) :-
        parents(Y,F,M),parents(M,X,GM),male(X).
?- grandfather(X,jan).
```

(b)
```
append(nil,X,X).
append(cons(K,X),Y,cons(K,Z)) :- append(X,Y,Z).
part(X,Y) :- append(W,B,Y), append(A,X,W).
?- part(cons(1,cons(2,nil)),
        cons(1,cons(2,cons(3,nil)))).
```

7: Suppose we are given the following logic program P:

```
path(a,b).
path(c,b).
path(X,Z) :- path(X,Y), path(Y,Z).
path(X,Y) :- path(Y,X).
```

and the query A:

```
?- path(a,c).
```

Show that:
(a) If a clause is removed from P then $P \cup \{A\}$ has no refutation for any search rule.
(b) Regardless of the computation rule and the sequence of the clauses in P, a logic programming system with a fixed search rule never finds a refutation to $P \cup \{A\}$.

8: Translate the following terms into unification instructions using the *code_U* function. Use the address environment $[X \rightarrow 5]$.
(a) `f(1,2)`
(b) `g(X,1,X)`
(c) `h(f(1,X),X)`

9: Translate the following program into WiM code.

```
delete(X,nil,nil).
delete(X,cons(X,Xs),Ys) :- delete(X,Xs,Ys).
delete(X,cons(K,Xs),cons(K,Ys)) :- delete(X,Xs,Ys).
```

10: Show that when the given compilation of unification is used there exists at most one chain of length two from a variable to an object (term, atom) to which it is bound.

11: Give definitions of the **pusharg**, **setbp**, **saveargs** and **restoreargs** instructions for the WiM after the introduction of argument registers and D frames.

12: Define the **getatom**, **getvar**, **getref** and **getstruct** instructions and alter the *code_C* and the *code_U* scheme so that unification with an argument term always expects the pointer to the root in an argument register.

13: Define new versions of the **restore** and **popenv** instructions and a new **execute** instruction and modify the code generation so that last goals are optimized.

4.10 Literature

Introductory books on programming with Prolog include Clocksin and Mellish (1994) and Bratko (1990). In addition to a description of programming techniques, Sterling and Shapiro (1994) and Maier and Warren (1988) also include sections on the interpretation and compilation of Prolog programs. The foundations of logic programming are described, for example, in Lloyd (1987), Apt (1990) and Bezem (1988).

In Warren (1977), David H.D. Warren describes a first abstract machine for Prolog. This uses structure sharing instead of structure copying. The WAM (Warren Abstract Machine), the basis of most available commercial Prolog implementations, was defined in Warren (1983). An accomplished step-by-step tutorial explanation of it is given in Aït-Kaci (1991).

5

Compilation of object-oriented languages

- Concepts of object-oriented languages

- The compilation of methods

- Schemes for compilation of inheritance

- Genericity

- Exercises

- Literature

Software systems are becoming increasingly complex and large. Thus, there is a growing need to make the development of such systems more efficient and more transparent. The ultimate objective is to construct software systems, like present-day hardware systems (including most products of day-to-day life such as cars, washing machines, and so on), from ready-made standard building blocks. Attempts to progress towards this objective cover the following areas (among others):

- Modularization
- Reusability of modules
- Extensibility of modules
- Abstraction

Object-oriented languages afford new possibilities in these areas. Thus, object orientation is viewed as an important paradigm in relation to management of the complexity of software systems.

In this chapter, we outline the most important new concepts of object-oriented languages and the compilation schemes that may be used to implement them.

5.1 Concepts of object-oriented languages

Object-oriented languages are far more closely related to imperative languages than to functional or even logic programming languages. For example, they (typically) use the same execution model: a version of the von Neumann computer in which a complex *structured* state is modified under explicit software control. Object-oriented languages may be viewed as imperative languages that introduce a number of new concepts in addition to the known concepts such as variables, arrays, structures and functions. We shall only discuss some of these '*new*' concepts (in fact, not all these concepts are brand new; some of them were previously used in modern imperative languages or in languages used in the artificial-intelligence area) in this chapter. At the centre is the specification of an appropriate unit of modularization.

5.1.1 Objects

The main modularization unit of imperative languages is the function (or procedure) (in what follows, we shall always speak of functions, although we are not dealing with functions in the mathematical sense, but with procedures with or without a return value). Functions may encapsulate or represent abstractions of highly complex processes such as solving optimization problems, linear or nonlinear systems of equations and differential equations. This is an appropriate level of abstraction and modularization provided that the complexity of the data is negligible in comparison with that of the processes. Functions alone are not sufficient as a modularization unit for tasks whose description and efficient solution requires the use of complex data structures. A suitable level of abstraction for efficient processing of these tasks should permit the encapsulation of both the data structures and the associated functions operating on these structures in a single unit.

The fundamental concept of object-oriented languages is the **object**. An object comprises an object state, expressed in terms of the actual values of a set of **attributes**, together with functions, called **object methods**, operating on this state. The attributes and methods together form the **features** of an object. Thus, an object encapsulates both data and the operations on this data. One of the most important basic operations of object-oriented languages is the activation of a method m for an object o, written as o.m. Here, the object plays the major role; the method, being a component of the object, is subordinate to it. This object orientation has given its name to the class of languages.

We shall illustrate the use of object orientation with the example of building blocks for processing (two-dimensional) graphical objects. There are many types of graphical object, including circles, ellipses, rectangles, triangles, polygons, points, lines, polylines, and so on. The grouping of graphical objects leads to a further type: compound graphical objects. Each of these different types has its own particular properties; but there are some commonalities. Thus, a usable building kit for work with graphical objects permits at least the following operations for each type:

- copying
- translation
- deletion
- and possibly scaling.

For many processes, the exact type is irrelevant and thus need not be given. Thus, the appropriate description for the copying of a compound object is: 'copy the subobjects of the compound object and group the copies into a new compound object'. The exact types of the subobjects are irrelevant for the description of the process. In an object-oriented implementation of this problem (object orientation can sometimes also be realized with an imperative language; this is true, for example, for C, although the type system of this language must be circumvented at at least one point by explicit type conversion), every graphical object contains its own copy function which can be activated without knowledge of the exact object type. To achieve this with a function-oriented implementation, we have to define a single copy function which can copy graphical objects of *all* types. This function has to determine the object type and then call the corresponding type-specific function. One disadvantage of this is that *all* types of graphical object are linked to each other by this function and the data structure for representing graphical objects interpreted by it. Consequently, a program contains all the copy functions, even if many types of graphical object are not actually required. This can lead to an unnecessarily large code size for the program. Another consequence is that extensions become more complicated. For example, if we need another basic type in our building kit, the above copy function must be extended, as must the data structures it interprets. In the worst case, all the building blocks have to be recompiled; this happens when they depend on the general data structure interpreted by the copy function. In an object-oriented implementation, the new basic type will simply be added. The remainder of the building kit can remain unchanged and continue to be used without recompilation; this represents a considerable improvement as far as modularizability and extensibility are concerned.

5.1.2 Object classes

To make program development more reliable and more efficient, it is desirable that inconsistencies and errors in programs should be recognized as soon as possible. Compilers can contribute to this since they analyse certain program parts in depth. However, their checking for consistency and freedom from errors is not necessarily complete, since they only work with partial specifications. Type information plays an important role here.

(Static) type information states abstract properties of program entities, indicating the values they can take at run time. Thus, a type stands for a set of permissible values; to a great extent, the type determines how the bit pattern stored in the runtime object should be decoded. Compilers can use type information to:

- generate code more efficiently,
- resolve ambiguities in the use of an operator,
- introduce automatic type conversions,
- detect inconsistencies.

Type information is thus an important prerequisite for generating efficient and reasonably reliable programs.

Object-oriented languages extend the known type concept of imperative languages such as Pascal or C (not all object-oriented languages use static typing, as the example of Smalltalk-80 shows). Their types are usually called **object classes**. An object class specifies attributes and methods together with their types and prototypes (that is, types of return values and parameters), respectively. In order to belong to the class, objects must contain these features, but they may also contain others. Some object-oriented languages such as Eiffel permit further specifications for the methods, such as pre- and post-conditions. This provides a means of restricting the meaning of the methods (semantics). Frequently, the class also defines the methods; however, under certain conditions, these definitions can be overwritten.

The object class forms the modularization unit of object-oriented languages. Thus, we can realize our building kit for implementing graphical objects as described in the last section as a class library with object classes for the different types of graphical object.

In what follows, we shall use the terms '*class*' and '*type*' synonymously.

5.1.3   Inheritance

Inheritance is defined as the incorporation of all features of a class A into a new class B. B may also define other features and, under certain conditions, overwrite methods inherited from A. Some languages permit the renaming of the inherited features to avoid name conflicts or simply to allow more meaningful names in the new context.

If B inherits from A then the class B is **derived** from A and A is called a **base class** for B.

Inheritance is one of the most important concepts of object-oriented languages. It makes extensions and the formation of variants very easy. The resulting inheritance hierarchies also permit a structuring of class libraries and the introduction of different levels of abstraction.

We again illustrate this using our example of graphical objects. Figure 5.1 shows a section of the inheritance hierarchy of this class library with the object classes graphical object, closed graphical, ellipse, polyline, polygon, rectangle and triangle.

In this figure, object classes are shown by ellipses. The ellipses contain the name of the object class together with a selection of the methods introduced by this class. Inheritance is represented by an arrow. For example, the class graphical object introduces the methods translate and scale: all graphical objects can be translated and scaled. The classes closed graphical and polyline inherit

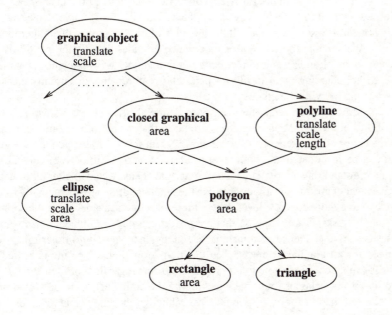

Figure 5.1   Inheritance hierarchy of graphical objects.

these methods from `graphical object`. In `polyline` the inherited methods `translate` and `scale` are overwritten and the method `length` (the length of the polyline) is introduced. `closed graphical` introduces the new method `area` which gives the area enclosed by the closed graphical object. The class `polygon` inherits from both `closed graphical` and `polyline`; `area` is overwritten. Finally, `rectangle` inherits from `polygon` and overwrites `area`.

While the methods `translate` and `scale` are introduced in the class `graphical object` they are not yet definable there. The methods for translation and scaling can only be defined when graphical objects are first given a concrete representation (in our example, in the classes `ellipse` and `polyline`). The fact that these methods are nevertheless introduced in `graphical object` is intended to indicate that every graphical object must possess these methods, although nothing can be said about their implementation. Classes that contain undefined methods are said to be **abstract**. They do not contain any objects of their own, that is, objects that do not come from a proper subclass.

Analogously, the class `closed graphical` introduces the method `area`, without being able to define it. `area` is first definable in the classes `ellipse` and `polygon`. However, the surface-area calculation for general polygons is complex and is based on a triangulation of the surface area enclosed by the polygon and a summation of the surface areas of the resulting triangles. On the other hand, the surface-area calculation for a rectangle is trivial. If rectangles are frequently used (and furthermore, in the application area under consideration, their surface areas often have to be determined) it is expedient to implement `area` in `rectangle` in a new and more efficient way, as we have done in our example. However, for polygons, it is best to take over all the methods of `polyline` without alteration.

We see that the concept of inheritance provides us with the possibility of reusing parts of an existing implementation in a simple way, extending them and, if need be, adapting them locally to particular requirements or circumstances by overwriting individual methods.

Moreover, we retain the facility to define abstract classes. This leads to a flexibility in programming languages similar to that achieved in natural languages by means of abstract concepts: we retain different levels of abstraction. Anything that can be formulated at a high level of abstraction tends to have a wide area of application and thus is to a large extent reusable. Thus, we shall attempt to use as high a level of abstraction as possible. On the other hand, we are occasionally forced to move to a more concrete level, where more structure is available for the solution of specific tasks. Let us suppose that a transformation of a graphical object can be described by a sequence of translations, scalings and (possibly) other operations defined for all graphical objects; then this transformation can be implemented by a single function, applicable to all graphical objects regardless of their type. If we had no abstract classes (but type checking by the compiler), then we would need a separate function for each specific class, although the implementations of these functions would always have the same appearance.

Thus, typed object-oriented languages take account of the inheritance hierarchy in their type system. If a class B inherits from a class A then the type assigned to B is a subtype of the type assigned to A. Every object of a subtype is automatically also an element of the supertype; an inheriting class is a subclass of the class from which it inherits. This has the following effect:

Subtype rule   When an object of a certain type is required at an input position (function input parameter, right-hand side of assignments) or as a function return value, objects of any subtype are allowed.

We shall call objects of B that are not also objects of a proper subclass of B the **proper objects** of B or the **proper** B objects. We refer to B as the **runtime type** of the **proper B** objects. Thus, each object has a uniquely determined runtime type, which is the smallest type to which that object belongs. In addition, it is an element of every supertype of its runtime type.

By virtue of the subtype rule, methods and functions in object-oriented languages can accept objects with different runtime types and thus different structures, for example in a parameter position. This is a form of **polymorphism**.

The subtype rule of inheritance together with the possibility that inheriting classes may overwrite an inherited method have an interesting consequence which is important for compilers. By way of example, let us consider a function f which permits objects of the class closed graphical as a parameter and let us suppose that it calls the area method of this parameter. Since closed graphical cannot define the area method, it is evident that the area method of the parameter and not that of the class closed graphical must be called in f. The following is generally true:

Method-selection rule   If class B inherits from class A and overwrites method **m** then for B objects b the definition of **m** given by B (or a subclass) *must* be used even if b is used as an A object.

This rule presents a compiler with a problem; it has to generate code to activate a method it does not know at compile time. Consequently, for example, in generating code for f, the compiler cannot bind the method name area to a specific method. This binding can only be performed when the actual parameter is known; that is, generally, at program run time. We therefore speak of **dynamic binding** in contrast to **static binding** where the compiler carries out the binding itself. Thus, we can also formulate the method-selection rule as follows:

Dynamic-binding rule   A method of an object o, which can potentially be overwritten in a subclass, has to be bound dynamically if the compiler cannot determine the runtime type of o.

The major part of this section is concerned with an efficient implementation of inheritance.

5.1.4 Genericity

Strongly typed languages often force one to reimplement the same function for different type instantiations. Often, the functions only differ in the type of their parameters and their name. These multiple instances of functions complicate the implementation, making it more difficult to understand and maintain.

We have seen that the type concept of object-oriented languages, based on inheritance, in some cases saves us from duplicating function implementations. However, inheritance alone does not lead to elegant solutions for one important class of problems, namely the implementation of container types such as lists, sets, stacks, queues, ... These containers have a natural parameter, namely the type of their contents. **Genericity** enables us to avoid multiple implementation for these data structures and their methods. It allows us to parametrize type definitions; types themselves are again permitted as parameters. For example, a single definition for the parametrized class `List<T>` may describe lists with an arbitrary element type. Lists with a specific element type are generated by **instantiation** of the generic class. For example, `List<int>` and `List<List<int>>` describe lists of integers and lists of such lists. Just as procedures describe a whole class of computations rather than a single computation, a generic type describes a whole class of types rather than a single type. Just as a computation is implemented by calling a procedure with actual parameters, so a special class is implemented by the instantiation of a generic class with actual parameters. Generic types are the *procedures of the type world*.

Genericity is supported by some object-oriented languages. However, it is not an invention of object-oriented languages. For example, the imperative language `Ada` already had a polished genericity concept.

5.1.5 Encapsulation of information

Most object-oriented languages provide constructs that can be used to classify the features of a class as `private` or `public`. Private features are either totally invisible or at least inaccessible in certain contexts. Some object-oriented languages distinguish between the scope in different contexts: for example, *within the class*, *in derived classes*, *in foreign classes*, *in certain classes*, and so on. Language constructs or general rules can specify the contexts in which features are visible, readable, writable or callable.

The implementation of these constructs by a compiler is simple and obvious. Thus, we shall not discuss it further in this section, although the encapsulation of information is very important (it provides a clear separation between the abstract view of the meaning of a class and the concrete view of its implementation).

5.1.6 Summary

We now summarize the most important results of our previous discussion.

- Object-oriented languages introduce a new modularization unit: **object classes**. Object classes may encapsulate both data and functions operating on this data. The consideration of both data *and* functions in one unit permits the implementation of natural, self-contained modularization units which are easy to integrate and to extend.

- The concept of **inheritance** is a powerful and convenient method for extending and constructing variants of existing modules (object classes).

- The type system of object-oriented languages uses the inheritance concept: inheriting classes become subtypes of the base classes and their objects can be used almost everywhere where objects of the base class are permissible. Considered strictly from the point of view of their functionality, they thus inherit the application area of their parents and are therefore very easy to integrate into existing systems.

- **Inheritance hierarchies** introduce different levels of abstraction into programs. This means that at various points within a program or system, it is possible to work at different levels of abstraction, as required: for example, at the `graphical object` level for the implementation of general graphical functions such as `zoom` (magnify and centre) or `group` and at the `closed graphical` level for the implementation of functions involving surface-area computations.

- **Abstract classes** can be used in specifications, refined by gradual inheritance and, finally, implemented. This provides a seamless transition from specification through design to various implementation variants.

- **Genericity** permits the parametrization of class definitions. For example, algorithms and associated data structures such as lists, stacks, queues, sets, ..., can be implemented in this way, independently of the element data type.

Examples of object-oriented languages include C++ and Eiffel. In this section, we shall mainly draw upon these two languages as examples. Some more recent C++ implementations support all the concepts described, although not always in full. They are fully supported by Eiffel. In addition, Eiffel provides a number of other interesting constructs which support the development of more reliable, reusable modules: for example, class invariants, pre- and post-conditions for methods, loop invariants and exception handling. The forefather of object-oriented languages is Simula 67, which extended Algol 60 by object classes, simple inheritance, co-routines and primitives to support discrete simulations. Another well-known representative is Smalltalk-80, a language which is normally interpreted without static typing, with simple inheritance, and in which classes themselves are again objects which can be altered under software control. Other representatives include Objective-C, an extension of C by the Smalltalk-80 concepts and, the object-oriented extensions of LISP, Loops, Flavors and Ceyx.

5.2   The compilation of methods

We begin this section with a concrete example. For this, we implement a subsection of the graphical object class hierarchy of the previous section in the object-oriented language C++. (This section and all other examples in it were processed using the GNU C++ Compiler Version 2.5.6. This compiler is *'free software'*. It can run on a large number of UNIX platforms and, with a special extender, under DOS and Windows 3.x. It can be obtained (including sources) over the Internet. Its use and distribution is covered by the **GNU General Public Licence** which accompanies any legal distribution.)

First, we define the class graphical object:

```
struct graphical_object {
   virtual void translate(double x_offset, double y_offset);
   virtual void scale(double factor);
   // possibly other general methods of the class
};
```

The class graphical object.

We note that the methods translate and scale were declared as virtual; in C++ this is a prerequisite for the possible overwriting of a method by a derived class.

One particularly important subclass of graphical objects is that of points. Points are used in one way or another in the implementation of almost every concrete class of graphical objects. The class of points is defined as follows:

```
class point : public graphical_object {
   double xc, yc;
public:
   void translate(double x_offset, double y_offset) {
     xc+= x_offset;
     yc+= y_offset;
   }
   void scale(double factor) {
     xc*= factor;
     yc*= factor;
   }
point(double x0=0, double y0=0) { xc= x0; yc= y0; }
   void set(double x0, double y0) { xc= x0; yc= y0; }
   double x(void) { return xc; }
   double y(void) { return yc; }
   double dist(point &);
};
```

The class point.

Table 5.1   Compilation of the method **m** of class C into a function **fm**.

	Method	Function
Prototype	`<returntype>m(<args>)`	`<returntype>fm(C&this,<args>)`
Call	`o.m(<args>)`	`fm(o,<args>)`
Feature access	`k`	`this.k`

Points contain their *x* and *y* coordinates xc and yc. These two coordinates specify the position of the point in the two-dimensional space. They are private data for the point and can only be accessed within methods of the class (or by so-called friend functions). The methods defined by point are public, that is, they can be used by anyone who *knows* a point. If p is a point, then, for example, p.x() activates the method x of p and returns the *x* coordinate of p, and p.translate(1,2) translates p by one unit in the *x* direction and two units in the *y* direction by altering the coordinates contained in p correspondingly.

In general, for an object o, the method m of o with arguments arg1, arg2, ...is activated by o.m(arg1, arg2, ...).

Methods are essentially compiled like functions in imperative languages. The difference is that methods can access the features of *their* objects directly. We now show how methods can be implemented by equivalent functions. As shown in the chapter on the compilation of imperative programming languages, the resulting functions can be compiled into the language of an abstract machine or a real machine.

If m is a method of the class C with the prototype `<Returntype>m(<Arguments>)` then fm, the function equivalent to m, has the prototype `<Returntype>fm(C &this, <Arguments>)` (in C++ & denotes references and &this denotes a formal parameter with name this which is passed 'by reference'). Thus, the information about o is passed to fm as a new additional first argument. Correspondingly, a call o.m(<args>) is compiled into fm(o,<args>) and an access from m to a feature k of o is implemented in fm by this.k. These compilation rules are summarized in Table 5.1.

The method x in the class point is compiled into the equivalent function x_5point with definition `double x_5point(point &this) { return this.xc; }`. The method activation p.x() is compiled into x_5point(p). The method translate of point compiles to the function translate_5pointdd.

```
void translate_5pointdd(point &this, double x_offset,
                        double y_offset) {
  this.xc+= x_offset; this.yc+= y_offset;
}
```

Definition of `translate_5pointdd`.

The name of the method itself is not used as the name for the implementing function; instead, the method name is extended by encoding the associated class and possibly the parameter types. The encoding of the class in the function name is necessary because different classes may contain methods with the same name; each class has its own name space and there is no conflict *between* these name spaces. On the other hand, the name space for the functions is global: the program as a whole should not contain different functions with the same name. The encoding of the class name in the function name ensures that the function name generated is unambiguous. (This unambiguity is not fully achieved by the encoding scheme described above (in C++): m__5a in class a and m in class a__1a lead to the same function name. The problem is easily solved: it suffices to use a character which is invalid in a name as a separator between method names and extensions.) Moreover, in C++, different methods even in the same class may have the same name, provided they can be distinguished by their parameter types. Therefore, for the C++ implementation, the parameter types are also encoded in the name. For example, the name `translate__5pointdd` has the following five components:

(1) `translate` – the method name

(2) `__` – the separator

(3) `5point` – encoding of the method name. The leading figure indicates how many of the following characters belong to this entry. All names taken directly from programs are prefixed by their length.

(4) `d` – encoding for `double` (type of the first parameter)

(5) `d` – encoding for `double` (type of the second parameter).

5.3 Schemes for compilation of inheritance

Inheritance is the most important of the concepts introduced by object-oriented languages. In this section, we deal with it in detail.

If B inherits directly or indirectly from A then A is a superclass of B and B objects can be used almost everywhere where A objects can be used. For reasons of efficiency, the compiler requires objects of a given type to have a certain structure. In order that B objects may be used as A objects, the compiler must therefore be able to generate an A view of B objects in an efficient manner. In this view, the compiler's assumptions about the structure of A objects must be satisfied.

The dynamic binding rule on page 177 requires that a method of an A object o which is overwritten in a derived class B should be dynamically bound if the compiler is unable to determine the runtime type of o directly. For example, if o has runtime type B then the method introduced in B should be used and not that in A. For such cases, the compiler must be able to make preparations so that at program run time the view expected by the method to be activated (that is, the original B view) can be efficiently generated from the A view.

As previously mentioned, many object-oriented languages (and, in particular, older object-oriented languages) only support simple inheritance. In Section 5.3.1, we shall consider a suitable scheme for compiling this concept. In Section 5.3.2, we shall turn to the considerably more complex problem of compiling multiple inheritance.

5.3.1   A compilation scheme for simple inheritance

In a language with simple inheritance, each class can inherit from at most one class; that is, it has at most one direct superclass. The inheritance hierarchies of such languages are trees or forests.

The mechanisms outlined in this section for compiling simple inheritance can also be used relatively simply and directly in imperative languages such as C. This also makes it possible to use object-oriented structuring (including simple inheritance) in imperative languages.

We begin with an example. The following program describes the class polyline and the derived class rectangle.

```
#include "graphical_object.h" /* imported "graphical_object" */
#include "list.h"              /* imported lists */
#include "point.h"             /* imported points */

class polyline : public graphical_object {
  List<point> points;
public:
  void translate(double x_offset, double y_offset);
  virtual void scale(double factor);
  virtual double length(void);
};
```

The class polyline.

```
#include "polyline.h"

class rectangle : public polyline {
  double side1_length, side2_length;
public:
  rectangle(double s1_len, double s2_len, double x_angle = 0);
  void scale(double factor);
  void length(void);
};
```

The class rectangle.

This definition of rectangle assumes that, for efficiency reasons, the lengths of the two sides of a rectangle are stored in the rectangle itself and do not have to be determined from the corner points whenever they are required. This definition permits an efficient redefinition of length; scale has to be redefined because the lengths of the sides are altered by scaling, and therefore the definition of scale cannot be taken over directly from polyline; on the other hand, translate can be taken over directly from polyline because the additional state is unaltered by translation.

The overall attributes of class rectangle comprise the attributes of class polyline and the additional attributes side1_length and side2_length introduced in rectangle.

We still have to explain how the compiler can implement the dynamic binding efficiently. In our example, for efficiency reasons, the class rectangle incorporates the two lengths of the sides of the rectangle in its objects. Consequently, the scale method of polyline cannot be used to scale a rectangle, since it knows nothing about the additional attributes which must also be changed by the scaling; the method defined by rectangle must be used (here we see a concrete example of the reason why the method-selection rule of page **??** was formulated). Now, an object of the class rectangle may generally be passed as an argument of a function or method if an object of the superclass polyline is permissible there. In particular, this applies to the function zoom which first translates a graphical object so that the point center comes to lie at the origin and then scales the result by the value zoom_factor.

```
void zoom(graphical_object &obj, double zoom_factor,
         point &center){
  obj.translate(-center.x,-center.y); // move "center"
                                        // to "(0,0)"
  obj.scale(zoom_factor);              // scale
}
```

The function zoom: center **and** scale.

If applied to a rectangle, the body of zoom must call the scaling function of rectangle and not that of polyline or even that of graphical_object. However, zoom may already be compiled and stored in a library before the class rectangle is even defined. Thus, when compiling zoom, the compiler may not even know the method to be activated in the body of zoom. Consequently, the compiler cannot bind scale to a concrete method. scale has to be dynamically bound, that is, bound at run time, to a method within zoom.

Compilers may use the following scheme to handle this dynamic binding efficiently. For each class, the compiler creates a method table which includes all the methods defined in the class that may have to be dynamically bound. For evident reasons, these method tables are called **virtual function tables** in C++. They contain entries for all methods of a class or its superclass that are defined to be **virtual**. Each object includes as its first component a pointer to the method table corresponding to its proper class. The compiler binds method names to indices in the method table.

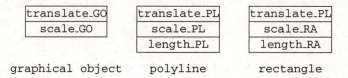

translate_GO	translate_PL	translate_PL
scale_GO	scale_PL	scale_RA
	length_PL	length_RA

graphical object   polyline   rectangle

Figure 5.2   Method tables for different subclasses of graphical objects.

To call the method it activates the function stored under the corresponding index in the method table. The method table of an inheriting class is generated as follows. We begin with a copy of the method table of the base class. In this copy, redefined methods are overwritten by the new definition. Then, the methods newly introduced are appended to the table. This ensures that the names of methods previously defined in the base class are assigned the same index in the new class.

If B is a class and A is a superclass of B then an A view of an object b of B consists of an initial section of b and an initial section of the method table referenced by b. The initial section of b belonging to the A view comprises precisely the pointer to the method table and the attributes inherited from A. The section of the method table belonging to the A view covers the indices for the methods introduced in A or a superclass. All views of b are represented in the same way by a pointer to b. Thus, the transition between different views is trivial.

We shall explain the scheme for our example in Figures 5.2 and 5.3.

Figure 5.2 shows the method tables for graphical object, polyline and rectangle. The method table for polyline is derived from that for graphical object; first the methods translate_PL and scale_PL which are redefined in polyline replace the corresponding methods of graphical object and second the newly defined (virtual) method length_PL is appended. In turn, the method table for rectangle is derived from that of polyline;

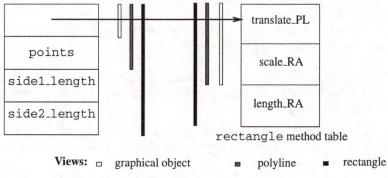

rectangle method table

Views: □ graphical object   ▨ polyline   ■ rectangle

Figure 5.3   Representation of rectangle objects.

the methods redefined in `rectangle` replace the corresponding methods of `polyline`. The method `translate_PL`, which is not redefined, is passed on. The compiler binds `translate` to the index 0, `scale` to the index 1 and `length` to the index 2.

Figure 5.3 shows the representation of `rectangle` objects. In addition to its own state, each such object contains a pointer to the method table of the class `rectangle`.

Thus, the implementation of simple inheritance with dynamic binding is associated with a storage overhead of one pointer per object. In addition, the method table associated with each class has to be stored. The dynamic binding leads to an increase in the run time for a method call, because of dereferencing a pointer to find the method table and indexing to locate the method to be activated.

5.3.2 Compilation scheme for multiple inheritance

In the last section, we saw that simple inheritance is easy to compile. On the other hand, multiple inheritance represents a greater challenge as far as both a clean language definition and the compiler design are concerned.

In languages with multiple inheritance, a class may inherit from not just one, but arbitrarily many classes. Thus, a class may have a number of direct superclasses. The resulting inheritance hierarchies are no longer trees but directed acyclic graphs.

The availability of multiple inheritance supports a programming style in which the elementary capabilities are implemented in small base classes, which can easily be acquired by inheritance to construct more complex classes. The application of multiple inheritance to abstract classes corresponds to a form of integration of multiple specifications corresponding to the abstract classes into a new specification corresponding to the inheriting class. Finally, multiple inheritance can be used, for example, to integrate a specification given by an abstract class with a concrete class as its implementation. One example might be a stack with a predefined maximum size. Such a class can be realized by inheritance from the abstract class `stack` and the concrete class `array` as its implementation.

All problems and possible solutions can be illustrated for the case of double inheritance. Thus, in the remainder of this section, we assume that a class C is derived from the two base classes B1 and B2.

The following lead to problems as far as the language definition and to some extent the compiler design are concerned:

(1) Conflicts and contradictions between B1 and B2. For example, if the same name is used for methods or attributes in the two base classes, inheritance may lead to a conflict.

(2) Repeated inheritance. If, for example, B1 and B2 inherit directly from A then C will inherit repeatedly from A; this produces a very interesting conflict situation, as we shall see.

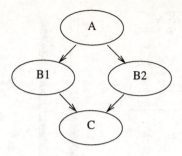

Figure 5.4   Repeated inheritance.

Problem (1) is primarily a problem of language definition. The following solutions, which can also be combined, are available when designing the language:

(1) B1 is defined to be the main ancestor. Conflicts are resolved in B1's favour. This approach is mainly used by interpreted object-oriented extensions of LISP. Typically, they bind names dynamically by searching the class hierarchy for an appropriate definition in a predefined order (in our case: C then B1 then B2); the first suitable definition wins.

   The approach is not totally without danger, since potential contradictions need not be apparent, and thus it might not always be clear to the program developer when the above strategy for resolving conflicts is used (possibly when he or she did not intend it).

(2) The language permits renaming of inherited features and thus allows the programmer to resolve potential conflicts by explicit intervention. This approach is used, for example, by Eiffel.

(3) The language provides constructs that may be used to resolve a conflict explicitly.

   For example, if definitions of a name n in B1 and B2 are contradictory, then constructs of the form B1::n or B2::n unambiguously specify that the definition of B1 or B2 should be used. This approach is used, for example, in C++.

The approach followed by the language has consequences on the management and organization of the compiler's symbol table. However, all the approaches permit a relatively simple implementation. We shall not go into this further.

   As far as problem (2) is concerned (see Figure 5.4) there are two diametrically opposite approaches.

(1) The repeated inheritance may be multiply instantiated (see Figure 5.5).

(2) The repeated inheritance is instantiated once (see Figure 5.6).

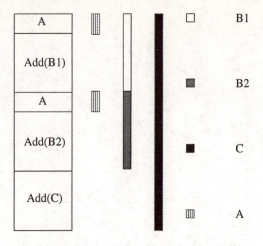

Figure 5.5 Multiple instantiation of repeated inheritance.

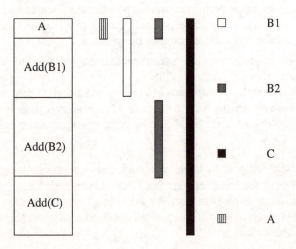

Figure 5.6 Single instantiation of repeated inheritance.

Both approaches have advantages and disadvantages.

Let us consider our class library of graphical objects as a first example. As we see in Figure 5.1, the class polygon inherits from both closed graphical and polyline since polygons are closed polylines. polygon inherits from the class graphical object via both routes. However, this does not mean that polygons should contain two independent object instances of graphical object as subobjects, as would be the case in Figure 5.5. We shall explain this with an extension of our example. For efficiency reasons, in many visualizations of object movements, it is not the movement of the object itself that is visualized but a simplified form of the object, usually its bounding rectangle. Against this background, we specify that every graphical object must contain a pointer to a bounding rectangle. This pointer is added to graphical object as a new attribute. When repeated inheritance is multiply instantiated, polygons contain two different pointers to the bounding rectangle and the consistency of these must be maintained. In this example, with a little luck, it may be possible to keep both pointers constant: they always point to the same rectangle; the pointers remain unchanged while the rectangle is altered in accordance with the operations on the main object. We would be lost if instead of a *pointer* to the bounding rectangle the coordinates of its corners were incorporated in graphical object. In this case, we would have to redefine all the methods inherited from polyline in polygon to ensure that the entries in the copies of graphical object inherited via closed graphical remained consistent with the copy inherited via polyline. In addition, all methods defined in polyline or subclasses would have to maintain the consistency of the two copies, which is an unnatural complication. Thus, we see that a multiple instantiation of the common inheritance is unnatural for our example of graphical objects and only appropriate under certain conditions.

We now construct an example for which multiple instantiation gives exactly the required result. The GNU C++ class library contains two classes for statistical evaluations: SampleStatistics and SampleHistogram. SampleStatistics includes services to determine the mean value, the variance and the standard deviation of series of measurements. SampleHistogram includes services to determine histograms. Let us suppose that we have to define a class to determine means and variances for a series of temperature measurements together with histograms for a series of pressure measurements. One obvious approach is to inherit from the two classes SampleHistogram and SampleStatistics and rename their methods (renaming is not possible in C++, although it is possible, for example, in Eiffel) so that the names indicate whether they relate to temperature or pressure measurements. Now, in the C++ class library SampleHistogram is defined as inheriting from SampleStatistics. Thus, our pressure/temperature class inherits twice from SampleStatistics. For this example, it is crucial that the common inheritance be multiply instantiated, otherwise the two series of measurements for the statistical evaluations would not be separated.

We see that, in some cases, it is desirable that the common inheritance be multiply instantiated, while in other cases we require a single instance of the common inheritance. In certain cases, it may even be desirable to have a single instance for certain features of the repeated inheritance while other features are multiply instantiated. Eiffel provides this flexibility.

Next we consider compilation schemes that only permit multiple instantiation of repeated inheritance. These schemes are simpler and generate more efficient code than schemes that also permit single instantiation of repeated inheritance.

Compilation of independent multiple inheritance

In the case of independent multiple inheritance, the inheritance from the base classes is mutually independent. Correspondingly, objects of the inheriting class C contain complete copies of the base classes B1 and B2, as shown in Figure 5.7.

The language C++ takes this view of multiple inheritance.

Thus, repeated inheritance, as illustrated in Figure 5.5, leads to conflicts and ambiguities, as follows:

- when the multiply instantiated features are referenced for access, calls or overwriting;
- when an A view of C objects is created, since C objects contain several A subobjects.

Visibility rules may in certain cases help to avoid the difficulties. For example, C++ allows a class to hide its own inheritance from its heirs: for example, B1 can inherit privately from A (in this case, B1 is not a subclass of A) without C being aware of this; in this case no ambiguities arise in C due to the multiple instantiation of A. (However, the designers of C++ decided not to use invisibility for disambiguation.) Where visibility rules are insufficient to eliminate the ambiguities, additional language constructs are needed: in C++ the qualification operator :: can be used in the form B1 : : f to denote that the feature f is of class B1. Additionally,

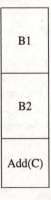

Figure 5.7   Object structure for independent multiple inheritance (program view).

type conversion can be used, for example, for explicit conversion of a C object into a B1 object.

We now try to extend the compilation scheme for simple inheritance to the case of independent double inheritance. We recall (see Figure 5.3) that, for efficient implementation of the dynamic binding of methods, we have incorporated in every object a pointer to the method table for its class as the first component. We try to keep to this approach.

Note that for every superclass B of C, the compiler must be able to generate a B view of C objects. Since the B1 subobject lies at the beginning of the C object, we can again use the simple-inheritance approach for B1: the B1 view of C objects is an initial section of the C view (for both the object components and the method table). Unfortunately, we cannot use an initial section of the C view for a B2 view, because a B2 view of an object must contain as its first component a pointer to a method table with a structure predefined by B2, followed by the attribute values for B2. This leads to the following approach: we incorporate in C objects a pointer to another method table before the B2 attribute values. This method table is derived from a copy of the B2 method table by overwriting the methods that are redefined in C. Thus, the B2 view is represented by a B2 reference which points to the beginning of the B2 subobject. Its first component is the pointer to the method table of the B2 subobject. For every instance of a superclass A, the compiler knows the offset of the corresponding subobject within the C object. It generates the corresponding A reference by adding this offset to the C reference. We obtain the structure shown in Figure 5.8.

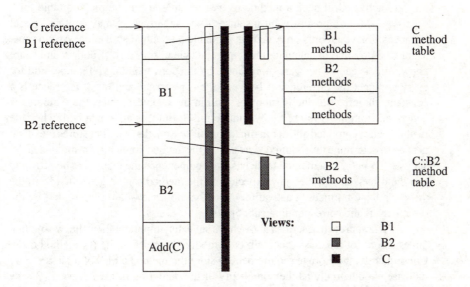

Figure 5.8   Object structure for independent multiple inheritance (implementation view).

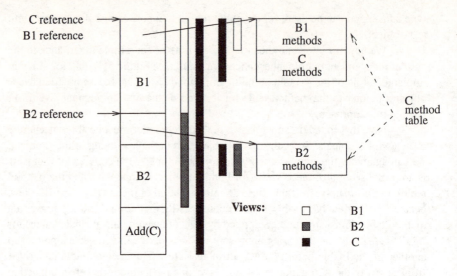

Figure 5.9   Object structure for independent multiple inheritance (actual implementation).

Thirdly, C methods (methods defined in C) expect a C view of the objects for which they are activated. If such a method overwrites an entry in the method table for a supertype A (more precisely, an instance of the supertype; C may contain several instances of A) then only an A view is available on method activation. At run time, it must be possible to calculate the required C view from this. If both A and C are known this is easy: views are represented by the corresponding references and for every C object the difference d between the A reference and the C reference is a constant: the offset of the A subobject within the C object. Thus, the C reference is derived from the A reference by subtracting d. But C is unknown both when the method call is compiled and at run time. For this reason, the compiler stores the offset needed to determine the required view next to the method pointer in the method table. Thus, every entry in a method table has two components: the method to be activated and the offset, so that the view expected by the method can be generated from the view available on method activation. Note that both views are represented by the references to the corresponding subobjects.

   The approach described above has a small but important flaw: the two method tables stored for the class C contain two (modified) copies of the B2 method table. Consequently, the storage requirement to store the method tables of a class C may increase exponentially as the complexity of the definition of C increases! (By the complexity of a class definition, we mean the size of the unfolded definition of the class. The unfolded definition of a class is derived from its definition by replacing the base classes by their unfolded definitions.)

To avoid exponential growth, we must use only a single copy of the B2 method table. We achieve this by storing the C method table in a *distributed* manner, as shown in Figure 5.9. This figure hides an interesting detail: the copies of the method tables for B1 and B2 may, of course, also be stored in a distributed manner.

Next we turn to a semi-formal description of this compilation scheme. We shall simplify matters by assuming that all ambiguities have already been resolved. The resolution of ambiguities is in no way trivial, but the techniques needed for this are described in Chapters 8 and 9 on syntax analysis and semantic analysis, respectively. Assuming a clean language design, the resolution of ambiguities is not a specific problem of the compilation of multiple inheritance.

For the description, we require a set of symbols which is introduced below:

- $\mathbb{N}$: the set of natural numbers,

- $\mathcal{N}$: a set of names (representations),

- $\mathcal{F}$: a set of specially coded function names (see Section 5.2); the corresponding functions implement methods,

- $\mathcal{T}$: a set of representations for types.

At our chosen level of abstraction a class definition for C with inheritance from B1 and B2 is given by:

- B1, B2: the base classes;

- $DM_1 \subset M_{B1} \times \mathcal{F}$: the overwritten B1 methods together with the new functions implementing them;

- $DM_2 \subset M_{B2} \times \mathcal{F}$: the overwritten B2 methods together with the new functions implementing them;

- $DM \subset \mathcal{N}$: the list of methods first introduced by C;

- $DMF: DM \rightarrow \mathcal{F}$: this function assigns to the newly introduced methods the functions implementing them;

- $DA \subset \mathcal{N}$: the list of attributes first introduced by C;

- $DAT: DA \rightarrow \mathcal{T}$: this function assigns the type to the newly introduced attributes; it can be used to determine, for example, the size of the storage area they occupy.

Based on this information, the compiler determines the following quantities for C (corresponding quantities are already available for B1 and B2):

- OC_C: the object components of C. These are the components which are stored in C objects at run time; in addition to the attributes, they include the pointers to the method tables, but not the methods themselves.

- M_C: the methods of C, including inherited methods.

- S_C: the superclasses of C.

- MT_C: the method table for C, represented as a sequence of method-table sections $MT_C^1 \ldots MT_C^{n_C}$, where each individual section is a table indexed by small numbers, with pairs consisting of function names and offsets as components: $MT_C^i : [0 \ldots n_C^i] \rightarrow \mathcal{F} \times \mathbb{N}$.

- $BC_C : C_C \rightarrow \mathbb{N}$: the binding function for object components which assigns to object components of C their offset within C objects.

- $BM_C : M_C \rightarrow \mathbb{N} \times \mathbb{N}$: the binding function for methods, which assigns pairs (i, j) to methods m of C. Meaning: m is described in the ith method-table section under index j.

- $BMT_C : [1 \ldots n_C] \rightarrow \mathbb{N}$: the binding function for method-table sections, which assigns to the method-table sections for C the offset within C objects at which the pointer to the method-table section is stored.

- $BS_C : S_C \rightarrow [1 \ldots n_C]$: the binding function for superclasses, which assigns to the superclasses A of C the method-table section in which the method table of A begins.

- $Size_C$: the size of C objects.

These quantities are determined as follows:

Object components

$OC_C := \{C\} \cup (OC_{B1} - \{B1\}) \cup OC_{B2} \cup DA$, that is, the object components of C include:

- C as a component for the pointer to the C method table,

- the object components of B1, but not B1 itself, since the pointer to the B1 method table coincides with that to the C method table,

- the object components of B2,

- the attributes newly introduced by C.

Methods

$M_C := M_{B1} \cup M_{B2} \cup DM$

Superclasses

$S_C := \{C\} \cup O_{B1} \cup O_{B2}$

The superclasses of C are C itself and the superclasses of B1 and B2 (which themselves contain B1 and B2).

Method tables

$MT_C := MT_C^1, MT'^2_{B1}, \ldots, MT'^{n_{B1}}_{B1}, MT'^1_{B2}, \ldots, MT'^{n_{B2}}_{B2}$ where

$MT_C^1 := MT'^1_{B1} \cdot DMF(DM) \times \{0\}$

$$MT'^i_{B1}(j) := \begin{cases} MT^i_{B1}(j) & \text{if the } j\text{th entry is not overwritten,} \\ & \text{that is, } \not\exists\, (m, f) \in DM_1 \text{ with} \\ & BM_{B1}(m) = (i, j); \\ (f, BMT_C(i)) & \text{otherwise.} \end{cases}$$

$$MT'^i_{B2}(j) := \begin{cases} MT^i_{B2}(j) & \text{if the } j\text{th entry is not overwritten,} \\ & \text{that is, if } \not\exists\, (m, f) \in DM_2 \text{ with} \\ & BM_{B2}(m) = (i, j); \\ (f, BMT_C(i + n_{B1})) & \text{otherwise.} \end{cases}$$

Thus, the method table of C is essentially a sequence of modified copies MT'^i_{Bx} of the method-table sections MT^i_{Bx} for B1 and B2; MT'^1_{B1}, the first of these sections, is extended at the end by entries for the methods newly introduced by C. These new methods use the offset 0. An entry $MT^i_{Bx}(j)$ is transferred unaltered to $MT'^i_{Bx}(j)$ if C does not contain a redefinition (m, f) for the associated method m; otherwise the entry (in the copy) is overwritten by (f, o) where o is the offset of the pointer to the corresponding method-table section within C objects: that is, $BMT_C(i)$ for Bx = B1 and $BMT_C(i + n_{B1})$ for Bx = B2. This definition is motivated by the following observations. If f is overwritten by C, the overwriting function is coded with a C view as object reference. If, on the other hand, f is referenced through a method-table section MT^i_C, a view corresponding to MT^i_C is available. This view is offest by $BMT_C(i)$ from the C view.

Binding of object components to their offsets in C objects

$BC_C(C) : 0$

for $c \in C_{B1} : BC_C(c) := BC_{B1}(c)$

for $c \in C_{B2} : BC_C(c) := BC_{B2}(c) + Size_{B1}$

for $c \in DA : BC_C(c) := o(c) + Size_{B1} + Size_{B2}$

Here, $o(c)$ is the offset of c in the storage area made available for the new attributes of C; it is determined in the same way we saw for the storage of records in Chapter 2 on the compilation of imperative programming languages.

Binding of methods to their position in the method table

for $m \in M_{B1} : BM_C(m) := BM_{B1}(m)$

for $m \in M_{B2} : BM_C(m) := (i + n_{B1}, j)$ where $(i, j) = BM_{B2}(m)$

for $m \in DM : BM_C(m) := (1, j + |MT^1_{B1}|)$ where j is the position of m in DM and $|MT^1_{B1}|$ is the number of entries in this section.

Binding of superclasses to method-table sections

$BS_C(C) := 0$

$BS_C(A) := BS_{B1}(A)$ for $A \in O_{B1}$

$BS_C(A) := BS_{B2}(A) + n_{B1}$ for $A \in O_{B2}$

Binding of method-table sections to offsets

for $1 \le i \le n_{B1} : BMT_C(i) := BMT_{B1}(i)$

for $i > n_{B1} : BMT_C(i) := BMT_{B2}(i - n_{B1}) + Size_{B1}$

Sizes of C objects

$Size_C := Size_{B1} + Size_{B2} + Size(C)$ where $Size(C)$ denotes the size of the storage area needed to store the attributes newly introduced in C.

The various binding functions and the method-table sections are the most important of the quantities determined above. The others are auxiliary quantities which enable us to determine these.

We now consider how the compiler uses this information.

Method tables   The method-table sections are stored once as data in the target program generated.

Object initialization BMT_C is used to initialize a C object. Code is generated to store a pointer to the method-table section MT_C^i at the offset $BMT_C(i)$.

Method call $BM_C(m)$ and BMT_C are used to generate code for a method call c.m. If $BM_C(m) = (i, j)$, then m is described in the jth entry of the ith method-table section. The pointer to this method-table section lies at offset $oi := BMT_C(i)$ in the associated object, given by its C reference c, whence at the address $mtv := c + oi$. mtv is also the object view of c to which the offset entries in the method-table section refer as starting point. Thus, $mta := *mtv$ is the starting address of the method-table section (in the languages C and C++, $*$ is the dereferencing symbol, which denotes the contents of a storage location with a given address (and a given type); $*$ is used in this form here). $f := mta[j].f$ is the function which implements the method m of the object c, and $o := mta[j].o$ is the offset which can be used to determine the object view required by f from the view mtv of the method-table section. Thus, the compiler generates the following code for the method call c.m(args).

```
mtv= c + oi;          // View of the ith method-table section
mta= *mtv;            // Starting address of this section
f=    mta[j].f;       // The function implementing 'm'
v=    mtv - mta[j].o; // The object view required by 'f'
(*f)(v,args);         // The method call
```

Compilation of the method activation c.m(args).

The quantities oi and j are known to the compiler at the time the method call is compiled; they are constants in the code generated. mtv, mta, v and f are temporary auxiliary variables.

Views   To generate an A view for a superclass A of C from a C view, the compiler uses BS_C and BMT_C. The A reference is obtained from the C reference by adding $BMT_C(BS_C(A))$ to the C reference.

We end this presentation with a brief consideration of the overheads generated by the scheme.

Runtime cost for method activation   The important method activation gives rise to a runtime overhead of one addition, one dereferencing, two indexed accesses and one subtraction. For many target machines, this amounts to six machine instructions.

Storage overhead per object   Each object contains the pointers to the method-table sections as overhead. We shall refer to a class which does not arise through inheritance from another class, and thus has no (true) predecessors in the inheritance hierarchy, as a **basic class**. Then, the number of instances of basic classes occurring in the definition of C is precisely the number of C method-table sections. This number increases at most linearly with the complexity of the definition of C and, moreover, will in practice almost always be small in comparison with the overall size of the object.

Storage overhead per class   The method table must be stored once per class. The size of this table increases linearly with the size of the class definition.

Runtime overhead for object initialization   When objects are newly initialized or created the pointers to the method-table sections must be initialized. The overhead is linear in the storage overhead per object. In many practical cases, it will not be very crucial. Nevertheless, it will be desirable for the language to be economical in its handling of automatically created and initialized temporary object instances and for the programmer to be able to control the initialization of objects explicitly. This is not fully the case for C++ at present.

Compilation of dependent multiple inheritance

Here, we refer to multiple inheritance where there may exist dependencies between the inheritance of B1 and that of B2. These dependencies are restricted to the common inheritance of B1 and B2 which is passed to C as a repeated inheritance. The most important special case arises when the repeated inheritance in C is only instantiated once and the B1 and B2 subobjects share this instance, as illustrated in Figure 5.5.

Many of the conflicts and contradictions which arise for independent inheritance, such as the ambiguities associated with access to the repeated inheritance or the occurrence of several instances of the same superclass in the derived class, do not arise in this special case: the repeated inheritance is only instantiated once. Other ambiguities and problems arise instead:

(1)   When a method m of the common inheritance A is overwritten by both B1 and B2, then it is not clear which of these methods should be incorporated in the A view of C objects. Renaming of the overwriting method is no solution: the A view only knows a single method m, but we have two competitors, independently of their names. Instead, we must require C itself to overwrite the two overwriting methods in B1 and B2 by the same method.

(2) Another problem is associated with class invariants. A class invariant for a class C is a statement which applies to all C objects. For example, let us suppose that we have a class List, which implements a list in the conventional manner by a list header where the linked list elements begin. Let us suppose that we also have an attribute NumberofElements in List; then, the meaning of NumberofElements is formally described by a class invariant, which states that in every List object NumberofElements contains the number of elements appended to the list header. Class invariants are an important aid to the formal description of the meaning of classes and their attributes. They are useful for correctness checking. Their checking at run time is an important aid to testing which increases the reliability of the modules generated. Of course, the invariants cannot be satisfied all the time; for example, while we are introducing an element into a List the assertion must be briefly violated. However, the class invariant must be satisfied again when a class method called from outside the class returns. That is an appropriate point to check its validity.

Single instantiation of common inheritance may lead to the following problem with class invariants: B2 methods may, for example, modify the single instance of the common inheritance and thereby alter parts of B1 objects, possibly violating their B1 invariants in an unnoticed manner.

The scheme developed in this section allows us to handle more than the special case of a single instantiation of the common inheritance: in fact for every individual feature of the common inheritance, we can determine whether it is singly or multiply instantiated. Thus, in addition to the extreme cases of multiple instantiation of the whole of the repeated inheritance, as in independent inheritance on the one hand, and single instantiation of the whole of the repeated inheritance on the other, hybrid forms can also be handled. This represents the flexibility which Eiffel offers the programmer. In Eiffel, differentiation between single and multiple instantiation of a feature of the common inheritance (attribute or method) is linked to renaming: if the feature was renamed at least once on an inheritance path, then it is multiply instantiated, otherwise it is singly instantiated.

Of course, for all hybrid forms we inherit the problems of both extreme cases (even the highly developed Eiffel does not contain sufficient language tools for full solution of the problems arising). I am therefore not convinced that the ability to distinguish between single and multiple instantiation for every individual feature is of practical importance. Instead, I expect that distinction at the level of complete superclasses would be sufficient; however, the general compilation scheme is only slightly more complex and may even lead to shorter program run times. Therefore, we describe this general compilation scheme. Figure 5.10 shows a possible object structure which is supported by this scheme.

The B2 subobject of a C object uses several sections in common with the B1 subobject. The important thing is that the B2 subobject no longer occupies a contiguous storage area: it contains gaps. Worse still, the gaps only arise when C inherits from B2, long after the compiler has had to determine what a B2 view

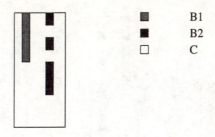

▧	B1
■	B2
▢	C

Figure 5.10   Object structure for general dependent multiple inheritance (program view).

looks like. Furthermore, the gaps may be of different sizes, depending on the context in which B2 arises; for example, they are not present in proper B2 objects. Consequently, it follows that the offsets of components within objects are no longer constant and thus can no longer be bound statically.

We met a similar problem in the compilation of simple inheritance, where the compiler had to generate code to call functions it did not yet know; now, it must generate code for access to components whose offset it does not know. In fact, for this (and many similar problems), the compiler can use the technique that helped in the dynamic binding of functions, namely, the inclusion of an indirection step via a table. The compiler binds the components of a class to fixed indices in an index table; a separate index table is created for every different context to contain the offsets valid for that context. The objects contain a pointer to the relevant index table. Thus, we implement the dynamic binding of component offsets in an analogous manner to the dynamic binding of methods. The resulting structure is shown in Figure 5.11.

The figure shows the structure of a C object with its two pointers C-index and C::B2-index to the index table which is stored only once. C-index assigns to every component of C its offset relative to a C reference; similarly, C::B2-index assigns to every component of the B2 subobject its offset relative to a B2 reference. In the figure, the offsets in the index table are shown by dotted arrows.

Just like the first approach to the implementation of independent multiple inheritance, this approach also has a crucial flaw. The two mapping tables for C contain two copies of the index table of B2; consequently there is a potentially exponentially increasing storage requirement as the size of the class definition increases. To avoid this, we must eliminate one of the copies. As the figure correctly shows, the two copies are almost identical. The only difference is that the offsets in C::B2-index relate to B2 references, while the copies in C-index contain offsets relating to C references. The difference between the two references is constant for all proper C objects and is already stored in the C index table at the beginning of its copy of the B2 index table. Provided we always take this offset into account when interpreting an index table, we can use the copy of the B2 index table in the C index table as the index table for B2 subobjects of C objects. The resulting object

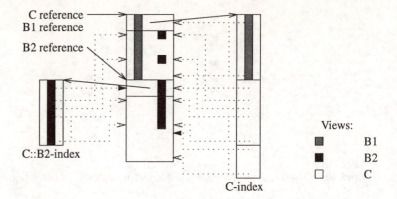

Figure 5.11 Object structure for general dependent multiple inheritance (implementation view).

structure is shown in Figure 5.12. In addition to offsets, we also include the method information known from the previous section in the index table.

As in the previous section, we shall now describe our scheme in a semi-formal way. Again, for simplicity, we assume that only the features that B1 and B2 may use in a common instance have identical names, while other names are pairwise distinct. It is guaranteed that none of the potential ambiguities or contradictions described above will occur (for example, a singly instantiated feature having two contradictory definitions).

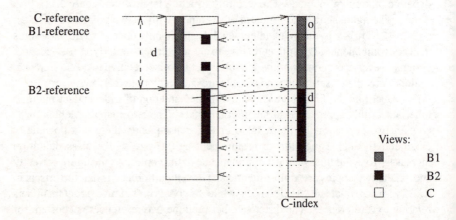

Figure 5.12 Object structure for general dependent multiple inheritance (actual implementation).

At our chosen level of abstraction, a class definition for C with inheritance from B1 and B2 is again given, as in the case of independent inheritance, by:

- B1, B2: the base classes;

- $DM_1 \subset M_{B1} \times \mathcal{F}$: the overwritten B1 methods together with the new functions implementing them;

- $DM_2 \subset M_{B2} \times \mathcal{F}$: the overwritten B2 methods together with the new functions implementing them;

- $DM \subset \mathcal{N}$: the list of methods first introduced by C;

- DMF: $DM \rightarrow \mathcal{F}$: this mapping assigns to the newly introduced methods the functions implementing them;

- $DA \subset \mathcal{N}$: the list of attributes first introduced by C;

- DAT: $DA \rightarrow \mathcal{T}$: this mapping assigns the type to the newly introduced attributes; it can be used to determine, for example, the size of the storage area they occupy.

Based on this information, the compiler determines the following quantities for C (corresponding quantities are already available for B1 and B2):

- F_C: the features of C, that is, its methods and attributes.

- S_C: the superclasses of C.

- OC_C: the object components. These are the components which are stored in C objects at runtime; in addition to the attributes, they include the pointers to the index sections, but not the methods.

- IC_C: the components in C indices: attributes, methods and superclasses with disambiguated names if they occur in both B1 and B2.

- IMC_C: the methods under the index components.

- IOC_C: the object components (attributes, superclasses) under the index components; thus IC_C splits into the two subsets IMC_C and IOC_C.

- $IS_C \subset S_C$: the sections of the C index table represented by classes using it.

- I_C: the index table for C. A table with indices from $0 \ldots |IC_C| - 1$ and as values (function, offset) pairs for methods and offsets for object components.

- $BF_C : F_C \rightarrow IC_C$: the binding function for features of C which assigns to each feature of C its index component.

- $BS_C : S_C \rightarrow IC_C$: the binding function for superclasses which assigns to each superclass of C its index component.

- $BOC_C : OC_C \rightarrow \mathbb{N}$: the binding function for object components which assigns to the elements of OC_C their offsets within proper C objects (that is, C objects which do not belong to a proper subclass).

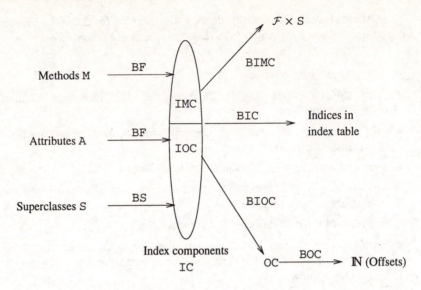

Figure 5.13 Relationship between the quantities defined for class compilation.

- $BIC_C : IC_C \rightarrow \mathbb{N}$: the binding function for index components which assigns to index components their position within the index table.

- $BIOC_C : IOC_C \rightarrow OC_C$: the binding function for object components in C indices. It assigns to the index components representing object components the corresponding object components in the C runtime objects.

- $BIMC_C : IMC_C \rightarrow \mathcal{F} \times S_C$: the binding function for methods under the C index components, which assigns to the method components pairs consisting of the functional implementation of the method and the class defining the method.

The relationship between these quantities is depicted in Figure 5.13.

Features of C

$$F_C := F_{B1} \cup (F_{B2} - F_{B1}) \cup DA \cup DM$$

Superclasses

$$S_C := \{C\} \cup S_{B1} \cup (S_{B2} - S_{B1})$$

Object components and their binding

$OC_C := \{C\} \cup (OC_{B1} - \{B1\}) \cup (OC_{B2} - OC_{B1}) \cup DA$, that is, the object components of C include:

- C as a component for the pointer to the C index table;

- the object components of B1, but not B1 itself, since the pointer to the B1 method table coincides with that to the C index table;
- the object components of B2, provided that they do not occur in B1;
- the attributes newly introduced by C.

For the determination of BOC_C the elements of OC_C are stored as components of a record, as we saw in Chapter 2 on the compilation of imperative languages. Thereby, the classes in OC_C represent the pointers to the associated index-table sections. The components of C must be stored from offset 0. BOC_C is defined as the offset of the component c within the record.

Note that BOC_C is only valid for actual C objects.

Index components and their binding

$$IC_C := \{C\} \cup B1::(IC_{B1} - \{B1\}) \cup B2::IC_{B2} \cup \{B1::B1\} \cup DA \cup DM$$

BIC_C assigns a sequence of consecutive numbers to the elements of IC_C in the order specified in the definition of IC_C. The relevant assignments are:

$$BIC_C(C) := 0$$
$$BIC_C(B1::c) := BIC_{B1}(c) \text{ for } c \neq B1$$
$$BIC_C(B2::c) := BIC_{B2}(c) + |IC_{B1}|$$
$$BIC_C(B1::B1) := |IC_{B1}| + |IC_{B1}|$$

The precise assignment of indices for the new features of C is of less importance.

These two definitions specify the structure of the C index tables. The index tables for C must each contain a (modified) copy of the index tables for B1 and B2. Thus, we would expect IC_C to include the union of IC_{B1} and IC_{B2}. But these two sets are not necessarily disjoint. This is the reason why we denote the two union operands by B1:: and B2:: and thus make their elements distinguishable from one another.

Note also that we do *not* assign the index 0 to B1 but have chosen an index after the other components of IC_{B1}. This was done for the following reasons: the first entry in an index-table section *must* always describe the associated class: it contains the offset of the subobject belonging to the class in the main object. Thus, the first entry in a C index table must describe C. If we had assigned the elements of IC_{B1} consecutive numbers beginning with 1, we would not have been able to use the index table of C for the B1 subobject. This would have necessitated another pointer to this index section in the runtime representation of C objects. By removing B1 and assigning the remaining elements the same index they obtain from BIC_{B1}, we can use an initial section of the C index table as the B1 index table. This is possible while the B1 object is actually instantiated within the C object. If this is not the case (this can only occur for C subobjects in objects of derived classes) then there is another copy of the B1 index table at another point in the index table for this derived class and the objects of this class contain a pointer to this index table; our B1 entry in the C index table is always set in such a way that we find the valid pointer to the B1 index table to be used via it. Thus, unlike the B1 object component, the B1 index component cannot be combined with the corresponding C component.

Index sections
$$\text{IS}_C := \{C\} \cup (\text{IS}_{B1} - \{B1\}) \cup (\text{IS}_{B2} - \text{IS}_{B1})$$

Binding of the features of C to their index components
$$\text{BF}_C(c) := B1::c \text{ for } c \in C_{B1}$$
$$\text{BF}_C(c) := B2::c \text{ for } c \in C_{B2} - C_{B1}$$
$$\text{BF}_C(c) := c \text{ otherwise}$$

Binding of the superclasses to their index components
$$\text{BS}_C(C) := C$$
$$\text{BS}_C(A) := B1::A \text{ for } A \in S_{B1}$$
$$\text{BS}_C(A) := B2::A \text{ for } A \in S_{B2} - S_{B1}$$

Binding of the index-object components to object components
$$\text{BIOC}_C(c) := \text{BIOC}'_C(c) \text{ if } \text{BIOC}'_C(c) \neq B1$$
$$\text{BIOC}_C(c) := C \text{ otherwise}$$
$$\text{BIOC}'_C(C) := C$$
$$\text{BIOC}'_C(B1::c) := \text{BIOC}_{B1}(c)$$
$$\text{BIOC}'_C(B2::c) := \text{BIOC}_{B1}(c) \text{ if } c \in \text{IOC}_{B1}$$
$$\text{BIOC}'_C(B2::c) := \text{BIOC}_{B2}(c) \text{ if } c \notin \text{IOC}_{B1}$$
$$\text{BIOC}'_C(B2::c) := c \text{ otherwise}$$

This definition takes account of the following consideration: if c belongs to B1 and B2 the binding function BIOC_{B1} should also be used for B2::c rather than the binding function BIOC_{B2}. BIOC_{B2} is only used to bind B2::c when c belongs to B2 but not to B1. In particular, this affects the common superclasses of B1 and B2. Under this method, a superclass A for B2 which previously shared the pointer to the index-table section with B2 may now have its pointer in a B1 component.

The auxiliary function BIOC'_C takes care of this. However, it can map components onto B1 which was replaced in the C object components by C; the given definition of BIOC_C corrects this.

Binding of method components to function–class pairs
$$\text{BIMC}_C(B1::m) := \text{BIMC}_{B1}(m) \text{ if there are no } (m, f) \text{ in DM1, otherwise}$$
$$\text{BIMC}_C(B1::m) := (f, C).$$
$$\text{BIMC}_C(B2::m) := \text{BIMC}_{B2}(m) \text{ if there are no } (m, f) \text{ in DM2, otherwise}$$
$$\text{BIMC}_C(B2::m) := (f, C).$$
$$\text{BIMC}_C(m) := (f, C) \text{ for } (m, f) \text{ in DM.}$$

Index table   Every component j of I_C corresponds under BIC_C to a component c of IC_C.

If c is an object component, then

$$I_C(j) := \text{BOC}_C(\text{BIOC}_C(c))$$

is the offset of c within (proper) C objects.

If c is a method, $(f, A) := BIMC_C(c)$ is the function implementing c and the class defining it, then $I_C(j)$ is given by:

$$I_C(j) := (f, BOC_C(BIOC_C(BS_C(A))))$$

The most important of the quantities determined above are the various binding functions, and the set of index sections and index tables. The others are auxiliary quantities used to determine these.

We now consider how the compiler uses this information.

Index table   The index table is stored once as data in the target program generated.

Object initialization   For the initialization of a proper C object, for each element A of S_C code is generated to store a pointer to the $BIC_C(BS_C(A))$th entry in the index table at offset $BOC_C(BIOC_C(BS_C(A)))$.

Method call   Assume a method m is to be activated for a C object, given by its C reference c. $i := BIC_C(BF_C(m))$ is the index corresponding to m in the C index table. The pointer at the address c points to an index table with the structure of a C index table. The first entry of this index table contains the offset co of the C subobject in question within its main object o := c − co. The ith entry of the index table contains a pair (f, fo) which describes the function implementing m and the object view expected by it. This view is obtained by adding fo to o. Thus, to activate c.m(args) the compiler generates the following code:

```
it= *c;              // Start of the index table
o=  c - *it;         // Reference to the main object
f=  it[i].f;         // The function implementing 'm'
v=  o + it[i].fo;    // The object view required by 'f'
(*f)(v,args);        // The method call
```

Compilation of the method activation c.m(args).

i is known to the compiler; it is a constant in the code generated. it, o, f and v are temporary auxiliary variables.

Access to attributes   If a is an attribute of a C object given by its reference c and $i := BIC_C(BF_C(a))$, then the pointer at the address c points to an index table with the structure of a C index table. The first entry in this table contains the offset co of the C subobject in question within its main object o := c − co. The ith entry of the index table contains the offset ao of a within o. To access c.a the compiler generates the following code:

```
it= *c;        // Start of the index table
o=  c - *it;   // Reference to the main object
ao= it[i];     // Offset of 'a' in 'o'
...o[ao]...;   // Access
```

Compilation of the attribute access c.a.

i is known to the compiler; it is a constant in the code generated. it, o and ao are temporary auxiliary variables.

Views To obtain an A view of a C object given by its C reference c for a supertype A of C, the compiler generates the following code:

```
it= *c;        // Start of the index table
o=  c - *it;   // Reference to the main object
ao= it[i];     // Offset of the 'A' subobject in 'o'
a=  o + ao;    // 'A' view of 'c'
```

Computation of an A view of c.

$i := \text{BIC}_C(\text{BS}_C(\text{A}))$ is known to the compiler; it is a constant in the code generated. it, o, ao and a are temporary auxiliary variables.

We end our presentation with a brief consideration of the overheads generated by the scheme.

Runtime overhead for attribute access The important attribute access gives rise to a runtime overhead of two dereferencings, one assignment and one subtraction to determine it and o. This amounts to four instructions on many target machines. Additional overheads are incurred in the form of an indexed access with variable index, which amounts to a further one or two instructions. Attribute accesses are usually only made to the current object (the current object is the object called this in the implementation of methods by functions). For this case, we may expect that an optimizing compiler would already hold the frequently used quantities it and o in its registers. Thus, normally, we can reckon on an overhead of one indexed access (with variable index), amounting to one or two machine instructions per attribute access.

Runtime overhead for method activation The method activation gives rise to a runtime overhead of one addition, two dereferencings, two indexed accesses and one subtraction. This amounts to seven machine instructions for many target machines.

Storage overhead per object Each object contains the pointers to the index sections as overhead. The number of these pointers corresponds, as for independent inheritance, to the number of basic-class instances in the definition of C. This number increases at most linearly with the complexity of the definition of C and is typically negligible.

Storage overhead per class   The index table must be stored once per class. The size of this table increases linearly with the size of the class definition.

Runtime overhead for object initialization   When objects are initialized or created, pointers to the index sections must be initialized. The overhead is linear in the storage overhead per object.

5.4   Genericity

Strongly typed languages with compiler type checking have considerable advantages over languages with dynamic type checking in terms of reliability and efficiency. For, based on type information, the compiler can recognize many potential inconsistencies at a time when they do not yet seriously affect our human world. Moreover, the compiler can use the information about the structure of the runtime objects provided by the types to generate efficient target programs. For example, we saw in the previous section how the compiler can access object methods and attributes very efficiently (with an overhead of 5–7 machine instructions), based on knowledge of the object types and thus also their structure. Without type information, a method would have to be sought dynamically, with an overhead of hundreds of instructions.

On the other hand, strongly typed languages place shackles on their programs. These shackles often mean that the same algorithm has to be implemented in many instances of functions. One of the simplest examples is the exchange operator, which interchanges its two arguments. In a typeless language, it can be implemented as follows:

```
exchange(inout x, inout y)
  local t;
  t:= x; x:= y; y:= t
```

Implementation of exchange.

It exchanges the values of an arbitrary x and y. In a strongly typed language, the exchange operator has to be implemented by a separate function for each type, for example:

```
exchange_integer(inout integer x, inout integer y)
  local integer t;
  t:= x; x:= y; y:= t
```

Implementation of exchange_integer.

for integers and

```
exchange_real(inout real x, inout real y)
  local real t;
  t:= x; x:= y; y:= t
```

Implementation of `exchange_real`.

for floating-point numbers. The operations to be executed are the same (at least, at the level of abstraction of the algorithm description), but nevertheless strongly typed languages require two different function definitions.

At first sight, it might seem as though inheritance, as introduced earlier, could solve the problem if we were to define a class `object` to be a superclass of every other class. This class defines general operations available for all objects: assignment, and test for identity. The `exchange` function could then be defined over `object` and inherited by all subclasses.

```
exchange_object(inout object x, inout object y)
  local object t;
  t:= x; x:= y; y:= t
```

Implementation of `exchange_object`.

Unfortunately, this function is completely unusable. This is a consequence of a property of the type system associated with inheritance, which we have only hinted at until now. There *are* places at which an object *cannot* be replaced by an object of a subclass. One very important example is the target of an assignment. A precisely converse rule applies for this.

Assignment type rule   An assignment b:= ... remains type correct if the variable of type B is replaced by a variable of a *super*type A. An assignment ... := a remains type correct if the object a of type A is replaced by an object b of a *sub*type B.

Let us briefly consider the reason for this rule. An assignment to a variable of type B is permissible if it is certain that the object assigned is actually a B object, that is, has all the features required by B. If we replace the assignment target by a variable of a supertype, we weaken the requirements (since superclasses require fewer features) and the assignment remains permissible. On the other hand, a change to a variable of a subtype would tighten the requirements and might make the assignment illegal. Therefore the type system forbids this sort of change. We use the assignment type rule directly to derive rules for the different sorts of parameters.

Type compatibility of actual and formal parameters   Only objects of a subtype of A can be passed to an input parameter with declared type A. Only variables of a supertype of A can be passed to an output parameter with declared type A. Only variables with a declared type A can be passed to an input/output parameter with declared type A.

These rules follow from the assignment rule since parameter passing to an input parameter may be viewed as an assignment of the actual parameter to the formal parameter on entry to the function, while parameter passing to an output parameter may be viewed as an assignment of the formal parameter to the actual parameter on exiting the function. It follows that the operator defined above can only be applied to objects with declared type object, and we have gained nothing.

Remark   The type system of Eiffel supports a concept whereby dependencies between the types of different variables can be formulated. Such dependencies in the form of 'y has the same type as x' and associated type rules in certain cases enable one to prove that an assignment remains valid when the target variable is changed to a subtype (because it demonstrably also tightens the type of the object assigned). If Eiffel had input/output parameters, the exchange operator could be implemented with a single function for all descendants of object. The possibility of specifying types by referring to the types of other objects and thereby formulating dependencies between the types of different objects provides the already powerful inheritance mechanism with even greater flexibility.   □

Were the problem restricted to such simple cases as the exchange operator, no one would give a solution any thought. But the exchange operator is only an example of a giant class of algorithms which includes very commonly used basic algorithms such as manipulating lists, sets, queues, directories and trees. Thus, it affects data types which can be referred to in a broad sense as *containers*. In typed languages, these containers have a natural parameter, namely the type of their content. **Genericity** allows one to define types parametrized in such a way.

A **generic data type**, or a **generic class**, is a type/class prototype with formal parameters. It defines a data type or a class when supplied with appropriate actual parameters. The application of a generic class to actual arguments is normally called **instantiation**: it generates an instance of a class. Abstraction by means of generic classes in the type area may be seen as analogous to abstraction by means of procedures in the area of computations. Instantiation in one area corresponds to procedure activation in the other area.

By way of example, we consider a part of the definition of a generic class of lists in C++. C++ introduces generic definitions with the keyword template followed by the formal parameter specifications enclosed in '<...>'. Instantiations also use '<...>' to enclose the actual parameters. Two generic classes are defined here. First, we have the class Listlink<T> which defines the link elements for constructing lists. Each link element contains two attributes: the stored value value and the pointer next to the next link element. The type of value is T, the formal parameter of the class.

The generic class List defines lists containing objects of type T as elements.

```
// Listlinks --- the links to form lists
template <class T>
struct Listlink {
  T               value; // value of this element
  Listlink        *next; // link to next element


 // Constructor
 Listlink(T val, Listlink *link) { value= val; next= link; }
};


// Lists --- implemented as head to linked listlinks
template <class T>
class List {
    Listlink<T> *head; // list head


  public:
    // Constructor
      List(void) { head= 0; }


    // check for emptiness
      int empty(void) { return head == 0; };


    // get an element (returns the first one)
      Listlink<T> *elem(void) { return head; };


    // push a value
      void push(T value) {
        Listlink<T>     *elem= new Listlink<T>(value,head);
        head=           elem;
      }


    // pop first element and return its value
    //    requires the list to be nonempty (not checked!)
      T pop(void) {
        Listlink<T> *elem= head;
        T value= elem->value;
        head= elem->next;
        delete elem;
        return value;
      }


    // ...
};
```

The generic class List.

They are implemented as a list head head which points to the start of a chain of link elements of the type T. The class definition refers to the formal parameter T and the corresponding instance List1ink<T> at several points.

This single definition can be instantiated for each required type of list elements: List<int> comprises lists of integers, List<List<int>> comprises lists whose elements are lists of integers, ... The definition of polylines uses lists of points:

```
class polyline : public graphical_object {
  List<point> points;
public:
  void translate(double x_offset, double y_offset);
  virtual void scale(double factor);
  virtual double length(void);
};
```

Polylines.

Genericity can also be used to solve the problem of our exchange operator.

```
template <class T> void exchange(T &x, T &y) {
  T t;
  t= x; x= y; y= t;
}
```

Generic implementation of the exchange operator in C++.

This involves the definition of a generic function which can be applied to any arguments provided their types are the same and they can be used as the target of assignments. For example, the following uses are permissible and lead to the expected result:

```
struct S {int i; int f[20]; } s1, s2;
int i1, i2;

void f(void) {
  // ...
  exchange(s1,s2); // s1 <-> s2
  exchange(i1,i2); // i1 <-> i2
  // ...
}
```

Use of exchange.

The compiler instantiates the generic function as required. For this it uses the concept of **overloading** which is supported by C++. C++ allows several functions to have the same name provided they can be distinguished from each other by the type of their arguments. Thus, function names may have an overloaded or multiple meaning. Conceptually, the generic function `exchange` defines an infinite family of functions which are all called `exchange` but which differ in the type of their arguments.

The typical C++ implementation of genericity is not very interesting from the point of view of compiler design. When instances of a generic definition are referenced, for example, by explicit instantiation as in `List<int>` or indirectly, for example, by a call to `exchange`, the generic definition is used as a pattern from which to generate a concrete class or a concrete function given the actual parameters: the generic definition is *expanded*. The result is a class or function definition such as a programmer might have defined. The compiler takes the tedious copying work away from the programmer and saves him or her from having to find new artificial names and introduce them at the right points in the copy. If a generic definition is multiply instantiated with *different* parameters then the program generated contains multiple instances of the class or function. Each instance of a class has its own method implementations. This means that when intense use is made of large generic classes the program size may increase dramatically.

Before we consider genericity in Eiffel, where a *generic* class is compiled directly into the target code and the implementation of its methods can be used for *all* instantiations of the generic class, we shall first explain why in many cases a C++ compiler actually *has to generate* different instantiations of the same function/method. The simple `exchange` operator again provides a good example. Although `exchange<int>` and `exchange<S>` have the same function body they are *actually* different functions: in `exchange<int>` one integer is exchanged between the two arguments, while 21 integers are exchanged in `exchange<S>`. If the corresponding actual parameters of two instantiations of a generic definition have the same size (here, by the size of a type, we mean the size of the objects of this type) then a single instance can carry out both tasks (the same would be true if either the object size were stored in the runtime object or the size information were passed to the function or method by other parameters; it is difficult, however, to reconcile these two approaches with other features of C++).

It is precisely this property that enables Eiffel to implement each of its instantiations with a single instance of a generic definition. In fact, in Eiffel, all variables, parameters, return values and object attributes have one of the following *runtime* types: INTEGER, CHARACTER, BOOLEAN, REAL or REFERENCE. The corresponding values are uniformly represented, typically by a machine word each. Objects are never manipulated directly, but always indirectly via references. For objects whose type is specified by a formal parameter of a generic definition, only the assignment and test-for-identity operations are available inside the generic definition. They operate only on runtime values and not on the objects themselves and can be uniformly realized for all runtime values. Thus, a single instance of a generic class can take over the implementation of all instantiations.

In C++, the genericity concept is interpreted much more broadly than we have indicated previously: in addition to types, all forms of parameters known from function definitions are allowed as formal parameters of a generic definition. The following example shows a fragment from the definition of **associative arrays**. These are arrays whose indices are not restricted to integers but may be of an arbitrary type.

```
template <class Indextype, class Valuetype>
class assoc {     // Abstract definition of an
                  // 'associative array',
                  // with values in 'Valuetype' and
                  // indices in 'Indextype'
public:
   // Access to components with given index
      virtual
      Valuetype operator [] (Indextype const &index);

   // Query, whether the 'index' component exists
      virtual
      bool exists(Indextype const &index);

   // Remove the 'index' component
      virtual
      void remove(Indextype const &index);

   // ...
};
template <class Indextype, class Valuetype, int maxsize>
class fixed_assoc: public assoc<Indextype,Valuetype> {
               // associative array
               // with maximal 'maxsize' entries
               // implemented as normal array
   pair<Indextype,Valuetype> vec[maxsize];
               // Vector with 'maxsize' elements
   int used; // Number of elements occupied
};
```

Fragment of the definition of associative arrays.

The example first defines the abstract class assoc which specifies the methods common to every associative array. The next definition shows a fragment from an implementation of this abstract class by arrays of a predefined maximum size maxsize, which is included as a parameter in the generic definition. The array used for the implementation contains pairs of the form (index, value). If an index component is accessed the array is searched for a corresponding component and a reference to the associated value is returned. If it does not yet exist, it is automatically created. An instantiation fixed_assoc<STRING, STRING, 100> defines a class in which standard arrays of size 100 are used to implement associative arrays with strings as indices and values.

So far, we have still not learnt about all the possibilities arising from the genericity supported by C++. The following example introduces another such possibility: for vectors of the same length, we can define an addition if we can add their components. Thus, the following definition cannot be arbitrarily instantiated:

```
template <class component: group, int size>
class vectorgroup: public vector<component,size> {
  // Addition of two vectors
  vectorgroup operator+ (vectorgroup y) {
    int i;
    vectorgroup result;

    for (i=0; i<size; i++) result[i]= this[i] + y[i];

    return result;
  }   // ...
}
```

Fragment of the definition of vectorgroup.

A prerequisite for an instantiation of the form

```
vectorgroup<comptype,size>
```

is that the component type comptype should define an operation +. The formal parameter specification class component: group entry used above expresses such a restriction. The actual parameter of an instantiation for vectorgroup must be a subclass of group (a group, in mathematics, is a set with operations +, − and an element 0 satisfying the so-called group axioms). Here, we have a kind of restricted genericity. The restriction is that the formal type parameters must be subclasses of predefined classes. The earlier forms will be referred to as unrestricted genericity.

Eiffel only supports unrestricted genericity using special language constructs, where only type parameters can be used as formal parameters of generic class definitions. However, the very flexible inheritance and type concept of Eiffel does permit *emulation* of restricted genericity.

5.5 Exercises

1: The following example shows another fragment of the class library of graphical objects of Figure 5.1.

```
class closed_graphical: public graphical_object {
 public:
  // Surface area enclosed by object
    virtual double area(void);
};

class ellipse: public closed_graphical {
   point _center; // Centre of the ellipse
   double _x_radius, _y_radius;
                   // Radii of the ellipse
   double _angle; // Rotation from x-axis

 public:
   // Constructor
     ellipse(point &center,
             double x_radius, double y_radius,
             double angle= 0) {
        _center= center;
        _x_radius= x_radius; _y_radius= y_radius;
        _angle= angle;
     }

   // Ellipse area ---'closed_graphical::area'
     double area(void) { return PI * _x_radius * _y_radius; }

   // Distance to a point --- expensive!
     virtual double dist(point &);

   // Center
     const point& center(void) { return _center; }

   // Translate --- overwrites'graphical_object::translate'
     void translate(double x_offset, double y_offset){
        _center.translate(x_offset, double y_offset);
     }

   // Scale --- overwrites'graphical_object::scale'
     void scale(double scale_factor) {
        _x_radius *= scale_factor;
        _y_radius *= scale_factor;
     }

   // ...
};

class circle: public ellipse {
 public:
   // Constructor
     circle(point &center, double radius){
        ellipse(center,radius,radius);
     }
```

```
           // Distance to a point --- overwrites'ellipse::dist'
           virtual double dist(point &p) {
             double center_dist= _center.dist(p);
             if (center_dist <= radius) return 0;
             else return center_dist - radius;
           }

// ...
};
```

The classes `closed graphical`, `ellipse` **and** `circle`.

Compile the method `ellipse::translate` in the function implementing it.

2: Determine the method tables and the method indices according to Section 5.3.1 for the classes defined in the previous exercise.

3: Determine the method table and the method indices according to the compilation scheme for independent multiple inheritance of page 190 for `circle` and compile a method call of the form `c.dist(p)`, where `c` is a circle and `p` is a point.

4: Determine the index table and the binding functions according to the compilation scheme for dependent multiple inheritance for the class `polygon`.

```
class polygon: public polyline, public closed_graphical {};
```

Polygon.

`polyline` is defined on page 183.

5: The definition of a new class should not affect the existing class structure. However, because of the subtype rule methods of existing classes must be able to operate with objects of the new class. Overwriting of features of inherited classes may mean that their view of the new objects becomes inconsistent. Thus, only limited redefinitions are permitted. Three different aspects must be taken into account:

- The meaning (semantics) of the feature. Every attribute and every method has a meaning or task which should not be affected by overwriting. For example, the method `scale` has the task of scaling a graphical object. A redefinition must carry out this same task, considered both at the actual level and at the level of a superclass.

- The restrictions due to the type system. Redefinition should not lead to type inconsistencies.

- The restrictions due to the compilation scheme. Redefinitions may mean that assumptions made in the compilation become invalid, and should not be allowed in this case.

The first aspect is very important, but a compiler does not typically have access to the necessary specification in order to check the semantic legality. In this exercise, we consider restrictions due to the type system.

The transition from a type to a subtype is called **type tightening** and the transition from a type to a supertype is called **type weakening**. A prototype (of a method) is tightened when the types of the return value and the output parameters are tightened and the types of the input parameters are weakened.

(a) Show that, from the point of view of the type system, there are no obstacles to the tightening of the prototype of a redefined model. Use examples to show that the prototype of public methods, that is, methods callable by arbitrary classes, can at best be tightened; any other change may lead to type errors in calls which were previously correct. Show that a non-tightening change of a prototype is also only permissible under very restricted conditions for redefined private methods, that is, methods callable only by this class and its heirs but not by foreign classes. Does verification of the legality require information about the superclasses going beyond a knowledge of the types of their attributes and prototypes of their methods? If so, what?

(b) The Eiffel language permits the tightening of the type of an inherited attribute in a derived class. Show that this implies that attributes can necessarily only be read by a foreign class. Use an example to show that the tightening of an attribute type is only permissible under very restricted conditions. Does verification of the legality require information about the superclasses going beyond a knowledge of the types of their attributes and prototypes of their methods? If so, what?

6: This exercise investigates the restrictions on redefinition due to the compilation scheme used.

(a) Our compilation scheme for simple inheritance permits the tightening of the prototype by redefinition of methods; this is not the case for our compilation schemes for multiple inheritance. Determine the conditions under which the two schemes can be harmed by a prototype tightening.

Look for an extension of our schemes that permits unrestricted tightening of prototypes of redefined methods. Hint: the redefined method is entered in the method table in two different ways. The new definition is used directly for views from the newly defined class; views from superclasses, on the other hand, do not use the new definition directly but are embedded in a wrapper function which converts between old and new types for parameters and return values.

(b) Our compilation scheme for simple inheritance permits the tightening of attribute types (provided the tightening does not lead to type inconsistencies), whereas the schemes for the multiple inheritance do not. Can you explain the reason for this?

(c) The Eiffel language permits a class to redefine an inherited parameterless method as an attribute. Show how our compilation scheme could be extended to handle such a redefinition.

7: Our compilation schemes for multiple inheritance have a comparatively high storage overhead per object. In this quite difficult exercise, we develop a compilation

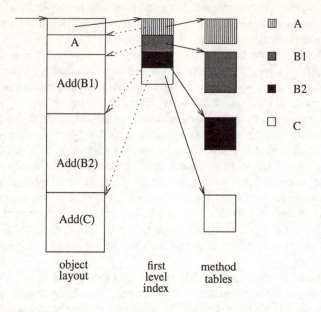

object
layout

first
level
index

method
tables

Figure 5.14   Object and index structure for class-related feature access.

scheme which reduces this overhead drastically.

(a) For every superclass A of a class C, there is an A view of C objects. However, our compilation schemes need not represent each view separately; the representations for different views often coincide. For each different representation of a view the objects contain one pointer as overhead. Therefore, to reduce the overhead we have to decrease the number of different representations of views.

In what follows, we suppose that repeated inheritance is only instantiated once. In this case, a C object contains precisely one A subobject for every supertype A. This enables us to represent *all* views uniformly using a pointer to the object, provided that when we access the features we specify the corresponding class as well as the attribute or method. Thus, the compiler binds attributes and methods to (Class ID, Offset) or (Class ID, Method index) pairs. Here, Class ID is a well-defined identification of the class that has introduced the feature (within the inheritance hierarchy). The pointer at the beginning of an object points to a two-level index. The first-level index table is indexed with the Class ID and gives the offset of the subobject belonging to this class together with the pointer to its method table. Figure 5.14 shows the corresponding structure for the situation of Figure 5.6.

For this procedure to be efficient, it is crucial that the indexing of the first-level indices with the Class IDs can be carried out efficiently. The use of very small integers as Class IDs would be desirable, for then the first-level index can be implemented using conventional tables. Class IDs must have the following properties:

- A class must retain the same Class ID within a program.
- If a program contains the class C then all superclasses of C must have different Class IDs.

A compiler usually has only a limited knowledge of the classes built into a program. Thus, it cannot allocate the Class IDs. The program binder binds pre-compiled classes into a program and thus knows all classes relevant to a program. It is an appropriate entity to bind the Class ID names used by the compiler to the Class IDs themselves (very small integers). Its tasks also include the construction of the first-level index table based on information in the form of lists of triples (Class ID name, Offset, Method name) prepared for each class by the compiler. Elaborate the details.

(b) When a repeated inheritance A is (partially or completely) multiply instantiated the above procedure is no longer applicable, since the specification of A alone when accessing features is insufficient to distinguish between the different instances of A.

For the situation of Figure 5.5, show that the views of B1 and B2 necessarily have different representations (if C must distinguish between two A instances and three B instances, then three differently represented views will be required).

(c) Combine the approach outlined in the first part of the exercise with our earlier compilation schemes. In this way, you should obtain new compilation schemes for independent and general dependent multiple inheritance, for which the number of differently represented views of C objects is given by the maximum number of distinguishable instances of *the same* object type.

8: Propose a generic definition for first-in-first-out queues.

5.6   Literature

Simula 67, the forefather of object-oriented languages, is described in Dahl *et al.* (1984) and Svensk Standard 636114 (1987). Goldberg and Robson (1983) describe Smalltalk 80. C++ is defined in Stroustrup (1990). ANSI (1990) is the basis for the standardization of C++ by ANSI, while Meyer (1993) provides a good introduction to Eiffel (Eiffel is defined in Meyer (1991)). Cox (1986) describes Objective-C. Object-oriented language extensions of LISP are described in Bobrow and Stefik (1982), Cannon (1980) and Hullot (1984).

6

The structure of compilers

- Compiler subtasks

- Lexical analysis

- Screening

- Syntax analysis

- Semantic analysis

- Machine-independent optimization

- Address assignment

- Generation of the target program

- Machine-dependent code improvement

- Real compiler structures

- Formal specification and generation
  of compiler modules

- Literature

Compilers for high-level programming languages are large, complex software systems. The development of large software systems should always begin with the decomposition of the overall system into subsystems (modules) with a well-defined and understood functionality. The division used should also involve sensible interfaces between the modules. This structuring task is in general not simple and frequently requires good intuition on the part of the engineer. Fortunately, compilers are very well-understood software systems with tried and tested structuring principles which, with certain adaptations, can be applied to almost all high-level programming languages.

The compiler structure described in what follows is a **conceptual** structure, that is, it identifies the subtasks of the compilation of a source language into a target language and specifies possible interfaces between the modules implementing these subtasks. The real module structure of the compiler will be derived from this conceptual structure later. At that time, modules of the conceptual structure may be combined, if the subtasks they implement permit this, or a module may be broken up into a number of submodules if the subtask it implements is very complex.

The first coarse structuring of the compilation process is the division into an **analysis phase** and a **synthesis phase**. In the analysis phase the syntactic structure and some of the semantic properties of the source program are computed. The semantic properties that can be computed by a compiler are called the **static** semantics. This includes all semantic information that can be determined solely from the program in question, without executing it with the input data. The results of the analysis phase comprise either messages about syntax or semantic errors in the program (that is, a rejection of the program) or an appropriate representation of the syntactic structure and the static semantic properties of the program. This phase is (ideally) independent of the properties of the target language and the target machine.

The synthesis phase for a compiler takes this program representation and converts it (possibly in several steps) into an equivalent target program.

6.1   Compiler subtasks

Figure 6.1 shows a conceptual compiler structure. Here, the compilation process decomposes into a sequence of subprocesses. Each subprocess receives a representation of the program and produces a further representation of a different type or of the same type but with a modified content. The subprocesses are shown by boxes containing the name of the compiler subtask performed by the process together with the name of a corresponding module, when one is introduced. We shall now follow the sequence of subprocesses step by step to explain their tasks and the structure of the program representation. A simple example program leads us through most of the steps.

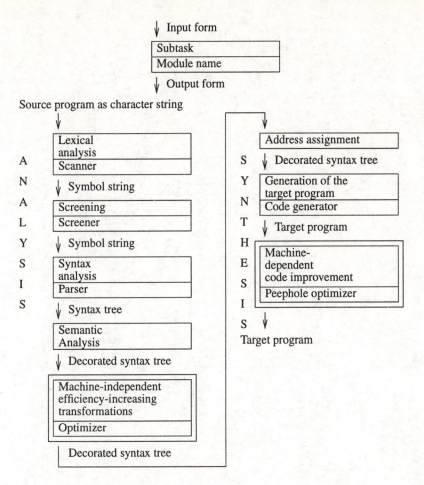

Figure 6.1 Conceptual compiler structure showing the intermediate program representations. The modules in double-framed boxes are optional.

6.2   Lexical analysis

A module, usually called a **scanner**, carries out the lexical analysis of a source program. It reads the source program in from a file in the form of a character string and decomposes this character string into a sequence of lexical units of the programming language, called **symbols**. Typical lexical units include the standard representations for objects of type integer, real, char, boolean and string, together with identifiers, comments, punctuation symbols and single or multiple character operators such as =, <=, >=, <, >, :=, (,), [,], and so on. The scanner can distinguish between sequences of space characters and/or line feeds, which only

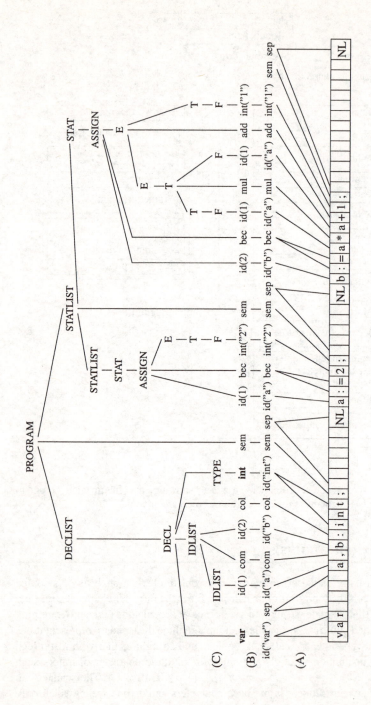

Figure 6.2 Analysis of a program section. (A) lexical analysis. (B) screening (C) syntax analysis.

have a meaning as separators and can subsequently be ignored, and relevant sequences of such characters, for example in strings. The output of the scanner, if it does not encounter an error, is a representation of the source program as a sequence of symbols or encoded symbols. Figure 6.2(a) shows the conversion of a character string into a symbol string by the scanner.

6.3   Screening

The task of the screener is to recognize the following symbols in the symbol string produced by the scanner:

- Symbols that have a special meaning in the programming language, for example among the identifiers, the reserved symbols of the language such as begin, end, var, int, and so on.
- Symbols that are irrelevant for the subsequent processing and will be eliminated, for example strings of space characters and line feeds, which have been used as separators between symbols, and comments.
- Symbols that are not part of the program but directives to the compiler (pragmas), for example the type of diagnosis to be performed, the type of compilation protocol desired, and so on.

In addition, the screener is often given the task of encoding the symbols of certain classes of symbols (such as the identifiers) in a unique way and replacing each occurrence of a symbol by its code. Thus, for example, if all the occurrences of an identifier in a program are replaced by the same natural number, the character-string representation of the identifier need only be stored once and thus the problem of having to store identifiers of different lengths is concentrated in a specialized part of the program.

Figure 6.2(b) shows the transformation of the scanner output by the screener. The reserved symbols found are shown in bold and the identifiers are numbered from 1 upwards. In practice, the scanner and the screener are usually combined into a single procedure (which is then simply called the scanner). Conceptually, however, they should be separated, because the task of the scanner can be accomplished by a finite automaton, while that of the screener must necessarily (sensibly) be carried out by other functions.

6.4   Syntax analysis

The syntax analysis should determine the structure of the program over and above the lexical structure. It knows the structure of expressions, statements, declarations and lists of these constructs and attempts to recognize the structure of a program in the given symbol string. The corresponding module, called the **parser**, must also be able to detect, locate and diagnose errors in the syntax structure. There is a wealth of methods for syntax analysis. A number of versions of the two methods of syntax analysis which are most important in practice are described in Chapter 8.

There are various equivalent forms of parser output. In our conceptual compiler structure and in Figure 6.2(c), we use the syntax tree of the program as output.

6.5 Semantic analysis

The task of semantic analysis is to determine those properties of programs, above and beyond the (context-free) syntactic properties, that can be computed using only the program text. These properties are often called **static semantic** properties, unlike **dynamic** properties, which are properties of programs that can only be determined when the compiled program is run. Thus, the two terms, static and dynamic, are associated with the two times, compile time and run time.

The static semantic properties include:

- The type correctness or incorrectness of programs in strongly typed languages such as Pascal. A necessary condition for type correctness is that every identifier must be declared (implicitly or explicitly) and there should be no double declarations.

- The existence of a consistent type assignment to all functions of a program in (functional) languages with polymorphism. Here, a function whose type is only partially defined, for example, using type variables, can be applied to combinations of arguments of a different type and essentially do the same thing. A type inference algorithm uses the partial type information to calculate a (most general) type assignment for the functions of the program, if such a thing exists.

Example 6.1 In the program of Figure 6.2, the semantic analysis, as illustrated in Figure 6.3(d), would collect declarative information in the DECLIST subtree and construct a list for this:

((id(1), (var,int)), (id(2), (var,int)))

In the statements of the STATLIST subtree, this declarative information can be used for type checking. For example, for the first statement $a := 2$ one checks whether there is a variable name on the left side and whether the type of the right side matches that of the left side. These two questions are answered positively, since a is declared as a variable and lexically, the character string '2' is recognized as a representation of an integer constant.

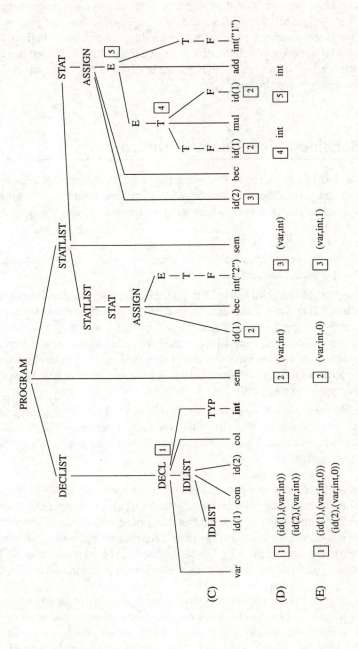

Figure 6.3 Analysis of a program segment, (D) semantic analysis, (E) address assignment.

227

In the second statement $b := a * a + 1$, the type of the right side has to be computed. This computation involves the types of the terminal operands (all integer) and rules that compute the type of a sum or a product from the types of the operands. Here, we note that the arithmetic operators in most programming languages are 'overloaded', that is, they stand for the operations they designate over both integer and real numbers, possibly even with different precision. In the type computation this overloading is eliminated. In our example, it is established that an integer multiplication and an integer addition are involved. Thus, the result of the whole expression is of type integer.   □

6.6   Machine-independent optimization

Further static analysis of the source program may uncover evidence of expected runtime errors and possibilities for efficiency-increasing transformations. Data flow analysis or abstract interpretation can be used to investigate, for example, the following properties:

- There may exist an execution path on which the value of a variable is used without it having been previously initialized.

- Properties of program parts that point to possibilities for improving efficiency. If program parts cannot be reached or defined functions are never called, these superfluous parts need not be compiled. If it is clear that a certain program variable in an imperative program always has the same known value in a statement, then the variable can be replaced there by its value; the same is true for a function for which a formal parameter always has the same known value on every call.

- The property of a Prolog predicate, that it is used in a Prolog program as a function, that is, with the same input/output parameter specification whenever it is called. This information can be exploited to produce a more efficient translation.

A further analysis of the program would provide information about the values of variables, with the possibility of transforming the program to improve efficiency. Such an analysis would bring to light the fact that whenever the second statement $b := a*a+1$ is executed, the variable a has value 2. Replacement of both occurrences of a by 2 leads to the expression $2*2+1$, whose value 5 can be calculated at compile time. This type of analysis and transformation is called propagation and folding of constants.

It belongs to the class of **efficiency-increasing program transformations**, traditionally referred to as **code optimization**. This name is inappropriate, since in many cases at best local and never global optimality with respect to a predefined criterion is achievable. Where optimality for a particular task can be defined in isolation, for example, for the global allocation of the machine registers to program quantities, the complexity of the problem (NP completeness) stands in the way of efforts to achieve optimality.

In addition to calculating (sub)expressions whose values are known at compile time, so-called optimizing compilers also carry out program transformations of the following type:

- Extraction of loop-invariant computations from loops. If an expression in the body of a loop is unaffected by any of the variables that may possibly be changed in the loop, it can be removed from the loop and computed just once outside the loop.

- A similar transformation exists in the compilation of functional programs when the *fully lazy* property has to be achieved. Here, expressions that only contain variables that are bound outside a function are removed from the function body and passed to calls of the function through an additional formal parameter.

- The elimination of redundant computations. When different occurrences of the same expressions are computed one after the other without the components of the expression being modified in the interim, these redundant computations can be avoided.

- The elimination of 'dead' code, that is, program segments that are known never to be executed.

The assignment of this optional phase (that is, it does not exist in all compilers) to the analysis phase appears somewhat arbitrary. It does not necessarily belong to either the analysis phase or the synthesis phase. However, it uses information computed by semantic analysis and, unlike the subtasks of the synthesis phase, it is machine independent.

6.7   Address assignment

The synthesis phase of the compilation begins with storage allocation and address assignment. This involves properties of the target machine such as the word length, the address length, the directly addressable units of the machine and the existence or non-existence of instructions giving efficient access to parts of directly accessible units. These machine parameters determine the assignment of storage units to the elementary types and the possibility of packing objects of 'smaller' types (for example, Boolean or character objects) into larger storage units. In this assignment, attention must be paid to the fact that in most machines the instructions have certain addressing restrictions, for example that an integer can only be loaded, stored or operated on if it is aligned on a full word boundary. These constraints on storage assignment are called **alignment conditions**.

Example 6.2 (see Figure 6.3)   We assume we have a machine with full-word addressing, that is, the addresses of consecutive full words differ by 1. Integer variables are assigned to full words in the order in which they are declared, starting at address 0. Thus, the variable *a* takes the address 0 and *b* is assigned the address 1.

□

6.8   Generation of the target program

The code generator generates the instructions of the target program. For this, it uses the addresses assigned in the previous step to address variables. However, the time efficiency of the target program can often be increased if it is possible to hold the values of variables and expressions in machine registers. Access to these is generally faster than access to memory locations. Since each machine has only a limited number of such registers the code generator must use them to the greatest advantage to store frequently used values. This task is called **register allocation**.

Another task of the code generator is **code selection**, that is, the selection of the 'best possible' instruction sequences for the expressions and statements of the source program. Most computers provide several instruction sequences for compiling a source language statement. Thus, the best possible instruction sequences should be selected based on execution time, storage space requirements and/or instruction length.

Example 6.3   Let us suppose that the target machine has the following instructions:

LOAD	*addr, reg*	Load contents of location with address *addr* into register *reg*
STORE	*reg, addr*	Store correspondingly
LOADI	*int, reg*	Load constant *int* into register *reg*
ADDI	*int, reg*	Add constant *int* to contents of register *reg*
MUL	*addr, reg*	Multiply contents of location with address *addr* by contents of register *reg*.

Suppose the machine registers are $R_1, R_2, \ldots, R_N$. Then one possible translation of our example program is:

LOADI	2, R_1
STORE	$R_1, 0$
LOAD	0, R_1
MUL	0, R_1
ADDI	1, R_1
STORE	$R_1, 1$

□

6.9   Machine-dependent code improvement

The procedures for machine-independent code improvement mostly use global information about the computations carried out by the program. On the other hand, machine-dependent code improvement usually manages with local views of parts of the target program. The name **peephole optimizer** is based on the image of passing a small window over the target program and attempting to replace the instruction sequence visible underneath by a better one.

Subtasks of this phase include:

- elimination of useless instructions;
- replacement of general instructions by more efficient ones for special cases.

The last task could equally well be allocated to the code generator. However, it is allocated to the peephole optimizer, to keep the code generator simple.

Example 6.4 (continuation of Example 6.3)   One sees, when one passes the window over the second and third instructions, that the third, LOAD 0, R_1, is redundant since the value loaded into the register is already there. If the computer has an INC *reg* instruction, which increases the content of the register *reg* by 1, the instruction ADDI 1, R_1 can be replaced by the (possibly) cheaper instruction INC R_1.   □

6.10   Real compiler structures

So far, we have considered a conceptual compiler structure. Its modular structure was characterized by the following properties:

- The compilation process is divided into a sequence of subprocesses.
- Each subprocess communicates with its successor without feedback; the information flows in one direction only.
- The intermediate representations of the source program can, as we shall see in more detail later, in part be described by mechanisms from the theory of formal languages, such as regular expressions, context-free grammars, attribute grammars, and so on.
- The distribution of tasks among subprocesses is in part based on the correspondence between the description mechanisms referred to above and automaton models and is in part carried out pragmatically in order to split a complex task into two separate, more manageable subtasks.

What spoils this conceptual compiler structure, that is, why is it not a good real compiler structure? In the design of a real compiler (one that is to be implemented), the structure is influenced by the complexity of the subtasks, the requirements on the compiler and the constraints of the computer and the operating system.

If a number of consecutive subtasks are not too complex and the requirements and the constraints permit, the work of these subtasks can be interleaved, that is, complete intermediate representations of the program will not be produced and instead partial representations will be passed to the next module, while the modules will not run sequentially one after the other but will be related by a main-program–subprogram or co-routine relationship.

Here is an example. We mentioned previously that scanners and screeners are usually integrated; the scanner recognizes the next symbol and the integrated screener determines whether it should be eliminated, whether it is a reserved word symbol or whether it should be or has been encoded, if it belongs to corresponding symbol classes. The work of this integrated program is usually interleaved with that of the parser, from which it is called as a subprogram. On every call, it returns the next relevant symbol found. Thus, the first three subtasks are implemented in one module, and the construction and storage of two intermediate forms of the program is suppressed. The transformation of the character string into the syntax tree is carried out in one **pass** through the program.

If the semantic analysis is simple and no optimization is called for by the compiler, the remaining subtasks can also be accomplished by subprograms of the parser. Then we have a so-called **one-pass** compiler.

On the other hand, the complexity of a subtask or the need for code-improving transformations may necessitate several passes through the program or possibly even the decomposition of an individual phase into several passes. For example, in Algol 68, defining and applied occurrences of identifiers may occur in an arbitrary order. Thus, the compiler designer is forced to implement one pass to collect the declarative information followed by a number of others for type checking.

6.11 Formal specification and generation of compiler modules

We know from the theory of formal languages and automata that a part of the compiler's tasks includes recognition problems for certain types of grammar and that these problems can be solved by automata of corresponding type. The automata corresponding to grammars used here can be generated automatically.

The lexical units, the symbols of the language, can be described by regular expressions. Procedures for constructing a non-deterministic finite automaton from a regular expression R, recognizing the regular sets described by R and converting these into a deterministic finite automaton are known from the (constructive) proofs of the equivalence of regular expressions, non-deterministic and deterministic finite automata.

The correspondence between context-free grammars and pushdown

Table 6.1   Compiler subtasks, specification mechanisms and automaton types.

Compiler subtask	Specification mechanism	Automaton type
Lexical analysis	Regular expressions	Deterministic finite automata
Syntax analysis	Context-free grammars	Deterministic pushdown automata
Semantic analysis	Attribute grammars	
Efficiency-increasing transformations	Tree → tree transformations	Finite tree transductors
Code selection in code generation	Regular tree grammars	Finite tree automata

automata and the construction of a pushdown automaton from a context-free grammar so that the latter recognizes the language defined by the grammar are equally well known. Unfortunately, here, the deterministic pushdown automata are less powerful than the non-deterministic pushdown automata. However, since compiler designers prefer deterministic types of automata, the class of context-free grammars permitted for the specification of the syntax of programming languages is restricted to the deterministically analysable subclasses (or perhaps even more restricted).

These two applications of results from the theory of formal languages and automata to the construction of compilers led to the idea that it might also be possible to generate other compiler modules automatically, if they could be specified formally by appropriate mechanisms. This idea of **compiler generation** led to the development of other description mechanisms and generation procedures which are discussed in the following chapters. Table 6.1 shows the subtasks of the conceptual compiler structure that can be described (in part) by formal specifications and for which generation procedures exist. In the next chapter, we shall first outline the task. Then we shall introduce the description mechanism for this task and the necessary theoretical foundations; finally, we shall describe generation procedures for modules that accomplish the task according to the formal specification.

6.12   Literature

The structuring of compilers was well understood at a relatively early date. It was dealt with in three articles by McKeeman and DeRemer (1974), McKeeman (1974) and Ganzinger and Wilhelm (1975), respectively.

7

Lexical analysis

- The task of lexical analysis

- Theoretical foundations

- A language for specifying the lexical analysis

- The generation of a scanner

- The screener

- Flex, a scanner generator under UNIX

- Exercises

- Literature

In this chapter, we first discuss the task of lexical analysis, then the formal specification of this task and finally a generation procedure for lexical analysers (scanners); at the end of the chapter we give a number of implementation-related tips. Under the last heading, we also discuss the screener, which on its own could only fill a very small section. We note that another generation procedure of greater practical relevance is described in Chapter 8, Syntax Analysis, in connection with the generation procedures for LR(k) analysers.

7.1   The task of lexical analysis

The lexical analysis implemented in the **scanner** module decomposes the source program, read in from a file as a string of characters, into a sequence of lexical units, called **symbols**. The scanner reads this character string from left to right. If the work of the scanner, the screener and the parser is interleaved the parser calls the scanner–screener combination to obtain the next symbol. The scanner begins the analysis with the character following the end of the last symbol found and searches for the longest string at the beginning of the remaining input that is a symbol of the language. It returns a representation of this symbol to the screener, which determines whether this symbol is relevant for the parser or should be ignored. If it is not relevant, the screener triggers the scanner again. Otherwise, it returns a (possibly altered) representation of the symbol to the parser.

In general, the scanner should be able to recognize infinitely many or at least, very many different symbols. It deliberately divides this set into a finite number of classes. Symbols with a related structure (for example, the same syntactic role) fall into the same **symbol class**. Thus, we now distinguish between:

- **Symbols** or words over an alphabet of characters, Σ, for example, xyz12, 125, begin, "abc",

- **Symbol classes** or sets of symbols such as the set of identifiers, the set of integer constants and that of character strings identified by the names id, intconst, string, and

- **Representations of symbols**. For example, the scanner might pass the word xyz12 to the screener in the representation (id, xyz12), which the latter enters in its symbol table as (1,17) and passes to the parser, where the code for the symbol class id is 1 and xyz12 is the 17th identifier found.

7.2   Theoretical foundations

Words and languages   We briefly review a number of important basic terms relating to formal languages, where Σ denotes an arbitrary **alphabet**, that is, a finite non-empty set of characters:

Word x over Σ of length n	$x : \{1, \ldots, n\} \to \Sigma$ denoted $x_1 x_2 \ldots x_n$	Finite sequence of characters of Σ
empty word	$\varepsilon : \emptyset \to \Sigma$	Word consisting of no characters
Σ^0	$\{x \mid x : \emptyset \to \Sigma\} = \{\varepsilon\}$	
Σ^n	$\{x \mid x : \{1, \ldots, n\} \to \Sigma\}$	Set of words of length n
Σ^*	$\bigcup_{n \geq 0} \Sigma^n$	Set of all words over Σ
Σ^+	$\bigcup_{n \geq 1} \Sigma^n$	Set of all non-empty words over Σ
$x.y$	$x_1 \ldots x_n y_1 \ldots y_m$, if $x = x_1 \ldots x_n, y = y_1 \ldots y_m$	Concatenation of x and y

Remarks

- The empty word ε is the neutral element for the concatenation of words, that is, $x.\varepsilon = \varepsilon.x = x$ for all $x \in \Sigma^*$.
- Concatenation is associative, that is, $x.(y.z) = (x.y).z$.
- In what follows, we write xy for $x.y$. $\square$

Other terms:

    Suppose $w = xyz$ with $x, y, z \in \Sigma^*$. Then

x is a **prefix** of w;	if $yz \neq \varepsilon \neq x$,	then x is a **proper prefix** of w;
z is a **suffix** of w;	if $xy \neq \varepsilon \neq z$,	then z is a **proper suffix** of w;
y is a **subword** of w;	if $xz \neq \varepsilon \neq y$,	then y is a **proper subword** of w.

Formal languages over Σ are subsets of Σ^*. We need a number of operations on formal languages $L, L_1, L_2, \ldots$

$L_1 \cup L_2$		Union of languages
$L_1 L_2$	$\{xy \mid x \in L_1, y \in L_2\}$	Concatenation of languages
$\overline{L}$	$\Sigma^* - L$	Complement of a language
L^n	$\{x_1 \ldots x_n \mid x_i \in L, 1 \leq i \leq n\}$	
L^*	$\bigcup_{n \geq 0} L^n$	Closure of a language

Regular languages, regular expressions and finite automata The lexical units recognized by a scanner form a non-empty regular language. Regular languages can be described by regular expressions. Thus, these form the basis for all languages for specifying the lexical analysis. Regular languages can be recognized by finite automata. These terms will now be introduced. In what follows, we shall always assume an underlying alphabet Σ.

Definition 7.1 (regular language)

The **regular languages** are defined inductively over Σ by:

$\emptyset$, $\{\varepsilon\}$ are regular languages over Σ.

For all $a \in \Sigma$, $\{a\}$ is a regular language.

If R_1 and R_2 are regular languages over Σ then so are $R_1 \cup R_2$, $R_1 R_2$ and R_1^*. □

Definition 7.2 (regular expression)

Regular expressions (RE) over Σ and the regular languages they describe can also be defined inductively:

$\underline{\emptyset}$ is a regular expression over Σ and describes the regular language $\emptyset$.

$\underline{\varepsilon}$ is a regular expression over Σ and describes the regular language $\{\varepsilon\}$.

a (for $a \in \Sigma$) is a regular expression over Σ and describes the regular language $\{a\}$.

If r_1 and r_2 are regular expressions, which describe the regular languages R_1 and R_2, then

$\underline{(}r_1\underline{|}r_2\underline{)}$ is a regular expression over Σ and describes the regular language $R_1 \cup R_2$,

$\underline{(}r_1r_2\underline{)}$ is a regular expression over Σ and describes the regular language $R_1 R_2$, and

$\underline{(}r_1\underline{)}^{\underline{*}}$ is a regular expression over Σ and describes the regular language R_1^*.

There are no other regular expressions. □

Remarks on the notation

- To save brackets, we set the following precedences: $\underline{*}$, the so-called Kleene star, has the highest precedence, followed by concatenation and the alternative character $\underline{|}$.

- The underlined characters $\underline{(}$, $\underline{)}$, $\underline{|}$, $\underline{*}$, $\underline{\emptyset}$ and $\underline{\varepsilon}$ are characters of the 'regular expression' description mechanism and not of the regular language described by regular expressions. Thus, they are called **meta-characters**. Every system that accepts descriptions of regular languages by regular expressions has to solve the following problem. Because of the limited supply of displayable characters, meta-characters coincide with characters from Σ. In addition, a representation must be found for the non-displayable characters $\emptyset$ and ε. We shall return to this problem in the practical section. In the examples, there is no possibility of confusion between meta-characters and characters of Σ. Thus, we shall not underline the meta-characters. In addition, in what follows, we no longer consider the empty set and the symbol $\emptyset$ representing it, since there is no sensible use for it in our context. □

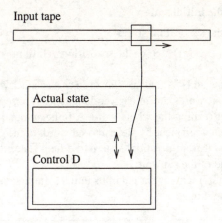

Figure 7.1   Finite automaton.

Example 7.1

Regular expression	Regular language described	Elements of the regular language
$a\vert b$	$\{a, b\}$	a, b
ab^*a	$\{a\}\{b\}^*\{a\}$	$aa, aba, abba, abbba, \ldots$
$(ab)^*$	$\{ab\}^*$	$\varepsilon, ab, abab, \ldots$
$abba$	$\{abba\}$	$abba$

$\square$

Acceptors, that is, mathematical machines that recognize regular languages, are finite automata. They are characterized by a very restricted memory, realized by one variable, which can only have a finite number of states. As Figure 7.1 shows, a finite automaton also has a read head with which it can scan the input tape from left to right. The transition relation Δ forms the control for the automaton.

Definition 7.3 (non-deterministic finite automaton)
A **(non-deterministic) finite automaton (NFA)** is a tuple

$$M = (\Sigma, Q, \Delta, q_0, F)$$

where

- Σ is an alphabet, the **input alphabet,**
- Q is a finite set of **states,**

- $q_0 \in Q$ is the **initial state,**
- $F \subseteq Q$ is the set of **final states,**
- $\Delta \subseteq Q \times (\Sigma \cup \{\varepsilon\}) \times Q$ is the **transition relation.** □

We now explain how an NFA and an NFA used as a scanner work. An NFA checks whether or not input words are in a given language. It accepts a word if it lands in a final state after reading the whole word. A finite automaton used as a scanner decomposes an input word piece by piece into subwords of the given language. Thus, each subword takes it from its initial state into a final state. It may have problems determining the end of the subword.

The finite automaton is started in its initial state. Its read head is then at the beginning of the input tape.

> When a finite automaton is used as a scanner it begins with the first character that has not yet been 'consumed'.

Then it takes a sequence of steps. Each step depends on the actual state and possibly on the next input character. This involves entering a new state and, when the input character has been read, moving the read head to the next character. The automaton accepts the input word when the input is exhausted and the actual state is a final state.

> The scanner reports that it has found a symbol when it is in a final state and has no transition to the next input character. If it has no transition from the actual state, and the actual state is not a final state, it must backtrack to the last final state it passed through. If there is no such state for the actual symbol then an error has occurred.

The future behaviour of an NFA is determined by the actual state and the remainder of the input. These two together form the actual configuration of the automaton.

Definition 7.4 (configuration, step, accepted language)
Let $M = (\Sigma, Q, \Delta, q_0, F)$ be an NFA. A pair (q, w) with $q \in Q$ and $w \in \Sigma^*$ is called a **configuration** of M, (q_0, w) is an **initial configuration** and (q_f, ε) with $q_f \in F$ is a **final configuration.**

The **step**-relation is a binary relation $\vdash_M$ on $(Q \times \Sigma^*) \times (Q \times \Sigma^*)$. We have $(q, aw) \vdash_M (p, w)$ if and only if $(q, a, p) \in \Delta$ for $q, p \in Q$ and $a \in \Sigma \cup \{\varepsilon\}$. $\vdash_M^*$ denotes the reflexive, transitive closure of this relation $\vdash_M$. The **language accepted** by the NFA M is

$$L(M) = \{w \in \Sigma^* | (q_0, w) \vdash_M^* (q_f, \varepsilon) \text{ where } q_f \in F\}$$ □

Thus, the finite automaton M accepts words through which it has a path from an initial configuration to a final configuration.

Table 7.1   NFA for recognizing integer and real constants. The alphabet is $\{0, \cdots, 9, ., E\}$. The first column represents 10 identical columns each under one of the numbers $0, 1, \ldots, 9$.

	$0,1,\ldots,9$	.	E	ε
0	$\{1,2\}$	$\emptyset$	$\emptyset$	$\emptyset$
1	$\{1\}$	$\emptyset$	$\emptyset$	$\emptyset$
2	$\{2\}$	$\{3\}$	$\emptyset$	$\emptyset$
3	$\{4\}$	$\emptyset$	$\emptyset$	$\emptyset$
4	$\{4\}$	$\emptyset$	$\{5\}$	$\{7\}$
5	$\{6\}$	$\emptyset$	$\emptyset$	$\emptyset$
6	$\{7\}$	$\emptyset$	$\emptyset$	$\emptyset$
7	$\emptyset$	$\emptyset$	$\emptyset$	$\emptyset$

$q_0 = 0, F = \{1, 7\}$.

The scanner is in a final configuration whenever it is in a final state. Correspondingly, it accepts as symbols all those words that take it from its initial state to a final state.

Example 7.2   In Table 7.1, the transition relation of an NFA M_0 is represented in the form of a two-dimensional matrix T_{M_0}. The rows correspond to the states represented by integers, the columns to the elements of $\Sigma \cup \{\varepsilon\}$. The element $T_{M_0}[q, a]$ contains the set of states p, for which $(q, a, p) \in \Delta$. The automaton recognizes integer and real constants, the latter with optional two-digit exponents.   □

An equivalent mechanism to the non-deterministic finite automaton, which is often used to represent it, is the (finite) transition diagram.

Definition 7.5 (transition diagram)
A **transition diagram** is a finite, directed, edge-labelled graph $TD = (V, E, T, v_0, V_f)$, where V is a finite set of nodes, E is a finite set of labelled edges, $v_0 \in V$ is a special node, the **start node**, and $V_f \subseteq V$ is the set of end nodes. Here, the labels for the edges come from the set T. For $w \in T^*$ a **w path** in TD is a path from a node q to a node p, for which the concatenation of the node labels is w. The **language accepted by the transition diagram** is

$$L(TD) = \{w \in T^* | \text{ there exists a } w \text{ path from } v_0 \text{ to a } v_f \in V_f \text{ in } TD \}$$ □

The correspondence between the two mechanisms is clear. Beginning with an NFA M, we take the nodes of the transition diagram of M TD_M to be the states, the initial node to be the initial state and the end nodes to be the final states. An edge

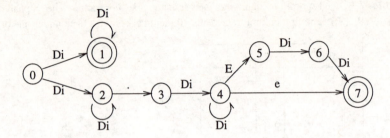

Figure 7.2 Transition diagram for the NFA of Example 7.2. Di stands for the set $\{0, 1, \ldots, 9\}$. An edge labelled by Di replaces 10 edges labelled $0, 1, \ldots, 9$ with the same input and output nodes.

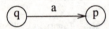

is drawn when $(q, a, p) \in \Delta$. Conversely, any transition diagram TD is associated with a well-defined NFA M_{TD}.

Example 7.3 The transition diagram associated with the NFA of Example 7.2 is shown in Figure 7.2. □

Theorem 7.1 *For every regular expression r, there is a non-deterministic finite automaton that accepts the regular set described by r.*

Proof: The proof is constructive and describes a part of the scanner generation procedure. The following algorithm **RE → NFA** describes the construction of the transition diagram of an NFA from a regular expression r over an alphabet Σ. It begins with the initial state and the final state with an edge between them labelled by r. Then r is decomposed according to its syntactic structure and the current transition diagram is refined. This decomposition and refinement continues until only edges labelled by characters from Σ or ε remain.

Algorithm RE → NFA
Input: Regular expression r over Σ.
Output: Transition diagram of an NFA.
Method: Start:

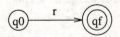

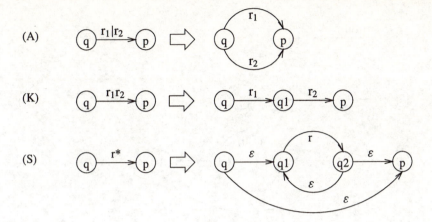

Figure 7.3   Rules for the algorithm **RE** → **NFA**.

Apply the rules of Figure 7.3 to the current transition diagram until all the edges are labelled by characters from Σ or ε. The nodes on the left sides of the rules are identified with nodes in the current transition diagram. All newly occurring nodes on the right side of a rule correspond to newly created nodes, whence to new states.

□

Example 7.4   Let $\Sigma = \{a, 0\}$. The regular expression $a(a|0)^*$ describes the set of the words over $\{a, 0\}$ that begin with an a. The construction of the NFA that accepts this language is as described in Figure 7.4.

□

Definition 7.6 (deterministic finite automaton, DFA)
Suppose $M = (Q, \Sigma, \Delta, q_0, F)$ is an NFA. M is said to be a **deterministic finite automaton** (DFA), if Δ is a partial function $\delta : Q \times \Sigma \to Q$.

□

Thus a DFA has no transitions via ε and at most one successor state for every pair (q, a) with $q \in Q$ and $a \in \Sigma$. Thus, for every word $w \in \Sigma^*$, there is at most one w path in the transition diagram for M. If w is in the language of M then this path leads from the initial state to a final state, without M having to employ the 'guesswork' of a non-deterministic automaton. Thus, DFAs are preferred for practical use. Fortunately, Theorem 7.2 holds.

Theorem 7.2   *If a language L is accepted by an NFA then there is a DFA that accepts L.*

Proof: The proof is constructive and describes another part of the generation procedure for scanners. It uses the so-called **subset construction**. The states of the

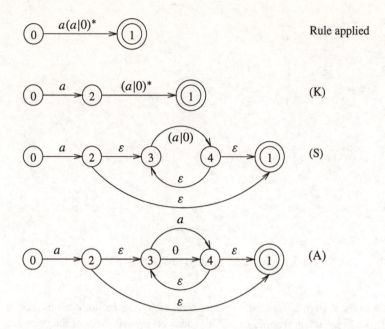

Rule applied

(K)

(S)

(A)

Figure 7.4 Construction of an NFA from a regular expression $a(a|0)^*$.

DFA constructed are subsets of the set of states of the initial NFA, and, moreover, two NFA states p and q lie in the same subset if there exists a word w that takes the NFA from its initial state to both p and q. This construction is described in the **NFA** $\rightarrow$ **DFA** algorithm in Figure 7.5. It uses the following terms. □

Definition 7.7 (ε successor state)
Suppose $M = (Q, \Sigma, \Delta, q_0, F)$ is an NFA, and let $q \in Q$. The set of ε **successor states** of q is

$$\varepsilon\text{-SS}(q) = \{p | (q, \varepsilon) \vdash_M^* (p, \varepsilon)\}$$

or the set of all states p, including q, for which there exists a ε path from q to p in the transition diagram for M. We extend ε-SS to sets of states $S \subseteq Q$.

$$\varepsilon\text{-SS}(S) = \bigcup_{q \in S} \varepsilon\text{-SS}(q)$$

The deterministic finite automaton M' associated with a non-deterministic finite automaton M is defined by:

Algorithm NFA → DFA
Input: NFA $M = (Q, \Sigma, \Delta, q_0, F)$.
Output: DFA $M' = (Q', \Sigma, \delta, q'_0, F')$ according to Definition 7.8.

Method: States in M' are sets of states of M. The starting state of M' is ε-SS(q_0). The additional states generated for Q' are marked, as soon as their successor states or transitions under all the symbols of Σ have been generated. The marking of generated states is determined in the partial function *marked*: $\mathcal{P}(Q) \to$ **bool**.

$q'_0 := \varepsilon$-SS(q_0); $Q' := \{q'_0\}$; *marked*$(q'_0) = $ **false**; $\delta := \emptyset$;
while there exists $S \in Q'$ and *marked*$(S) = $ **false do**
    marked$(S) := $ **true**;
    foreach $a \in \Sigma$ **do**
        $T := \varepsilon$-SS$(\{p \in Q | (q, a, p) \in \Delta$ and $q \in S\})$;
        if $T \notin Q'$
        then $Q' := Q' \cup \{T\}$; (∗ new state ∗)
            marked$(T) := $ **false**
        fi;
        $\delta := \delta \cup \{(S, a) \mapsto T\}$ (∗ new transition ∗)
    od
od;

Figure 7.5   Algorithm NFA → DFA.

Definition 7.8 (the DFA associated with an NFA)
Suppose $M = (Q, \Sigma, \Delta, q_0, F)$ is an NFA. The **DFA associated with** M $M' = (Q', \Sigma, \delta, q'_0, F')$ is defined by:

$Q' \subseteq \mathcal{P}(Q)$ (power set of Q),
$q'_0 = \varepsilon$-SS(q_0),
$F' = \{S \subseteq Q | S \cap F \neq \emptyset\}$ and
$\delta(S, a) = \varepsilon$-SS$(\{p | (q, a, p) \in \Delta$ for $q \in S\})$ for $a \in \Sigma$. □

Thus, the successor state of a state S under a character a in M' is obtained by combining the successor states of all states $q \in S$ under a and adding their ε successor states.

Example 7.5 The algorithm **NFA → DFA**, applied to the NFA of Example 7.4 (see Figure 7.4), runs with the steps described in Figure 7.6. The states of the DFA to be constructed are 'primed' natural numbers $0', 1', \ldots$. The initial state is $0'$. The labelled states in Q' are underlined. The state $\emptyset$ is the error state. It is the successor state of a state q under a, if there is no transition from q under a. □

$0' = \{0\}; \; Q' = \{0'\}$

Selected state	New Q'	New (sub) DFA

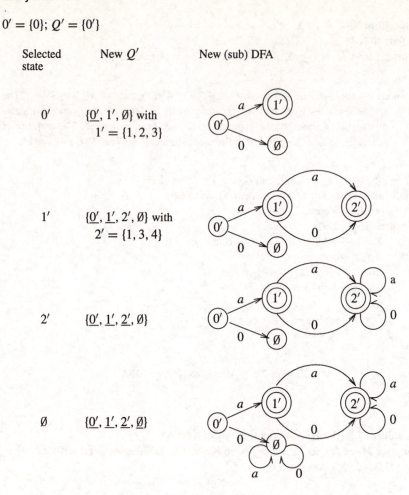

$0'$	$\{\underline{0'}, 1', \emptyset\}$ with $1' = \{1, 2, 3\}$	
$1'$	$\{\underline{0'}, \underline{1'}, 2', \emptyset\}$ with $2' = \{1, 3, 4\}$	
$2'$	$\{\underline{0'}, \underline{1'}, \underline{2'}, \emptyset\}$	
$\emptyset$	$\{\underline{0'}, \underline{1'}, \underline{2'}, \underline{\emptyset}\}$	

Figure 7.6   Construction steps for Example 7.5.

The deterministic finite automata generated from regular expressions in the two steps are in general not the smallest possible accepting the language. There may also be states with the same 'acceptance behaviour'. This applies to states p and q if for all input words, the automaton always or never moves to a final state from p and q. The procedure shown in Figure 7.7 produces a DFA for the same language with a minimal number of states.

Algorithm MinDFA

Input: DFA $M = (Q, \Sigma, \delta, q_0, F)$.

Output: DFA $M_{min} = (Q_{min}, \Sigma, \delta_{min}, q_{0,min}, F_{min})$ with $S(M) = S(M_{min})$ and Q_{min} minimal.

Method: The set of states of M is divided into a partition which is gradually refined. We already know that two states in different classes of a partition exhibit different 'acceptance behaviour', that is, that there is at least one word w, under which a final state is reached from one of the states, but not from the other. Thus, we begin with the partition $\Pi = \{F, Q - F\}$. The algorithm stops when in some step the partition is not refined further. The procedure terminates since in each iteration step only classes of the current partition may be decomposed into unions of new classes, but Q and thus $\mathcal{P}(Q)$ are finite. The classes of the partition then found are the states of M_{min}. There exists a transition between two new states P and R under a character $a \in \Sigma$, if there exists a transition $\delta(p, a) = r$ with $p \in P$ and $r \in R$ in M. This leads to the program.

$\Pi := \{F, Q - F\};$
do changed := **false**;
   $\Pi' := \Pi;$
   foreach $K \in \Pi$ **do**
      $\Pi' := (\Pi' - \{K\}) \cup \{\{K_i\}_{1 \leq i \leq n}\}$, where the K_i are maximal with
      $K = \bigcup_{1 \leq i \leq n} K_i$; and $\forall a \in \Sigma : \exists K_i' \in \Pi : \forall q \in K_i : \delta(q, a) \in K_i'$
      if $n > 1$ **then** changed := **true** **fi** (* K was split up *)
   od;
$\Pi := \Pi'$
until not changed ;
$Q_{min} = \Pi - (\text{Dead} \cup \text{Unreachable});$

$q_{0,min}$	the class in Π containing q_0.
F_{min}	the classes, containing an element of F.
$\delta_{min}(K, a) = K'$,	if $\delta(q, a) = p$ with $q \in K$ and $p \in K'$ for one and thus for all $a \in \Sigma$.
$K \in \text{Dead}$,	if K is not a final state and only contains transitions to itself.
$K \in \text{Unreachable}$,	if there is no path from the initial state to K.

Figure 7.7   Algorithm MinDFA.

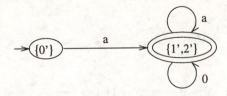

Figure 7.8   Minimal finite automaton of Example 7.6.

Example 7.6   Minimization of the DFA of Example 7.5.

Partition	Class	Division
$\{\{0', \emptyset\}, \{1', 2'\}\}$		
	$\{0', \emptyset\}$	$\{0'\}, \{\emptyset\}$
	$\{1', 2'\}$	no
$\{\{0'\}, \{\emptyset\}, \{1', 2'\}\}$	no further division	

$\{1', 2'\}$	together form a new state
$\{\emptyset\}$	is a dead state, since it is not a final state, and all transitions from it return to it.

The resulting minimal automaton is shown in Figure 7.8.   □

7.3   A language for specifying the lexical analysis

The regular expressions provide the main description formalism for the lexical analysis. But this alone is too unwieldy for practical purposes.

Example 7.7   A regular expression of the language accepted by NFA or transition diagrams in Examples 7.2 and 7.3 which describes integer or real constants is:

$$(0|1|2|3|4|5|6|7|8|9)(0|1|2|3|4|5|6|7|8|9)^*$$
$$(\varepsilon|.(0|1|2|3|4|5|6|7|8|9)(0|1|2|3|4|5|6|7|8|9)^*$$
$$(\varepsilon|E(0|1|2|3|4|5|6|7|8|9)(0|1|2|3|4|5|6|7|8|9)))$$

Note that the concatenation of the three subexpressions stretches over the three lines.   □

In the following sections, we shall carry out gradual extensions of the description formalism; these extensions increase the user friendliness but do not extend the power (that is, the class of languages that can be described).

7.3.1   Character classes

A specification of the lexical analysis should enable us to combine sets of characters into classes, if they can be exchanged in symbols without the resulting symbols being assigned to different symbol classes.

Example 7.8

> le = a–z A–Z
> di = 0–9
> or = |
> $open$ = (
> $close$ =)
> $star$ = ∗   □

The first two definitions of character classes meet the purpose outlined above. They define sets of characters by specifying intervals in the underlying character code, for example ASCII. We can now give the usual definition of the symbol class of identifiers:

> $id = le\ (\ le\ |\ di\ )^*$

The remaining four definitions of character classes (partially) solve the meta-character problem. When the character class definitions are syntactically separate from the definition of the symbols in the scanner specification, the characters, which should be both meta-characters and usable characters at the same time, may be provided with character class names. In the symbol definitions these names are then used for the usable characters to distinguish them from the meta-characters. In the character class definitions, we manage with only three meta-characters, namely '=', '-' and the space character. For this, we accept a certain type violation.

Example 7.9   The regular expression for the integer and real constants is simplified by the definition of the character class di = 0–9, to

> $di\ di^*(\ \varepsilon\ |.di\ di^*(\ \varepsilon\ |Edi\ di))$ □

7.3.2   Sequences of regular definitions

Symbols of a programming language may contain symbols of other symbol classes as subwords. Thus, it is desirable to be able to give names to regular expressions that define the symbol classes so that these names can be used in other regular expressions for abbreviation.

Definition 7.9 (sequence of regular expressions)
A **sequence of regular expressions** over Σ is a sequence of definitions

$$A_1 = R_1$$
$$A_2 = R_2$$
$$\vdots$$
$$A_n = R_n$$

where $A_1, \ldots, A_n$ are pairwise distinct identifiers and R_i are regular expressions over $\Sigma \cup \{A_1, \ldots, A_{i-1}\}$ $(1 \leq i \leq n)$.

The regular expression over Σ corresponding to R_i is

$$R'_i = [R_1/A_1][[R'_2/A_2][\ldots [R'_{i-1}/A_{i-1}]R_i]\ldots]$$

where $[R_j/A_j]R$ denotes the replacement of all occurrences of A_j by R_j in R. □

Example 7.10

$$intconst = di\ di^*$$
$$realconst = intconst.intconst\ (E di\ di\ |\varepsilon)$$

The definition of the integer constants can be used in the definition of the real constants. □

The restriction that R_i should only contain identifiers from the set $\{A_1, \ldots, A_{i-1}\}$ is important and requires an explanation. The boundary between lexical and syntax analysis, which both analyse the syntactic structure of a program, is fluid and can be moved for pragmatic reasons. However, it is important that the tasks assigned to lexical analysis can be carried out by a finite automaton, since the latter can be more efficiently implemented than the pushdown automata used for syntax analysis. Thus, the symbol classes of lexical analysis must be regular languages. Without the above restriction for sequences of regular definitions, it is also possible to give a definition $A = (aAb|\varepsilon)$ which describes the language $\{a^n b^n | n \geq 0\}$ which is known to be non-regular.

7.3.3 Non-recursive bracketing

Programming languages contain lexical units which are characterized by the brackets delimiting them, for example character strings and comments. In the case of comments, the brackets may consist of a number of characters: (* and *), /* and */, **cobegin** and **coend**, -- and NL (new line). Almost any words may lie between the opening and the closing bracket. This is not very easy to describe. An abbreviating notation for this is:

$$R_1\ until\ (R_2)$$

Here, the regular language described by R_2 must not contain the empty word. The regular language defined in this way is

$$R_1\ \overline{\Sigma^* R_2 \Sigma^*}\ R_2$$

7.4   The generation of a scanner

The generation of a minimal deterministic finite automaton from a regular expression was discussed in Section 7.2. The steps described there form the core of a possible scanner-generation procedure. It remains to explain the extensions to the description formalism that were mentioned in the previous section.

7.4.1   Character classes

Character classes were introduced to reduce the notation and the size of the automata produced. The class definitions

$$le = \text{a–z}$$
$$di = \text{0–9}$$

enable us to replace 26 transitions under letters between two states of the automaton for $id = le(le|di)^*$ by one under le.

The implementation is not difficult. An array is created, with components indexed by the machine representations of the characters. The content of an array component is the code for the character class to which the character belongs. A separate class is implicitly defined for characters that do not occur explicitly in a character class and for those that occur explicitly in a symbol definition. A problem arises when two classes A and B are not disjoint. Then the generator replaces these by three classes $A - B$, $B - A$ and $A \cap B$. Thus, in the automaton, everywhere there was a transition under A or B, respectively, there are now two transitions under $A - B$ and $A \cap B$ and $B - A$ and $A \cap B$, respectively, provided the classes produced are non-empty. This process is carried out until all the classes are pairwise disjoint.

Example 7.11   If we had defined the two classes

$$le\ \ = \text{a–z}$$
$$ledi = \text{a–z 0–9}$$

in order to define the symbol class

$$id = le\ ledi^*$$

the generator would have to implement a division into the character classes

$$di' = ledi\text{–}le$$
$$le' = le \cap ledi = le$$

This would result in the above (clearly sensible) division into classes.   □

7.4.2   Sequences of regular definitions

Suppose we are given a sequence of regular definitions.

$$A_1 \; = \; R_1$$
$$A_2 \; = \; R_2$$
$$\vdots$$
$$A_n \; = \; R_n$$

The generation of a scanner for this sequence involves the following steps:

(1)   Generation of NFAs $M_i = (Q_i, \Sigma, \Delta_i, q_{0,i}, F_i)$ for the regular expressions R_i' (obtained by replacement), where the Q_i are pairwise disjoint.

(2)   Construction of the NFA $M = (Q, \Sigma, \Delta, q_0, F)$ with
$Q = \bigcup_{i=1}^{n} Q_i \cup \{q_0\}, \quad q_0 \notin \bigcup_{i=1}^{n} Q_i, \quad F = \bigcup_{i=1}^{n} F_i$
$\Delta = \bigcup_{i=1}^{n} \Delta_i \cup \{(q_0, \varepsilon, q_{0,i}) \mid 1 \leq i \leq n\}$.
Thus, we obtain the NFA M for the sequence, by providing the new initial state q_0 with a ε transition to all initial states $q_{0,i}$.

(3)   Application of the algorithm **NFA** $\to$ **DFA** (see Figure 7.5) to M, result DFA M'.

(4)   Possible minimization of M'. We start with the **MinDFA** algorithm with a partition $\Pi = \{F_1', F_2', \ldots, F_n', Q' - \bigcup_{i=1}^{n} F_i'\}$, where the F_i' are the final states of M' belonging to the symbol class A_i. More precisely: $F_i' = \{S \mid S \cap F_i \neq \emptyset \text{ and } S \cap F_j = \emptyset \; (1 \leq j < i)\}$ (this means that a symbol that takes the automaton M' into two former final states of the M_i is assigned to the class occurring earlier in the definition list).

Example 7.12   Suppose we are given the individual character classes:

$di \;\; = 0\text{--}9$
$hex = \text{A--F}$

The sequence of regular definitions

$intconst \; = di \; di^*$
$hexconst = \text{h} \; (di|hex) \; (di|hex)^*$
$realconst = intconst \; . \; intconst \; (\text{e} \; di \; di|\varepsilon)$

is processed in the following steps:

- Replacement of both occurrences of the symbol class name *intconst* by its definition:

$intconst \; = di \; di^*$
$hexconst = \text{h} \; (di|hex) \; (di|hex)^*$
$realconst = di \; di^* \; . \; di \; di^* \; (\text{e} \; di \; di|\varepsilon)$

- Generation of NFAs for the regular expressions:

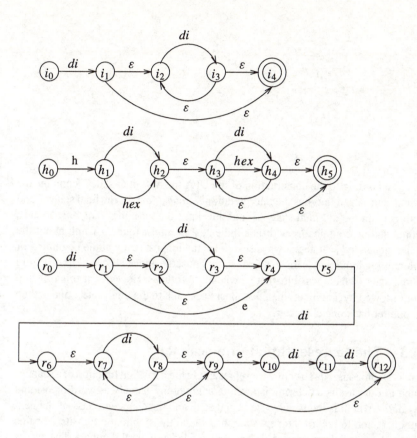

Note that the three final states have the following interpretation: '*intconst* found' (i_4), '*hexconst* found' (h_5) and '*realconst* found' (r_{12}).

- Combination of the three NFAs using a new initial state q_0:

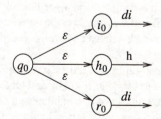

- Make this NFA deterministic.

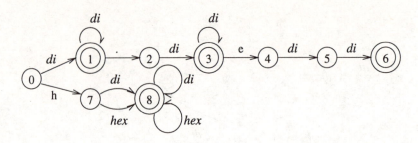

According to the construction of the DFA the new final state 1 contains the old final state i_4 and thus has the interpretation '*intconst* found'; the final states 3 and 6 both contain the old final state r_{12} and thus have the meaning '*realconst* found'; the final state 8 contains h_5 and thus indicates '*hexconst* found'. Think about the fact that generated scanners always search for the longest string at the beginning of the remaining input that leads to a final state. Thus, the above DFA will transit from the final state 1 when possible, that is, when a '.' follows. However, if this full stop is not followed by a number, the DFA must backtrack to the final state 1 and set the read pointer back one character. □

7.4.3 The representation of a scanner

There is an obvious data structure for representing the transition function of a scanner (which in our case is a deterministic finite automaton), namely a two-dimensional array *delta*, which is indexed by the actual state and the character class of the next input character, to record the new state into which the automaton transits. For this both the states and the character classes are encoded as natural numbers. The access to *delta[actstate, nextcl]* is extremely fast. However, the size of the array *delta*, which is the product of the number of states and the number of character classes, may be a problem. Since this array is also generally sparsely populated, various procedures for compressing sparse matrices may be applied to it. These generally save much space at the cost of a small increase in access time. However, since the empty entries correspond to undefined transitions which are significant for analysis and error detection, the information they contain must remain available.

Let us consider such a compression algorithm. We represent the transition function in a somewhat different way than via the above array *delta*, namely via an array *RowPtr* which is indexed by states and whose components are the addresses of the rows of *delta*, see Figure 7.9.

We have still gained nothing, and indeed have forfeited a little access speed. The rows which are pointed to by *RowPtr* are by and large almost empty. Thus, the individual rows are arranged on top of one another in a common one-dimensional array *Delta* in such a way that non-zero entries do not collide. This can be done for

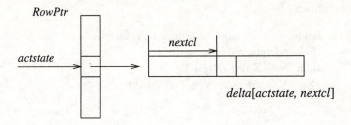

Figure 7.9   Representation of the transition function of a DFA.

the individual rows consecutively using a first fit strategy. The next row to be stored is moved over the array *Delta* until no collisions occur between non-zero entries in this row and non-zero entries in the rows already stored. The non-zero entries are then stored in *Delta*. The index in *Delta* at which the ith row is stored is then stored in *RowPtr[i]*, see Figure 7.10.

However, now this automaton has lost its ability always to recognize undefined transitions, for example when $delta(i, a)$ is undefined but $Delta[RowPtr[i] + a]$ contains a non-zero entry from the state $j \neq i$ (here, we use character classes and their numbers equivalently). Thus, we have to provide a second array *Check* of the same length as *Delta*, which indicates the states to which entries in *Delta* belong; that is, $Check[RowPtr[i] + a] = i$, if $delta(i, a)$ is defined.

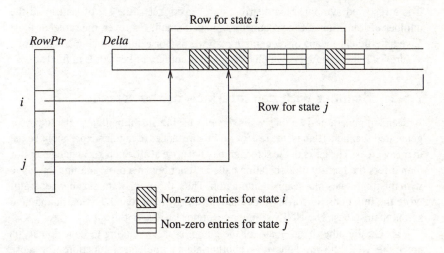

Figure 7.10   Compressed representation of the transition function of a DFA.

The DFA's transition function can then be implemented as follows by a function *nextstate*:

> **function** *nextstate* (*i*: *state*, *a*: *charclass*) **returns** state;
>   **if** *Check*[*RowPtr*[*i*] + *a*] = *i*
>   **then** *Delta*[*Row Ptr*[*i*] + *a*]
>   **else** −1   (∗ stands for undefined ∗)
>   **fi**

7.5 The screener

There are many possibilities for the distribution of tasks between the scanner and the screener and for the functionality of the screener, and the advantages and disadvantages of these are not always easy to judge. We shall discuss a number of these alternatives below.

7.5.1 The recognition of keywords

According to the distribution of tasks in the last chapter, the screener knows the set of reserved names or keywords. This presupposes that the scanner has one or more symbol classes containing these symbols. This is the case when, as for example in Pascal, C and Ada, the keywords have the same structure as identifiers. In the task as described above, for every identifier, whether reserved or not, the scanner will report the presence of an identifier. The screener will then determine whether it is a reserved symbol. This distribution of tasks keeps the set of states and the number of transitions of the scanner automaton small. However, the screener must have an efficient means of recognizing keywords, for example, using a hash table. Figure 7.11 shows an NFA which recognizes a number of keywords in final states.

7.5.2 Scanner with call interface to the screener

A scanner generator is a fairly universally usable instrument. Applications for generated scanners (that is, the task of finding instances of regular expressions) exist in many areas. The tasks of the screener may not arise at all. Such a scanner generator then offers the facility of associating calls of functions in a programming language with the final states of a scanner automaton. Thus, the users of the scanner generator write the functions for further processing of the symbol found, for journaling, and so on, themselves. The UNIX scanner generator LEX is of this type.

On the other hand, many of the compiler tasks relating to lexical analysis are quite well known. Thus it is appropriate to implement functions for these in a screener. Such a design, as implemented in the POCO compiler generator (Eulenstein, 1988), is described in the next section.

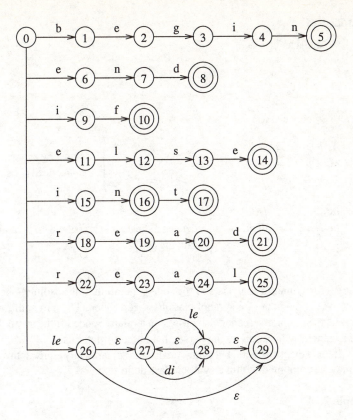

Figure 7.11   An NFA for recognizing identifiers and the keywords begin, end, if, else, int, in, read, real.

7.5.3   Symbol classes

Symbol classes are sets of symbols that are equivalent for the 'consumer' in the compiler, that is, the parser. Two symbols are equivalent if in every state the parser makes the same transition (takes the same decision) under each of the symbols. Typical symbol classes include the various classes of constants, the identifiers (without the reserved symbols), comments, arithmetic operators of the same precedence and relational operators.

The designer of a scanner–screener combination will define such classes. A well-defined class code will be assigned to each class either explicitly by the designer or implicitly by the generator. This class code is passed to the parser when a symbol of the class is found by the generated scanner.

Example 7.13

% Character classes

le = a–z
di = 0–9

% Symbol classes

$AddOp$ = $+\,|\,-$ ⎫
$MulOp$ = $*\,|\,/$ ⎬ defined by enumeration
$CompOp$ = $<\,|\,>\,|\,=\,|\,<>\,|\,>=\,|\,<=$ ⎭ 'enumerated classes'

Id = $le(le\,|\,di)^*$ ⎫
$IntConst$ = $di\ di^*$ ⎬ defined by regular expression with iteration
⎭ 'infinite class'

□

Of course, for semantic analysis and for code generation, it is absolutely necessary to know which element of a symbol class has been found. Thus, in addition to the class code, the scanner/screener also passes on a relative code for the symbol found, which is generally not used by the parser, but noted for later use.

If there exist different, but syntactically and semantically equivalent symbols, these may be combined within a symbol class definition.

Example 7.14

CompOp = $(<,\text{lt})\,|\,(>,\text{gt})\,|\,(=,\text{eq})\,|\,(<>,\text{neq})\,|\,(>=,\text{ge})\,|\,(<=,\text{le})$

□

The relative codes for elements of enumerated classes, which are classes whose finitely many elements are given by enumeration in the class definition, are determined by the position of the elements in this enumeration. Elements of infinite classes are numbered consecutively in the order in which they occur in a program to be analysed. Here, a user-friendly scanner generator may offer the user the following options:

- to assign a unique relative code to every element of the class; the scanner/screener must then identify different occurrences of the same symbol;

- to assign a unique relative code to every occurrence of a symbol.

The first option is typically chosen for the symbol class of identifiers. For a symbol class such as that of character strings, one would probably choose the second option, because the cost of comparing every newly found character string with all existing strings would be considerable and the gain tiny.

However, it is clear that such a screener has the task of logging the elements of infinite classes. Thus, it will store the symbols found in an appropriate data structure, which must permit the following operations: enter a new symbol allocating a new relative code; and test for an existing entry, returning the relative code if successful; find the external representation of the symbol using the class code and the relative code. Such a data structure would be initialized with predefined symbols from enumerated classes, for example the reserved symbols.

There are other directives for a screener for handling the elements of a symbol class. For example, it should be possible to specify that each element of a certain class should be ignored, that is, not passed to the parser.

Example 7.15

% Single-character classes

open = (
close =)
star = *

% Symbol classes

− Comment   =   open star until (star close)
− Separator =   (Blank | NL)$^+$

The minus sign in front of the class name indicates that all elements of the class should be ignored.   □

7.6 Flex, a scanner generator under UNIX

In this section, we shall describe the important properties of a scanner generator which is available as public domain software under UNIX.

7.6.1 The mode of operation of Flex-generated scanners

The core of the generator is the generation of a deterministic finite automaton to recognize a regular language. The DFA generated, like the DFA described previously, recognizes maximal length strings at the beginning of the remaining input as symbols (tokens). There are a number of facilities for influencing the 'consumption pattern' of the DFA, for example reinserting characters that have already been read before the remaining input or consuming of additional start characters before the remaining input.

There is no screener as described in the last section. Instead, there is an interface to C; user-defined C functions can be called whenever a final state is reached. These are responsible for the further processing of the symbols found. The last symbol found can be accessed via a global pointer (yytext), and its length is in a global integer variable (`yyleng`). The generated scanner is a C function `yylex`, which can be called from other programs such as a parser.

7.6.2 Flex specifications

Flex input is divided into three sections each separated by '%%':

> Definitions
> %%
> Rules
> %%
> The user's C programs

To simplify the description of the rules the **definitions** section introduces names for regular expressions. These names may be enclosed in curly brackets and are replaced by regular expressions in later definitions and in rules.

Example:

```
DI [0-9]
LE [a - z]
ID {LE} ({LE} | {DI})*
```

These definitions should be self-explanatory.

The **rules** each consist of a *pattern*, a regular expression, and an *action*, a piece of C code. This C code is executed when the generated scanner recognizes a symbol as belonging to this pattern.

Example:

```
{DI}+ printf ("An integer: %s (%d)\n", yytext, atoi(yytext));
"+"|"-"|"*"|"/" {
        printf( An operator: %s\n", yytext);
        }
if|then|else|while|do|begin|end {
        printf ("A keyword: %s\n", yytext);
        }
{ID} printf ("A name: %s\n", yytext);
[ \t\n] /* consumes spaces, tabs and ends of lines */
}
```

Here are some remarks on this example.

- Character classes can also be listed using square brackets '[' and ']', as in the definition part and in the form of ranges. Single characters and character classes may also occur in negated form.
- '*', '+' and '−' as meta-characters have the usual meaning. If they occur as

characters of the specified input they will be protected by double quotation marks.

- The keywords `if, ..., end` are of course members of the class `ID`. The conflict between the final states for these regular expressions is resolved in favour of the keywords, since they come earlier in the specification.

Another simplification of the description is possible using *conditional rules*. Rules prefixed by the name of a condition will only be used if the corresponding condition is activated.

Example:

```
<STRING>[^"]* {/* Code constructing a string constant */}
```

This rule must be activated when the introductory double quotation marks of a string constant are found. It then continues to read while no other double quotation marks are found. Conditional rules can be switched on and off, individually or in groups.

7.7   Exercises

1:   Let Σ be an alphabet and for sets $P \subseteq \Sigma^*$ let $P^* = \{p_1 \ldots p_k \mid k \geq 0, \ p_i \in P\}$; in addition $\emptyset^* = \{\varepsilon\}$.

Show that:

(a) $L \subseteq L^*$

(b) $\varepsilon \in L^*$

(c) $u, v \in L^* \Rightarrow uv \in L^*$ for all words $u, v \in \Sigma^*$

(d) L^* is the smallest set with the properties (a)–(c), that is, whenever for a set M we have:

$$L \subseteq M, \ \varepsilon \in M \text{ and } (u, v \in M \Rightarrow uv \in M)$$

then $L^* \subseteq M$

(e) $L \subseteq M \Rightarrow L^* \subseteq M^*$

(f) $L^{**} = L^*$

2:   Construct the minimal deterministic finite automaton for the sequence of regular definitions:

$$
\begin{aligned}
id &= le \ (le \mid di)^* \\
sysid &= le \ \& \ (le \mid di)^* \\
comid &= le \ le \ \& \ (le \mid di)^*
\end{aligned}
$$

3: (a) Give a sequence of regular definitions for the Roman numerals.

(b) Generate a deterministic finite automaton from this.

(c) Supplement this automaton as follows to include the possibility of calculating the decimal value of a Roman numeral. On every state transition, the automaton may execute an assignment statement to **one** variable w. The value is determined from an expression involving w and constants. w is initialized to 0. Give an appropriate assignment statement for each state transition, so that in each final state w has the value of the number recognized.

4: Make the NFA of Figure 7.11 deterministic.

5: Extend the algorithm **RE**$\rightarrow$ **NFA** of Figure 7.3 so that it also processes regular expressions r^+ and $[r]$. r^+ stands for rr^* and $[r]$ for $(\varepsilon|r)$.

6: Extend the algorithm **RE**$\rightarrow$ **NFA** to process numerical iteration, that is, by regular expressions of the form:

$r\{l-u\}$ at least l and at most u consecutive instances of r

$r\{l-\}$ at least l consecutive instances of r

$r\{-u\}$ at most u consecutive instances of r

7: Fortran permits the implicit declaration of identifiers by their initial letters. Give definitions for the symbol classes *realid* and *intid*.

8: Suppose we are given the following definitions of character classes:

$$le \;=\; a\text{--}z$$
$$di \;=\; 0\text{--}9$$

and the symbol class definitions

$$bin \;=\; b\,(0|1)^+$$
$$oct \;=\; o\,(0|1|2|3|4|5|6|7)^+$$
$$hex \;=\; h\,(di|A|B|C|D|E|F)^+$$
$$intconst \;=\; di^+$$
$$id \;=\; le\,(le\mid di)^+$$

(a) Give the division into character classes computed by the scanner generator.

(b) Describe the NFA generated using this division into character classes.

(c) Make this NFA deterministic.

9: Give an implementation of the *until* construct, R_1 *until* R_2.

10:   Compress the tables of the deterministic finite automaton you generated 'manually' for Exercise 8 using the procedure of Section 7.4.3.

7.8   Literature

The conceptual separation between scanner and screener was proposed by F. DeRemer (DeRemer, 1974). The generation of scanners from regular expressions is supported in many so-called compiler generators. Johnson *et al.* (1968) describe such a system. The corresponding service program under UNIX, LEX, was developed by M. Lesk (Lesk, 1975). Flex was written by Vern Paxson. The concept described in this chapter is based on the scanner generator of the POCO compiler generator (Eulenstein, 1988).

Compression methods for sparsely occupied tables, such as those typically generated by the scanner and parser, are analysed and compared in Dencker *et al.* (1984).

8

Syntax analysis

- The task of syntax analysis

- Theoretical foundations

- Top-down syntax analysis

- Bottom-up syntax analysis

- Bison, an LALR(1)-parser generator

- Exercises

- Literature

8.1   The task of syntax analysis

The parser implements the syntax analysis of programs. It receives the programs in the form of a sequence of symbols generated by the scanner/screener. Its task is to find the syntax structure of the program in this sequence of symbols, that is, to combine subsequences into ever larger syntactic units.

Syntactic units in imperative languages are variables, expressions, statements, statement sequences, declarations and specifications; in functional languages, they are variables, expressions, patterns, definitions and declarations, while in logic languages they are variables, terms, lists of terms, goals and clauses.

In the conceptual view of the compiler, the parser recognizes the syntactic structure of a program and represents this structure accordingly so that other compiler parts can work with it. One possible representation is the syntax tree of the program. This can be decorated with static semantic information, transformed to increase efficiency and finally compiled into a machine program.

Sometimes, the compilation task for a programming language is so easy that the program can be compiled in one pass. Then, the parser does not have to supply an explicit representation of the syntactic structure. Instead, it functions as a main program which calls subprograms for semantic analysis and code generation at appropriate points during syntax analysis.

The recognition of the syntactic structure involves another important task, namely the recognition and good 'handling' of syntax errors. Most programs presented to a compiler contain errors, including many syntax errors, which often arise as a result of typing errors such as unmatched brackets. Every compiler is expected to locate syntax errors as precisely as possible. In so doing, it cannot generally determine the location of the error itself, but only the earliest point where the error has led to a situation in which it is impossible to extend the input previously analysed to a correct program. If the compiler runs in batch mode, it is expected not to terminate on finding an error but to progress as soon as possible to a state in which it can analyse the remainder of the program and detect more errors.

If it operates in an interactive environment, it is sufficient for it to report a small number of errors and provide the attached editor with information about the error locations to which the editor then directs the programmer.

The syntactic structure of the programs of a programming language can be described by a context-free grammar. An associated syntax analyser, a pushdown automaton, can be generated automatically from such a grammar. For efficiency and unambiguity, compiler designers confine themselves mainly to deterministically analysable context-free grammars, for which tried and tested parser generators exist. However, as we shall see later, it is possible to write a parser for a given context-free grammar manually. But this is not to be recommended if changes may be made to the syntax of the language. In general, it is easier to alter the grammar input to the parser generator and perform a new generation run than to modify a hand-written parser. This argument is even more applicable when the syntax error detection and handling is also generated automatically.

The syntax analysis procedures implemented in practice fall into two classes.

They operate deterministically and read programs from left to right. **Top-down analysers** begin the analysis and construct the syntax tree with the start symbol of the grammar, the label of the root of the syntax tree. They predict what the program or program part will look like and then try to confirm it. Technically, this prediction is a sentential form, or, more precisely, a left sentential form of the grammar. Thus, the first, completely unconfirmed prediction consists of the start symbol of the grammar. Let us assume that some part of it is confirmed by the input which has already been read. If the unconfirmed part of the prediction begins with a nonterminal, the top-down parser deterministically chooses one of the productions for this nonterminal using the next unconsumed input symbols and generates a new prediction. If the current prediction begins with a terminal symbol, the parser compares this with the next input symbol. If they agree, another symbol of the prediction is confirmed, otherwise, an error has occurred. The top-down parser has finished when all the input is confirmed.

Deterministic **bottom-up parsers** begin the analysis and the construction of the syntax tree with the input word of the program to be analysed. They attempt to find the syntax structure for ever longer initial pieces of the input. They succeed in this when they discover occurrences of productions of the context-free grammar. When a right production side is found, reduction to the nonterminal of the left side takes place. Bottom-up parsers alternate between the actions of reading the next input symbol and executing as many reductions as are adequate. The number of adequate reductions, if any, is determined from the already reduced initial piece, or, more precisely, from what it is reduced to together with a fixed-length section of the remaining input. The bottom-up parser has finished when it has read all its input and reduced it to the start symbol.

The handling of syntax errors

Most programs that a compiler sees have errors, for while programs with errors are generally compiled several times, error-free programs are only compiled after they are modified or ported to another computer. Thus, a compiler should handle the 'normal case', the incorrect source program, in an adequate manner. Lexical errors and also errors in the static semantics, such as type errors, are simpler to diagnose and handle locally. Syntax errors, particularly in the bracket structure of the program, are difficult to diagnose and repair. In this section, we shall describe the desired reactions of a parser to syntax errors and the reactions possible in practice.

According to the above task description, a compiler should not only accept correct programs but also react appropriately to syntactically incorrect programs. The desired reactions of the parser can be classified as follows:

(1)   Report and locate the error

(2)   Diagnose the error

(3)   Correct the error

(4)   Recover to discover more (possible) errors.

The first reaction should be expected from every parser; no syntax error should slip through unnoticed. However, we must make two qualifications. An error may remain unnoticed near another syntax error. The second restriction is weightier. In general, a parser discovers an error when no legal continuation exists for its current configuration. However, this may be only a symptom of the presence of an error rather than the error itself.

Example 8.1

$$a := a * (b + c * d \qquad ;$$
$$\uparrow$$

Symptom of error: $')'$ missing

There are many possible errors here; either the opening bracket is surplus or a closing bracket is missing after c or after d. The meanings of each of the three possible expressions are different. □

For other bracket errors with surplus or missing **begin, end, if,** and so on, the error location and the location of the symptom of the error may be far apart. However, the parsers considered below, LL(k)- and LR(k)-parsers, have the **valid prefix property**. Given a context-free grammar G, if the parser processes a prefix u of a word without reporting an error then there exists a word w such that uw is a sentence of G.

Thus, parsers with this property report errors (symptoms) at the earliest possible time. Although in general we can only detect the symptom of the error and not the error itself we shall in the future speak mostly of errors. In this sense, the parsers described below satisfy requirement (1). They report and locate syntax errors.

That requirement (2) is not fully satisfiable should now be clear; the parser will only attempt a diagnosis of the error (symptom). This diagnosis should contain at least the following information:

- Location of the error symptom in the program
- Description of the parser configuration (state, symbol expected, symbol found), and so on.

To meet requirement (3), the correction of errors, the parser must guess the programmer's intention. This is generally impossible. The next more realistic requirement would be for a globally optimal error correction. This is defined as follows. The parser is extended by the facility to insert or delete one symbol in an input word. The **globally optimal** error correction for an invalid input word w is a word w' which is derived from w by a minimal number of insertions or deletions. We say that w and w' are the **least distance** apart. Such procedures have been proposed, but because of their costs have not found their way into practice.

Instead, local solutions, insertions or replacements, which meet at least the following requirement, are usually found to be satisfactory. Such a local correction should lead the parser from the error configuration into a new configuration in which it can at least read the next input symbol. This ensures that the parser does not get into an infinite loop as a result of these local changes. In addition, it should avoid the appearance of follow-on errors, as far as possible.

Why is no consideration given to corrections to the stack contents of the parser? The valid-prefix property says that the stack contents up to the time the error is discovered give no grounds for complaint. Thus, it is in general difficult to locate the possible cause of an error based on the symptoms of the error in the stack. In addition, parsers frequently control the semantic analysis by initiating semantic routines. Changes in the parser's stack would require the undoing of the effects of these semantic routines.

The structure of this chapter

In Section 8.2 we describe the foundations of syntax analysis from the theory of formal languages and automata. We deal with context-free grammars and pushdown automata, the associated detection mechanisms. A special non-deterministic pushdown automaton for a given context-free grammar G is constructed, which accepts the language defined by G. We shall later derive deterministic top-down and bottom-up pushdown automata from this pushdown automaton. The technique of grammar flow analysis is introduced. It can be used to compute properties of context-free grammars and attribute grammars.

Top-down and bottom-up syntax analysis are described in Sections 8.3 and 8.4. For this, we characterize the corresponding classes of grammars, describe generation procedures and present error-handling algorithms.

8.2   Theoretical foundations

Like lexical analysis, syntax analysis is based on the theory of automata and formal languages. The important theorem is the equivalence of the two mechanisms of context-free grammars and pushdown automata, in the sense that:

(1)   for every context-free grammar we can construct a pushdown automaton which accepts the language defined by the grammar;

(2)   the language accepted by a pushdown automaton is context free, and therefore has a context-free grammar (which is even effectively constructible).

Perhaps we still need to explain why regular expressions are not sufficient to describe the syntax of programming languages. It is known from the theory of formal languages that regular expressions are not suitable for describing embedded recursions. However, these occur in the form of nested blocks, statements and expressions in programming languages. Therefore, we have to move from regular expressions to context-free grammars, which are capable of describing such recursive structures.

In Sections 8.2.1 and 8.2.2, we briefly review the most important terms relating to context-free grammars and pushdown automata. Readers familiar with these may skip these sections and continue with Section 8.2.3, where for a context-free grammar we define a (somewhat unusual) pushdown automaton which accepts the language defined by the grammar.

8.2.1 Context-free grammars

Context-free grammars are used to describe the syntactic structure of programs of a programming language. This shows how programs are composed from subprograms, or, more precisely, which elementary constructs there are and how composite constructs can be built from other constructs.

The following production rules describe the structure of statements in a Pascal-like language, where nothing further is said about the form of a condition (*Con*), an expression (*Expr*) or a name.

Example 8.2

Stat	→	If_Stat |
		While_Stat |
		Repeat_Stat |
		Proc_Call |
		Assignment
If_Stat	→	**if** Con **then** Stat_Seq **else** Stat_Seq **fi** |
		if Con **then** Stat_Seq **fi**
While_Stat	→	**while** Con **do** Stat_Seq **od**
Repeat_Stat	→	**repeat** Stat_Seq **until** Con
Proc_Call	→	Name (Expr_Seq)
Assignment	→	Name := Expr
Stat_Seq	→	Stat |
		Stat_Seq; Stat
Expr_Seq	→	Expr |
		Expr_Seq, Expr

□

The first rule says that there are five different types of statement. The second should be read as follows: an *If* statement (a word for *If_Stat*) either consists of the word **if** followed by a word for *Con*, followed by the word **then**, followed by a statement sequence (more precisely, a word for *Stat_Seq*), followed by the word **else**, followed by another statement sequence, followed by the word **fi** or it consists of the word **if** followed by a condition, the word **then** and a statement sequence followed by the word **fi**.

Definition 8.1 (context-free grammar)
A **context-free grammar** (cfg) is a quadruple $G = (V_N, V_T, P, S)$ where V_N and V_T are alphabets, V_N is the set of **nonterminals**, V_T is the set of **terminals**, $P \subseteq V_N \times (V_N \cup V_T)^*$ is the set of **production rules** and $S \in V_N$ is the start symbol.

□

The nonterminal symbols of the grammar stand for sets of words, namely for the words they produce (see Definition 8.2). The terminals are the symbols that actually occur in the program to be analysed. Whereas in our treatment of lexical analysis we spoke of an alphabet of characters, which in practice comprises the **characters** of the ASCII or EBCDIC character sets allowed in a program, in this chapter we shall speak of **symbols**. According to the division of work between lexical analysis (scanner) and syntax analysis (parser) which we described in the introductory chapter, the scanner recognizes certain character strings as lexical units and passes them to the parser as symbols. Such symbols, for example keywords in bold type or **id** for the symbol class of identifiers, will often occur as elements of the terminal alphabet in example grammars.

Notation   In the following definitions, theorems, remarks and algorithms, we shall adhere consistently to the following notation. Upper case Roman letters, for example A, B, C, X, Y, Z, stand for elements of V_N; lower case letters at the beginning of the Roman alphabet, for example $a, b, c, \ldots$, stand for terminals, that is, elements of V_T; lower case letters at the end of the Roman alphabet, for example u, v, w, x, y, z, stand for terminal words, that is, elements of V_T^*; lower case Greek letters, for example $\alpha, \beta, \gamma, \varphi, \psi$, stand for words in $(V_T \cup V_N)^*$.

These specifications of notation should be understood in the sense of a declaration in a program. Thus, A is declared as a variable of type 'nonterminal' and α as of type 'word over $V_N \cup V_T$'. This is generally no longer stated explicitly. As in programming languages with nested scopes, characters will be redefined locally from time to time. Thus, the global convention will be concealed. In examples, nonterminals and terminals given are constants and as such are not subject to the above conventions, for example STAT and **if, id, +**.

The relation P has already been used to denote the set of production rules; we write every element of the relation (A, α) as $A \rightarrow \alpha$. We write multiple production rules $A \rightarrow \alpha_1, A \rightarrow \alpha_2, \ldots, A \rightarrow \alpha_n$ for a nonterminal A as $A \rightarrow \alpha_1 \mid \alpha_2 \mid \ldots \mid \alpha_n$. The $\alpha_1, \alpha_2, \ldots, \alpha_n$ are then called the *alternatives* for A.

Example 8.3

$G_0 = (\{E, T, F\}, \{+, *, (,)\, , \textbf{id}\}, \{E \rightarrow E+T \mid T, T \rightarrow T*F \mid F, F \rightarrow (E) \mid \textbf{id}\}, E)$
$G_1 = (\{E\}, \{+, *, (,)\, , \textbf{id}\}, \{E \rightarrow E + E \mid E * E \mid (E) \mid \textbf{id}\}, E)$

□

A production rule of a cfg describes how to '*produce*' or '*derive*' new words by replacing left sides (nonterminals) by right sides (words of $(V_T \cup V_N)^*$). The relation '*produces directly*' on $(V_T \cup V_N)^*$ is induced by the relation P.

Definition 8.2 (directly produced, produced, derivation)
Suppose $G = (V_N, V_T, P, S)$ is a context-free grammar. φ **produces** ψ **directly according to** G, denoted by $\varphi \underset{G}{\Longrightarrow} \psi$, whenever there exist words σ, τ, α and a nonterminal A, such that $\varphi = \sigma A \tau$, $\psi = \sigma \alpha \tau$ and $A \to \alpha \in P$. We say that φ **produces** ψ **according to** G (or ψ is **derivable from** φ **according to** G), denoted by $\varphi \underset{G}{\overset{*}{\Longrightarrow}} \psi$, whenever there exists a finite sequence of words $\varphi_0, \varphi_1, \ldots \varphi_n$, ($n \geq 0$) with the property that $\varphi = \varphi_0$, $\psi = \varphi_n$ and $\varphi_i \underset{G}{\Longrightarrow} \varphi_{i+1}$ for $0 \leq i < n$. $\varphi_0, \varphi_1, \ldots, \varphi_n$ is then called a **derivation** of ψ from φ according to G. In the above case, we also write $\varphi \underset{G}{\overset{n}{\Longrightarrow}} \psi$. $\qquad\square$

Remark $\underset{G}{\overset{*}{\Longrightarrow}}$ is the reflexive and transitive closure of $\underset{G}{\Longrightarrow}$. $\qquad\square$

Example 8.4 (continuation of Example 8.3)
$$E \underset{G_0}{\Longrightarrow} E + T \underset{G_0}{\Longrightarrow} T + T \underset{G_0}{\Longrightarrow} T * F + T \underset{G_0}{\Longrightarrow} T * \text{id} + T \underset{G_0}{\Longrightarrow} F * \text{id} + T \underset{G_0}{\Longrightarrow}$$
$$F * \text{id} + F \underset{G_0}{\Longrightarrow} \text{id} * \text{id} + F \underset{G_0}{\Longrightarrow} \text{id} * \text{id} + \text{id}, \quad \text{whence} \quad E \underset{G_0}{\overset{*}{\Longrightarrow}} \text{id} * \text{id} + \text{id},$$
$$E \underset{G_1}{\Longrightarrow} E + E \underset{G_1}{\Longrightarrow} E * E + E \underset{G_1}{\Longrightarrow} \text{id} * E + E \underset{G_1}{\Longrightarrow} \text{id} * E + \text{id} \underset{G_1}{\Longrightarrow} \text{id} * \text{id} + \text{id},$$
whence $E \underset{G_1}{\overset{*}{\Longrightarrow}} \text{id} * \text{id} + \text{id}$. $\qquad\square$

Definition 8.3 (defined language, sentence, sentential form)
Suppose $G = (V_N, V_T, P, S)$ is a cfg. The **language defined (generated)** by G is $L(G) = \{u \in V_T^* | S \overset{*}{\Longrightarrow} u\}$. A word $x \in L(G)$ is called a **sentence** of G. A word $\alpha \in (V_T \cup V_N)^*$ with $S \underset{G}{\overset{*}{\Longrightarrow}} \alpha$ is called a **sentential form** of G. $\qquad\square$

Example 8.5 (continuation of Example 8.4)
$\text{id} * \text{id} + \text{id} \in L(G_0)$ and $\text{id} * \text{id} + \text{id} \in L(G_1)$, because E is the start symbol of G_0 and G_1, and Example 8.4 showed that $E \underset{G_0}{\overset{*}{\Longrightarrow}} \text{id} * \text{id} + \text{id}$ and $E \underset{G_1}{\overset{*}{\Longrightarrow}} \text{id} * \text{id} + \text{id}$. $\qquad\square$

Notation We shall omit the index G in $\underset{G}{\Longrightarrow}$, when G is clear from the context.

A context-free grammar may contain nonterminals that do not contribute to the generation of the language and are also troublesome in some definitions and sentences. Thus, we shall eliminate these.

Definition 8.4 (unproductive, unreachable NT, reduced cfg)
A nonterminal A is said to be **unreachable** if there are no words α, β with $S \stackrel{*}{\Rightarrow} \alpha A \beta$. A is said to be **unproductive** if there is no word u with $A \stackrel{*}{\Rightarrow}$ u. A cfg G is said to be **reduced** if it contains neither unreachable nor unproductive nonterminals. □

Thus, an unreachable nonterminal cannot occur in any derivation beginning with the start symbol in a sentential form, while an unproductive nonterminal cannot produce a terminal word. If these two kinds of nonterminals and all productions in which they occur are eliminated, the language defined by the grammar is clearly unaltered. In what follows, we always assume that grammars are reduced.

The syntactic structure of a program, as obtained as a result of syntax analysis, is a tree. This tree is of theoretical and practical interest. It is used to define terms such as ambiguity (see Definition 8.6) and to describe analysis strategies (see Sections 8.3 and 8.4); however, it is also used within compilers as an interface between different compiler phases. Most procedures for evaluating semantic attributes in Chapter 9 'Semantic Analysis' work on this tree structure.

Definition 8.5 (syntax tree)
Suppose $G = (V_N, V_T, P, S)$ is a cfg. Let B be an ordered tree, that is, a tree in which the output edges from every node are ordered. Suppose its leaves are labelled with symbols from $V_T \cup \{\varepsilon\}$ and its internal nodes with symbols from V_N. B is called a **syntax tree** (synonym: **parse tree**) for a word $x \in V_T^*$ and $X \in V_N$ according to G, if the following hold:

(a) If n is any internal node, labelled by the nonterminal A, then either its children are labelled from left to right by $N_1, N_2, \ldots, N_k \in V_N \cup V_T$ and $A \rightarrow N_1 N_2 \ldots N_k$ is a production in P, or its only child is labelled by ε and $A \rightarrow \varepsilon$ is a production in P.

(b) The leaf word of B, that is, the word obtained by concatenating the labels of the leaves from left to right, is x.

(c) The root is labelled by X. A syntax tree for a word x and the start symbol S is simply called a syntax tree for x. □

Example 8.6 (continuation of Example 8.3)
Figure 8.1 shows two syntax trees according to the grammar G_1 for the word **id** $*$ **id** + **id**. □

Definition 8.6 (ambiguous, unambiguous)
A sentence $x \in L(G)$ is said to be **ambiguous** if it has more than one syntax tree. A cfg G is said to be **ambiguous** if $L(G)$ contains at least one ambiguous sentence. A cfg that is not ambiguous is said to be **unambiguous**. □

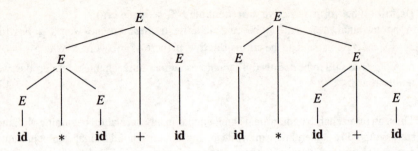

Figure 8.1 Syntax trees for **id * id + id**.

Example 8.7 (continuation of Example 8.3)
(1) G_1 is ambiguous, since the sentence **id * id + id** is ambiguous.
(2) G_0 is not ambiguous. □

Outline of proof of (2):
The following auxiliary assertions should be proved:

(a) If $u \in L(G_0) \cap \{*, \textbf{id}\}^*$, that is, u contains neither '+' nor brackets, then there is precisely one syntax tree for u and T. This is shown by induction over the number of occurrences of '*' in u. The induction step is as follows: Every syntax tree for u and T has the form shown in Figure 8.2(a), if u contains at least one '*'. t contains one fewer occurrences of '*'. t is therefore unambiguously determined by the inductive assumption.

(b) If $u \in L(G_0) \cap \{+, *, \textbf{id}\}^*$, that is, u does not contain any brackets, then there is precisely one syntax tree for u and E. Again, we use induction over the number of occurrences, this time of '+'.

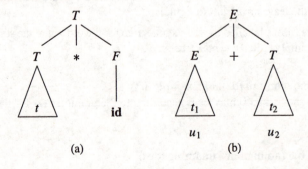

Figure 8.2 Syntax trees for * and +.

The induction step is similar to the above. Every syntax tree for u and E has the form shown in Figure 8.2(b), if u contains at least one '+'. Here, t_2 contains no '+'. According to (a) there is precisely one syntax tree t_2 for u_2 and T. By virtue of the inductive assumption there is precisely one tree t_1 for u_1 and E. Assertion (b) now follows.

Now it can be shown that for all $u \in L(G_0)$ and E there exists precisely one syntax tree. The proof follows by induction over the number of pairs of brackets. In the induction step, we take an innermost pair of brackets and apply (b). If this innermost bracket expression is replaced by **id**, we obtain a word to which the inductive assumption is applicable. □

Remarks

(1) Every sentence x of a language has at least one derivation, or, more precisely, a derivation from S. This follows from Definition 8.3.

(2) Every derivation for a sentence x is associated with a syntax tree for x.

(3) Every sentence x has at least one syntax tree. This is a consequence of (1) and (2). It can also be shown by giving a procedure which constructs a syntax tree for x from a derivation for x (see Exercise 1).

(4) Every syntax tree for x is associated with at least one derivation for x. The proof of this statement requires a procedure, which operates in the opposite direction to (2). But that is easy to define. □

Example 8.6 (continuation of Example 8.3)
On remark (1):
The word **id** + **id** has two derivations according to G_1.

$$E \Rightarrow E + E \Rightarrow \mathbf{id} + E \Rightarrow \mathbf{id} + \mathbf{id}$$
$$E \Rightarrow E + E \Rightarrow E + \mathbf{id} \Rightarrow \mathbf{id} + \mathbf{id}$$

On remark (2):
Both the above derivations are associated with the syntax tree of Figure 8.3.

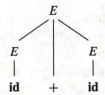

Figure 8.3 Syntax tree for **id** + **id**.

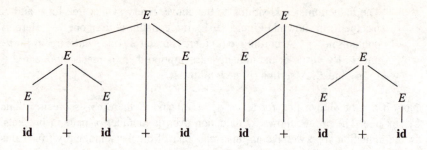

Figure 8.4 Two different syntax trees for **id** + **id** + **id**.

Here we see that the syntax tree shows the structure of the sentence, but abstracts from the rather unimportant order in which the productions are applied, which is different for the two derivations. For the derivation according to G_1,

$$E \underset{G_1}{\Longrightarrow} E + E \underset{G_1}{\Longrightarrow} E + E + E \underset{G_1}{\Longrightarrow} \mathbf{id} + E + E$$
$$\underset{G_1}{\Longrightarrow} \mathbf{id} + \mathbf{id} + E \underset{G_1}{\Longrightarrow} \mathbf{id} + \mathbf{id} + \mathbf{id}$$

the two are associated with different syntax trees which are shown in Figure 8.4.

One cannot tell from the above derivation which of the occurrences of E is replaced in the second derivation step. Thus, if only in the case of ambiguous grammars, the awkward situation may arise where two different syntax structures are associated with one derivation. □

In the above example, we have seen that (also for unambiguous words) a number of derivations may correspond to a single syntax tree. These arise from the various possible ways of selecting a nonterminal in a sentential form for the next application of a production. If we specify that the leftmost or rightmost nonterminal is replaced, we obtain special derivations, namely the so-called leftmost or rightmost derivations.

Definition 8.7 (leftmost derivation, rightmost derivation)
Suppose that $\varphi_1, \varphi_2, \ldots, \varphi_n$ is a derivation of $\varphi = \varphi_n$ from $\varphi_1 = S$. $\varphi_1, \varphi_2, \ldots, \varphi_n$ is called a **leftmost derivation** of φ, $S \underset{lm}{\overset{*}{\Longrightarrow}} \varphi$, if in the step from φ_i to φ_{i+1} the leftmost nonterminal in φ_i is always replaced, that is, $\varphi_i = uA\tau$, $\varphi_{i+1} = u\alpha\tau$ and $A \to \alpha \in P$. $\varphi_1, \varphi_2, \ldots, \varphi_n$ is called a **rightmost derivation** of φ, $S \underset{rm}{\overset{*}{\Longrightarrow}} \varphi$, if the rightmost nonterminal is always replaced, that is, $\varphi_i = \sigma Au$, $\varphi_{i+1} = \sigma\alpha u$ and $A \to \alpha \in P$. A sentential form which occurs in a leftmost derivation (rightmost derivation) is called a **left sentential form (right sentential form)**. □

Remarks

(5) For every syntax tree there is precisely one leftmost and precisely one rightmost derivation.

(6) For every unambiguous sentence there is precisely one leftmost and precisely one rightmost derivation. This is a consequence of the definition of ambiguity and remark (5). □

Example 8.9 (continuation of Example 8.3)

On remark (5):

According to G_1, the word $\mathbf{id} * \mathbf{id} + \mathbf{id}$ has the leftmost derivations

$$E \underset{lm}{\Longrightarrow} E + E \underset{lm}{\Longrightarrow} E * E + E \underset{lm}{\Longrightarrow} \mathbf{id} * E + E \underset{lm}{\Longrightarrow} \mathbf{id} * \mathbf{id} + E$$
$$\underset{lm}{\Longrightarrow} \mathbf{id} * \mathbf{id} + \mathbf{id}$$

and

$$E \underset{lm}{\Longrightarrow} E * E \underset{lm}{\Longrightarrow} \mathbf{id} * E \underset{lm}{\Longrightarrow} \mathbf{id} * E + E \underset{lm}{\Longrightarrow} \mathbf{id} * \mathbf{id} + E$$
$$\underset{lm}{\Longrightarrow} \mathbf{id} * \mathbf{id} + \mathbf{id}$$

It has the rightmost derivations

$$E \underset{rm}{\Longrightarrow} E + E \underset{rm}{\Longrightarrow} E + \mathbf{id} \underset{rm}{\Longrightarrow} E * E + \mathbf{id} \underset{rm}{\Longrightarrow} E * \mathbf{id} + \mathbf{id}$$
$$\underset{rm}{\Longrightarrow} \mathbf{id} * \mathbf{id} + \mathbf{id}$$

and

$$E \underset{rm}{\Longrightarrow} E * E \underset{rm}{\Longrightarrow} E * E + E \underset{rm}{\Longrightarrow} E * E + \mathbf{id} \underset{rm}{\Longrightarrow} E * \mathbf{id} + \mathbf{id}$$
$$\underset{rm}{\Longrightarrow} \mathbf{id} * \mathbf{id} + \mathbf{id}$$

On remark (6):

In G_1, the word $\mathbf{id} + \mathbf{id}$ has only one leftmost derivation, namely

$$E \underset{lm}{\Longrightarrow} E + E \underset{lm}{\Longrightarrow} \mathbf{id} + E \underset{lm}{\Longrightarrow} \mathbf{id} + \mathbf{id}$$

and one rightmost derivation, namely

$$E \underset{rm}{\Longrightarrow} E + E \underset{rm}{\Longrightarrow} E + \mathbf{id} \underset{rm}{\Longrightarrow} \mathbf{id} + \mathbf{id}$$

□

Context-free grammars that describe the syntax of programming languages are required to be unambiguous. Then, for every syntactically correct program, that is, for every sentence of the grammar, there is precisely one syntax tree, precisely one leftmost derivation and precisely one rightmost derivation.

8.2.2   Pushdown automata

In this section we shall deal with the acceptors belonging to the class of context-free grammars, namely the pushdown automata. The equivalence of the two concepts was mentioned at the beginning of Section 8.2. One of the two directions, namely the constructibility of a pushdown automaton for an arbitrary context-free grammar, is already almost redolent of what we need for compiler construction. If the syntax of a programming language has a context-free description, we could obtain an acceptor for the programming language by such a constructive procedure.

In fact, in Section 8.2.3, we shall describe the construction of a pushdown automaton for an arbitrary cfg, which accepts the language defined by the cfg. However, this pushdown automaton still has flaws: it is in general non-deterministic, even when the output grammar (like the grammars used in practice) has a deterministic acceptor.

Sections 8.3 and 8.4 describe how, based on this non-deterministic pushdown automaton, deterministic automata can be generated for certain subclasses of context-free grammars.

Unlike the finite automata considered in the last chapter, a pushdown automaton has an unlimited storage capacity. In fact, it has a stack, which is a potentially infinitely long array of cells with a last-in-first-out discipline for storage and retrieval. An illustration of a pushdown automaton is given in Figure 8.5.

The read head moves from left to right only; a transition of the automaton is determined by the topmost stack symbols and (possibly) the current input symbol. The transition alters the content of the stack at its topmost end.

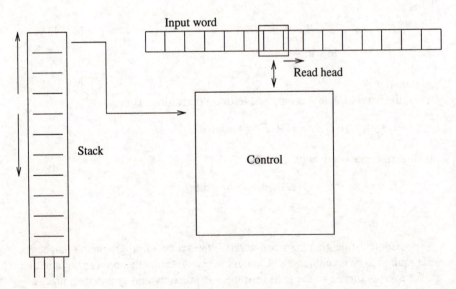

Figure 8.5   A pushdown automaton.

Definition 8.8 (pushdown automaton)
A **pushdown automaton** (PA) is a tuple $P = (V, Q, \Delta, q_0, F)$, where

- V is the **input alphabet**
- Q is the finite set of **states**
- $q_0 \in Q$ is the **initial state**
- $F \subseteq Q$ is the set of **final states**
- Δ is a finite relation between $Q^+ \times (V \cup \{\varepsilon\})$ and Q^*, the **transition relation**. Δ can also be viewed as a finite partial function δ from $Q^+ \times (V \cup \{\varepsilon\})$ to the finite subsets of Q^*. □

Note that this definition is somewhat unusual, since the sets of states and stack symbols are identified. The content of the stack is therefore always a sequence of states. We shall call the topmost state in the stack the **current** state. The transition relation defines the computations of the pushdown automaton. It defines sets of possibilities for continuation for finitely many combinations of non-empty words over Q and input characters from V or the empty word ε. The possibilities for continuation are sequences of states that replace the sequence of states inspected in the stack. If the current input character is inspected, it is also consumed, that is, the read head moves one field to the right. Transitions that do not inspect the next input character are called ε-**transitions**.

In a pushdown automaton there are several sources of non-deterministic behaviour. For example, a pair $(\gamma, a) \in Q^+ \times V$ may give several continuations in accordance with Δ. In addition, pairs $(\gamma', a) \in Q^+ \times V$, where γ' is a suffix of γ, and possible pairs (γ', ε) compete with the pair (γ, a), that is, if a transition for (γ, a) matches a configuration of the automaton, then so do they.

As usual for an automaton, the term configuration is defined so as to cover all components relevant to the future steps of the automaton. For our kind of pushdown automata, this means the stack contents and the remaining input.

Definition 8.9 (configuration)
A **configuration** of the PA P is a pair $(\gamma, w) \in Q^+ \times V^*$. A **transition** from P is represented by the binary relation $\vdash_P$ between configurations, which is defined as follows: $(\gamma, aw) \vdash_P (\gamma', w)$ if and only if $\gamma = \gamma_1\gamma_2$, $\gamma' = \gamma_1\gamma_3$ and $(\gamma_2, a, \gamma_3) \in \Delta$ for $\gamma, \gamma_1, \gamma_3 \in Q^*$, $\gamma_2 \in Q^+$, $a \in (V \cup \{\varepsilon\})$.

As usual for configurations, C and C', we define $C \vdash_P^n C'$, if there exist configurations $C_1, \ldots, C_{n+1}$ such that $C_1 = C, C_{n+1} = C'$ and $C_i \vdash_P C_{i+1}$ for $1 \leq i \leq n$. $\vdash_P^*$, the reflexive transitive closure of $\vdash_P$, then stands for $\bigcup_{n \geq 0} \vdash_P^n$, $\vdash_P^+$ for $\bigcup_{n \geq 1} \vdash_P^n$. For an arbitrary $w \in V^*$, (q_0, w) is called an **initial configuration**, (γ, ε) for $q \in F$ is called a **final configuration**. A word $w \in V^*$ is **accepted** by P, if $(q_0, w) \vdash_P^* (\gamma q, \varepsilon)$ for some $q \in F$. The **language** of P, $L(P)$, is the set of words accepted by P:

$$L(P) = \{w \in V^* | w \text{ is accepted by } P\}$$

□

Note that a word is accepted by a pushdown automaton when there exists *at least one* sequence of configurations leading from the corresponding initial configuration to a final configuration. There may, however, be several successful sequences and also many unsuccessful ones that can only read the beginning of the word. Since it would be undesirable in practice to discover these sequences by trial and error, only deterministic pushdown automata are important there.

Definition 8.10 (deterministic pushdown automaton)
A pushdown automaton P is said to be **deterministic** (DPA), if the following holds: For $(\gamma_1, a, \gamma_2), (\gamma_1', a', \gamma_2') \in \Delta$ where γ_1' is a suffix of γ_1 or vice versa and a' is a prefix of a or vice versa, it follows that $\gamma_1 = \gamma_1', a = a', \gamma_2 = \gamma_2'$. $\qquad\square$

Thus, all competition between transitions is excluded. For every configuration there is at most one transition, and for an accepted word there is precisely one sequence of configurations.

8.2.3 The item pushdown automaton of a context-free grammar

In this section, we are interested in *one* direction of the equivalence between context-free grammars and pushdown automata. We present a procedure which can be used to construct a (non-deterministic) pushdown automaton from any context-free grammar, which accepts the language defined by the grammar.

Because it is non-deterministic, this automaton is of no interest for practical purposes, but of greater didactic interest; based on it, we can derive firstly the LL-analysers of Section 8.3 and secondly the LR-analysers of Section 8.4 by employing clear design decisions (instead of by magic).

The concept of the context-free item plays a crucial role. As always, when we speak of items, we consider syntactic patterns of a particular type (in this case, context-free productions) and identify the extent to which the existence of a pattern has already been confirmed. The interpretation placed on a context-free item $[A \to \alpha.\beta]$ is the following: 'In an attempt to recognize a word for A, a word for α has already been recognized'.

Definition 8.11 (context-free item)
Suppose G is a cfg and $A \to \alpha\beta$ is a production of G. Then the triplet (A, α, β) is called a **context-free item** of G. We write the item (A, α, β) as $[A \to \alpha.\beta]$. α is called the **history** of the item. An item $[A \to \alpha.]$ is said to be **complete**. We denote the set of all context-free items of G by It_G. If $\rho \in It_G^*$, that is, it is a sequence of items $[A_1 \to \alpha_1.\beta_1] [A_2 \to \alpha_2.\beta_2] \dots [A_n \to \alpha_n.\beta_n]$, then $hist(\rho)$ denotes the concatenation of the histories of the items of ρ, that is, $hist(\rho) = \alpha_1\alpha_2\dots\alpha_n$. $\qquad\square$

We now define the item pushdown automaton associated with a context-free grammar. Its states and thus its stack symbols are items of the grammar. The current state is the item on whose right side the automaton is currently working. Below on the stack are the items for which the processing on the right side has already begun but not yet been completed.

First, we wish to ensure that the pushdown automaton constructed terminates cleanly. What are the candidates for the final states? They will of course include all completed items $[S \to \alpha.]$, where S is the start symbol of the grammar. If S also occurs on the right side of a production, these complete items may occur at the top of the stack without the automaton having to terminate, because items whose processing is not yet complete lie below. We therefore extend the grammar by a new start symbol S', which does not occur on a right side, and a production $S' \to S$, which forms the basis for the initial and final states of the item pushdown automaton. The grammars that occur in what follows are extended in this way.

Definition 8.12 (item pushdown automaton of a cfg)
Let $G = (V_N, V_T, P, S)$ be an extended cfg. The pushdown automaton

$$K_G = (V_T, It_G, \delta, [S' \to .S], \{[S' \to S.]\})$$

is called the **item pushdown automaton** for G.
Here, δ consists of all transitions of the following three types:

(E) $(\delta([X \to \beta.Y\gamma], \varepsilon) = \{[X \to \beta.Y\gamma][Y \to .\alpha] | Y \to \alpha \in P\}$
(L) $\delta([X \to \beta.a\gamma], a) = \{[X \to \beta a.\gamma]\}$
(R) $\delta([X \to \beta.Y\gamma][Y \to \alpha.], \varepsilon) = \{[X \to \beta Y.\gamma]\}$ □

The above interpretation of context-free items does not depend on a particular context in which the items occur. In the item pushdown automaton they occur as states in the stack. We can give a more precise interpretation of an item as a state in a configuration of the item pushdown automaton and a sequence of items as stack contents. The following assertion (I) about configurations of the item pushdown automaton is also the main auxiliary assertion for the proof that $L(K_G) \subseteq L(G)$.

Lemma
(I)   If $([S' \to .S], uv) \vdash^*_{K_G} (\rho, v)$ then $hist(\rho) \overset{*}{\underset{G}{\Longrightarrow}} u$.

The following discussion attempts to explain how the automaton K_G works and at the same time prove by induction (over the length of computations) that the assertion (I) is satisfied for all configurations reachable from an initial configuration.

Let us consider the initial configuration for the input w to determine whether it satisfies the assertion. This initial configuration is $([S' \to .S], w)$. Nothing, that is, ε, has already been read, $hist([S' \to .S]) = \varepsilon$, and $\varepsilon \overset{*}{\Longrightarrow} \varepsilon$.

Let us consider the transitions in accordance with (E), the so-called **expansion transitions**. Suppose the current configuration reached from the initial configuration $([S' \to .S], uv)$ is $(\rho[X \to \beta.Y\gamma], v)$. According to the induction hypothesis, this configuration satisfies the assertion (I); that is, $hist(\rho)\beta \overset{*}{\Longrightarrow} u$.

The item $[X \rightarrow \beta.Y\gamma]$, as the current state, suggests deriving a prefix for v from Y. Then the automaton should try out the alternatives for Y non-deterministically. The transitions in accordance with (E) describe precisely this. All possible subsequent configurations $(\rho[X \rightarrow \beta.Y\gamma][Y \rightarrow .\alpha], v)$ for $Y \rightarrow \alpha \in P$ also satisfy the assertion (I); because $hist(\rho[X \rightarrow \beta.Y\gamma][Y \rightarrow .\alpha]) = hist(\rho)\beta \stackrel{*}{\Longrightarrow} u$.

The next transitions considered are those in accordance with (L), the so-called **shift transitions**. Suppose the current configuration reached from $([S' \rightarrow .S], uav)$ is $(\rho[X \rightarrow \beta.a\gamma], av)$. According to the induction hypothesis, it satisfies (I), that is, $hist(\rho)\beta \stackrel{*}{\Longrightarrow} u$. Then we have $hist(\rho)\beta a \stackrel{*}{\Longrightarrow} ua$. Thus, the successor configuration $(\rho[X \rightarrow \beta a.\gamma], v)$ also satisfies (I).

A **reduction transition**, that is, a transition of type (R), involves a configuration $(\rho[X \rightarrow \beta.Y\gamma][Y \rightarrow \alpha.], v)$ reached from the initial configuration $([S' \rightarrow .S], uv)$. According to the induction hypothesis, it satisfies (I), that is, $hist(\rho)\beta\alpha \stackrel{*}{\underset{G}{\Longrightarrow}} u$, where u is the input already consumed.

The current state is the complete item $[Y \rightarrow \alpha.]$. Its processing (in the form $[Y \rightarrow .\alpha]$) was begun when $[X \rightarrow \beta.Y\gamma]$ was the current state and the alternatives from Y had to be tested. One alternative $Y \rightarrow \alpha$ can therefore now be 'crossed off' as successful.

The successor configuration $(\rho[X \rightarrow \beta Y.\gamma], v)$ also satisfies the assertion (I), since it follows naturally from $hist(\rho)\beta\alpha \stackrel{*}{\underset{G}{\Longrightarrow}} u$ that $hist(\rho)\beta Y \stackrel{*}{\underset{G}{\Longrightarrow}} u$. $\square$

Theorem 8.1   *Suppose* $G = (V_N, V_T, P, S)$ *is a context-free grammar. Then* $L(K_G) = L(G)$.

Proof: "$\subseteq$"
$L(K_G) = \{w \in V_T^* | ([S' \rightarrow .S], w) \vdash_{K_G}^* ([S' \rightarrow S.], \varepsilon)\}$
(I) says that $S \stackrel{*}{\underset{G}{\Longrightarrow}} w$, if $w \in L(K_G)$. Thus, w is also in $L(G)$.
"$\supseteq$"
The following assertion can be proved by induction over m, the length of the derivation: if $A \stackrel{m}{\underset{G}{\Longrightarrow}} w$ for $m \geq 1$, $A \in V_N$ and $w \in V_T^*$, then there exists a production $A \rightarrow \alpha$, such that $(\rho[A \rightarrow .\alpha], wv) \vdash_{K_G}^* (\rho[A \rightarrow \alpha.], v)$ for any $\rho \in It_G^*$ and any $v \in V_T^*$. $\square$

Example 8.10
Suppose $G' = (\{S, E, T, F\}, \{+, *, (,), \mathbf{id}\}, P, S)$ is the extension of G_0, where $P = \{S \rightarrow E, E \rightarrow E + T \mid T, T \rightarrow T * F \mid F, F \rightarrow (E) \mid \mathbf{id}\}$. The transition relation Δ for K_{G_0} is given in Table 8.1. $\square$

Example 8.11
A sequence of configurations of K_{G_0}, leading to the acceptance of the word $\mathbf{id}+\mathbf{id}*\mathbf{id}$, is shown in Table 8.2. $\square$

Table 8.1 Tabular representation of the transition relation of Example 8.10. The middle column gives the input consumed.

Top of stack	Input	New top of stack
$[S \to .E]$	ε	$[S \to .E][E \to .E + T]$
$[S \to .E]$	ε	$[S \to .E][E \to .T]$
$[E \to .E + T]$	ε	$[E \to .E + T][E \to .E + T]$
$[E \to .E + T]$	ε	$[E \to .E + T][E \to .T]$
$[F \to (.E)]$	ε	$[F \to (.E)][E \to .E + T]$
$[F \to (.E)]$	ε	$[F \to (.E)][E \to .T]$
$[E \to .T]$	ε	$[E \to .T][T \to .T * F]$
$[E \to .T]$	ε	$[E \to .T][T \to .F]$
$[T \to .T * F]$	ε	$[T \to .T * F][T \to .T * F]$
$[T \to .T * F]$	ε	$[T \to .T * F][T \to .F]$
$[E \to E + .T]$	ε	$[E \to E + .T][T \to .T * F]$
$[E \to E + .T]$	ε	$[E \to E + .T][T \to .F]$
$[T \to .F]$	ε	$[T \to .F][F \to .(E)]$
$[T \to .F]$	ε	$[T \to .F][F \to .id]$
$[T \to T * .F]$	ε	$[T \to T * .F][F \to .(E)]$
$[T \to T * .F]$	ε	$[T \to T * .F][F \to .id]$
$[F \to .(E)]$	(	$[F \to (.E)]$
$[F \to .id]$	**id**	$[F \to id.]$
$[F \to (E.)]$	)	$[E \to (E).]$
$[E \to E. + T]$	+	$[E \to E + .T]$
$[T \to T. * F]$	*	$[T \to T * .F]$
$[T \to .F][F \to id.]$	ε	$[T \to F.]$
$[T \to T * .F][F \to id.]$	ε	$[T \to T * F.]$
$[T \to .F][F \to (E).]$	ε	$[T \to F.]$
$[T \to T * .F][F \to (E).]$	ε	$[T \to T * F.]$
$[T \to .T * F][T \to F.]$	ε	$[T \to T. * F]$
$[E \to .T][T \to F.]$	ε	$[E \to T.]$
$[E \to E + .T][T \to F.]$	ε	$[E \to E + T.]$
$[E \to E + .T][T \to T * F.]$	ε	$[E \to E + T.]$
$[T \to .T * F][T \to T * F.]$	ε	$[T \to T. * F]$
$[E \to .T][T \to T * F.]$	ε	$[E \to T.]$
$[F \to (.E)][E \to T.]$	ε	$[F \to (E.)]$
$[F \to (.E)][E \to E + T.]$	ε	$[F \to (E.)]$
$[E \to .E + T][E \to T.]$	ε	$[E \to E. + T]$
$[E \to .E + T][E \to E + T.]$	ε	$[E \to E. + T]$
$[S \to .E][E \to T.]$	ε	$[S \to E.]$
$[S \to .E][E \to E + T.]$	ε	$[S \to E.]$

Table 8.2   The sequence of configurations of K_G leading to the acceptance of $\mathbf{id}+\mathbf{id}+\mathbf{id}$. No other sequences of configurations lead to the acceptance of this word.

Stack contents	Remaining input
$[S \to .E]$	$\mathbf{id} + \mathbf{id} * \mathbf{id}$
$[S \to .E][E \to .E + T]$	$\mathbf{id} + \mathbf{id} * \mathbf{id}$
$[S \to .E][E \to .E + T][E \to .T]$	$\mathbf{id} + \mathbf{id} * \mathbf{id}$
$[S \to .E][E \to .E + T][E \to .T][T \to .F]$	$\mathbf{id} + \mathbf{id} * \mathbf{id}$
$[S \to .E][E \to .E + T][E \to .T][T \to .F][F \to .\mathbf{id}]$	$\mathbf{id} + \mathbf{id} * \mathbf{id}$
$[S \to .E][E \to .E + T][E \to .T][T \to .F][F \to \mathbf{id}.]$	$+\mathbf{id} * \mathbf{id}$
$[S \to .E][E \to .E + T][E \to .T][T \to F.]$	$+\mathbf{id} * \mathbf{id}$
$[S \to .E][E \to .E + T][E \to T.]$	$+\mathbf{id} * \mathbf{id}$
$[S \to .E][E \to E. + T]$	$+\mathbf{id} * \mathbf{id}$
$[S \to .E][E \to E + .T]$	$\mathbf{id} * \mathbf{id}$
$[S \to .E][E \to E + .T][T \to .T * F]$	$\mathbf{id} * \mathbf{id}$
$[S \to .E][E \to E + .T][T \to .T * F][T \to .F]$	$\mathbf{id} * \mathbf{id}$
$[S \to .E][E \to E + .T][T \to .T * F][T \to .F][F \to .\mathbf{id}]$	$\mathbf{id} * \mathbf{id}$
$[S \to .E][E \to E + .T][T \to .T * F][T \to .F][F \to \mathbf{id}.]$	$*\mathbf{id}$
$[S \to .E][E \to E + .T][T \to .T * F][T \to F.]$	$*\mathbf{id}$
$[S \to .E][E \to E + .T][T \to T. * F]$	$*\mathbf{id}$
$[S \to .E][E \to E + .T][T \to T * .F]$	$\mathbf{id}$
$[S \to .E][E \to E + .T][T \to T * .F][F \to .\mathbf{id}]$	$\mathbf{id}$
$[S \to .E][E \to E + .T][T \to T * .F][F \to \mathbf{id}.]$	
$[S \to .E][E \to E + .T][T \to T * F.]$	
$[S \to .E][E \to E + T.]$	
$[S \to E.]$	

Pushdown automaton with output

The pushdown automata discussed hitherto are only acceptors, that is, they only decide whether or not a given word is a sentence of the language. When one uses a pushdown automaton for syntax analysis in a compiler, the syntax structure of accepted words is also of interest. This can be represented in the form of syntax trees, derivations or even sequences of productions applied in a right or left derivation. Therefore, we shall now provide pushdown automata with output facilities.

Definition 8.13 (pushdown automaton with output)
A **pushdown automaton with output** is a tuple $P = (V, Q, O, \Delta, q_0, F)$, where V, Q, q_0 and F are as previously defined and O is the output alphabet. Δ is now a finite relation between $Q^+ \times (V \cup \{\varepsilon\})$ and $Q^* \times (O \cup \{\varepsilon\})$. A **configuration** is an element of $Q^+ \times V^* \times O^*$. $\square$

On every transition the automaton can print a character of O. If we use a pushdown automaton with output as a parser, its output alphabet consists of the productions of the cfg or their indices.

Definition 8.14 (left parser)
A **left parser** for a cfg $G = (V_N, V_T, P, S)$ is an item pushdown automaton with output $K_G^l = (V_T, It_G, P, \Delta_l, [S' \to .S], \{[S' \to S.]\})$, where Δ_l at (E) transitions prints the production applied; that is,

$$\Delta_l([X \to \beta.Y\gamma], \varepsilon) = \{([X \to \beta.Y\gamma][Y \to .\alpha], Y \to \alpha) | Y \to \alpha \in P\}$$

The other transitions print nothing.

A **configuration** of a left parser is an element of $It_G^+ \times V_T^* \times P^*$. The output for an expansion transition is appended to the right of the output that has already been produced, that is,

$$(\rho[X \to \beta.Y\gamma], w, o) \vdash_{K_G^l} (\rho[X \to \beta.Y\gamma][Y \to .\alpha], w, o(Y \to \alpha))$$

□

Definition 8.15 (right parser)
A **right parser** for a cfg $G = (V_N, V_T, P, S)$ is an item pushdown automaton with output $K_G^r = (V_T, It_G, P, \Delta_r, [S' \to .S], \{[S' \to S.]\})$, where Δ_r at (R) transitions gives the production applied as output, that is,

$$\Delta_r([X \to \beta.Y\gamma][Y \to \alpha.], \varepsilon) = ([X \to \beta Y.\gamma], Y \to \alpha)$$

The other transitions print nothing. In the case of a reduction the production applied is appended after the output that has already been produced, that is,

$$(\rho[X \to \beta.Y\gamma][Y \to \alpha.], w, o) \vdash_{K_G^r} (\rho[X \to \beta Y.\gamma], w, o(Y \to \alpha))$$

□

The production sequence output by a left parser corresponds to the sequence of the substitutions in a leftmost derivation. The output of a right parser is the reversed sequence of the rules which are applied in a rightmost derivation.

Deterministic parsers

We have already proved a crucial property of the item pushdown automaton in Theorem 8.1, namely that the item pushdown automaton K_G for a context-free grammar G accepts precisely its language $L(G)$.

Another rather unpleasant property is that it does this non-deterministically. Where is the source of the non-determinism of K_G? It is easy to see that it lies in the transitions of type (E). The problem is that K_G has to guess which of the alternatives it should choose for the current nonterminal, that is, the nonterminal after the period.

In the case of a grammar that is not ambiguous at most one of the alternatives can be applied to derive a prefix of the remaining input.

In Sections 8.3 and 8.4, we shall attempt to eliminate this non-determinism in two ways. The LL-analysers of Section 8.3 choose an alternative for the current nonterminal deterministically by means of a limited lookahead at the remaining input. Thus, if the grammar is of a certain type, called LL(k), then precisely one (E) transition will be chosen, when the input that has already been read, the nonterminal to be expanded and the next k input symbols are taken into account. Of course, this is not true for faulty inputs. There, no transition exists in some configuration. LL-analysers are left parsers.

The LR-analysers work differently. They defer the decision, which the LL-analyser takes on expansion, by pursuing all possibilities that could lead to a (rightmost) derivation for the input word in parallel. Only when such a situation forces a decision (that is, to select or reject possibilities) do they take this decision, again based on their stack contents and a lookahead at a limited number of symbols. LR-analysers are right parsers.

8.2.4 Grammar flow analysis

In what follows we frequently require information about properties of context-free grammars, for example about the set of all syntax trees for a cfg. We often associate this information with nonterminals of the grammar. In general, a nonterminal X has infinitely many subtrees with X as the root label. Moreover, there are in general infinitely many so-called upper tree fragments for X, which are obtained by separating out from a syntax tree a subtree for X without the root X (see Figure 8.6). Using grammar flow analysis (GFA), one attempts to compute finite or finitely representable information about these two infinite sets.

Example 8.12
The problem of determining whether a nonterminal X is productive is equivalent to that of determining whether the set of subtrees for X is non-empty. On the other hand, X is reachable when there exists at least one upper tree fragment for X. □

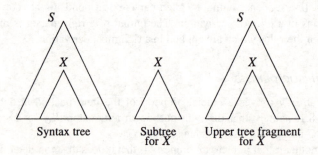

| Syntax tree | Subtree for X | Upper tree fragment for X |

Figure 8.6 Syntax tree, subtree, upper tree fragment for X.

Information about the set of all subtrees for X can be computed by using information about the sets of all subtrees for the nonterminals in productions for X recursively.

Since information from the right sides of productions (in illustrations, usually at the bottom) is used here to obtain information for left sides (in illustrations, usually at the top), we speak of a **bottom-up problem**. After all, a bottom-up parser also combines trees for a right side of a production into a tree for the nonterminal of the left side.

Conversely, information about the set of the upper tree fragments of X is computed using information about the nonterminals in whose productions X occurs on the right. Since in this case information about the left side is used to compute information for the right side, we speak of a **top-down problem**.

We shall introduce two techniques for solving these two classes of problem, namely **bottom-up** and **top-down grammar flow analysis**.

In the following sections we use a notation for context-free productions appropriate for the representation of grammar flow problems. Each production is given a name. The generic names are p, q, r, and so on. The **arity** of a production, which is the number of occurrences of nonterminals on the right side, is always assigned the name n_p, n_q, n_r, and so on. If $p = (X_0 \rightarrow u_0 X_1 u_1 \ldots X_{n_p} u_{n_p})$ with $X_i \in V_N, u_i \in V_T^*$, then $p[i]$ stands for $X_i, 0 \leq i \leq n_p$. An **occurrence** of a nonterminal X in p at the position i, that is, $p[i] = X$, is denoted by (p, i). In addition, we assume that the grammars are extended. Thus, S does not occur on a right side.

Let us again consider the productivity of nonterminals. $X \in V_N$ is **productive** if and only if there exists a terminal word w with $X \overset{*}{\Longrightarrow} w$. A suitable recursive definition leading to an algorithm is the following:

(1) X is **productive over the production** p if and only if $p[0] = X$ and all $p[i]$ for $1 \leq i \leq n_p$ are productive. In particular, X is productive over a production $X \rightarrow u, u \in V_T^*$ if such a production exists.

(2) X is **productive** if X is productive over at least one of its alternatives.

The two-level nature of the definition is typical for all problems, which we shall solve by grammar flow analysis:

(1) represents a dependence of the information for a nonterminal X on the information about the symbols on the right side of a production for X; (2) indicates how the information obtained from the various alternatives for X is to be combined.

We now consider the analysis of the reachability of nonterminals. Again, a two-level recursive definition helps.

(1) A nonterminal X is **reachable** at its occurrence (p, i) for some i with $1 \leq i \leq n_p$, if $p[0]$ is reachable.

(2) X is reachable if it is reachable at one of its occurrences.

(3) The start symbol is reachable.

The last specification ensures that the analysis starts properly. (1) specifies that the reachability of left sides of productions carries over to right sides. (2) says that even one occurrence of X on a right side with a reachable left side is sufficient. Here, we are concerned with a combination of the information obtained for all occurrences of X on the right sides of productions.

We shall now abstract from these two examples, to come to our algorithm schemes. The following can now be identified as parameters of the schemes:

- Domains for the information to be computed;
- **Transfer functions** for all productions of the cfg; these describe the dependence between information from the left and right sides of productions;
- A **combination function**; this describes how a set of information for a nonterminal is to be combined into a single piece of information.

The corresponding components in the definition of the bottom-up grammar flow analysis problem have an '↑' appended to their names, in the top-down case – a '↓'. The objective of a grammar flow analysis is to compute a function $I : V_N \rightarrow D$ which assigns to every nonterminal X information from the domain D, so that I satisfies a system of equations constructed from the grammar, the transfer functions and the combination function.

Definition 8.16 (bottom-up grammar flow analysis problem)
Let G be a cfg. A **bottom-up grammar flow analysis problem** for G and I consists of:

- A domain $D\uparrow$; this domain is the set of possible information for nonterminals;
- A **transfer function** $F_p\uparrow : D\uparrow^{n_p} \rightarrow D\uparrow$ for each production $p \in P$;
- A **combination function** $\nabla\uparrow : 2^{D\uparrow} \rightarrow D\uparrow$.

For a given cfg, this specification is used to define a recursive system of equations:

$$I(X) = \nabla\uparrow\{F_p\uparrow(I(p[1]), \ldots, I(p[n_p])) \mid p[0] = X\} \; \forall X \in V_N \qquad (I\uparrow)$$

$\square$

Example 8.13 (productivity of nonterminals)

$D\uparrow$	$\{true, false\}$	*true* for productive
$F_p\uparrow$	$\wedge$	(*true* for $n_p = 0$, i.e. for terminal productions)
$\nabla\uparrow$	$\vee$	(*false* for nonterminals without alternatives)

The system of equations for the problem of the productivity of nonterminals is:

$$Pr(X) = \bigvee\{\bigwedge_{i=1}^{n_p} Pr(p[i]) \mid p[0] = X\} \text{ for all } X \in V_N \qquad (Pr)$$

□

Definition 8.17 (top-down grammar flow analysis problem)
Let G be a cfg. A **top-down grammar flow analysis problem** for G and I consists of:

- A domain $D\downarrow$;
- n_p **transfer functions** $F_{p,i}\downarrow : D\downarrow \to D\downarrow$, $1 \le i \le n_p$, for each production $p \in P$;
- A **combination function** $\nabla\downarrow : 2^{D\downarrow} \to D\downarrow$;
- A value I_0 for S under the function I.

For a given cfg, this is again used to define a recursive system of equations for I; for ease of understanding, we define I for nonterminals and for occurrences of nonterminals:

$$
\begin{aligned}
I(S) &= I_0 \\
I(p, i) &= F_{p,i}\downarrow(I(p[0])) \text{ for all } p \in P,\ 1 \le i \le n_p \\
I(X) &= \nabla\downarrow\{I(p, i) \mid p[i] = X\},\ \text{for all } X \in V_N - \{S\}
\end{aligned}
\qquad (I\downarrow)
$$

□

Example 8.14 (reachable nonterminals)

$D\downarrow$	$\{true, false\}$	*true* for reachable
$F_{p,i}\downarrow$	*id*	identity mapping
$\nabla\downarrow$	*false*	if no nonterminal occurs
I_0	*true*	

This leads to the recursive system of equations for Re:

$$
\begin{aligned}
Re(S) &= true \\
Re(X) &= \bigvee\{Re(p[0]) \mid p[i] = X,\ 1 \le i \le n_p\}\ \forall X \in V_N - \{S\}
\end{aligned}
\qquad (Re)
$$

□

Thus, for both schemes and both examples, we obtain recursive equations, whose solution will give us the desired information about the nonterminals of the given grammar. Naturally, a number of questions now arise:

- Are there any solutions for the resulting systems of equations?

- Which solution is the desired one when there are several solutions to a system of equations?

- How does one compute solutions and in particular the desired solution?

To answer these questions we first discuss an obvious approach and then study the necessary assumptions for this system of equations.

Suppose we are given a recursive system of equations:

$$x_1 = f_1(x_1, \ldots, x_n)$$
$$x_2 = f_2(x_1, \ldots, x_n)$$
$$\vdots$$
$$x_n = f_n(x_1, \ldots, x_n)$$

It is to be solved over a domain D. If D has a smallest element (usually denoted by $\perp$), we could try the following. For all $x_1, \ldots, x_n$ we use the value $\perp$ and apply all the f_i to this $(\perp, \ldots, \perp)$ tuple, which we denote by $\overline{x}^0$. We then obtain a new tuple $\overline{x}^1$, to which we again apply all the f_i, and so on. Thus, we obtain a sequence $(\overline{x}^0, \overline{x}^1, \overline{x}^2, \ldots)$. In general, this leads to nothing. In all cases considered by us we can however guarantee that this procedure converges to a desired solution. First, we know something about the domains that occur in what follows:

- They are all finite;

- A partial order, represented by the symbol $\sqsubseteq$, is defined on all of them;

- They all contain a unique smallest element, $\perp$, read bottom, required above;

- The least upper bound, $\sqcup$, is defined for every two elements of the domain.

These domains together with their operation $\sqcup$ and their partial order $\sqsubseteq$ form finite, **complete $\sqcup$ semi-lattices**, written as $(D, \sqsubseteq, \perp, \sqcup)$.

Second, all functions are monotonic. The fact that $\overline{x}^0$ is the smallest element ensures that $\overline{x}^0 \sqsubseteq \overline{x}^1$. From the monotonicity of the functions f_i it thus follows by induction that $\overline{x}^0 \sqsubseteq \overline{x}^1 \sqsubseteq \overline{x}^2 \sqsubseteq \cdots$. Since the domain D is finite there exists n such that $\overline{x}^n = \overline{x}^{n+1}$. Then for all $m > n$, we have $\overline{x}^m = \overline{x}^n$. This $\overline{x}^n$ is a solution of the system of equations. It can be easily shown that this is the smallest solution, which is called the smallest fixed point.

In GFA problems the functions f_i are composed from the transfer and the combination functions in such a way that the monotonicity of the transfer and combination functions implies that the composite function is monotonic.

Thus, for every flow analysis problem, we have to prove that its domain is a finite complete $\sqcup$ semi-lattice, and that the transfer functions and the combination function are monotonic.

If $V_N = \{X_1, \ldots, X_n\}$, we order the nonterminals in the order $X_1, X_2, \ldots, X_n$ and use the system of equations $(I \uparrow)$ in an obvious way to construct a function $F\uparrow : D\uparrow^n \to D\uparrow^n$, the so-called **total step function** (analogously for top-down problems); in one (total) step, $F\uparrow$ computes new information for all nonterminals using the functions $F_p\uparrow$ assigned to the productions. $F\uparrow$ is defined by $F\uparrow(d_1, \ldots, d_n) = (d'_1, \ldots, d'_n)$ with

$$d'_i = \nabla\uparrow\{F_p\uparrow(d_{i_1}, \ldots, d_{i_{n_p}}) \mid p[0] = X_i, p[j] = X_{i_j} \text{ for } 1 \le j \le n_p\}$$

If the $F_p\uparrow$ and $\nabla\uparrow$ are monotonic, then $F\uparrow$ is also monotonic. If $D\uparrow$ is finite, then so too is $D\uparrow^n$. The bottom element $\perp^n$ of $D\uparrow^n$ is equal to $(\perp, \ldots, \perp)$. Thus, we begin the iteration for $F\uparrow$ with $\perp^n$. The iteration converges to the smallest fixed point.

Now we must return to our two examples and show that they satisfy the sufficient conditions for the fixed point computation.

Example 8.15 (productive nonterminals)
$D = \{true, false\}$ with $false \sqsubseteq true$, whence $\perp = false$ and $\top = true$, is a finite complete $\sqcup$ lattice. Here, $Pr(X) = true$ is interpreted as 'X has already been recognized as productive'. $Pr(X) = false$ during the iteration means 'productivity still unknown'; after the convergence to the smallest fixed point $Pr(X) = false$ means that X is unproductive. The transfer functions assigned to the productions, that is, the conjunctions, are monotonic, as is the combination function, the disjunction. Thus, the function constructed from them, $pr : D^n \to D^n$, is also monotonic. The iterative computation of the smallest fixed point of pr begins with the bottom element in D^n, that is, $(false, \ldots, false)$. $\square$

Example 8.16 (productive nonterminals)
Suppose we are given the following grammar:

$$G = (\{S', S, X, Y, Z\}, \{a, b\}, \left\{ \begin{array}{rcl} S' & \to & S \\ S & \to & aX \\ X & \to & bS \mid aYbY \\ Y & \to & ba \mid aZ \\ Z & \to & aZX \end{array} \right\}, S')$$

The system of equations (Pr) was given by:

$$Pr(A) = \bigvee_{\{p \mid p[0] = A\}} \left(\bigwedge_{i=1}^{n_p} Pr(p[i]) \right) \quad \text{(for all } A \in V_N)$$

Thus, for the above grammar we obtain the following system of equations (we do not consider S', since $Pr(S') = Pr(S)$):

$$\begin{array}{rcl} Pr(S) & = & Pr(X) \\ Pr(X) & = & Pr(S) \vee Pr(Y) \\ Pr(Y) & = & true \vee Pr(Z) = true \\ Pr(Z) & = & Pr(Z) \wedge Pr(X) \end{array}$$

We choose the order S, X, Y, Z on V_N and obtain the total step function pr : $\{true, false\}^4 \rightarrow \{true, false\}^4$ defined by

$$pr(s, x, y, z) = (x, s \vee y, true, z \wedge x)$$

The fixed point iteration starts with $p = (false, false, false, false)$.

$$pr(p) = (false, \ false, \ true, \ false)$$
$$pr^2(p) = (false, \ true, \ true, \ false)$$
$$pr^3(p) = (true, \ true, \ true, \ false)$$
$$pr^4(p) = (true, \ true, \ true, \ false)$$

Thus the result has the interpretation that Z is unproductive, while all other nonterminals are productive. □

Example 8.17 (reachable nonterminals)

The ⊔ semi-lattice assigned to all nonterminals is again $D = \{true, false\}$ with $false \sqsubseteq true$. The transfer functions are the identity, the combination function is the disjunction. Both are monotonic. Thus, the total step function constructed from them, $re : D^n \rightarrow D^n$, is also monotonic. The iteration again starts with $(false, \ldots, false)$.
□

Example 8.18 (reachable nonterminals)

Suppose we are given the following grammar:

$$G = (\{S, U, V, X, Y, Z\}, \{a, b, c, d\}, \left\{ \begin{matrix} S & \rightarrow & Y \\ Y & \rightarrow & YZ \mid Ya \mid b \\ U & \rightarrow & V \\ X & \rightarrow & c \\ V & \rightarrow & Vd \mid d \\ Z & \rightarrow & ZX \end{matrix} \right\}, S)$$

The system of equations (Re) was given by:

$$Re(X) = \bigvee\{Re(p[0]) \mid p[i] = X, \ 1 \le i \le n_p\} \text{ for all } X \in V_N - \{S\} \text{ and}$$
$$Re(S) = true$$

For the example grammar we have:

$$Re(S) = true$$
$$Re(U) = false$$
$$Re(V) = Re(U) \vee Re(V) = Re(V)$$
$$Re(X) = Re(Z)$$
$$Re(Y) = Re(S) \vee Re(Y)$$
$$Re(Z) = Re(Y) \vee Re(Z)$$

We choose the order S, U, V, X, Y, Z on the nonterminals and obtain the total step function

$$re(s, u, v, x, y, z) = (true, false, v, z, s \lor y, y \lor z)$$

The iteration starts with the value $e = (true,\ false,\ false,\ false,\ false,\ false)$.

$$re(e) = (true,\ false,\ false,\ false,\ true,\ false)$$
$$re^2(e) = (true,\ false,\ false,\ false,\ true,\ true)$$
$$re^3(e) = (true,\ false,\ false,\ true,\ true,\ true)$$
$$re^4(e) = (true,\ false,\ false,\ true,\ true,\ true)$$

The result has the interpretation that U, V are not reachable but all other nonterminals are reachable. Note however that Z is unproductive, and that after elimination of Z and the productions in which Z occurs, X is no longer reachable. If one wishes to obtain a reduced grammar by eliminating unproductive and non-reachable nonterminals, it is advisable to eliminate the unproductive nonterminals first and then the non-reachable nonterminals.   □

We can also express this by defining a new stronger definition of reachability and thus also a new top-down GFA problem. According to this, a nonterminal X in its occurrence (p, i) is only reachable if $p[0]$ is reachable and if all $p[j]$ with $1 \leq j \leq n_p$ and $i \neq j$ are productive. Thus, the resulting top-down problem is based on the previously computed information of the bottom-up problem of the productivity of nonterminals. This is the case for most top-down GFA problems. The system of equations for the new reachability problem is:

$$
\begin{aligned}
Re(S) &= true \\
Re(X) &= \bigvee \left\{ Re(p[0]) \land \bigwedge_{1 \leq j \leq n_p, i \neq j} Pr(p[j]) \mid p[i] = X, \right. \\
&\qquad \left. 1 \leq i \leq n_p \right\} \text{ for all } X \in V_N - \{S\}
\end{aligned}
\qquad (Re)
$$

Instead of iterating via the total step procedure, various single-step procedures can be used to compute the smallest fixed point. In each single-step procedure, only the information for one nonterminal is recomputed at each step. Otherwise, the information is passed on. Thus, it is a sensible strategy only to visit a nonterminal after all its predecessors, that is, nonterminals on its right side, have been visited (since the last pass through this node), and, in the case of recursive nonterminals, to begin with the 'topmost' in this recursion. In addition, a record should be kept of whether information has changed, so that further computations are required. As soon as all nonterminals have been consecutively visited once without the information having been altered, a stable solution, the smallest fixed point, is obtained.

In what follows, we shall summarize the elements that characterize a GFA problem in small boxes of the following type:

Bottom-up/top-down GFA problem ⟨Name⟩
S-lattice
Transfer function
Combination function

The productivity problem is described as follows:

Bottom-up GFA problem PRODUCTIVE	
S-lattice	$(\{false, true\}, \{false \sqsubseteq true\}, false, \vee)$
Transfer function	$\wedge$
Combination function	$\vee$

Algorithm: PRODUCTIVE
Input: A context free grammar G
Output: The solution of the system of equations (Pr) for G
Method: Bottom-up-traversal of the grammar starting with the terminal productions. After an initialization phase, the main loop processes the elements of *toprocess* maintaining the following invariant: (a) If $Pr[X] = true$, then X is productive. (b) If $restNT[p] = 0$, then $Pr[p[0]] = true$. (c) $restNT[p]$ is the number of nonterminal occurrences $p[i] = X$ $(i > 0)$ with $Pr[X] = false$ or $X \in toprocess$.

   After termination with $toprocess = \emptyset$ follows $Pr[X] = true$ iff X is productive. (Additionally, the unproductive productions p are characterized by the condition $restNT[p] > 0$.) Linearity of the algorithm can be achieved if the occurrences of the nonterminals are maintained in lists, which are efficiently computable from the grammar.

var Pr: **array**$[V_N]$ **of boolean initially false**;
      $restNT$: **array**$[P]$ **of integer**;
      $toprocess$: **set of** V_N **initially** $\emptyset$;
begin
      for each production p **do**
            (*n_p occurrence on the right side of p not yet recognized as productive *)
            $restNT[p] := n_p$;
            if $restNT[p] = 0$ **then** (* terminal production *)
                  $Pr[p[0]] := $ **true**;
                  $toprocess := toprocess \cup \{p[0]\}$
            fi
      od;
      while $toprocess \neq \emptyset$ **do**
            select $X \in toprocess$;
            for each *occurrence of* $p[i] = X$ $(i > 0)$ **do**
                  $restNT[p] := restNT[p] - 1$;
                  if $restNT[p] = 0$ **then**
                        (* recognized as productive *)
                        if not $Pr[p[0]]$ **then**
                              $Pr[p[0]] := $ **true**;
                              $toprocess := toprocess \cup \{p[0]\}$
                        fi
                  fi
            od;
            $toprocess := toprocess - \{X\}$
      od
end;

Figure 8.7   Algorithm PRODUCTIVE.

8.2.5   A linear procedure

'Productive nonterminals' and 'reachable nonterminals' are among the simplest problems that can reasonably be described as GFA problems. Thus, it is not surprising that there exist much more efficient special procedures for them than the total step procedure and the iteration over the grammar. In fact, a skilful scanning of the grammar, which processes each nonterminal at most once, is sufficient for both problems (Figure 8.7).

What are the special features of the 'productive nonterminal' problem that permit this efficient algorithm?

(1)   Its lattice only has height two, that is, the longest increasing chain has length two. Monotonicity ensures that a $Pr(X)$ set to *true* cannot be set to *false* again. Thus, every $Pr(X)$ set to *true* has attained its final value.

(2)   Why need one not iterate over cycles? If the situation arises in which an element of the cycle is found to be productive, the cycle can be interrupted at this point. If this situation never occurs, all nonterminals in this cycle are unproductive.

8.2.6   *FIRST* and *FOLLOW*

Let us consider the item pushdown automaton K_G for a cfg G with an expansion, an (E) transition. Suppose its current state is $[X \rightarrow \alpha.Y\beta]$. K_G must choose non-deterministically from among the alternatives $Y \rightarrow \alpha_1 \mid \ldots \mid \alpha_n$. It could possibly take this decision deterministically if it knew the set of words produced by the α_i or at least the beginnings of them. If the beginning of the remaining input can be produced by just one of the α_i, for example by α_{i_0}, then the alternative $Y \rightarrow \alpha_{i_0}$ would have to be chosen. If at least one of the α_i can also produce ε, then the set of words (or their beginnings) that can follow Y is of interest.

Thus, when generating parsers for context-free grammars, it is frequently necessary to know the set of prefixes of a certain length of all words for each nonterminal. The parsers generated then base decisions on a comparison of a prefix of the remaining input with the elements of this precomputed set. If a nonterminal can produce ε then a prefix of the remaining input is also 'good' for the decision if it can follow this nonterminal in a sentential form. These two concepts are formalized by the functions $FIRST_k$ and $FOLLOW_k$.

Definition 8.18 (k **prefix**, k **concatenation**)
Suppose V is an alphabet and let $w = a_1 \ldots a_n$, $a_i \in V$ for $(1 \leq i \leq n)$, $n \geq 0$.

$$k : w = \begin{cases} a_1 \ldots a_n & \text{if } n \leq k \\ a_1 \ldots a_k & \text{otherwise} \end{cases} \quad \text{is the } k \text{ \textbf{prefix} of } w$$

$\oplus_k : V^* \times V^* \rightarrow V^{\leq k}$, defined by $u \oplus_k v = k : uv$, is called the k **concatenation**.

We extend this to sets of words.
Let $L_1, L_2 \subseteq V^*$. $L_1 \oplus_k L_2 = \{x \oplus_k y \mid x \in L_1, y \in L_2\}$. We write $V^{\leq k}$

for $\bigcup_{i=0}^{k} V^i$ and $V_{\#}^{\leq k}$ for $V^{\leq k} \cup V^{\leq k-1}\{\#\}$, where $\#$ is a symbol that is not contained in V. □

Definition 8.19 ($FIRST_k$, $FOLLOW_k$)
Suppose $G = (V_N, V_T, P, S)$ is a context-free grammar.
$$FIRST_k : (V_N \cup V_T)^* \to 2^{V_T^{\leq k}} \text{ defined as}$$

$$FIRST_k(\alpha) = \{k : u \mid \alpha \overset{*}{\Longrightarrow} u\}$$

is the set of prefixes of length at most k of terminal words for α.
$$FOLLOW_k : V_N \to 2^{V_{T\#}^{\leq k}} \text{ defined as}$$

$$FOLLOW_k(X) = \{w \mid S \overset{*}{\Longrightarrow} \beta X \gamma \text{ and } w \in FIRST_k(\gamma)\}$$

is the set of terminal words of length less than or equal to k that may follow X directly in a sentential form. $\#$ is an end symbol that does not belong to the sentence, such as the end-of-file symbol, **EOF**.
$FIRST_k$ is easily generalized to sets of words: suppose $L \subseteq (V_N \cup V_T)^*$, then

$$FIRST_k(L) = \bigcup_{\alpha \in L} FIRST_k(\alpha) \qquad \square$$

The following lemma describes some properties of k concatenation and of $FIRST_k$ and $FOLLOW_k$:

Lemma 8.1   *Suppose $L_1, L_2, L_3 \subseteq V^*$ and $k \geq 1$. Then*

(a) $L_1 \oplus_k (L_2 \oplus_k L_3) = (L_1 \oplus_k L_2) \oplus_k L_3$

(b) $L_1 \oplus_k \{\varepsilon\} = \{\varepsilon\} \oplus_k L_1 = FIRST_k(L_1)$

(c) $L_1 \oplus_k L_2 = \emptyset$, *iff* $L_1 = \emptyset$ *or* $L_2 = \emptyset$

(d) $\varepsilon \in L_1 \oplus_k L_2$, *iff* $\varepsilon \in L_1$ *and* $\varepsilon \in L_2$

(e) $FIRST_k(X_1 \ldots X_n) = FIRST_k(X_1) \oplus_k \ldots \oplus_k FIRST_k(X_n)$

The proofs of (b), (c) and (d) are trivial. (a) follows by distinguishing between cases for the length of words $x \in L_1, y \in L_2, z \in L_3$. The proof of (e) uses a number of auxiliary claims, namely:

(1) $X_1 \ldots X_n \overset{*}{\Longrightarrow} u$ iff $\exists u_1, \ldots, u_n : X_1 \overset{*}{\Longrightarrow} u_1, \ldots, X_n \overset{*}{\Longrightarrow} u_n$ and $u = u_1 \ldots u_n$.

(2) $k : u_1 \ldots u_n = u_1 \oplus_k \ldots \oplus_k u_n$. □

The computations of the functions $FIRST_k(X)$ and $FOLLOW_k(X)$ for nonterminals X can again be formulated as GFA problems. $FIRST_k(X)$ consists of the k prefixes of the leaf words of all trees for X and $FOLLOW_k(X)$ of the k prefixes of the second part of the tree words of all upper tree fragments for X, as shown in Figure 8.8.

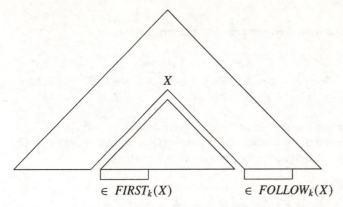

$\in FIRST_k(X)$ $\in FOLLOW_k(X)$

Figure 8.8 $FIRST_k$ and $FOLLOW_k$ in parse trees.

Before we can formulate the $FIRST_k$ grammar flow analysis problem, we must first determine the recursion over the grammar which underlies the definition of $FIRST_k$. All productions for a nonterminal X contribute to the $FIRST_k$ set for X. The combination function is the set theoretic union. In a production $p = (X \to u_0 X_1 u_1 \ldots X_{n_p} u_{n_p})$ for X the terminal words $u_0, u_1, \ldots, u_{n_p}$ and the words from the $FIRST_k$ sets of the nonterminals of the right side have to be concatenated into words of $FIRST_k(X)$. Concatenation proceeds from left to right until the length k is reached.

Figure 8.9 defines the bottom-up GFA problem $FIRST_k$ together with the associated system of equations for a given context-free grammar G. The underlying semi-lattice is $(2^{V_T^{\leq k}}, \subseteq, \emptyset, \cup)$. $V_T^{\leq k}$ is finite, and $\{Fir_p\}_{p \in P}$ is clearly a set of monotonic functions.

Bottom-up GFA problem $FIRST_k$
S-lattice $(2^{V_T^{\leq k}}, \subseteq, \emptyset, \cup)$

Transf. fct. $Fir_p(d_1, \ldots, d_{n_p}) = \{u_0\} \oplus_k d_1 \oplus_k \{u_1\} \oplus_k d_2 \oplus_k \ldots \oplus_k d_{n_p} \oplus_k \{u_{n_p}\},$
        if $p = (X_0 \to u_0 X_1 u_1 X_2 \ldots X_{n_p} u_{n_p})$;
        $Fir_p = k : u$, if $p = (X_0 \to u)$;

Comb. fct. $\cup$

The recursive system of equations for $FIRST_k$ is

$$Fi_k(X) = \cup_{\{p \mid p[0] = X\}} \; Fir_p(Fi_k(p[1]), \ldots Fi_k(p[n_p])) \; \forall X \in V_N \qquad (Fi_k)$$

Figure 8.9   GFA problem $FIRST_k$.

Example 8.19

Suppose G_2 is the context-free grammar with the productions:

$$
\begin{array}{lll}
0: \ S \ \rightarrow \ E & \quad 3: \ E' \ \rightarrow \ +E & \quad 6: \ T' \ \rightarrow \ *T \\
1: \ E \ \rightarrow \ TE' & \quad 4: \ T \ \rightarrow \ FT' & \quad 7: \ F \ \rightarrow \ (E) \\
2: \ E' \ \rightarrow \ \varepsilon & \quad 5: \ T' \ \rightarrow \ \varepsilon & \quad 8: \ F \ \rightarrow \ \mathbf{id}
\end{array}
$$

G_2 generates the same language of arithmetic expressions as G_0 and G_1.

Let $k = 1$, that is, we consider the bottom-up GFA problem $FIRST_1$ for G_2. The transfer functions assigned to the productions 0–8 are then:

$$Fir_0(d) = d$$
$$Fir_1(d_1, d_2) = Fir_4(d_1, d_2) = d_1 \oplus_1 d_2$$
$$Fir_2 = Fir_5 = \{\varepsilon\} \quad Fir_3(d) = \{+\} \quad Fir_6(d) = \{*\} \quad Fir_7(d) = \{(\}$$
$$Fir_8 = \{\mathbf{id}\}$$

An iterative computation of the smallest solution of the $FIRST_1$ problem for this context-free grammar follows. The information $\emptyset$ is initially associated with all nonterminals. $\quad\square$

Example 8.20 (continuation of Example 8.19)

The following three columns describe the computation of Fi_1 for the nonterminals of the grammar. The steps in the computation are listed columnwise. For example, the second entry in the first column says that after the visit to the production nodes 8 and subsequently 7, the Fi_1 set in the nonterminal F receives the symbols $\mathbf{id}$ and $($.

Prod.	Fi_1						
8	$F:$	$\{\mathbf{id}\}$	5	$T': \ \{*, \varepsilon\}$	2	$E': \ \{+, \varepsilon\}$
7	$F:$	$\{\mathbf{id}, (\}$	4	$T: \ \{\mathbf{id}, (\}$	1	$E: \ \{\mathbf{id}, (\}$
6	$T':$	$\{*\}$	3	$E': \ \{+\}$	0	$S: \ \{\mathbf{id}, (\}$

$\quad\square$

Figure 8.10 defines $FOLLOW_k$, the top-down GFA problem for a context-free grammar G, and the associated recursive system of equations. The semi-lattice is similar to that for $FIRST_k$. Let us consider the contribution of the occurrence (p, i) of X to $FOLLOW_k(X)$. After this occurrence of X in the production $p = (X_0 \rightarrow u_0 X_1 u_1 \ldots X_{n_p} u_{n_p})$ is $u_i X_{i+1} \ldots X_{n_p} u_{n_p}$. Thus, we obtain the set of words that can follow this occurrence of X by the concatenation, in the correct order, of the $\{u_i\}, \{u_{i+1}\}, \ldots, \{u_{n_p}\}$ with the previously computed sets $FIRST_k(X_{i+1}), \ldots, FIRST_k(X_{n_p})$, where the resulting words are truncated after the kth symbol. If a word computed in this way is less than k symbols long we append words from $FOLLOW_k(X_0)$. This is how the function $Fol_{p,i}$ works. It is easy to see that $\{Fol_{p,i}\}_{p \in P, 1 \le i \le n_p}$ is a set of monotonic functions.

Top-down GFA problem $FOLLOW_k$	
S-lattice	$(2^{V_{T\#}^{\leq k}}, \subseteq, \emptyset, \cup)$
Transf. fct.	$Fol_{p,i}(d) = \{u_i\} \oplus_k Fi_k(X_{i+1}) \oplus_k \{u_{i+1}\} \oplus_k \cdots$
	$\oplus_k Fi_k(X_{n_p}) \oplus_k \{u_{n_p}\} \oplus_k d$
	if $p = (X_0 \to u_0 X_1 u_1 X_2 \ldots X_{n_p} u_{n_p})$;
Comb. fct.	$\cup$

The recursive system of equations for $FOLLOW_k$ is

$$Fo_k(X) = \bigcup\nolimits_{\{p \mid p[i]=X, 1 \leq i \leq n_p\}} Fol_{p,i}(Fo_k(p[0])) \;\; \forall X \in V_N - \{S\}$$
$$Fo_k(S) = \{\#\}$$

(Fo_k)

Figure 8.10   GFA problem $FOLLOW_k$.

Example 8.21 (continuation of Example 8.19)
We consider the top-down GFA problem $FOLLOW_1$ for the context-free grammar
G_2 of Example 8.19. A transfer function is assigned to each occurrence (p, i) of a
nonterminal X on a right side, that is, $p[i] = X$. We list these:

$$Fol_{0,1}(d) = d$$
$$Fol_{1,1}(d) = Fi_1(E') \oplus_1 d \; = \; \{+, \varepsilon\} \oplus_1 d, \; Fol_{1,2}(d) \; = \; d$$
$$Fol_{3,1}(d) \; = \; d$$
$$Fol_{4,1}(d) \; = \; Fi_1(T') \oplus_1 d \; = \; \{*, \varepsilon\} \oplus_1 d, \; Fol_{4,2}(d) \; = \; d$$
$$Fol_{6,1}(d) \; \doteq \; d$$
$$Fol_{7,1}(d) \; = \; \{)\}$$

To compute Fo_1 for all nonterminals, S is initialized with $\{\#\}$ and all other
nonterminals with $\emptyset$. One possible iteration computes the $FOLLOW_1$ information
in the following order, again read columnwise.

Pos.	Fo_1					
(0, 1)	E :	$\{\#\}$	(4, 1)	F :	$\{*, +, \#\}$	(4, 2) T' : $\{+, \#,)\}$
(1, 2)	E' :	$\{\#\}$	(7, 1)	E :	$\{\#,)\}$	(4, 1) F : $\{*, +, \#,)\}$
(1, 1)	T :	$\{+, \#\}$	(1, 2)	E' :	$\{\#,)\}$	
(4, 2)	T' :	$\{+, \#\}$	(1, 1)	T :	$\{+, \#,)\}$	

□

8.3 Top-down syntax analysis

8.3.1 Introduction

The mode of operation of parsers can intuitively be best understood if one considers how the syntax tree for an input word is constructed. Top-down parsers begin the construction of the syntax tree at the root. The initial situation is shown in Figure 8.11: the first fragment of the syntax tree consists of the root, labelled by the start symbol S of the context-free grammar; the input word w is given, and the input pointer is in front of the first symbol of w.

Now (as described later) we choose an alternative for S for expansion. The symbols of the right side of this alternative are appended below the root in their order. This creates a new fragment of the syntax tree. The choice of a nonterminal (here, always the leftmost), the choice of one of its alternatives and its incorporation in the current syntax tree are repeated. When a production is appended, terminal symbols may occur in the leaf word of the tree fragment. If there are no nonterminals to the left of these, we compare them with the next unconsumed symbols in the input word, and if they agree, we cross them off as confirmed by moving the read pointer forwards.

Thus, the top-down analysis involves a sequence of the following two kinds of activities: 'incorporate production in current tree fragment' and 'check agreement between incorporated and input symbols'.

A sequence of syntax-tree fragments constructed in this way for the arithmetic expression grammar G_2 is shown in Figure 8.12. Note that the sequence of the leaf words is a leftmost derivation for the generated sentence **id** $+$ **id** $*$ **id**. The choice of the alternatives for each nonterminal to be expanded was always taken so as to ensure that the analysis was successful. In the next section, we show that this does not always require a 'higher intuition'.

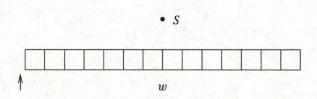

Figure 8.11   Start of a top-down analysis.

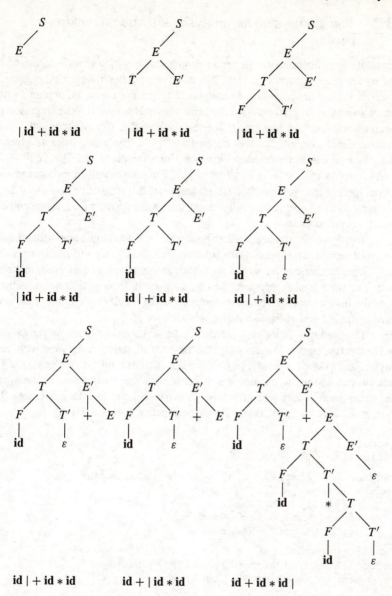

Figure 8.12   Steps in a top-down analysis; the position of the read pointer is shown by the character |.

8.3.2 Top-down syntax analysis with backtracking in Prolog

A possible specification of a parser in Prolog consists of a representation of the context-free grammar and a 'driver', that is, a program that interprets the grammar (however, Prolog has a built-in formalism, the 'definite clause grammars', which permits a notation for grammars similar to our previous notation). When representing grammars, we use the functors t (for terminal) and n (for nonterminal). Some of the terminal symbols have to be enclosed in ''. The input word is given as a list of terminals represented in this way, for example [t(id), t('+'), t(id), t('*'), t(id), t('#')]. The productions of the grammar are given as facts of the Prolog parser, for example rule(n(factor), [t('('), n(expr), t(')')]), that is, the right side of the production is represented as a list of its components.

Top-down parsers are predictive parsers; by expanding a nonterminal using its alternatives the parser predicts the structure it expects for a prefix of the remaining input. These predictions are stored on a stack and removed when a confirmation is found. The stack is also represented as a list. Since in Prolog it is only possible to access the first, that is, the leftmost element of a list efficiently, the top of the stack is now at the left end of the list, unlike the stack for K_G.

The predicate predict(Input, Stack) has as input the (remaining) input list and the current stack content. On the first call, these are the input word to be analysed, and as stack content n(s), where s is the start symbol of the grammar. The predicate has no output, because we dispense with the construction of the syntax tree. Acceptance occurs when the input is exhausted and the stack is empty. The driver, given here by three clauses for the predicate predict, is:

```
% accept
predict([], []).

% expand nonterminal using one of its alternatives
predict(Input, [n(X) | Stack]) :-
        rule(n(X), Rhs),
        append(Rhs, Stack, Newstack),
        predict(Input, Newstack).

% verify terminal
predict([t(A) | Restinput], [t(A) | Stack]) :-
        predict(Restinput, Stack).
```

The parser uses the production rules in the sequence in which they are written. It backtracks if a terminal occurs at the top of the stack but not at the beginning of the remaining input and when all alternatives for a nonterminal have been unsuccessfully tested. A left recursive production may lead to an infinite computation. This Prolog parser can exhibit a non-acceptable run time due to backtracking even if the grammar allows for a very fast syntax analysis (using a procedure from the next section). We shall return later to procedures for top-down syntax analysis in Prolog that operate without backtracking.

Example 8.22   Suppose we are given the above parser driver and the set of productions as facts:

```
rule(n(expr),    [n(term), n(expr1)]).
rule(n(expr1),   []).
rule(n(expr1),   [ t('+'), n(expr)]).
rule(n(term),    [n(factor), n(term1)]).
rule(n(term1),   []).
rule(n(term1),   [t('*'), n(term)]).
rule(n(factor),  [t(id)]).
rule(n(factor),  [t('('), n(expr), t(')')]).
```

The query

```
?- predict([t(id), t('*'), t(id)], [n(expr)]).
```

leads to the following trace:

```
C-Prolog version 1.5


Spy-point placed on predict/2.
Debug mode switched on.
No leashing.
*    (4)  2 Call: predict([t(id),t(*),t(id)],[n(expr)])
*    (9)  3 Call: predict([t(id),t(*),t(id)],[n(term),n(expr1)])
*   (14)  4 Call: predict([t(id),t(*),t(id)],[n(factor),n(term1),
                  n(expr1)])
*   (18)  5 Call: predict([t(id),t(*),t(id)],[t(id),n(term1),
                  n(expr1)])
*   (19)  6 Call: predict([t(*),t(id)],[n(term1),n(expr1)])
*   (22)  7 Call: predict([t(*),t(id)],[n(expr1)])
*   (25)  8 Call: predict([t(*),t(id)],[])
*   (25)  8 Fail: predict([t(*),t(id)],[])
*   (29)  8 Call: predict([t(*),t(id)],[t(+),n(expr)])
*   (29)  8 Fail: predict([t(*),t(id)],[t(+),n(expr)])
*   (22)  7 Back to: predict([t(*),t(id)],[n(expr1)])
*   (22)  7 Fail: predict([t(*),t(id)],[n(expr1)])
*   (33)  7 Call: predict([t(*),t(id)],[t(*),n(term),n(expr1)])
*   (34)  8 Call: predict([t(id)],[n(term),n(expr1)])
*   (39)  9 Call: predict([t(id)],[n(factor),n(term1),n(expr1)])
*   (43) 10 Call: predict([t(id)],[t(id),n(term1),n(expr1)])
*   (44) 11 Call: predict([],[n(term1),n(expr1)])
*   (47) 12 Call: predict([],[n(expr1)])
*   (50) 13 Call: predict([],[])
*   (50) 13 Exit: predict([],[])
*   (47) 12 Exit: predict([],[n(expr1)])
```

further exiting from successful clause applications

```
*   (4) 2 Exit: predict([t(id),t(*),t(id)],[n(expr)])
```

yes

Let us consider the steps this parser takes when analysing **id** $*$ **id**. In steps (4), (9), (14), (18) and (19) it determines the start of a left derivation

$$expr \Rightarrow term\ expr1 \Rightarrow factor\ term1\ expr1 \Rightarrow \text{id}\ term1\ expr1$$

and verifies the agreement of the symbol **id** in the input and in the sentential form produced. In step (22) it uses the first (empty) alternative for *term1* and in step (25) the first (empty) alternative for *expr1*. Thus, it has an empty stack, but the input $*$**id** remains. It then cancels the last choice. These and the following steps can be represented as follows:

$$\textbf{id } term1\ expr1 \overset{(22)}{\Rightarrow} \textbf{id } expr1 \overset{(25)}{\Rightarrow} \textbf{id}$$
$$\overset{(25)}{\Leftarrow}$$
$$\overset{(29)}{\Rightarrow} \textbf{id} + expr$$
$$\overset{(22)}{\Leftarrow} \qquad \overset{(29)}{\Leftarrow}$$
$$\overset{(33)}{\Rightarrow} \textbf{id} * term\ expr1$$

From then on the analysis runs successfully.

8.3.3   LL(k): definition, examples, properties

The item pushdown automaton K_G for a context-free grammar G works in principle like a top-down parser; its (E) transitions predict which alternative should be chosen for the current nonterminal, to derive the input word. The nuisance is that K_G makes this choice non-deterministically. All the non-determinism of K_G lies in the (E) transitions. If the current state is $[X \rightarrow \beta.Y\gamma]$ and Y has the alternatives $Y \rightarrow \alpha_1 \mid \ldots \mid \alpha_n$, then under δ we have the n transitions

$$\delta([X \rightarrow \beta.Y\gamma], \varepsilon) = \{[X \rightarrow \beta.Y\gamma][Y \rightarrow .\alpha_i] \mid 1 \leq i \leq n\}$$

To create a deterministic automaton from K_G, we shall permit a limited lookahead at the remaining input. More precisely, we choose a natural number k and for every (E) transition we let K_G use the first k symbols of the remaining input to help it take its decision. If it is certain that the length of this lookahead k is always sufficient to choose the correct alternative, the resulting grammar G is called an LL(k)-grammar.

Let us look at a corresponding configuration which K_G has reached from an initial configuration:

$$([S' \rightarrow .S], uv) \vdash^*_{K_G} (\rho[X \rightarrow \beta.Y\gamma], v)$$

Assertion (I) of Section 8.2.3 says that $hist(\rho)\beta \overset{*}{\Rightarrow} u$. Suppose $\rho = [\ X_1 \longrightarrow \beta_1.Y_1\gamma_1\ ]\ldots[\ X_n \longrightarrow \beta_n.Y_n\gamma_n\ ]$ is a sequence of items. We define the **future** of

$\rho, fut(\rho)$, as $\gamma_n \dots \gamma_1$. Let $\delta = fut(\rho)$. If the previously found leftmost derivation $S' \xRightarrow[lm]{*} uY\gamma\delta$ can be extended to a derivation of the terminal word uv, that is, $S' \xRightarrow[lm]{*} uY\gamma\delta \xRightarrow[lm]{*} uv$, then in an LL($k$)-grammar the choice of the alternative to use for Y can always be made by considering u, Y and $k : v$.

Definition 8.20 (LL(k)-grammar)
Let $G = (V_N, V_T, P, S)$ be a context-free grammar and k a natural number. G is an **LL(k)-grammar** if for any two leftmost derivations

$$S \xRightarrow[lm]{*} uY\alpha \xRightarrow[lm]{} u\beta\alpha \xRightarrow[lm]{*} ux \text{ and } S \xRightarrow[lm]{*} uY\alpha \xRightarrow[lm]{} u\gamma\alpha \xRightarrow[lm]{*} uy$$

$k : x = k : y$ implies $\beta = \gamma$. □

This definition says that the choice of the alternative for the current nonterminal Y for a fixed left context u is uniquely determined by the first k symbols of the remaining input. Note that the choice does not depend on Y and the next k symbols only, but also, in general, on the prefix u of the input that has already been consumed.

The above definition does not provide a way of testing for the LL(k)-property of a context-free grammar. In what follows, we shall introduce simple tests for the membership of subclasses of LL(k)-grammars, including, in particular, a practical test for the class of strong LL(k)-grammars. In this class, the choice of an alternative for the current nonterminal does not depend on the left-context consumed.

Example 8.23
Let G_1 be the context-free grammar with the productions:

$$STAT \rightarrow \quad \textbf{if id then } STAT \textbf{ else } STAT \textbf{ fi } \mid$$
$$\textbf{while id do } STAT \textbf{ od} \qquad \mid$$
$$\textbf{begin } STAT \textbf{ end} \qquad \mid$$
$$\textbf{id} := \textbf{id}$$

G_1 is an LL(1)-grammar. If $STAT$ occurs as a leftmost nonterminal in a sentential form, the next input symbol determines the alternative to be used. More precisely:

$$STAT \xRightarrow[lm]{*} w\, STAT\alpha \xRightarrow[lm]{} w\,\beta\,\alpha \xRightarrow[lm]{*} w\,x$$
$$STAT \xRightarrow[lm]{*} w\, STAT\alpha \xRightarrow[lm]{} w\,\gamma\,\alpha \xRightarrow[lm]{*} w\,y$$

If $1 : x = 1 : y$, then it follows that $\beta = \gamma$. For example, it follows from $1 : x = 1 : y = \textbf{if}$ that $\beta = \gamma = \textbf{if id then } STAT \textbf{ else } STAT \textbf{ fi}$. □

Definition 8.21 (simple LL(1)-grammar)
Let G be a context-free grammar with no ε productions. If the alternatives for each nonterminal N each begin with a different terminal symbol then G is said to be a **simple LL(1)-grammar**. □

This is a first, easily checkable test criterion for a special case. The grammar G_1 of Example 8.23 is a simple LL(1)-grammar.

Definition 8.22

Suppose G_1 of Example 8.23 is extended by the productions

$$STAT \rightarrow \textbf{id}: STAT \mid \qquad (* \text{ labelled statement } *)$$
$$\textbf{id}\,(\textbf{id}) \qquad (* \text{ procedure call } *)$$

to the grammar G_2. G_2 is no longer LL(1); in particular, it is no longer simple LL(1), since:

$$STAT \underset{lm}{\overset{*}{\Rightarrow}} w\, STAT\alpha \underset{lm}{\Rightarrow} w\, \overbrace{\textbf{id} := \textbf{id}}^{\beta}\, \alpha \underset{lm}{\overset{*}{\Rightarrow}} w\, x$$

$$STAT \underset{lm}{\overset{*}{\Rightarrow}} w\, STAT\alpha \underset{lm}{\Rightarrow} w\, \overbrace{\textbf{id} : STAT}^{\gamma}\, \alpha \underset{lm}{\overset{*}{\Rightarrow}} w\, y$$

$$STAT \underset{lm}{\overset{*}{\Rightarrow}} w\, STAT\alpha \underset{lm}{\Rightarrow} w\, \overbrace{\textbf{id}(\textbf{id})}^{\delta}\, \alpha \underset{lm}{\overset{*}{\Rightarrow}} w\, z$$

and $1 : x = 1 : y = 1 : z =$ '**id**', and β, γ and δ are pairwise distinct. However, G_2 is an LL(2)-grammar, since the following holds for the above three leftmost derivations: $2 : x =$ '**id**' $:=$, $2 : y =$ '**id**' $:$ and $2 : z =$ '**id**'$($ are pairwise distinct and these are the only critical cases.

$\qquad$ We recall that a scanner, as described in the last chapter, always combines the characters of the longest prefix of the remaining input into the next symbol. Thus, if the input contains the assignment operator ':=', it will not deliver the colon as the next symbol. $\qquad\qquad\square$

Example 8.24

Suppose G_3 contains the productions

$$
\begin{array}{lll}
STAT & \rightarrow \textbf{if id then } STAT \textbf{ else } STAT \textbf{ fi} & \mid \\
& \textbf{while id do } STAT \textbf{ od} & \mid \\
& \textbf{begin } STAT \textbf{ end} & \mid \\
& VAR := VAR & \mid \\
& \textbf{id}(IDLIST) & (* \text{ Procedure call } *) \\
VAR & \rightarrow \textbf{id} \mid \textbf{id}\,(IDLIST) & (* \text{ indexed variable } *) \\
IDLIST & \rightarrow \textbf{id} \mid \textbf{id}, IDLIST &
\end{array}
$$

G_3 is not an LL(k)-grammar for any k.

$\qquad$ Assume G_3 is LL(k) for some $k > 0$.

Let $\quad STAT \Rightarrow \beta \underset{lm}{\overset{*}{\Rightarrow}} x$ and $STAT \underset{lm}{\overset{*}{\Rightarrow}} \gamma \underset{lm}{\overset{*}{\Rightarrow}} y$ with

$$x = \textbf{id}\, \underbrace{(\textbf{id}, \textbf{id}, \dots, \textbf{id})}_{\lceil \frac{k}{2} \rceil \text{ times}} := \textbf{id} \text{ and } y = \textbf{id}\, \underbrace{(\textbf{id}, \textbf{id}, \dots, \textbf{id})}_{\lceil \frac{k}{2} \rceil \text{ times}}$$

Then $k : x = k : y$, but $\beta = VAR := VAR \neq \gamma = \textbf{id}\,(IDLIST)$. $\qquad\square$

However, there is an LL(2)-grammar for $L(G_3)$. This is obtained from G_3 by a transformation called factorization. The critical productions are those for the assignment and the procedure call. Since both the dimension of arrays and the number of procedure parameters are unrestricted, an LL(k)-parser cannot check whether a ':=' is present after the closing bracket by means of a k symbol lookahead. Factorizing combines common beginnings of such productions under a new nonterminal. Therefore, the productions

$$STAT \qquad \rightarrow VAR := VAR \mid \textbf{id}(IDLIST)$$

are replaced by

$$
\begin{aligned}
STAT &\rightarrow ASSPROC \mid \textbf{id} := VAR \\
ASSPROC &\rightarrow \textbf{id}(IDLIST)\ APREST \\
APREST &\rightarrow := VAR \mid \varepsilon
\end{aligned}
$$

Now, an LL(2)-parser can decide between the critical alternatives for $STAT$ via the combinations '**id**:=' and '**id**('. If it chooses the nonterminal $ASSPROC$, it processes its beginning up to $APREST$. Since a $STAT$ cannot be followed by a ':=', looking ahead one symbol leads to the correct decision for one of the alternatives of $APREST$. We shall shortly introduce the basis for these arguments in detail.

Example 8.25
Let

$$
\begin{aligned}
G_4 &= (\{S, A, B\}, \{0, 1, a, b\}, P_4, S); \\
P_4 &= \left\{
\begin{array}{ccl}
S &\rightarrow& A \mid B \\
A &\rightarrow& aAb \mid 0 \\
B &\rightarrow& aBbb \mid 1
\end{array}
\right\} \\
L(G_4) &= \{a^n 0 b^n \mid n \geq 0\} \cup \{a^n 1 b^{2n} \mid n \geq 0\}
\end{aligned}
$$

Then G_4 is not LL(k) for any k.
With the notation of Definition 8.20, we choose $u = \alpha = \varepsilon$, $\beta = A$, $\gamma = B$, $x = a^k 0 b^k$, $y = a^k 1 b^{2k}$. We then obtain the two leftmost derivations:

$$
\begin{aligned}
S \xRightarrow[lm]{0} S \xRightarrow[lm]{} A \xRightarrow[lm]{*} a^k 0 b^k \\
S \xRightarrow[lm]{0} S \xRightarrow[lm]{} B \xRightarrow[lm]{*} a^k 1 b^{2k}
\end{aligned}
$$

We have $k : x = k : y$, but $\beta \neq \gamma$. Since k can be arbitrarily chosen, G_4 is not LL(k) for any k. It can also be shown that there is no LL(k)-grammar for $L(G_4)$ for any k. □

Theorem 8.2 *Suppose $G = (V_N, V_T, P, S)$ is a context-free grammar. G is LL(k) if and only if the following condition is satisfied:*
if $A \rightarrow \beta$ and $A \rightarrow \gamma$ are different productions in P then

$$FIRST_k(\beta\alpha) \cap FIRST_k(\gamma\alpha) = \emptyset \quad \text{for all } \alpha \text{ with } S \xRightarrow[lm]{*} wA\alpha$$

Proof:

"⇒" Suppose G is LL(k). Assume there exists $x \in FIRST_k(\beta\alpha) \cap FIRST_k(\gamma\alpha)$. From the definition of $FIRST_k$ and since G is reduced there exist derivations:

$$S \underset{lm}{\overset{*}{\Rightarrow}} wA\alpha \underset{lm}{\Rightarrow} w\beta\alpha \underset{lm}{\overset{*}{\Rightarrow}} wxy$$

$$S \underset{lm}{\overset{*}{\Rightarrow}} wA\alpha \underset{lm}{\Rightarrow} w\gamma\alpha \underset{lm}{\overset{*}{\Rightarrow}} wxz, \text{(if } |x| < k, \text{ then } y = z = \varepsilon)$$

Since $\beta \neq \gamma$ it follows that G is not LL(k).

"⇐" Suppose G is not LL(k). Then there exist two derivations

$$S \underset{lm}{\overset{*}{\Rightarrow}} wA\alpha \underset{lm}{\Rightarrow} w\beta\alpha \underset{lm}{\overset{*}{\Rightarrow}} wx$$

$$S \underset{lm}{\overset{*}{\Rightarrow}} wA\alpha \underset{lm}{\Rightarrow} w\gamma\alpha \underset{lm}{\overset{*}{\Rightarrow}} wy \text{ with } k : x = k : y$$

where $A \to \beta$ and $A \to \gamma$ are different productions. But $k : x = k : y$ lies in $FIRST_k(\beta\alpha) \cap FIRST_k(\gamma\alpha)$. Thus, we have obtained a contradiction. □

Theorem 8.2 states that in an LL(k)-grammar, the application of two different alternatives to a left sentential form always leads to different k-prefixes of the rest of the input.

Theorem 8.2 can be used to derive good criteria for membership of certain subclasses of the LL(k)-grammars. The first relates to the case $k = 1$. For all left sentential forms $wA\alpha$ and every two different alternatives $A \to \beta$ and $A \to \gamma$, the set $FIRST_1(\beta\alpha) \cap FIRST_1(\gamma\alpha)$ can be simplified to $FIRST_1(\beta) \cap FIRST_1(\gamma)$, provided neither β nor γ produces the empty word ε. This is the case if no nonterminal of G is ε productive.

Theorem 8.3 *Suppose G is an ε-free context-free grammar, that is, with no productions of the form $X \to \varepsilon$. Then G is an LL(1)-grammar if and only if for every nonterminal X with the alternatives $X \to \alpha_1 | \ldots | \alpha_n$ the sets $FIRST_1(\alpha_1), \ldots,$ and $FIRST_1(\alpha_n)$ are pairwise disjoint.* □

For practical purposes, it would be too strong a restriction to forbid ε productions. What can we say if in Theorem 8.2 one of the two right sides can produce ε? If both β and γ produce the empty word, G is clearly not LL(k). Let us assume, without loss of generality, that $\beta \overset{*}{\Rightarrow} \varepsilon$. Then the condition of Theorem 8.2 requires:

$$FIRST_1(\alpha) \cap FIRST_1(\gamma) = \emptyset$$

for all left sentential forms $wA\alpha$. This can be equivalently reformulated into

$$\bigcup \{FIRST_1(\alpha) \mid S \underset{lm}{\overset{*}{\Rightarrow}} wA\alpha\} \cap FIRST_1(\gamma) = \emptyset$$

But the first part is equal to $FOLLOW_1(A)$. Thus, we have:

Theorem 8.4   *G is LL(1) if and only if for any two different productions $A \to \beta$ and $A \to \gamma$*

$$FIRST_1(\beta) \oplus_1 FOLLOW_1(A) \cap FIRST_1(\gamma) \oplus_1 FOLLOW_1(A) = \emptyset \quad \square$$

Corollary 8.1   *G is LL(1) if and only if for all alternatives $A \to \alpha_1 | \ldots | \alpha_n$ we have:*

(1)   *$FIRST_1(\alpha_1), \ldots, FIRST_1(\alpha_n)$ are pairwise disjoint; in particular, at most one of the sets contains ε, and*

(2)   *It follows from $\alpha_i \overset{*}{\Longrightarrow} \varepsilon$ that:*

$$FIRST_1(\alpha_j) \cap FOLLOW_1(A) = \emptyset \; for \; 1 \leq j \leq n, \; j \neq i \quad \square$$

Definition 8.23 (strong LL(k)-grammar)
Suppose $G = (V_N, V_T, P, S)$ is a context-free grammar. If for any two distinct productions $A \to \beta$ and $A \to \gamma$ of a nonterminal A we have:

$$FIRST_k(\beta) \oplus_k FOLLOW_k(A) \cap FIRST_k(\gamma) \oplus_k FOLLOW_k(A) = \emptyset$$

then G is called a **strong LL(k)-grammar**. $\quad \square$

Remark:

- There exist context-free grammars that are LL(k)-grammars but not strong LL(k)-grammars, that is, the condition of Theorem 8.4 cannot be generalized from 1 to k, $k > 1$. The reason for this is that $FOLLOW_k(A)$ contains the successor word of **all** left sentential forms with A; in the LL(k) condition only successor words in right sentential form occur.

- Every LL(1)-grammar is strong (Theorem 8.4). $\quad \square$

Example 8.26   Suppose G is the context-free grammar with the productions

$$S \; \to \; aAaa \mid bAba$$
$$A \; \to \; b \mid \varepsilon$$

Then G is LL(2).

Case 1   The derivation begins with $S \Rightarrow aAaa$.

$$FIRST_2(baa) \cap FIRST_2(aa) = \emptyset$$

Case 2   The derivation begins with $S \Rightarrow bAba$.

$$FIRST_2(bba) \cap FIRST_2(ba) = \emptyset$$

Thus G is LL(2) by Theorem 8.2. G is not strong LL(2), because
$FIRST_2(b \, FOLLOW_2(A)) \cap FIRST_2(\varepsilon \, FOLLOW_2(A)) =$
$FIRST_2\{baa, bba\} \cap FIRST_2\{aa, ba\} = \{ba\}$. $\quad \square$

Thus, *FOLLOW* is too simplistic, since it combines the terminal successor words that are possible in **all** sentential forms.

Definition 8.24 (left recursive)

Suppose G is a context-free grammar. A production of G is said to be **directly recursive** if it has the form $A \rightarrow \alpha A \beta$. It is **directly left recursive** if $\alpha = \varepsilon$ and **directly right recursive** if $\beta = \varepsilon$. A nonterminal A is said to be **recursive** if there exists a derivation $A \overset{+}{\Rightarrow} \alpha A \beta$. A is **left recursive** if $\alpha = \varepsilon$ and **right recursive** if $\beta = \varepsilon$. A context-free grammar G is **left recursive** if G contains at least one left recursive nonterminal. $\qquad \square$

Theorem 8.5 *Suppose G is a context-free grammar.*

(a) *If G is left recursive, then G is not LL(k) for all k.*

(b) *If G is an LL(k)-grammar, then G is not ambiguous.*

Proof:

(a): G is left recursive, thus there is at least one left recursive nonterminal X. For simplicity, we assume that X has a directly left recursive production. Suppose $X \rightarrow X\alpha$. Since we have implicitly assumed that G is reduced, there is also another production $X \rightarrow \beta$. If X occurs in a left sentential form, that is, $S \overset{*}{\underset{lm}{\Rightarrow}} wX\gamma$, then the alternative $X \rightarrow X\alpha$ can be applied arbitrarily often.

We obtain $S \overset{*}{\underset{lm}{\Rightarrow}} wX\gamma \overset{n}{\underset{lm}{\Rightarrow}} wX\alpha^n\gamma$. Let us suppose that G is LL(k). Then, by Theorem 8.2 $FIRST_k(X\alpha^{n+1}\gamma) \cap FIRST_k(\beta\alpha^n\gamma) = \emptyset$. Since $X \rightarrow \beta$ we have $FIRST_k(\beta\alpha^{n+1}\gamma) \subseteq FIRST_k(X\alpha^{n+1}\gamma)$. Thus, we also have $FIRST_k(\beta\alpha^{n+1}\gamma) \cap FIRST_k(\beta\alpha^n\gamma) = \emptyset$. If α produces ε, we have an immediate contradiction. If α does not produce ε, we choose $n \geq k$ and again obtain a contradiction. Thus, G is not LL(k). The general case of indirect left recursion is not a great deal harder. We leave this to the reader.

(b): follows from the definition of LL(k). $\qquad \square$

What are the consequences of the fact that a possible LL(k)-parser generator does not accept any left recursive grammars? The user has to transform his grammar so that it is no longer left recursive and the resulting grammar is LL(k). This transformation is always possible and can be carried out automatically, but it has a number of serious disadvantages:

(1) The size of the grammar increases greatly.

(2) The structure of the grammar may be greatly changed.

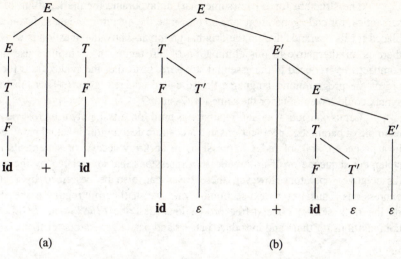

Figure 8.13   Syntax tree for **id** + **id**.

Example 8.27   We consider two versions of the expression grammar.

$$G_0: \quad E \to E + T \mid T \qquad G_1: \quad E \to TE' \qquad T' \to \varepsilon \mid * T$$

$$T \to T * F \mid F \qquad \qquad E' \to \varepsilon \mid + E \quad F \to (E) \mid \mathbf{id}$$

$$F \to (E) \mid \mathbf{id} \qquad \qquad T \to FT'$$

3 nonterminals   5 nonterminals

6 productions   8 productions

The syntax tree for **id** + **id** according to G_0 is shown in Figure 8.13(a), that according to G_1 in Figure 8.13(b).

As can be seen in the example, the tree structure for a subexpression $e_1 \; op \; e_2$ in G_0 is as shown in Figure 8.14(a) and in G_1 as shown in Figure 8.14(b).   □

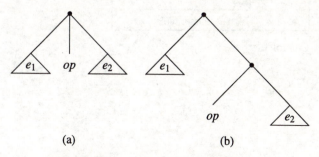

Figure 8.14.   Tree structure for $e_1 \; op \; e_2$.

The structure for G_1 is (somewhat) unfavourable for the handling of the semantics, for code generation, and so on, since the operator *op* is less favourably placed for its operands than in the original grammar. Thus, the question is whether there is an alternative to this elimination of left recursion. Compilers use more compact trees reduced to the essential structure, instead of the syntax trees for the cfg of the programming language, the so-called concrete syntax. This 'abstract' syntax could look similar or the same for G_0 and G_1.

Let us consider what left recursion is used for. It is mainly used for lists, for example of parameter specifications in a procedure declaration or actual parameters in a procedure call, of index expressions in an array access, of statements in a statement sequence or of arithmetic subexpressions that are related by the same (associative) operator. However, these cases can also be described by regular expressions. Thus, in the next section but one, we shall permit regular expressions on the right side of context-free productions, describe $FIRST_1$ and $FOLLOW_1$ computations for them and introduce parsers and parser generators for them.

8.3.4 (Strong) LL(k)-parsers

The structure of a parser for (strong) LL(k)-grammars is shown in Figure 8.15. The prefix w has already been read from the input on the input tape. The remaining

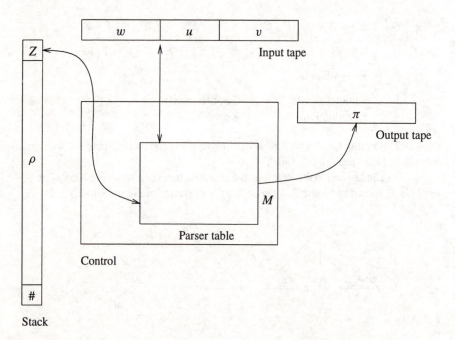

Figure 8.15 LL-parser.

input begins with a prefix u of length k. Above an end-of-stack character # the stack contains a sequence of items of the context-free grammar. The topmost item, the current state Z, determines whether the next action should be to:

- read the next symbol
- test for the end of the analysis
- expand the current nonterminal.

In the last case the parser consults the parser table, to select the correct alternative for the nonterminal with the aid of the next k symbols. The parser table M is a 2-dimensional array, whose rows are indexed by nonterminals and columns by words of length k. It represents a choice function $m : V_N \times V_T^{\leq k}{}_\# \to P \cup \{error\}$. Let $[X \to \beta.Y\gamma]$ be the topmost stack item and u the prefix of length k of the remaining input. $m(Y, u) = Y \to \alpha$ implies that $[Y \to .\alpha]$ becomes the new topmost stack item and $(Y \to \alpha)$ is written to the output tape. $m(Y, u) = error$ means that in this situation the current nonterminal and the prefix of the remaining input do not go together. A syntax error has occurred. Thus, an error diagnosis and handling routine is started, which should allow the analysis to be continued. These procedures are described in Section 8.3.6, 'Error handling in LL(k)-parsers'.

   We shall now restrict ourselves to the practically relevant case, $k = 1$. An **LL(1)-parser generator** expects a context-free grammar G as input. It computes $FIRST_1$ and $FOLLOW_1$ sets for the nonterminals of G and uses them to carry out the LL(1) test in accordance with Theorem 8.4. If the outcome of the test is positive, that is, G is an LL(1)-grammar, the parser table is generated using the algorithm which now follows. If the parser generator rejects G, that is, G is not an LL(1)-grammar, the user must try to obtain an LL1(1)-grammar for the same language by transforming G, for example by factorizing.

Algorithm LL(1)-GEN
Input: LL(1) grammar G, $FIRST_1$ and $FOLLOW_1$ for G.
Output: parser table M for LL(1) parser for G.
Method: M is constructed as follows:
For all $X \to \alpha \in P$ and for all terminal symbols $a \in FIRST_1(\alpha)$
set $M[X, a]$ to $(X \to \alpha)$. If $eps(\alpha) = true$, then set $M[X, b]$ to $(X \to \alpha)$ for all $b \in FOLLOW_1(X)$. All other entries of M are set to *error*.

A possible alternative to the LL(1) test according to Theorem 8.4 is provided by the LL(1)-GEN algorithm: if a component $M[X, a]$ receives two different entries while M is being filled, the grammar is not LL(1).

Example 8.28 Table 8.3 shows the LL(1)-parser table for the grammar of Example 8.19; Table 8.4 shows a run of the associated parser for the input **id** $*$ **id**#.

□

Table 8.3   LL(1)-parser table for the grammar of Example 8.19.

	(	)	+	*	id	#
E	$(E \to TE')$	error	error	error	$(E \to TE')$	error
E'	error	$(E' \to \varepsilon)$	$(E' \to +E)$	error	error	$(E' \to \varepsilon)$
T	$(T \to FT')$	error	error	error	$(T \to FT')$	error
T'	error	$(T' \to \varepsilon)$	$(T' \to \varepsilon)$	$(T' \to *T')$	error	$(T' \to \varepsilon)$
F	$(F \to (E))$	error	error	error	$(F \to \mathbf{id})$	error
S	$(S \to E)$	error	error	error	$(S \to E)$	error

Table 8.4   Parser run for the input **id** $*$ **id**#.

Stack contents	Input
$\#[S \to .E]$	**id** $*$ **id**#
$\#[S \to .E][E \to .TE']$	**id** $*$ **id**#
$\#[S \to .E][E \to .TE'][T \to .FT']$	**id** $*$ **id**#
$\#[S \to .E][E \to .TE'][T \to .FT'][F \to .\mathbf{id}]$	**id** $*$ **id**#
$\#[S \to .E][E \to .TE'][T \to .FT'][F \to \mathbf{id}.]$	$*$**id**#
$\#[S \to .E][E \to .TE'][T \to F.T']$	$*$**id**#
$\#[S \to .E][E \to .TE'][T \to F.T'][T' \to . * T]$	$*$**id**#
$\#[S \to .E][E \to .TE'][T \to F.T'][T' \to *.T]$	**id**#
$\#[S \to .E][E \to .TE'][T \to F.T'][T' \to *.T][T \to .FT']$	**id**#
$\#[S \to .E][E \to .TE'][T \to F.T'][T' \to *.T][T \to .FT'][F \to .\mathbf{id}]$	**id**#
$\#[S \to .E][E \to .TE'][T \to F.T'][T' \to *.T][T \to .FT'][F \to \mathbf{id}.]$	#
$\#[S \to .E][E \to .TE'][T \to F.T'][T' \to *.T][T \to F.T']$	#
$\#[S \to .E][E \to .TE'][T \to F.T'][T' \to *.T][T \to F.T'][T' \to \varepsilon.]$	#
$\#[S \to .E][E \to .TE'][T \to F.T'][T' \to *.T][T \to FT'.]$	#
$\#[S \to .E][E \to .TE'][T \to F.T'][T' \to *T.]$	#
$\#[S \to .E][E \to .TE'][T \to FT'.]$	#
$\#[S \to .E][E \to T.E']$	#
$\#[S \to .E][E \to T.E'][E' \to \varepsilon.]$	#
$\#[S \to .E][E \to TE'.]$	#
$\#[S \to E.]$	#
$\#$	#

Output

$(S \to E)\,(E \to TE')\,(T \to FT')\,(F \to \mathbf{id})\,(T' \to *T)\,(T \to FT')\,(F \to \mathbf{id})$
$(T' \to \varepsilon)\,(E' \to \varepsilon)$

LL(1)-parsers in Prolog

The top-down parser of Section 8.3.2, written in Prolog, is made deterministic using calculated $FIRST_1$ and $FOLLOW_1$ sets. The parser table is represented in the form of a set of facts. An entry $M[X, a] = (X \to \alpha)$ is represented by the fact $parstab(t(a), n(x), <\text{List of elements of } \alpha >)$. The parser driver is modified to:

```
predict([],[]).
predict( [ t(A) | Input], [n(X) | Stack]) :-
   parstab(t(A),n(X), Rhs),
   append( Rhs, Stack, Newstack),
   predict( [t(A) | Input], Newstack).
predict( [ t(A) | Restinput], [t(A) | Stack] ) :-
   predict( Restinput, Stack).
```

Example 8.29
The $FIRST_1$ and the $FOLLOW_1$ sets for the grammar in Example 8.19 were calculated in Examples 8.20 and 8.21. Thus, we can exhibit the parser table for this grammar as a sequence of Prolog facts:

```
parstab( t(id),    n(s),     [n(expr),t('#')]).
parstab( t('('),   n(s),     [n(expr),t('#')]).
parstab( t(id),    n(expr),  [n(term), n(expr1)]).
parstab( t('('),   n(expr),  [n(term), n(expr1)]).
parstab( t('+'),   n(expr1), [t('+'), n(expr)]).
parstab( t(')'),   n(expr1), []).
parstab( t('#'),   n(expr1), []).
parstab( t(id),    n(term),  [n(factor), n(term1)]).
parstab( t('('),   n(term),  [n(factor), n(term1)]).
parstab( t('*'),   n(term1), [t('*'), n(term)]).
parstab( t('+'),   n(term1), []).
parstab( t('#'),   n(term1), []).
parstab( t(')'),   n(term1), []).
parstab( t('('),   n(factor),[t('('), n(expr), t(')')]).
parstab( t(id),    n(factor),[t(id)]).
```

Now the query

```
?- predict([t(id), t('*'), t(id), t(#)], [n(s)]).
```

gives the trace:

```
C-Prolog version 1.5

Spy-point placed on predict/2.
```

```
Debug mode switched on.
No leashing.
*   (4)   2 Call:  predict([t(id),t(*),t(id),t(#)],[n(s)])
*   (9)   3 Call:  predict([t(id),t(*),t(id),t(#)],[n(expr),
                     t(#)])
*   (14)  4 Call:  predict([t(id),t(*),t(id),t(#)],[n(term),
                     n(expr1),  t(#)])
*   (19)  5 Call:  predict([t(id),t(*),t(id),t(#)],[n(factor),
                     n(term1),n(expr1),t(#)])
*   (23)  6 Call:  predict([t(id),t(*),t(id),t(#)],[t(id),
                     n(term1),  n(expr1),t(#)])
*   (24)  7 Call:  predict([t(*),t(id),t(#)],[n(term1),n(expr1),
                     t(#)])
*   (29)  8 Call:  predict([t(*),t(id),t(#)],[t(*),n(term),
                     n(expr1),  t(#)])
*   (30)  9 Call:  predict([t(id),t(#)],[n(term),n(expr1),
                     t(#)])
*   (35) 10 Call:  predict([t(id),t(#)],[n(factor),n(term1),
                     n(expr1),  t(#)])
*   (39) 11 Call:  predict([t(id),t(#)],[t(id),n(term1),n(expr1),
                     t(#)])
*   (40) 12 Call:  predict([t(#)],[n(term1),n(expr1),t(#)])
*   (43) 13 Call:  predict([t(#)],[n(expr1),t(#)])
*   (46) 14 Call:  predict([t(#)],[t(#)])
*   (47) 15 Call:  predict([],[])
*   (47) 15 Exit:  predict([],[])
*   (46) 14 Exit:  predict([t(#)],[t(#)])
*   (43) 13 Exit:  predict([t(#)],[n(expr1),t(#)])
```

other successful applications are exited

```
*   (4)  2 Exit: predict([t(id),t(*),t(id),t(#)],[n(s)])
```

yes

The crucial difference from the backtracking parser in Section 8.3.1 can be seen in step (29). Here, the parser uses the information from the table *parstab* to choose the correct alternative *term1* → *∗term* for *term1*.

8.3.5   LL-parser for regular right part context-free grammars

Left recursive nonterminals destroy the LL-property of context-free grammars. We shall now permit regular expressions on the right sides of productions, so that we have a replacement for the left recursion in lists. These are the most frequent uses of left recursion in the description of programming languages.

Definition 8.3.5 (regular right part grammar)
A **regular right part grammar** (rrpg) is a tuple $G = (V_N, V_T, p, S)$, where V_N, V_T and S are defined as usual, and $p : V_N \rightarrow RE$ is a mapping of the nonterminals into the set RE of the regular expressions over $V_N \cup V_T$. □

It is possible to view p as a mapping, since different alternatives for a nonterminal can be brought together in a regular expression using the alternative operator.

Example 8.30
$G_e = (\{S, E, T, F\}, \{\mathbf{id}, (,), +, -, *, /\}, p, S)$, is a regular right part grammar for arithmetic expressions where p is the following mapping ('{' and '}' are used as meta-characters to avoid the conflict with the terminal symbols '(' and ')'):

$$S \rightarrow E$$
$$E \rightarrow T\{\{+\,|-\}\,T\}^*$$
$$T \rightarrow F\{\{*\,|/\}\,F\}^*$$
$$F \rightarrow (E)\,|\,\mathbf{id}$$

□

Definition 8.26 (regular derivation)
Suppose G is an rrpg. The relation $\underset{R,lm}{\Longrightarrow}$ on RE, 'derives regularly directly leftmost', is defined by:

(a) $w\,X\,\beta$ $\underset{R,lm}{\Longrightarrow}$ $w\,\alpha\,\beta$ with $\alpha = p(X)$

(b) $w\,(r_1\,|\ldots|\,r_n)\,\beta$ $\underset{R,lm}{\Longrightarrow}$ $w\,r_i\,\beta$ for $1 \leq i \leq n$

(c) $w\,(r)^*\,\beta$ $\underset{R,lm}{\Longrightarrow}$ $w\,\beta$

(d) $w\,(r)^*\,\beta$ $\underset{R,lm}{\Longrightarrow}$ $w\,r\,(r)^*\,\beta$

Let $\underset{R,lm}{\overset{*}{\Longrightarrow}}$ be the reflexive, transitive closure of $\underset{R,lm}{\Longrightarrow}$. The language defined by G is then $L(G) = \{w \in V_T^* \mid S \underset{R,lm}{\overset{*}{\Longrightarrow}} w\}$. □

Example 8.31
A regular left derivation for the word $\mathbf{id} + \mathbf{id} * \mathbf{id}$ of the grammar G_e of Example 8.30 is:

$$S \underset{R,lm}{\Longrightarrow} E \underset{R,lm}{\Longrightarrow} T\{\{+|-\}T\}^*$$
$$\underset{R,lm}{\Longrightarrow} F\{\{*|/\}F\}^*\{\{+|-\}T\}^*$$
$$\underset{R,lm}{\Longrightarrow} \{(E)|\mathbf{id}\}\{\{*|/\}F\}^*\{\{+|-\}T\}^*$$

$$\underset{R,lm}{\Longrightarrow} \quad \mathbf{id}\{\{*|/\}F\}^*\{\{+|-\}T\}^*$$

$$\underset{R,lm}{\Longrightarrow} \quad \mathbf{id}\{\{+|-\}T\}^*$$

$$\underset{R,lm}{\Longrightarrow} \quad \mathbf{id}\{+|-\}T\{\{+|-\}T\}^*$$

$$\underset{R,lm}{\Longrightarrow} \quad \mathbf{id}+T\{\{+|-\}T\}^*$$

$$\underset{R,lm}{\Longrightarrow} \quad \mathbf{id}+F\{\{*|/\}F\}^*\{\{+|-\}T\}^*$$

$$\underset{R,lm}{\Longrightarrow} \quad \{(E)|\mathbf{id}\}\{\{*|/\}F\}^*\{\{+|-\}T\}^*$$

$$\underset{R,lm}{\Longrightarrow} \quad \mathbf{id}+\mathbf{id}\{\{*|/\}F\}^*\{\{+|-\}T\}^*$$

$$\underset{R,lm}{\Longrightarrow} \quad \mathbf{id}+\mathbf{id}\{*|/\}F\{\{*|/\}F\}^*\{\{+|-\}T\}^*$$

$$\underset{R,lm}{\Longrightarrow} \quad \mathbf{id}+\mathbf{id}*F\{\{*|/\}F\}^*\{\{+|-\}T\}^*$$

$$\underset{R,lm}{\Longrightarrow} \quad \{(E)|\mathbf{id}\}\{\{*|/\}F\}^*\{\{+|-\}T\}^*$$

$$\underset{R,lm}{\Longrightarrow} \quad \mathbf{id}+\mathbf{id}*\mathbf{id}\{\{*|/\}F\}^*\{\{+|-\}T\}^*$$

$$\underset{R,lm}{\Longrightarrow} \quad \mathbf{id}+\mathbf{id}*\mathbf{id}\{\{+|-\}T\}^*$$

$$\underset{R,lm}{\Longrightarrow} \quad \mathbf{id}+\mathbf{id}*\mathbf{id}$$

$\square$

Our aim is to develop an RLL parser, that is, a deterministic top-down parser for regular right part grammars. This will produce a regular leftmost derivation for a correct input. It is clear from the above definition that the case of expansion (a) (a nonterminal is replaced by its (only) right side) is now no longer critical. Instead, the cases (b), (c) and (d) must now be made deterministic. Thus, we shall call a parser for an rrpg an RLL(1), if it can select the correct alternative when a regular left sentential form $w(r_1|\ldots|r_n)\beta$ occurs and it can decide to continue or end the iteration when a left sentential form $w(r)^*\beta$ occurs using the next input symbol. We now carry a number of concepts over to the case of rrpgs.

Definition 8.27 (regular subexpression)
r_i is a **direct regular subexpression** of $(r_1|\ldots|r_n)$ and $(r_1 \ldots r_n)$, $1 \le i \le n$; r is a **direct regular subexpression** of $(r)^*$ and of r itself; r_1 is a **regular subexpression** of r_2, if $r_1 = r_2$ or if r_1 is a direct regular subexpression of r_2 or a regular subexpression of a direct regular subexpression of r_2. $\square$

Definition 8.28 (rrpg item)
A tuple $(X, \alpha, \beta, \gamma)$ is an **rrpg item** of an rrpg $G = (V_N, V_T, p, S)$, if $X \in V_N$, $\alpha, \beta, \gamma \in (V_N \cup V_T \cup \{(,), ^*, |, \varepsilon\})^*$, $p(X) = \beta\alpha\gamma$ and α is a regular subexpression of $\beta\alpha\gamma$. This item is written as $[X \to \beta.\alpha\gamma]$. $\square$

The generation of an RLL(1)-parser from an rrpg again uses $FIRST_1$ and $FOLLOW_1$ sets, in this case, of regular subexpressions of right sides of productions.

FIRST$_1$ *and FOLLOW*$_1$ *calculation for regular right part grammars*

The computation of *FIRST*$_1$ for rrpgs is done in two steps. First, the ε-productivity of regular subexpressions is determined. Then, the ε-free first function ε-*ffi* is calculated. The equations for the ε-productivity can be defined over the structure of the regular expressions. In addition, the ε-productivity of right sides carries over to the nonterminal on the left side.

$$
\begin{array}{l}
eps(a) = false, \quad \text{for } a \in V_T \\[4pt]
eps(\varepsilon) = true \\[4pt]
eps(r^*) = true \\[4pt]
eps(X) = eps(r), \text{ if } p(X) = r \text{ for } X \in V_N \\[4pt]
eps((r_1|\ldots|r_n)) = \bigvee_{i=1}^{n} eps(r_i) \\[4pt]
eps((r_1\ldots r_n)) = \bigwedge_{i=1}^{n} eps(r_i)
\end{array}
\qquad (eps)
$$

Example 8.32 (continuation of Example 8.30)
For all nonterminals of G_e we have: $eps(X) = false$ □

If the ε-productivity has been calculated, one can now calculate the ε-free first function. The following equations are obtained for this.

$$
\begin{array}{l}
\varepsilon\text{-}ffi(\varepsilon) = \emptyset \\[4pt]
\varepsilon\text{-}ffi(a) = \{a\} \\[4pt]
\varepsilon\text{-}ffi(r^*) = \varepsilon\text{-}ffi(r) \\[4pt]
\varepsilon\text{-}ffi(X) = \varepsilon\text{-}ffi(r), \text{ if } p(X) = r \\[4pt]
\varepsilon\text{-}ffi((r_1|\ldots|r_n)) = \bigcup_{1 \le i \le n} \varepsilon\text{-}ffi(r_i) \\[4pt]
\varepsilon\text{-}ffi((r_1\ldots r_n)) = \bigcup_{1 \le j \le n} \{\varepsilon\text{-}ffi(r_j) \mid \bigwedge_{1 \le i < j} eps(r_i)\}
\end{array}
\qquad (\varepsilon\text{-}ffi)
$$

Example 8.33 (continuation of Example 8.30)
The ε-*ffi* and thus also the *FIRST*$_1$ sets for the nonterminals of the grammar G_e are
$FIRST_1(S) = FIRST_1(E) = FIRST_1(T) = FIRST_1(F) = \{(, \textbf{id}\}$ □

ε-productivity and ε-free first functions can be defined inductively over the structure of regular expressions. The *FIRST*$_1$ set of a regular expression is independent of its context. This is not so for the *FOLLOW*$_1$ set; two different occurrences of a regular (sub) expression in general have different *FOLLOW*$_1$ sets. For the generation of

RLL(1)-parsers we are interested in the $FOLLOW_1$ sets of occurrences of regular (sub) expressions. A certain occurrence of a regular expression in a right side corresponds to precisely one rrpg item with the period just in front of this regular expression. In the following equations for $FOLLOW_1$, we assume that concatenations and lists of alternatives have brackets around them and no surplus internal brackets.

(1) $FOLLOW_1([S' \rightarrow .S]) = \{\#\}$ The end symbol '#' follows every sentence.

(2) $FOLLOW_1([X \rightarrow \cdots (r_1|\cdots|.r_i|\cdots|r_n) \cdots]) =$
$\qquad FOLLOW_1([X \rightarrow \cdots .(r_1|\cdots|r_i|\cdots|r_n) \cdots])$ for $1 \leq i \leq n$

(3) $FOLLOW_1([X \rightarrow \cdots (\cdots .r_i r_{i+1} \cdots) \cdots]) =$

$$\varepsilon\text{-}ffi(r_{i+1}) \cup \begin{cases} FOLLOW_1([X \rightarrow \cdots (\cdots r_i.r_{i+1} \cdots) \cdots]), \\ \quad \text{if } eps(r_{i+1}) = true \\ \emptyset \quad \text{otherwise} \end{cases}$$

(4) $FOLLOW_1([X \rightarrow \cdots (r_1 \cdots r_{n-1}.r_n) \cdots]) =$ $(FOLLOW_1)$
$\qquad FOLLOW_1([X \rightarrow \cdots .(r_1 \cdots r_{n-1}r_n) \cdots])$

(5) $FOLLOW_1([X \rightarrow \cdots (.r)^* \cdots]) =$
$\qquad \varepsilon\text{-}ffi(r) \cup FOLLOW_1([X \rightarrow \cdots .(r)^* \cdots])$

(6) $FOLLOW_1([X \rightarrow .r]) = \bigcup FOLLOW_1([Y \rightarrow \cdots .X \cdots])$

Example 8.34 (continuation of Example 8.30)   The $FOLLOW_1$ sets for the items for the grammar G_e are:

$$FOLLOW_1([S \rightarrow .E]) = \{\#\}$$
$$FOLLOW_1([E \rightarrow T.\{\{+|-\}T\}^*]) \overset{(4)}{=}$$
$$FOLLOW_1([E \rightarrow .T\{\{+|-\}T\}^*]) \overset{(6)}{=}$$
$$FOLLOW_1([S \rightarrow .E]) \cup FOLLOW_1([F \rightarrow (.E)]) =$$
$$(\{\#\} \cup FOLLOW_1([F \rightarrow (.E)])) \overset{(3)}{=} \{), \#\}$$
$$FOLLOW_1([T \rightarrow F.\{\{*|/\}F\}^*]) = \{+, -,), \#\}$$

$\square$

Definition 7.29 (RLL(1)-grammar)
An rrpg $G = (V_N, V_T, p, S)$ is called an **RLL(1)-grammar**, if for all rrpg items $[X \rightarrow \cdots .(r_1|\cdots|r_n) \cdots]$ we have:

$\qquad FIRST_1(r_i) \oplus_1 FOLLOW_1([X \rightarrow \cdots .(r_1|\cdots|r_n) \cdots]) \cap$
$\qquad FIRST_1(r_j) \oplus_1 FOLLOW_1([X \rightarrow \cdots .(r_1|\cdots|r_n) \cdots]) = \emptyset$ for all $i \neq j$

and for all rrpg items $[X \rightarrow \cdots .(r)^* \cdots]$ we have:

$\qquad FIRST_1(r) \cap FOLLOW_1([X \rightarrow \cdots .(r)^* \cdots]) = \emptyset$ and $eps(r) = false$ $\square$

If the $FIRST_1$ and $FOLLOW_1$ sets for an rrpg have been calculated, and the RLL(1)-property has been shown to be satisfied, then an RLL(1)-parser for the grammar can be generated. There are two quite different representations of the parser. The first comprises a driver which is fixed for all grammars and a table for each individual grammar. The driver indexes the table with the current item and the next input symbol, or, more precisely, with integer codes for these two objects. The component selected in the table either indicates the next item or signals a syntax error. The second possible representation is via a program. The program essentially consists of a set of simultaneously recursive procedures, one for each nonterminal. The procedure for the nonterminal X is responsible for the analysis of words for X. We begin with the table version of RLL(1)-parsers.

RLL(1)-parser for regular right part grammars (table version)

The RLL(1)-parser is a deterministic pushdown automaton. The parser table M represents a mapping $m : It_G \times V_T \rightsquigarrow It_G \cup \{error\}$. The parser table is consulted whenever a decision has to be taken by looking ahead at the remaining input. Thus, M must only contain rows for:

- items, in which an alternative must be chosen, and
- items, in which an iteration must be processed;

that is, the mapping m is defined for items of the form $[X \rightarrow \cdots.(r_1| \cdots |r_n) \cdots]$ and of the form $[X \rightarrow \cdots.(r)^* \cdots]$.

The RLL(1)-parser is started in an initial configuration $(\#[S' \rightarrow .S], w\#)$. The current item, the topmost in the stack, determines whether or not the parser table must be consulted. If the table has to be consulted, then $M[\rho, a]$ (if not equal to *error*) gives the next current item for the current item ρ and the current input symbol a. If $M[\rho, a] = error$, then a syntax error has occurred. The parser finally accepts the input read in the configuration $(\#[S' \rightarrow S.], \#)$.

The remaining transitions are:

$$\delta([X \rightarrow \cdots.a \cdots], a) \qquad = [X \rightarrow \cdots a. \cdots]$$

$$\delta([X \rightarrow \cdots.Y \cdots], \varepsilon) \qquad = [X \rightarrow \cdots.Y \cdots][Y \rightarrow .p(Y)]$$

$$\delta([X \rightarrow \cdots.Y \cdots][Y \rightarrow p(Y).], \varepsilon) = [X \rightarrow \cdots Y. \cdots]$$

In addition, there will be a number of transitions, for example from $[X \rightarrow \cdots(\cdots |r_i.| \cdots) \cdots]$ to $[X \rightarrow \cdots(\cdots |r_i| \cdots). \cdots]$, which do not read symbols, do not expand nonterminals, and do not reduce to nonterminals. These may be executed once and for all at generation time, by modifying the transition function in accordance with the following table:

(1) $[X \rightarrow \cdots(\cdots |r_i.| \cdots) \cdots] \qquad \Rightarrow \qquad$ (2) $[X \rightarrow \cdots(\cdots |r_i| \cdots). \cdots]$

(3) $[X \rightarrow \cdots(r.)^* \cdots] \qquad \qquad \Rightarrow \qquad$ (4) $[X \rightarrow \cdots.(r)^* \cdots]$

(5) $[X \rightarrow \cdots.(r_1 \cdots r_n) \cdots] \qquad \Rightarrow \qquad$ (6) $[X \rightarrow \cdots(.r_1 \cdots r_n) \cdots]$

If a transition δ leads to (1), then it is transferred to item (2). If it leads to (3) then it is transferred to (4) and from (5) directly to (6).

Here now is the algorithm to generate the RLL(1)-parser tables.

Algorithm RLL(1)-GEN

Input: RLL(1)-grammar G, $FIRST_1$ and $FOLLOW_1$ for G.

Output: parser table M for RLL(1)-parser for G.

Method: For all items of the form $[X \rightarrow \cdots.(r_1|\cdots|r_n)\cdots]$ set
$$M([X \rightarrow \cdots.(r_1|\cdots|r_n)\cdots], a) = [X \rightarrow \cdots(\cdots|.r_i|\cdots)\cdots], \text{ for}$$
$a \in FIRST_1(r_i)$ and if in addition $\varepsilon \in FIRST_1(r_i)$, then also for
$a \in FOLLOW_1([X \rightarrow \cdots.(r_1|\cdots|r_n)\cdots])$

For all items of the form $[X \rightarrow \cdots.(r)^* \cdots]$ set
$M([X \rightarrow \cdots.(r)^* \cdots], a) =$

$$\begin{cases} [X \rightarrow \cdots(.r)^* \cdots] & \text{if } a \in FIRST_1(r) \\ [X \rightarrow \cdots(r)^*.\cdots] & \text{if } a \in FOLLOW_1([X \rightarrow \cdots.(r)^* \cdots]) \end{cases}$$

Set all entries which have not been filled to *error*.

Example 8.35 (continuation of Example 8.30)
The parser table for the grammar G_e (for reasons of makeup, rows and columns are interchanged):

	$[E \rightarrow T.\{\{+|-\}T\}^*]$	$[T \rightarrow F.\{\{*|/\}F\}^*]$
+	$[E \rightarrow T\{\{.+|-\}T\}^*]$	$[T \rightarrow F\{\{*|/\}F\}^*.]$
−	$[E \rightarrow T\{\{+|.-\}T\}^*]$	$[T \rightarrow F\{\{*|/\}F\}^*.]$
#	$[E \rightarrow T\{\{+|-\}T\}^*.]$	$[T \rightarrow F\{\{*|/\}F\}^*.]$
)	$[E \rightarrow T\{\{+|-\}T\}^*.]$	$[T \rightarrow F\{\{*|/\}F\}^*.]$
*	*error*	$[T \rightarrow F\{\{.*|/\}F\}^*]$
/	*error*	$[T \rightarrow F\{\{*|./\}F\}^*]$

Note that the presentation of the table has involved a compression. From the item $[E \rightarrow T.\{\{+|-\}T\}^*]$ we transferred directly under + to the item $[E \rightarrow T\{\{.+|-\}T\}^*]$. Analogously for − and for the item $[T \rightarrow F.\{\{*|/\}F\}^*]$ under * and /. Thus, we can spare ourselves all items of the form $[E \rightarrow T\{.\{+|-\}T\}^*]$ or $[T \rightarrow F\{.\{*|/\}F\}^*]$ and a corresponding derivation step for each at compile time.
□

Recursive descent RLL(1)-parser

One popular representation for RLL(1)-parsers is in the form of a program. This representation can be generated automatically from an RLL(1)-grammar and its $FIRST_1$ and $FOLLOW_1$ sets, as we shall soon see, or programmed 'manually'.

The latter is an obvious method of implementing a parser if no parser generator is available.

Suppose we are given an rrpg $G = (V_N, V_T, p, S)$ with $V_N = \{X_0, \ldots, X_n\}$, $S = X_0$, $p = \{X_0 \mapsto \alpha_0, X_1 \mapsto \alpha_1, \ldots, X_n \mapsto \alpha_n\}$. Recursive functions *p_progr* and *progr* of the parser are now used to generate a so-called recursive-descent parser from the rrpg G and the calculated $FIRST_1$ and $FOLLOW_1$ sets. A procedure with name X is generated for each production, that is, for each nonterminal X. The constructors for regular expressions are compiled into constructs such as case, while and repeat statements, tests for the presence of terminal symbols and recursive procedure calls for nonterminals. Here, the $FIRST_1$ and $FOLLOW_1$ sets of occurrences of regular expressions are needed, for example to choose the correct one of several alternatives. Thus, an occurrence of a regular (sub) expression corresponds to precisely one rrpg item. Therefore, the function *progr* is defined recursively over rrpg items of the grammar G. The following function *FiFo* is used in distinguishing between cases for alternatives; $FiFo([X \rightarrow \cdots.\beta\cdots]) = FIRST_1(\beta) \oplus_1 FOLLOW_1([X \rightarrow \cdots.\beta\cdots])$.

program *parser;*
    var *nextsym: symbol;*
    proc *scan;*
        (* reads next input symbol in *nextsym* *)
    proc *error* (*message:* **string**);
        (* issues error message and stops parser run *)
    proc *accept;*
        (* reports end of the analysis, stops parser run *)
    p_progr$(X_0 \rightarrow \alpha_0)$;
    p_progr$(X_1 \rightarrow \alpha_1)$;
        $\vdots$
    p_progr$(X_n \rightarrow \alpha_n)$;
    begin
        scan;
        X_0;
        if *nextsym* = "#"
        then *accept*
        else *error* ("...")
        fi
    end

p_progr$(X \rightarrow \alpha) =$
    proc *X;*
    begin
        progr$([X \rightarrow .\alpha])$
    end;

$progr([X \rightarrow \cdots .(\alpha_1|\alpha_2|\ldots\alpha_{k-1}|\alpha_k)\cdots]) =$

    case *nextsym* **in**

        $FiFo([X \rightarrow \cdots (.\alpha_1|\alpha_2|\cdots\alpha_{k-1}|\alpha_k)\cdots]) :$

            $progr([X \rightarrow \cdots (.\alpha_1|\alpha_2|\cdots\alpha_{k-1}|\alpha_k)\cdots]);$

        $FiFo([X \rightarrow \cdots (\alpha_1|.\alpha_2|\cdots\alpha_{k-1}|\alpha_k)\cdots]) :$

            $progr([X \rightarrow \cdots (\alpha_1|.\alpha_2|\cdots\alpha_{k-1}|\alpha_k)\cdots]);$

      $\vdots$

        $FiFo([X \rightarrow \cdots (\alpha_1|\alpha_2|\cdots.\alpha_{k-1}|\alpha_k)\cdots]) :$

            $progr([X \rightarrow \cdots (\alpha_1|\alpha_2|\cdots.\alpha_{k-1}|\alpha_k)\cdots]);$

    otherwise $progr([X \rightarrow \cdots (\alpha_1|\alpha_2|\cdots\alpha_{k-1}|.\alpha_k)\cdots]);$

    endcase

$progr([X \rightarrow \cdots .(\alpha_1\alpha_2\cdots\alpha_k)\cdots]) =$

    $progr([X \rightarrow \cdots (.\alpha_1\alpha_2\cdots\alpha_k)\cdots]);$

    $progr([X \rightarrow \cdots (\alpha_1.\alpha_2\cdots\alpha_k)\cdots]);$

    $\vdots$

    $progr([X \rightarrow \cdots (\alpha_1\alpha_2\cdots.\alpha_k)\cdots]);$

$progr([X \rightarrow \cdots .(\alpha)^*\cdots]) =$

    while *nextsym* **in** $FIRST_1(\alpha)$ **do**

        $progr([X \rightarrow \cdots .\alpha\cdots])$

    od

$progr([X \rightarrow \cdots .(\alpha)^+\cdots]) =$

    repeat $progr([X \rightarrow \cdots .\alpha\cdots])$

    until *nextsym* **not in** $FIRST_1(\alpha)$

$progr([X \rightarrow \cdots .\varepsilon\cdots]) = ;$

For $a \in V_T$ we have

$progr([X \rightarrow \cdots .a\cdots]) =$

    if *nextsym* $= a$

    then *scan*

    else *error*

    fi

For $Y \in V_N$ we have

$progr([X \rightarrow \cdots .Y\cdots]) = Y$

How does such a parser work? The procedure X for a nonterminal X is responsible for recognizing words for X. When it is called, the first symbol of the word to be recognized has already been read by the integrated scanner/screener, the *scan* procedure. When it finds a word for X and returns it has already read the symbol following this word. In the next section we shall describe a possible modification for error-handling purposes.

    The recursive descent parser for the above extended context-free grammar G is now generated.

Example 8.36 (continuation of Example 8.30)

The following parser is obtained for the extended expression grammar. Here, a standard string representation is used for terminal symbols. However, the remarks on symbols and representations of symbols in Chapter 7 should be noted.

```
program parser;
var nextsym: string;
proc scan; {reads next input symbol in nextsym}
proc error (message: string); {issues error message and stops parser run}
proc accept; {reports successful analysis, stops parser run}
proc S;
    begin E end;
proc E;
    begin
        T;
        while nextsym ∈ {" + "|" − "} do
            case nextsym in
                {" + "} :   if nextsym = " + " then scan else error ("'+' expected") fi;
                otherwise if nextsym = " − " then scan else error ("'−' expected") fi;
            endcase;
            T
        od;
    end;
proc T;
    begin
        F;
        while nextsym ∈ {" * "|"/"} do
            case nextsym in
                {" * "} :   if nextsym = " * " then scan else error ("'*' expected") fi;
                otherwise if nextsym = "/" then scan else error ("'/' expected") fi;
            endcase;
            F
        od;
    end;
proc F;
    begin
            case nextsym in
                {"("} :     E;
                            if nextsym = ")" then scan else error ("')' expected") fi;
                otherwise if nextsym =" id" then scan else error ("id expected") fi;
            endcase;
    end;
begin
    scan; S;
    if nextsym = "#"
    then accept
    else error ("'#' expected")
    fi
end.
```

The schematic generation of this program is inefficient in a number of ways. This can to some extent be avoided by a less naive generation scheme, see Exercise 17.

□

8.3.6 Error handling in LL(k)-parsers

LL(k)-parsers have the valid prefix property; that is, whenever the beginning of an input word is confirmed by an LL(k)-parser there exists at least one continuation to a sentence of the language. Although, in general, parsers only find symptoms of errors and not the errors themselves, the above property suggests that one should not correct the part of the input that has already been read but instead search for another parser configuration from which an analysis of the remaining input is possible by modifying or skipping parts of the remaining input. By skilfully skipping an initial part of the remaining input, the procedure described endeavours to generate another suitable combination from the stack contents and the remaining input.

One obvious approach would be to look for a closing bracket or a separator symbol for the current nonterminal and skip all intermediate input symbols, or, when a characteristic end symbol for a construct is found, to delete entries in the stack until a nonterminal corresponding to this end symbol appears at the top of the stack. In Pascal or similar languages, this might involve searching for:

- a semicolon when analysing a statement;
- a comma or a semicolon when analysing a declaration;
- a **fi** or an **od** (if these symbols exist in the language) when analysing conditional statements or loops;
- an **end** corresponding to an open **begin** in a statement sequence.

However, this so-called **panic mode** has a number of serious disadvantages. The parser might skip long sequences of words without analysing them. If the symbol is missing or does not belong to the current incarnation of the current nonterminal, the parser usually gets out of step.

Thus, the error-handling mechanism described is more subtle. It has two modes, the **parser mode** and the **error mode**. In the parser mode for a nonterminal X it is in the middle of analysing a word for X and has not detected errors since the beginning of this analysis or has (supposedly) completed the handling of an error it detected. It leaves the parser mode for X when a word for X is found. If the parser mode was started in the initial configuration, whence $X = S$, the end of the syntax analysis is now reached, assuming the input is exhausted. However, the parser mode may also have been started recursively in the error mode, in which case it returns there. It enters the error mode when an error occurs. It then skips the next input symbols until it finds an end symbol that matches the actual analysis situation. To avoid skipping large parts of the input without analysis, which was criticized above, it transfers recursively to the parser mode for a nonterminal X when it finds a

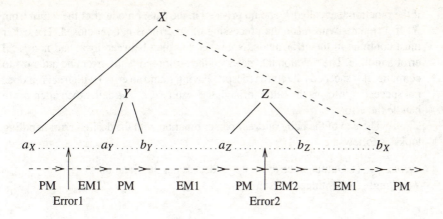

Figure 8.16   Error handling: EM stands for error mode, PM for parser mode.

characteristic start symbol for X. Figure 8.16 shows how it switches between parser and error mode. In the figure a_X, a_Y and a_Z are start symbols and b_X, b_Y and b_Z are end symbols for the nonterminals X, Y and Z.

Switching back from the error mode to the parser mode when a characteristic end symbol is found is called **continuation on a continuation symbol**; recursive switching from the error mode to the parser mode when a characteristic start symbol is found is called **restarting on a restart symbol**.

We shall now introduce two classes of restart symbols and continuation symbols and modify the generation scheme for recursive descent RLL(1)-parsers in stages for these four classes, so that the RLL(1)-parsers generated control the continuation and restarting in the case of errors. Here, the generator uses user input to determine the nonterminals and/or occurrences of nonterminals for which this error handling should take effect.

This generation scheme generates a Boolean function X for a nonterminal X. The function is responsible for recognizing words for X, and for handling errors detected by tests in the body of X. One aim of the modification of the generation scheme is the following.

An error message is only issued in X, that is, subsequent error messages for the same error from different parser procedures should be avoided. The parser functions that called X will be informed if an error that may also affect them is discovered and reported in X. This would mean that the error mode was entered in X and persists after X has been exited. To achieve this aim, the parser procedures are converted into Boolean functions. A parser function X returns with the result *true*, if the function that called X should proceed in the parser mode after the return from X. If X returns with *false*, the processing of an error is not yet closed. The caller must continue in the error mode. Note this interplay between local and non-local error handling. The function that detected the error reports the error and attempts to continue. If it succeeds, it returns (despite having found an error) with *true*; if it does not succeed it informs the caller through the result *false*. The caller then attempts to handle the error.

The end of the body of every parser function with the desired error handling looks as follows:

> *error*:   (∗ Output an error message identifying the situation ∗)
> *handling*:   (∗ Continue or restart ∗)

Continuation on LAST symbols

Let us suppose that the parser is in the middle of analysing a word for a nonterminal X when it encounters an error, that is, a situation where the next input symbol does not match the current state. One obvious way of handling the error would be to report the error and skip the next input symbols until a symbol that can be the last symbol in a word for X is found. In a Pascal statement sequence, one would search for the symbol **end** or, in a parameter list, for the bracket ')', and so on. For this, by analogy with $FIRST_1$, we must define the set valued function $LAST_1$.

Definition 8.30 (*LAST*)
For $w \in V_T^*$ and $k \in \mathbb{N}$ let $w : k$ be the k **suffix** of w. Then let $LAST_k(X) = \{w : k \mid X \underset{R}{\overset{*}{\Longrightarrow}} w\}$ for a nonterminal X.   □

To calculate $LAST_k$ for the rrpgs handled here, we again need to find an inductive definition, that is, a definition over the structure of the regular expressions. This is an easy exercise for the reader.

The implementation of this continuation on *LAST* symbols is easy; the error handling part in the function X is:

> *error:*   (∗ *report error* ∗)
> *handling:*   **while** *nextsym* **not in** $LAST_1(X)$ **do**
>   *scan*
>   **od**;
>   *scan*;
>   **return**(**true**)

After a *LAST* symbol for X is found it is assumed that a successful continuation in the parser mode is possible and that no further error handling by the caller of X is required.

The user of the RLL(1)-parser generator or the author of the input grammar must state the nonterminals for which a continuation via *LAST* symbols should be attempted, namely those that have characteristic *LAST* symbols. Brackets are ideal for this, since they can be uniquely assigned to a nonterminal; for example, **if–fi** bracketing for conditional statements, **do–od** for loop bodies, **begin–end** for statement lists, '(' and ')' for lists of expressions and formal parameter specifications, and so on. Care is required for recursive nonterminals. Here, it may happen that an end bracket is assigned to the wrong incarnation of the nonterminal. Thus, recursive nonterminals should only be designated for continuation on *LAST* symbols if the start of their words can also be recognized.

In what follows, we denote the set of nonterminals for which the author of the grammar *G* desires a continuation on *LAST* symbols by *LAST(G)*.

Non-local continuation on LAST symbols

The kind of error handling outlined above clearly places far too much trust in the presence of the *LAST* symbol for the current nonterminal. There are two problems with this. First, the syntax error itself may consist of the fact that this *LAST* symbol is missing. Second, the current nonterminal might not have a characteristic *LAST* symbol (for example, the nonterminal for an arithmetic expression).

The next improvement also enables parser functions to search for *LAST* symbols 'surrounding' nonterminals; that is, we now consider nonterminals (more precisely, occurrences of nonterminals), which have produced the current nonterminal in the actual left derivation. The associated incarnations of the parser functions are not yet fully processed and will now be included in the error handling, if this is not possible 'locally' in the actual function. For this, every parser function is extended by a parameter of type *set of symbol*. This parameter is used to tell each of its incarnations which *LAST* symbols the surrounding occurrences of nonterminals expect. In the case of error, the parser function stops skipping the input symbols on finding one of the *LAST* symbols. If it is its own *LAST* symbol it returns with the result *true*, otherwise it returns with the result *false*. The callers then test (in the order of the returns) whether the symbol found is a *LAST* symbol for them.

Thus, we have a new generation scheme for RLL(1)-parsers with continuation on *LAST* symbols. A few preparatory remarks on this and the following generation schemes are required. We use two functions *p_progr* and *progr*. *p_progr* is applied to productions and calls *progr*. *progr* is defined inductively over rrpg items. *p_progr*$(X \rightarrow \alpha)$ generates the 'framework' for the function X, that is, the head of the function declaration and one or more variable declarations, and the error handling part. In the text generated, a number of names of variables and labels are defined or declared, which are used in the body part of X generated by *progr*. These are the variables s (and later b) and the labels *err* and *handling*. Thus, the (free) names used in the various cases of the definition of *progr* always refer to the declaration in the function declaration currently generated.

The set-valued function *FiFo* is again used in the generation scheme. We recall that it is defined by:

$$FiFo\left([X \rightarrow \alpha.\beta\gamma]\right) = FIRST_1(\beta) \oplus_1 FOLLOW_1([X \rightarrow \alpha.\beta\gamma])$$

The corresponding sets, like the sets $LAST_1(X)$, which occur in the generated text, are always precomputed, that is, constant sets.

(a) For a nonterminal $X \in LAST(G)$

$p\_progr(X \rightarrow \alpha) =$
 func X (*lasts:* **set of symbol**) **bool***;*
  var $s:$ **set of symbol***;*
  begin
    $s := lasts \cup LAST_1(X);$
    $progr([X \rightarrow .\alpha]);$
    return(true)*;*
 err: *error*(" ... ")*;*
 handling: **while** *nextsym* **not in** s **do** *scan* **od***;*
    if *nextsym* **in** $LAST_1(X)$
    then *scan;* **return(true)**
    else return(false)
    fi*;*
  end

(b) For nonterminal $X \notin LAST(G)$

$p\_progr(X \rightarrow \alpha) =$
 func X (*lasts:* **set of symbol**) **bool***;*
  var $s:$ **set of symbol***;*
  begin
    $s := lasts;$
    $progr([X \rightarrow .\alpha]);$
    return(true*);*
 err: *error*(" ... ")*;*
 handling: **return(false***)*
  end

(c) For $X \in LAST(G)$

$progr'([Y \rightarrow \cdots.X \cdots]) =$
 if *nextsym* **in** $Fi\,Fo([Y \rightarrow \cdots.X \cdots])$
 then
  if not $X(s)$
  then goto *handling*
  fi
 else goto *err*
 fi*;*
 $progr([Y \rightarrow \cdots X. \cdots])$

(d) For $X \notin LAST(G)$

$progr([Y \rightarrow \cdots.X \cdots]) =$
 if not $X(s)$
 then goto *handling*
 fi*;*
 $progr([Y \rightarrow \cdots X. \cdots])$

(e) For $a \in V_T$

$progr([X \rightarrow \cdots.a \cdots]) =$
 if *nextsym* $=$ " a "
 then *scan*
 else goto *err*
 fi

(f) $progr([X \rightarrow \alpha.]) = \varepsilon$

The main program of the RLL(1)-parser is:

program *parser;*
    var *nextsym:* **symbol***;*
    proc *scan;*
        (∗reads next input symbol into *nextsym*∗)
    proc *error (message:* **string***);*
        (∗issues error message; no longer stops the parser run.∗)
    proc *accept;*
        (∗reports end of the analysis; stops the parser run∗)
    $p\_progr(X_0 \to \alpha_0)$;
    $p\_progr(X_1 \to \alpha_1)$;
    $\vdots$
    $p\_progr(X_n \to \alpha_n)$;
    begin
        scan;
        if *nextsym* **in** $FIRST_1(X_0)$ (∗only generated if $X_0 \in LAST(G)$∗)
        then
            if not $X_0(\{ \text{ "#"}\})$
            then goto *handling*
            fi
        else goto *err*
        fi*;*
        if *nextsym* = "#"
        then *accept*
        else goto *err*
        fi*;*
    err: *error(" . . . ");*
    handling: **while** *nextsym* **not in** $\{ \text{ "#" } \}$ **do** *scan* **od**
    end

Continuation on *FOLLOW* symbols

Error handling based solely on continuation on *LAST* symbols is insufficient. Expressions in general have no characteristic end symbols. However, they occur in different contexts, in which they must be followed by symbols that carry a lot of meaning as far as the syntax position is concerned. These include conditions in if statements (followed by **then**), in while loops (followed by **do**), nested, bracketed expressions (followed by ')'), expressions in parameter lists (followed by ',' or ')') and statements in statement sequences (followed by ';', **end**, **fi** or **od**). Thus, we add continuation on successor symbols; here the successor symbols for an occurrence of a nonterminal are the symbols that can follow this occurrence in sentential forms. The author of the grammar again defines those occurrences of nonterminals for which he or she desires continuation on successor symbols. The corresponding set is denoted by *FOLLOW(G)*.

    The generation scheme for RLL(1)-parsers is now changed for the second time to incorporate the continuation on successor symbols. Every parser function

X is given another parameter with which to pass sets of successor symbols for the associated applied occurrence of X. The parser function X for an extended context-free production $X \rightarrow \alpha$ is then generated as follows:

(a) For a nonterminal $X \in LAST(G)$:

$p\_progr(X \rightarrow \alpha) =$

    func X (*lasts, follows:* **set of symbol**) **bool**;

      var *s:* **set of symbol**;

      begin

              $s := lasts \cup LAST_1(X) \cup follows$;

              $progr([X \rightarrow .\alpha])$;

              return(**true**);

    err: *error*(" ... ");

    handling: **while** *nextsym* **not in** *s* **do** *scan* **od**;

              if *nextsym* **in** $LAST_1(X)$

              then *scan;* **return**(**true**)

              fi;

              if *nextsym* **in** *follows*

              then return(**true**)

              fi;

              return(**false**)

    end

(b) For a nonterminal $X \notin LAST(G)$:

$p\_progr(X \rightarrow \alpha) =$

    func X (*lasts, follows:* **set of symbol**) **bool**;

      var *s:* **set of symbol**;

      begin

               $s := lasts \cup follows$;

              $progr([X \rightarrow .\alpha])$;

              return(**true**);

    err: *error*(" ... ");

    handling: **if** *follows* $\neq \emptyset$

              then while *nextsym* **not in** *s* **do** *scan* **od**;

                  if *nextsym* **in** *follows*

                  then return(**true**)

                  fi

              fi;

              return(**false**)

    end

(c) For an occurrence of a nonterminal $X \notin FOLLOW(G)$.

$progr([Y \rightarrow \cdots.X\cdots]) =$

    if *nextsym* **in** $FiFo([Y \rightarrow \cdots.X\cdots])$

    then

        if not $X(s, \emptyset)$

then goto *handling*
    fi
else goto *err*
fi;
$progr([Y \rightarrow \cdots X. \cdots])$

(c′) For an occurrence of $X \in FOLLOW(G)$:
$progr([Y \rightarrow \cdots .X \cdots]) =$
    if *nextsym* **in** $FiFo([Y \rightarrow \cdots .X \cdots])$
    then
        if not $X(s, FOLLOW_1([Y \rightarrow \cdots .X \cdots]))$
        then goto *handling*
        fi
    else goto *error*
    fi;
    $progr([Y \rightarrow \cdots X. \cdots])$

Restart on start symbols

One problem with the solution of the error handling problem we have now obtained is that in a number of situations, when searching for a *LAST* or *FOLLOW* symbol, too much is skipped. Whole statements or even statement sequences may be skipped in a search for the end of a conditional statement or the body of a loop. There is also a particular problem with recursive nonterminals for which continuation on *LAST* symbols is specified. If the corresponding constructs occur nested, the strategy previously developed will always use the first end symbol after the error position for continuation even if it belongs to a deeper nesting. This leads to follow-on errors.

Example 8.37

    ... **while** ... **do** $a := a + 1$ ↑**while** ... **do** ... **od**; ... **od** ...

The error consists of the missing semicolon after the assignment statement. Error handling based only on continuation on *LAST* symbols would take the **od** symbol of the inner loop for the end of the outer loop and thus produce a follow-on error. A continuation on successor symbols would make the same mistake or would use a semicolon from the body of the inner loop as successor symbol for the assignment statement, with essentially the same consequences. This incorrect error handling can be avoided if the beginning of the inner loop is detected and the parser is reset to the parser mode there.   □

We shall now modify the error handling so that, on skipping, a switch to the parser mode for a nonterminal X takes place if a characteristic start symbol for X is found. Here, only nonterminals reachable from the current nonterminal will be taken into consideration. In other words, the error handling only restarts for a start symbol for a nonterminal X, if there exists a possible connection in the syntax tree from the new X node to an **open nonterminal node**. An open nonterminal node is a leaf with a nonterminal label in a fragment of the syntax tree which has already been constructed.

In the above example, the nonterminal *whilestat* would be derivable from the open nonterminal *statement*. Thus, a restart on the start symbol **while** of the nonterminal *whilestat* would be possible and would lead to good error handling.

Here a remark on the nature of the error handling executed by the algorithm described is appropriate. It appears that the error mode solely involves skipping symbols, which would be equivalent to deleting the symbols from the input. However, restarting, which is now added, frequently corresponds to the introduction of one or more symbols, for example, the introduction of a semicolon in the above example.

What requirements must start symbols satisfy if one wishes to restart on them in an error situation?

- They should only occur as first symbols of words for nonterminals.

- If the current nonterminal is X and $Y_1, \ldots, Y_n$ are the nonterminals derivable from X, then every start symbol of X must belong to a unique Y_j $(1 \leq j \leq n)$.

We assume that the author of the grammar has specified a subset $BEG(G)$ of the nonterminals for restarting on start symbols.

In order to formalize the set of start symbols, we need a couple of definitions.

Definition 8.31 (start symbol)   Suppose $G = (V_N, V_T, p, S)$ is an rrpg. Suppose $X \in V_N$ and let $prod(X) = \{Y \mid X \overset{*}{\underset{R}{\Longrightarrow}} \ldots Y \ldots\}$ be the set of nonterminals producible from X and $prod\_b(X) = prod(X) \cap BEG(G)$, the set of those nonterminals for which 'restart on start symbols' is defined. Let

$$BEGSYMBS(X)_Y = FIRST_1(Y) - \bigcup_{Z \in prod\_b(X), Z \neq Y} FIRST_1(Z)$$

be the set of all **start symbols for Y in the context X** and

$$BEGSYMBS(X) = \bigcup_{Y \in prod\_b(X)} BEGSYMBS(X)_Y$$

the set of all **start symbols in the context X**.   □

Thus, the start symbols of Y in the context X form a subset of the set $FIRST_1(Y)$. All symbols that occur in the $FIRST_1$ sets of other nonterminals derivable from X are eliminated. If, somewhat unluckily, the specifier of the grammar G specifies that the nonterminals *STAT* and *IFSTAT* should both be in $BEG(G)$, then **if** ceases to be a start symbol, since it lies in the $FIRST_1$ sets of both nonterminals. Subsequently, the **if** symbol is never used for restarting.

Let X be the current nonterminal. Because of an error, the parser switches to the error mode and starts the error handling. As before, it searches for *LAST* or *FOLLOW* symbols. However, in the next refinement it starts a continuation on every symbol of *BEGSYMBS(X)*. Thus, it transfers recursively to the parser mode, in particular, for the nonterminal $Y \in prod(X)$, for which *nextsym* is in $BEGSYMBS(X)_Y$. According to the construction $BEGSYMBS(X)_Y$ and $BEGSYMBS(X)_Z$ are disjoint for $Y \neq Z$, and *BEGSYMBS(X)* is given by the union of all sets $BEGSYMBS(X)_Y$. Thus, each symbol of *BEGSYMBS(X)* determines the continuation with precisely one nonterminal. This happens via the following program fragment (a macro):

recover(X):

case *nextsym* **in**
    $BEGSYMBS(X)_{Y_1} : Y_1(s, \emptyset, b)$
    $BEGSYMBS(X)_{Y_2} : Y_2(s, \emptyset, b)$
    $\vdots$
    $BEGSYMBS(X)_{Y_n} : Y_n(s, \emptyset, b)$
endcase

when $prod\_b(X) = \{Y_1, \ldots, Y_n\}$. As can be clearly seen, s is again the set of end symbols accumulated by the calls and b is the set of start symbols accumulated. The fact that the context for the chosen nonterminal Y_i is not clear is expressed by the empty set of successor symbols.

    The generation scheme for RLL(1)-parsers incorporating continuation on start symbols now follows. First, we have the statement list of the main program:

```
begin     scan;
          if nextsym in FiFo([S' → .S])
          then
                if not S(∅, {#}, BEGSYMBS(S))
                then goto handling
                fi
          else goto err
          fi;
          if nextsym = "#"
          then accept
          else goto err
          fi;
err:      error(" ... ");
handling: while nextsym ≠ "#" do
                if nextsym in BEGSYMBS(S)
                then recover(S)
                else scan
                fi
          od
end
```

This is followed by the definitions of the functions *p_progr* and *progr* for the productions of the rrpg. They are again defined recursively over rrpg items of the grammar.

(a) For a nonterminal $X \in LAST(G)$:
$p\_progr(X \to \alpha) =$
    func X (*lasts, follows, begins:* **set of symbol) bool***;*
    var *s,b:* **set of symbol***;*
    begin $s := lasts \cup LAST_1(X) \cup follows;$
                $b := begins \cup BEGSYMBS(X);$
                $progr([X \to .\alpha]);$
                return(true)*;*
    err: *error(" ...");*
    handling: **while** *nextsym* **not in** *s* **do**
                  if *nextsym* **in** *b*
                  then **if** *nextsym* **in** $BEGSYMBS(X)$
                        then $recover(X)$
                        else return(false)
                        fi*;*
                  else *scan*
                  fi
              od*;*
              if *nextsym* **in** $LAST_1(X)$ **then** *scan;* **return(true) fi***;*
              if *nextsym* **in** *follows* **then return(true) fi***;*
              return(false)
    end

(b) For a nonterminal $X \notin LAST(G)$:
$p\_progr(X \to \alpha) =$
    func X (*lasts, follows, begins:* **set of symbol) bool***;*
    var *b,s:* **set of symbol***;*
    begin $s := lasts \cup follows;$
                $b := begins;$
                if *follows* $\neq \emptyset$ **then** $b := b \cup BEGSYMBS(X)$ **fi***;*
                $progr([X \to .\alpha]);$
                return(true)*;*
    err: *error(" ... ");*
    handling: **if** *follows* $\neq \emptyset$
                then while *nextsym* **in** *s* **do**
                    if *nextsym* **in** *b*
                    then **if** *nextsym* **in** $BEGSYMBS(X)$
                        then $recover(X)$
                        else return(false)
                        fi
                    else *scan*
                    fi*;*
                od*;*
                if *nextsym* **in** *follows* **then return(true) fi***;*
          fi*;*
              return(false)
    end

(c) For an occurrence of a nonterminal $X \notin FOLLOW(G)$:

$progr([Y \rightarrow \cdots .X \cdots]) =$
   if *nextsym* **in** $FiFo([Y \rightarrow \cdots .X \cdots])$
   then
      if not $X(s, \emptyset, b)$
      then goto *handling*
      fi
   else goto *err*
   fi
   $prog([Y \rightarrow \cdots X. \cdots])$

(c') For an occurrence of $X \in FOLLOW(G)$:

$progr([Y \rightarrow \cdots .X \cdots]) =$
   if *nextsym* **in** $FiFo([Y \rightarrow \cdots .X \cdots])$
   then
      if not $X(s, FOLLOW_1([Y \rightarrow \cdots .X \cdots]), b)$
      then goto *handling*
      fi
   else goto *err*
   fi;
   $progr([Y \rightarrow \cdots X. \cdots])$

Restart on predecessor symbols

In the last section, we extended the error handling so that it restarted in the error mode, that is, switched to the parser mode for a nonterminal Y if a characteristic start symbol for Y was found. However, frequently, nonterminals have no characteristic start symbols that satisfy the requirements described above. In this case, there may exist symbols that always precede a special occurrence of these nonterminals. Such symbols are called **predecessor symbols** for an occurrence of a nonterminal. By analogy with *FOLLOW* we call them *PRECEDE* symbols. For example, the two occurrences of type descriptions in Pascal declarations are preceded once by a colon and once by an equals sign. In the conditional statement the occurrence of the nonterminal statement is preceded once by **then** and once by **else**.

Definition 8.32 (*PRECEDE*)
Let $[X \rightarrow \alpha.\beta\gamma]$ be an rrpg item. Then

$$PRECEDE([X \rightarrow \alpha.\beta\gamma]) = \{a \in V_T \mid S \underset{R,lm}{\overset{*}{\Rightarrow}} wX\delta \underset{R,lm}{\Rightarrow} w\alpha\beta\gamma\delta$$
$$\text{and } a \in LAST_1(w\alpha)\}$$

is the set of all terminal symbols that can precede this occurrence of β in a regular left sentential form.   □

The recursive definition of *PRECEDE* needed for the calculation is constructed in an analogous way to that of $FOLLOW_1$. It is left to the reader as an exercise.

The specifier of the grammar again specifies a set of occurrences of regular subexpressions, that is, rrpg items, for restarting on predecessor symbols. We call this set $PREC(G)$.

The following conditions must be satisfied in the calculation of the restart symbols, that is, the start symbols and the predecessor symbols.

- If the specifications of the grammar mean that a symbol would at the same time be both a start and a predecessor symbol, then this symbol is not chosen as a restart symbol; every restart symbol should uniquely support a restart on a start symbol or on a predecessor symbol.

- Every restart symbol should determine a unique nonterminal, for which the parser mode is recursively entered.

We now determine the sets $BEGS(X)_Y$ and $PRECS(X)_Y$ of start symbols and predecessor symbols for Y in the context X in several steps.

(1) Calculate $B1(X)_Y = \begin{cases} FIRST_1(Y) & , \quad \text{if } Y \in prod\_b(X) \\ \emptyset & , \quad \text{otherwise} \end{cases}$

(2) Calculate $P1(X)_Y = \bigcup_{Z \in prod(X) \cup \{X\}} \{PRECEDE([Z \to \cdots .Y \cdots]) \mid [Z \to \cdots .Y \cdots] \in PREC(G)\}$
    $P1(X)_Y$ contains all predecessor symbols for occurrences of Y in $PREC(G)$, for those nonterminals which are reachable from X.

(3) $B2(X)_Y = B1(X)_Y - \bigcup_Y P1(X)_Y$.
    Eliminate all $FIRST$ symbols that are also $PRECEDE$ symbols.

(4) $P2(X)_Y = P1(X)_Y - \bigcup_Y B1(X)_Y$.
    Eliminate all $PRECEDE$ symbols that are also $FIRST$ symbols.

(5) $BEGS(X)_Y = B2(X)_Y - \bigcup_{Z \neq Y} B2(X)_Z$.
    Eliminate all start symbols occurring more than once.

(6) $PRECS(X)_Y = P2(X)_Y - \bigcup_{Z \neq Y} P2(X)_Z$.
    Eliminate all predecessor symbols occurring more than once.

(7) $BEGSYMBS(X) = \bigcup_Y (BEGS(X)_Y \cup PRECS(X)_Y)$.
    This is the new final definition of the restart symbols in the context X.

The generation scheme for RLL(1)-parsers, now with restarting on start and predecessor symbols, remains unchanged, except for the program fragment (macro) $recover(X)$. This changes to:

recover(X):
case *nextsym* **in**
    $BEGS(X)_{Y_1}$: $Y_1(s, \emptyset, b)$
        $\vdots$
    $BEGS(X)_{Y_n}$: $Y_n(s, \emptyset, b)$
    $PRECS(X)_{Z_1}$:   **begin** *scan;* $Z_1(s, \emptyset, b)$ **end**

$\vdots$

$PRECS(X)_{Z_m}$:   **begin** *scan;* $Z_m(s, \emptyset, b)$ **end**
endcase

This completes the description of the error handling for RLL(1)-parsers. Based on an rrpg G, given the sets $LAST(G), FOLLOW(G), BEG(G)$ and $PREC(G)$, the error handling is generated by a modified RLL(1)-parser generator.

8.4   Bottom-up syntax analysis

8.4.1   Introduction

Parsers of the class discussed in this section also read their input from left to right; before they read another input symbol they carry out all necessary reductions in the part that has already been read and analysed. To construct the syntax tree they begin with the leaf word of the tree, the input word, and construct subtrees of the tree for ever larger pieces of the input. At reductions they append subtrees under the new nonterminal nodes. Finally, they generate and incorporate the node labelled by the start symbol of the grammar as the root node of the whole syntax tree. In the analysis they use a stack, on which two operations are possible:

- storing the next input symbol (shift), and
- locating a right side of a production at the top of the stack and replacing by the nonterminal of the corresponding left side (reduce).

The name **shift–reduce parsers** comes from these two operations. The specification that reduction may only take place at the top of the stack means that such a shift–reduce parser is a right parser, that is, as a result of a successful analysis it delivers a right derivation in reversed order. How can this be made clear?

A shift–reduce parser can never miss a 'necessary' reduction, that is, 'cover it up' by a symbol read into the stack. Here, a reduction is said to be necessary if it must be made to obtain a right derivation up to the start symbol. Once a right side is covered up it will never appear again at the top of the stack, unless one permits the undoing of previously executed reductions and read actions. The covered-up, necessary reduction can no longer be executed. A right side at the top of the stack which must be reduced to obtain a derivation will be called a **handle**.

However, not all occurrences of right sides at the top of the stack are handles. Sometimes, reductions at the top of the stack lead to dead ends, that is, not to a right derivation.

Table 8.5 A successful analysis of the sentence **id** * **id**.

Stack	Input	Remarks
	id * **id**	
id	* **id**	
F	* **id**	
T	* **id**	Reduction of T to E would lead to a dead end
$T*$	**id**	
$T*$ **id**		
$T*F$		Reduction of F to T would lead to a dead end
T		
E		
S		accepted

Example 8.38

Suppose G_0 is again our expression grammar with the productions:

$$
\begin{aligned}
S &\rightarrow E \\
E &\rightarrow E + T \mid T \\
T &\rightarrow T * F \mid F \\
F &\rightarrow (E) \mid \mathbf{id}
\end{aligned}
$$

Table 8.5 shows a successful bottom-up analysis of the sentence **id** * **id** of G_0. The table also shows the other possible reductions in two of the steps; however, these would lead to dead ends, that is, not to right sentential forms.

8.4.2 Bottom-up backtrack parsing with Prolog

As in top-down syntax analysis we shall use Prolog here to carry out a very inefficient kind of bottom-up syntax analysis, bottom-up backtrack parsing. The bottom-up parser in Prolog described below attempts to find a derivation by trial and error. Through the arrangement of the clauses for *parse* it has a preference for reduction, that is, it always reduces as much as possible before it reads. The predicate *parse* has two arguments, the remaining input and the analysis stack. Both are represented by lists. Since the stack operations can only be efficiently realized on the beginnings of lists, we use the mirror image of the stack contents; thus, the topmost stack symbol lies at the beginning of the list. The parser again splits into the parser driver, which is independent of the grammar, that is, the predicate *parse*, and the representation of the production rules, that is, the clauses for the predicate *reduce*. The complete parser for the grammar for arithmetic expressions now follows:

```
% Parser driver

% Accept
parse([$], [n(s) ]).
```

```
% Reduction
parse(Input, Stack) :-  reduce(Stack, Newstack),
                        parse(Input, Newstack).
% Shift
parse([NextSym | Rest], Stack) :- parse(Rest,
                                      [NextSym | Stack]).

% Production rules

reduce( [n(expr) | R], [n(s) | R]).
reduce( [n(term), t('+'), n(expr) | R ], [n(expr) | R]).
reduce( [n(term) | R], [n(expr) | R]).
reduce( [n(factor), t('*'), n(term) | R], [n(term) | R]).
reduce( [n(factor) | R], [n(term) | R]).
reduce( [t(')'), n(expr), t('(') | R], [n(factor) | R]).
reduce( [t(id) | R], [n(factor) | R]).
```

Applied to the query

```
?- parse ([t('('), t(id), t(')'), $], []).
```

it executes the following computation:

```
C-PROLOG version 1.5

| ?- parse([t('('), t(id), t(')'), $], []).
   (1) 1 Call: parse([t((),t(id),t()),$],[])
   (2) 2 Call: reduce([],_65637)
   (2) 2 Fail: reduce([],_65637)
   (1) 1 Back to: parse([t((),t(id),t()),$],[])
   (3) 3 Call: parse([t(id),t()),$],[t(())])
   (4) 4 Call: reduce([t(()],_65645)
   (4) 4 Fail: reduce([t(()],_65645)
   (3) 3 Back to: parse([t(id),t()),$],[t(())])
   (5) 5 Call: parse([t()),$],[t(id),t(())])
   (6) 6 Call: reduce([t(id),t(()],_65653)
   (6) 6 Exit: reduce([t(id),t(()],[n(factor),t(()])
   (7) 6 Call: parse([t()),$],[n(factor),t(())])
   (8) 7 Call: reduce([n(factor),t(()],_65672)
   (8) 7 Exit: reduce([n(factor),t(()],[n(term),t(()])
   (9) 7 Call: parse([t()),$],[n(term),t(())])
  (10) 8 Call: reduce([n(term),t(()],_65691)
  (10) 8 Exit: reduce([n(term),t(()],[n(expr),t(()])
  (11) 8 Call: parse([t()),$],[n(expr),t(())])
  (12) 9 Call: reduce([n(expr),t(()],_65710)
  (12) 9 Exit: reduce([n(expr),t(()],[n(s),t(()])
```

```
(13)  9 Call: parse([t()),$],[n(s),t(())])
(14) 10 Call: reduce([n(s),t(())],_65729)
(14) 10 Fail: reduce([n(s),t(())],_65729)
(13)  9 Back to: parse([t()),$],[n(s),t(())])
(15) 11 Call: parse([$],[t()),n(s),t(())])
(16) 12 Call: reduce([t()),n(s),t(())],_65737)
(16) 12 Fail: reduce([t()),n(s),t(())],_65737)
(15) 11 Back to: parse([$],[t()),n(s),t(())])
(17) 13 Call: parse([],[$,t()),n(s),t(())])
(18) 14 Call: reduce([$,t()),n(s),t(())],_65745)
(18) 14 Fail: reduce([$,t()),n(s),t(())],_65745)
(17) 13 Back to: parse([],[$,t()),n(s),t(())])
(17) 13 Fail: parse([],[$,t()),n(s),t(())])
(15) 11 Fail: parse([$],[t()),n(s),t(())])
(13)  9 Fail: parse([t()),$],[n(s),t(())])
(12)  9 Back to: reduce([n(expr),t(())],_65710)
(12)  9 Fail: reduce([n(expr),t(())],_65710)
(11)  8 Back to: parse([t()),$],[n(expr),t(())])
(19) 15 Call: parse([$],[t()),n(expr),t(())])
(20) 16 Call: reduce([t()),n(expr),t(())],_65718)
(20) 16 Exit: reduce([t()),n(expr),t(())],[n(factor)])
(21) 16 Call: parse([$],[n(factor)])
(22) 17 Call: reduce([n(factor)],_65737)
(22) 17 Exit: reduce([n(factor)],[n(term)])
(23) 17 Call: parse([$],[n(term)])
(24) 18 Call: reduce([n(term)],_65756)
(24) 18 Exit: reduce([n(term)],[n(expr)])
(25) 18 Call: parse([$],[n(expr)])
(26) 19 Call: reduce([n(expr)],_65775)
(26) 19 Exit: reduce([n(expr)],[n(s)])
(27) 19 Call: parse([$],[n(s)])
(27) 19 Exit: parse([$],[n(s)])
```

... other successful exits

```
(3)  3 Exit: parse([t(id),t()),$],[t(())])
(1)  1 Exit: parse([t(()),t(id),t()),$],[])
```

yes

8.4.3   LR(k)-analysers

In this section, we consider the most powerful deterministic bottom-up syntax-analysis procedure, LR(k)-analysis. Here, L denotes the fact that the analysers of this class read their input from left to right, and R denotes that it is a right parser; k indicates the number of symbols in the input that may be looked ahead at in the decision taking.

We begin with the item pushdown automaton K_G for a context-free grammar G, in order to find an LR(k)-analyser for G. In the LL(k) approach, we used the grammar to compute lookahead words for the expansion transitions of K_G, which will permit the choice of a uniquely determined alternative. LR(k)-analysers attempt to avoid such early decisions and to pursue all possibilities in *parallel* for as long as possible. A decision whether to read or reduce and which production to use for reduction, based on looking ahead at k symbols, will only be taken when necessary, that is, when further reading and reduction or reductions using several productions are possible.

After the more didactically motivated derivation of the LR(0)-analyser and a practical method for constructing it given in this section, in Section 8.4.4 we present the so-called LR(k)-parser and its properties. In Section 8.4.5 we introduce canonical and weaker versions of the LR(1)-analysis, which are usually sufficiently powerful for practical purposes. Finally, we explain an error-handling procedure for LR(k)-parsers.

The characteristic finite automaton for the item pushdown automaton

Instead of the tabular representation of the transition relation for K_G (as in Table 8.1), we can also represent K_G by a non-deterministic finite automaton, its characteristic finite automaton. Since this representation should, of course, contain the same information, we must associate stack operations with a number of states and transitions of this NFA.

Definition 8.33 (characteristic finite automaton)
Suppose G is a context-free grammar. The following non-deterministic finite automaton $char(K_G) = (Q_c, V_c, \Delta_c, q_c, F_c)$ is called the **characteristic finite automaton** for K_G if:

- $Q_c = It_G$; its states are the items of the grammar;
- $V_c = V_T \cup V_N$; its input alphabet consists of the nonterminal and terminal symbols;
- $q_c = [S' \rightarrow .S]$; the start state results from the additional production $S' \rightarrow S$;
- $F_c = \{[X \rightarrow \alpha.] | X \rightarrow \alpha \in P\}$; final states are the complete items;
- $\Delta_c = \{([X \rightarrow \alpha.Y\beta], Y, [X \rightarrow \alpha Y.\beta]) | X \rightarrow \alpha Y\beta \in P$ and $Y \in V_N \cup V_T\}$ $\cup \{([X \rightarrow \alpha.Y\beta], \varepsilon, [Y \rightarrow .\gamma]) | X \rightarrow \alpha Y\beta \in P$ and $Y \rightarrow \gamma \in P\}$;
- $char(K_G)$ includes transitions within a production, under both terminals and nonterminals, and transitions that correspond to the expansion transitions of K_G. □

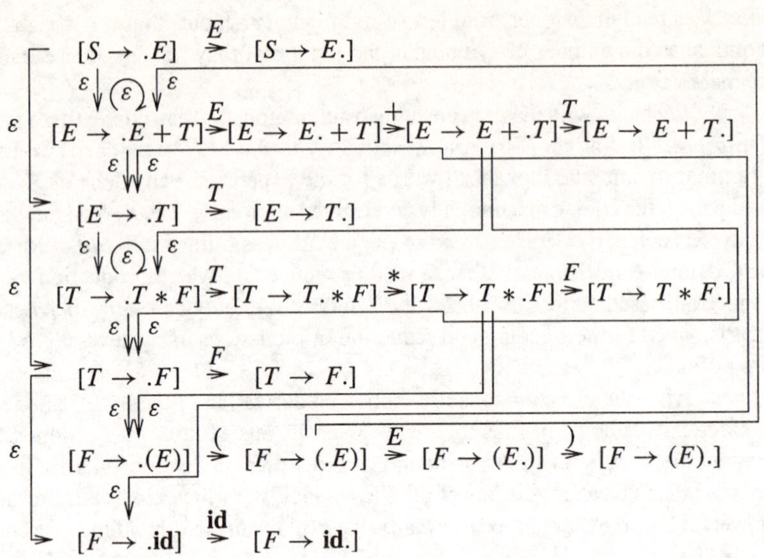

$$[S \rightarrow .E] \xrightarrow{E} [S \rightarrow E.]$$

$$[E \rightarrow .E + T] \xrightarrow{E} [E \rightarrow E. + T] \xrightarrow{+} [E \rightarrow E + .T] \xrightarrow{T} [E \rightarrow E + T.]$$

$$[E \rightarrow .T] \xrightarrow{T} [E \rightarrow T.]$$

$$[T \rightarrow .T * F] \xrightarrow{T} [T \rightarrow T. * F] \xrightarrow{*} [T \rightarrow T * .F] \xrightarrow{F} [T \rightarrow T * F.]$$

$$[T \rightarrow .F] \xrightarrow{F} [T \rightarrow F.]$$

$$[F \rightarrow .(E)] \xrightarrow{(} [F \rightarrow (.E)] \xrightarrow{E} [F \rightarrow (E.)] \xrightarrow{)} [F \rightarrow (E).]$$

$$[F \rightarrow .\mathbf{id}] \xrightarrow{\mathbf{id}} [F \rightarrow \mathbf{id}.]$$

Figure 8.17 The characteristic finite automaton $char(K_{G_0})$ for the grammar G_0.

Example 8.39

Suppose that G_0 is again the grammar for arithmetic expressions with the productions

$$
\begin{aligned}
S &\rightarrow E \\
E &\rightarrow E + T \mid T \\
T &\rightarrow T * F \mid F \\
F &\rightarrow (E) \mid \mathbf{id}
\end{aligned}
$$

The characteristic finite automaton for K_{G_0} is illustrated in Figure 8.17 through its transition diagram. □

How can we describe a pushdown automaton completely by means of a finite automaton? This does not work in general. But it works for K_G because of its particular structure.

With every ε-transition in $char(K_G)$ we associate a push operation in K_G, which pushes the new state of $char(K_G)$ onto the stack of K_G.

The transitions of $char(K_G)$ under terminal symbols correspond precisely to the shift transitions that K_G executes on its current state, that is, its topmost item. If $char(K_G)$ reaches a final state $[X \rightarrow \alpha.]$, this corresponds to the following actions in K_G: K_G removes the $[X \rightarrow \alpha.]$ item from the top of its stack and makes a transition described by Δ_c out of the new topmost item under X. The result is the new state of *char*(K_G) (and of K_G). Thus, we have described how the pushdown automaton K_G works by presenting the finite automaton *char*(K_G). *char*(K_G) is a more compact representation of K_G because it avoids some of the redundancies in the definition of K_G. More detailed inspection shows that because of the construction of K_G all (R) transitions contain redundancies:

- According to the definition of δ, an (R) transition is only possible if the top of the stack has the form $[Y \rightarrow \beta.X\gamma][X \rightarrow \alpha.]$, that is, if the second highest item permits a transition via the left side of the topmost item. However, by construction, that is always the case.

- What happens in an (R) transition? The current state $[X \rightarrow \alpha.]$ is forgotten, and the topmost stack item is installed as the new current state after the period is moved past the X. This is done independently of which special item (with X after the period) is at the top of the stack.

char(K_G) eliminates these two types of redundancy. The characteristic finite automaton for an item pushdown automaton also has other interesting properties. If all its states are considered to be final states it then accepts an extremely interesting language for the LR-analysis.

Definition 8.34 (handle, viable prefix)

Suppose $S \overset{*}{\underset{rm}{\Rightarrow}} \beta X u \underset{rm}{\Rightarrow} \beta \alpha u$ is a rightmost derivation for a context-free grammar G. Then α is called a **handle** for the right sentential form $\beta \alpha u$. Each prefix of $\beta \alpha$ is called a **viable prefix** of G.   □

Example 8.40   In the grammar G_0 we have

Right sentential form	Handle	Viable prefix	Reason
$E + F$	F	E, $E+$, $E + F$	$S \underset{rm}{\Rightarrow} E \underset{rm}{\Rightarrow} E + T \underset{rm}{\Rightarrow} E + F$
$T * \mathbf{id}$	$\mathbf{id}$	T, $T*$, $T * \mathbf{id}$	$S \overset{3}{\underset{rm}{\Rightarrow}} T * F \underset{rm}{\Rightarrow} T * \mathbf{id}$

□

In an unambiguous grammar the handle of a right sentential form is the unique subword which, in a bottom-up analyser, must be replaced in the next reduction step by a nonterminal in order to obtain a rightmost derivation. A viable prefix is a prefix of a right sentential form which does not extend beyond the handle. Thus, in a viable prefix no reductions are possible, except maybe at the end. Apart from this (possible) reduction at the end of the viable prefix, it is thus reduced as far as possible.

Definition 8.35 (valid item)
An item $[X \to \alpha.\beta]$ is said to be **valid** for the viable prefix $\gamma\alpha$ if there exists a rightmost derivation $S \overset{*}{\underset{rm}{\Rightarrow}} \gamma X w \underset{rm}{\Rightarrow} \gamma\alpha\beta w$. □

Definition 8.36
We introduce two viable prefixes of G_0 together with a number of valid items for these. To show that these items are valid according to Definition 8.35, we in each case introduce a right sentential form and the corresponding bindings of the variables of Definition 8.35:

Viable prefix	Valid items	Reason	γ	w	X	α	β
$E+$	$[E \to E + .T]$	$S \underset{rm}{\Rightarrow} E \underset{rm}{\Rightarrow} E + T$	ε	ε	E	$E+$	T
	$[T \to .F]$	$S \overset{*}{\underset{rm}{\Rightarrow}} E + T \underset{rm}{\Rightarrow} E + F$	$E+$	ε	T	ε	F
	$[F \to .id]$	$S \underset{rm}{\Rightarrow} E + F \underset{rm}{\Rightarrow} E + id$	$E+$	ε	F	ε	id
$(E + ($	$[F \to (.E)]$	$S \overset{*}{\underset{rm}{\Rightarrow}} (E + F)$ $\underset{rm}{\Rightarrow} (E + (E))$	$(E+$	$)$	F	$($	$E)$

□

Let us regard an attempt to construct a rightmost derivation for a word. The existing prefix x of the word (as read to date) is reduced to a viable prefix $\gamma\alpha$. Then every valid item for $\gamma\alpha$, $[X \to \alpha.\beta]$, describes a possible interpretation of the analysis situation. Thus, there exists a rightmost derivation in which $\gamma\alpha$ is the prefix of a right sentential form and $X \to \alpha\beta$ is one of the possible productions just being 'processed'. All such productions are candidates for later reductions.

Let us consider the rightmost derivation $S' \overset{*}{\underset{rm}{\Rightarrow}} \gamma X w \underset{rm}{\Rightarrow} \gamma\alpha\beta w$. Since it is to be continued as a rightmost derivation, a number of steps must be carried out to derive a terminal word v from β, followed by a number of steps to derive a terminal word u from α, that is, $S' \overset{*}{\underset{rm}{\Rightarrow}} \gamma X w \underset{rm}{\Rightarrow} \gamma\alpha\beta w \overset{*}{\underset{rm}{\Rightarrow}} \gamma\alpha v w \overset{*}{\underset{rm}{\Rightarrow}} \gamma u v w$. The valid item $[X \to \alpha.\beta]$ for the viable prefix $\gamma\alpha$ describes the situation, in which the reduction from u to α has already taken place, while the reduction from v to β has not yet begun. One possible long-term goal in this situation is the application of the production $X \to \alpha\beta$.

Theorem 8.6 *For every viable prefix γ there is at least one valid item.*

We now return to the question of which languages are accepted by the characteristic finite automaton of K_G. Theorem 8.7 says that under a viable prefix it transfers to a state that is a valid item for this prefix. Final states, which are complete items, are only valid for viable prefixes of maximal length, that is, prefixes with a possible reduction at the end.

Theorem 8.7 *If $\gamma \in (V_T \cup V_N)^*$ and $q \in Q_c$, then $(q_c, \gamma) \vdash^*_{char(K_G)} (q, \varepsilon)$ if and only if γ is a viable prefix and q is a valid item for γ.*

Corollary 8.2 *The language of the viable prefixes of a context-free grammar is regular.*

Proof:
If all the states in $char(K_G)$ are assumed to be final states, we obtain a finite automaton, which, according to Theorem 8.7, accepts the language of the viable prefixes. □

LR-DFA (G)

In Chapter 6, we described a procedure, namely the **NFA** $\rightarrow$ **DFA** algorithm, for generating an equivalent deterministic finite automaton from a non-deterministic finite automaton. This deterministic finite automaton pursues all the paths in parallel through which the non-deterministic automaton could pass for a given input. Its states are sets of states of the non-deterministic automaton. We now apply this so-called subset construction to the characteristic finite automaton $char(K_G)$ of the item pushdown automaton of K_G of a context-free grammar G.

Definition 8.37 (LR-DFA)
The deterministic finite automaton resulting from the application of the algorithm **NFA** $\rightarrow$ **DFA** to $char(K_G)$, $(Q_d, V_N \cup V_T, \delta_d, q_d, F_d)$, is called the **LR-DFA(G)**. □

Example 8.41
The LR-DFA(G_0), where G_0 is the grammar of Example 8.2, is obtained by applying the algorithm **NFA** $\rightarrow$ **DFA** to $char(K_{G_0})$. It is shown in Figure 8.18. □

We shall now list a number of interesting properties of the LR-DFA(G) for a context-free grammar G.

Theorem 8.8 *Suppose that γ is a viable prefix, and that $p(\gamma) \in Q_d$ is the uniquely determined state to which the LR-DFA(G) transfers from the initial state on reading γ, that is, $(q_d, \gamma) \vdash^*_{LR-DFA(G)} (p(\gamma), \varepsilon)$. Then the following assertions hold:*

(a) $p(\varepsilon) = q_d$

(b) $p(\gamma) = \{q \in Q_c \mid (q_c, \gamma) \vdash^*_{char(K_G)} (q, \varepsilon)\}$

(c) $p(\gamma) = \{i \in It_G \mid i \text{ valid for } \gamma\}$

(d) *Suppose Γ is the (in general, infinite) set of all viable prefixes of G. Then the mapping $p : \Gamma \rightarrow Q_d$ defines a finite partition on Γ.*

(e) $L(LR\text{-}DFA(G))$ *is the set of the viable prefixes of G that end with a handle.*

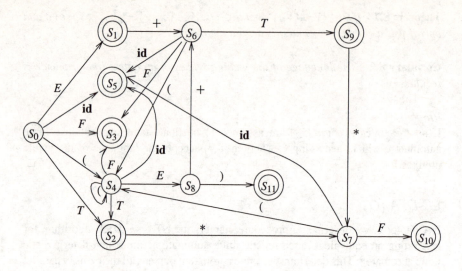

$$
\begin{aligned}
S_0 \;=\;&\{\quad [S \to .E], \\
&\;\;[E \to .E + T], \\
&\;\;[E \to .T], \\
&\;\;[T \to .T * F], \\
&\;\;[T \to .F], \\
&\;\;[F \to .(E)], \\
&\;\;[F \to .\mathbf{id}]\} \\[4pt]
S_1 \;=\;&\{\quad [S \to E.], \\
&\;\;[E \to E. + T]\} \\[8pt]
S_2 \;=\;&\{\quad [E \to T.], \\
&\;\;[T \to T. * F]\} \\[4pt]
S_3 \;=\;&\{\quad [T \to F.]\} \\[4pt]
S_4 \;=\;&\{\quad [F \to (.E)], \\
&\;\;[E \to .E + T], \\
&\;\;[E \to .T], \\
&\;\;[T \to .T * F] \\
&\;\;[T \to .F] \\
&\;\;[F \to .(E)] \\
&\;\;[F \to .\mathbf{id}]\}
\end{aligned}
\qquad
\begin{aligned}
S_5 \;=\;&\{\quad [F \to \mathbf{id}.]\} \\[8pt]
S_6 \;=\;&\{\quad [E \to E + .T], \\
&\;\;[T \to .T * F], \\
&\;\;[T \to .F], \\
&\;\;[F \to .(E)], \\
&\;\;[F \to .\mathbf{id}]\} \\[4pt]
S_7 \;=\;&\{\quad [T \to T * .F], \\
&\;\;[F \to .(E)], \\
&\;\;[F \to .\mathbf{id}]\} \\[8pt]
S_8 \;=\;&\{\quad [F \to (E.)], \\
&\;\;[E \to E. + T]\} \\[4pt]
S_9 \;=\;&\{\quad [E \to E + T.], \\
&\;\;[T \to T. * F]\} \\[4pt]
S_{10} \;=\;&\{\quad [T \to T * F.]\} \\[4pt]
S_{11} \;=\;&\{\quad [F \to (E).]\}
\end{aligned}
$$

Figure 8.18   The LR-DFA(G_0) resulting from $char(K_{G_0})$ in Figure 8.17.

Proof:

(a): This follows from the construction of $q_d = \{q \in Q_c \mid (q_0, \varepsilon) \vdash^*_{char(K_G)} (q, \varepsilon)\}$.

(b): This is a property of the subset construction. It is proved by induction.

(c): This assertion follows from (b) together with Theorem 8.7.

(d): Trivial.

(e): The final states of LR-DFA(G) contain at least one complete item. Every such complete item determines a handle at the end of the prefix. □

We recall what it means for an item to be valid for a viable prefix. Viable prefixes are prefixes of right sentential forms, as they occur during the reduction of an input word. A reduction in them leading to another right sentential form is only possible at the extreme right end. A valid item for such a viable prefix describes one possible view of the actual analysis situation.

Theorem 8.8 says precisely that the states of the LR-DFA(G) are constructed in such a way that they decompose the set of the viable prefixes into finitely many disjoint subsets, and that the state $p(\gamma)$ assigned to a viable prefix γ consists of all valid items for γ, that is, all possible descriptions of the actual analysis situation.

Example 8.42

$\gamma = E + F$ is a viable prefix of G_0. The following viable prefixes are also assigned to the state $p(\gamma) = S_3$:

$$F, \ (F, \ ((F, \ (((F, \ldots$$
$$T * (F, \ T * ((F, \ T * (((F, \ldots$$
$$E + F, \ E + (F, \ E + ((F, \ldots$$

□

Example 8.43

Let us consider the state S_6 in the LR-DFA(G_0). It contains precisely all valid items for the viable prefix $E+$, namely the items $[E \rightarrow E + .T], [T \rightarrow .T * F], [T \rightarrow .F], [F \rightarrow .id], [F \rightarrow .(E)]$.

Now $E+$ is a prefix of the right sentential form $E + T$;

$$S \underset{rm}{\Longrightarrow} E \underset{rm}{\Longrightarrow} \qquad E + T \qquad \underset{rm}{\Longrightarrow} \qquad E + F \qquad \underset{rm}{\Longrightarrow} \qquad E + id$$
$$\uparrow \qquad\qquad\qquad \uparrow \qquad\qquad\qquad \uparrow$$

whence, for example $\quad [E \rightarrow E + .T] \qquad\qquad [T \rightarrow .F] \qquad\qquad [F \rightarrow .id]$

are valid. □

According to Theorem 8.8(a), the LR-DFA(G) for a context-free grammar G accepts, as a deterministic finite automaton, a language of viable prefixes of G. However, we can again interpret it as a description of a pushdown automaton as follows. Let $K_0 = (\Gamma, V_T, \Delta, q_0, \{q_f\})$ be the following pushdown automaton.

Γ, the stack alphabet, is the set Q_d of the states of the LR-DFA(G). Each state consists of a set of context-free items of G.

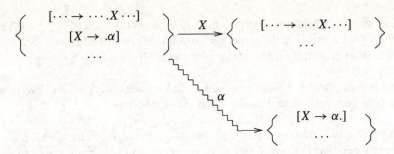

Figure 8.19 Section from the transition diagram of the LR-DFA(G).

$q_0 = q_d$ is the initial state with which the stack of K_0 is initialized.

q_f is the final state of the LR-DFA(G) containing the item $[S' \rightarrow S.]$.

$\Delta \subseteq \Gamma^* \times (V_T \cup \{\varepsilon\}) \times \Gamma^*$ is the transition relation. It is defined by:

(Shift)
$(q, a, q\delta_d(q, a)) \in \Delta$, if $\delta_d(q, a)$ is defined. In this transition the next input symbol a is read and the successor state of q under a is pushed. It is only possible if at least one item of the form $[X \rightarrow \cdots .a \cdots]$ is present in q.

(Reduce)
$(qq_1 \ldots q_n, \varepsilon, q\delta_d(q, X)) \in \Delta$, if $[X \rightarrow \alpha.] \in q_n$, $|\alpha| = n$. The complete item $[X \rightarrow \alpha.]$ in the topmost stack entry indicates a possible reduction. After that, as many entries are removed from the stack as the right side is long. Then the X successor of the new topmost stack entry is pushed onto the stack. Figure 8.19 shows a section from the transition diagram for the LR-DFA(G), which reflects this situation. Entries at the top of the stack correspond to the α path in the transition diagram. These entries are removed by the reduction. The underlying new topmost state has a transition under X which is now taken.

The special case $[X \rightarrow \varepsilon.]$ merits attention. According to the above representation a reduction would remove $|\varepsilon| = 0$ topmost stack entries, and a transition would be made from the new (and old) current state under X. This is precisely the case; for every item $[\cdots \rightarrow \cdots .X \cdots]$ the complete item $[X \rightarrow \varepsilon.]$ is in the same state. A transition under X is possible from this state.

The stack content, that is, the sequence of the stacked states of the LR-DFA(G), uniquely determines an associated viable prefix; for, by the construction of the LR-DFA(G), each of its states has precisely one 'entry symbol', that is, a symbol under which all transitions in it take place. Thus, for a stack content $q_0, \ldots, q_n$ with $q_0 = q_d$ a unique word $\alpha = X_1 \ldots X_n \in (V_N \cup V_T)^*$ can be read, such that $\delta_d(q_i, X_{i+1}) = q_{i+1}$. α is a viable prefix and q_n is the state assigned to α, which contains all valid items for α.

When is the pushdown automaton K_0 described above non-deterministic? Clearly if a state q has

- both a shift transition under a symbol $a \in V_T$ and a reduced transition (**shift–reduce conflict**), or
- two different reduce transitions (for two different productions) (**reduce–reduce conflict**).

In the first case, there is at least one shift item $[X \rightarrow \alpha.a\beta]$ and at least one complete item $[Y \rightarrow \gamma.]$ in q, while in the second case there are at least two different complete items $[Y \rightarrow \alpha.]$ and $[Z \rightarrow \beta.]$ in q.

Definition 8.38 (inadequate states)
Let $(Q_d, V_N \cup V_T, \Delta, q_d, \{q_f\})$ be the LR-DFA(G) for a context-free grammar G. A state $q \in Q_d$ is said to be **inadequate** if it contains a shift–reduce or a reduce–reduce conflict.   □

Thus, an inadequate state either contains only incomplete items or consists of just one complete item.

Thus, inadequate states make an LR-DFA(G) non-deterministic. In what follows, we shall develop parsers that determine the action to be chosen in inadequate states deterministically by looking ahead at the remaining input.

Example 8.44   The LR-DFA(G) of Figure 8.18 has three inadequate states, namely the states S_1, S_2 and S_9. In state S_1, E can be reduced to S (complete item $[S \rightarrow E.]$) or a '+' may be read (shift item $[E \rightarrow E. + T]$); in S_2, T can be reduced to E (complete item $[E \rightarrow T.]$) or a '*' may be read (shift item $[T \rightarrow T. * F]$); finally, in S_9 the parser may reduce $E + T$ to E (complete item $[E \rightarrow E + T.]$) or read a '*' (shift item $[T \rightarrow T. * F]$).   □

Direct construction of the LR-DFA(G)

The LR-DFA(G) for a context-free grammar G does not have to be generated via the item pushdown automaton K_G, its characteristic finite automaton $char(K_G)$ and the subset construction. It can be generated directly from G using the algorithm shown in Figure 8.20.

Here, the semantics of the foreach statement in the *Succ* function are such that each element of the (dynamically growing) set Q_d is combined precisely once with each element of $V_N \cup V_T$.

8.4.4   LR(k): definition, properties, examples

Suppose $S' = \alpha_0 \underset{rm}{\Longrightarrow} \alpha_1 \underset{rm}{\Longrightarrow} \alpha_2 \cdots \underset{rm}{\Longrightarrow} \alpha_m = v$ is an arbitrary rightmost derivation for a context-free grammar G. G will be called an LR(k) grammar, if

Algorithm LR-DFA:

Input: context-free grammar $G = (V'_N, V_T, P', S')$.

Output: LR-DFA$(G) = (Q_d, V_N \cup V_T, q_d, \delta_d, F_d)$.

Method: The states and transitions of the LR-DFA(G) are constructed in steps using the following three auxiliary functions *Start, Closure* and *Succ*.

var q, q': **set of item**;
function *Start:* **set of item**;
   return($\{[S' \rightarrow .S]\}$);
        (∗ if S' and S are the new and old start symbols of G, respectively ∗)
function *Closure*(s : **set of item**) : **set of item**;
        (∗ corresponds to the ε successor states of Def. 7.7 ∗)
begin
   $q := s$;
   while *exist.* $[X \rightarrow \alpha.Y\beta]$ **in** q **and** $Y \rightarrow \gamma$ **in** P
      and $[Y \rightarrow .\gamma]$ **not in** q **do**
     add $[Y \rightarrow .\gamma]$ to q
   od;
   return(q)
end;

function *Succ*(s : **set of item**, $Y : V_N \cup V_T$) : **set of item**;
        (∗ corresponds to the (S) transitions in K_G ∗)
   return($\{[X \rightarrow \alpha Y.\beta] \mid [X \rightarrow \alpha.Y\beta] \in s\}$);

begin
   $Q_d := \{Closure(Start)\}$;
   $\delta_d := \emptyset$;
   foreach q **in** Q_d **and** X **in** $V_N \cup V_T$ **do**
     let $q' = Closure(Succ(q, X))$ **in**
       if $q' \neq \emptyset$
       then
         if q' **not in** Q_d
         then $Q_d := Q_d \cup \{q'\}$
         fi;
         $\delta_d := \delta_d \cup \{q \xrightarrow{X} q'\}$
       fi
     tel
   od
end

Figure 8.20   Algorithm LR-DFA.

in each such rightmost derivation and each right sentential form α_i occurring in that derivation,

- the handle can be localized, and
- the production to be applied can be determined,

by considering α_i from the left to at most k symbols beyond the handle. Thus, in an LR(k)-grammar, the division of α_i into $\gamma\beta w$ and the determination of $X \to \beta$, so that $\alpha_{i-1} = \gamma X w$ are uniquely determined by $\gamma\beta$ and $k : w$.

Definition 8.39 (LR(k)-grammar)

Suppose $G = (V_N, V_T, P, S)$ is a context-free grammar and $G' = (V'_N, V_T, P', S')$ the extended context-free grammar for G obtained by extending G by the new start symbol S' and the additional production $S' \to S$. Then G' is said to be an **LR(k)-grammar** if it follows from

$$S' \underset{rm}{\overset{*}{\Longrightarrow}} \alpha X w \underset{rm}{\Longrightarrow} \alpha\beta w$$
$$S' \underset{rm}{\overset{*}{\Longrightarrow}} \gamma Y x \underset{rm}{\Longrightarrow} \alpha\beta y \text{ and}$$
$$k : w = k : y \text{ that}$$
$$\alpha = \gamma, X = Y \text{ and } x = y \qquad \square$$

Example 8.45

Let G be the grammar with the productions

$$\begin{aligned}
S &\to A \mid B \\
A &\to aAb \mid 0 \\
B &\to aBbb \mid 1
\end{aligned}$$

$L(G) = \{a^n 0 b^n \mid n \geq 0\} \cup \{a^n 1 b^{2n} \mid n \geq 0\}$. We already know that G is not LL(k) for all k.

G is an LR(0)-grammar. The right sentential forms for G have the forms (the handle is underlined in each case): $S, \underline{A}, \underline{B}, a^n \underline{aAbb}^n, a^n \underline{aBbbb}^{2n}, a^n a\underline{0}bb^n, a^n a\underline{1}bbb^{2n}$. There would be two different possible reductions only in the case of the right sentential forms $a^n aAbb^n$ and $a^n aBbbb^{2n}$. $a^n aAbb^n$ could be reduced to $a^n Ab^n$ and to $a^n aSbb^n$. The former belongs to the rightmost derivation $S \underset{rm}{\overset{*}{\Longrightarrow}} a^n Ab^n \underset{rm}{\Longrightarrow}$ $a^n aAbb^n$, the latter does not belong to a rightmost derivation. The prefix a^n of $a^n Ab^n$ unambiguously determines whether A is the handle, namely in the case $n = 0$, or whether aAb is the handle, namely in the case $n > 0$. The right sentential forms $a^n Bb^{2n}$ are handled analogously. $\qquad \square$

Example 8.46

The grammar G_1 with the productions

$$\begin{aligned}
S &\to aAc \\
A &\to Abb \mid b
\end{aligned}$$

and the language $L(G_1) = \{ab^{2n+1}c \mid n \geq 0\}$ is an LR(0)-grammar. In a right sentential form $aAbbb^{2n}c$ only the reduction to $aAb^{2n}c$ exists as part of a rightmost derivation. The prefix $aAbb$ determines this uniquely. For the right sentential form $abb^{2n}c$, b is the handle, and the prefix ab determines this uniquely. $\qquad\square$

Example 8.47
The grammar G_2 with the productions

$$S \rightarrow aAc$$
$$A \rightarrow bbA \mid b$$

with the language $L(G_2) = L(G_1)$ is an LR(1)-grammar. The critical right sentential forms have the form $ab^n w$. If $1 : w = b$, then the handle lies in w; if $1 : w = c$, then the last b in b^n forms the handle. $\qquad\square$

Example 8.48
The grammar G_3 with the productions

$$S \rightarrow aAc$$
$$A \rightarrow bAb \mid b$$

and with $L(G_3) = L(G_1)$ is not an LR(k)-grammar for any k. Suppose that an arbitrary but fixed k is chosen. Consider the two rightmost derivations

$$S \underset{rm}{\overset{*}{\Longrightarrow}} ab^n Ab^n c \underset{rm}{\Longrightarrow} ab^n bb^n c$$
$$S \underset{rm}{\overset{*}{\Longrightarrow}} ab^{n+1} Ab^{n+1} c \underset{rm}{\Longrightarrow} ab^{n+1} bb^{n+1} c \quad \text{with } n \geq k$$

Here, with the notation of Definition 8.39 we have: $\alpha = ab^n$, $\beta = b$, $\gamma = ab^{n+1}$, $w = b^n c$, $y = b^{n+2}c$. Then $k : w = k : y = b^k$. Since $\alpha \neq \gamma$ it follows that G_3 is not an LR(k)-grammar. $\qquad\square$

Theorem 8.9   *A context-free grammar G is an LR(0)-grammar if and only if LR-DFA(G) has no inadequate states.*

Proof:
"$\Rightarrow$"
Suppose G is an LR(0)-grammar;
Assumption: LR-DFA(G) has an inadequate state p.

Case 1: p has a reduce–reduce conflict; then p has at least two different reduce items $[X \rightarrow \beta.]$ and $[Y \rightarrow \delta.]$. A non-empty set of viable prefixes is assigned to p. Let γ be one such viable prefix. Both reduce items are valid for $\gamma\beta$; that is, there are two different rightmost derivations

$$S' \underset{rm}{\overset{*}{\Longrightarrow}} \gamma X w \underset{rm}{\Longrightarrow} \gamma\beta w \quad \text{and}$$
$$S' \underset{rm}{\overset{*}{\Longrightarrow}} vY y \underset{rm}{\Longrightarrow} v\delta y \quad \text{with } v\delta = \gamma\beta$$

But this contradicts the LR(0)-property.

Case 2: p has a shift–reduce conflict; the contradiction is obtained analogously.

"$\Leftarrow$"

LR-DFA(G) has no inadequate states.
Consider the two rightmost derivations

$$S' \overset{*}{\underset{rm}{\Rightarrow}} \alpha X w \underset{rm}{\Rightarrow} \alpha \beta w$$

$$S' \overset{*}{\underset{rm}{\Rightarrow}} \gamma Y x \underset{rm}{\Rightarrow} \alpha \beta y$$

We need to show that $\alpha = \gamma$, $X = Y$, $x = y$.

After reading $\alpha \beta$, LR-DFA(G) is in a state p. p is not inadequate. Thus $p = \{[X \rightarrow \beta.]\}$. Thus, p contains all valid items for $\alpha \beta$, whence $\alpha = \gamma$, $X = Y$ and $x = y$.   □

Thus, we have recognized the following interrelations. Based on a context-free grammar G, we could construct LR-DFA(G) either directly or in a roundabout way using the item pushdown automaton K_G. This LR-DFA(G) describes the behaviour of a pushdown automaton K_0 uniquely. K_0 is deterministic, if LR-DFA(G) has no inadequate states. Theorem 8.9 says that this is the case if the original grammar G is an LR(0)-grammar. Thus, we have met a parser generation procedure for the case of LR(0)-grammars which seldom arise in practice.

We now turn to the more relevant cases $k > 0$. In LR(0)-parsers, the current state, a set of context-free items, determines the next action, that is, read or reduce. LR(k)-parsers also have states, which consist of sets of items, in this case LR(k)-items; that is, context-free items extended by a set of words of length k.

Definition 8.40 (LR(k)-item)
Let G' be an extended context-free grammar. $[X \rightarrow \alpha_1.\alpha_2, L]$ is called an **LR(k)-item** of G', if $X \rightarrow \alpha_1\alpha_2 \in P$ and $L \subseteq V_{T\#}^{\leq k}$. $[X \rightarrow \alpha_1.\alpha_2]$ is the **kernel** of the LR(k)-item $[X \rightarrow \alpha_1.\alpha_2, L]$, L is its **lookahead set**. This LR(k)-item is **valid** for a viable prefix $\alpha\alpha_1$, if for all $u \in L$ there exists a rightmost derivation $S'\# \overset{*}{\underset{rm}{\Rightarrow}} \alpha X w \underset{rm}{\Rightarrow} \alpha\alpha_1\alpha_2 w$ with $u = k : w$.   □

Thus, we can view the previously considered context-free items as LR(0)-items if we identify $[X \rightarrow \alpha_1.\alpha_2, \{\varepsilon\}]$ with $[X \rightarrow \alpha_1.\alpha_2]$.

Example 8.49
Let us again consider the grammar G_0.

(1) $[E \rightarrow E + .T, \{\}, +\}]$ is a valid LR(1)-item for $(E+$ in G_0

(2) $[E \rightarrow T., \{*\}]$ is not a valid LR(1)-item for any viable prefix

because:

(1) $S' \overset{*}{\underset{rm}{\Rightarrow}} (E) \underset{rm}{\Rightarrow} (E+T) \overset{*}{\underset{rm}{\Rightarrow}} (E+T+\mathbf{id})$ where $\alpha = ($, $\alpha_1 = E+$, $\alpha_2 = T$, $u = +$, $w = +\mathbf{id})$;

(2)   the subword $E*$ cannot occur in any right sentential form.   □

Theorem 8.10   *A context-free grammar G is an LR(k)-grammar if and only if the following holds: Let $\alpha\beta$ be a viable prefix. If the LR(k)-item $[X \to \beta., L_1]$ is valid for $\alpha\beta$, then there is no other LR(k)-item $[Y \to \beta_1.\beta_2, L_2]$ valid for $\alpha\beta$ such that $L_1 \cap FIRST_k(\beta_2 L_2) \neq \emptyset$.*   □

8.4.5   LR(k)-parsers

The LR(k) definition says the following. Assume the parser has on reading a right sentential form found a candidate for reduction. It is then able to use the associated viable prefix together with the next k symbols of the input to decide whether or not this candidate is actually the handle, and if it is, what it has to be reduced to. If we wished to tabulate all combinations of viable prefixes and words of length k, we would have problems, because in general there are infinitely many viable prefixes. However, Theorem 8.8 says that the states of the LR-DFA(G) induce a finite partition on this set of viable prefixes. Every viable prefix γ belongs to precisely one state of the LR-DFA(G), namely that to which the LR-DFA(G) transfers when, beginning in its initial state, it reads γ. This state associated with γ together with the next k symbols are sufficient to take the decision whether to read on or reduce. Thus, a table of an LR(k)-parser, the so-called **action table**, will specify one of the following actions for each combination of a state and k input symbols:

shift: read the next input symbol;
reduce $(X \to \alpha)$:   reduce using the production $X \to \alpha$;
error: report error
accept: report successful end of the parser run.

A second table, called the **goto table**, contains the representation of the transition function of the LR-DFA(G). Thus, it describes the transitions between states under terminals and nonterminals of the grammar. It is consulted when a *shift* action or a *reduce* action has occurred, to compute the new state. In the case of a *shift* it determines the transition from the current state under the symbol read; in the case of a reduction by $X \to \alpha$ it determines the transition under X from the state, which appears at the top of the stack after the removal of the stack states associated with α. These two tables are shown in Figure 8.21.

We see not only that the current state, the topmost in the stack, contains all the important information about the current viable prefix, but also that this state need not be recomputed with an analysis of γ' by the LR-DFA(G) on every change from one actual viable prefix γ to the next γ'. The new state for γ' is obtained by local calculations at the top of the stack.

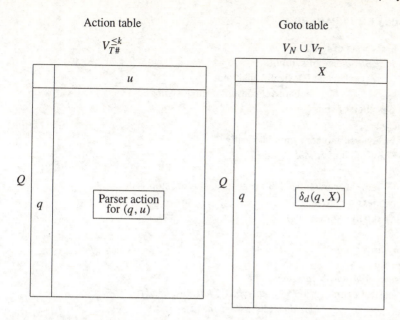

Action table

$V_{T\#}^{\leq k}$

Goto table

$V_N \cup V_T$

Figure 8.21   LR(k)-parser control consisting of the action table and the goto table. The set of states of the LR(k)-parser is Q.

An LR(k)-parser for an LR(k)-grammar G consists of the two tables, which are generated from G as described below, and a program that interprets these tables. This program is independent of G and can thus be used for all LR(k)-grammars. It is called the **LR(k)-parser** here (Figure 8.22).

The construction of LR(k)-parsers

In what follows, we shall meet three different ways of constructing an LR(k)-parser for the language defined by a context-free grammar G. The resulting LR(k)-parsers are similar insofar as in each case their states consist of sets of LR(k)-items of the grammar, but they differ in the number of their states and/or in the size of their lookahead sets. We would expect to obtain more precise information with more states. For this reason, more powerful methods, capable of generating LR(k)-parsers for a larger class of grammars, in general construct parsers with larger sets of states. The behaviour is the opposite for the lookahead sets; the most powerful parser generation methods equip the items in their states with smaller lookahead sets. This can be understood as follows. Each word u in the set L of an LR(k)-item $[X \to \alpha., L]$ in the state q means: if the parser is in state q and the next k input symbols form the word u, then reduce by $X \to \alpha$. If there is a second complete item $[Y \to \beta., L']$ in q, L and L' must be disjoint, for the parser to be deterministic. However, the smaller the two sets L and L' are, the earlier they are disjoint. A similar behaviour is found when shift and reduce items are simultaneously present in a state.

Algorithm LR(k)-PARSER:

type   *state* = **set of item;**
var   *lookahead:* **seq of symbol;**
            (∗ the next k lexically analysed,
                  but not yet consumed input symbols ∗)
        S : **stack of state;**
proc *scan*;
        (∗ analyse another symbol lexically,
          append it after *lookahead* ∗)
proc *acc*;
        (∗ report successful end of the syntax analysis; stop ∗)
proc *err*(*message*: **string**);
        (∗ report error; stop ∗)
$scan^k$;
$push(S, q_0)$;
forever do
    case *action*[*top*(S), *lookahead*] **of**
        shift: **begin** $push(S, goto(top(S), hd(lookahead)))$;
                        lookahead := $tl(lookahead)$;
                        scan
            end;
        reduce ($X \rightarrow \alpha$): **begin** $pop^{|\alpha|}(S)$; $push(S, goto(top(S), X))$;
                            $output("X \rightarrow \alpha")$
                    end;
        accept: *acc*;
        error: *err*(" ... ");
    end case
od

Figure 8.22   Algorithm LR(k)-PARSER.

The most powerful method is the canonical LR(k)-method. If a grammar G is an LR(k)-grammar, there exists a canonical LR(k)-parser for G. The two other methods are the SLR(k)-method and the LALR(k)-method.

The scheme for the three types of parser is the same: there exists a set of states, which are however computed in different ways, and items in the states, (some of) which are provided with sets of lookahead words of maximal length k. The action table is constructed from the states. The states and the lookahead words are used as indices for this table.

In what follows, we again restrict ourselves to the case of practical relevance, $k = 1$. This case is in principle sufficient, since for every language with an LR(k)-parser there is also an LR(1)-parser. But a non-LR(1)-grammar for the language must be transformed into an LR(1)-grammar.

How does the LR(k)-PARSER algorithm change? The variable *lookahead* now has the type *symbol*, and the method *scan* analyses the following input and stores the next symbol in *lookahead*.

If an LR(1)-parser state contains several complete items there is still no reduce–reduce conflict, if their lookahead sets are pairwise disjoint. When it is in this state, the parser will choose the reduction whose lookahead set contains the next input symbol.

If a parser state contains both a complete item $[X \rightarrow \alpha., L]$ and a shift item $[Y \rightarrow \beta.a\gamma, L']$ simultaneously, there is no shift–reduce conflict between these, if L does not contain the symbol a. When it is in this state the parser will reduce if the next input symbol is in L, and read if it is equal to a. In all situations in which the next input symbol is neither in the lookahead set of a complete item nor the symbol to be read by a shift item of the current state the parser must report a syntax error.

Definition 8.41 (conflict)

Let I be a set of LR(1)-items. I has a **shift–reduce conflict**, if it contains an item $[X \rightarrow \alpha.a\beta, L_1]$ and an item $[Y \rightarrow \gamma., L_2]$ and $a \in L_2$. I has a **reduce–reduce conflict**, if it contains two items $[X \rightarrow \alpha., L_1]$ and $[Y \rightarrow \beta., L_2]$ with $L_1 \cap L_2 \neq \emptyset$. If a set of items with a conflict occurs as a state in the construction of an LR(1)-parser this state is said to be **inadequate**. □

The construction of an LR(1)-parser is successful, if it does not involve the generation of any inadequate states.

Algorithm LR(1)-Table:
Input: set of LR(1)-states Q
Output: Action table
Method:

foreach $q \in Q$ **do**
    foreach *LR(1) item* $[K, L] \in q$ **do**
        if $K = [S' \rightarrow S.]$ **and** $L = \{\#\}$
        then   *action*$[q, \#] :=$ *"accept"*
        elseif $K = [X \rightarrow \alpha.]$
        then   **foreach** $a \in L$ **do**
                action$[q, a] :=$ *" reduce $X \rightarrow \alpha$"*
            od
        elseif $K = [X \rightarrow \alpha.a\beta]$
        then *action*$[q, a] :=$ *" shift"*
        fi
    od
od;
foreach $q \in Q$ **and** $a \in V_T$ with *action*$[q, a]$ *undef.* **do**
    action$[q, a] :=$ *" error"*
od;

Figure 8.23   Construction of an LR(1)-table.

Construction of an LR(1)-action table

The last step in the construction of an LR(1)-parser is the construction of the action table. It is identical for the different types of LR-parsers. The input for this step is the set of LR(1)-states. For a given grammar, this is in general dependent on the LR-analysis method chosen. The algorithm is given in Figure 8.23.

Algorithm LR(1)-GEN:
Input: context-free grammar G.
Output: characteristic finite automaton of a canonical LR(1)-parser for G
Method: The states and transitions of the LR(1)-parser for G are constructed
       in steps using the following three auxiliary functions *Start, Closure* and *Succ*.

var q, q': **set of item**;
var Q: **set of set of item**;
var δ: **set of item** $\times (V_N \cup V_T) \to$ **set of item**;
function *Start*: **set of item**;
    return $(\{[S' \to .S, \{\#\}]\})$;
function *Closure*$(q :$ **set of item**$) :$ **set of item**;
begin
    foreach $[X \to \alpha.Y\beta, L]$ **in** q **and** $Y \to \gamma$ **in** P **do**
        if *exists* $[Y \to .\gamma, L']$ **in** q
        then *replace* $[Y \to .\gamma, L']$ *by* $[Y \to .\gamma, L' \cup \varepsilon\text{-}\mathit{ffi}(\beta L)]$
        else $q := q \cup \{[Y \to .\gamma, \varepsilon\text{-}\mathit{ffi}(\beta L)]\}$
        fi
    od;
    return(q)
end;
function *Succ*$(q :$ **set of item**, $Y : V_N \cup V_T) :$ **set of item**;
    return$(\{[X \to \alpha Y.\beta, L] \mid [X \to \alpha.Y\beta, L] \in q\})$
begin
    $Q := \{Closure(Start)\}$; $\delta := \emptyset$;
    foreach q **in** Q **and** X **in** $V_N \cup V_T$ **do**
        let $q' = Closure(Succ(q, X))$ **in**
            if $q' \neq \emptyset$
            then
                if q' **not in** Q
                then $Q := Q \cup \{q'\}$
                fi;
                $\delta := \delta \cup \{q \xrightarrow{X} q'\}$
            fi
        tel
    od
end.

Figure 8.24   Algorithm LR(1)-GEN.

Computation of sets of LR(1)-states

We now present three different methods for computing sets of LR(1)-states. We begin with the computation of the sets of canonical LR(1)-states (Figure 8.24).

We should compare the algorithm LR(1)-GEN with the algorithm LR-DFA in Section 8.4.3. What has changed? In the auxiliary function *Start* we construct the set consisting of LR(1)-item $[S' \to .S, \{\#\}]$, where # stands for the end of text or end of file symbol. We assume that every input is followed by an end symbol.

A call *Succ* (Y, q) generates the set of all Y successor items for state q. The lookahead set is carried over in each case. This is clear if we consider the validity of LR(k)-items. If $[X \to \alpha.Y\beta, L]$ is valid for any viable prefix $\gamma\alpha$, then $[X \to \alpha Y.\beta, L]$ is valid for the viable prefix $\gamma\alpha Y$.

The function *Closure* calculates new lookahead sets for the LR(1)-items which it appends to its argument. In fact, if $[X \to \alpha.Y\beta, L]$ is valid for the arbitrary viable prefix $\delta\alpha$ and $Y \to \gamma$ is an alternative for Y, the appended item with kernel $[Y \to .\gamma]$ must also be valid for $\delta\alpha$. Then in a right sentential form any symbol from $\varepsilon\text{-}\mathit{ffi}(\beta L)$ can follows $\delta\alpha\gamma$. These are the symbols from $\varepsilon\text{-}\mathit{ffi}(\beta)$, together with those from L, if $\beta \stackrel{*}{\Longrightarrow} \varepsilon$.

The test 'q' **not in** Q' uses an equality relation on LR(1)-items, under which two LR(1)-items are only equal if they coincide in the kernel and the lookahead set.

Example 8.50

In this example, we describe a number of LR(1)-states for the context-free grammar G_0. The indexing of the states is as in Figure 8.17. We see that after extension by lookahead sets, the previously inadequate states S_1, S_2 and S_9 no longer contain any conflicts. In the state S_1' the next input symbol '+' leads to a shift, '#' a reduction. In S_2' '$*$' leads to a shift, '#' and '+' to a reduction; likewise in S_9'.

$$
\begin{aligned}
S_0' \;&=\; \textit{Closure(Start)}\\
&=\{\; [S \to .E, \{\#\}]\\
&\qquad [E \to .E + T, \{\#, +\}],\\
&\qquad [E \to .T, \{\#, +\}],\\
&\qquad [T \to .T * F, \{\#, +, *\}],\\
&\qquad [T \to .F, \{\#, +, *\}],\\
&\qquad [F \to .(E), \{\#, +, *\}],\\
&\qquad [F \to .\mathbf{id}, \{\#, +, *\}] \;\}
\end{aligned}
$$

$$
\begin{aligned}
S_1' \;&=\; \textit{Closure(Succ}(S_0', E))\\
&=\{\; [S \to E., \{\#\}],\\
&\qquad [E \to E. + T, \{\#, +\}]\}
\end{aligned}
$$

$$
\begin{aligned}
S_2' \;&=\; \textit{Closure(Succ}(S_1', T))\\
&=\{\; [E \to T., \{\#, +\}],\\
&\qquad [T \to T. * F, \{\#, +, *\}] \;\}
\end{aligned}
$$

$$
\begin{aligned}
S_6' \;&=\; \textit{Closure(Succ}(S_1', +))\\
&=\{\; [E \to E + .T, \{\#, +\}],\\
&\qquad [T \to .T * F, \{\#, +, *\}],\\
&\qquad [T \to .F, \{\#, +, *\}],\\
&\qquad [F \to .(E), \{\#, +, *\}],\\
&\qquad [F \to .\mathbf{id}, \{\#, +, *\}]\}
\end{aligned}
$$

$$
\begin{aligned}
S_9' \;&=\; \textit{Closure(Succ}(S_6', T))\\
&=\{\; [E \to E + T., \{\#, +\}],\\
&\qquad [T \to T. * F, \{\#, +, *\}]\}
\end{aligned}
$$

□

Table 8.6 Some of the cells of the action table of the canonical LR(1)-parser for G_0. s stands for shift, ri for reduce by production i, acc for accept. All unoccupied entries are error entries.

	id	(	)	*	+	#
S_0'	s	s				
S_1'					s	acc
S_2'				s	$r3$	$r3$
S_6'	s	s				
S_9'				s	$r2$	$r2$

Numbering of the productions
1: $S \to E$
2: $E \to E + T$
3: $E \to T$
4: $T \to T * F$
5: $T \to F$
6: $F \to (E)$
7: $F \to \mathbf{id}$

Table 8.6 shows the rows of the action table of the canonical LR(1)-parser for our grammar G_0 associated with the above states.

SLR(1)- and LALR(1)-parser generation

Two LR-analysis methods which are frequently used in practice are the SLR(1) (simple LR) and LALR(1) (lookahead LR) methods. There does not exist an SLR(1) (LALR(1))-parser for every canonical LR(1)-grammar. Conversely, every grammar that has an SLR(1) (LALR(1))-parser is an LR(1)-grammar. One advantage of SLR- and LALR-parsers over the canonical LR-parsers is that their set of states for a grammar G is only as large as that for the LR(0)-parser for G.

The starting point for the (practical) construction of SLR(1)- and LALR(1)-parsers is an LR(0)-parser that has already been constructed. To eliminate inadequate states, the complete items in LR(0)-states are extended by lookahead sets. Let q be an LR(0)-state and $[X \to \alpha.\beta]$ an item in q. Then $LA(q, [X \to \alpha.\beta])$ denotes the lookahead set to be appended to the item $[X \to \alpha.\beta]$ in q. Thus, LA is a function $LA : Q_d \times It_G \to 2^{V_T}$. It is defined in different ways for the SLR(1) and the LALR(1) cases.

- **SLR(1)**

Every reduce item $[X \to \alpha.]$ (in all states) is assigned the set $FOLLOW_1(X)$ as lookahead set.

$$LA_S(q, [X \to \alpha.]) = \{a \in V_T \mid S' \stackrel{*}{\Longrightarrow} \beta X a \gamma\} = FOLLOW_1(X)$$

for all q with $[X \to \alpha.] \in q$.

Definition 8.42 (SLR(1)-grammar)
Suppose the complete items of the LR-DFA(G) for a grammar G are extended in the way described above by lookahead sets. A state is said to be **SLR(1) inadequate**, if it contains two items $[X_1 \to \alpha_1., L_1]$ and $[X_2 \to \alpha_2., L_2]$ with $L_1 \cap L_2 \neq \emptyset$ or two items $[X \to \alpha.a\beta]$ and $[Y \to \gamma., L]$ with $a \in L$. If there are no SLR(1) inadequate states, then G is an **SLR(1)-grammar**. □

Example 8.51

We again consider the grammar G_0 of Example 8.38. Its LR-DFA(G_0) had the inadequate states S_1, S_2 and S_9. We extend their complete items by the following $FOLLOW_1$ sets. We obtain

$$
\begin{aligned}
S_1'' &= \{ & [S \rightarrow E., \{\#\}], & \qquad \text{conflict eliminated,} \\
& & [E \rightarrow E. + T]\} & \qquad \text{'+' is not in } \{\#\} \\[1em]
S_2'' &= \{ & [E \rightarrow T., \{\#, +,)\}], & \qquad \text{conflict eliminated,} \\
& & [T \rightarrow T. * F]\} & \qquad \text{'*' is not in } \{\#, +,)\} \\[1em]
S_9'' &= \{ & [E \rightarrow E + T., \{\#, +,)\}], & \qquad \text{conflict eliminated,} \\
& & [T \rightarrow T. * F]\} & \qquad \text{'*' is not in } \{\#, +,)\}
\end{aligned}
$$

Thus, G_0 is an SLR(1)-grammar.   □

Example 8.52   The following grammar (from Aho, Sethi, Ullman: Principles of Compiler Design, Addison-Wesley) describes a simplification of the C assignment statement. As we shall show later, it is an LALR(1)-grammar, but not an SLR(1)-grammar.

$$
\begin{aligned}
S' &\rightarrow S \\
S &\rightarrow L = R \mid R \\
L &\rightarrow *R \mid \mathbf{id} \\
R &\rightarrow L
\end{aligned}
$$

The sets of items, which form the states of the LR-DFA, are:

$$
\begin{aligned}
S_0 = \{ & [S' \rightarrow .S], & \qquad S_5 = \{ & [L \rightarrow \mathbf{id}.] \} \\
& [S \rightarrow .L = R], & \qquad S_6 = \{ & [S \rightarrow L = .R], \\
& [S \rightarrow .R], & & [R \rightarrow .L], \\
& [L \rightarrow . * R], & & [L \rightarrow . * R], \\
& [L \rightarrow .\mathbf{id}], & & [L \rightarrow .\mathbf{id}] \} \\
& [R \rightarrow .L] \} & & \\
& & \qquad S_7 = \{ & [L \rightarrow *R.] \} \\
S_1 = \{ & [S' \rightarrow S.] \} & & \\
& & \qquad S_8 = \{ & [R \rightarrow L.] \} \\
S_2 = \{ & [S \rightarrow L. = R], & \qquad S_9 = \{ & [S \rightarrow L = R.] \} \\
& [R \rightarrow L.] \} & & \\[1em]
S_3 = \{ & [S \rightarrow R.] \} & & \\[1em]
S_4 = \{ & [L \rightarrow *.R], & & \\
& [R \rightarrow .L], & & \\
& [L \rightarrow . * R], & & \\
& [L \rightarrow .\mathbf{id}] \} & &
\end{aligned}
$$

S_2 is the only inadequate state. $FOLLOW_1(R) = \{\#, =\}$. When the complete item $[R \rightarrow L.]$ is extended by the lookahead set $\{\#, =\}$ the shift–reduce conflict remains, since the symbol to be read '=' is contained in the lookahead set of the complete item. $\qquad\square$

• LALR(1)

$FOLLOW_1(X)$ collects together all symbols that can follow X in sentential forms of the grammar. In the construction of the SLR(1)-parser $FOLLOW_1(X)$ is used as lookahead set for $[X \rightarrow \alpha.]$ in all states in which this complete item occurs. For an occurrence of $[X \rightarrow \alpha.]$ in a state q we now construct a frequently smaller lookahead set depending on q.

$$LA_L(q, [X \rightarrow \alpha.]) = \{a \in V_T \cup \{\#\} \mid S'\# \overset{*}{\underset{rm}{\Longrightarrow}} \beta X a w \text{ and } \delta_d^*(q_d, \beta\alpha) = q\}$$

Here, δ_d is the transition function of the LR-DFA(G). Now only the terminal symbols that can follow X in a right sentential form $\beta X a w$ are in $LA_L(q, [X \rightarrow \alpha.])$, so that $\beta\alpha$ brings the characteristic finite automaton LR-DFA(G) into the state q.

Definition 8.43 (LALR(1) grammar)
Suppose the complete items of the LR-DFA(G) of a grammar G are extended by the LA_L lookahead sets. A state is said to be **LALR(1) inadequate**, if it contains two items $[X_1 \rightarrow \alpha_1., L_1]$ and $[X_2 \rightarrow \alpha_2., L_2]$ with $L_1 \cap L_2 \neq \emptyset$ or two items $[X \rightarrow \alpha.a\beta]$ and $[Y \rightarrow \gamma., L_2]$ with $a \in L$. A grammar with no LALR(1) inadequate states is called an **LALR(1)-grammar**. $\qquad\square$

This definition is not constructive, since, in general, infinite sets of right sentential forms occur in it.

The following computational method for LALR(1)-parsers is conceivable, but unnecessarily time-consuming. We attempt to construct a canonical LR(1)-parser. If its states do not contain any conflicts, such states p and q are merged into a new state p', if the set of the kernels of the items in p is equal to the set of the kernels of the items of q, that is, if the difference between the two sets of items consists solely of the difference between lookahead sets. The new state p' is created by combining the lookahead sets of items with the same kernel. If there are no conflicts after this merging the grammar is an LALR(1)-grammar.

Example 8.53
The grammar of Example 8.52 is an LALR(1)-grammar. The transition diagram of its LALR(1)-parser is given in Figure 8.25. $\qquad\square$

8.4.6 Error handling in LR-parsers

Like LL-parsers, LR-parsers have the valid prefix property; that is, every error-free prefix of the input analysed by an LR-parser can be continued to a correct input word, a sentence of the language. In what follows, we shall write configurations of

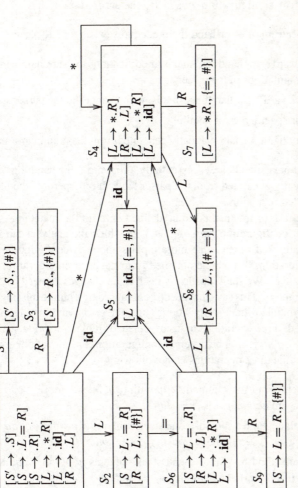

Figure 8.25 Transition diagram of the LALR(1)-parser for the grammar of Example 8.52.

an LR-parser as $(\varphi q, a_i \dots a_n)$; that is, the stack content is φq, the current state q, and the remaining input is $a_i \dots a_n$. If an LR-parser is in the configuration $(\varphi q, a_i \dots a_n)$ with $action(q, a_i) = error$, this is the earliest possible situation in which an error can be detected.

Definition 8.44 (error configuration)
A configuration $(\varphi q, a_i \dots a_n)$ of an LR(1)-parser with $action(q, a_i) = error$ is called an **error configuration**. q is called the **error state** of this configuration. $\square$

A whole spectrum of error-handling procedures exists for LR-parsers:

- Forward error handling; that is, modifications to the remaining input without manipulations in the parser stack, or
- Backward error handling, that is, with changes to the parser stack;
- User-specified error handling, or
- Error handling automatically generated from the grammar or the LR-parser.

The method presented below is essentially a forward error-handling method which is automatically generated from the parser table. It only permits the undoing of the last completed reduction.

The task of the method to be defined is to find a 'matching' configuration for the error configuration $(\varphi q, a_i \dots a_n)$, in which the analysis can be continued with the reading of at least one more input symbol. A configuration matches the error configuration, if it can be obtained from the error configuration by as few as possible changes. We shall drastically restrict the changes allowed by assuming the 1-error hypothesis. This says that the error is caused by **a single** missing, superfluous or wrong symbol at the error position. Thus, the error handling algorithm must be provided with three operations to insert, delete or replace *a single* symbol.

Let $(\varphi q, a_i \dots a_n)$ be the error configuration. The aim of our error correction using one of the three operations is the following:

- **Delete**: Find stack contents $\varphi' p$ with $(\varphi q, a_{i+1} \dots a_n) \vdash^* (\varphi' p, a_{i+1} \dots a_n)$ and with $action[p, a_{i+1}] = shift$.
- **Replace**: Find a symbol a and stack contents $\varphi' p$ with $(\varphi q, a a_{i+1} \dots a_n) \vdash^* (\varphi' p, a_{i+1} \dots a_n)$ and $action[p, a_{i+1}] = shift$.
- **Insert**: Find a symbol a and stack contents $\varphi' p$ with $(\varphi q, a a_i \dots a_n) \vdash^* (\varphi' p, a_i \dots a_n)$ and $action[p, a_i] = shift$.

The stack contents we seek, $\varphi' p$, may result from the fact that under the new next input symbol reductions are possible which were not possible in the error configuration.

One important property of the three operations is already apparent; they guarantee that the error handling procedure terminates, for in the case of success, each of the three steps moves the read pointer on by at least one symbol.

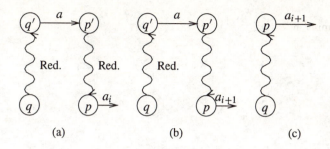

Figure 8.26 Closing of bridges in error correction, (a) at insertion, (b) at replacement, (c) at deletion of a symbol.

Error handling methods with backtracking also allow the undoing of a most recently applied production of the form $X \to \alpha Y$ and $Ya_i \ldots a_n$ to be considered as input, if the other correction attempts have failed.

The 1-symbol correction operations are too expensive, if they are executed as described above. The search for (a symbol and) a configuration, in which a restart is possible, might possibly require reductions, then a test, of whether a symbol can be read, and a reproduction of the error configuration if it failed, and so on. Such a procedure would test various possibilities dynamically, that is, at compile time. We shall now see how precomputations on the parser can be made at the time of parser generation in order to handle errors more efficiently.

Let $(\varphi q, a_i \ldots a_n)$ again be the error configuration. Let us consider the **insertion** of a symbol $a \in V_T$. The error handling may comprise the following sequence of steps (see Figure 8.26(a)):

(1) a sequence of reductions for lookahead symbol a, followed by

(2) an action shifting a, followed by

(3) a sequence of reductions for lookahead symbol a_i.

The subsequences (1)–(3) can be efficiently carried out by precomputation.

(1) For all $q \in Q_d$ and all $a \in V_T$ compute the set $Succ(q)_a$ of the **reduction successors** of q under a. These are all states which the parser can only reach from q by reduction under the lookahead symbol a and in which it can read a (see Figure 8.27) and also q itself.

(2) For all $a \in V_T$ calculate the set $Sh(a)$ of states in which a can be read. These are the states q, for which $action[q, a] = shift$.

(3) For all $p \in Q_d$ and all $a \in V_T$, calculate the set $Pred(q)_a$ of the **reduction predecessors** of p under a. These are all the states from which the parser can only reach the state p by reduction under the lookahead symbol a (see Figure 8.28) together with p itself.

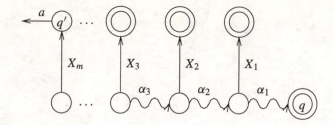

Figure 8.27 $Succ(q)_a$. The possible reductions from q under a in q' use the productions $X_1 \to \alpha_1, X_2 \to \alpha_2 X_1, \ldots, X_m \to \alpha_m X_{m-1}$.

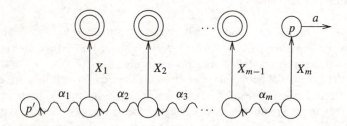

Figure 8.28 $Pred(p)_a$. The reductions from p' under a to p use the productions $X_1 \to \alpha_1, X_2 \to \alpha_2, X_1, \ldots, X_m \to \alpha_m X_{m-1}$.

Theorem 8.11 $q \in Pred(p)_a$ if and only if $p \in Succ(q)_a$. $\qquad\qquad$ □

Correction by the insertion of a symbol a is promising if there exists a state q' in $Succ(q)_a$, a state p in $Sh(a_i)$ and a state p' in $Pred(p)_{a_i}$, such that $\delta_d(q', a) = p'$. This can be represented as:

$$
\begin{array}{ccc}
q' & \xrightarrow{\ a\ } & p' \\
\in Succ(q)_a & & \in Pred(p)_{a_i}
\end{array}
$$

a closes the bridges in the error configuration.

If it is desired to extend the precomputation the set

$$
Bridge(q)_{a_i} = \{a \in V_T \mid \ \exists q' \in Succ(q)_a \text{ and } \delta_d(q', a) = p' \text{ and }
$$
$$
Sh(a_i) \cap Succ(p')_{a_i} \neq \emptyset\}
$$

can be computed for q and a_i.

Example 8.54

We now consider the grammar of Example 8.52 with the LALR(1)-parser of Figure 8.25 which was calculated for it. First, we calculate the sets $Sh(a)$ of states in which a can be read.

$Sh(a)$:

$$
\begin{array}{rcl}
Sh(=) & = & \{S_2\} \\
Sh(*) & = & \{S_0, S_6, S_4\} \\
Sh(\text{id}) & = & \{S_0, S_6, S_4\}
\end{array}
$$

Then the reduction successors $Succ(q)_a$ of q under a and the sets $Bridge(q)_a$ are calculated.

$Succ(q)_a$:

	$=$	$*$	id
S_0	S_0	S_0	S_0
S_1	S_1	S_1	S_1
S_2	S_2	S_2	S_2
S_3	S_3	S_3	S_3
S_4	S_4	S_4	S_4
S_5	S_2, S_5	S_5	S_5
S_6	S_6	S_6	S_6
S_7	S_2, S_7	S_7	S_7
S_8	S_2, S_8	S_8	S_8
S_9	S_9	S_9	S_9

$Bridge(q)_a$:

	$=$	$*$	id
S_0	$\{\text{id}\}$	$\{*\}$	$\{*\}$
S_1	$\emptyset$	$\emptyset$	$\emptyset$
S_2	$\emptyset$	$\{=\}$	$\{=\}$
S_3	$\emptyset$	$\emptyset$	$\emptyset$
S_4	$\{\text{id}\}$	$\{*\}$	$\{*\}$
S_5	$\emptyset$	$\{=\}$	$\{=\}$
S_6	$\{\text{id}\}$	$\{*\}$	$\{*\}$
S_7	$\emptyset$	$\{=\}$	$\{=\}$
S_8	$\emptyset$	$\emptyset$	$\emptyset$
S_9	$\emptyset$	$\emptyset$	$\emptyset$

We can now consider which error corrections the error handler generated would make.

Input	Error configuration	Bridge	Correction
$* =$ id #	$(S_0 S_4, = \text{ id } \#)$	$Bridge(S_4)_= = \{\text{id}\}$	Insertion of **id**
id $==$ id #	$(S_0 S_2 S_6, = \text{ id } \#)$	$Bridge(S_6)_{\text{id}} = \{*\}$	Replacement of $=$ by $*$

Here is an example of a correction by deletion:

Input	Error configuration	Bridge	Correction
id id $=$ **id** #	$(S_0 S_5, \text{id} = \text{ id } \#)$	$Sh(=) \cap Succ(S_5)_= \\ = \{S_2\}$	Deletion of **id**, Replacement of S_5 by S_2

$\square$

Based on these precomputed sets, we can attempt an efficient 1-symbol **correction by replacement**. The difference is that symbols of $Bridge(q)_{a_{i+1}}$ have to be considered, see Figure 8.26(b).

The test for whether a 1-symbol **deletion correction** is sensible can now also be carried out efficiently. The deletion of a symbol a is clearly a possibility for the error handling, when there exists a state p in $Sh(a_{i+1}) \cap Succ(q)_{a_{i+1}}$, see Figure 8.26(c). For every combination of a state q and a symbol a it is possible to precompute whether there exists such a state p. If this predicate is tabulated, a simple lookup is all that remains.

Until now, we have ignored a special case, namely corrections when the input is exhausted. Since the end symbol '#' is not read, $Sh(\text{'#'}) = \emptyset$. Delete and replace actions are not possible, since there is nothing to delete or replace. Only insert actions remain.

The insertion of a symbol a is sensible if, after possible reductions from q under a, a state p is reached from which a state p' is reached after reading a, from which via '#' reductions into *accept* configurations are possible. Here, for every state q, the set $Acc(q)$ which contains all the terminal symbols which guarantee this can be precomputed.

Forward movement

A few questions about the mechanism presented above are still open and a few improvements are still possible. First, it is not clear which correction should be made if several are possible. Associated with this is the question of how to judge the quality of a correction. In order to check the quality of corrections efficiently, the error handling moves forward over the remaining input, reducing a prefix of the remaining input in all possible ways. This 'condensed' right context is then used to test whether the correction allows a continuation over more than one symbol. The parser starts a forward movement in the error configuration $(\varphi q, a_i \ldots a_n)$. It then attempts to reduce as long a prefix of $a_i \ldots a_n$ as possible. Since the parser cannot begin this analysis in a uniquely determined state (q does not match $a_i \ldots a_n$) it begins it in the set of states $Sh(a_{i+1})$, namely the states in which it can read a_{i+1}. Subsequently, its configurations consist of sequences of **sets of states** Q in an error stack ES and the remaining input. If the parser is in the set of states Q for the next input symbol a, then for all $q \in Q$ it makes all non-error transitions in accordance with $action[q, a]$,

- if they all agree, that is, they are either all *shift* or all *reduce*($X \to \alpha$) with the same production $X \to \alpha$, and
- in the case of *reduce*($X \to \alpha$) the error stack is not shorter than $|\alpha|$.

The forward movement stops

- if for all $q \in Q$ $action[q, a] = error$ (this is called 'second error found'),

- if the *action* table for Q and a indicates more than one action,
- if it indicates a single action with *accept*, and
- if it requires a reduction, where the length of the right side is greater than the depth of the error stack (this is called 'reduction beyond the error position').

As a result the forward movement returns the word α to which it has reduced the prefix of the remaining input read up to then, together with the remaining input. We denote this by $FM(a_i \ldots a_n) = (\alpha, a_{i+k} \ldots a_n)$.

Thus, error handling with forward movement can be described as follows.

Suppose the error configuration is $(\varphi q, a_i \ldots a_n)$; $FM(a_i \ldots a_n) = (\alpha, a_{i+k} \ldots a_n)$.

- **Attempt to delete**:
  if there exists $p \in Sh(a_{i+1}) \cap Succ(q)_{a_{i+1}}$, then *test* $(\varphi q, \alpha a_{i+k} \ldots a_n)$;
- **Attempt to replace**:
  if there exists $a \in Bridge(q)_{a_{i+1}}$ with $\begin{array}{ccc} q' & \xrightarrow{a} & p' \\ \in Succ(q)_a & & \in Pred(p)_{a_{i+1}} \end{array}$,
  then *test* $(\varphi q, a\alpha a_{i+k} \ldots a_n)$;
- **Attempt to insert**:
  if there exists $a \in Bridge(q)_{a_i}$ with $\begin{array}{ccc} q' & \xrightarrow{a} & p' \\ \in Succ(q)_a & & \in Pred(p)_{a_i} \end{array}$, then
  test $(\varphi q, a a_i \alpha a_{i+k} \ldots a_n)$;

Correction attempts are evaluated in the procedure *test*. In each case, precisely one of the configurations considered in parallel during the forward movement is assumed. The error correction tested is confirmed if an *accept* configuration occurs, or, if in the case of a reduction beyond the error position, the missing begin of the production is now found on the stack during the test.

Unlike the forward movement, which operates without a left context, that is, without the contents of the parser stack, the contents of the parser stack are now available when testing the proposed correction.

False reductions in SLR(1)- and LALR(1)-parsers

Canonical LR-parsers detect errors at the earliest possible time; they do not read any symbols beyond the error position and do not reduce via a wrong lookahead symbol. While SLR(1)- and LALR(1)-parsers also never read any symbols beyond the error position, they may make reductions before detecting the error in a later *shift* state because the lookahead sets are less diverse. An additional stack is provided for this, on which all the reductions performed since the last read are stored. This stack is emptied at a read action. In case of error, the reductions stacked are cancelled in reverse order.

8.4.7   Scanner generation using LR techniques

The techniques for LR-parser generation described above permit the direct generation of deterministic finite automata for the lexical analysis, without the detour via non-deterministic finite automata. When an LR-parser generator is used, as a result one would first expect a deterministic pushdown automaton. However, we shall assume, as before, a specification of the lexical analysis by a sequence of **regular** definitions. We also know that the language described by such a sequence can be recognized by a finite automaton. Thus, the LR automaton generated must be able to do without a stack. What is the stack used for in LR-parsers? It is used to store consumed terminals and nonterminals resulting from reductions, together with the corresponding states. If the topmost state, possibly in combination with lookahead symbols, orders a reduction using a production $X \rightarrow \alpha$, $|\alpha|$ entries are removed from the stack and the result of the reduction is stored on the stack.

The specification of a scanner involves a sequence of regular definitions:

$$X_1 \rightarrow r_1$$
$$\vdots$$
$$X_n \rightarrow r_n$$

We assume that the names X_i have already been eliminated from $r_1, \ldots, r_{i-1}$ by substitution. We can then consider this sequence as a set of regular right part productions. Nonterminals no longer occur in its right side. Thus, reductions followed by transitions under nonterminals do not arise. If an instance of r_i is found (the automaton generated signals a reduction) and a read transition is not possible, this is reported as 'an X_i found'. After this the automaton starts again in the start state with the next input symbol. If there is a read transition, it has to record the final state reached and the current state of the read pointer in two global variables (it should deliver the longest prefix of the remaining input which leads to a final state as the next symbol). Overall, there is no need to use a stack.

The states of the scanner constructed using the LR method consist of sets of rrpg items. Every item in a state describes a possible interpretation of the analysis situation. In the construction of LR automata the closure formation must be extended to regular right sides. This is done using the following function *replace*:

replace(I **set of item**) **set of item**;

produces the set of items which results from repeated application of the following substitution rules to I (repeat until no further substitution is possible):

replace	$\alpha.(r)^*\beta$	by	$\alpha(.r)^*\beta, \alpha(r)^*.\beta$
replace	$\alpha(r.)^*\beta$	by	$\alpha(.r)^*\beta, \alpha(r)^*.\beta$
replace	$\alpha.(r_1| \cdots |r_n)\beta$	by	$\alpha(.r_1| \cdots |r_n)\beta, \ldots, \alpha(r_1| \cdots |.r_n)\beta$
replace	$\alpha(r_1| \cdots |r_i.| \cdots |r_n)\beta$	by	$\alpha(r_1| \cdots |r_i| \cdots |r_n).\beta$ for $1 \le i \le n$

This leads to the algorithm LR-SCANGEN for direct construction of a scanner from a sequence of regular definitions.

Algorithm LR-SCANGEN:
Input: Sequence of regular definitions
(after substitution of r_i for X_i): $X_1 \rightarrow r_1, \ldots, X_n \rightarrow r_n$
Output: Deterministic finite automaton $(Q, \Sigma, \delta, q_0, Q_f)$ for the union of the languages $r_1, \ldots, r_n$; there are one or more definitions for every end state.
Method:

```
type state = set of item;
var q, q': state;
var S : set of state; (* set of the states still to be processed*)
var Q : set of state; (* set of the states already generated*)
function succ(I :  set of item, a : Σ) set of item;
var I': set of item;
begin
        I' := {[X → αa.β] | [X → α.aβ] ∈ I};
        return(replace(I'))
end;
begin
    q0 := replace({[X1 → .r1], ..., [Xn → .rn]});
    S := {q0};  Q := {q0};
    repeat
        choose q ∈ S;
        foreach a ∈ Σ with: exist [X → α.aβ] in q  do
            q' := succ(q, a);
            if q' not in Q then Q := Q ∪ {q'};  S := S ∪ {q'} fi;
            δ := δ ∪ {q, a, q'}    (* new transition q →a q' *)
        od;
        S := S − {q};    (* q completed *)
    until S = ∅
end.
```

Q_f is the set of all states with at least one complete item.

Example 8.55
Iconst $\rightarrow$ Di(Di)*
Rconst $\rightarrow$ Di(Di)*.Di(Di)*$(e(+|-)$ Di Di $|\varepsilon)$
The corresponding LR scanner is shown in Figure 8.29.   □

Theorem 8.12 *Suppose $X_1 \rightarrow r_1, \ldots, X_n \rightarrow r_n$ is a sequence of regular definitions (after substitution). Let M be the DFA generated according to the LR-SCANGEN algorithm. Then every regular set of M described by the r_i will be recognized through halting in a final state which contains the item $[X_i \rightarrow r_i.]$.*   □

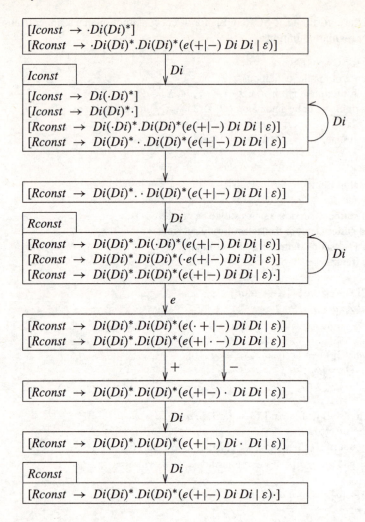

Figure 8.29   Finite deterministic automaton generated using LR techniques. For final states, the names of the corresponding definitions are given above the boxes.

This theorem says that M is in fact an acceptor for the regular languages described, and that final states of M can be assigned to the regular languages.

Corollary 8.3   *The regular sets described by r_i and r_j are not disjoint if and only if there exists a final state of M which contains both complete items $[X_i \rightarrow r_i.]$ and $[X_j \rightarrow r_j.]$.*   □

If the regular sets are pairwise disjoint, then M can uniquely assign each accepted word to a regular set by interpretation of the final state.

8.5   Bison, an LALR(1)-parser generator

Bison is an LALR(1)-parser generator which is part of the Open Software Foundation's GNU system. It is upwards compatible with the LALR(1)-parser generator Yacc, a UNIX utility program. Like Yacc, Bison allows one to input ambiguous grammars and eliminate the resulting parser conflicts, in particular for operators, by specifying precedences and associativity rules. In addition, Bison has a rudimentary mechanism for handling syntax errors.

Parsers generated by Bison have an interface to C. The call of a user-defined C function can be associated with the reduction of a production. There is a predefined s-attribution; for every symbol of the grammar there is precisely one synthesized attribute. Its occurrence on the left side of a production is indicated by '$$', its occurrence for the ith symbol on a right side is indicated by '$i'. The standard type of this attribute for all symbols is *int*, but other type conventions exist, including different conventions for different symbols.

Parsers generated by Bison are called yyparse. They expect to find a scanner called yylex. This may be generated by Flex or written by hand.

8.5.1   Bison – input

The input file for Bison has the following format:

```
%{
C declarations
%}
Bison declarations
%%
Grammar rules
%%
User-defined C code
```

The *C declarations part* introduces types and variables, which are used in the semantic rules. The macro definitions and the necessary includes are also found here.

The *Bison declarations part* lists the terminal and nonterminal alphabets and may assign individual types to the attributes of grammar symbols. The precedences of and associativity rules for operators can also be given here. Example:

```
%token NUM     /* Symbol class of integers */
%left '-' '+' /* Left associative operators */
```

```
%left '*' '/"
%left NEG       /* Unary minus */
%right '^'      /* Right associative power operator */
```

The listing of the operators determines the precedences; operators in the same line have the same precedence, those introduced later have higher precedences than those introduced earlier. NEG is introduced as a level of precedence, in order to include the unary minus. This can only be distinguished from the binary minus by virtue of its syntactic position.

We now give an example of the use of different attribute types. Let us suppose that an abstract syntax tree is to be constructed under the control of the syntax analysis. Then the node for a statement would have pointers to its component trees, the node for an identifier a pointer to the symbol table and the node for a constant a pointer to a representation of the constant. The attributes of the corresponding nonterminals would then be `structs` with pointers to the necessary components. A *union* declaration in the Bison declarations part will then introduce the set of possible attribute types.

```
%union{
    symrec *tptr;
    snode  *nptr;
    value  *vptr;
}
```

One of the attribute types introduced in this way will then be assigned to each attribute of the nonterminals.

```
%type <tptr> identifier
%type <nptr> statement, ifstat, whilestat
%type <vptr> const
```

The *grammar rules* list the productions and their associated semantic actions.

Example: A grammar for variable-free, arithmetic expressions with semantic rules for evaluating them.

```
expr    NUM                       { $$ = $1;          }
        | exp '+' exp             { $$ = $1 + $3; }
        | exp '-' exp             { $$ = $1 - $3; }
        | exp '*" exp             { $$ = $1 * $3; }
        | exp '/' exp             { $$ = $1 / $3; }
        | '-' exp %prec NEG { $$ = - $2;       }
        | exp '^' exp             { $$ = pow ( $1, $3 );}
        | '(' exp ')'             { $$ = $2;          }
```

As previously stated, the ambiguities of this grammar are resolved using the associativity rules and the precedences.

The *user-defined C code* contains the definitions of the actions, which occur in the grammar rules, which may include the definition of a scanner `yylex` and other necessary functions.

8.5.2   Error handling

If a parser generated by Bison finds a syntax error it calls a routine `yyerror`, which issues an error message and normally ends the syntax analysis.

However, like Yacc, Bison supports the following simple mechanism for handling syntax errors. There is a predefined symbol `error`. This symbol may occur at any position on the right sides of productions. The parser generated by Bison reports an occurrence of this symbol if it has no legal transition. If the current state contains an item in which an `error` follows the period then a transition under `error` is executed. If this production leads to a reduction, the associated action can be used for error handling. The predefined routine `yyerrok` authorizes the parser to continue the analysis.

8.6   Exercises

1:   Give a definition of the future of a sequence of items, $fut(\gamma)$, such that you can prove the following invariant (I'):

(I')   For all sentences $uv \in L(G)$ there exists $\gamma \in It_G^*$ with the property:
$$(q_0, uv) \vdash_{K_G}^* (\gamma, v) \text{ implies } fut(\gamma) \overset{*}{\Longrightarrow} v.$$

2:   Define $LAST_k$ inductively.

3:   Define $PRECEDE_k$ inductively.

4:   A pushdown automaton with output (Definition 8.13) outputs the indices of the productions applied. The syntax tree for an analysed word can be generated from this output. In many applications the syntax tree has to be generated simultaneously with the analysis. Suppose we have the following definition of the signature of syntax trees for the context-free grammar:

$$G = (\{N_1, \ldots, N_k\}, \{t_1, \ldots, t_l\}, P, N_1)$$

syntaxtree$(G) =$
      sorts: V_N
             V_T
             syntree(G)

$$
\begin{aligned}
\textbf{opns:} \quad & N_1, \ldots, N_k : && \to V_N \\
& t_1, \ldots, t_l : && \to V_T \\
& \textit{LEAF:} && V_T \to \textit{syntree} \\
& \forall p \in P, p \equiv N_i \to b_1 \ldots b_n, b \in V_T \cup V_N : \\
& \textit{NODE}_p : V_N \, \textit{syntree}^n \to \textit{syntree}
\end{aligned}
$$

Suppose X is a countably infinite set of variables for $\textit{syntaxtree}(G)$. $T_{\textit{syntaxtree}(G)}$ is the set of all syntax trees (ground term), $T_{\textit{syntaxtree}(G)}(X)$ is the set of all syntax trees with variables. Give the definition, the transition relation of Example 8.10 and the sequence of configurations according to Table 8.2 of the pushdown automaton with tree output for

(a) left parsers
(b) right parsers

5: (a) Construct the item pushdown automaton for

$$
G = (\{S\}, \{\textbf{if, then, else, } a, b\}, \left\{ \begin{array}{lll} S & \to & a \\ S & \to & \textbf{if } b \textbf{ then } S \\ S & \to & \textbf{if } b \textbf{ then } S \textbf{ else } S \end{array} \right\}, S)
$$

(b) Give an accepting sequence of configurations for

if b **then if** b **then** a **else** a

(c) Show that G is ambiguous.
(d) Give an unambiguous grammar G' with $L(G') = L(G)$.

6: (a) Construct the item pushdown automaton for

$$
G = (\{S, A, B, C\}, \{a, b\}, \left\{ \begin{array}{lll} S & \to & AB \mid BC \\ A & \to & BA \mid a \\ B & \to & CC \mid b \\ C & \to & AB \mid a \end{array} \right\}, S)
$$

(b) How many accepting configurations are there for $babaab$?

7: (a) Give an efficient algorithm to determine the reachable nonterminals of a grammar.

(b) Use this procedure to check
(i) the productivity and
(ii) the reachability

of the nonterminals of the grammar

$$G = (\{S, A, B, C, D, E\}, \{a, b, c\}, \begin{cases} S &\to& aAa \mid bS \\ A &\to& BB \mid C \\ B &\to& bC \\ C &\to& B \mid c \\ D &\to& aAE \\ E &\to& Db \end{cases}, S)$$

8: Suppose we are given the following grammar:

$$G = (\{S', S, B, E, J, L\}, \{;, , :=, (,), , \}, \begin{cases} S' &\to& S \\ S &\to& LB \\ B &\to& ; S; L \mid := L \\ E &\to& a \mid L \\ J &\to& , E J \mid) \\ L &\to& (E J \end{cases}, S')$$

(a) Compute $FIRST_1$ and $FOLLOW_1$ using the total step procedure given in Section 8.2.4.

(b) Compute $FIRST_1$ and $FOLLOW_1$ using appropriate single-step procedures.

9: Example 8.18 shows that after removing the non-reachable nonterminals and then the unproductive nonterminals, one does not in general obtain a reduced grammar.

Show that by inverting the sequence of removals, one always obtains a reduced grammar.

10: Prove that $\oplus_k$ is associative.

11: Test the LL(1) property of

(a) G of Exercise 5.

(b) G of Exercise 6.

(c) G of Exercise 8.

(d)

$$G = (\{E, E', D, D', F\}, \{a, (,), +, *\}, \begin{cases} E &\to& DE' \\ E' &\to& +DE' \mid \varepsilon \\ D &\to& FD' \\ D' &\to& *FD' \mid \varepsilon \\ F &\to& (E) \mid a \end{cases}, E)$$

12: (a) Draw up the LL(1)-parser table for G of Exercise 11(d).

(b) Describe a run of the corresponding parser for the input $(a + a) * a + a$.

13: Give the LL(1)-table for the following grammar:

$$
\begin{aligned}
E &\rightarrow -E|(E)|VE' \\
E' &\rightarrow -E|\varepsilon \\
V &\rightarrow \text{id } V' \\
V' &\rightarrow (E)|\varepsilon
\end{aligned}
$$

Sketch a run of the parser for the input $-\text{id}\,(-\text{id}) - \text{id}$.

14: Calculate the ε-productivity, the ε-free first function and $FOLLOW_1$ for the following regular right part grammars:

(a) the regular right part grammar for arithmetic expressions (Example 8.30)

(b) the grammar

$$
G = (\{S, A, B\}, \{c, d, e\}, \left\{ \begin{aligned}
S &\rightarrow c\{A \mid \varepsilon\} \\
A &\rightarrow \{B\}^* Sd \\
B &\rightarrow S \mid Ae
\end{aligned} \right\}, S)
$$

Are these two grammars RLL(1)?

15: (a) Calculate the ε-productivity, the ε-free first function and $FOLLOW_1$ for the following regular right part grammar:

$$
\begin{aligned}
S &\rightarrow E \\
E &\rightarrow T(+T)^* \\
T &\rightarrow F(*F)^* \\
F &\rightarrow -E|\text{ if } E \text{ then } E \text{ else } E|CC^* \\
C &\rightarrow \text{id }|'('E')'|[(E(','E)^*)|\varepsilon]
\end{aligned}
$$

(b) Check whether it is an RLL(1)-grammar.

(c) Give the RLL(1)-parser in the table form.

(d) Give the RLL(1)-parser as a program.

16: We define the $LAST_1$ set of a nonterminal X by

$$
LAST_1(X) = \{w : 1 | X \stackrel{*}{\Longrightarrow} w\}
$$

Here, $w : 1$ denotes the 1-suffix of the word w, which is defined analogously to the 1-prefix.

Describe the GFA problem for $LAST_1$ for a regular right part grammar G.

17: Describe a modified scheme for generating recursive descent RLL(1)-parsers, which avoids immediately consecutive checks for the same symbol.

18: Investigate whether a cfg with the following productions can be an LR(k)-grammar. Justify your answer.

> object-declaration → identifier-list : subtype-indication
> renaming-declaration → identifier : type-mark **renames** object-name
> identifier-list → identifier | identifier-list , identifier
> subtype-indication → type-mark

19: Which of the following grammars are not LR(0)-grammars. Justify your answer.

$S \rightarrow L$	$S \rightarrow L$	$S \rightarrow L$	$S \rightarrow L$
$L \rightarrow L; A \mid A$	$L \rightarrow A; L \mid A$	$L \rightarrow L; L \mid A$	$L \rightarrow aT$
$A \rightarrow a$	$A \rightarrow a$	$A \rightarrow a$	$T \rightarrow \varepsilon \mid ; L$
(a)	(b)	(c)	(d)

20: Show that the following grammar is SLR(1), and give the action table:

$$S \rightarrow E$$
$$E \rightarrow T \mid E + T$$
$$T \rightarrow P \mid T * P$$
$$P \rightarrow F \mid F \uparrow P$$
$$F \rightarrow id \mid (E)$$

21: Show that the following grammar is LL(1), but not SLR(1):

$$S \rightarrow Aa Ab \mid BbBa$$
$$A \rightarrow \varepsilon$$
$$B \rightarrow \varepsilon$$

22: Show that the following grammar is LALR(1), but not SLR(1):

$$S \rightarrow Aa \mid bAc \mid dc \mid bda$$
$$A \rightarrow d$$

23: Show that the following grammar is LR(1), but not LALR(1):

$$S \rightarrow Aa \mid bAc \mid Bc \mid bBa$$
$$A \rightarrow d$$
$$B \rightarrow d$$

24: Suppose we are given the following grammar:

$$S \rightarrow A$$
$$A \rightarrow bB$$
$$B \rightarrow cC$$
$$B \rightarrow cCe$$
$$C \rightarrow dA$$
$$A \rightarrow a$$

(a) Calculate the set of LR(1)-items.
(b) Is the grammar SLR(1)?
(c) Is the grammar LALR(1)?
(d) Is the grammar LR(1)?

25: Suppose we are given the following grammar:

$$S \rightarrow A$$
$$B \rightarrow \varepsilon$$
$$C \rightarrow \varepsilon$$
$$A \rightarrow BCA$$
$$A \rightarrow a$$

(a) Calculate the set of LR(1)-items and try to construct the set of LALR(1)-items from this by merging. Is the grammar LALR(1)?
(b) Construct the LR-DFA for the above grammar.

8.7 Literature

Comprehensive presentations of the theory of formal languages and automata are given in the books by Hopcroft and Ullman (1979) and Harrison (1983). These books are completely devoted to the area of syntax analysis.

Grammar flow analysis was first described in Möncke and Wilhelm (1982) and developed further in Möncke (1985) and Möncke and Wilhelm (1991). A related approach was followed in several works by Courcelle, for example Courcelle (1986).

LL(k)-grammars were introduced by Lewis and Stearns (1966, 1968).

The error-handling procedure in RLL(1)-procedures described here is a refinement of the procedure used by Ammann in the Zurich Pascal P4 compiler (Ammann, 1978; Wirth 1987). It is described in Lewi *et al.* (1982).

LR(k)-grammars were introduced by Knuth. The important subclasses for practical purposes, SLR(k) and LALR(k), were discovered by DeRemer (1969, 1971).

The error-handling procedure for LR(k)-parsers described here follows Penello and DeRemer (1978).

Nijholt (1983) provides a very comprehensive bibliography of works on deterministic syntax-analysis procedures appearing up to 1983.

Various syntax-analysis procedures, with and without backtracking, are presented in Cohen and Hickey (1987) in the form of Prolog programs.

9

Semantic analysis

- Task of the semantic analysis

- Attribute grammars

- Examples of attribute grammars

- The generation of attribute evaluators

- Exercises

- Literature

9.1 Task of the semantic analysis

A number of the necessary properties of programs cannot be described by a context-free grammar. These properties are described by predicates on context information, so-called context conditions. These include the declaration-related properties and the type consistency. Both depend on the scoping and visibility rules of the programming language.

For identifiers declared in the program, the **scoping rules** may specify the part of the program in which their declaration takes effect. The **visibility rules** specify where an identifier is visible or hidden within its scope.

The **declaration-related properties** specify that, for example, for every identifier with an applied occurrence, there must exist an explicit declaration, and that duplicate declarations are forbidden.

The **type consistency** of a program guarantees that at execution time no operation (except for input operations) is applied to operands that do not match its argument types.

Static semantic properties

A (non-context-free) property of a programming-language construct is said to be a **static semantic** property, if

(1) for every occurrence of this construct in a program, the 'value' of this property is valid for all (dynamic) executions of the construct (the type of an expression, that is, the 'value of the type property', indicates the type (possibly only the most general type) of all values that can arise dynamically when this expression is evaluated), and if

(2) this property can be calculated for every occurrence of the construct in a correct program (in both strongly and polymorphically typed languages, the/a type can be calculated for every expression in a correct program).

The first condition describes the relationship between static and dynamic semantics. Dynamic semantic properties are in general first known at program run time. Static semantic properties describe common properties of all dynamic executions which can be calculated at compile time. Condition (1) also covers those properties that are usually computed by abstract interpretation (data flow analysis). The second condition excludes such properties since abstract interpretation only attempts to compute the best possible static approximations to dynamic properties of program constructs, where the 'empty' information item is, in general, a possible information item.

Let us consider, for example, the property 'value of variables', that is, for every statement in a program the information giving the values each program variable has before the execution of this statement. This information is, of course, a dynamic property. It can, however, be calculated approximately. An approximation to this

Table 9.1   Type calculation for simple operators.

Operator	Type of 1st operand	Type of 2nd operand	Type of result
$+, -, *$	*int*	*int*	*int*
	int	*real*	*real*
	real	*int*	*real*
	real	*real*	*real*
/	*int* | *real*	*int* | *real*	*real*
$\div$	*int*	*int*	*int*

dynamic property consists of the fact that the value of some program variables can be calculated for some statements.

For example, if the information 'variable x has the value 5' is computed for one statement, this holds for all executions of this program and this statement. In this respect, condition (1) is satisfied. On the other hand, one possible piece of information for a statement is: 'for no variable is it known what value it will have on entry to this statement'. Thus, we shall not define the property 'value of variables' to be a static semantic property. This and similar properties are calculated by abstract interpretation.

As another example, let us consider the calculation of the type property for arithmetic expressions. We assume that we already know the type of all terminal operands, variables and constants, and that this is either integer or real. Then the type calculation for expressions formed using the operators $+, -, *, /$ and $\div$ (integer division) can be given as in Table 9.1.

Under the above assumptions the type property described in this way satisfies the two conditions for static semantic properties. Namely, if an expression e is calculated to have type t, it is certain that in every error-free execution of the program containing e the evaluation of e gives a value of type t. The only critical case here is the possibility of division by 0 at run time. If the underlying domains of the integers and the real numbers contain the undefined element of the respective type then, in the case of the expression of type real, the result of division by 0 is the undefined element of the domain of real numbers. In addition, as required by condition (2), for any correct program, the type of each expression can be calculated. In the case of a type error the function defined by Table 9.1 is not defined for a combination of arguments.

We therefore stress that the type property for expressions using the operators introduced above is a static semantic property. A number of other standard operators, such as unary minus, the modulo function, the absolute value and the rounding of real numbers up or down to the next integer, can be included without difficulty.

Now, however, we would like to extend the above by the power operator and define the type calculation for power expressions as in Algol 60, see Table 9.2.

Now, the type of the expression $e_1 \uparrow e_2$ depends not only on the types of e_1 and

Table 9.2 Type calculation for the power operator.

Operator	Type, size of 1st Operand	Type, size of 2nd operand	Type of result
↑	int | real	int > 0	int | real as 1st Op.
	int | real ≠ 0	int = 0	int | real as 1st Op.
	int | real ≠ 0	int < 0	real
	int | real > 0	real	real
	int | real = 0	real > 0.0	real = 0.0

e_2 but also on the value of e_2. This value is not a static property, but is only available at run time. If e_1 and e_2 are of type integer, then we cannot, in general, determine statically whether the result of the evaluations of $e_1 \uparrow e_2$ will be of type integer or real. Thus, the type property is no longer a static semantic property for the arithmetic expressions extended by exponentiation. A compiler will generate instructions that check at run time whether the operations following an exponentiation are using operands of the right type. As in the case of division by 0, runtime errors due to illegal values of e_1 and e_2 are also possible here.

Terminology

We use the following terms to describe a number of tasks of the semantic analysis. Here, using the contractions (i), (f) and (l), we list examples from imperative, functional and logic languages, respectively.

An **identifier** is a symbol (in the lexical analysis sense), which can be used in a program to name an object. Objects that can be named include variables in imperative, functional and logic languages, constants, types, procedures, functions, predicates and functors.

The **declaration** of an identifier introduces the identifier as the name of an object (usually given in the declaration). Its occurrence in a declaration is a **defining occurrence**, all other occurrences are **applied occurrences**.

Every programming language contains constructs that delimit the validity of identifiers. These constructs, for example

(i)   procedure declarations, blocks, packages, modules,

(f)   function definitions, let, letrec, and where constructs, and

(l)   clauses

are called **scope constructs**. Occurrences of scope constructs in programs are called **blocks**. Thus, in this usage, a procedure declaration in a Pascal program is a block, as are a function definition and a local definition with a let expression in a function program and a clause in a logic program.

The **type** of an object indicates what can be done with the object during the execution of the corresponding program. Thus, an integer value may become involved with other values in appropriate operations; for example, it may be (i) assigned to an integer variable, or (f) bound to an integer variable. (f) An object of type $(t_1 \times t_2 \times \cdots \times t_n \to t)$ can be applied to an n-tuple of objects of the types $t_1, \ldots, t_n$, to produce a result of type t.

Concrete and abstract syntax

The input for the semantic analysis of a program is a tree generated by the syntax analysis. This tree may represent the concrete or the abstract syntax of the program. The **concrete syntax** of the program is represented by the syntax tree in accordance with the context-free grammar defining the language. The context-free grammar for a language contains much information that is not important for the further processing of programs. This includes all terminal symbols, which are important for the syntax analysis and for reading programs, but are of no semantic importance, for example all keywords. In addition, precedences of operators are expressed in the nesting of nonterminals, one nonterminal per precedence depth. These nonterminals and associated productions are no longer relevant if the syntax structure is known. Thus, compilers use the **abstract syntax** for an explicit representation of the syntax structure of programs. It contains only the important part of the syntax structure of the program, namely the constructs occurring in the program and their nesting relationship.

Example 9.1   The program fragment

> **if** $x + 1 > y$
> **then** $z := 1$
> **else** $z := 2$
> **fi**

has (for a correspondingly conceived context-free grammar) trees for the concrete and the abstract syntax, as shown in Figures 9.1 and 9.2.   □

In what follows, we shall use the concrete or the abstract syntax, depending on which is the more advantageous. However, we stress that compilers always use the abstract syntax for semantic analysis and code generation.

9.1.1   Scoping and visibility rules

Since programming languages usually permit several declarations of the same identifier to denote different objects in a program, there is a need to determine the defining occurrence to which an applied occurrence relates. This is determined by the **scoping rules** and the **visibility rules**.

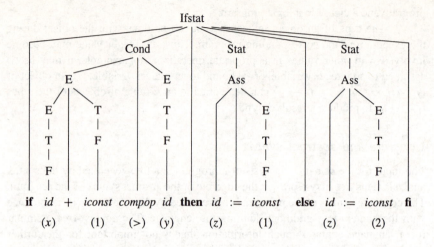

Figure 9.1   Tree for the concrete syntax.

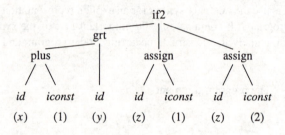

Figure 9.2   Tree for the abstract syntax.

The **scope or range of validity** of a defining occurrence of an identifier x is the part of the program (or several programs) in which an applied occurrence of x can relate to this defining occurrence.

The task of assigning corresponding defining occurrences (or the corresponding defining occurrence) to each applied occurrence of an identifier in accordance with the scoping and visibility rules is called the **identification of identifiers**. We shall see later that in programming languages that permit the **overloading** of identifiers, an applied occurrence of an identifier can actually relate to several defining occurrences.

The scoping and visibility rules of a programming language depend heavily on the nature of the nesting of scope constructs allowed by the language.

Scoping

Cobol does not allow nesting of scope constructs; all identifiers are valid and visible everywhere. Fortran only allows nesting depth 1, that is, blocks (procedure/function declarations) in a main program; no nesting beyond this is allowed. Identifiers defined in a block are only visible within that block. An identifier declared in the main program is visible everywhere, beginning with the declaration, except in procedure declarations that contain a new declaration of the identifier.

Algol 60, Algol 68, PL/I, Pascal, Ada, C and functional programming languages allow arbitrarily deep nesting of blocks. The scope and visibility of defining occurrences of identifiers are then controlled by additional specifications.

For a let construct **let** $v_1 == e_1; \ldots; v_n == e_n$ **in** e_0 the identifiers $v_1, \ldots, v_n$ are valid in e_0, the **body** of the let construct. Thus, applied occurrences of the v_i in the expressions $e_1, \ldots, e_n$ relate to defining occurrences in surrounding blocks. The same holds for the where construct.

The scope of the identifiers $v_1, \ldots, v_n$ for a letrec construct **letrec** $v_1 == e_1; \ldots; v_n == e_n$ **in** e_0 consists of the expressions $e_0, e_1, \ldots, e_n$. The same rule also holds for Algol 60 and Algol 68 blocks. Every identifier declared in a block is valid throughout the block.

This regulation makes it impossible to compile programs of such a programming language in one pass; for, in order to compile a declaration, the compiler may need information about an identifier whose definition has not yet been processed. Thus, Pascal and Ada (and C, see above) contain rules which avoid this problem. In Ada, the scope of an identifier begins with the end of the declaration and ends at the end of the block. In Pascal, the scope is the whole block, but an applied occurrence cannot come before the end of the declaration.

Prolog has several classes of identifiers, which are characterized by their syntactic position. The identifiers from the different classes have the following scoping rules (since there is no hiding, scope and visibility coincide):

- Predicates and functors are valid globally; they are valid throughout the Prolog program and in associated queries.
- Identifiers of clause variables are only valid in the clause in which they occur.

An analogue to declarations only exists for predicates, namely the set of alternatives for a predicate. Variables are untyped and therefore do not have to be declared. The concept of 'defining and applied occurrences of variables' also exists but has another meaning: a defining occurrence of a clause variable is the one that is the first to be bound in the sequential execution; an applied occurrence is one for which the binding has already been generated.

Visibility

It is not true that at every point in the scope of a defining occurrence of x an applied occurrence of x actually means this defining occurrence. If the defining occurrence is **global** to the actual block, that is, not in its declaration part, then a local declaration of x may **hide** it. It is then not **directly visible**. However, there are several ways of making a defining occurrence of an identifier x visible if it is not already directly visible within its scope. The visibility rules of a programming language specify the defining occurrences of an identifier to which an applied occurrence may relate. Here are some visibility rules from existing programming languages:

- **Extension of an identifier** by the identifier of a construct containing the declaration permits reference to a hidden defining occurrence. In Pascal, it is possible to make a name of a hidden record component visible by extending it by the name of the record. Ada permits extension by the identifier of the program unit containing the desired declaration.

- Some directives can be used to make a hidden defining occurrence of an identifier visible in a part of the scope (a **region**) without extending the identifier. These directives are usually also called statements, but are part of the static rather than the dynamic semantics.
  The boundaries of the region are either determined by special 'open and close' brackets as in the Pascal 'with' directive, or they are the same as the boundaries of the immediately surrounding program unit. The 'use' directive in Ada lists identifiers of surrounding program units, whose declarations are thus made visible. Such an identifier is visible from the end of the **use** directive to the end of the surrounding program unit.

- If a variable (and not just its implementation) includes the concept of separate compilation of program units, then there exist directives which make the definitions from separately compiled units visible. Each separately compilable program unit can offer its own definitions for use, for example an Ada package (a module) can offer the definitions of its public part, and a procedure can offer its formal parameters. We assign a scope to these identifiers which covers all programs which are linked together after separate compilation. Thus, the Ada 'with' directive makes visible identifiers provided by separately compiled units and mentioned in the 'with list'.

In summary, the scope of a defining occurrence of an identifier x is the part of a program in which the identifier can be used to address the object assigned to it in the definition. Within the scope, the definition is either directly visible or can be made visible.

9.1.2 Checking the context conditions

We shall now outline how the adherence to the context conditions can be verified in compilers. For this, we consider a simple case of a programming language with nested scope constructs but with no modules and no overloading.

The task is split into two subtasks. The first may be solved by a module called the declaration analyser. It solves the problem of the identification of identifiers and at the same time checks whether the declaration-related properties are satisfied. This involves the scoping and visibility rules of the programming language. The second subtask checks the type consistency.

Identification of identifiers

According to the scoping and visibility rules (in our simple case) there is precisely one defining occurrence for every applied occurrence of an identifier in a correct program. The identification of identifiers involves establishing this relationship between applied occurrences and defining occurrences or determining that no such (well-defined) relationship exists. The result of the identification is used by the type checking and code generation. Thus, it must survive beyond this phase. There are a number of ways of representing the correspondence between applied and defining occurrences. Traditionally, a compiler builds a so-called **symbol table**, in which the associated declarative information is stored for every defining occurrence of an identifier. This symbol table usually has an organization analogous to the block structure of the program, so that from any applied occurrence the corresponding defining occurrence can be (rapidly) reached. Such a symbol table is not the result of the identification but is used to perform it. The result of the identification is that for every node for an applied occurrence of an identifier, either

(1)   a pointer to the node for the declaration, or

(2)   the address of the symbol-table entry for the defining occurrence, or

(3)   the declarative information for the defining occurrence

is stored. In the case of alternatives (1) and (3) the symbol table can be released at the end of the identification phase. The syntax tree, supplemented by non-context-free information, remains the only data structure. Alternative (1) has the additional advantage that all applied occurrences for a defining occurrence share this. Thus we decide on alternative (1).

What operations must the symbol table offer? When the declaration analyser encounters a declaration, it has to enter the declared identifier together with a pointer to the associated declaration node of the syntax tree in the symbol table. Such a declaration occurs in some block. Another operation has to record the opening of blocks, and another the closing of blocks. The latter can remove the entries for declarations of the blocks closed from the symbol table. Thus, at any given time, the symbol table contains precisely the entries for declarations of all blocks that have been opened but are not yet closed. If the declaration analyser encounters an applied occurrence of an identifier it searches the symbol table according to the scoping and visibility rules for the entry for the corresponding defining occurrence. If it finds it, it copies the pointer to the declaration to the node for the applied occurrence.

Thus, overall, the following operations on the symbol table are required:

(a)   *create_symb_table*   creates an empty symbol table.

(b)   *enter_block*   records the opening of a new block.

(c)   *exit_block*   resets the symbol table to the
                                 state it was in before the last *enter_block*.

(d)   *enter_id(id, decl_ptr)*   adds an entry for identifier *id* to the symbol
                                 table. This contains the pointer to the declaration
                                 passed on in *decl_ptr*.

(e)   *search_id(id)*   searches for the defining occurrence for *id* and
                                 returns the pointer to the declaration,
                                 if it exists.

The last two operations or functions operate relative to the last block opened, the actual block.

Before we describe the implementation of the symbol table, that is, the procedures and functions listed above, we shall discuss their use in the declaration analysis. For this, we assume Ada-like scoping rules; that is, a defining occurrence of an identifier is only valid after the end of its declaration.

```
proc analyse_decl (k : node);
    proc analyse_subtrees (root: node);
    begin
        for i := 1 to #descs(root) do      (* #descs: Number of children *)
            analyse_decl(root.i)           (* ith child of root *)
        od
    end;

begin
    case symb(k) of        (* Label of k *)
    block:      begin
                    enter_block;
                    analyse_subtrees(k);
                    exit_block
                end;
    decl:       begin
                    analyse_subtrees(k);
                    foreach identifier id declared here do
                        enter_id(id, ↑k)
                    od
                end;
    appl_id:    (* applied occurrence of identifier id *)
                store search_id(id) at k;
    otherwise: if k not leaf then analyse_subtrees(k) fi
    od
end
```

The Ada scoping rules are expressed by the fact that in the *decl* case of the case statement all declarations are first processed recursively before the local declarations are entered. The modifications of this algorithm for Algol-like and Pascal-like scoping rules are left to the reader (see Exercise 4).

Checking of type consistency

The type consistency can be checked by a bottom-up pass over expression trees. For constant terminal operands the type is already fixed; for identifiers the type is obtained from the point where they are declared. For each operator a table lookup is performed (see Figure 9.4), to see whether the types of the operands fit and what the type of the result is. If built-in operators are overloaded the correct operation is also selected.

If the programming language permits type conversion, for example from integer to real, then for each operator and each invalid combination of operand types, a check is made to see whether the operand types can be converted to a valid combination of operand types for the operator.

Implementation of the symbol table

When implementing a symbol table, one must ensure that at any given time the *search_id* function finds the correct entry (among several possible entries) for an identifier, in accordance with the visibility rules.

A first solution might be a linear list of *enter_block* and *enter_id* entries. New entries are appended and *exit_block* deletes all previous *enter_id* entries from the end up to and including the last *enter_block* entry. *search_id* searches through the list from the end and in so doing will find all identifiers currently valid according to the Ada scoping rule. Since this linear list is clearly managed like a stack, it can also be organized as a stack.

This solution is marred by the cost of *search_id*, which depends linearly on the number of identifiers declared. A logarithmic search time in each block is achieved, if the entries for each block are managed in a binary search tree. The search then begins with the search tree of the actual block, and continues through the search tree of the surrounding block until a defining occurrence is found or it is determined that there is no such occurrence.

If we assume that each identifier defined has several applied occurrences, then *search_id* should be very efficient; at best it should run in constant time. This can be realized with the following data structure. The entries for all currently valid defining occurrences of an identifier are linearly linked; a new entry is appended to the end of this chain. An array component indexed by the identifier points to the last entry added. In addition, all entries belonging to the same block are linked, to support the *exit_block* procedure. A list header assigned to the block points to this chain. These list headers can be managed like stacks.

Example 9.2   The symbol table shown in Figure 9.4 is obtained for the program of Figure 9.3 and the point labelled ∗.   □

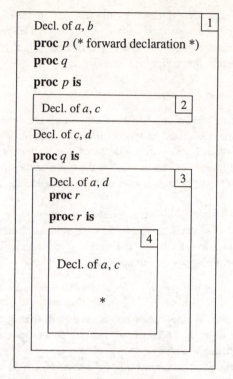

Figure 9.3 Example program.

The implementation of the symbol table operations is as follows:

```
proc create_symb_table;
    begin
        create empty stack of block entries
    end;

proc enter_block;
    begin
        push new entry for the new block
    end;

proc exit_block;
    begin
        foreach declaration entry of the current block do
            delete entry
        od;
        pop block entry from the stack
    end;
```

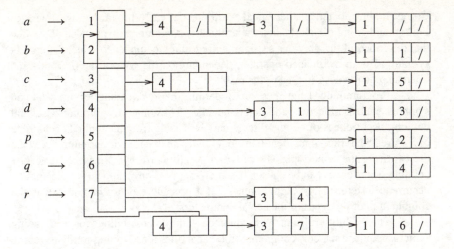

Figure 9.4   Symbol table for the program of Figure 9.3. For clarity, the chaining of the entries for a block is only shown for block 4. Otherwise, the 'addresses' of the boxes, numbers 1–7, are given. The empty box in each entry contains the pointer to the subtree for the declaration.

proc *enter_id* (*id: Idno; decl:* ↑ *node*);
    begin
        if an entry for *id* already exists in this block
        then *error*("Duplicate declaration")
        fi;
        create new entry with *decl* and no. of current block;
        add this entry to end of the linear list for *id*;
        add this entry to end of the linear list for this block
    end;

function *search_id* (*id: idno*) ↑ *node*;
    begin
        if list for *id* is empty
        then *error*("undeclared identifier")
        else return (Value of the decl. comp. from first entry in list for *id*)
        fi
    end

9.1.3   Overloading of identifiers

A symbol is said to be **overloaded** if it can have more than one meaning at a point in the program. Overloaded operators, such as the arithmetic operators, which may denote operations on the integers, the real numbers or the complex numbers, or even on rings or fields, depending on the context, are already known in mathematics.

Corresponding to the mathematical tradition, the early programming languages Fortran and Algol 60 overloaded the arithmetic operators. A type calculation, like that described in the previous section, is used in the compiler to select the correct operation for an overloaded operator, depending on the type of the operands and often also on the desired type of the result.

Programming languages often permit the overloading of user-defined symbols, such as procedure and function names. Thus, in correct programs, several defining occurrences of an identifier x may be visible from an applied occurrence of x. A redeclaration of an identifier x only hides an external declaration of x when the two have the same type. The program is only correct if precisely one of the defining occurrences can be chosen based on the 'type environment' of the applied occurrence. Here, the type environment of a procedure or a function call is the combination of the types of the actual parameters.

The visibility rules of Ada combined with the possibilities for overloading symbols require a scarcely comprehensible set of rules for resolving conflicts, for the cases where non-overloaded operators, which are visible or have been made visible in various ways, are in competition.

Example 9.3 (Ada program (Istvan Bach))

```
procedure BACH is
    procedure put (x: boolean) is begin null; end;
    procedure put (x: float)   is begin null; end;
    procedure put (x: integer) is begin null; end;
    package x is
       type boolean is (false, true);
       function f return boolean;                        -- (D1)
    end x;
    package body x is
       function f  return boolean is begin null; end;
    end x;
    function f return float is begin null; end;          -- (D2)
    use x;
begin
    put (f);                                             -- (A1)
    A: declare
       f: integer;                                       -- (D3)
    begin
       put (f);                                          -- (A2)
       B: declare
          function f return integer is begin null; end; -- (D4)
          begin
             put (f);                                    -- (A3)
          end B;
    end A;
end BACH;
```

In its public part, the package x declares two new identifiers, namely the type identifier boolean and the function identifier f. These two identifiers are (potentially) made visible by the 'use' statement use x; (see below (D2)) from the semicolon onwards. Function identifiers may be overloaded in Ada. Since the two declarations of f in (D1) and (D2) have different 'parameter profiles', in this case different result types, they are both (potentially) visible at the point (A1).

The declaration f: integer in the program unit A (see (D3)) hides the external declaration (D2) of f, since variable identifiers cannot be overloaded in Ada. For this reason, the declaration (D1) is not visible. The declaration (D4) of f in the program unit B again hides the declaration (D3), and since this hides the declaration (D2), by transitivity (D4) also hides (D2). However, the declaration (D1), which was (potentially) made visible by the use statement, is not hidden and remains potentially visible. In the context of put(f) (see (A3)), f can only relate to the declaration (D4), since the first declaration of put uses a different type, boolean, from the result type of f in (D1).   □

The selection of the correct defining occurrence of an overloaded symbol is called **overload resolution**. The overload resolution takes place after the identification of identifiers within certain constructs of the language, that is, it is restricted to expressions, (composite) identifiers, and so on.

The resolution algorithm runs on the representation of the Ada program as an abstract syntax tree. Conceptually, this involves four passes over an expression tree. However, the first and second and the third and fourth passes can be merged.

To formulate the algorithm, we introduce the following notation. For every node k of the abstract syntax tree, we speak of

$\#descs(k)$	the number of child nodes of k,
$symb(k)$	the symbol with which k is labelled,
$vis(k)$	the set of definitions of $symb(k)$ visible to k,
$ops(k)$	the set of current candidates for the overloaded symbol $symb(k)$ and
$k.i$	as usual, the ith child of k.

For every defining occurrence of an overloaded symbol op with type $t_1 \times \cdots \times t_m \to t$ we let

$rank(op)$	$=$	m
$res\_type(op)$	$=$	t
$par\_type(op, i)$	$=$	$t_i \quad (1 \leq i \leq m)$

We extend the last two definitions to sets of operators. For every expression in which the overloading of operators is to be resolved, a type, the so-called a priori type, is calculated from its context.

proc *resolve_overloading* (*root: node, a_priori_type: type*);

func *pot_res_types* (*k: node*): **set of** *type*;
　　　　　　(∗ potential type of the result ∗)
　　return {*res_type(op)* | *op* ∈ *ops(k)*}

func *act_par_types* (*k: node, i:* **integer**): **set of** *type*;
　　return {*par_type(op, i)* | *op* ∈ *ops(k)*}

proc *init_ops*
begin
　　foreach *k*
　　　　ops(k) := {*op* | *op* ∈ *vis(k)* **and** *rank(op)* = #*descs(k)*}
　　od;
　　ops(root) := {*op* ∈ *ops(k)* | *res_type(op)* = *a_priori_type*}
end;

proc *bottom_up_elim* (*k: node*);
begin
　　for *i* := 1 **to** #*descs(k)* **do**
　　　　bottom_up_elim (*k.i*);
　　　　ops(k) := *ops(k)* − {*op* ∈ *ops(k)* | *par_type(op, i)* ∉ *pot_res_types(k.i)*}
　　　　　　(∗ eliminate the operators, whose *i*th parameter type does not
　　　　　　match any of the possible result types for the *i*th operands ∗)
　　od;
end;

proc *top_down_elim* (*k: node*);
begin
　　for *i* := 1 **to** #*descs(k)* **do**
　　　　ops(k.i) := *ops(k.i)* − {*op* ∈ *ops(k.i)* | *res_type(op)* ∉ *act_par_types(k, i)*};
　　　　　　(∗ eliminate the operators, whose result type does not match
　　　　　　a type of the associated parameter ∗)
　　　　top_down_elim(k.i)
　　od;
end;

begin
　　init_ops;
　　bottom_up_elim(root);
　　top_down_elim(root);
　　check that all *ops* sets now consist of a single element;
　　otherwise error message
end

The bottom-up elimination and the top-down elimination appear to do the same thing. That is almost true. Figure 9.5 shows a combination of nodes labelled op_1 and op_2. Every node is associated with a set of possible definitions of the operator. The bottom-up elimination deletes candidates from the definition set for op_1, the top-down elimination from that for op_2.

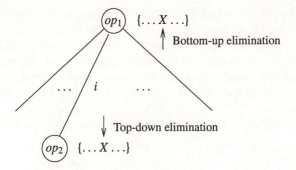

Figure 9.5   Bottom-up and top-down elimination.

9.1.4   Polymorphism

Overloading of operators, which was informally introduced in the last section, allows different definitions to be visible at an application. One of the definitions must be chosen, based on the combination of the operand and result types. The overloading of operators is also referred to as **ad hoc polymorphism**. On the other hand, **parametric polymorphism**, which occurs in functional programming languages and in the form of generic packages in Ada, allows one to give **one** definition of a function which does essentially the same thing for a set of combinations of operand and result types. This flexibility is not paid for by poorer error detection, for part of any compiler for a programming language with polymorphic types is a type inference algorithm, which computes the right type for every application of a polymorphically typed function and determines whether all these computed types have a common type scheme, which is then the type of the function.

To every function defined in a type-correct program, the type inference module assigns its most general type, that is, the least specified operand and result types, for which no type error in an application of the function can occur in any dynamic execution of the program. Thereby, different applications of the function may be statically assigned different instances of this most general type.

As an example, we use the LaMa language of Section 3.3.2. We recall the representation of the (abstract) syntax of LaMa programs in Table 9.3. A let construct has been added.

Type terms (**types** for short) are constructed from type variables, $\alpha, \beta, \gamma, \ldots$, which stand for arbitrary types (note that we have now overloaded the term 'type': types are both the built-in and the user-definable types of the programming language, that is, semantic concepts, and the representation of these by type terms) and from operators. The built-in types *int* and *bool* are represented by the placeless operators **int** and **bool**. **list** is a one-place operator. $\rightarrow$, the constructor for function types, and $\times$, the constructor for pair types, are two-place operators. The most general forms of list, pair and function types are **list** α, $\alpha \times \beta$ and $\alpha \rightarrow \beta$. The substitution of types for the type variables, known as instantiation, produces more special types, such as **list int**, **int** $\rightarrow$ **bool**, **list** $\alpha \rightarrow$ **int** and $(\gamma \rightarrow \delta) \rightarrow \beta$. Types that contain type variables are said to be **polymorphic**, those without type variables are **monomorphic**. The polymorphic identity function $\lambda x.x$ has the type $\alpha \rightarrow \alpha$. This has the monomorphic instantiations **int** $\rightarrow$ **int**, **bool** $\rightarrow$ **bool**, **list int** $\rightarrow$ **list int**, and so on.

The assignment of built-in LaMa operators to types is as follows:

true, false : bool	**pair:** $\alpha \rightarrow \beta \rightarrow (\alpha \times \beta)$
$0, 1, \ldots :$ **int**	**fst:** $(\alpha \times \beta) \rightarrow \alpha$
succ, pred, neg : int $\rightarrow$ **int**	**snd:** $(\alpha \times \beta) \rightarrow \beta$
plus, sub, mul, div : int $\rightarrow$ **int** $\rightarrow$ **int**	
cons : $\alpha \rightarrow$ **list** $\alpha \rightarrow$ **list** α	
head : list $\alpha \rightarrow \alpha$	
tail : **list** $\alpha \rightarrow$ **list** α	
null : list $\beta \rightarrow$ **bool**	

This defines an initial **type environment**, with which the type inference begins. Type combination rules are assigned to the composite LaMa constructs, which describe conditions on the types of the constituents. The application of the rules introduces new type variables.

The conditional expression **if** e **then** e_1 **else** e_2 **fi** has the type α and gives the type conditions e : **bool** and e_1 : α and e_2 : α with a newly introduced type variable α. Thus, the types t, t_1 and t_2 calculated for e, e_1 and e_2 must satisfy these conditions. These calculated types and the above types are matched by unification. Here, both α and type variables in the t, t_1 and t_2 can be bound. Of course, all occurrences of α must be bound to the same type.

The **function application** $e_1 e_2$ requires e_1 to have a type $\alpha \rightarrow \beta$ and e_2 to have the type α, and the result of the application is of type β, again with new type names α and β.

The **abstraction** $\lambda v.e$ has the type $\alpha \rightarrow \beta$, where α is a new type variable for the type of v and β is of the type that results for e if **all** free occurrences of v in e are assigned the type α. It seems that the specification that all free occurrences of v in e should be assigned the same type is an unnecessary restriction of the flexibility of the type system, since it should be possible to assign different types to different occurrences of a polymorphically typed identifier. Let us consider the following example: $g = \lambda f.\textbf{pair} \ (f \ 5) \ (f \ \textbf{true})$. The subexpression $f \ 5$ gives f the type **int** $\rightarrow \alpha$ and the expression f **true** then gives it the type **bool** $\rightarrow \beta$; the types **int** $\rightarrow \alpha$ and **bool** $\rightarrow \beta$ cannot be unified with each other. Thus, the above expression cannot be assigned a type. Of course, there exist type assignments that work correctly in some cases, for example the assignment g : $(\alpha \rightarrow \textbf{int}) \rightarrow \textbf{int}$ for the application $g \ (\lambda x.0)$. The application $g \ (\lambda x.0)$ would not lead to a type error at run time. The result would be **pair** $(\lambda x.0 \ 5) \ (\lambda x.0 \ \textbf{true}) = \textbf{pair} \ 0 \ 0$. But this only says that an application to **this** function, $\lambda x.0$, would be dynamically type correct; however, it requires that no application of g should lead to type errors. Even the application

Table 9.3   The syntax of LaMa.

Element name	Domain	
b	B	Set of basic values, e.g. Boolean values, integer, character,... The empty list, [ ]
op_{bin}	Op_{bin}	Set of binary operators, e.g. $+, -, =, \neq,$ **and, or, cons, pair,** ...
op_{un}	Op_{un}	Set of unary operators, e.g. $-,$ **not, head, tail, fst, snd,** ...
v	V	Set of variables
e	E	Set of expressions

$e = b \mid v \mid (op_{un}\ e\ ) \mid (e_1\ op_{bin}\ e_2)$

$\quad \mid$ (**if** e_1 **then** e_2 **else** e_3)

$\quad \mid (e_1 e_2)$ function application

$\quad \mid (\lambda v.e)$ functional abstraction

$\quad \mid$ (**letrec** $v_1 == e_1;$ simultaneously recursive definitions

                    $v_2 == e_2;$

                       $\vdots$

                    $v_n == e_n$

    in e_0)

$\quad \mid$ (**let** $v_1 == e_1;$ non-recursive definition

                       $v_2 == e_2;$

                       $\vdots$

                    $v_n == e_n$

    in e_0)

to the identity function, $(\lambda x.x)$, would lead to a type error, since at run time **one** monomorphic version of the identity function, for example of the type **int** $\rightarrow$ **int** or **bool** $\rightarrow$ **bool**, would be passed to g. But every monomorphic version will lead to a type error. Thus, type inference is not concerned with whether a type can be assigned to a term in a particularly favourable context; instead, the type assignment must result in correct typing under all circumstances.

Thus, we require that all occurrences of an identifier bound by a λ-abstraction should be assigned the same type. The type variables in the type of an identifier bound by a λ-abstraction are said to be **non-generic** within the scope of this binding.

In **let expressions let** $v == e_1$ **in** e_2 one can be more liberal and assign different types to different occurrences of v in e_2, since more information is available than in the case of the λ-abstraction. The binding of v, to e_1, is already visible. Thus, in

$$\textbf{let } f == \lambda x.x \textbf{ in pair } (f\ 5)\ (f\ \textbf{true})$$

f can be assigned the type $\alpha \rightarrow \alpha$. The type variables in the types of identifiers bound by **let**, which do not occur in the types of λ-bound identifiers in the neighbourhood of the **let**, are said to be **generic**. Different occurrences of the **let**-bound identifier are assigned different 'versions' of the type of the identifier, where two versions differ only in the consistent renaming of all generic identifiers in the type. The generic identifiers are fixed and must therefore be the same in all versions.

The type of a **let** expression

$$\textbf{let } v_1 == e_1 \ldots;\ v_n == e_n \quad \textbf{in } e$$

is therefore calculated as follows. First, all equations are type checked, resulting in n pairs $v_i : t_i$ where t_i is the type of e_i. Different versions of t_i $(1 \leq i \leq n)$ are then used for all occurrences of v_i in e and the type of e is calculated.

In a **letrec expression**

$$\textbf{letrec } v_1 == e_1;\ \ldots;\ v_n == e_n \quad \textbf{in } e$$

the occurrences of the v_i in the e_i are assigned non-generic type variables and those in e generic type variables.

The type checking first creates a type environment $\{v_1 : \alpha_1, \ldots, v_n : \alpha_n\}$ with non-generic type variables $\alpha_1, \ldots, \alpha_n$. Then, in this type environment it computes the types t_i of the e_i. These types t_i are then unified with the α_i and/or their instances.

Example 9.4 (type calculation for a LaMa expression)

$$\textbf{letrec } \textit{append} == \lambda l_1\ l_2.$$
$$\textbf{if null } l_1$$
$$\textbf{then } l_2$$
$$\textbf{else}$$
$$\textbf{let} \quad x == \textbf{head } l_1$$
$$y == \textbf{tail } l_1$$
$$\textbf{in} \quad \textbf{cons } x\ (\ \textit{append } y\ l_2)$$
$$\textbf{in} \ldots$$

This results in type assignments $(a : t)$ for subterms of the program, and type equations $(\alpha = t)$ for type variables α introduced.

(1)	**null** $:$ **list** $\alpha \rightarrow$ **bool**	the type assignments of the built-in
(2)	**cons** $: \beta \rightarrow$ **list** $\beta \rightarrow$ **list** β	operators occurring in
(3)	**head** $:$ **list** $\gamma \rightarrow \gamma$	the definition of *append*.
(4)	**tail** $:$ **list** $\delta \rightarrow$ **list** δ	

(5)	$append : \varepsilon$	new type variables for the
(6)	$l_1 \qquad : \zeta$	letrec- and λ-bound names.
(7)	$l_2 \qquad : \eta$	

(8)	$(\textbf{head } l_1) \; \gamma$	Unification between **list** γ as argument type
	$\zeta = \textbf{list } \gamma$	of **head** and ζ as type of l_1.
(9)	$(\textbf{tail } l_1) : \textbf{list } \gamma$	Unification between **list** δ and the new
	$\delta = \gamma$	type, **list** γ, of l_1.
(10)	$x : \gamma$	Left sides inherit the calculated type
(11)	$y : \textbf{list } \gamma$	of the right sides.

(12)	$append: \vartheta \to \iota$	Function type, since on left in an application.
	$\varepsilon = \vartheta \to \iota$	
	$\vartheta = \textbf{list } \gamma$	Unification with type of y.
(13)	$(append\, y) : \iota$	Type of the application.

(14)	$(append\, y) : \kappa \to \mu$	Function type, since applied to l_2.
	$\iota = \kappa \to \mu$	
	$\kappa = \eta$	Unification with type of l_2.
(15)	$(append\, y\, l_2): \mu$	

(16)	$\textbf{cons}: \gamma \to \textbf{list } \gamma \to \textbf{list } \gamma$	Unification of β with γ.
	$\beta = \gamma$	
(17)	$(\textbf{cons } x): \textbf{list } \gamma \to \textbf{list } \gamma$	
	$\mu = \textbf{list } \gamma$	Unification with type of $(append\, y\, l_2)$
	$\iota = \eta \to \textbf{list } \gamma$	according to (14).
	$\varepsilon = \textbf{list } \gamma \to \eta \to \textbf{list } \gamma$	
(18)	$\textbf{cons } x\, (append\, y\, l_2): \textbf{list } \gamma$	
	$\eta = \textbf{list } \gamma$	**then** and **else** part
	$\varepsilon = \textbf{list } \gamma \to \textbf{list } \gamma \to \textbf{list } \gamma$	must have same type.

Thus, the polymorphic type of *append* is given by:

$$\textbf{list } \gamma \to \textbf{list } \gamma \to \textbf{list } \gamma \qquad\qquad \square$$

9.2   Attribute grammars

Attribute grammars are used to describe the static semantic analysis in most compiler generating systems. They associate attributes, as carriers of static semantic information, with the symbols of a context-free grammar, the so-called **underlying grammar**. In addition, they show what the **functional dependencies** between the values of **occurrences of attributes** in the productions of the grammar are. Such a functional dependency can be viewed as a computational prescription, which specifies how the value of the occurrence of an attribute is calculated from the values of other occurrences of attributes of the same production.

Appropriate conditions for the functional dependencies ensure that all **instances of attributes** in every syntax tree for a syntactically and semantically correct program can be **evaluated**, that is, can be assigned a value from their **domain of attribute values**.

Definition 9.1 (attribute grammar)

Suppose $G = (V_N, V_T, P, S)$ is a context-free grammar. As before, we write the pth production in P as $p : X_0 \rightarrow X_1 \ldots X_{n_p}$, $X_i \in V_N \cup V_T$, $0 \leq i \leq n_p$. An **attribute grammar AG** over G consists of

- an association of two disjoint sets, $Inh(X)$, the set of the **inherited** attributes and $Syn(X)$, the set of the **synthesized** attributes, with each symbol of $V_N \cup V_T$. We let $Attr(X) = Inh(X) \cup Syn(X)$ denote the set of all attributes of X; if $a \in Attr(X_i)$, then a has an **occurrence** in production p at the occurrence of X_i, which we write as a_i. Let $V(p)$ be the set of all attribute occurrences in production p.

$$Inh = \bigcup_{X \in V_N} Inh(X); \quad Syn = \bigcup_{X \in V_N \cup V_T} Syn(X); \quad Attr = Inh \cup Syn$$

- the specification of a **domain** D_a for each attribute $a \in Attr$, that is, the set of its potential values;

- a **semantic rule**

$$a_i = f_{p,a,i}(b_{j_1}^1, \ldots, b_{j_k}^k) \quad (0 \leq j_l \leq n_p)(1 \leq l \leq k)$$

  for each attribute $a \in Inh(X_i)$ for $1 \leq i \leq n_p$ and each $a \in Syn(X_0)$ in every production p, where $b_{j_l}^l \in Attr(X_{j_l})$ $(0 \leq j_l \leq n_p)$ $(1 \leq l \leq k)$. Thus, $f_{p,a,i}$ is a function from $D_{b^1} \times \ldots \times D_{b^k}$ to D_a. $\qquad\square$

We always view an attribute as an attribute of **one** nonterminal or terminal; that is, the assignments Inh and Syn can be viewed as injective functions from the set $V_N \cup V_T$ into the set of attributes. We stress this because several attributes for different nonterminals and terminals may have the same name. This is sensible when they are carriers of the same type of information.

Definition 9.2 (defining, applied occurrence, normal form)

Let AG be an attribute grammar and p a production. The attribute occurrences a_i with $a \in Inh(X_i)$ and $1 \leq i \leq n_p$ and with $a \in Syn(X_0)$ are called **defining** occurrences. All others are called **applied** occurrences. AG is in **normal form** if all arguments of semantic rules are applied occurrences. $\qquad\square$

We have also allowed synthesized attributes for the terminal symbols of the grammar. However, the occurrences of these attributes are applied, whence there are no

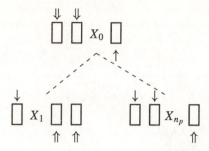

Figure 9.6 A production (with attributes). Inherited attribute occurrences are shown as boxes to the left of syntactical symbols, synthesized occurrences as boxes to the right of symbols. Simple arrows denote semantic rules of the production, double arrows the flow of information from outside into the rules.

semantic rules for them. How then do they obtain their values? In a formal definition of the attribute grammars, so-called **external rules** are used to calculate the values of instances of synthesized attributes for terminal symbols 'from nothing'. In practice, that is, in a compiler, the semantic analysis is performed after the lexical and syntax analysis. Typical synthesized attributes for terminals include the value of constants, the external representation or a unique identification of names, the address of string constants, and so on. The values of these attributes are usually provided by the scanner, at least, if it is extended by a number of bookkeeping functions. Thus, in practice, the synthesized attributes play a major role for (some) terminal symbols. Later, in our description of the generation procedure, they upset the representation somewhat, without causing difficulties as far as the implementation is concerned. We shall omit them then.

In an attribute grammar in normal form, for each defining attribute occurrence in a production, there exists precisely one semantic rule, and all its arguments are applied attribute occurrences. Let us consider an instance of the production in a syntax tree. Then, the instances of applied attribute occurrences must obtain their values from outside (the instance of) the production, inherited attributes on the left side of the production from the upper tree fragment and synthesized attributes on the right side from the underlying subtrees and/or via 'external rules', see Figure 9.6.

9.2.1 The semantics of an attribute grammar

What are the semantics of an attribute grammar? Under certain conditions, for each syntax tree t of the underlying context-free grammar they specify an assignment of attribute values to nodes of t as follows. Let n be a node of t. We view n as a word over $\mathbb{N}$ and define the concatenation $n.j$ (also nj for short) in the usual way, except that we specify that $n.0 = n$. Let $symb(n) \in V_N \cup V_T$ be the symbol, labelling

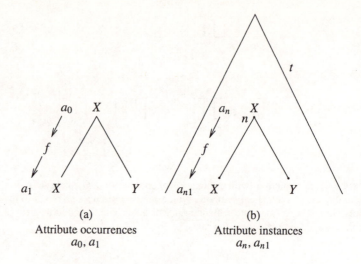

(a)   (b)
Attribute occurrences   Attribute instances
a_0, a_1 a_n, a_{n1}

Figure 9.7   (a) Attribute occurrences, semantic rules at generation time, (b) attribute instances, induced semantic relation at compile time.

n. If $symb(n) \in V_N$, then let $prod(n)$ be the production applied at n. For every attribute $a \in Attr(symb(n))$ there exists an **attribute instance** a_n at n. This instance should be assigned a value from within its domain D_a. The values of the different attribute instances for the instance of $prod(n)$ must be related as follows. Let $val(a_m)$ be the value of the instance of a for the node m. If $a_i = f_{p,a,i}(b^1_{j_1}, \ldots, b^k_{j_k})$ is a semantic rule of $prod(n) = p$, then it induces the following relation between values of attribute instances:

$$val(a_{ni}) = f_{p,a,i}(val(b^1_{nj_1}), \ldots, val(b^k_{nj_k}))$$

Thus, attributes and attribute occurrences 'exist' from the moment the attribute grammar is written, whence, in any case, whenever an attribute evaluator is to be generated. Attribute instances first exist at compile time, when a syntax tree has been constructed, that is, at the time that the attribute instances are evaluated. Suppose $a \in Inh(X)$ is an attribute of a nonterminal X, and $p : X \longrightarrow XY$ is a production. Then a has two occurrences in a_0 and a_1 in p. Suppose p contains the semantic rule $a_1 = f(a_0)$. Figure 9.7(a) shows this relationship between the attribute occurrences of p; Figure 9.7(b) shows the relationship this induces between the corresponding attribute instances of an application of p in a syntax tree.

Let $V(t) = \{a_m\}_{m \in t, \, a \in Attr(symb(m))}$ be the set of all attribute instances in t. There exists a system of equations in the unknowns a_m induced in this way by the attribute grammar. If this system of equations is recursive (cyclic), then it may have several solutions or even no solutions. If it is not recursive, then it has precisely one solution, that is, precisely one value per attribute instance. An attribute grammar is said to be **well formed** if none of these systems of equations is recursive. In this case, the semantics of the attribute grammar are represented by the well-defined assignment of attribute values to the nodes of the syntax trees of the underlying context-free grammar.

9.2.2   A notation for attribute grammars

In what follows, we shall present a number of example grammars in the following syntax:

AttrGramm	$\longrightarrow$	*GrammName: Nonts; Attrs; Rules; Functions*
GrammName	$\longrightarrow$	**attribute grammar** *Name*
Nonts	$\longrightarrow$	**nonterminals** *NonEmptyNamList*
Attrs	$\longrightarrow$	**attributes** *AttrDeclList*
AttrDeclList	$\longrightarrow$	*AttrDeclList; AttrDecl* | ε
AttrDecl	$\longrightarrow$	*Direction Name* **with** *NonEmptyNamList DomSpec*
Direction	$\longrightarrow$	**inh** | **syn**
DomSpec	$\longrightarrow$	**domain** *Domain*
Rules	$\longrightarrow$	**rules** *RuleList*
RuleList	$\longrightarrow$	*RuleList Rule* | *Rule*
Rule	$\longrightarrow$	*CfRule SemRuleList*
CfRule	$\longrightarrow$	*Name* $'\to'$ *NamList*
SemRuleList	$\longrightarrow$	*SemRuleList SemRule* | ε
SemRule	$\longrightarrow$	*Attr* $'='$ *Name (AttrList)* | *Attr* $'='$ *Attr* |
		Attr $'='$ *Const*
AttrList	$\longrightarrow$	*AttrList Attr* | *Attr*
Attr	$\longrightarrow$	*Name.Name* | *Name Index.Name*
Functions	$\longrightarrow$	**functions** *FunctDefList*
FunctDefList	$\longrightarrow$	*FunctDefList FunctDef* | ε
NamList	$\longrightarrow$	*NonEmptyNamList* | ε
NonEmptyNamList	$\longrightarrow$	*NonEmptyNamList Name* | *Name*

Of course, context conditions must also hold for the language in which attribute grammars are written; we list the most important of these:

- Only names which are listed after **nonterminals** may occur on the left side of Cfrules (context-free production rules).

- $X.Y$ and $X_i.Y$ are allowed as attribute names, where X is a nonterminal from the preceding context-free production and Y is an attribute name, which is associated with X according to the **attributes** specification. $X_i.Y$ denotes the attribute occurrence of Y for the ith occurrence of X on the right side, for $i > 0$, and for the occurrence of X on the left side, for $i = 0$.

- Each defining occurrence of an attribute in a production must occur in precisely one semantic rule of the production on the left, and only defining occurrences may occur on the left side. Only applied occurrences of attributes of the production may occur on the right side of semantic rules (normal form).

- For every occurrence of a function symbol in a semantic rule there must exist precisely one definition in the function part.

9.3 Examples of attribute grammars

The following attribute grammars describe several versions of the type-calculation problem for arithmetic expressions. They are used later as examples of members of certain classes of attribute grammars and to demonstrate the implementation problems and techniques.

To define the functional relationship between attribute occurrences we use a functional programming language with the following properties:

- The different cases for the function are given by the permissible combinations of argument values and variables.

- Arguments irrelevant for a case are denoted by an anonymous variable '_'.

- If an actual argument tuple falls under several cases the 'special' case is selected; here constants are more special than variables and a tuple t_1 is more special than a tuple t_2, if t_1 is obtained from t_2 by a substitution of constants for variables (the case of incomparable cases which overlap in the above way does not arise here).

- Variables which occur several times in a tuple must have the same value for the corresponding case to be chosen.

Example 9.5 (attribute grammar AG$_1$)

attribute grammar AG$_1$:
nonterminals E, T, F, P, Aop, Mop;
attributes   **syn** *type* **with** E, T, F, P, c, v **domain** {*int*, *real*};
                 syn *op* **with** Aop, Mop **domain** {$'+',' -',' *',' /',' \div'$};

rules

1 : $E \to E\ Aop\ T$ 2 : $E \to T$
      $E_0.type = f_1(E_1.type, T.type)$ $E.type = T.type$

3 : $T \to T\ Mop\ F$ 4 : $T \to F$
      $T_0.type = f_3(\ Mop.op, T_1.type, F.type\ )$ $T.type = F.type$

5 : $F \to P$ 6 : $P \to c$
      $F.type = P.type$ $P.type = c.type$

7 : $P \to v$ 8 : $P \to (E)$

        $P.type = v.type$ $P.type = E.type$

9 : $Aop \to +$ 10 : $Aop \to -$

        $Aop.op = {}'+'$ $Aop.op = {}'-'$

11 : $Mop \to *$ 12 : $Mop \to /$

        $Mop.op = {}'*'$ $Mop.op = {}'/'$

13 : $Mop \to \div$

        $Mop.op = {}'\div'$

functions:

$f_1\ int\ int$ $=$ int $f_3\ '*'\ int\ int$ $=$ int

$f_1\ \_\ \_$ $=$ $real$ $f_3\ '\div'\ int\ int$ $=$ int

                                 $f_3\ '*'\ \_\ \_$ $=$ $real$

                                 $f_3\ '/'\ \_\ \_$ $=$ $real$ □

The first attribute grammar, **AG**$_1$, shown in Example 9.5, describes the type calculation for expressions with the operators $+, -, *, /$ and $\div$ and variables and constants of the type *integer* or *real*.

We consider the problem in isolation from the rest of the semantic analysis, that is, we assume that for the terminal operands, constants and variables, the type has already been calculated. We shall see later how this can be done using attribute grammars.

This observation forms the basis for a statistically very well-founded observation; a large part of the semantic rules are equations (copying actions) between two attribute occurrences. It is typical of attribute grammars that attributes are calculated at certain 'places' in the grammar and their values are then transported over long distances before being used at other places in the grammar. Thus, we introduce a new convention for defining attribute grammars, which frees them from most copying actions. If there is no semantic rule for an inherited attribute occurrence on the right side (synthesized occurrence on the left side), a copying action of an inherited attribute occurrence on the left side of the same name is assumed (synthesized attribute occurrence on the right side).

Of course, in the case of a copying action to a synthesized attribute on the left side, precisely one synthesized attribute with the same name must occur on the right side. The following examples already use this convention.

We now consider two versions of the type calculation for arithmetic expressions, which permit a better localization of type errors. For if according to **AG**$_1$ in an expression $e_1 \div e_2$ the type of e_2 is calculated to be *real*, an error message will be issued because the function f_3 is not defined for this combination of arguments. However, it is not clear where the cause of this error lies, for example, in a real terminal operand or in a division in e_2. The next attribute grammar, **AG**$_2$, in Example 9.6, describes how the cause of this type error can be localized in right operands of $'\div'$. It passes the information that the result type *integer* is required to subexpressions in an attribute, *obltype*.

Example 9.6 (attribute grammar AG_2)

attribute grammar AG_2:
nonterminals S, E, T, F, P, Aop, Mop;
attributes   **syn** *type* **with** E, T, F, P, c, v **domain** $\{int, real\}$;
    syn *op* **with** Aop, Mop **domain** $\{'+', '-', '*', '/', '\div'\}$;
    inh *obltype* **with** E, T, F, P **domain** $\{int, unspec\}$;

rules

$$1: \quad E \to E\ Aop\ T$$
$$E_0.type = f_1(E_1.type, T.type)$$
$$3: \quad T \to T\ Mop\ F$$
$$T_0.type = f_3^1(Mop.op, T_0.obltype, T_1.type, F.type)$$
$$F.obltype = f_3^2(Mop.op, T_0.obltype)$$
$$5: \quad F \to P$$
$$7: \quad P \to v$$
$$P.type = f_6(P.obltype, v.type)$$
$$9: \quad Aop \to +$$
$$Aop.op = '+'$$
$$11: \quad Mop \to *$$
$$Mop.op = '*'$$
$$13: \quad Mop \to \div$$
$$Mop.op = '\div'$$

$$0: \quad S \to E$$
$$E.obltype := unspec$$
$$2: \quad E \to T$$
$$4: \quad T \to F$$
$$6: \quad P \to c$$
$$P.type = f_6(P.obltype, c.type)$$
$$8: \quad P \to (E)$$
$$10: Aop \to -$$
$$Aop.op = '-'$$
$$12: Mop \to /$$
$$Mop.op = '/'$$

functions:

$$f_3^1\ '*'\ int\ int\ int \quad = \quad int \qquad f_3^2\ '\div'\ \_ \quad = \quad int$$
$$f_3^1\ '/'\ unspec\ \_\ \_ \quad = \quad real \qquad f_3^2\ \_\ int \quad = \quad int$$
$$f_3^1\ '\div'\ \_\ int\ int \quad = \quad int \qquad f_3^2\ \_\ \_ \quad = \quad unspec$$
$$f_3^1\ '*'\ \_\ \_\ \_ \quad = \quad real$$

$$f_1\ int\ int \quad = \quad int \qquad f_6\ int\ int \quad = \quad int$$
$$f_1\ \_\ \_ \quad = \quad real \qquad f_6\ unspec\ t \quad = \quad t \qquad \qquad \Box$$

The attribute grammar AG_2 has a somewhat unnatural asymmetry (those in the know are aware of why it was constructed in this way). Only right operands of $'\div'$ are explicitly assigned the type they require. This asymmetry will now be removed, by replacing production 3 by the new production 3' as in Example 9.7. The resulting grammar will be denoted by AG_3.

Example 9.7 (attribute grammar AG_3)
This is obtained from AG_2 by replacing production 3 by 3'.

attribute grammar AG_3:
nonterminals S, E, T, F, P, Aop, Mop;
attributes   **syn** $type$ **with** E, T, F, P, c, v **domain** $\{int, real\}$;
                  syn op **with** Aop, Mop **domain** $\{'+',' -',' *'y,' /',' \div'\}$;
                  inh $obltype$ **with** E, T, F, P **domain** $\{int, unspec\}$;

rules

0 : $S \rightarrow E$
       $E.obltype := unspec$

1 : $E \rightarrow E\, Aop\, T$ 2 : $E \rightarrow T$
       $E_0.type = f_1(E_1.type, T.type)$ 4 : $T \rightarrow F$

3' : $T \rightarrow T\, Mop\, F$ 6 : $P \rightarrow c$
       $T_0.type = f_3^1(Mop.op, T_0.obltype,$ $P.type = f_6(P.obltype, c.type)$
       $\qquad\qquad\qquad T_1.type, F.type)$ 8 : $P \rightarrow (E)$
       $T_1.obltype = f_3^2(Mop.op, T_0.obltype)$ 10 : $Aop \rightarrow -$
       $F.obltype = f_3^2(Mop.op, T_0.obltype)$

5 : $F \rightarrow P$ $Aop.op = '-'$

7 : $P \rightarrow v$ 12 : $Mop \rightarrow /$
       $P.type = f_6(P.obltype, v.type)$ $Mop.op = '/'$

9 : $Aop \rightarrow +$ 13 : $Mop \rightarrow \div$
       $Aop.op = '+'$ $Mop.op = '\div'$

11 : $Mop \rightarrow *$
       $Mop.op = '*'$

functions:

$$f_3^1 \,'*'\, int\ int\ int\ =\ int \qquad f_3^2 \,'\div'\, \_\ =\ int$$
$$f_3^1 \,'/'\, unspec\,\_\_\ =\ real \qquad f_3^2 \,\_\, int\ =\ int$$
$$f_3^1 \,'\div'\, \_\, int\ int\ =\ int \qquad f_3^2 \,\_\_\ =\ unspec$$
$$f_3^1 \,'*'\, \_\_\_\ =\ real$$

$$f_1\ int\ int\ =\ int \qquad f_6\ int\ int\ =\ int$$
$$f_1\ \_\_\ =\ real \qquad f_6\ unspec\ t\ =\ t \qquad\qquad \square$$

We obtain the next grammar by introducing the power operator as an additional operator. In the introduction we showed that in this case the type property is no longer a static property because the type of $e_1 \uparrow e_2$ for integer expressions e_1 and e_2 depends on the size of e_2. Thus, for **AG$_4$** we add the constraint that integer exponents for an integer basis must have non-negative values. As additional attributes **AG$_4$** contains a *value* attribute for constants and an *oblsize* attribute for the E, T, F and P. The latter is used to specify the possible magnitude of the value of the expression (of type *int*). The value of the attribute can be used to generate runtime tests with the corresponding condition.

Example 9.8 (attribute grammar AG$_4$)

attribute grammar AG$_4$:
nonterminals S, E, T, F, P, Aop, Mop;
attributes   **syn** *type* **with** E, T, F, P, c, v **domain** {*int, real*};
           syn *op* **with** Aop, Mop **domain** {$'+','-','*','/','\div'$};
           syn *value* **with** c **domain** $int \cup real$;
           inh *obltype* **with** E, T, F, P **domain** {*int, unspec*};
           inh *oblsize* **with** E, T, F, P **domain** {*unspec, nonneg*}

rules

0 : $S \to E$
    $E.obltype := unspec$
    $E.oblsize := unspec$

1 : $E \to E\ Aop\ T$
    $E_0.type = f_1(E_1.type, T.type)$

2 : $E \to T$

3' : $T \to T\ Mop\ F$

    $T_0.type = f_3^1(Mop.op, T_0.obltype,$
                    $T_1.type, F.type)$
    $T_1.obltype = f_3^2(Mop.op, T_0.obltype)$
    $F.obltype = f_3^2(Mop.op, T_0.obltype)$

4 : $T \to F$

5' : $F \to P \uparrow F$
    $F_1.oblsize = f_{5'}^2(P.type)$
    $P.oblsize = f_{5'}^3(F_1.type)$
    $F_0.type = f_{5'}^1(F_0.obltype, P.type, F_1.type)$

6' : $P \to c$
    $P.type = f_{6'}(P.obltype, P.oblsize, c.type, c.value)$

7' : $P \to v$
    $P.type = f_{7'}(P.obltype,$
                       $v.type)$

8 : $P \to (E)$

9 : $Aop \to +$
    $Aop.op = '+'$

10 : $Aop \to -$
    $Aop.op = '-'$

11 : $Mop \to *$
    $Mop.op = '*'$

12 : $Mop \to /$
    $Mop.op = '/'$

13 : $Mop \to \div$
    $Mop.op = '\div'$

functions:

$f_3^1\ '*'\ int\ int\ int\ \ =\ int$ $f_3^2\ '\div'\ \_\ =\ int$
$f_3^1\ '/'\ unspec\ \_\_\ =\ real$ $f_3^2\ \_\ int\ =\ int$
$f_3^1\ '\div'\ \_\ int\ int\ \ =\ int$ $f_3^2\ \_\_\ =\ unspec$
$f_3^1\ '*'\ \_\_\_\ \ =\ real$

$f_1\ int\ int\ \ \ =\ int$
$f_1\ \_\_\ \ \ \ \ \ \ \ =\ real$

$f_{5'}^1\ int\ int\ int\ \ =\ int$ $f_{5'}^2\ int\ \ \ =\ nonneg$
$f_{5'}^1\ \_\_\_\ \ \ \ \ =\ real$ $f_{5'}^2\ real\ \ =\ unspec$

$f_{5'}^3$ *int* $= unspec$ $f_{6'}$ *int nonneg int nonneg* $= int$
$f_{5'}^3$ *real* $= nonneg$ $f_{6'}$ *int unspec int* _ $= int$
                                 $f_{6'}$ *unspec* _ t _ $= t$

$f_{7'}$ *int int* $= int$
$f_{7'}$ *unspec* t $= t$

$\square$

Another example is the following attribute grammar **Bin_to_Dec**, which describes the computation of the value of binary numbers.

Example 9.9 (attribute grammar Bin_to_Dec)

attribute grammar Bin_to_Dec:
nonterminals   *N, BIN, BIT;*
attributes   syn *l* with *BIN* **domain int;**
           syn *v* with *N, BIN, BIT* **domain real;**
           inh *r* with *BIN, BIT* **domain int;**

rules

1 : $N \to BIN. BIN$ 3 : $BIN \to$
      $N.v = BIN_1.v + BIN_2.v$ $BIN.v = 0$
      $BIN_1.r = 0$ $BIN.l = 0$
      $BIN_2.r = -BIN_2.l$ 4 : $BIT \to 1$
2 : $BIN \to BIN\ BIT$ $BIT.v = 2^{BIT.r}$
      $BIN_0.v = BIN_1.v + BIT.v$ 5 : $BIT \to 0$
      $BIN_0.l = BIN_1.l + 1$ $BIT.v = 0$
      $BIN_1.r = BIN_0.r + 1$
      $BIT.r = BIN_0.r$

Here is a short explanation of the way the grammar evaluates binary numbers. The values are computed into the attribute v. The rules for v are straightforward. Only the rule for production 4 requires that the 'rank' r of the position of a BIT is known. The rank is related to the position of a BIT relative to the binary period. Positions to the left of the period have rank $0, 1, 2, \ldots$, those to the right of the period have ranks $-1, -2, -3, \ldots$, each time starting from the period. We use the inherited attribute r to tell a BIN what the rank of its rightmost BIT is.

      Let us now look at strings of BITs to the left of the period. The rightmost BIT has rank 0. Given this initial value it is simple to calculate the r-attribute in the recursive production 2. BIT strings on the right side are more difficult to treat. The rank of their rightmost BIT is equal to the length of the string. Therefore, the synthesized attribute l is used to compute the length of BIT strings and to initialize the r-attribute on the right side of the period. $\square$

The attribute grammar BoolExp given below describes the code generation for the so-called short-circuit evaluation of Boolean expressions. The code generated for a Boolean expression has the following properties:

- only load instructions and conditional jumps are generated;
- no instructions are generated for the Boolean operators **and, or** and **not** ;
- the subexpressions of the expression are evaluated from left to right;
- for each (sub)expression, only the smallest subexpressions which uniquely determine the value of the whole (sub)expression are evaluated.

The following instruction sequence is generated for the Boolean expression $(a$ **and** $b)$ **or not** c where a, b and c are Boolean variables:

	LOAD a	
	JUMPF L1	jump on false
	LOAD b	
	JUMPT L2	jump on true
L1:	**LOAD** c	
	JUMPT L3	
L2:	Code for the successor in the true case	
L3:	Code for the successor in the false case	

The attribute grammar BoolExp describes the code generation, including in particular the generation of jump destinations (labels) for subexpressions and the transfer of these labels to the primitive subexpressions from which these labels can be jumped to. Every subexpression is given two labels, the label of the successor in the 'false case' and that of the successor in the 'true case'.

In addition, *jcond*, the correlation of the value of the whole expression with the value of its rightmost identifier, is calculated for each expression. If *jcond* has the value *true* for an expression *e* this means that when during the execution of the translation of *e* the last identifier is loaded, its value is equal to the value of *e*.

If *jcond* has the value *false*, then the value of the last identifier of *e* and that of *e* are the negation of each other. The same holds for the code generation: when a **LOAD** is generated for the last identifier of an expression *e*, the *jcond* value of *e* determines whether the jump to the true successor is a **JUMPT** (in the case *jcond* = *true*) or a **JUMPF** (in the case *jcond* = *false*).

To obtain a context for Boolean expressions, we add another production for the two-sided conditional statement. The successor in the true case is the then part and the successor in the false case is the else part. As usual, at the end of the condition, we generate a conditional jump to the else part. This tests whether the condition E is *false*. Thus, **not** *jcond* is used as the first parameter of the gencjump function.

attribute grammar BoolExp:
nonterminals *IFSTAT, STATS, E, T, F;*
attributes inh *tsucc, fsucc* **with** *E,T,F* **domain string;**
           syn *jcond* **with** *E,T,F* **domain bool;**
           syn *code* **with** *IFSTAT, E,T,F* **domain string**
rules

IFSTAT → **if** *E* **then** *STATS* **else** *STATS* **fi**
    E.tsucc = *t*
    E.fsucc = *e*
    IFSTAT.code = *E.code* ++ *gencjump* (**not** *E*. *jcond*, *e*) ++
    t: ++ *STATS$_1$.code* ++ *genujump* (*f*) ++ *e:* ++ *STATS$_2$.code* ++ *f:*

E → *T*
E → *E* **or** *T*
E$_1$.fsucc = *t*
E$_0$.jcond = *T.jcond*
E$_0$.code = *E$_1$.code* ++ *gencjump* (*E$_1$.jcond*, *E$_0$.tsucc*) ++ *t:* ++ *T.code*

T → *F*
T → *T* **and** *F*
    T$_1$.tsucc = *f*
    T$_0$.jcond = *F.jcond*
    T$_0$.code = *T$_1$.code* ++ *gencjump* (**not** *T$_1$.jcond*, *T$_0$.fsucc*) ++ *f:* ++ *F.code*

F → (*E*)
F → **not** *F*
    F$_1$.tsucc = *F$_0$.fsucc*
    F$_1$.fsucc = *F$_0$.tsucc*
    F$_0$.jcond = **not** *F$_1$.jcond*

F → **id**
    F.jcond = *true*
    F.code = **LOAD id**.*identifier*

Auxiliary functions used:

genujump (*l*) = **JUMP** *l*
gencjump (*jc*, *l*) = **if** *jc* = *true*
                then JUMPT *l*
                else JUMPF *l*
                fi

9.4   The generation of attribute evaluators

In this section we are concerned with the evaluation of attributes or, more precisely, instances of attributes in syntax trees. For every syntax tree of the underlying context-free grammar, the attribute grammar defines a system of equations. The unknowns in this system are the attribute instances at the nodes of the syntax tree. Let us suppose that the system of equations is not recursive. Then we could solve it by an elimination procedure and thus assign values to the attribute instances. In each elimination step, we would have to look for the next attribute instance that did not depend on the instances already computed and calculate its value. This would be a totally dynamic process since no information about the origin of this system of equations is used in the elimination procedure.

Static attribute evaluation procedures use information about the attribute grammar. Every attribute grammar describes dependencies between the attribute occurrences of the productions. Here, an attribute occurrence a_i depends on an occurrence b_j, if b_j is an argument of the semantic rule for a_i. These dependencies determine the dependencies between attribute instances in the system of equations referred to above. If a corresponding generator analyses the dependencies in the attribute grammar, it can if necessary generate an attribute evaluator which does not have to look for the next attribute instance to be evaluated, but evaluates the attribute instances according to a statically determined 'sequence of visits'. Let us look again at Figure 9.6. Suppose this production, p, is applied somewhere within a tree t. The attribute analysis then requires an interplay of calculations which are local to the occurrence of the production and those in the neighbourhood. A local calculation of (an instance of) a defining occurrence in X_0 is provided by the next production q, in addition to a new value. A calculation of an attribute instance at the same node, which takes place locally in q, makes a new value available to p, which may then permit new local calculations in p. There is a similar interplay between this occurrence of p and the productions applied below it. Static planning of this interplay generally requires an analysis of global dependencies. For a nonterminal X, these dependencies describe the attributes whose values are provided by the context if the latter provides the values of certain attributes. Here, the context may be a subtree for X or an upper tree fragment for X. The production-local dependencies form a natural starting point for the calculation of the global dependency relationships.

We must introduce a number of terms, algorithms and properties for our treatment of this generation procedure.

9.4.1 Attribute dependencies

The semantic rules for the production p of an attribute grammar induce a relation on the set $V(p)$ of the attribute occurrences of the production.

Definition 9.3 (production-local dependency)
The **production-local dependency relation for a production** p $Dp(p) \subseteq V(p) \times V(p)$ is defined as follows:

$$b_j \; Dp(p) \; a_i \qquad \text{if and only if} \qquad a_i = f_{p,a,i}(\ldots, b_j, \ldots)$$

for a semantic rule of p. Thus, the occurrence of the attribute b in X_j is related to the occurrence of a in X_i, or a_i **depends on** b_j, if b_j is an argument in the semantic rule for a_i. We shall always represent relations by their graphs, the **production-local dependency graphs**, which we also denote by $Dp(p)$. □

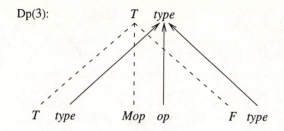

Dp(3): T type

T type   Mop op   F type

Figure 9.8   The production-local dependency graph for production 3 of AG_1.

Example 9.10 (continuation of Example 9.5)
The production-local dependency graphs for the attribute grammar AG_1 all have a
very simple structure; the only edges are from occurrences of synthesized attributes
on the right side to those on the left side. For clarity, we always present dependency
graphs together with the underlying syntax structure, that is, the production of the
syntax tree (see Figure 9.8).   □

Example 9.11 (continuation of Example 9.7)
The calculation of obligatory types reveals more complicated dependencies for the
productions in AG_3. This is illustrated in Figure 9.9.   □

Example 9.12 (continuation of Example 9.9)
The production-local dependencies for the attribute grammar **Bin_to_Dec** are shown
in Figure 9.10.   □

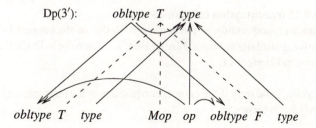

Dp(3′): obltype T type

obltype T type   Mop op   obltype F type

Figure 9.9   The production-local dependency graph for production 3′ of AG_3.

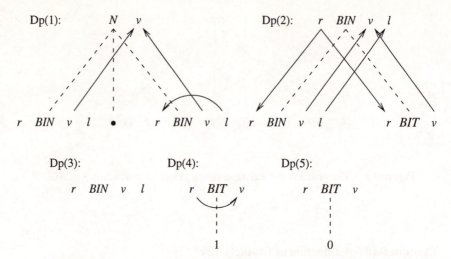

Figure 9.10   The production-local dependencies of the AG Bin_to_Dec.

In attribute grammars in normal form the arguments of the semantic rules of the defining occurrences are always applied attribute occurrences. Thus $Dp(p)$ is non-reflexive for all p, that is, the graph is not cyclic, and all paths in $Dp(p)$ have length 1. Assuming that grammars are in normal form simplifies a number of considerations; thus, in what follows, we shall always assume that attribute grammars are in normal form.

As previously noted, the production-local dependencies induce dependencies between the argument instances in the trees of the grammar.

Definition 9.4 (individual dependency graph)
Let t be a tree of the underlying context-free grammar. The **individual dependency graph** for the attribute instances of t, $Dt(t)$, is obtained by 'gluing together' the production-local dependency graphs for the productions applied in t.   ☐

Example 9.13 (continuation of Example 9.9)
For the tree t corresponding to the sentence '10.01' of the context-free grammar with underlying attribute grammar **Bin_to_Dec**, we obtain the individual dependency graph shown in Figure 9.11.   ☐

$Dt(t)$ is cyclic if and only if the system of equations in the unknowns a_m introduced in Section 9.2.1 is recursive.

Definition 9.5 (non-circular attribute grammar)
An attribute grammar is **non-circular**, if $Dt(t)$ is not cyclic for any tree t of the underlying context-free grammar.   ☐

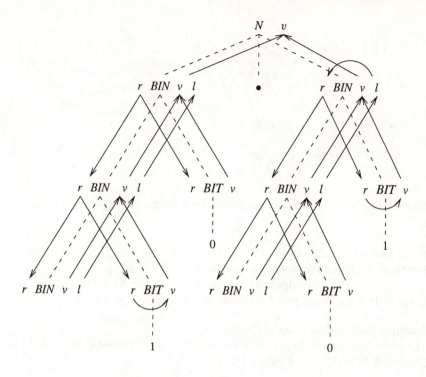

Figure 9.11 Syntax tree with individual dependency graphs for the sentence '10.01'.

Theorem 9.1 *An attribute grammar is well-formed if and only if it is non-circular.*

□

Let us consider a tree t with root label X in Figure 9.12. The instances of its inherited attributes are, as it were, input to t and the instances of synthesized attributes output from t. The instance of d depends (transitively) only on the instance of c. Thus, if the value of the instance of c is known, an attribute evaluator can descend into t and return with the value for the instance of d; there are no other dependencies on instances from outside t which do not go through c. The instance of e depends on the instances of a and b. Both values are needed before one can successfully descend into t to evaluate the instance of e (here, we assume that the semantic functions are strict, that is, require their arguments). The lower characteristic graph of X induced by t describes this situation.

Example 9.14 (lower characteristic graph)
Let t be a tree of the underlying context-free grammar with root label X, that is, $symb(\varepsilon) = X$. By restricting the transitive closure of $Dt(t)$ to the attribute instances

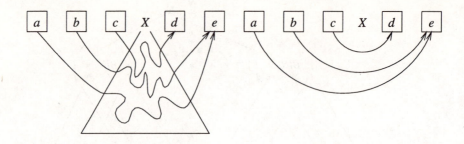

Figure 9.12   Attribute dependencies in a tree for X and the induced lower characteristic graph.

of the root, we obtain a relation $Dt\!\uparrow_t(X) \subseteq Inh(X) \times Syn(X)$, whose graph we refer to as the **lower characteristic graph** for X induced by t.

Thus, there is an **edge** from $a \in Inh(X)$ to $b \in Syn(X)$ in $Dt\!\uparrow_t(X)$, if there is a path from the instance of a at the root to the instance of b in $Dt(t)$.   □

Example 9.15 (continuation of Example 9.14)
The lower characteristic graph for *BIN* induced by the left subtree of the root of t in Example 9.14 is shown in Figure 9.13(a).   □

We now consider an upper tree fragment for X, see Figure 9.14.

The transitive dependencies of the inherited instances of X on the synthesized instances of X are also important for an attribute evaluator. When it goes into the upper tree fragment to evaluate an inherited attributed instance a in X, it is successful if and only if it knows the values of the synthesized instances of X on which a depends. This situation is described by the upper characteristic graph of X induced by an upper tree fragment.

Definition 9.6 (upper characteristic graph)
Suppose n is an internal node of the tree t, $symb(n) = X \in V_N$. Let us consider the upper tree fragment of t at n, $t \backslash n$, which is the tree obtained from t by removing

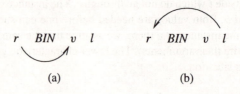

(a)   (b)

Figure 9.13   (a) lower and (b) upper characteristic graph for *BIN*.

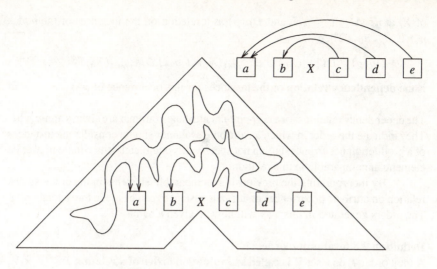

Figure 9.14   Attribute dependencies in an upper tree fragment for X and the induced upper characteristic graph.

the subtree at n, t/n, except for n itself. The restriction of the transitive closure of $Dt(t\backslash n)$ to the attribute instances of n yields a relation $Dt\downarrow_{t,n}(X) \subseteq Syn(X) \times Inh(X)$, whose graph we refer to as the **upper characteristic graph** for X induced by t at n.   □

$Dt\downarrow_{t,n}(X)$ contains an **edge** from $a \in Syn(X)$ to $b \in Inh(X)$, if the upper tree fragment in question contains a **path** leading from the instance of a at n to the instance of b at n.

Example 9.16 (continuation of Example 9.14)
The upper characteristic graph for *BIN* induced by the tree t of Example 9.14 at the node 3.1.1 is shown in Figure 9.13(b).   □

Let us consider a node n in a tree t. Suppose the production p is applied at n. We are now interested to learn everything there is to know about the dependencies between the instances of the attribute occurrences of p. For this, we combine the upper characteristic graph at n and the lower characteristic graphs at the children of n with the production-local dependency graph.

Definition 9.7 (dependency relation for an instance of a production)
Let n be an interior node of t with label X and applied production p. Let us consider $Dt\downarrow_{t,n}(X_0)$, the upper characteristic graph induced by t at n, as a relation on the attribute instances of X at n, $Dt\uparrow_{t/ni}(X_i)$ as a relation on the attribute instances

of X_i at ni $(1 \leq i \leq n_p)$, and $Dp(p)$ as a relation on the instances of the nodes $n, n1, \ldots, nn_p$. Then

$$Dp(p) \cup Dt\!\downarrow_{t,n}(X_0) \cup Dt\!\uparrow_{t/n1}(X_1) \cup \ldots \cup Dt\!\uparrow_{t/nn_p}(X_{n_p})$$

is the **dependency relation** of the instances for this occurrence of p.   □

The dependency relations for a non-circular attribute grammar are always non-cyclic. They indicate the order in which an attribute evaluator should consider the instances of a production occurrence, but do not specify this completely since there may exist elements incomparable in this relation.

By incorporating the previously incomparable elements in the order, such a relation on attribute occurrences or attribute instances can be made into a total order. The orders generated in this way will now be given a name.

Definition 9.8 (evaluation order)
A total order T on a set V is called an **evaluation order of a relation** $R \subseteq V \times V$, if $R \subseteq T$. Let $Dt(t)$ be the individual dependency graph for a tree t. A total order $T(t)$ on the set $V(t)$ of all attribute instances of t is called an **evaluation order** for t, if $Dt(t) \subseteq T(t)$.   □

Every evaluation order describes one sequence for the evaluation of the attribute instances in t, where the attribute dependencies are respected.

Different trees (and different nodes in the tree) may induce different relations $Dt\!\uparrow_t(X)$ and $Dt\!\downarrow_{t,n}(X)$, but only finitely many since the number of attributes for each symbol is finite and fixed. If $n = |Inh(X)|$ and $m = |Syn(X)|$, then there are $2^{n \cdot m}$ different possible relations. Unfortunately, this theoretical upper bound is responsible for the complexity of several problems relating to the generation of attribute evaluators.

Efficient computation of the upper and lower characteristic graphs in syntax trees

We have already explained how lower and upper characteristic graphs can help an attribute evaluator to plan its visits to subtrees and upper tree fragments. For this, for every tree on which the attributes are to be evaluated, the compiler has to calculate the graphs induced at its nodes. Let t be a tree for X. The calculation of the induced lower characteristic graphs $Dt\!\uparrow_t(X)$ was previously described as follows: calculate $Dt(t)$, the individual dependency graphs for t, form the transitive closure and restrict it to the attribute instances of the root. But this method of calculation is too expensive. However, it is easy to see how these graphs can be computed for **all** nodes in a single bottom-up pass over the tree.

For this, we consider an interior node n at which the production p is applied. If p is a terminal production for X, we obtain $Dt\!\uparrow_{t/n}(X)$ by restricting $Dp(p)$ to the attribute instances at n. If p is not a terminal production, we assume that the lower characteristic graphs at the nonterminal children of n have already been calculated.

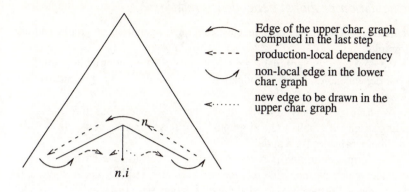

← ⌒	Edge of the upper char. graph computed in the last step
←- - - -	production-local dependency
⌣↗	non-local edge in the lower char. graph
←·······	new edge to be drawn in the upper char. graph

Figure 9.15   The calculation of an upper characteristic graph.

Then $Dt\uparrow_{t/n}(X)$ can be calculated by appending these graphs to the production-local dependency graphs $Dp(p)$ and restricting the transitive closure of the resulting graph to the instances in X. Thus, we have calculated the lower characteristic graphs at all nodes of the tree in a single pass. However, there remains the disadvantage that expensive graph operations have to be used at every step.

Therefore, we now use the fact that for every nonterminal there are only finitely many lower characteristic graphs. As we shall see, these can be precomputed, for example using grammar flow analysis. Thus, let $Dt\uparrow(X_0), Dt\uparrow(X_1), \ldots, Dt\uparrow(X_{n_p})$ be the sets of the lower characteristic graphs for the nonterminals in the production p. Then we can precompute a function lc_p, which for every n_p tuple $(d_1, \ldots, d_{n_p}) \in Dt\uparrow(X_1) \times \ldots \times Dt\uparrow(X_{n_p})$ calculates the graph $d_0 \in Dt\uparrow(X_0)$, corresponding to this tuple. To this end, the $d_1, \ldots, d_{n_p}$ are again appended to $Dp(p)$ and the transitive closure is restricted to the attributes of X_0, but now at generation time. For a terminal production this function is a nullary constant function. The application of these functions in a bottom-up pass over the tree corresponds, as we shall see in a later chapter, to the calculation performed by a bottom-up tree automaton on a tree. This device has finitely many states, namely the lower characteristic graphs in $\bigcup_{X \in V_N} Dt\uparrow(X)$. Every time a production is applied, it makes a transition from the states at the children (in this case, the lower characteristic graphs there) to the state at the parent (the corresponding lower characteristic graph there). The state is left at the node for the information of the attribute evaluator.

The calculation of the upper characteristic graphs is performed correspondingly by a finite top-down tree automaton. However, there is one important difference. As Figure 9.15 shows, for the calculation of the upper characteristic graph at a node $n.i$ the upper characteristic graph at the node n and all **lower** characteristic graphs at the children of n must be known. Thus, this calculation is described by functions $uc_{p_i} : Dt\downarrow(X_0) \times Dt\downarrow(X_1) \times \ldots \times Dt\downarrow(X_{n_p}) \to Dt\downarrow(X_i)$, $(1 \leq i \leq n_p)$.

The calculation of global dependency relations

To calculate global attribute dependencies we require operations on graphs and on sets of graphs.

We now omit the terminals in productions since they contribute nothing to the global dependencies. For the production $p : X_0 \rightarrow X_1 \dots X_{n_p}$ this means that $X_i \in V_N$ for all $1 \leq i \leq n_p$.

We have previously referred to the first two operations informally as 'appending of global graphs to local graphs' and 'restricting the transitive closure to the attribute instances for a node'.

The formal definition is somewhat complex because we have a 'typing' problem. The operations combine relations on attributes, attribute occurrences and attribute instances, respectively, and produce relations on attributes and attribute occurrences, respectively.

Definition 9.9 $(Dp(p)[\ ])$
Suppose $R_0, R_1, \dots, R_{n_p}$ are relations on the sets $Attr(X_0), Attr(X_1), \dots$ and $Attr(X_{n_p})$. Then $Dp(p)[R_0, R_1, \dots, R_{n_p}]$ is the following relation on $V(p)$, the set of the attribute **occurrences** of p:

$$Dp(p) \cup R_0^0 \cup R_1^1 \cup \dots \cup R_{n_p}^{n_p}$$

where $b_i\ R_i^i\ a_i$, if $b\ R_i\ a$. The relations (graphs) on the attributes of the $X_0, X_1, \dots, X_{n_p}$ will be viewed as relations (graphs) on attribute occurrences and then combined (their union is formed).

For $Dp(p)[\emptyset, R_1, \dots, R_{n_p}]$ we write $Dp(p)[R_1, \dots, R_{n_p}]$. □

Example 9.17
Let $\{(r, v)\} \in Inh(BIT) \times Syn(BIT)$, $\{(l, r)\} \in Syn(BIN) \times Inh(BIN)$. $Dp(2)[\{(l, r)\}, \emptyset, \{(r, v)\}]$ is the graph of Figure 9.16(a). $Dp(2)[\emptyset, \{(r, v)\}]$ is the graph of Figure 9.16(b). □

The next two definitions describe functions which combine graphs of attribute occurrences or instances, form their transitive closure, restrict this to the attribute occurrences or instances for a single node and return the result as a relation on attributes.

Definition 9.10 $(R\uparrow(p)[\ ])$
$R\uparrow(p)[R_1, \dots, R_{n_p}]$ is the following relation on $Attr(X_0)$:

$$b\ R\uparrow(p)[R_1, \dots, R_{n_p}]\ a \text{ if and only if } b_0\ Dp(p)[R_1, \dots, R_{n_p}]^+\ a_0 \qquad □$$

Example 9.18
$R\uparrow(2)[\emptyset, \{(r, v)\}]$ is the graph of Figure 9.16(c) □

Definition 9.11 $(R\downarrow_i(p)[\ ])$
$R\downarrow_i(p)[R_0, R_1, \dots, R_{n_p}]$ for $(1 \leq i \leq n)$ is defined by

$$b\ R\downarrow_i(p)[R_0, R_1, \dots, R_{n_p}]\ a$$

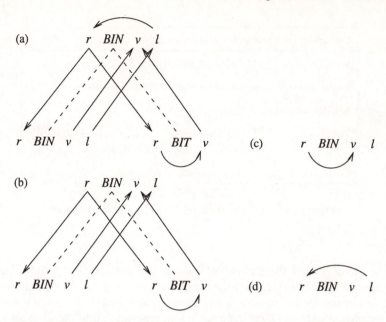

Figure 9.16   The graph operations $Dp(2)[\dots]$, $R{\uparrow}(2)[\dots]$ and $R{\downarrow}_1(2)[\dots]$.

if and only if

$$b_i \; Dp(p)[R_0, R_1, \dots, R_{i-1}, \emptyset, R_{i+1}, \dots, R_{n_p}]^+ \; a_i \qquad \square$$

Example 9.19

$R{\downarrow}_1(2)[\{\{(l, r)\}, \emptyset, \{(r, v)\}\}]$ is the graph of Figure 9.16(d) $\square$

If $\mathcal{R}_1, \dots, \mathcal{R}_{n_p}$ are sets of relations over $Attr(X_1), \dots, Attr(X_{n_p})$, then we define

$$R{\uparrow}(p)[\mathcal{R}_1, \dots, \mathcal{R}_{n_p}] = \{R{\uparrow}(p)[R_1, \dots, R_{n_p}] \mid R_i \in \mathcal{R}_i, (1 \leq i \leq n_p)\}$$

and

$$R{\downarrow}_i(p)[\mathcal{R}_0, \mathcal{R}_1, \dots, \mathcal{R}_{n_p}] = \{R{\downarrow}_i(p)[R_0, R_1, \dots, R_{n_p}] \mid R_j \in \mathcal{R}_j \; (0 \leq j \leq n_p)\}$$

for all i in $(1 \leq i \leq n_p)$. $\square$

Let us again consider the inductive calculation of the lower characteristic graphs $Dt{\uparrow}_t(X_0)$ for a tree t with root labelled X_0, introduced in the last section. Suppose the production applied at the root is $p : X_0 \rightarrow X_1 \dots X_{n_p}$. If the relations $Dt{\uparrow}_{t/1}(X_1)$, $\dots, Dt{\uparrow}_{t/n_p}(X_{n_p})$ have already been calculated, we can calculate $Dt{\uparrow}_t(X_0)$ locally as

$$Dt{\uparrow}_t(X_0) = R{\uparrow}(p)[Dt{\uparrow}_{t/1}(X_1), \dots, Dt{\uparrow}_{t/n_p}(X_{n_p})] \qquad (Dt{\uparrow}_t)$$

that is, by substituting the lower characteristic graphs for the X_i in the production-local dependency graph for the production p and restricting the transitive closure of

Bottom-up GFA problem 'lower characteristic graphs'	
S-lattices	$\{D(X) = \mathcal{P}(\mathcal{P}(Inh(X) \times Syn(X)))\}_{X \in V_N}$
Partial order	$\subseteq$ (subset relation on sets of relations)
Smallest element	$\emptyset$
Transf. fct.	$\{Lc_p : D(p[1]) \times \ldots \times D(p[n_p]) \rightarrow D(p[0])\|$ $Lc_p(\mathcal{R}_1, \ldots, \mathcal{R}_{n_p}) = R{\uparrow}(p)[\mathcal{R}_1, \ldots, \mathcal{R}_{n_p}]\}_{p \in P}$
Comb. fct.	$\cup$ (union on sets of relations)

Figure 9.17   GFA problem for 'lower characteristic graphs'.

the resulting graph to the attributes of the root. The equation $(Dt{\uparrow}_t)$ shows how at the **time of attribute evaluation** the lower characteristic graph for the attributes of the root nonterminal induced by a tree t can be calculated on the tree in a bottom-up manner. In addition $(Dt{\uparrow})$ indicates how at **generation time** the set of **all** lower characteristic graphs for each nonterminal can be calculated from the grammar alone. This finds expression in the following system of equations whose smallest fixed-point solution comprises the sets $Dt{\uparrow}(X)$ of all lower characteristic graphs for the nonterminals X of the grammar.

$$Dt{\uparrow}(X) = \bigcup_{p:p[0]=X} R{\uparrow}(p)[Dt{\uparrow}(p[1]), \ldots, Dt{\uparrow}(p[n_p])] \qquad (Dt{\uparrow})$$

This system of equations, which is in general recursive, suggests a calculation of the fixed point using grammar flow analysis. In this case the iteration step for a production p looks as follows. Insert all combinations of graphs, which have already been calculated for the nonterminals of the right side, in the local dependency graph $Dp(p)$ and 'project' the resulting paths onto the attributes of the left side. The resulting set of graphs is associated with the production p. In the iteration step for nonterminals X the alternatives obtained in this way for X are unioned together. The grammar flow problem for 'lower characteristic graphs' for an attribute grammar **AG** is illustrated in Figure 9.17.

This leads to the recursive system of equations $(Dt{\uparrow})$ for $Dt{\uparrow}$. In this GFA problem, the case in which nonterminals of the grammar are assigned individual domains arises for the first time.

We can now give a statically verifiable criterion for non-circularity.

Theorem 9.2   *An attribute grammar AG is non-circular if and only if all graphs in $Dp(p)[Dt{\uparrow}(X_1), \ldots, Dt{\uparrow}(X_{n_p})]$ are non-cyclic for all productions p of the attribute grammar.* $\square$

Top-down GFA problem 'upper characteristic graphs'	
S-lattices	$\{D(X) = \mathcal{P}(\mathcal{P}(Syn(X) \times Inh(X)))\}_{X \in V_N}$
Partial order	$\subseteq$ (subset relation on sets of relations)
Smallest element	$\emptyset$
Transf. fct.	$\{Uc_{p,i} : D(p[0]) \rightarrow D(p[i]) \mid 1 \leq i \leq n_p,$ $Uc_{p,i}(\mathcal{R}) = R\downarrow_i(p)[\mathcal{R}, Dt\downarrow(p[1]), \ldots, Dt\downarrow(p[n_p])]\}_{p \in \mathcal{P}, 1 \leq i \leq n_p}$
Comb. fct.	$\cup$ (union on sets of relations)

Figure 9.18   GFA problem 'upper characteristic graphs'.

As previously mentioned, it is possible to construct attribute grammars in which the number of lower characteristic graphs increases exponentially with the number of attributes per nonterminal. Jazayeri has shown that the problem of the non-circularity test for attribute grammars has an exponential complexity in terms of storage and time requirements. This means that there is no significantly cheaper way of testing for non-circularity than that given in Theorem 9.2, namely the insertion of all combinations of lower characteristic graphs in the production-local dependency graphs. In practice, it turns out that real grammars are considerably easier to test for non-circularity. Moreover, we shall meet other sufficient conditions for non-circularity, which can be decided polynomially.

The calculation of the upper characteristic graphs on a tree, whence at the time the attributes are evaluated, can be developed in a similar manner. Let us consider an occurrence of the production p at the node n in t. We shall calculate the graph $Dt\downarrow_{t,ni}(X_i)$ $(1 \leq i \leq n_p)$. This can be done locally for this occurrence of p, if the upper characteristic graph $Dt\downarrow(X_0)$ and the lower characteristic graphs $Dt\uparrow_{t/n1}(X_1), \ldots, Dt\uparrow_{t/nn_p}(X_{n_p})$ are known. For this, we use the operation $R\downarrow_i(p)[\ldots]$.

At generation time the set of all upper characteristic graphs for each nonterminal is calculated from the grammar. For this we use the operation $R\downarrow_i(p)$ on sets of graphs.

$$Dt\downarrow(S) = \emptyset$$
$$Dt\downarrow(X) = \bigcup_{p:p[i]=X} R\downarrow_i(p)[Dt\downarrow(p[0]), Dt\uparrow(p[1]), \ldots, Dt\uparrow(p[n_p])] \qquad (Dt\downarrow)$$

The associated GFA problem 'upper characteristic graphs' for an attribute grammar AG is illustrated in Figure 9.18. Note that the sets of lower characteristic graphs which occur in the definition of the $Uc_{p,i}$ are precomputed. They are involved in the calculation of the set of upper characteristic graphs for X_i.

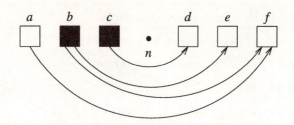

Figure 9.19 A characteristic graph.

Approximate global dependencies

The lower characteristic graph at the root of a subtree t/n represents the global dependencies of the synthesized attributes at n on the inherited attributes at n in the subtree t/n exactly; the same is true of the upper characteristic graph at n for the global dependencies in this tree fragment. Thus, an attribute evaluator has perfect strategic information.

If it visits the node n, as shown in Figure 9.19, with values for the instances of b and c, it then knows

- that after visiting t/n it will return with the values of d and e, and
- that it will never return with the value for f since it is missing the value of a on which f is (globally) dependent.

Thus, if after visiting t/n the instances of d and e are evaluated, it is only advisable to revisit this subtree when the value of a is also known.

The characteristic graphs appear to be the right tools for efficient evaluation of attributes. But, because there are so many of them, cheaper alternatives are sought. Graphs (relations) which represent the global dependencies approximately are found to be satisfactory. What can such an approximate dependency relation for a nonterminal look like in comparison with a characteristic graph? One might omit edges from the characteristic graph or add edges.

Let us be clear what it means for an attribute evaluator, when the characteristic graph of Figure 9.19 is approximated by removing the edge from a to f from the graph. The attribute evaluator would then assume that for a known value of b and an unknown value of a a visit to the subtree t/n would provide the value of f; however, this is of course not so. This type of approximation would therefore in general lead to futile visits to subtrees.

What happens when characteristic graphs are approximated by adding edges? Let us suppose that the dependency relation used for X were also to contain the dependencies of the instances d and e on a (see Figure 9.20). Then on visiting

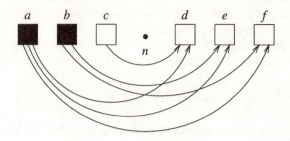

Figure 9.20   Approximated dependencies.

n with known values of b and c and an unknown value of a, an attribute evaluator would not visit the subtree t/n, since the attribute dependencies promise no success for this. It would wait until the value of a also became available.

We see that missing edges would in general lead to futile visits to subtrees. Thus, this is not an acceptable approximation. Added edges may delay a visit, although the dependency actually present would show it to be meaningful. Moreover, additional edges can also cause an attribute evaluator to wait for an infinite time, namely if they introduce cycles in dependency graphs.

Additional edges which do not correspond to a global dependency in an individual dependency graph may arise, for example, if several or all characteristics graphs are superimposed (union of relations).

The GFA problem 'I/O graphs' (Figure 9.21) assigns precisely one dependency graph in $Inh(X) \times Syn(X)$ to each nonterminal of an attribute grammar; it describes a hypothetical case of dependencies, and thus in general contains more

Bottom-up GFA problem 'I/O graphs'	
S-lattices	$\{D(X) = \mathcal{P}(Inh(X) \times Syn(X))\}_{X \in V_N}$
Partial order	$\subseteq$ (subset relation on relations)
Smallest elem.	$\emptyset$
Transf. fct.	$\{Io : D(p[1]) \times \ldots \times D(p[n_p]) \to D(p[0]) \mid$
	$Io(g_1, \ldots, g_{n_p}) = R{\uparrow}(p)[g_1, \ldots, g_{n_p}]\}_{p \in P}$
Comb. fct.	$\cup$ (union of relations)

Figure 9.21   GFA problem 'I/O graphs'.

edges than an individual tree with a corresponding root label would exhibit. We obtain the I/O graphs for all nonterminals by superimposing the different possible graphs calculated for a nonterminal (union of the relations).

The GFA problem 'I/O graphs' leads to the recursive system of equations (IO), whose smallest solution is the desired I/O graphs:

$$IO(X) = \bigcup_{p:p[0]=X} R{\uparrow}(p)[IO(p[1]), \ldots, IO(p[n_p])] \qquad (IO)$$

The I/O graphs in general contain more dependencies than actually occur in any tree. Thus, it is no surprise that there exist grammars which are non-circular but in which the I/O graphs signal a cycle. Example 9.20 presents such a grammar.

Example 9.20
Non-circular, but not absolutely non-circular attribute grammar.

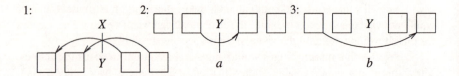

The two possible trees have non-cyclic individual dependency graphs.

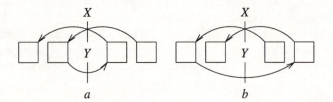

In the calculation of $IO(X)$, $Dp(2)$ and $Dp(3)$ are unioned and inserted in $Dp(1)$. This gives a cycle.

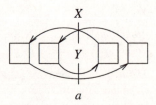

□

Definition 9.12 (absolutely non-circular)
An attribute grammar is said to be **absolutely non-circular**, if the graph $Dp(p)[IO(p[1]), \dots, IO(p[n_p])]$ is not cyclic for any production p. $\qquad$ $\square$

Analogously to the definition and construction, it is also possible to construct O/I graphs which approximate the upper characteristic graphs. Various versions exist, depending on what sort of lower dependencies are used, see Exercise 9.

9.4.2 Attribute evaluation

We consider the tree t of the underlying context-free grammar, extended by storage locations for attribute instances. At every node n there is something like a record with components for all attributes of $symb(n)$. The task of the attribute evaluation is to calculate the values of the attribute instances and store them at the nodes (some attribute evaluators store attribute values only partially (if at all) in the tree, and mainly in stacks and/or in global variables).

The first requirement on an attribute grammar is that every tree should have an evaluation order.

Theorem 9.3 *For every tree t of an attribute grammar AG an evaluation order exists if and only if AG is non-circular.* $\qquad$ $\square$

Phases of the attribute evaluation

The evaluation of the attribute instances in a tree t can be conceptually divided into two phases:

(1) The strategy phase. This determines an evaluation order $T(t)$.

(2) The evaluation phase proper. Here, the attribute evaluation is performed in accordance with $T(t)$.

Variants of each of these two phases exist. The choice of a variant defines a particular class of evaluator.

Let us consider the **evaluation phase**. The evaluation may begin with the minimal elements ($a \in V$ is said to be **minimal (maximal)** for a relation R, if there does not exist $b \in V$ with $b \, R \, a \, (a \, R \, b)$) or with the maximal elements of $Dt(t)$.

- **Demand-driven** attribute evaluation begins with the maximal elements; that is, the evaluator is called with a set of attribute instances, whose values are sought. It in turn then recursively calls the evaluation of the arguments it needs.

- **Data-driven** attribute evaluation begins with the evaluation of the minimal elements of $V(t)$, namely those attribute instances that do not depend on any others. It only evaluates an instance when all the arguments needed to calculate it have already been calculated.

Algorithm cfA
Input: $Dt(t)$
Output: an evaluation order for $Dt(t)$
Method:

$completed := \emptyset$;
while $completed \neq V(t)$ **do**

   choose a $v \in V(t) - completed$, which is minimal w.r.t. $Dt(t)\Big|_{V(t)-completed}$;

   print(v);   (∗ Output is the order of evaluation ∗)
   $completed := completed \cup \{v\}$
od

Figure 9.22   Construction of an evaluation order and an attribute evaluation for non-circular attribute grammars. A data-driven evaluator is obtained by replacing **print**(v) by **evaluate**(v).

Now for the **strategy phase**, the determination of an evaluation order $T(t)$ for the tree t. There are many variants of this, and we shall present three such; the first is dynamic, the second static and the third partially static and partially dynamic.

(1)   **Dynamic determination of the evaluation order**. The individual dependency graphs $Dt(t)$ are topologically sorted to obtain a total order $T(t)$ on $V(t)$. This is guaranteed to be successful if the grammar is non-circular. A corresponding evaluator is shown in Figure 9.22. This is expensive in terms of time and storage at evaluation time and should not be used in practice.

(2)   **Induced evaluation order**. There is a restricted class of attribute grammars, which is sufficiently large for practical purposes, the so-called **l-ordered attribute grammars**. They have the following nice property: for every nonterminal X, there exists a total order T_X on the set $Attr(X)$, such that for any tree t: $b_n \, Dt(t) \, a_n$ and $symb(n) = X$ imply $b \, T_X \, a$; that is, the individual dependency graphs of all trees are compatible with the precomputed total orders on the attribute sets of the nonterminals. Based on these total orders on attribute sets, total orders, so-called **visit sequences**, can be constructed on the sets $V(p)$ of attribute occurrences in productions p. These in turn induce a well-defined evaluation order $T(t)$ for each tree t. Thus, at evaluation time there is nothing left for the strategy phase to do.

(3)   **Choice between visit sequences**. If an attribute grammar is not l-ordered, there exist productions to which different visit sequences must be assigned in different tree contexts. The calculation of the set of all visit sequences for each production can take place at *generation time*. For the given tree, the selection of the right visit sequence for every application of a production is then made dynamically, that is, at evaluation time.

In what follows, we shall meet a number of subclasses of attribute grammars. They will be denoted by a prefix X-AG (attribute grammar with property X). There is always a dynamic and a static test for the property, that is, the membership of the class:

- the **dynamic test** determines whether a certain kind of attribute evaluation works for all trees. Here, a defining attribute evaluator for this class is given.
- The **static test** checks dependency properties of the attribute grammar.

In this sense, we have already met a dynamic and a static test for the class **NC-AG** of non-circular attribute grammars. The dynamic test uses topological sorting of the individual dependency graphs $Dt(t)$ for the trees of the grammar. If it is always successful, the grammar is clearly non-circular. This topological sorting of the individual dependency graphs and the subsequent or simultaneous evaluation of the attribute instances in the resulting total order describes the defining evaluator (data driven) for the class NC-AG.

The static test for the membership of NC-AG is given by Theorem 9.2. It uses only finite, statically computable dependency information about the grammar.

The static tests for membership of other classes will mostly be very similar to the test in Theorem 9.2. Time and again, for all productions p of the grammar, graphs for the nonterminals $X_0, X_1, \ldots, X_{n_p}$ will be inserted in the production-local dependency graph $Dp(p)$, and a check will be made to see whether the resulting graph has a cycle. Here, the graphs for the nonterminals for the smaller classes contain more and more additional edges which are not contained in the characteristic graphs. These additional edges usually describe predetermined visit sequences.

Complexity of generation and evaluation procedures

We now briefly discuss the complexity of the tests for membership of the grammar classes. The tests are usually constructive in the following sense. When one has constructed the graphs for the static test, one has essentially also generated an attribute evaluator. The order of magnitude of the effort of the test for membership is the same as that of the generation of the evaluator. This is not the case for the defining evaluator for the class NC-AG. It has no generation costs. On the other hand, the static test is exponential.

If the 'drive' is fixed, that is, demand driven or data driven, and the class membership of the grammar is known, a certain kind of attribute evaluation is appropriate. In certain respects, the smallest class containing the grammar gives the most efficient kind of evaluation.

First, however, the efficiency criteria for the attribute evaluation must be specified.

The time complexity is measured, in general, by the number of semantic rules applied. The cost of walking the tree is also relevant but more difficult to calculate. It can be relevant in practice because a local behaviour puts less load on the operating system's memory management.

There are various optimality criteria. According to one very commonly used criterion an evaluation is optimal if it evaluates every instance precisely once. If one only has to evaluate a subset of $V(t)$, for example some synthesized attributes at the root, this criterion is unusable. In this case, an evaluation is defined to be optimal if it evaluates precisely once the instances on which the desired instances depend. This optimality criterion can only be met by demand-driven evaluators.

The time taken to construct the evaluation order should also be added to the overall run time.

Example 9.21

The defining interpreter for the class NC-AG is time-optimal by the first criterion, since it evaluates every instance precisely once. However, it also requires at least $|V(t)| + |Dt(t)|$ steps for the topological sorting of $Dt(t)$. □

The storage-space requirements for the attribute evaluation divide into:

- the **static size**, that is, the size of the evaluator, namely the programs and/or tables, measured as a function of the size of the grammar, and

- the **dynamic size**, that is, the space for attribute values and the evaluation state components, measured in terms of the size of the tree or the number of attribute instances.

Example 9.22

The complexity of the storage requirements of the ncA attribute evaluator (**A**ttribute evaluator for **n**on-**c**ircular AG) for the grammars in NC-AG is calculated as follows. For the construction of the evaluation order, $Dt(t)$ must be given. Let *maxattr* denote the maximum number of attributes for a nonterminal, and *maxnont* the maximum number of nonterminals on the right side of a production. Then the production-local dependency graph of a production p in an attribute grammar in normal form has maximum size $((maxnont + 1) \cdot \frac{1}{2}maxattr)^2$. Thus, an upper bound for the size of $Dt(t)$ is $ap \cdot ((maxnont + 1) \cdot \frac{1}{2}maxattr)^2$, where ap is the number of productions applied in t. This worst case actually arises if only one production with *maxnont* nonterminals with *maxattr* attributes each is applied ap times. This gives the order of the space complexity for the topological sorting of $Dt(t)$. It clearly increases quadratically with the number of attributes per nonterminal. □

Example 9.23

Suppose we are given the following attribute grammar:

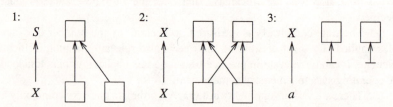

The dynamic size required by a demand-driven evaluator, which saves storage by storing the attributes in its calling stack, is a stack of maximum depth $O(\text{height}(t))$ and t itself. However, the run time is exponential in the height of t, or, more precisely, $O(4^{\text{height}(t)})$ or $O(2^{|V(t)|})$.

If the demand-driven evaluator stores the attribute values in the tree, it requires $|V(t)| + |t|$ space for the dynamic part and time $O(|V(t)|)$. □

9.4.3   Visit-oriented evaluators

Although the evaluation phase of the compilation process takes place after the strategic phase, we discuss it first. As a starting point for the attribute evaluation, we suppose that for each node n there exists a total order T_n on the set *Attr* (*symb* (*n*)) (either such a total order exists for every nonterminal, when the case of Section 9.4.4 applies, or a total order has already been selected in a preceding strategy phase and then the case of Section 9.4.5 applies). The attribute instances for n should be evaluated in the order given by T_n.

Visit-oriented evaluators take their name from the concept of a **visit** at a production occurrence. The evaluation of the attribute instances at a production occurrence happens during a sequence of such visits. The production occurrence is entered from its upper or lower tree context, some attribute instances are evaluated, and the production occurrence is left for a visit to the upper or the lower tree context. The visiting strategy is generated from the attribute grammar.

Figure 9.23 describes the program of this section, namely the generation and use of a visit-oriented evaluator. Total orders on the attribute sets provide the initial information for the generation. They are generated during the strategy phase. They

Generation time	Execution time
Total orders $T_x \subseteq Attr\ (X) \times Attr\ (X)$ for all $X \in V_N$	Tree t with $\{T_n\}_{n \in \text{nodes}}\ (t)$ $prod(n) = p, (T_0, T_1, \ldots, T_{n_p})$
↓	⇓
Ordered partition for $Attr(X)$	$B(p; T_{n0}, T_{n1}, \ldots, T_{nn_p})$
↓	⋮
Seq. of visits $B(p; T_0, T_1, \ldots, T_{n_p})$	⋮ ∨
for $p \in P$, T_i total order on $Attr\ (p[i]) \rightarrow$	rvE, recursive visit-oriented evaluator

$B\ \rightarrow\ A$ stands for 'A is calculated from B at generation time',
$A\ \Rightarrow\ B$ stands for 'A determines B uniquely',
$A\ \cdots\!\!>\ B$ stands for 'A is used in B'.

Figure 9.23   The evaluation phase, generation and execution.

can be used to calculate ordered partitions for the attributes of the nonterminals. A $(n_p + 1)$ tuple of total orders or ordered partitions, respectively, for the nonterminals of a production p determines a visit sequence for the attribute occurrences in p. This visit sequence is divided into the components for the consecutive visits to the production. Procedures for the individual visits are generated from this.

At evaluation time total orders exist on the attribute instances at all nodes of the tree t. The total orders for the occurrence of a production p determine uniquely one visit sequence for p according to the precomputation at generation time. It is used in case statements for selection of the visiting procedures.

Definition 9.13 (induced local order)
Let $T(t)$ be an evaluation order for $Dt(t)$. $T(t)$ **induces** the total orders $\{T_n\}_{n \in \text{nodes}(t)}$ if and only if for all $a, b \in Attr(symb(n))$: $a_n\ T(t)\ b_n \Leftrightarrow a\ T_n\ b$. $\qquad \square$

We now give a dynamic and a static criterion for the possibility of performing attribute evaluation for a grammar AG in accordance with the $\{T_n\}$.

> (l1) There exists an evaluator for AG, which for all trees t computes the attributes of t in accordance with an evaluation order $T(t)$ for $Dt(t)$, which induces the $\{T_n\}_{n \in \text{nodes}(t)}$.
>
> (l2) For every node n with $prod(n) = p$: $Dp(p)[T_{n_0}, T_{n_1}, \ldots, T_{n_{n_p}}]$ is acyclic.

The two conditions are equivalent. The proof for the direction $(l2) \Rightarrow (l1)$ given below involves the derivation of an evaluator.

Definition 9.14 (ordered partition)
Suppose T is a total order on $Attr(X)$. We consider T as a word over $Attr(X)$. An **ordered partition** for T is a division of T into a sequence $\iota^1 \sigma^1 \iota^2 \sigma^2 \ldots \iota^k \sigma^k$ with

- $\iota^j \in Inh(X)^*$, $\sigma^j \in Syn(X)^*$ for all $1 \leq j \leq k$,
- $\iota^j \neq \varepsilon$ for all $1 < j \leq k$,
- $\sigma^j \neq \varepsilon$ for all $1 \leq j < k$.

ι^j is called the jth **downwards visit**, σ^j is the jth **upwards visit**, $\iota^j \sigma^j$ is the jth **visit**. $\qquad \square$

The conditions $\iota^j \neq \varepsilon$ and $\sigma^j \neq \varepsilon$ guarantee that maximally long sequences of inherited respectively synthesized attributes are always cut out of T.

Note that in what follows the upper index is a 'visit index', while the lower index always denotes a position of a nonterminal occurrence in a production.

Example 9.24 (continuation of Example 9.9)
We consider the following total orders on $Attr(BIN)$ and $Attr(BIT)$.

$$T_{BIN} = l \quad r \quad v \qquad T_{BIT} = r \quad v$$

Then the ordered partitions are:

$$\text{of } BIN \quad \begin{matrix} \varepsilon & l & r & v \\ \iota^1 & \sigma^1 & \iota^2 & \sigma^2 \end{matrix}$$

$$\text{of } BIT \quad \begin{matrix} r & v \\ \iota^1 & \sigma^1 \end{matrix} \qquad\qquad\qquad\qquad \square$$

At a node n with total order T_n and associated ordered partition $\iota^1\sigma^1 \ldots \iota^k\sigma^k$ the visit evaluator we shall describe evaluates the instances of ι^j on the jth visit to the node n 'from above' and the instances of σ^j on the return from the subtree t/n. The visits to a node belonging to an instance of the production p are given by a visit sequence. These visit sequences can be precomputed for a given combination of total orders $T_0, T_1, \ldots, T_{n_p}$.

Definition 9.15 (visit sequence)
Let T_i be a total order on $Attr(X_i)$ for all i with $(0 \le i \le n_p)$, such that $D = Dp(p)[T_0, T_1, \ldots, T_{n_p}]$ is not cyclic. Let $\iota_j^1\sigma_j^1 \ldots \iota_j^{k_j}\sigma_j^{k_j}$ be the ordered partitions of T_j $(0 \le j \le n_p)$. A **visit sequence** for p and $T_0, T_1, \ldots, T_{n_p}$ is an evaluation order for D of the following form:

$$B(p; T_0, T_1, \ldots, T_{n_p}) = \iota_0^1\delta^1\sigma_0^1\iota_0^2\delta^2\sigma_0^2 \ldots \iota_0^k\delta^k\sigma_0^k$$

and δ^l is a sequence of visits $\iota_j^l\sigma_j^l$ $(1 \le j \le n_p)$ to nonterminals X_j of the right side. $\qquad\qquad \square$

Thus, a visit sequence $B(p; T_0, T_1, \ldots, T_{n_p})$ consists of a sequence of triples, comprising a downwards visit ι_0^l to X_0, a visit sequence δ^l to nonterminals of the right side and an upwards visit σ_0^l to X_0. One such sequence is constructed by the algorithm **Visit sequence**.

Algorithm Visit sequence:

Input: production-local dependency graph $Dp(p)$,
total orders $T_0, T_1, \ldots, T_{n_p}$ on $Attr(X_0), Attr(X_1), \ldots, Attr(X_{n_p})$.

Output: a visit sequence $B(p; T_0, T_1, \ldots, T_{n_p})$.

Method:

(1) Construct a graph of visits $\tilde{D}$ from $D = Dp(p)[T_0, T_1, \ldots, T_{n_p}]$

  ● the nodes of $\tilde{D}$ are:

   — $\iota_j^r\sigma_j^r$ $(1 \le j \le n_p)$, $\iota_j^r\sigma_j^r$ is a visit to X_j in T_j (on the right side)

   — $\sigma_0^l\iota_0^{l+1}$ $(0 \le l < k_0)$ (visit to the parent) and

   — ι_0^1 and $\sigma_0^{k_0}$ first downwards and last upwards visit to the parent

  ● there exists an edge from x to y in $\tilde{D}$, if there exist attribute occurrences a_i in x and b_j in y with a_i D b_j.

(2) Construct an evaluation order for $\tilde{D}$, beginning with ι_0^1 and ending with $\sigma_0^{k_0}$. This evaluation order is a visit sequence for $p, T_0, T_1, \ldots, T_{n_p}$. $\qquad \square$

Step (2) in the **Visit sequence** algorithm is possible because $\tilde{D}$ is not cyclic and ι_0^1 is a minimal element of $\tilde{D}$ and $\sigma_0^{k_0}$ is a maximal element of $\tilde{D}$.

Thus, the **Visit sequence** algorithm can be used at generation time to generate one or more visit sequences for p from one or more combinations of total orders $T_0, T_1, \ldots, T_{n_p}$.

Example 9.25 (continuation of Example 9.9)

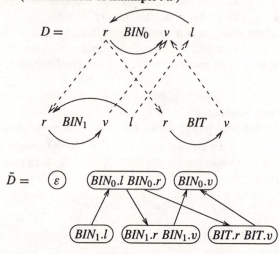

Evaluation order for $\tilde{D}$ with ι_0^1 as first and σ_0^2 as last element.

$$
\begin{array}{ccccccccc}
\iota_0^1 & \iota_1^1 & \sigma_1^1 & \sigma_0^1 & \iota_0^2 & \iota_1^2 & \sigma_1^2 & \iota_2^1 & \sigma_2^1 & \sigma_0^2 \\
\varepsilon & \varepsilon & BIN_1.l & BIN_0.l & BIN_0.r & BIN_1.r & BIN_1.v & BIT.r & BIT.v & BIN_0.v
\end{array} \quad \square
$$

The evaluation of the attribute instances for an application of production 2: $BIN \rightarrow BIN\ BIT$ begins, without values of attributes of BIN_0 being brought in. The first child visited is also visited without evaluated inherited attributes. The evaluator returns from this visit with the value of the attribute l. The attribute l can then be calculated for BIN_0. This completes the first visit to the production. It is exited in an upwards direction. The second visit then brings the value of r with it. Now, the evaluator visits the first child for the second time, taking the value of r with it. On return the value of v is available. Since the value of its inherited attribute r has already been calculated the second child (BIT) can be visited. The evaluator returns from this subtree with the value of v. The second visit to the production is then completed with the calculation of v for BIN_0. Alternatively, the evaluator could visit the second child for the first time and then the first child for the second time.

Thus, the evaluation of the instance for applications of this production requires two visits. Subtrees for BIN_1 are visited twice and subtrees for BIT once.

The visit sequence must now be used to construct another evaluator. From among several possibilities, we choose a **recursive evaluator**. It moves through the tree recursively and visits every node n as often as specified by the length of its ordered partition. On the ith visit to n it brings the value of the inherited attribute ι_0^i with it and again leaves n in an upwards direction after calculating the value of the synthesized attribute σ_0^i. In the interim, it undertakes a visit sequence to children of n. Suppose this sequence is $\iota_{j_1}^{i_1}\sigma_{j_1}^{i_1} \ldots \iota_{j_l}^{i_l}\sigma_{j_l}^{i_l}$. The visit $\iota_{j_r}^{i_r}\sigma_{j_r}^{i_r}$ is the i_rth visit to the node nj_r. Thus, the evaluator is very flexible; on the ith visit to n it may visit a child several times or not at all. A program is now generated from the visit sequence in the following way:

$eval\,(\alpha)$ stands for the evaluation of the attribute instance in α.

proc $visit\_i\,(n : node)$ is a procedure, which carries out the ith visit to the node n; here i ranges over $1, \ldots, maxvisit$, where $maxvisit$ is the maximum number of visits in an ordered partition. The body of $visit\_i$ consists of a case statement over all visit sequences $B(p; T_0, T_1, \ldots, T_{n_p})$. The selection for this case statement uses the visit sequence $vs(n)$ found at the node n (the production suffices as the selector if there is only one total order for each nonterminal and hence only one visit sequence for each production). The following part of the visit sequence: $\iota_0^i\iota_{j_1}^{i_1}\sigma_{j_1}^{i_1} \ldots \iota_{j_l}^{i_l}\sigma_{j_l}^{i_l}\sigma_0^i$ is used to construct the case components for $B(p; T_0, T_1, \ldots, T_{n_p})$ as follows:

$$
\begin{aligned}
&eval\,(\iota_{nj_1}^{i_1});\ visit\_i_1(nj_1);\\
&eval\,(\iota_{nj_2}^{i_2});\ visit\_i_2(nj_2);\\
&\quad\vdots\\
&eval\,(\iota_{nj_l}^{i_l});\ visit\_i_l(nj_l);\\
&eval\,(\sigma_0^i)
\end{aligned}
$$

Let us call this block of calls $B_i(p; T_0, T_1, \ldots, T_{n_p})$. It contains $eval$ calls for all instances belonging to defining occurrences and evaluatable in the ith visit to nodes n with $\mathrm{prod}(n) = p$. The recursive visit-oriented evaluator is shown in Figure 9.24. The visit sequences relevant to production 2 of the grammar **Bin_to_Dec** are shown in Figure 9.25.

The recursive visit-oriented evaluator is used in the following context:

- Every node has an associated total order on the attribute instances; if there is more than one per nonterminal, one of them is selected beforehand.

- The total orders associated with the nodes determine the visit sequence for the production applied at this node.

- This visit sequence is then used to control the evaluator.

Example 9.26 (continuation of Example 9.9)
We consider the evaluation order of Example 9.25. According to the above scheme,

```
program rvE;
proc visit_1(n : node);
  ⋮
proc visit_i(n : node);
begin
    case vs(n) of
      ⋮
    B(p; T₀, T₁, ..., Tₙₚ) : Bᵢ(p; T₀, T₁, ..., Tₙₚ)
      ⋮
    endcase
end
  ⋮
begin
    visit_1(ε)
end
```

Figure 9.24   The recursive visit-oriented evaluator, rvE.

the program parts for the two visits for production 2 are derived from the evaluation order.

The static size of the evaluator **rvE** is linear in the size of the attribute grammar. The dynamic size is made up of $|t|$, $|V(t)|$ and $|\text{height}(t)|$ for the recursion stack.   □

9.4.4   *l*-ordered attribute grammars

We now consider the completely static case of the strategy phase, outlined above. Here, at generation time, one total order is calculated on the attributes of each nonterminal; these total orders associated with nonterminals in a tree induce an evaluation order for the tree. The attribute evaluator described in the last section then expects the total orders in the tree.

Definition 9.16 (*l*-ordered attribute grammar)
An attribute grammar AG is *l*-ordered (is in *l*-ordered-AG), if there exists a family of total orders $\{T_X\}_{X \in V_N}$, such that every tree t with the total orders $\{T_{symb(n)}\}_{n \in \text{nodes } n(t)}$ satisfies one of the criteria (*l*1) or (*l*2) of Definition 9.13.   □

If (*l*2) is satisfied, it follows that there exists a family $\{T_X\}_{X \in V_N}$, such that $Dp(p)[T_{X_0}, T_{X_1}, \ldots, T_{X_{n_p}}]$ is acyclic for every production p. Since there is precisely one total order for every nonterminal in p, exactly one visit sequence is sufficient to control the visits to all applications of p. We then call this visit sequence to p $B(p)$.

The *test* for whether the criterion (*l*2) is satisfied for a given family $\{T_X\}_{X \in V_N}$ has only ever polynomial cost. The problem of *finding* the total orders for an

```
program rvE_xmp;
proc visit_1(n : node);
begin
      case vs(n) of
        ⋮
      B(2; ...) :  begin
                      eval(ε);  visit_1(n1);
                      eval(l_n);
                  end

        ⋮
      endcase
end;
proc visit_2(n : node);
begin
      case vs(n) of
        ⋮

      B(2; ...) :  begin
                      eval(r_{n1});  visit_2(n1);
                      eval(r_{n2});  visit_1(n2);
                      eval(v_n);
                  end

        ⋮
      endcase
end;
begin
      visit_1(ε)
end
```

Figure 9.25   Section of the recursive visit-oriented evaluator for the attribute grammar 'Bin_toDec'.

attribute grammar is NP complete. This is because one does not look for an arbitrary total order on the attribute set of each nonterminal, but one has to find total orders which when used in all relevant production-local dependency graphs lead to acyclic graphs. This can (probably) only be achieved deterministically by trying out all possible combinations of total orders. Thus, we implement a subclass of the l-ordered attribute grammars in which the total orders $\{T'_X\}_{X \in V_N}$ can be constructed in polynomial time.

The starting point comprises relations $\{R_X\}_{X \in V_N}$ on $Attr(X)$ with the following property. The R_X are the smallest relations R'_X for which:

$$a_j \ Dp(p)[R'_{X_0}, R'_{X_1}, \ldots, R'_{X_{n_p}}]^+ \ b_j \Rightarrow a \ R'_{X_j} \ b$$

for all productions p and all attributes a and b of X_j $(0 \leq j \leq n_p)$. This means, if the relations R_{X_i} $(0 \leq i \leq n_p)$ are attached to the production-local dependency graph $D_p(p)$, there may not result new (transitive) dependencies for any X_i in addition to R_{X_i}. How are these relations obtained? We have: $IO(X) \cup OI(X) \subseteq R_X$. That can be seen from the equations (IO) in Section 9.4.1. Starting with the $IO(X) \cup OI(X)$, the R_X can be obtained by the following iterative process. Insert the actual relations into all production-local dependency graphs and check whether new edges result for any nonterminal. In this case, add them to the corresponding relations and repeat the process until no further changes occur. This process terminates, since edges are only added and since the relations are finite. If the attribute grammar is l-ordered by the total orders $\{T_X\}_{X \in V_N}$, then $R_X \subseteq T_X$ for all $X \in V_N$. In this case, the R_X are also all acyclic. These relations clearly form a good starting point for the construction of total orders for the nonterminals, for, as previously stated, they must be contained in each corresponding total order. From these relations R_X we obtain total orders T'_X as evaluation orders, by alternately combining and artificially ordering the largest possible sets of inherited and applied attributes. More precisely, T'_X is a sequence $\iota^1 \sigma^1 \iota^2 \sigma^2 \ldots \iota^k \sigma^k$, such that ι^j consists of the minimal inherited attributes with respect to

$$R_X\big|_{Attr(X)} - \bigcup_{l=1}^{j-1} (\iota^l \cup \sigma^l)$$

consisting of the inherited attributes of X, which can be evaluated when the attributes in the $\iota^1 \sigma^1 \iota^2 \sigma^2 \ldots \iota^{j-1} \sigma^{j-1}$ are calculated.

σ^j consists of the minimal synthesized attributes with respect to

$$R_X\big|_{Attr(X)} - \bigcup_{l=1}^{j-1} (\iota^l \cup \sigma^l) \cup \iota^j$$

In this way, the R_X are made totally in isolation, that is, no consideration is given as to whether the introduced edges cause cycles at production level. Thus, on the one hand the class of grammars is smaller, but on the other hand the complexity is polynomial.

Definition 9.17 (ordered attribute grammar)
An attribute grammar is **ordered** (is in **ordered AG**), if for the total orders $\{T'_X\}_{X \in V_N}$ calculated as above, for each production p: $Dp(p)[T'_{X_0}, T'_{X_1}, \ldots, T'_{X_{n_p}}]$ is acyclic. □

If an attribute grammar is ordered by the total orders $\{T'_X\}_{X \in V_N}$, then it is also l-ordered. Thus, the evaluator **rvE** can be used to evaluate the attributes for every tree of the grammar.

9.4.5 Absolutely non-circular attribute grammars

We now consider the third variant of the strategy phase. This deals with the case in which there exist several order partitions for a nonterminal and several visit

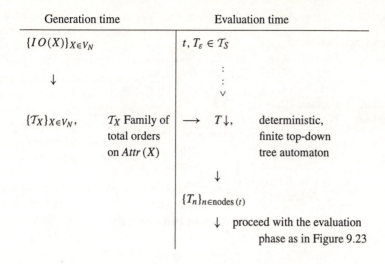

Figure 9.26   Strategy phase, generation and execution.

sequences for a production. The starting point comprises the relations $\{I\,O_{(X)}\}_{X\in V_N}$, whose calculation was described in Section 9.4.1. They provide an approximate description of the dependencies of the synthesized attributes of X on the inherited attributes of X, that is, lower dependencies in subtrees for X. Thus, all lower dependencies are precomputed (approximated) statically, and the same applies for all occurrences of nonterminals in trees. In contrast, the $IO(X)$ contain no upper dependencies. However, we need these to calculate total orders for the nodes of the tree from which we determine the visit sequences for the recursive visit-oriented evaluator.

The procedure at evaluation time is now as follows, see Figure 9.26:

(1)   Calculation of total orders at the nodes of the tree; here, the total order at a node depends on its upper context.

(2)   Selection of the visit sequences for all occurrences of productions; the selection function is precomputed statically.

(3)   Evaluation with the **rvE** evaluator.

Steps (2) and (3) are the same as in the case of the l-ordered grammars. Step (1) involves the construction of a deterministic finite top-down tree automaton $T\!\downarrow$. This tree automaton $T\!\downarrow$ uses as input alphabet the productions, which are applied at the nodes of a syntax tree. Its (finitely many) states are the total orders on the attribute sets of the nonterminals. For each production p it has a transition function $\delta_p : \mathcal{T}_0 \rightarrow \mathcal{T}_1 \times \ldots \times \mathcal{T}_{n_p}$, where $\mathcal{T}_i$ is the set of the total orders on $Attr(X_i)$. δ_p determines total orders $T_1, \ldots, T_{n_p}$ on $Attr(X_1), \ldots, Attr(X_{n_p})$

Algorithm Gen Delta

Input: Productions $\{p : X_0 \to X_1 \ldots X_{n_p}\}_{p \in P}$.
Relations $\{IO(X)\}_{X \in V_N}$ with the property
that $Dp(p)[IO(X_1), \ldots, IO(X_{n_p})]$ is acyclic.

Output: Functions $\{\delta_p : T_0 \to T_1 \times \ldots \times T_{n_p}\}_{p \in P}$.

Method: For all T_0, total order on $Attr(X_0)$ with $IO(X_0) \subseteq T_0$:
1. Construct an evaluation order T for
$Dp(p)[T_0, IO(X_1), \ldots, IO(X_{n_p})]$;
2. The restriction of T to the $Attr(X_j)$ $(1 \le j \le n_p)$
gives total orders $\{T_j\}_{1 \le j \le n_p}$.
3. Define $\delta_p(T_0) = (T_1, \ldots, T_{n_p})$.

Figure 9.27   Gen Delta algorithm.

from a total order T_0 for $Attr(X_0)$. These were determined at generation time in such a way that

- $Dp(p)[T_0, T_1, \ldots, T_{n_p}]$ is acyclic, and
- $IO(X_j) \subseteq T_j$ for $(1 \le j \le n_p)$.

The set of transition functions $\{\delta_p\}_{p \in P}$ is constructed using the algorithm **Gen Delta** shown in Figure 9.27. This algorithm requires some explanation. Step (1) operates in such a way that for each production p $Dp(p)[T_0, IO(X_1), \ldots, IO(X_{n_p})]$ is acyclic; for $Dp(p)[IO(X_1), \ldots, IO(X_{n_p})]$ is acyclic by assumption, and the edges, added to $IO(X_0)$ to obtain T_0, cannot result in further cycles since otherwise T_0 would have to have been cyclic already.

The total orders T_j $(1 \le j \le n_p)$ constructed in step (2) have the property that $Dp(p)[T_0, T_1, \ldots, T_{n_p}]$ is acyclic, and that $IO(X_j) \subseteq T_j$ $(1 \le j \le n_p)$. T is also an evaluation order of $Dp(p)[T_0, T_1, \ldots, T_{n_p}]$. Since this also provides an evaluation order of $Dp(p)$ $[T_0, T_1, \ldots, T_{n_p}]$, this must be acyclic, according to Theorem 9.2.

For the deterministic finite top-down tree automaton to be completely determined, an initial state, that is, a total order, must be specified for the root. Every total order T_0 with the property $IO(S) \subseteq T_0$ is suitable for this.

The tree automaton constructed in this way executes step (1) in the evaluation of attributes of an absolutely non-circular grammar. The construction of the transition functions $\{\delta_p\}_{p \in P}$ uses the graphs $\{IO(X)\}_{X \in V_N}$. This kind of attribute evaluation can be generalized to an evaluation for all non-circular grammars. In this case, an earlier bottom-up pass through this tree must be made in which acyclic relations R_n, for example, the lower characteristic graphs, are calculated for each node n. These can again be used to calculate suitable total orders $\{T_n\}_{n \in nodes(t)}$ by means of a top-down tree automaton. However, this automaton now has transitions under $(p, r_1, \ldots, r_{n_p})$, where p is the production applied and the $r_1, \ldots, r_{n_p}$ are the precomputed lower dependencies. In this way a **Gen Delta** algorithm for general non-circular attribute grammars would calculate several transition functions $\delta_{(p,r_1,\ldots,r_{n_p})}$ for a production p.

The complexity of the tests for absolute non-circularity, whose cost is determined by that of the calculation of the $\{IO(X)\}$, is polynomial. But the static size of the evaluator generated is exponential, since the number of possible total orders increases exponentially with the number of attributes.

9.4.6 Parser-driven attribute evaluation

In this section we consider a class of attribute grammars which is very restricted but of practical interest due to time and space efficiency. They are characterized by the fact that the attributes can be evaluated in parallel with the syntax analysis under the control of the parser. The attribute values are managed in a stack-like fashion, either in a dedicated attribute stack or in the syntax stack together with the parser states and grammar symbols. In each case, the values are addressed with fixed relative addresses in their stack, so that a more efficient access is possible. The construction of the syntax tree is redundant, at least for the purposes of the later attribute evaluation. All this makes classes of grammars with parser-driven attribute evaluation interesting for languages which are easier to implement.

Since the attribute evaluation is parser driven the values of synthesized attributes must be delivered punctually to terminal symbols by the scanner. To deal with this, we now once again consider productions with terminals.

L-attributed grammars

All parsers for controlling attribute evaluation that we consider here process their input from left to right. Thus, the first class of grammars we introduce is a superclass of all classes of attribute grammars for which the attribute evaluation can be parser driven. It contains all grammars in which in every syntax tree the attributes can be evaluated in **one** left-to-right depth-first search. The evaluation of attributes in a left-to-right depth-first search uses the algorithm **L-AA** of Figure 9.28.

This algorithm provides a dynamic test for the membership of the class L-AG. An attribute grammar **AG** is in **L-AG** if and only if in every tree for **AG** the attributes (attribute instances) can be evaluated using the **L-AA** algorithm.

As always, the static test is based on an analysis of the attribute dependencies. We formulate it as the definition of the class of grammars.

Definition 9.18 (L-attributed grammar)
An attribute grammar **AG** is said to be **L-attributed, is in L-AG**, if for every production of the grammar $p : X_0 \rightarrow X_1 \ldots X_{n_p}$ and every semantic rule $a_i = f_{p,a,i}(b_{j_1}^1, \ldots, b_{j_k}^k)$ for p: if $a \in Inh(X_i)$ and $1 \leq i \leq n_p$, then $j_l < i$ for all l ($1 \leq l \leq k$), that is, inherited occurrences on the right side depend only on occurrences to the left of themselves. □

```
            program L-AA;
      proc    visit (n : node)
               case    prod (n) of
                ⋮
                  p :  begin
                           eval (Inh (X₁)); visit (n1);
                           eval (Inh (X₂)); visit (n2);
                            ⋮
                           eval (Inh (Xₙₚ)); visit (nnₚ);
                           eval (Syn (X₀));
                       end;
                ⋮
               endcase
      end;
      begin
      visit(ε)         (∗Start at the root; any inherited attributes of the root,
                        must have predefined values∗)
      end.
```

$$\text{visit}(\varepsilon)$$

Figure 9.28   L-AA algorithm.

Thus, the productions of an L-attributed grammar have no right–left dependencies. It is easy to see that in each tree for an L-attributed grammar the attributes can be evaluated using the L-AA algorithm. Conversely, it is clear that the grammar must be L-attributed if in each tree the attributes can be evaluated using the L-AA algorithm.

Example 9.27   The attribute grammars AG_1 and AG_2 of Examples 9.5 and 9.6 are both L-attributed. AG_1 is even **S-attributed**, that is, it has only synthesized attributes. Every S-attributed grammar is also L-attributed.   □

Let us consider the actions needed for a parser-driven attribute evaluation.

$eval(Inh(X))$ at the beginning of the analysis of a word for X,

$eval(Syn(X))$ at the end of the analysis of a word for X,
          that is, on the reduction to X,

$get(Syn(X))$ on reading a terminal.

An LL-parser, as described in Chapter 8, 'Syntax Analysis', could trigger these evaluations on expansion, on reduction, and on reading a terminal, respectively.

Definition 9.19 (LL-attributed grammar)
An attribute grammar AG is **LL-attributed**, in **LL-AG**, if

- it is L-attributed, and
- the underlying context-free grammar is an LL-grammar.   □

Example 9.28
Neither $\mathbf{AG}_1$ nor $\mathbf{AG}_2$ is LL-attributed, since the underlying context-free grammars are left recursive and therefore not LL.   □

Example 9.26   The attribute grammar BoolExp in Section 9.3 is of interest for a number of reasons. First, it describes a relevant compiler task. Of course, it is not LL-attributed, since it is left recursive. However, it can even be shown that there is no LL-attributed grammar which solves the given problem in this way, that is, by propagating two jump destinations to each subexpression.   □

The implementation of LL-attributed grammars

The fact that an attribute grammar is LL-attributed means that the syntax analysis can be carried out using an LL-parser and that whenever the LL-parser expands a nonterminal all arguments of its inherited attributes are calculated or, more precisely, can be calculated.

Figure 9.29 shows an LL-parser-driven attribute evaluation. It uses a parse stack PS, whose entries are extended by pointers to a second stack, the attribute stack AS. Every LL state $[A \rightarrow \alpha.\beta]$ in the parse stack points to the start of the AS section, containing the values for this application of the production $A \rightarrow \alpha\beta$. All attribute occurrences of a production are addressed relative to this start address. In addition, the attributes of each nonterminal and terminal are listed in a fixed order. For this, we use the notation:

$LInh(X)$ List of the inherited attributes of the symbol X
$LSyn(X)$ List of the synthesized attributes of the symbol X

If α is a sequence of terminals and nonterminals, then we extend $LInh$ and $LSyn$ to α. $LInh(\alpha)$ is then correspondingly defined as the result of concatenating the sublists for the symbols in α.

It is clearly possible to formulate an assertion about the contents of the attribute stack as a function of the contents of the parse stack. If $[A_1 \rightarrow \alpha_1.\beta_1]$ $[A_2 \rightarrow \alpha_2.\beta_2] \ldots [A_n \rightarrow \alpha_n.\beta_n]$ represent the contents of the parse stack, then the contents of the attribute stack comprise the list of the attribute values for $LInh(A_1)$ $LSyn(\alpha_1)$ $LInh(A_2)$ $LSyn(\alpha_2) \ldots LInh(A_n)$ $LSyn(\alpha_n)$.

LR-attributed grammars

We shall now investigate how an LR-parser can control the evaluation of attributes. Let us compare the possibilities offered by the LL- and LR-parsers in this respect. When expanding a nonterminal, an LL-parser already knows which production will be chosen and thus also knows the addressing of the attribute occurrences for this alternative. The LR-parser usually has several items in its state which describe the possible situations being analysed. Things only become clear on reduction. Thus,

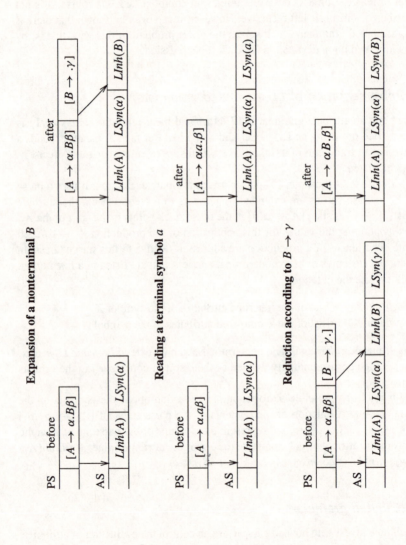

Figure 9.29 Actions of an LL-parser-driven attribute evaluation (PS = parse stack, AS = attribute stack).

one approach might be to associate all attribute-evaluation actions with reductions of the LR-parser. We shall now follow this approach.

The following problems must be resolved in the case of LR-parser-driven attribute evaluation:

- The upper tree fragment, containing the transport paths for inherited attribute values, is not yet known. However, if we assume that the grammar is in L-AG then we know that all attributes on which an inherited attribute of a nonterminal depends have already been calculated.

- When the LR-parser begins to analyse a word for a nonterminal, the values of its inherited attributes must be made available. How can this be done when the LR-parser may not even be able to determine the time at which this happens?

- For the same reason a positive addressing of the attributes relative to a base pointer in the parse stack cannot work. The LR-parser has no means of knowing when to set this base pointer.

Let us consider the context-free item $[X_0 \rightarrow X_1 \cdots . X_i \cdots X_{n_p}]$ with a nonterminal X_i. If this item occurs in an LR-state, one possible interpretation of the state is that a word for X_i is next to be analysed. To evaluate the attributes in the subtree for X_i which must then be constructed the values of the inherited attributes of X_i must be available. Since, by assumption, the attribute grammar is L-attributed, we may suppose that all arguments of the inherited attributes of X_i are available in the attribute stack. We shall shortly see how this is guaranteed and how they are addressed.

Then, a new nonterminal N with the production $N \rightarrow \varepsilon$ and $LSyn(N) = LInh(X_i)$ is introduced before X_i. If reduction to this nonterminal N occurs, the attribute evaluator obtains the arguments for the attributes in $LInh(X_i)$ at stack positions addressed relative to the top of the stack, evaluates the attributes and leaves the values behind at the top of the stack. The reduction from ε to N is associated with the calculation of the attributes in $LInh(X_i)$ and the storage of the values at the top of the attribute stack.

The reduction to a nonterminal in the original grammar is linked with the stacking of the values of the synthesized attributes. Similarly, when a terminal is read, its synthesized attributes are stored at the top of the attribute stack.

In this way, one possible situation in the attribute stack for the item resulting from the original item $[X_0 \rightarrow X_1 \cdots . X_i \cdots X_{n_p}]$ by the transformation is:

$$\cdots \left| LInh(X_0) \right| LInh(X_1) \left| LSyn(X_1) \right| \cdots \left| LInh(X_{i-1}) \right| LSyn(X_{i-1}) \left| LInh(X_i) \right|$$

More precisely, if one can guarantee that when a production p is entered the inherited values of X_0, which come 'from outside', occur in the correct order at the top of the stack, then the transformation described above would create this stack situation.

However, this transformation has several disadvantages. The usage of stack space is high and too many new nonterminals are introduced. The latter could even lead to the transformed grammar losing the LR-property, for example a left-recursive original grammar would never lead to a transformed grammar with the LR-property, since a new ε-terminal would be introduced at the beginning of every left-recursive production N. The parser would then have to introduce a number of reductions to N equal to the recursion depth in the right side before entry. However, that is not known at the start and cannot be determined by a fixed-length lookahead. Thus, the transformation described above is improved upon. Let us consider a left-recursive production

$$X \rightarrow X\alpha \qquad \text{with } LInh(X) = (a, b)$$
$$X_1.a = X_0.a$$
$$X_1.b = X_0.b$$

This form of identical transfer for inherited attributes is very frequent. The transformation of the grammar outline above would destroy a possible LR-property, since a new ε-nonterminal N would be introduced at the beginning of the right side. Only the copying of the values of a and b would be linked with a reduction from ε to N. The resulting situation in the attribute stack would be: $\boxed{\cdots |a|b|a|b}$. But, this copying of the values of a and b would be almost unnecessary since they are already at the top of the stack in the order expected by X_1. However, in the reduction to X the values of the inherited attributes should not be overwritten, since now they are shared by several nonterminals. Another example is the following:

$$X \rightarrow aY\alpha \qquad \text{with } LInh(X) = (a_1, a_2)$$
$$Y.a_1 = a.a_3 \qquad LSyn(a) = (a_3)$$
$$Y.a_2 = X.a_1 \qquad LInh(Y) = (a_1, a_2)$$

The stack situation after reading the terminal symbol a is $\boxed{\cdots |a_1|a_2|a_3}$. Here, it is only necessary to copy the value of $X.a_1$, to create the required stack situation for $[X \rightarrow a.Y\alpha]$. This gives a saving of one stack location.

The transformation of the grammar described as the **LR-AG Transformation** algorithm in Figure 9.30 only introduces an ε-nonterminal where the values of inherited attributes of a nonterminal do not form the top of the attribute stack. If a prefix of the list of values of the inherited attributes occurs at the top of the attribute stack only as much information is calculated or copied as is necessary to extend the prefix to the whole list.

Definition 9.19 (LR-attributed grammar)
An L-attributed grammar is said to be **LR-attributed (is in LR-AG)**, if the underlying context-free grammar resulting from the above transformation is an LR-grammar. □

No L-attributed grammar whose underlying context-free grammar before the transformation is not an LR-grammar is an LR-attributed grammar.

Algorithm	**LR-AG Transformation**
Input:	L-AG AG, lists $LInh(X)$ and $LSyn(X)$
	for all $X \in V_N \cup V_T$.
Output:	Transformed L-AG AG'.
Method:	New nonterminals N with single productions $N \longrightarrow \varepsilon$

are inserted in the right side of productions,
to control the copying of values of inherited attributes.
A list *LAttr* is used, to record the actual attribute-stack allocation
when passing through the right side of a production.

var *LAttr*: List of attribute occurrences;

foreach $p \in P$ **do**

    LAttr := *LInh* (X_0); (∗The values of inherited attributes on the
                                 left side are at the top of the stack∗)

    for $i := 1$ **to** n_p **do**

    case X_i **from**

    Terminal: *LAttr* := *LAttr.LSyn* (X_i) (∗describes storage of
                                   the scanner attributes∗)

    Nonterminal: let L be the longest prefix of $LInh(X_i)$, which
                 is a suffix of *LAttr*. Let L' be the remainder of $LInh(X_i)$

        if L' is non-empty

        then (∗attributes must be copied∗)
            introduce a new terminal N before X_i,
            and add a production $N \longrightarrow \varepsilon$.
            This production is associated with the copying
            of the attribute values of L'.
            LAttr := *LAttr.L'*

        fi
      endcase
      od
  od

Figure 9.30   Transformation for the LR-parser-driven attribute evaluation.

Example 9.30   The attribute grammar BoolExp in Section 9.3 is not LR-attributed. An ε-nonterminal must be inserted at the beginning of the right side of both productions 2 and 4 to provide the recursive nonterminal with a new attribute value.

                             □

9.5   Exercises

1:   Describe the contents of the symbol table in the body of the procedure q after the declaration of the procedure r in Example 9.2.

2: Suppose we are given the following operators:

$$+ \quad :int \longrightarrow int$$
$$+ \quad :real \longrightarrow int$$
$$+ \quad :int \times int \longrightarrow int$$
$$+ \quad :real \times real \longrightarrow real$$
$$/ \quad :int \times int \longrightarrow int$$
$$/ \quad :int \times int \longrightarrow real$$
$$/ \quad :real \times real \longrightarrow real$$

Use the algorithm from Section 9.1.3 to resolve the overloading in the assignment $A := 1/2 + 3/4$ to the *real* variable A.

3: Use the inference rules to derive the type of the following LaMa expression:
letrec *length* $=$ $\lambda l.$ **if** *null l* **then** 0 **else** *succ* (*length* (*tl l*))

4: Modify the algorithm for identifying identifiers given in Section 9.1.2 so that it implements (a) the Pascal scoping rules, (b) the Algol 60 scoping rules.

5: Suppose we are given the following grammar:

$$P \longrightarrow B$$
$$B \longrightarrow \textbf{begin } Ds; Sts \textbf{ end}$$
$$Ds \longrightarrow Ds; D \mid D$$
$$Sts \longrightarrow Sts; St \mid St$$
$$D \longrightarrow \textbf{id}: T$$
$$T \longrightarrow int \mid \textbf{list } T \mid \textbf{id} \mid \textbf{type } T$$
$$St \longrightarrow \textbf{id} \mid B$$

Give attributions which describe the identification of identifiers for Algol and Pascal scoping rules. Organize the symbol tables as linear lists at the head of which new entries are added by the operation *conc*.

6: Formulate the algorithm for resolving overloading described in Section 9.1.3 as an attribute grammar.

7: Evaluate the attributes for the inputs $5 \uparrow 2 + 0 \div 4$ and $(7 - 2) \uparrow 2 \div 4$ for the attribute grammar AG_4.

8: Consider the attribute grammar 'Exercise' (see below).

(a) Give the production-local dependency graphs for the individual productions.

(b) Construct the trees with their individual dependency graphs for the inputs *su*, *sv*, *tu* and *tv*.

(c) Give the lower characteristic graphs for *B* induced by these.

(d) Give an order of evaluation for one of the trees.

(e) Is this grammar *l*-ordered, absolutely non-circular?

(f) Construct an evaluator for this grammar in accordance with Sections 9.4.3 and 9.4.5.

attribute grammar Exercise:
nonterminals *L, A, B*;
attributes   **syn** *z* **with** *A, L*; **syn** *x, y* **with** *B*;
        inh *c* **with** *A*; **inh** *a, b* **with** *B*;
rules

1: $L \longrightarrow A$
        $L.z = A.z$
        $A.c = 0$
2: $A \longrightarrow s\ B$
        $B.a = B.y$
        $B.b = A.c$
        $A.z = B.x$

3: $A \longrightarrow t\ B$
        $B.a = A.c$
        $B.b = B.x$
        $A.z = B.y$

4: $B \longrightarrow u$
        $B.x = B.a$
        $B.y = B.b$
5: $B \longrightarrow v$
        $B.x = B.a$
        $B.y = 0$

9:   Define O/I graphs which approximate the upper characteristic graphs. Use the I/O graphs as lower dependencies. Give the corresponding grammar flow analysis problem.

10:

(a) Calculate an evaluation order for production 1 of the attribute grammar **Bin_to_Dec**. Use the ordered partition of **Bin_to_Dec** of Example 9.9.

(b) Give the program parts of the programs rvE_xmp associated with production 1.

9.6   Literature

The presentation of the context conditions follows Watt (1984) in parts. The data structure for the symbol table described in Section 9.1 was invented independently by a large number of compiler designers. An early source is Krieg (1971).

The algorithm for resolving overloading is that of Penello *et al.* (1980). Type inference for polymorphically typed languages is due to Hindley (1969), Milner (1978) and Damas and Milner (1982).

The concept of attribute grammar was introduced by Knuth (1968, 1971).

Jazayeri showed the exponential complexity of the non-circularity test for attribute grammars (Jazayeri *et al.*, 1975). The class of absolutely non-circular attribute grammars together with their evaluation procedure is due to Kennedy and Warren (1976). Ordered attribute grammars were defined by Kastens (1980), visit-oriented attribute evaluation by Riis–Nielson (1983). The concept of ordered partition is due to Engelfriet and Filé (1982). The attribute grammar for the short-circuit evaluation of Boolean expressions was taken from Giegerich and Wilhelm (1978). The LR-parser-driven attribute evaluation was developed by Watt (1977).

Lipps *et al.* (1988) describe an implementation of attribute grammars with data-driven and demand-driven evaluation and incremental re-evaluation after tree transformations. In addition, the same work uses 'uninterpreted' attribute values as an aid to the implementation of more complex data structures such as symbol tables. Here, certain semantic rules are used as constructors for terms. Thus, attributes may have terms as values, which are constructed according to the attribute dependencies. Other semantic rules can operate on these terms like functions of a functional language.

The following articles and books provide overviews of attribute grammars, classes of grammars, evaluation procedures and/or implemented systems: Courcelle (1984), Engelfriet (1984), Alblas (1991) and Deransart *et al.* (1988).

10

Abstract interpretation

- Introduction
- Abstract interpretation based on denotational semantics
- Abstract interpretation based on operational semantics
- Exercises
- Literature

10.1   Introduction

In this chapter we study a class of algorithms for obtaining information about a program to answer the following question:

> For a given program does there exist a program which is equivalent in terms of its input and output behaviour but with lower costs (time, space)? If so what is it?

Questions of this type are generally undecidable, that is, there is no algorithm that can generally answer them correctly and completely. In this book, we are interested in the above question, to enable us to generate better code for a given program (code with a lower space and/or time requirement). The improved code must have the input/output behaviour specified for the program; it *must* be correct in this sense. However, we can dispense with completeness, because it is not mandatory that the compiler recognizes and uses all possibilities for improvement.

To improve code, algorithms that answer questions of the following kind with a '*yes, definitely*' or an '*I cannot decide*' may be used in a compiler:

- Does an expression always have the same (constant) value at a point in the program? If yes, it can be evaluated at compile time and its value used in the target program. This saves the computation at run time.

- Can a computation be removed from a loop? Then the computation need be performed only once before entry into the loop instead of in each pass through the loop.

- Does an expression occur several times in a program and does the evaluation always give the same value at two places? In this case, the second evaluation can be dispensed with if the value of the first evaluation is remembered.

- Is the value of an expression subsequently no longer required? Then its evaluation can be omitted completely. While the original programs normally contain few such irrelevant computations, computations may become irrelevant due to other optimizations.

An answer '*Yes, definitely*' must apply to all permissible input values for the program. But, of course, the compiler cannot in general apply the program to all input values in order to obtain this answer. It must make appropriate simplifications, abstractions, to obtain the answers within a reasonable time, and even to ensure that it obtains an answer at all in finite time. The technique described in this chapter thus replaces the (concrete) data with which the program usually works by appropriate abstractions and then lets the program run with these abstract values. From the result of *one* such abstract program run it is frequently possible to draw conclusions about a whole set of program runs with concrete data, and, under certain circumstances, about all possible program runs. Corresponding to the data abstraction, we must also move to an abstraction of the meaning (semantics) of the language constructs.

By simplification, certain versions of problems, which were originally undecidable or could only be decided at considerable expense, become decidable or easy to solve. On the other hand, abstraction results in the loss of information, so that the solution of the simplified problem does not normally provide a complete solution of the original problem.

We shall explain this principle in what follows, initially using simple examples from mathematics and everyday life, before we return to its application in compilers.

10.1.1 Example 1: computation with residues

We begin with a simple example from mathematics which explains our principle very well, but which is of no further practical importance.

We shall show that for every integer z the expression $z^2(z+1)^2$ is divisible by four. One possible proof involves abstracting from the integers to represent them by their residues on division by four, and correspondingly abstracting from the operations of taking powers, multiplication and addition, to show that the expression interpreted over the residues modulo four always gives zero modulo four. Since there are only four distinct residues modulo four this simplified statement can be verified directly by substituting the four values for z and calculating the expression.

We now consider this example in detail. The residue modulo four of an integer z is the integer $\bar{z}$ between 0 and 3, for which $z - \bar{z}$ is divisible by 4. An integer is divisible by 4 if and only if it has residue 0 modulo four: 1, 5 and -3 have residue 1 modulo four; 2, 6 and -2 have residue 2 modulo four; 3, 7 and -1 have residue 3 modulo 4. In general z and $z + 4$ have the same residue modulo four.

We can define an addition $\overline{+}$ and a multiplication $\overline{*}$ on the residues modulo four by

$$\bar{z_1} \,\overline{+}\, \bar{z_2} \ := \ \overline{z_1 + z_2}$$
$$\bar{z_1} \,\overline{*}\, \bar{z_2} \ := \ \overline{z_1 z_2}$$

This definition leads to the following function tables:

$\overline{+}$	$\bar{0}$	$\bar{1}$	$\bar{2}$	$\bar{3}$
$\bar{0}$	$\bar{0}$	$\bar{1}$	$\bar{2}$	$\bar{3}$
$\bar{1}$	$\bar{1}$	$\bar{2}$	$\bar{3}$	$\bar{0}$
$\bar{2}$	$\bar{2}$	$\bar{3}$	$\bar{0}$	$\bar{1}$
$\bar{3}$	$\bar{3}$	$\bar{0}$	$\bar{1}$	$\bar{2}$

$\overline{*}$	$\bar{0}$	$\bar{1}$	$\bar{2}$	$\bar{3}$
$\bar{0}$	$\bar{0}$	$\bar{0}$	$\bar{0}$	$\bar{0}$
$\bar{1}$	$\bar{0}$	$\bar{1}$	$\bar{2}$	$\bar{3}$
$\bar{2}$	$\bar{0}$	$\bar{2}$	$\bar{0}$	$\bar{2}$
$\bar{3}$	$\bar{0}$	$\bar{3}$	$\bar{2}$	$\bar{1}$

The operations live up to their names: they represent the abstractions of addition and multiplication from integers to the residues modulo four, since for all integers z_1 and z_2 we have

$$\overline{z_1 + z_2} \ = \ \bar{z_1} \,\overline{+}\, \bar{z_2}$$

$$\overline{z_1 z_2} \;=\; \overline{z_1} * \overline{z_2}$$

When we interpret our expression $zz(z+1)(z+1)$ abstractly (over the residues modulo four with $\overline{+}$ as addition and $\overline{*}$ as multiplication) then we obtain the result 0 for each of the four possible residues modulo four. Taken together with the above property, this implies that for every integer $\overline{z^2(z+1)^2} = \overline{0}$, which is the desired property.

We note that the abstraction chosen is directly associated with our problem. In general, different problems will need to be answered with different abstractions. For example, our abstraction is inappropriate for proving that $z^5 - z$ is divisible by 5 for every integer z. However, this property can be proved using an abstraction based on residues modulo five.

10.1.2   Example 2: casting out of nine

For our second example, we consider the nine test. Before the introduction of pocket calculators this was an important procedure for obtaining indications of errors in complex calculations based on addition, subtraction and multiplication.

In the casting out of nine test the calculation to be checked is executed not with the concrete data but with the the 'sum of its digits'. Here, in summing the digits of a number, two-place interim results are immediately reduced to the sum of their digits. If the sum of the digits of the result based on the concrete data does not agree with the result obtained using sums of the digits, then an error has occurred in the execution of one of the calculations. If the two values agree, this does not necessarily mean that both calculations are actually correct. The nine test only provides a *sufficient* (but not a necessary) condition for the presence of an error. Abstraction, in this case, the formation of the sum of the digits, considerably simplifies the calculation used for the test but does not provide a complete answer.

The nine test is closely associated with residues modulo nine. Thus, the abstraction used is very similar to that used in our previous example.

10.1.3   Example 3: rules of sign

We now consider the sign rules for addition and multiplication as another example of an abstract interpretation. We are only interested in the signs *plus*, '**p**', (> 0) and *minus*, '**m**', (< 0) of numbers. To enable us to assign a sign to zero, we introduce '**z**' as an extra sign symbol. The formation of the sum of the digits in the nine-test example corresponds here to a function φ, which assigns every number its sign, whence

$$\varphi(z) = \begin{cases} \mathbf{p} & \text{if } z > 0 \\ \mathbf{z} & \text{if } z = 0 \\ \mathbf{m} & \text{if } z < 0 \end{cases}$$

Our abstract interpretation will not always be able to determine the sign of an expression; for example, the sign of an expression $E_1 + E_2$ cannot be determined if

$\overline{+}$	p	z	m	?
p	p	p	?	?
z	p	z	m	?
m	?	m	m	?
?	?	?	?	?

$\overline{*}$	p	z	m	?
p	p	z	m	?
z	z	z	z	z
m	m	z	p	?
?	?	z	?	?

Figure 10.1   Operation of $\overline{+}$ and $\overline{*}$ on sign symbols.

the first expression is positive and the second negative. We shall express the fact that we know nothing about the sign by another sign symbol '?'. We can now give function tables to describe how addition and multiplication operate on our sign symbols, see Figure 10.1. For example, $\mathbf{m} \overline{*} \mathbf{m} = \mathbf{p}$ is the well-known sign rule that *minus times minus gives plus*. These tables also contain all other sign rules for addition and multiplication.

These two function tables provide us with an easy way of obtaining information about the sign of expressions constructed from numbers using addition and multiplication. We simply replace all numbers by the sign symbol assigned to them by φ, replace '+' by '$\overline{+}$' and '$*$' by '$\overline{*}$' and evaluate the resulting expression using the above function tables. If the result is not equal to '?', then we have determined the sign of the original expression; if it is equal to '?' then (with this abstraction) we are unable to say anything about the sign of the original expression.

How can we convince ourselves that this statement is correct? We introduce an abstraction relation δ between the numbers and our sign symbols. $z \, \delta \, s$ says that s describes the sign of z correctly. Thus, δ is defined as follows:

$$z \, \delta \, s \; :\Longleftrightarrow \; s = \mathbf{p} \;\; \wedge \;\; z > 0 \;\; \vee$$
$$s = \mathbf{z} \;\; \wedge \;\; z = 0 \;\; \vee$$
$$s = \mathbf{m} \;\; \wedge \;\; z < 0 \;\; \vee$$
$$s = ?$$

The following statements are proved by direct inspection:

(1) $\forall z : z \, \delta \, \varphi(z)$

(2) $\forall s_1, s_2 \, \forall z_1, z_2 : z_1 \, \delta \, s_1 \, \wedge \, z_2 \, \delta \, s_2 \Longrightarrow z_1 + z_2 \, \delta \, s_1 \overline{+} s_2 \, \wedge \, z_1 * z_2 \, \delta \, s_1 \overline{*} s_2$

Here, (1) says that $\varphi(z)$ describes the sign of z correctly and (2) that $\overline{+}$ and $\overline{*}$ correctly reproduce the effect of $+$ and $*$ on the sign, or, in other words, that $\overline{+}$ and $\overline{*}$ are abstractions of $+$ and $*$ on the signs. It follows directly by structural induction on the structure of the expressions that the abstract value describes the sign of the concrete value correctly.

10.1.4   Components of an abstract interpretation

Although the above example is simple, it already shows us the important components of the abstract interpretation:

(1) Concrete data, in our example, the integers,

(2) Operations on the concrete data, in our example, addition and multiplication,

(3) Abstract data, in our example, the sign symbols,

(4) Abstract operations, in our example, $\overline{+}$ and $\overline{*}$,

(5) An abstraction relation, in our example, δ. It relates the abstract data to the concrete data. With respect to this abstraction relation, the abstract operations must be abstractions of the concrete operations.

If we apply the abstract interpretation to programs, then the semantics of the programming language (largely) specify the data and the operations. On the other hand, the abstract data, the abstract operations and the abstraction relation can be freely chosen from a wide range of possibilities, depending on the tasks in question and the acceptable computational costs. The only important prerequisites are that the abstract operations should be computable, that the abstract operations should be correct abstractions of the concrete operations with respect to the abstraction relation and that the abstraction relation should be appropriate for solving the problem.

The semantics of programming languages can be described in various ways. The most common formal methods include the so-called *denotational* and *operational* methods for defining semantics. We shall consider abstract interpretations based on these two definition methods.

10.2   Abstract interpretation based on denotational semantics

In this section, we consider the abstract interpretation based on a denotational definition of semantics in more detail.

10.2.1   The denotational method

Programs of a programming language are hierarchically structured objects; their structure, the *syntax*, is usually described by a context-free grammar. The denotational method assigns a meaning to programs and program fragments using structural induction over this structure. However, the starting point is not the context-free grammar which describes the character-string representation of programs. This grammar, called a *concrete* grammar, contains many details needed to represent programs as character strings in a clear manner, including parentheses, infix- and distfix-operator symbols and separator symbols. Such details are unimportant as far as the specification of the meaning of programs (their *semantics*) is concerned; a simplified grammar, the so-called *abstract syntax*, is used for this. The productions of such a grammar have a particularly simple form, namely $N \rightarrow T N_1 \ldots N_n$, where T is a terminal uniquely assigned to the production and the Ns are nonterminals. The abstract syntax is always unambiguous.

Example 10.1   As a simple example, we consider a grammar for the language of (simplified) arithmetic expressions. Its concrete syntax is described by the grammar G_c.

$$
\begin{aligned}
G_c : E &\rightarrow T \\
&\rightarrow E + T \\
T &\rightarrow F \\
&\rightarrow T * F \\
F &\rightarrow c \quad \text{constant} \\
&\rightarrow v \quad \text{variable} \\
&\rightarrow (E)
\end{aligned}
$$

In its derivation rules, it encodes the precedence rule for $*$ and $+$, the (left) associativity of $*$ and $+$ and the possibility of parenthesizing subexpressions to overrule precedence and associativity rules.

The associated abstract syntax is described by the grammar

$$
\begin{aligned}
G_a : E &\rightarrow *EE \\
&\rightarrow +EE \\
&\rightarrow v \\
&\rightarrow c
\end{aligned}
$$

This grammar expresses the fact that an expression can be formed in four ways. It may be a constant or a variable or it may arise from two other expressions by applying $+$ or $*$.

This grammar defines the language A of the arithmetic expressions. We shall refer to it in numerous examples.   □

The denotational method assigns a meaning to every program and program fragment by induction according to the structure of the abstract syntax. Here, the program fragments are assigned to *syntactic domains*, which correspond to the nonterminals in the abstract syntax. A program fragment lies in the syntactic domain N^X for the nonterminal N, if it is in the language of N and can thus be derived from N. For the assignment of meanings, for every nonterminal N a so-called *semantic domain* N^S of mathematical objects, so-called denotations, is specified, together with a so-called *semantic function* $[\![\,]\!]$, which maps the syntactic domain N^X into the semantic domain N^S. The semantic functions are defined by structural induction over the structure of the abstract syntax.

Example 10.2

$$E^S \quad := \quad \mathbf{Z}$$
$$[\![v]\!] \quad := \quad vb(v)$$
$$[\![c]\!] \quad := \quad I(c)$$
$$[\![+ E_1 E_2]\!] \quad := \quad [\![E_1]\!] + [\![E_2]\!]$$
$$[\![* E_1 E_2]\!] \quad := \quad [\![E_1]\!] * [\![E_2]\!]$$

defines a meaning for the arithmetic expressions (according to G_a) in the integers $\mathbf{Z}$. The syntactic domain E^X is mapped into the semantic domain $E^S = \mathbf{Z}$ by the semantic function $[\![\,]\!]$. $[\![\,]\!]$ interprets the symbols $+$ and $*$ of G_a as addition and multiplication of integers; constants c are interpreted by their value $I(c)$; the meaning of variables is assigned using a variable binding vb, a map from variables to the integers. In this way, every arithmetic expression is assigned a value in $\mathbf{Z}$. Thus, $*4 + 23 * 2\, 6$ is assigned the value $4 * (23 + 2 * 6) = 140$. □

As we see, the fundamental principle of the denotational method is very simple. However, for real programming languages a number of technical problems have to be solved before one can describe the meaning of the language constructs adequately. Almost all real programming languages have either a loop construct or a facility for recursive definitions. Such constructs give the programming language the power of Turing machines, thereby introducing the halting problem. In the definition of the corresponding semantic functions, the denotational method uses the formation of least fixpoints. For this, both the semantic domains and the semantic functions must have a special structure (complete partial orders and continuous mappings over these). In addition, the semantic domains are frequently defined recursively, that is, they themselves often occur on the right side of the equation defining them. The by no means simple mathematical theory behind the denotational method ensures that such definitions make sense. However, a discussion of these is beyond the scope of this book.

10.2.2   Basic principle of abstract interpretation

The semantic functions used for real programming languages are in general not computable. In particular, the formation of least fixpoints is only computable in exceptional cases. Since a compiler must necessarily derive its information about a program algorithmically, for this purpose it is convenient to turn to simplified non-standard semantics for the language, whose semantic functions are computable.

A non-standard semantics is specified in the same way as the actual meaning of a language, the so-called standard semantics: by defining (abstract) semantic domains and (abstract) semantic functions. However, the semantic domains and the functions are mostly highly simplified. By computing the meaning of a program using the non-standard semantics we would like to obtain information about the standard meaning of the program. Thus, the two meanings must be related to one another by a specific relation δ. δ is called an **abstraction relation** and describes

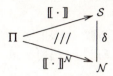

Figure 10.2   Commutative diagram: relationship between the set of program fragments and standard and non-standard semantics.

and describes the aspects from which we abstract and what properties we are able to ded$v$ the standard meaning of a probram $[[\pi]]$ from the non-standard $[[\pi]]^N$. Thus, programs and program fragments π, we require that:

$$[\![\pi]\!] \; \delta \; [\![\pi]\!]^N$$

This property follows easily by structural induction if for every production $N \rightarrow T N_1 \ldots N_n$ of the abstract syntax and $\omega_i \in N_i^X$ it follows from $[\![\omega_i]\!] \; \delta \; [\![\omega_i]\!]^N$ for $i = 1 \ldots n$ that $[\![T\omega_1\omega_2 \ldots \omega_n]\!] \; \delta \; [\![T\omega_1\omega_2 \ldots \omega_n]\!]^N$. This leads directly to the following definition.

Definition 10.1 (abstract interpretation)
Let L be a language with abstract syntax G and standard semantics S. An **abstract interpretation** for (L, S) is a non-standard semantics N together with a relation δ between the semantic domains of S and N, such that for all productions $N \Longrightarrow T N_1 \ldots N_n$:

$$\forall \omega_i \in N_i^X : (\forall i : [\![\omega_i]\!] \; \delta \; [\![\omega_i]\!]^N) \Rightarrow [\![T\omega_1 \ldots \omega_n]\!] \; \delta \; [\![T\omega_1 \ldots \omega_n]\!]^N$$

δ is called an **abstraction relation** for the abstract interpretation.   □

Theorem 10.1   *If (N, δ) is an abstract interpretation for (L, S), then for every program fragment π of L: $[\![\pi]\!] \; \delta \; [\![\pi]\!]^N$.*   □

Thus, the abstract meaning $[\![\pi]\!]^N$ is related to the standard meaning of π by the relation δ. If Π denotes the set of the program fragments of L, then the theorem can be illustrated by the commutative diagram of Figure 10.2.

Example 10.3
In the semantic definition of Example 10.2, all semantic functions are computable. Nevertheless, it may be sensible to move to an abstract consideration, for example to make the calculations easier. The example of the nine test presented in the introduction relates to this. The procedure can be easily described as abstract interpretation. The system

$$E^N \quad := \quad \{0, 1, \ldots, 8\}$$

$$
\begin{aligned}
\llbracket v \rrbracket^{\mathcal{N}} &:= Q(vb(v)) \\
\llbracket c \rrbracket^{\mathcal{N}} &:= Q(I(c)) \\
\llbracket + E_1 E_2 \rrbracket^{\mathcal{N}} &:= Q(\llbracket E_1 \rrbracket^{\mathcal{N}} + \llbracket E_2 \rrbracket^{\mathcal{N}}) \\
\llbracket * E_1 E_2 \rrbracket^{\mathcal{N}} &:= Q(\llbracket E_1 \rrbracket^{\mathcal{N}} * \llbracket E_2 \rrbracket^{\mathcal{N}}
\end{aligned}
$$

defines a non-standard semantics for arithmetic expressions; here, Q denotes the mapping which takes integers to the sum of their digits in $E_{\mathcal{N}}$ (9 is mapped to 0). If we define the relation δ between $\mathbf{Z} = E^{\mathcal{S}}$ and $E^{\mathcal{N}}$ by

$$
z \,\delta\, q :\Longleftrightarrow q = Q(z)
$$

we then see that for all variables v and constants c

$$
\llbracket v \rrbracket \,\delta\, \llbracket v \rrbracket^{\mathcal{N}} \quad \text{and} \quad \llbracket c \rrbracket \,\delta\, \llbracket c \rrbracket^{\mathcal{N}}
$$

Moreover,

$$
z_1 \,\delta\, q_1, \ \ z_2 \,\delta\, q_2, \quad \Rightarrow \quad
\begin{aligned}
&\llbracket + z_1 z_2 \rrbracket \,\delta\, \llbracket + z_1 z_2 \rrbracket^{\mathcal{N}} \\
&\llbracket * z_1 z_2 \rrbracket \,\delta\, \llbracket * z_1 z_2 \rrbracket^{\mathcal{N}}
\end{aligned}
$$

Thus, $(\mathcal{N}, \delta)$ is an abstract interpretation of $(A, \mathcal{S})$. Consequently, the value of all arithmetic expressions E in $\mathcal{S}$ is related to that in $\mathcal{N}$ by the relation δ: $\llbracket E \rrbracket \,\delta\, \llbracket E \rrbracket^{\mathcal{N}}$ or, equivalently, $\llbracket E \rrbracket^{\mathcal{N}} = Q(\llbracket E \rrbracket)$. $\qquad\square$

10.2.3 Use of auxiliary semantics

The use of abstract interpretations in the compiler-design area should help the compiler to transform the program to be compiled into a more efficient but semantically equivalent program. Verification that a transformation is permissible often requires *more* detailed information than that contained in the standard semantics. In this case, a move to an extended auxiliary semantics is necessary. This situation is very similar to the introduction of proof variables and associated statements when proving the correctness of programs using Hoare logic. Proof variables are often necessary even to formulate invariants used, for example, in induction proofs.

A typical example of the application of an extended auxiliary semantics is the determination of information at the individual program points of a program by means of abstract interpretation. We recall that we may view programs as hierarchically structured, that is, as trees. A **program point** is a node in this tree. Information at a program point can be used to check the permissibility of a local program transformation, that is, a program transformation at that program point.

The desirable information at a program point has two main components: the **lower context**, that is, the program fragment at the program point in question, and the **upper context**, that is, the rest of the program without this program fragment. The denotational method assigns the meaning to program fragments by structural induction; thus, the meaning is independent of the upper context. That makes it easy to assign information that depends only on the lower context to a program point (all our previous examples were of this type). However, the assignment of information from the upper context is not self-evident.

The alert reader of Chapter 9 will already have discovered that there is a great similarity between denotational semantic descriptions and S-attributed grammars. Both describe properties of programs by induction over the structure. These properties are calculated in a bottom-up manner. Attribute grammars also have inherited attributes which are calculated in a top-down manner. If something similar is to be expressed in a denotational semantics the necessary information must be transported, bottom up, to a common predecessor, to be fed into a calculation there.

Propagation of constants: the problem

We now consider this topic using a concrete example. Suppose that we are interested in relocating calculations from run time to compile time. We can evaluate an expression E at compile time if we can prove (for example, by abstract interpretation) that every evaluation in an execution of the program always gives the same value and that this value can be determined at compile time. In this case, the compiler can replace the expression by its value, a local program transformation. This is clearly possible if E does not contain any variables. However, if E contains variables which are defined outside E, then this property normally depends on the upper context of E.

To illustrate this further, we consider a simple language whose programs consist of sequences of assignments of the form $v := E$. Here, v is a variable and E an expression for our expression grammar of Example 10.2. We now extend the abstract syntax of the expressions by a nonterminal S (statement) and a nonterminal Q (statement sequence) and the following productions:

$$S \;\rightarrow\; v := E \quad \text{for variable } v$$
$$Q \;\rightarrow\; \varepsilon$$
$$Q \;\rightarrow\; ; S Q$$

$v := E$ describes an assignment to the variable v, ε is the empty statement sequence, $; S Q$ is a sequence of statements consisting of S followed by Q. In Example 10.2 we made the value of an expression dependent on a fixed variable binding vb. Since this variable binding alters when the program is executed we now consider the meaning of an expression explicitly as a mapping from variable bindings to values (we turn the implicit parameter vb into an explicit parameter). We define the meaning of a statement sequence to be the effect of its execution on an initial variable binding; that is, the meaning of a statement sequence is a mapping from variable bindings to variable bindings. This informal semantic description is formalized in Figure 10.3. Note that we still require (as an implicit parameter) a mapping I which maps a constant to a value in $\mathbf{Z}$. Let VB denote the set of variable bindings, that is, the set of mappings from variables to integers $V \rightarrow \mathbf{Z}$.

$$
\begin{array}{lcl}
[\![E]\!]^S & := & VB \to \mathbf{Z} \\[4pt]
[\![S]\!]^S & := & VB \to VB \\[4pt]
[\![Q]\!]^S & := & VB \to VB \\[4pt]
[\![v]\!](vb) & := & vb(v) \\[4pt]
[\![c]\!](vb) & := & I(c) \\[4pt]
[\![+E_1E_2]\!](vb) & := & [\![E_1]\!](vb) + [\![E_2]\!](vb) \\[4pt]
[\![*E_1E_2]\!](vb) & := & [\![E_1]\!](vb) * [\![E_2]\!](vb) \\[4pt]
[\![v := E]\!](vb) & := & vb[v \mapsto [\![E]\!](vb)] \\[4pt]
[\![\varepsilon]\!](vb) & := & vb \\[4pt]
[\![; S Q]\!](vb) & := & [\![Q]\!]([\![S]\!](vb))
\end{array}
$$

Figure 10.3   Semantic definitions for propagation of constants.

This definition makes use of the notation '$f[x \mapsto w]$'. It denotes a function, which takes the value w for x and agrees with f otherwise, that is:

$$
f[x \mapsto w](y) = \begin{cases} f(y) & \text{for } y \neq x \\ w & \text{for } y = x \end{cases}
$$

As an example, let us consider how the meaning of a program $Q = (v := E;\ Q')$ is determined (to increase readability, we use ';' as a right associative infix operator, as usual in programming languages; the abstract syntax represents this program as $;\ v := E\ Q'$). This meaning is a mapping $[\![Q]\!]$, which transforms an initial variable binding vb into a new variable binding $[\![Q]\!](vb)$. vb is initially transformed by $v := E$. Here, only its value for the variable v is changed, namely to $[\![E]\!](vb)$, the value of E in the variable binding vb. This gives the variable binding $vb[v \mapsto [\![E]\!](vb)]$. This variable binding is subsequently transformed by the statement sequence Q' to $[\![Q]\!](vb) = [\![Q']\!](vb[v \mapsto [\![E]\!](vb)])$.

We can transform a program $Q = (S_1; \ldots; S_n; v := E;\ Q')$ into a semantically equivalent program $Q' = (S_1; \ldots; S_n; v := c;\ Q')$, if it is certain that for every execution of Q, E is always evaluated to the same value, namely $I(c)$. For this, we essentially have to consider $S_1; \ldots; S_n$, that is, the upper context for the program point at which we wish to execute the program. If for all variable bindings vb we have: $[\![E]\!]([\![S_1; \ldots; S_n]\!](vb)) = I(c)$, then the above transformation of the program is permissible. Now, because of the right associativity of ';', Q' is a program fragment in Q, but the sequence $S_1; \ldots; S_n$ is not (in the abstract syntax, Q has the structure $;\ S_1\ ;\ \ldots\ ;\ S_n\ ;\ v := E\ Q'$). Thus, only $[\![Q']\!]$ is calculated when determining $[\![Q]\!]$, and not $[\![S_1; \ldots; S_n]\!]$ and an abstract interpretation of Q based on the given semantics cannot provide the information needed to check that the transformation is permissible.

Propagation of constants: extended auxiliary semantics

We shall now show that the necessary information can in principle be obtained by extending the semantics appropriately. Using a (computable) abstract interpretation of this extended semantics, we can then attempt to collect information to prove that such transformations are permissible.

First, we note that, in order to check that transformations of the type used above are permissible, it is sufficient to know a superset of the set $VB(s)$ of all variable bindings vb, which may arrive at a program point s for some program execution. Here, 'arrive' means the following: in our simple language, all meanings of program fragments are mappings with a variable binding as parameter. We say that vb arrives at a program point s, if for some program execution the meaning of the program fragment at the point s is applied to vb. If s is a program point, the program fragment at s is an expression E and $[\![E]\!](vb) = I(c)$ for all vb in $VB(s)$, then replacing E by c preserves the semantics, and is therefore permissible.

Thus, we extend the meaning of a program fragment by the set of variable bindings which occur at the program points. For technical reasons, the meaning of program fragments has a point as parameter. This point tells the program fragment where it is within the program as a whole. We obtain the semantic definition $\mathcal{A}$ from Figure 10.4. In the definition P denotes the set of program points and $\mathcal{P}VB$ the set of the sets of variable bindings. $arr \in (S \to \mathcal{P}VB)$ assigns a set of variable bindings to every program point.

In the definition, we have made use of a special representation of the program points: points within a tree can be represented by sequences of natural numbers. The root is represented by the empty sequence ε. If a node is represented by a sequence ω then its ith child is represented by $\omega.i$.

We note that (S, δ_S) is an abstraction of $\mathcal{A}$, where the abstraction relation δ_S is defined by:

$$f \; \delta_S \; \overline{f} :\Longleftrightarrow \forall vb, s, arr \exists arr' : f(vb, s, arr) = (\overline{f}(vb), arr')$$

Propagation of constants: abstract interpretation

We now briefly sketch an abstract interpretation $\mathcal{N}$ of $\mathcal{A}$, which is suitable for proving that the transformation described above is permissible. This abstract interpretation is based on an abstraction of $\mathbf{Z}$ by $(\overline{\mathbf{Z}}, \delta_{\mathbf{Z}})$, defined by: $\overline{\mathbf{Z}} := \mathbf{Z} \cup \{\bot, ?\}$ and

$$z \; \delta_{\mathbf{Z}} \; \overline{z} :\Longleftrightarrow (\overline{z} = ?) \; \vee \; (\overline{z} = z)$$

The choice of this abstraction is very appropriate for our example application:

- $\overline{z} \in \mathbf{Z}$ expresses the fact that the compiler knows the value (of an expression, a variable), it is $\overline{z}$;

- $?$ means that the compiler knows that it will not be able to determine the value;

$$E^A \quad := \quad VB \times P \times (P \to \mathcal{P}VB) \longrightarrow \mathbf{Z} \times (P \to \mathcal{P}VB)$$

$$S^A \quad := \quad VB \times P \times (P \to \mathcal{P}VB) \longrightarrow VB \times (P \to \mathcal{P}VB)$$

$$Q^A \quad := \quad VB \times P \times (P \to \mathcal{P}VB) \longrightarrow VB \times (P \to \mathcal{P}VB)$$

$$\llbracket v \rrbracket^A (vb, s, arr) \quad := \quad (vb(v), arr[s \mapsto arr(s) \cup \{vb\}])$$

$$\llbracket c \rrbracket^A (vb, s, arr) \quad := \quad (I(c), arr[s \mapsto arr(s) \cup \{vb\}])$$

$$\llbracket + E_1 E_2 \rrbracket^A (vb, s, arr) \quad := \quad (z_1 + z_2, arr_2)$$

$$\text{with} \quad \begin{array}{l} (z_1, arr_1) = \llbracket E_1 \rrbracket^A (vb, s.1, arr[s \mapsto arr(s) \cup \{vb\}]) \\ (z_2, arr_2) = \llbracket E_2 \rrbracket^A (vb, s.2, arr_1) \end{array}$$

$$\llbracket * E_1 E_2 \rrbracket^A (vb, s, arr) \quad := \quad (z_1 * z_2, arr_2)$$

$$\text{with} \quad \begin{array}{l} (z_1, arr_1) = \llbracket E_1 \rrbracket^A (vb, s.1, arr[s \mapsto arr(s) \cup \{vb\}]) \\ (z_2, arr_2) = \llbracket E_2 \rrbracket^A (vb, s.2, arr_1) \end{array}$$

$$\llbracket v := E \rrbracket^A (vb, s, arr) \quad := \quad (vb[v \mapsto z'], arr')$$

$$\text{with} \quad (z', arr') = \llbracket E \rrbracket^A (vb, s.1, arr[s \mapsto arr(s) \cup \{vb\}])$$

$$\llbracket \varepsilon \rrbracket^A (vb, s, arr) \quad := \quad (vb, arr[s \mapsto arr(s) \cup \{vb\}])$$

$$\llbracket ; SQ \rrbracket^A (vb, s, arr) \quad := \quad \llbracket Q \rrbracket^{\mathcal{H}} (vb', s.2, arr')$$

$$\text{with} \quad (vb', arr') = \llbracket S \rrbracket^A (vb, s.1, arr[s \mapsto arr(s) \cup \{vb\}])$$

Figure 10.4 Extended semantic definitions for propagation of constants.

- $\perp$ means not yet defined; as we shall see, it is used to define an initial value with which to start the abstract execution.

For sets B, D and M we can always lift an abstraction (B, δ) of D to the space of functions $M \to D$ by defining the new abstraction relation $M \to \delta$ between $M \to D$ and $M \to B$ pointwise, that is:

$$f \, M{\to}\delta \, \overline{f} :\Longleftrightarrow \forall x \in M : f(x) \, \delta \, \overline{f}(x)$$

This allows us to lift $\delta_{\mathbf{Z}}$ to $VB = \mathcal{V} \to \mathbf{Z}$; we obtain: $(\overline{VB}, \delta_{VB})$ with $\overline{VB} = (\mathcal{V} \to \overline{\mathbf{Z}})$ and $\delta_{VB} = \mathcal{V}{\to}\delta_{\mathbf{Z}}$, that is:

$$vb \, \delta_{VB} \, \overline{vb} :\Longleftrightarrow \forall v : vb(v) \, \delta_{\mathbf{Z}} \, \overline{vb}(v)$$

In the course of all program executions, more than one variable binding occurs at the program points, and we must in general also reckon with a set of possible variable bindings. Thus, we shall extend the above abstraction to sets of variable bindings: that is, the power set of VB, $\mathcal{P}VB$. To keep the abstract calculation simple, we represent a whole set M of concrete variable bindings by a single abstract variable binding $\overline{vb}$. The corresponding abstraction is given by $(\overline{VB}, \delta_{\mathcal{P}VB})$ with

$$M \; \delta_{\mathcal{P}VB} \; \overline{vb} :\Longleftrightarrow \forall vb \in M : vb \; \delta_{VB} \; \overline{vb}$$

This extension is also quite natural: the abstract variable binding $\overline{vb}$ abstracts from a set of concrete variable bindings (for $\delta_{\mathcal{P}VB}$), if it abstracts from every element of the set (for δ_{VB}).

We can again lift this abstraction to the space of functions $S \to \mathcal{P}VB$ and obtain the abstraction $((S \to \overline{VB}), \delta_{S \to \mathcal{P}VB})$ with $\delta_{S \to \mathcal{P}VB} = S \to \delta_{\mathcal{P}VB}$:

$$arr \; \delta_{S \to \mathcal{P}VB} \; \overline{arr} :\Longleftrightarrow \forall s : arr(s) \; \delta_{\mathcal{P}VB} \; \overline{arr}(s)$$

Our aim is ultimately to lift this abstraction to $E^{\mathcal{A}}$, $S^{\mathcal{A}}$ and $Q^{\mathcal{A}}$. For this, we need two more auxiliary results which enable us to lift abstractions to pairs and to function spaces. If D_1 and D_2 are sets and $(\overline{D_i}, \delta_i)$ is an abstraction of D_i, then $(\overline{D_1} \times \overline{D_2}, \delta_1 \times \delta_2)$ is an abstraction of $D_1 \times D_2$, if $\delta_1 \times \delta_2$ is defined component wise:

$$(d_1, d_2) \; \delta_1 \times \delta_2 \; (\overline{d_1}, \overline{d_2}) :\Longleftrightarrow d_1 \; \delta_1 \; \overline{d_1} \quad \text{and} \quad d_2 \; \delta_2 \; \overline{d_2}$$

Furthermore, $(\overline{D_1} \to \overline{D_2}, \delta_1 \to \delta_2)$ is an abstraction of the space of functions $D_1 \to D_2$, if $\delta_1 \to \delta_2$ is defined by:

$$f \; \delta_1 \to \delta_2 \; \overline{f} :\Longleftrightarrow \forall d_1 \in D_1, \overline{d_1} \in \overline{D_1} : d_1 \; \delta_1 \; \overline{d_1} \Rightarrow f(d_1) \; \delta_2 \; \overline{f}(\overline{d_1})$$

that is, $f \; \delta_1 \to \delta_2 \; \overline{f}$, if for an abstraction $\overline{d_1}$ of d_1 for δ_1, $\overline{f}(\overline{d_1})$ is also an abstraction of $f(d_1)$ for δ_2.

Using these auxiliary results, we can extend the previously defined abstraction relations to the data areas of the auxiliary semantics. For this, we use the following abstract data area:

$$E^{\mathcal{N}} := \overline{VB} \times P \times (P \to \overline{VB}) \longrightarrow \overline{\mathbf{Z}} \times (P \to \overline{VB})$$

$$S^{\mathcal{N}} := \overline{VB} \times P \times (P \to \overline{VB}) \longrightarrow \overline{VB} \times (P \to \overline{VB})$$

$$Q^{\mathcal{N}} := \overline{VB} \times P \times (P \to \overline{VB}) \longrightarrow \overline{VB} \times (P \to \overline{VB})$$

The associated abstraction relations are:

$$\delta_E := \delta_{VB} \times =_P \times \delta_{P \to \mathcal{P}VB} \longrightarrow \delta_{\mathbf{Z}} \times \delta_{P \to \mathcal{P}VB}$$

$$\delta_S := \delta_{VB} \times =_P \times \delta_{P \to \mathcal{P}VB} \longrightarrow \delta_{VB} \times \delta_{P \to \mathcal{P}VB}$$

$$\delta_Q := \delta_{VB} \times =_P \times \delta_{P \to \mathcal{P}VB} \longrightarrow \delta_{VB} \times \delta_{P \to \mathcal{P}VB}$$

We note that these abstractions have only two non-trivial components: the abstraction of $\mathbf{Z}$ by $\mathbf{Z} \cup \{\bot, ?\}$ with $\delta_{\mathbf{Z}}$ and the abstraction of $\mathcal{P}VB$ by $\overline{VB}$ with $\delta_{\mathcal{P}VB}$. The remaining components are obtained directly by lifting to structured types (a family of relations obtained by standard lifting to structured types is sometimes called a 'logical relation'). We explain this in what follows using the example of the abstraction of E^A:

$$E^A \;=\; VB \;\times\; P \;\times\; (P \;\to\; \mathcal{P}VB) \;\longrightarrow\; \mathbf{Z} \;\times\; (P \;\to\; \mathcal{P}VB)$$

$$\big|\qquad\big|\qquad\big|\qquad\big|\qquad\qquad\big|\qquad\big|\qquad\qquad\big|$$

$$\delta_{VB} \;\times\; =_P \;\times\; (P \;\to\; \delta_{\mathcal{P}VB}) \;\longrightarrow\; \delta_{\mathbf{Z}} \;\times\; (P \;\to\; \delta_{\mathcal{P}VB})$$

$$\big|\qquad\big|\qquad\big|\qquad\big|\qquad\qquad\big|\qquad\big|\qquad\qquad\big|$$

$$E^N \;=\; \overline{VB} \;\times\; P \;\times\; (P \;\to\; \overline{VB}) \;\longrightarrow\; \overline{\mathbf{Z}} \;\times\; (P \;\to\; \overline{VB})$$

The abstract semantic functions can be constructed in a similar way from the abstractions for addition $\overline{+}$, multiplication $\overline{*}$ and 'union' $\overline{\cup}$ over $\overline{\mathbf{Z}}$ by lifting.

$$\overline{z_1} \,\overline{+}\, \overline{z_2} \;:=\; \begin{cases} \bot, & \text{if } \overline{z_1} = \bot \text{ or } \overline{z_2} = \bot; \\ ?, & \text{otherwise and } (\overline{z_1} =? \text{ or } \overline{z_2} =?); \\ \overline{z_1} + \overline{z_2}, & \text{otherwise.} \end{cases}$$

$$\overline{z_1} \,\overline{*}\, \overline{z_2} \;:=\; \begin{cases} \bot, & \text{if } \overline{z_1} = \bot \text{ or } \overline{z_2} = \bot; \\ 0, & \text{otherwise and } (\overline{z_1} = 0 \text{ or } \overline{z_2} = 0); \\ ?, & \text{otherwise and } (\overline{z_1} =? \text{ or } \overline{z_2} =?); \\ \overline{z_1} * \overline{z_2}, & \text{otherwise.} \end{cases}$$

$$\overline{z_1} \,\overline{\cup}\, \overline{z_2} \;:=\; \begin{cases} \overline{z_1}, & \text{if } \overline{z_1} = \overline{z_2} \text{ or } \overline{z_2} = \bot, \\ \overline{z_2}, & \text{if } \overline{z_1} = \bot, \\ ?, & \text{otherwise.} \end{cases}$$

Lifting of these basic functions leads to the abstract semantic functions of Figure 10.5.

For $\overline{\cup}$ these equations use the definition of the union on $\overline{\mathbf{Z}}$ given above, lifted pointwise to the space of functions $\overline{VB} = V \to \overline{\mathbf{Z}}$, that is, $(vb_1 \,\overline{\cup}\, vb_2)(v) := vb_1(v) \,\overline{\cup}\, vb_2(v)$ for all variables v.

It is easy to check that the non-standard semantics defined above, together with the abstraction relation $\delta = (\delta_E, \delta_A, \delta_F)$, form an abstract interpretation of the extended auxiliary semantics. Whence we obtain the following property:

Theorem 10.2 *For every program* Q: $[\![Q]\!]^A \, \delta_Q \, [\![F]\!]^N$.
For a variable binding vb it follows that $arr' \, \delta_{P \to \mathcal{P}VB} \, \overline{arr'}$, *where*

$$(vb', arr') \;:=\; [\![Q]\!]^A(vb, \varepsilon, \lambda s.\emptyset)$$
$$(\overline{vb'}, \overline{arr'}) \;:=\; [\![Q]\!]^N(\lambda v.?, \varepsilon, \lambda s.\bot)$$

since $vb \, \delta_{VB} \, \lambda v.?$ *and* $\lambda s.\emptyset \, \delta_{P \to \mathcal{P}VB} \, \lambda s.\bot$.

Moreover, the set VB(s) of variable bindings occurring at a point s is the union of all the sets $arr'(s)$, where arr' is obtained in the above way. It follows that $VB(s) \, \delta_{\mathcal{P}VB} \, \overline{arr'}(s)$. □

$$[\![v]\!]^{\mathcal{N}}(\overline{vb}, s, \overline{arr}) \quad := \quad (\overline{vb}(v), \overline{arr}[s \mapsto \overline{arr}(s)\,\overline{\cup}\,\overline{vb}])$$

$$[\![c]\!]^{\mathcal{N}}(\overline{vb}, s, \overline{arr}) \quad := \quad (I(c), \overline{arr}[s \mapsto \overline{arr}(s)\,\overline{\cup}\,\overline{vb}])$$

$$[\![+E_1 E_2]\!]^{\mathcal{N}}(\overline{vb}, s, \overline{arr}) \quad := \quad (\overline{z_1}\,\overline{+}\,\overline{z_2}, \overline{arr_2})$$
$$\text{with} \quad \begin{aligned} (\overline{z_1}, \overline{arr_1}) &= [\![E_1]\!]^{\mathcal{N}}(\overline{vb}, s.1, \overline{arr}[s \mapsto \overline{arr}(s)\,\overline{\cup}\,\overline{vb}]) \\ (\overline{z_2}, \overline{arr_2}) &= [\![E_2]\!]^{\mathcal{N}}(\overline{vb}, s.2, \overline{arr_1}) \end{aligned}$$

$$[\![*E_1 E_2]\!]^{\mathcal{N}}(\overline{vb}, s, \overline{arr}) \quad := \quad (\overline{z_1}\,\overline{*}\,\overline{z_2}, \overline{arr_2})$$
$$\text{with} \quad \begin{aligned} (\overline{z_1}, \overline{arr_1}) &= [\![E_1]\!]^{\mathcal{N}}(\overline{vb}, s.1, \overline{arr}[s \mapsto \overline{arr}(s)\,\overline{\cup}\,\overline{vb}]) \\ (\overline{z_2}, \overline{arr_2}) &= [\![E_2]\!]^{\mathcal{N}}(\overline{vb}, s.2, \overline{arr_1}) \end{aligned}$$

$$[\![v := E]\!]^{\mathcal{N}}(\overline{vb}, s, \overline{arr}) \quad := \quad (\overline{vb}[v \mapsto \overline{z'}], \overline{arr'})$$
$$\text{with} \quad (\overline{z'}, \overline{arr'}) = [\![E]\!]^{\mathcal{N}}(\overline{vb}, s.1, \overline{arr}[s \mapsto \overline{arr}(s)\,\overline{\cup}\,\overline{vb}])$$

$$[\![\varepsilon]\!]^{\mathcal{N}}(\overline{vb}, s, \overline{arr}) \quad := \quad (\overline{vb}, \overline{arr}[s \mapsto \overline{arr}(s)\,\overline{\cup}\,\overline{vb}])$$

$$[\![; SQ]\!]^{\mathcal{N}}(\overline{vb}, s, \overline{arr}) \quad := \quad [\![Q]\!]^{\mathcal{N}}(\overline{vb'}, s.2, \overline{arr'})$$
$$\text{with} \quad (\overline{vb'}, \overline{arr'}) = [\![S]\!]^{\mathcal{N}}(\overline{vb}, s.1, \overline{arr}[s \mapsto \overline{arr}(s)\,\overline{\cup}\,\overline{vb}])$$

Figure 10.5   Abstract semantic functions for propagation of constants.

A single execution of the program for the semantics $[\![\,]\!]^{\mathcal{N}}$ is thus sufficient to obtain at all program points information with which to test the permissibility of replacing an expression E by a value c:

Theorem 10.3   *Suppose the assumptions of Theorem 10.2 hold. Let s be a point in Q with an expression E as program fragment at s. Then replacing E by c preserves the semantics, if $[\![E]\!]^{\mathcal{N}}(\overline{arr'}(s), \cdot, \cdot)$ has the form $(I(c), \cdot)$.*   □

In summary: for many applications in compilers, particularly when information about the *upper* context of program points is required, the information in the standard semantics is not sufficient for an effective decision as to the permissibility of program transformations. Thus, we move to an auxiliary semantics extending the standard semantics, which contains the information required. We then abstract from this semantics in an appropriate manner to compute, effectively and efficiently, information to prove that the transformation is permissible.

10.2.4   Case example: strictness analysis

In this section we consider a complete example of an application of the denotationally based abstract interpretation. Since a denotational semantic definition for common *imperative* programming languages is very complex because of side effects and branches we use a *functional* programming language as our starting point. Functional programming languages typically have a simple denotational semantic definition. To reduce the complexity of the example further, we begin with a very simple functional language, the so-called *typed λ-expressions*. Despite its simplicity, it contains important elements of functional programming languages: recursive definitions and higher-order functions. We shall use abstract interpretation to execute a so-called strictness analysis. The next section gives an introduction to this problem.

Motivation

Some functional programming languages, such as the LaMa language introduced in Chapter 3, use **delayed evaluation**, also known as **lazy evaluation**, as their evaluation strategy. This means that a function argument or a component of a data structure is only evaluated when the value is needed to determine the program value. For example, if the function f is defined by

$$f(x, y, z) == \textbf{if } P(x) \textbf{ then } E_1(y) \textbf{ else } E_2(z)$$

where $P(x)$, $E_1(y)$ and $E_2(z)$ are expressions which depend on x, y and z, respectively, but not on either of the other two variables, then this evaluation strategy ensures that when f is called, at most the second or the third parameter is evaluated, but not both. This allows the programmer to enter expensive calculations at a parameter position without having to worry whether the result is actually required. In addition, the evaluation strategy makes it easy to handle data objects which are very large or even infinite when completely evaluated, again because a data object is only evaluated to the extent to which this is necessary for the program evaluation. These two aspects mean that programs can be made clearer and easier to follow than in the case where delayed evaluation is not used.

This evaluation strategy is implemented, for example as in MaMa, in such a way that when evaluating a function application the arguments are not evaluated immediately but instead special data structures or **closures** are constructed which permit the later evaluation of an argument. The evaluation takes place when the value of the argument is first required to continue the calculation of the program result. After the evaluation, the value replaces the corresponding closure so that later references to the argument find the value there already and a further evaluation may be dispensed with. This type of parameter passing is called **call by need** parameter passing, because the value of an actual argument is only evaluated as needed. This contrasts with the **call by value** parameter passing of imperative programming languages, where the argument is always passed as evaluated when the function is called, even though its value may not be required. This can lead to redundant calculations. Since, under certain circumstances, these calculations do not terminate without errors, there exist cases in which a call by need evaluation terminates without errors but a call by value evaluation does not.

If the value of an actual argument is in fact required, passing it by value is more efficient than passing it by need since the former does not incur the additional expense of constructing the closure. If a compiler is able to determine by analysing a program that, for example, the actual value of E_i is in fact required for every evaluation of a function application $f(E_1, \ldots, E_n)$, then it can generate code to pass the parameters E_i by value instead of by need, thereby making it unnecessary to construct the closure for each evaluation. This optimization can reduce the program run time (Wray (Fairbairn and Wray, 1987) gives examples where the run time is reduced to a third) and its storage requirement (Burton *et al.* (1987) gives examples of a reduction by an order of magnitude) substantially. **Strictness analysis** is a technique which can be used to obtain such information.

Let us consider a function application $f(E_1, \ldots, E_n)$ in an error-free program, that is, a program whose evaluation terminates without errors. During the evaluation of the program, our function application may be evaluated several times, once or not at all. All these evaluations must terminate without errors, for otherwise the evaluation of the program would not terminate without errors. If we now knew that the evaluation of a function application would not terminate without errors if we were to replace the ith parameter E_i by an expression whose evaluation does not terminate without errors, then we could deduce that the value of the ith parameter is required, since otherwise our modification would have no effect at all. This is the motivation for the following definition of strictness.

Definition 10.2 Strictness
A mapping $f: D^n \to D$ is said to be **strict in the ith argument**, if whenever the ith argument is undefined it follows that the function value is undefined.   □

For example, the addition of two natural numbers is strict in both arguments. On the other hand, the 'conditional'

$$if(x, y, z) == \textbf{if } x \textbf{ then } y \textbf{ else } z$$

is strict in the first argument only and not in the second and third arguments. The 'conditional and'

$$cand(x, y) == \textbf{if } x \textbf{ then } y \textbf{ else } false$$

is strict in the first argument but not in the second.

If we know that the function f is strict in the ith argument then the value of E_i is required in every evaluation of a function application $f(E_1, \ldots, E_n)$ and E_i can be passed by value.

In general, the question whether a function f is strict in an argument is undecidable. This means that there do not exist algorithms which can always determine correct **and** complete strictness information. Thus, algorithms for strictness analysis have to be limited to the derivation of incomplete strictness information, since correctness is a *sine qua non*. For example, were a function to be wrongly determined as strict in an argument, a transformation based on this could transform a program that terminates without errors into a non-terminating program or one that terminates with errors. Conversely, the failure of a strictness-analysis algorithm to detect that a function is strict in an argument means only that a possibility for optimization is missed.

In what follows, we consider the strictness analysis for typed λ-expressions without structured data.

The language: typed λ-expressions

In this section, we give a complete semantic definition of typed λ-expressions based on the denotational method. In fact, for this, we have to formulate two languages and equip them with meaning: the first of these languages is that of the *types* and the second that of the *λ-expressions*.

First we consider the types. Our representation will be based on a very simple underlying type system. This system has only one basic type T and a facility for constructing new types from existing types, namely function-space formation $\rightarrow$. Generalizations to several basic types and other type constructors are possible. Our type system, or, more precisely, the *abstract* syntax of types, is shown in Figure 10.6. In the following, we use (in the string representation) right associativity for $\rightarrow$, that is, $\tau_1 \rightarrow \tau_2 \rightarrow \tau_3$ denotes the type $\tau_1 \rightarrow \tau$ with $\tau = \tau_2 \rightarrow \tau_3$. We shall now specify the meaning of our type language and begin with the meaning $[\![T]\!]$ of the basic type T. We assume that $[\![T]\!]$ contains the natural numbers and the Boolean values *true* and *false*, with which we calculate in the usual way. In addition, we would like to model nonterminating computations, or those that terminate with errors. For this, we introduce another element $\bot$ to $[\![T]\!]$; this models *undefined*.

To enable us to assign a value to, for example, recursions and loop constructs using the denotational method, we use an iterative procedure. This begins with the approximation 'undefined' which it gradually refines; the meaning of the construct is obtained by forming a limit, similar to the limits used in differential calculus. As an example, we consider the assignment of meaning for the factorial function

$$\mathbf{fac}(n) := \mathbf{if}\ n = 0\ \mathbf{then}\ 1\ \mathbf{else}\ n * \mathbf{fac}(n - 1)$$

The zeroth approximation $\mathbf{fac}^0$ is the function which assigns $\bot$, 'undefined', to all arguments. The first approximation is obtained by replacing $\mathbf{fac}$ on the right side of the above equation by its zeroth approximation:

$$\mathbf{fac}^1(n) := \mathbf{if}\ n = 0\ \mathbf{then}\ 1\ \mathbf{else}\ n * \mathbf{fac}^0(n - 1)$$

Defined sorts

τ	$\in$	T	Types

Structure

τ	$\rightarrow$	T	Basic type
	$\rightarrow$	$\tau_1 \rightarrow \tau_2$	Function-space formation

Figure 10.6   Abstract syntax of types.

It has value 1 for 0 and values $\bot$ for all other arguments. The $i+1$th approximation is obtained analogously:

$$\mathbf{fac}^{i+1}(n) := \mathbf{if}\ n = 0\ \mathbf{then}\ 1\ \mathbf{else}\ n * \mathbf{fac}^i(n - 1)$$

For $n \leq i$ it has value $n!$ (n factorial), while its value is 'undefined', $\bot$, for other n. The factorial function itself is obtained as the limiting value of these approximations.

To formalize the procedure, we must give a precise definition of what an approximation is, when one approximation is better than another and what kind of limiting value should be used. Thus, it is appropriate to compare various candidates with one another; we order these using a partial order $\leq$: intuitively, f should be less than f', $f < f'$, if f is less defined than f'. For this, we stipulate that $\bot$ should be smaller than all other elements of $[\![T]\!]$ and that the remaining elements are pairwise incomparable. Thus, $[\![T]\!]$ becomes a *partially ordered set, PO* (partial order), with least element $\bot$. By lifting this to the function space using point-wise definition, we can partially order the function space; it too has a smallest element, the constant function $\bot$. Its partial order formalizes the following: $f < f'$ if f is less defined than f'. The iterative process mentioned above defines an ascending chain: $f_0 \leq f_1 \leq \ldots$. The limiting value of such a chain is an f with the following two properties:

(1) $f_i \leq f$ for all i,

(2) if f' has property (1), that is, $f_i \leq f'$ for all i, then $f \leq f'$.

Property (1) says that f is an upper bound for the chain; property (2) says that it is the least such upper bound. Whenever the limiting value exists, it is unique and we denote it by $\bigvee_i f_i$. Limiting values of this type are of crucial importance for the denotational method; thus, the semantic domains used normally have the following properties:

(1) they are partially ordered

(2) they have a smallest element, $\bot$

(3) ascending chains $f_0 \leq f_1 \leq \ldots$ have a limiting value, $\bigvee_i f_i$.

Such domains are called *complete partial orders, CPO*. Not every function f between complete partial orders D_1 and D_2 is compatible with the order structure. Functions that commute with the formation of the limiting value of ascending chains, that is:

$$f(\bigvee_i d_i) = \bigvee_i f(d_i)$$

for every ascending chain $d_1 \leq d_2 \leq \cdots$, are said to be *continuous*. In particular, continuous functions are *monotonic*, that is, $f(d_1) \leq f(d_2)$ if $d_1 \leq d_2$. The space of continuous functions $[D_1 \rightarrow D_2]$ is again a complete partial order. A continuous function $f: D \rightarrow D$ has a *least fixpoint*, fix $f = \bigvee_i f^i(\bot)$, which satisfies

Imported sorts

$$\begin{array}{rcll}
\tau & \in & \mathcal{T} & \text{Types} \\
c_\tau & \in & \mathcal{C}_\tau & \text{Constants of type } \tau \\
v_\tau & \in & \mathcal{V}_\tau & \text{Variables of type } \tau
\end{array}$$

Defined sorts

$$\begin{array}{rcll}
E_\tau & \in & \Lambda_\tau & \lambda\text{-expressions of type } \tau
\end{array}$$

Structure

$$\begin{array}{rcll}
E_\tau & \to & c_\tau & \\
& \to & v_\tau & \\
& \to & \lambda v_{\tau_1}.E_{\tau_2} & \text{if } \tau = \tau_1 \to \tau_2 \\
& \to & E_{\tau' \to \tau} E_{\tau'} &
\end{array}$$

Figure 10.7   Abstract syntax of the λ-expressions of type τ.

$f(\text{fix } f) = \text{fix } f$. The denotational method assigns a least fixpoint to recursive definitions as meaning.

We are now in a position where we can specify the meaning of $\tau_1 \to \tau_2$:

$$[\![\tau_1 \to \tau_2]\!] := [\![[\![\tau_1]\!] \to [\![\tau_2]\!]]\!]$$

Thus, the meaning of $\tau_1 \to \tau_2$ is the space of continuous functions between $[\![\tau_1]\!]$ and $[\![\tau_2]\!]$.

We now come to the description of the typed λ-expressions. λ-expressions are recursively constructed from constants, variables, the so-called λ-abstraction and the function application. Every λ-expression has a uniquely determined type. In particular, this is true for the constants and variables. We assume that for each type τ $\mathcal{C}_\tau$ denotes the set of the constants and $\mathcal{V}_\tau$ that of the variables of type τ. Of course, we require these sets to be pairwise disjoint. The abstract syntax for typed λ-expressions is defined in Figure 10.7.

The construct $\lambda v_{\tau_1}.E_{\tau_2}$ is called λ-**abstraction**. It stands for an (unnamed) function with formal parameter v_{τ_1} and body E_{τ_2}. The function is of type $\tau_1 \to \tau_2$. The construct $E_{\tau_1 \to \tau_2} E_{\tau_1}$ is called **function application**. It stands for the application of the function $E_{\tau_1 \to \tau_2}$ to the (actual) argument E_{τ_1}.

It is noticeable that all functions have only one argument. But, the result of a function application can also have a functional type and may then be applied to another argument. In this framework, an n-ary function f of type $\tau_1 \times \cdots \times \tau_n \to \tau$ is modelled as a function $\overline{f}$ of type $\tau_1 \to \ldots \to \tau_n \to \tau$ with

$$f(E_1, \ldots, E_n) = \overline{f} \, E_1 \ldots E_n$$

Here, (in the string representation), we view the function application as a left-associative binary operation, that is, $E E_1 E_2$ stands for $(E E_1) E_2$. Furthermore, based on our string representation of λ-expressions, we assume that the function application binds more strongly than the abstraction. As usual, we use parentheses if these precedence rules do not give the desired result.

In what follows, the choice of the set of constants is unimportant. But to be able to write interesting programs using λ-expressions, the set of constants must satisfy certain conditions. Now we give an example set of constants.

Example 10.4 (example set of constants)

- C_T contains the natural numbers and the Boolean values *true* and *false*.

- $C_{T \to T \to T}$ contains the usual arithmetic operators such as addition, multiplication, subtraction, division, ..., together with comparators such as test for equality and inequality, test for less/greater than ....

- For every type τ $C_{T \to \tau \to \tau \to \tau}$ contains the conditional if_τ.

- For every type τ $C_{(\tau \to \tau) \to \tau}$ contains the fixed point operator Y_τ, which is used to express recursion.

Using these constants, we can, for example, 'define' the factorial function (the fact that this is actually a definition of the factorial function only becomes apparent after we have assigned a semantics to λ-expressions) as follows

$$Y_{T \to T}(\lambda f_{T \to T}.\lambda n_T.\, if_T\, (= n_T 0)\, 1\, (*n_T(f_{T \to T}(-n_T\, 1))))$$

or, if we use the usual infix notation for the arithmetic operators and the comparators and the distfix notation for the conditional and dispense with type specifications:

$$Y(\lambda f.\lambda n.\, \textbf{if}\ n = 0\ \textbf{then}\ 1\ \textbf{else}\ n * f(n-1)) \qquad \square$$

Let us now return to the task of assigning a meaning to each λ-expression. This meaning should assign an element of $[\![\tau]\!]$ to a λ-expression of type τ, when the values of all the variables are given. The values of the variables are modelled using a so-called **variable binding**, a mapping vb from the set $\mathcal{V} = \bigcup_\tau \mathcal{V}_\tau$ of all variables to the set $D = \bigcup_\tau [\![\tau]\!]$ of all values, such that for $v_\tau \in \mathcal{V}_\tau$: $vb(v_\tau) \in [\![\tau]\!]$. Thus, the meaning of a λ-expression E_τ is a mapping, which assigns an element of $[\![\tau]\!]$ to every variable binding, the **value of E_τ in the variable binding** vb. Here, we interpret the λ-abstraction and the application as function definition and function application.

Thus, we obtain the following semantic definition, where VB denotes the CPO of the variable bindings.

$$
\begin{aligned}
E_\tau^S &:= [VB \to [\![\tau]\!]] \\[4pt]
[\![c_\tau]\!](vb) &= I(c_\tau) \\[4pt]
[\![v_\tau]\!](vb) &= vb(v_\tau) \\[4pt]
[\![\lambda v_{\tau_1}.E_{\tau_2}]\!](vb) &= \lambda d_1 \in [\![\tau_1]\!].[\![E_{\tau_2}]\!](vb[v_{\tau_1} \mapsto d_1]) \\[4pt]
[\![E_{\tau_1 \to \tau_2} E_{\tau_1}]\!](vb) &= ([\![E_{\tau_1 \to \tau_2}]\!](vb))\,([\![E_{\tau_1}]\!](vb))
\end{aligned}
$$

Thus, the semantic definition is complete up to the specification of the constant-interpretation function I. For our example constants, we define I as follows:

Example 10.5 (semantics for example constants)

- For simplicity, we assume that all c_T are in $[\![T]\!]$ and that they are their own meaning:

  $C_\tau \subseteq [\![T]\!]$; $I(c_T) = c_T$;

- $I(+)$ is the usual addition of natural numbers:

  $$I(+)d_1 d_2 := \begin{cases} d_1 + d_2, & \text{if } d_1, d_2 \in \mathbb{N} \\ \bot_T, & \text{otherwise.} \end{cases}$$

  Analogously for the other arithmetic operators and the comparators;

- $I(if_\tau)$ is the usual choice of two:

  $$I(if_\tau)d_1 d_2 d_3 := \begin{cases} d_2, & \text{if } d_1 = true; \\ d_3, & \text{if } d_1 = false; \\ \bot_\tau, & \text{otherwise.} \end{cases}$$

- $I(Y_\tau)$ is the so-called fixed point operator:

  $$I(Y_\tau)f = \text{fix } f = \bigvee_{n \in \mathbb{N}} f^n(\bot_\tau)$$

Thus, we have specified the standard semantics for typed λ-expressions. For these standard semantics the λ-expressions are capable of expressing Turing computable functions. More precisely, there exists a computable mapping which assigns a λ-expression E_f (of type $\underbrace{T \to \cdots \to T}_{n \text{ times}} \to T$) to every recursive function f from $\mathbb{N}^n \to \mathbb{N}$ such that for $x_1, \ldots, x_n \in \mathbb{N}$:

$$(x_1, \ldots, x_n) \in \text{Def}(f) \iff [\![E_f]\!](vb)x_1 \cdots x_n \neq \bot_{D_T} \tag{10.1}$$
$$(x_1, \ldots, x_n) \in \text{Def}(f) \implies f(x_1, \ldots, x_n) = [\![E_f]\!](vb)x_1 \cdots x_n \tag{10.2}$$
$$[\![E_f]\!](vb) \text{ is independent of } vb. \tag{10.3}$$

□

Definition 10.3 (Strictness)
A function $f : [\![\tau_1]\!] \to [\![\tau_2]\!]$ is said to be **strict** if $f(\bot_{\tau_1}) = \bot_{\tau_2}$.   □

It follows immediately from the Turing-machine power of λ-expressions that strictness is undecidable. Thus, for example, there is no algorithm that can decide the strictness of λ-terms of the form

$\lambda v_T.$ **if** E_T **then** 1 **else** v_T

where v_T does not occur in E_T. In fact, such a term is strict in its argument if and only if $[\![E_T]\!] \neq true$. But if we could decide this problem, we could also decide whether a given argument lies in the domain of definition of a given recursive function, which is equivalent to the halting problem (if f is the function and x the argument, then we would (essentially) choose for E_T the λ-term corresponding to the zero-ary recursive function $TRUE(f(x))$; then $[\![E_T]\!] = true \iff x \in \mathrm{Def}(f)$).

An abstract interpretation for strictness analysis

In this section, we meet an abstract interpretation which provides us with correct, but usually incomplete information about the strictness of λ-expressions.

We repeat that the Turing power of the λ-expressions (for their standard semantics) leads directly to the undecidability of the strictness problem. One important prerequisite for the Turing power is the range of $[\![T]\!]$; it contains the natural numbers. If, for example, we interpret the types with a finite CPO $[\![T]\!]^{\mathcal{N}}$ as an interpretation of the basic type, then all type meanings $[\![\tau]\!]^{\mathcal{N}}$ are finite and consequently, all functions which occur are computable.

For the strictness analysis, we use as abstract interpretation for T the complete partial order with the two elements $\bot_T$ and $\top_T$. This abstraction is very coarse: it abstracts completely from the concrete value and only decides between 'defined', $\top_T$, and 'undefined', $\bot_T$. The associated abstraction relation δ_T is defined by:

$$d \; \delta_T \; \overline{d} :\iff d = \bot_T \text{ or } \overline{d} = \top_T$$

With respect to δ_T, $\top_T$ represents every $d \in [\![T]\!]$, $\bot_T$ only $\bot_T$. We define the abstract meaning of $\tau_1 \to \tau_2$ by analogy with page 478:

$$[\![\tau_1 \to \tau_2]\!]^{\mathcal{N}} := \left[[\![\tau_1]\!]^{\mathcal{N}} \to [\![\tau_2]\!]^{\mathcal{N}} \right]$$

The abstraction relations δ_{τ_1} between $[\![\tau_1]\!]$ and $[\![\tau_1]\!]^{\mathcal{N}}$ and δ_{τ_2} between $[\![\tau_2]\!]$ and $[\![\tau_2]\!]^{\mathcal{N}}$ are lifted as shown on page 470 for the abstraction relation $\delta_{\tau_1} \to \delta_{\tau_2}$ between $[\![\tau_1 \to \tau_2]\!]$ and $[\![\tau_1 \to \tau_2]\!]^{\mathcal{N}}$. Thus, using structural induction, for every type τ we obtain an abstract semantic domain $[\![\tau]\!]^{\mathcal{N}}$ and an abstraction relation δ_τ between $[\![\tau]\!]$ and $[\![\tau]\!]^{\mathcal{N}}$. We show by structural induction that the δ_τ have the following properties:

(E_1) there exists $\top_\tau \in [\![\tau]\!]^{\mathcal{N}}$, which is related to each $d \in [\![\tau]\!]$ by the relation δ_τ:
$$d \; \delta_\tau \; \top_\tau,$$

(E_2) $\bot_\tau$ is only related to $\bot_\tau$ by the relation δ_τ: $d \; \delta_\tau \; \bot_\tau$ iff $d = \bot_\tau$.

The property E_2 enables us to deduce the strictness of f from that of $\overline{f}$:

Theorem 10.4 *If $f \; \delta_\tau \; \overline{f}$ and $\overline{f}$ is strict, then f is strict.* $\square$

Now we only have to use these results to define a non-standard semantics for λ-expressions and lift the family δ_τ appropriately. For this, we define an abstract variable binding $\overline{vb}$ (analogous to a variable binding as before) as a mapping $\overline{vb}$ from the set of variables to the set of abstract values $\overline{D} = \bigcup_\tau [\![\tau]\!]^{\mathcal{N}}$ with $\overline{vb}(v_\tau) \in [\![\tau]\!]^{\mathcal{N}}$ for $v_\tau \in \mathcal{V}_\tau$. Then the specification of the semantics for λ-expressions carries over from D to $\overline{D}$: $\overline{VB}$ denotes the CPO of the abstract variable bindings.

$$
\begin{aligned}
[\![E_\tau]\!]^{\mathcal{N}} &:= [\overline{VB} \to [\![\tau]\!]^{\mathcal{N}}] \\
[\![c_\tau]\!]^{\mathcal{N}}(\overline{vb}) &= \overline{I}(c_\tau) \\
[\![v_\tau]\!]^{\mathcal{N}}(\overline{vb}) &= \overline{vb}(v_\tau) \\
[\![\lambda v_{\tau_1}.E_{\tau_2}]\!]^{\mathcal{N}}(\overline{vb}) &= \lambda \overline{d_1} \in [\![\tau_1]\!]^{\mathcal{N}}.[\![E_{\tau_2}]\!]^{\mathcal{N}}(\overline{vb}[v_{\tau_1} \mapsto \overline{d_1}]) \\
[\![E_{\tau_1 \to \tau_2} E_{\tau_1}]\!]^{\mathcal{N}}(\overline{vb}) &= ([\![E_{\tau_1 \to \tau_2}]\!]^{\mathcal{N}}(\overline{vb}))([\![E_{\tau_1}]\!]^{\mathcal{N}}(\overline{vb}))
\end{aligned}
$$

Thus, the definition of the abstract semantics is complete up to the specification of the abstract constant-interpretation function $\overline{I}$. For our example constants we define $\overline{I}$ as follows:

Example 10.6 (abstract semantics for example constants)

- $\overline{I}(c_T) = \overline{\top}_T$

- $\overline{I}(+)\,\overline{d_1}\,\overline{d_2} := \overline{d_1} \wedge \overline{d_2} = \begin{cases} \overline{\bot}_T, & \text{if } \overline{d_1} = \overline{\bot}_T \text{ or } \overline{d_2} = \overline{\bot}_T; \\ \overline{\top}_T, & \text{otherwise.} \end{cases}$

  This expresses the fact that $+$ is strict in both arguments. The abstract meaning of the remaining arithmetic operators and the comparators is specified in the same way.

- $\overline{I}(\text{if}_\tau)\,\overline{d_1}\,\overline{d_2}\,\overline{d_3} := \begin{cases} \overline{\bot}_\tau, & \text{if } \overline{d_1} = \overline{\bot}_T, \\ \overline{d_2} \vee \overline{d_3}, & \text{otherwise.} \end{cases}$

  $\overline{d_2} \vee \overline{d_3}$ denotes the least upper bound for $\{\overline{d_2}, \overline{d_3}\}$, that is, the smallest element $\overline{d}$, which is greater than or equal to $\overline{d_2}$ and $\overline{d_3}$. This is the sharpest strictness information which is expressed by both $\overline{d_2}$ and $\overline{d_3}$. It is also called the union of $\overline{d_2}$ and $\overline{d_3}$. Its use in the abstract semantics of *if* expresses the fact that we do not know which alternative will be chosen if all we can say about the first argument is that it is defined. If the first argument is undefined then the whole expression is also undefined. This expresses the fact that *if* is strict in the first argument.

- Y_τ is again interpreted as the fixed point operator:

$$
\overline{I}(Y_\tau)\overline{f} = \text{fix}\,\overline{f} = \bigvee_{n \in \mathbb{N}} \overline{f}^n(\overline{\bot}_\tau) \qquad \square
$$

We must also ensure that as far as our abstraction relations are concerned, our abstract semantic functions are abstractions of the semantic functions of the standard semantics. For all constants except the fixed-point operator, this can be seen directly. However, in the case of the fixed-point operator, it requires a new concept: a relation δ between complete partial orders D and $\overline{D}$ is said to be $\bigvee$-*closed*, if for increasing chains $d_1 \leq d_2 \leq \cdots$ in D and $\overline{d_1} \leq \overline{d_2} \cdots$ in $\overline{D}$, $d_i \; \delta \; \overline{d_i}$ for all i implies: $\bigvee_i d_i \; \delta$ $\bigvee_i \overline{d_i}$, that is, if δ (viewed as a subset of $D \times \overline{D}$) is closed with respect to the formation of limiting values. If $\delta \subseteq D \times \overline{D}$ is $\bigvee$-closed and $\perp \delta \; \overline{\perp}$ (in the literature a relation with these two properties is often said to be *admissible*), then for continuous functions $f: D \to D$ and $\overline{f}: \overline{D} \to \overline{D}$ with $f \; \delta \to \delta \; \overline{f}$, we have:

$$\bigvee_{n \in \mathbb{N}} f^n(\perp) \; \delta \; \bigvee_{n \in \mathbb{N}} \overline{f}^n(\overline{\perp})$$

The fixed-point operator over $\overline{D}$ is therefore an abstraction of the fixed-point operator over D. E_2 provides the second required property for δ_τ. It remains to show that all δ_τ are $\bigvee$-closed. A direct check shows that δ_T is $\bigvee$-closed. On the other hand, $\delta_1 \to \delta_2$ is $\bigvee$-closed, whenever δ_2 is $\bigvee$-closed. Consequently, all δ_τ are $\bigvee$-closed. Thus, $\overline{I}(Y_\tau)$ is an abstraction of $I(Y_\tau)$.

We obtain the following statement:

Theorem 10.5   *The non-standard semantics $\mathcal{N}$ of page 463 is an abstraction of the standard semantics of the typed λ-expressions with the abstraction relation $\delta :=$ $(\mathcal{V} \to \delta_D) \to \delta_D$, where $\delta_D \subseteq D \times \overline{D}$ is the union of the δ_τ. It follows that for all typed λ-expressions E_τ: $[\![E_\tau]\!] \; \delta \; [\![E_\tau]\!]^{\mathcal{N}}$.*
If $\overline{vb}$ is an abstraction of vb (for $\mathcal{V} \to \delta_D$) and if $[\![E_\tau]\!]^{\mathcal{N}}(\overline{vb})$ is strict, then $[\![E_\tau]\!](vb)$ is also strict. $\square$

According to property E_1, there exists $\overline{\top}_\tau$ in $[\![\tau]\!]^{\mathcal{N}}$ with $d \; \delta_\tau \; \overline{\top}_\tau$ for all d in $[\![\tau]\!]$. Thus, $\overline{vb}_\top := \lambda v_{\tau'}.\overline{\top}_{\tau'}$ represents each variable binding vb. To prove that $[\![E_\tau]\!](vb)$ is strict for $\tau = \tau_1 \to \tau_2$ we therefore only need to check that $[\![E_\tau]\!]^{\mathcal{N}}(\overline{vb}_\top)(\overline{\perp}_{\tau_1}) = \overline{\perp}_{\tau_2}$. Since $[\![E_\tau]\!](\overline{vb}_\top)(\overline{\perp}_{\tau_1})$ is computable, we have found a procedure which enables us to determine correct but generally incomplete (because of the abstraction) strictness information about $[\![E_\tau]\!]$.

We end with a simple example.

Example 10.7   On page 476 we saw the definition of the factorial function:

$$fac == Y(\lambda f.\lambda n. \text{ if } n = 0 \text{ then } 1 \text{ else } n * f(n-1))$$

As an interpretation over the abstract data domain, we obtain:

$$\overline{fac} == \text{fix}\left(\lambda \overline{f} \in [\![T \to T]\!]^{\mathcal{N}}.\lambda \overline{n} \in [\![T]\!]^{\mathcal{N}}.(\overline{n} \wedge \overline{\top}_T) \wedge \left(\overline{\top}_T \vee (\overline{n} \wedge \overline{f}(\overline{n} \wedge \overline{\top}_T))\right)\right)$$

After some simplification, we obtain:

$$\overline{fac} == \text{fix}\left(\lambda \overline{f}.\lambda \overline{n}.\overline{n}\right) = \lambda \overline{n}.\overline{n}$$

Consequently, we have $\overline{fac}(\overline{\perp}_T) = \overline{\perp}_T$. Thus, $\overline{fac}$ is strict and thereby the factorial function is shown to be strict. $\square$

10.3 Abstract interpretation based on operational semantics

In this section we consider the abstract interpretation based on operational semantics in more detail. In other words, we consider the abstract interpretation of programs of a programming language whose semantics are specified using the operational method.

10.3.1 The operational method

The operational method for semantics definition specifies a procedure which is used to obtain a mathematical machine and a set of possible initial states for a program and its input data. In addition, a specification of how the program result can be read off from calculations and/or terminal states of the mathematical machine is given.

A mathematical machine is characterized by

- a set of states Z,
- a transition relation between states $\rightarrow$,
- a set of initial states I,
- a set of final states F.

A *computational step* is a transition $z \rightarrow z'$, where z is not a final state; a *computation* $z_0 \rightarrow z_1 \rightarrow \cdots$ is a sequence of computational steps. A computation $z_0 \rightarrow \cdots \rightarrow z_n$ *terminates*, when there is no computational step of the form $z_n \rightarrow z$; if this is the case, if z_n is a final state, then the computation *terminates without errors*, otherwise it terminates *with errors*. z_n is the *result of the computation*.

The mapping of a program P and its input data i onto a mathematical machine M and a set of possible initial states enables us to describe possible 'runs of the program': every (possibly infinite) non-continuable computation of M, which begins in one of the permissible initial states, describes a possible behaviour of the given program for the given input data. Here, infinite computations model nontermination of the program. Terminated computations model termination of the program. The semantics definition specifies how the program result is obtained from the final state in this case.

We now illustrate the procedure with an example. For this, we extend the example language for arithmetic expressions of Example 10.2 by different types of statements and statement sequences to obtain a simple imperative language. Its abstract syntax is defined in Figure 10.8.

Imperative languages are typically *control oriented*. This means that at any time during the program execution the control is at a specific program point (possibly several points in parallel languages). The statement at this point is executed. The memory state may change and/or the control pass to another point. The states of a mathematical machine which specifies the meaning of a program for such a language may be expected to contain at least two components: one component specifies the

Imported sorts

c	$\in$	$\mathcal{C}$	Constants
v	$\in$	$\mathcal{V}$	Variables

Defined sorts

E	Expressions
S	Statements
Q	Statement sequences

Structure

E	$\rightarrow$	c	
	$\rightarrow$	v	
	$\rightarrow$	$+EE$	
	$\rightarrow$	$*EE$	
S	$\rightarrow$	$v := E$	Assignment $v := E$
	$\rightarrow$	**result** E	**result** statement
	$\rightarrow$	**if** EQQ	conditional statement
	$\rightarrow$	**while** EQ	**while** loop
Q	$\rightarrow$	ε	empty statement sequence
	$\rightarrow$	$; SQ$	non-trivial statement sequence

Figure 10.8   Abstract syntax of a simple imperative language.

program point where the control presently is, while the second component describes the actual state of the memory. Practical semantics definitions typically describe other components including the (as yet unconsumed) input, the output (already produced), a stack with function-call frames, a stack with values for the evaluation of expressions, and so on.

We model the first component using so-called *program items*. A program item is a program in which either a '↓' or a '↑' is introduced after a statement or statement sequence. The first case models the situation where the control is located directly before the statement which is the next to be executed; the second case is that where the control has just executed the statement. We model the second component as before, using variable bindings, and mappings of variables to integers. We shall not consider any other components for our example.

Before we can give the operational semantics definition, we require one more technical tool. As for a denotational semantics definition, we shall not assign a meaning directly to each individual program but will instead describe the meaning of the program constructs, so that we can derive the meaning of all programs in a systematic manner from these. For this, a notation which enables us to describe local transformations of program items in a simple way is very helpful: *contexts*.

Contexts for program items may be defined very generally: as a partial mapping of program items to program items. For our purposes, a context can be viewed as a program item from which a fragment is removed. We can introduce another program item at this point and obtain a new (or the old) program item. For this, the fragment removed should contain the special labels ↓ or ↑. We use the notation $P[]$ to denote contexts. For a program item P', $P[P']$ denotes the program item obtained by applying $P[]$ to P', that is, by inserting P' at the hole in $P[]$.

Operational semantics of the language of Figure 10.8

We are now in a position to specify the semantics of our example language. As program input we choose the initial variable binding.

$\mathcal{P}$ denotes the set of the program items; VB the set of the variable bindings, which are mappings from variables to values (integers in our example). $[\![E]\!]$ denotes the standard meaning of E as defined on page 467. The mathematical machine $M = (Z, \rightarrow, I, F)$ is defined by:

- $Z = \mathcal{P} \times VB$; that is, the actual point of activity and the actual variable binding are encoded in the state.

- $I = \{ (\downarrow p, vb) \mid p \text{ program}, vb \text{ variable binding} \}$; that is, initial states are the states in which the control is located at the start of the program.

- $F = \{ (P[\textbf{result } E \uparrow], vb) \mid P[] \text{ context}, E \text{ expression}, vb \text{ variable binding} \}$; that is, final states are the states in which a **result** statement has just been executed.

- $\rightarrow$ contains precisely the following transitions (for all $P[], E, Q, S, \ldots$):

Assignment

$$(P[\downarrow v := E], vb) \rightarrow (P[v := E \uparrow], vb[v \mapsto [\![E]\!](vb)])$$

Result statement

$$(P[\downarrow \textbf{result } E], vb) \rightarrow (P[\textbf{result } E \uparrow], vb)$$

Conditional statement

$$(P[\downarrow \textbf{if } E \textbf{ then } Q_1 \textbf{ else } Q_2 \textbf{ fi}], vb)$$
$$\rightarrow (P[\textbf{if } E \textbf{ then } \downarrow Q_1 \textbf{ else } Q_2 \textbf{ fi}], vb), \text{ if } [\![E]\!](vb) \in \mathbf{Z} - \{0\}$$
$$(P[\downarrow \textbf{if } E \textbf{ then } Q_1 \textbf{ else } Q_2 \textbf{ fi}], vb)$$
$$\rightarrow (P[\textbf{if } E \textbf{ then } Q_1 \textbf{ else } \downarrow Q_2 \textbf{ fi}], vb), \text{ if } [\![E]\!](vb) = 0$$
$$(P[\textbf{if } E \textbf{ then } Q_1 \uparrow \textbf{ else } Q_2 \textbf{ fi}], vb)$$
$$\rightarrow (P[\textbf{if } E \textbf{ then } Q_1 \textbf{ else } Q_2 \textbf{ fi } \uparrow], vb)$$
$$(P[\textbf{if } E \textbf{ then } Q_1 \textbf{ else } Q_2 \textbf{ fi } \uparrow], vb)$$
$$\rightarrow (P[\textbf{if } E \textbf{ then } Q_1 \textbf{ else } Q_2 \uparrow], vb)$$

While loop

$$(P[\downarrow \textbf{while } E \textbf{ do } Q \textbf{ od}], vb)$$
$$\rightarrow (P[\textbf{while } E \textbf{ do } \downarrow Q \textbf{ od}], vb), \text{ if } [\![E]\!](vb) \in \mathbf{Z} - \{0\}$$

$(P[\downarrow \textbf{ while } E \textbf{ do } Q \textbf{ od}], vb)$
$\quad \rightarrow (P[\textbf{while } E \textbf{ do } Q \textbf{ od } \uparrow], vb), \text{ if } [\![E]\!](vb) = 0$
$(P[\textbf{while } E \textbf{ do } Q \uparrow \textbf{ od}], vb)$
$\quad \rightarrow (P[\downarrow \textbf{ while } E \textbf{ do } Q \textbf{ od}], vb)$

Empty statement sequence

$(P[\downarrow \varepsilon], vb) \rightarrow (P[\varepsilon \uparrow], vb)$

Non-trivial statement sequence

$(P[\downarrow; (S, Q)], vb) \rightarrow (P[; (\downarrow S, Q)], vb)$
$(P[; (S \uparrow, Q)], vb) \rightarrow (P[; (S, \downarrow Q)], vb)$
$(P[; (S, Q \uparrow)], vb) \rightarrow (P[; (S, Q) \uparrow], vb)$

We note that this mathematical machine depends only on the programming language and not on a particular program. The program and its input data influence the choice of the initial state.

If p is a program and vb its input, then $(\downarrow p, vb)$ is the initial state of the mathematical machine associated with (p, vb). If the mathematical machine terminates for $(\downarrow p, vb)$ in a final state $(P[\textbf{result } E \uparrow], vb')$, then $[\![E]\!](vb')$ is the result of p with input vb.

We shall refer to this example time and again in what follows.

10.3.2   Basic principle of the abstract interpretation

Abstract interpretation for an operational semantics definition is defined in a natural manner by another mathematical machine. This machine, the so-called '*abstract*' machine (note that this machine is abstract in a different sense from the abstract machines of Chapters 2–4; it abstracts from the standard semantics, while the P-machine, the MaMa and the WiM abstract from real computers, but implement the standard semantics with the corresponding compiler) simulates the original 'concrete' machine by which the operational semantics was specified. Using simulation, we obtain partial information about the concrete machine, whence about the programs whose semantics it defines. With appropriate abstraction, we can use the results, for example, to check the permissibility of program transformations and so obtain more efficient equivalent programs. As in the abstract interpretation based on denotational semantics, we must take the relationship between the simulation and the computation itself formally into account. This is done using an abstraction or simulation relation, which establishes a relationship between the states of the concrete and the abstract machines.

Example: propagation of constants

We shall now explain this using the example of Section 10.2.3. Thus, our aim is again to find expressions in a program whose value is always the same for every execution of the program and can already be determined by the compiler. In these cases, the compiler can evaluate the expression itself and replace it by its value. As we saw in Section 10.2.3, we require (trivial cases apart) information about the upper context of the expression, or more precisely, which variable bindings can arrive at the expression. If the expression always has the same value c for all variable bindings arriving at the subexpression, it can be replaced by c, without changing the semantics. The 'arrival' of a variable binding at a program point can be formulated in an operational context as follows:

Suppose the concrete machine is given by $M = (Z, \to, I, F)$ as defined at the end of the previous section. We model a program point by a program item of the form $P[\downarrow P']$. We say that a variable binding vb arrives at the point $P[\downarrow P']$ if there exist a variable binding vb' and a computation

$$(\downarrow P[P'], vb') \to \cdots \to (P[\downarrow P'], vb)$$

that is, if $(P[\downarrow P'], vb)$ is reachable from an initial state $(\downarrow P[P'], vb')$ via $\to$. If Z' is a superset of the states which are reachable from an initial state of the form $(\downarrow P[E], vb)$, and $[\![E]\!](vb) = [\![c]\!](\cdot)$ for all $(P[\downarrow E], vb) \in Z'$, then E can be replaced by c without changing the semantics.

Thus, to check the permissibility of such a transformation it is sufficient to determine a superset of states reachable via $\to$ from the initial states for the program. We use an appropriate abstraction for this, which is analogous to that used in Section 10.2.3. As basis it has an abstract interpretation of $\mathbf{Z}$, the set of integers, by $\overline{\mathbf{Z}} := \mathbf{Z} \cup \{\bot, ?\}$ with the abstraction relation $\delta_{\mathbf{Z}}$, defined by:

$$z \; \delta_{\overline{\mathbf{Z}}} \; \overline{z} :\Longleftrightarrow (\overline{z} = ?) \vee (\overline{z} = z)$$

Here, $\overline{z} \in \mathbf{Z}$ expresses the fact that we know the value exactly, $?$, that we know nothing about the value; $\bot$ models 'still undefined'. It enables us to define an initial situation easily, as we shall see later.

Thus, $(\overline{VB}, \delta_{VB})$ with $\overline{VB} = \mathcal{V} \to \overline{\mathbf{Z}}$ and $\delta_{VB} = \mathcal{V} \to \delta_{\overline{z}}$ is an abstraction of the variable bindings $VB = \mathcal{V} \to \mathbf{Z}$. If we define $\overline{Z} = \mathcal{P} \times \overline{VB}$, then $\delta = (=_{\mathcal{P}}) \times (\delta_{VB})$ defines an abstraction relation between the 'concrete' states Z and the 'abstract' states $\overline{Z}$. If we define the 'abstract' transition relation $\Rightarrow$ as follows, then the set of reachable states in the abstract machine represents the reachable states in the concrete machine: $\Rightarrow$ contains precisely the following transitions (for all $P[]$, E, Q, $S, \dots$):

Assignment

$$(P[\downarrow v := E], \overline{vb}) \Rightarrow (P[v := E \uparrow], \overline{vb}[v \mapsto [\![E]\!]^{\mathcal{N}}(\overline{vb})])$$

Result statement

$$(P[\downarrow \mathbf{result} \; E], \overline{vb}) \Rightarrow (P[\mathbf{result} \; E \uparrow], \overline{vb})$$

Conditional statement

$$(P[\downarrow \mathbf{if} \; E \; \mathbf{then} \; Q_1 \; \mathbf{else} \; Q_2 \; \mathbf{fi}], \overline{vb})$$
$$\Rightarrow (P[\mathbf{if} \; E \; \mathbf{then} \downarrow Q_1 \; \mathbf{else} \; Q_2 \; \mathbf{fi}], \overline{vb}), \text{ if } [\![E]\!]^{\mathcal{N}}(\overline{vb}) \notin \{0, \bot\}$$

$(P[\downarrow$ **if** E **then** Q_1 **else** Q_2 **fi**$], \overline{vb})$
   $\Rightarrow(P[$**if** E **then** Q_1 **else** $\downarrow Q_2$ **fi**$], \overline{vb})$, if $[\![E]\!]^{\mathcal{N}}(\overline{vb}) \in \{0, ?\}$
$(P[$ **if** E **then** $Q_1 \uparrow$ **else** Q_2 **fi**$], \overline{vb})$
   $\Rightarrow(P[$ **if** E **then** Q_1 **else** Q_2 **fi** $\uparrow], \overline{vb})$
$(P[$ **if** E **then** Q_1 **else** Q_2 **fi** $\uparrow], \overline{vb})$
   $\Rightarrow(P[$ **if** E **then** Q_1 **else** Q_2 **fi** $\uparrow], \overline{vb})$

While loop

$(P[\downarrow$ **while** E**do** Q **od**$], \overline{vb})$
   $\Rightarrow(P[$**while** E **do** $\downarrow Q$ **od**$], \overline{vb})$, if $[\![E]\!]^{\mathcal{N}}(\overline{vb}) \notin \{0, \bot\}$
$(P[\downarrow$ **while** E **do** Q **od**$], \overline{vb})$
   $\Rightarrow(P[$**while** E **do** Q **od** $\uparrow], \overline{vb})$, if $[\![E]\!]^{\mathcal{N}}(\overline{vb}) \in \{0, ?\}$
$(P[$**while** E **do** $Q \uparrow$ **od**$], \overline{vb})$
   $\Rightarrow(P[\downarrow$ **while** E **do** Q **od**$], \overline{vb})$

Empty statement sequence

$(P[\downarrow \varepsilon], \overline{vb}) \Rightarrow (P[\varepsilon \uparrow], \overline{vb})$

Non-trivial statement sequence

$(P[\downarrow; (S, Q)], \overline{vb}) \Rightarrow (P[; (\downarrow S, Q)], \overline{vb})$
$(P[; (S \uparrow, Q)], \overline{vb}) \Rightarrow (P[; (S, \downarrow Q)], \overline{vb})$
$(P[; (S, Q \uparrow)], \overline{vb}) \Rightarrow (P[; (S, Q) \uparrow], \overline{vb})$

Here, expressions are interpreted abstractly by $[\![E]\!]^{\mathcal{N}}$, where $+$ and $*$ are interpreted by their abstractions on $\mathbf{Z} \cup \{\bot, ?\}$:

$$\overline{z}_1 \overline{+} \overline{z}_2 := \begin{cases} \bot, & \text{if } \overline{z}_1 = \bot \text{ or } \overline{z}_2 = \bot; \\ ?, & \text{otherwise and } (\overline{z}_1 = ? \text{ or } \overline{z}_2 = ?); \\ \overline{z}_1 + \overline{z}_2, & \text{otherwise.} \end{cases}$$

$$\overline{z}_1 \overline{*} \overline{z}_2 := \begin{cases} \bot, & \text{if } \overline{z}_1 = \bot \text{ or } \overline{z}_2 = \bot; \\ 0, & \text{otherwise and } (\overline{z}_1 = 0 \text{ or } \overline{z}_2 = 0); \\ ?, & \text{otherwise and } (\overline{z}_1 = ? \text{ or } \overline{z}_2 = ?); \\ \overline{z}_1 * \overline{z}_2, & \text{otherwise.} \end{cases}$$

We obtain the following interesting result: if z is reachable via $\rightarrow$ from $(\downarrow p, vb)$, then there exists a $\overline{z}$ with $z \, \delta \, \overline{z}$ which is reachable via $\Rightarrow$ from $\overline{z}_0 = (\downarrow p, \lambda v. \, ?)$. Or, in other words, the set of states reachable from $\overline{z}_0$ in the abstract machine represents (with respect to δ) a superset of the states in the concrete machine reachable from an initial state of the form $(\downarrow p, vb)$. If $[\![E]\!]^{\mathcal{N}}(\overline{vb}) = I(c) \in \mathbf{Z}$, for all states of the form $(p[\downarrow E], \overline{vb})$ reachable from $\overline{z}_0$, then E can be replaced by c without altering the semantics. This result follows from the following property of δ relating to $\rightarrow$ and $\Rightarrow$: If $z \rightarrow z'$ and $z \, \delta \, \overline{z}$, then there exists $\overline{z}'$ with $\overline{z} \Rightarrow \cdots \Rightarrow \overline{z}'$ and $z' \, \delta \, \overline{z}'$. In words: if z' is reachable from z in one step and z is represented by $\overline{z}$, then there exists a $\overline{z}'$ which is reachable from $\overline{z}$, which abstracts z'. This is illustrated in the following diagram, in which continuous lines represent 'for all' statements and dashed lines 'there exists' statements.

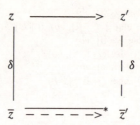

Despite our abstraction, the set of states reachable from $(\downarrow P, \lambda v.?)$ is in general not computable. We shall return to this problem in the next section and formulate a further abstraction which eliminates this problem.

Forwards and backwards problems

To obtain sufficient information to determine the applicability of a transformation, in the above example, we had to determine a superset of the reachable states. Other types of transformation occasionally require another type of information. We shall demonstrate this with another example.

If a program contains an assignment of the form $v := E$ and the value of v calculated in this way is not used again subsequently during the execution of the program, then the assignment can generally be omitted without altering the semantics of the program. In this case, we say that v is *dead* at the assignment. A normal program initially usually only contains a few, if any, dead variables. However, variables may 'die' as a result of the application of different program transformations. For example, if v is used in the **then** part of a conditional statement **if** E **then** Q_1 **else** Q_2 **fi**, but not in the **else** part, and it is discovered that E always takes the value **false**, then v may die upstream from the conditional statement if the value of v is not required again downstream from it.

We shall give a precise formulation of the 'dead variables' problem in Section 10.3.4. For this we shall require an extended auxiliary semantics. It should already be self-evident that, for this problem, the computations that begin in the initial states are less relevant that those that end in final states. In Section 10.3.4 we shall see that we actually have to determine a superset of the end fragments of computations in order to be able to eliminate assignments to dead variables.

While we had to determine a superset of the states reachable from initial states in order to recognize constant expressions, whence our analysis ran in a forwards direction, in order to recognize dead variables we require a superset of the end fragments of computations. Thus, our analysis must proceed in a backwards direction. Problems of the first type are called *forwards problems*, those of the second type *backwards problems*. We can also formulate a simple condition on the abstraction relation for the backwards analysis, which ensures that information determined using the abstract machine represents a superset of the states of the concrete machine leading to final states. This condition is described by the following diagram.

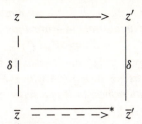

If the diagram is commutative and $Z' \subseteq \cdot \, \delta \, \overline{Z'}$ ($\cdot \, \delta \, \overline{Z'}$ denotes the set of states z represented by a z' in Z', that is, the set of z with $z \, \delta \, z'$), then for every state z leading to Z', there exists a state $\overline{z}$, which abstracts z and leads to $\overline{Z'}$. In other words, if the diagram is commutative and $L_M(Z')$ denotes the set of states of the concrete machine which lead to Z' and $L_{\overline{M}}(\overline{Z'})$ the set of states of the abstract machine which lead to $\overline{Z'}$, then $L_M(Z') \subseteq \cdot \, \delta \, L_{\overline{M}}(\overline{Z'})$ if $Z' \subseteq \cdot \, \delta \, \overline{Z'}$.

The backwards problem is completely dual to the forwards problem; we only need to reverse the transition relation. Thus, everything we say about forwards analysis also applies directly to backwards analysis.

Definitions

We now summarize the result of our previous discussion in the following definitions.

Definition 10.4 (reachable states)
If $M = (Z, \rightarrow, I, F)$ is a mathematical machine, $Z' \subseteq Z$ a set of states, then the smallest subset of Z, $R_M(Z')$ with the property:

$$Z' \subseteq R_M(Z') \;\; \wedge \;\; \forall z \in R_M(Z'), z' \in Z : z \rightarrow z' \Rightarrow z' \in R_M(Z')$$

is called the *set of states reachable from Z'*. Thus, $R_M(Z')$ is the smallest superset of Z' which is closed with respect to $\rightarrow$. $z' \in R_M(Z')$ is said to be *reachable from Z'*. □

Definition 10.5 (abstract interpretation)
Let $M = (Z, \rightarrow, I, F)$ be a mathematical machine. An abstract machine $\overline{M} = (\overline{Z}, \Rightarrow, \overline{I}, \overline{F})$ together with an abstraction relation δ between Z and $\overline{Z}$ is called an *abstract interpretation of M for forwards analysis*, if:

(1) $\forall z \in I : \exists \overline{z} \in \overline{I} : z \, \delta \, \overline{z}$,
(2) $\forall z, z' \in Z, \overline{z} \in \overline{Z} : z \, \delta \, \overline{z} \wedge z \rightarrow z' \;\Rightarrow\; \exists \overline{z'} : z' \, \delta \, \overline{z'} \wedge \overline{z} \Rightarrow^* \overline{z'}$.

$(\overline{M}, \delta)$ is called an *abstract interpretation of M for backwards analysis*, if:

(1) $\forall z \in F : \exists \overline{z} \in \overline{F} : z \, \delta \, \overline{z}$,
(2) $\forall z, z' \in Z, \overline{z} \in \overline{Z} : z' \, \delta \, \overline{z'} \wedge z \rightarrow z' \;\Rightarrow\; \exists \overline{z} : z \, \delta \, \overline{z} \wedge \overline{z} \Rightarrow^* \overline{z'}$.   □

Theorem 10.6 *If $M = (Z, \to, I, F)$ is a mathematical machine, $\overline{M} = (\overline{Z}, \Rightarrow, \overline{I}, \overline{F})$ and $(\overline{M}, \delta)$ is an abstract interpretation of M for forwards analysis, then for $Z' \subseteq Z, \overline{Z}' \subseteq \overline{Z}: Z' \subseteq \cdot \delta \overline{Z}' \Rightarrow R_M(Z') \subseteq \cdot \delta R_{\overline{M}}(\overline{Z}')$.*

In other words, if for every $z \in Z'$ there exists $\overline{z} \in \overline{Z}'$ with $z \, \delta \, \overline{z}$, then for every $z \in R_M(Z')$ there exists $\overline{z} \in R_{\overline{M}}(\overline{Z}')$ with $z \, \delta \, \overline{z}$. In this case, $R_{\overline{M}}(\overline{Z}')$ is a representation (correct with respect to δ) of a superset of $R_M(Z')$. □

By virtue of duality (replacing $\to$ by $\leftarrow$), a corresponding result also exists for the abstract interpretation for backwards analysis.

10.3.3 Construction of abstract interpretations

In this section we present several approaches to the construction of abstract interpretations. We begin with a number of remarks on the choice of the abstract set of states.

Typical properties of abstract sets of states

If $((\overline{Z}, \Rightarrow, \overline{I}, \overline{F}), \delta)$ is an abstraction of $(Z, \to, I, F)$, then every abstract state $\overline{z}$ represents a set of concrete states, namely $\cdot \, \delta \, \overline{z}$. Thus, $\overline{z}$ represents every set of states $Z' \subseteq \cdot \, \delta \, \overline{z}$. If Z' is represented by $\overline{z}$ and $\cdot \, \delta \, \overline{z} \subset \cdot \, \delta \, \overline{z}'$ (in this case, we write $\overline{z} \subset \overline{z}'$) then Z' is also represented by $\overline{z}'$. But the description by $\overline{z}$ is clearly better than that by $\overline{z}'$, since fewer elements which do not belong to Z' are described. If we require that for every set of states Z' there should exist a unique abstract state $\alpha(Z')$ which best describes Z', then we achieve the following advantages:

- $\subseteq$ makes $\overline{Z}$ into a complete lattice. In other words, with respect to $\subseteq$, every subset $\overline{Z}'$ of $\overline{Z}$ has a (uniquely determined) least upper bound (union), $\bigcup \overline{Z}'$, and a greatest lower bound (intersection), $\bigcap \overline{Z}'$.

- The mapping $\overline{z} \mapsto \gamma(\overline{z}) := \cdot \, \delta \, \overline{z}$ from the complete lattice $(\overline{Z}, \subseteq)$ to the complete lattice $(\mathcal{P}Z, \subseteq)$ is injective and commutes with arbitrary intersections. A slightly weaker property holds for unions: $\gamma(\bigcup \overline{Z}') = \alpha(\bigcup \gamma(\overline{Z}'))$.

- There exists an optimal abstract transition relation, namely $\overline{z} \Rightarrow \overline{z}' \iff \overline{z}' = \alpha(\gamma(\overline{z}) \to \cdot)$.

These results were described by Cousot and Cousot (1979). Although in practice the requirement that *every* set of states should have a best representation is not absolutely necessary, most abstract sets of states used for the abstract interpretation of an operational semantics have the above properties.

Accumulation property of abstract transition relations

In what follows we describe a special property of the abstract transition relation. Through the abstract interpretation, we would like (for forwards analysis) to obtain a representation for the set $R_M(Z_0)$ of states reachable from a set of states Z_0. For an appropriate abstraction $(\overline{M}, \delta)$ the set $R_{\overline{M}}(\overline{Z}_0)$ of abstract states reachable from a set of states $\overline{Z}_0$ with $Z_0 \, \delta \, \overline{Z}_0$ via $\overline{M}$ can be used. However, this set contains mainly elements which are not necessary for the representation of $R_M(Z_0)$. For example, if it contains $\overline{z}$ and $\overline{z}'$ with $\overline{z} \subseteq \overline{z}'$, then $\overline{z}$ can be omitted without altering the set represented. To enable us to use simplifications of this kind, it is convenient to define the abstract machine so that it simulates not only the concrete machine, but also, simultaneously, the possible extension of the set of the states (presently) reached associated with every transition in the concrete machine. This property is expressed in a very simple (accumulation) property of the abstract transition relation:

$$\mathbf{A} : \overline{z} \Rightarrow \overline{z}' \Rightarrow \overline{z} \subset \overline{z}'$$

In other words, the set of states represented is actually enlarged for every transition in the abstract machine.

 If M is abstracted from $(\overline{M}, \delta)$, if $\overline{M}$ has the property **A**, if $\overline{z}_0 \Rightarrow \cdots \Rightarrow \overline{z}_n$ is a terminated computation of $\overline{M}$ and if $Z_0 \, \delta \, \overline{z}_0$, then $R_M(Z_0) \, \delta \, \overline{z}_n$, that is, $\overline{z}_n$ represents all states reachable from Z_0 in M. Let us suppose that $\overline{M}$ terminates for all admissible initial states and that its transition relation is computable, then an explicit algorithm for determining a representation of $R_M(\cdot \, \delta \, \overline{z})$ can be given:

Algorithm 10.1

(1) $i := 0; \overline{z}_0 := \overline{z}$

(2) If there does not exist $\overline{z}'$ with $\overline{z}_i \Rightarrow \overline{z}'$, then $R_M(\cdot \, \delta \, \overline{z})$ is represented by $\overline{z}_i$.
    Otherwise, choose a $\overline{z}'$ with this property and set $i := i + 1$ and $\overline{z}_{i+1} := \overline{z}'$
    and repeat step (2). $\qquad\qquad\qquad\qquad\qquad\qquad\qquad\qquad\qquad\qquad\quad$ □

Since $\overline{M}$ terminates for $\overline{z}$, the above procedure ends after finitely many steps with the desired representation.

Typical features of an abstract interpretation

Thus, we have examined the typical features of an abstract interpretation based on an operational semantics definition. An abstract interpretation $(\overline{M}, \delta)$ of M typically has the following properties:

(1) $(\overline{Z}, \subseteq)$ is a complete lattice.

(2) The mapping $\gamma : \overline{z} \mapsto \cdot \, \delta \, \overline{z}$ of abstract states to the complete lattice of the sets of concretes states is injective and commutes with arbitrary intersections.

(3) $(\overline{M}, \delta)$ has the accumulation property: $\overline{z} \Rightarrow \overline{z}' \Rightarrow \overline{z} \subset \overline{z}'$.

(4) $\overline{M}$ terminates for every initial state $\overline{z} \in \overline{I}$.

Dataflow analysis: propagation of constants

We now return to the example of the previous section and apply the above rules to construct abstract interpretations for it.

To satisfy the accumulation property, an abstract state provides a description of all the knowledge obtained to date about the variable bindings arriving at the program points. Thus, it is now no longer restricted to information about the variable bindings arriving at a *single* program point. To limit the information sets, we keep to one variable binding per program point. If several variable bindings arrive at a program point we retain their union (the abstract variable bindings form a complete lattice; whence arbitrary unions are defined). For abstract states we choose the mappings π from program items (of a program) to abstract variable bindings. The set of abstract states thus defined is not quite a complete lattice; it lacks a largest and a smallest element. Introducing the two elements would give a complete lattice, but they are not of practical value.

The abstraction relation δ between concrete and abstract states is defined by:

$$(P, vb) \; \delta \; \pi \; :\Longleftrightarrow \; vb \; \delta_{VB} \; \pi(P)$$

that is, π represents the state (P, vb) if $\pi(P)$ represents the variable binding vb arriving at P.

To define the abstract transition relation we first rename the transition relation $\Rightarrow$ of page 488 to $\Rightarrow$. We now use $\Rightarrow$ to define the (new) abstract transition relation $\Rightarrow$ as follows:

$$\pi \Rightarrow \pi' \; :\Longleftrightarrow \; \pi' \supset \pi \; \wedge \; \exists \, (P, \pi(P)) \Rightarrow (P', \overline{vb}') : \pi' = \pi[P' \mapsto \pi(P') \cup \overline{vb}']$$

In other words, to determine a successor state to π we choose a program point P and a transition $(P, \pi(P)) \Rightarrow (P', \overline{vb}')$. We define π' by $\pi' = \pi[P' \mapsto \pi(P') \cup \overline{vb}']$. We derive π' from π by weakening the existing information at the point P' by the newly propagated increment $\overline{vb}'$. The formation of unions provides the sharpest information, which is compatible with both the existing information and the increment. π' is then a successor state for π, $\pi \Rightarrow \pi'$, if $\pi \subset \pi'$, that is, if the information at the point P' was actually weakened.

We next ensure that $\Rightarrow$ and δ define an abstraction of $\rightarrow$. For this, we have to show that:

$$\left.\begin{array}{c} (P, vb) \rightarrow (P', vb') \\[4pt] (P, vb) \; \delta \; \pi \end{array}\right\} \;\Longrightarrow\; \exists \pi' : \left\{\begin{array}{c} \pi \Rightarrow^* \pi' \\[4pt] (P', vb') \; \delta \; \pi' \end{array}\right\}$$

$(P, vb) \; \delta \; \pi$ means that $\pi(P)$ represents the variable binding at the point P: $vb \; \delta_{VB} \; \pi(P)$. Together with $(P, vb) \rightarrow (P', vb')$, this means that there exist $\overline{vb}'$ with $(P, \pi(P)) \Rightarrow (P', \overline{vb}')$ and $vb' \; \delta_{VB} \; \overline{vb}'$. Suppose $\pi' = \pi[P' \mapsto \pi(P') \cup \overline{vb}']$. Then $(P', vb') \; \delta \; \pi'$ and either $\pi = \pi'$ or $\pi \Rightarrow \pi'$. Thus, we have demonstrated the desired property.

We now investigate which abstract states are interesting as initial states for an abstract interpretation of a program p. Understandably, we are only interested in the values of variables which actually occur in p. Let V_p denote this set of variables, $\overline{vb}_{V_p \mapsto \perp}$ denote the abstract variable binding, which maps all variables in V_p to $\perp$ and all other variables to ?, and $\overline{vb}_?$ denote the abstract variable binding which maps all variables to ?. Then only one initial state π_p needs to be considered as far as the abstract interpretation of p is concerned. π_p is defined on the program items of p; $\pi_p(\downarrow p) = \overline{vb}_?$ and $\pi_p(P) = \overline{vb}_{V_p \mapsto \perp}$ for all other program items P. Clearly, $(\downarrow p, vb)$ δ π_p for every initial state of an execution of p. The information at the other program points was made as sharp as possible for the variables in p. It is weakened, if necessary, when the abstract computation is executed. For the variables which are not of interest, that is, those which do not occur in p, the initial information is already chosen to be as weak as possible so as not to complicate the computation unnecessarily.

Next, we shall show that the abstract machine defined above with initial state π_p for the analysis of a program p always terminates; that is, every computation $\pi_p \Rightarrow \cdots \Rightarrow \cdots$ is finite. The following observations are crucial to this:

(1)   It follows from $\pi_1 \Rightarrow \pi_2$ that $\pi_1 \sqsubset \pi_2$, that is, π_2 contains information which is strictly weaker than that in π_1.

(2)   All states π reachable from π_p have the following property: if P is a program item for p, then $\pi(P)$ maps all variables which do not occur in p onto ?; thus, the different $\pi(P)$ differ at most in their values for the finitely many variables referenced in p.

(3)   The lattice $\overline{Z} = Z \cup \{\perp, ?\}$ satisfies the *ascending chain condition*, that is, every strictly ascending chain is finite. All strictly ascending chains in $\overline{Z}$ have length at most three.

(4)   If D is a partial order with the ascending chain condition and V is a finite set, then $V \rightarrow D$ satisfies the ascending chain condition. Consequently, the partial order $\overline{VB}_p$ of the abstract variable bindings $\overline{vb}$ with $\overline{vb}(v) = ?$ for v not in the finite set V_p also satisfies the ascending chain condition. Consequently the partial order of the mappings of program points in p to $\overline{VB}_p$ also satisfies the ascending chain condition. Since every computation $\pi \Rightarrow \cdots \Rightarrow \cdots$ defines a strictly ascending chain in this partial order, every computation must be finite.

Thus, we have shown that our abstract interpretation defined above has almost all the features of a typical abstract interpretation, except that our set of states is not quite a complete lattice, although it could be extended to one by (artificially) introducing smallest and greatest elements. In particular, it satisfies the conditions for Algorithm 10.1. If the algorithm gives the result π for the input π_p then π represents each state reachable from a $(\downarrow p, vb)$ (for arbitrary vb). For each of these states (P, vb'), (P, vb') δ π, that is, vb' δ_{VB} $\pi(P)$. Thus, $\pi(P)$ provides information about all variable bindings which may possibly arrive at program point P in an 'execution' of p.

As an example, we consider the analysis of a small program p:

$$p: \qquad i := 5; \quad j := 0; \quad k := 0;$$
$$\textbf{while } j \leq i \textbf{ do}$$
$$k := k + j; \quad j := j + 1$$
$$\textbf{od}$$

We visualize an abstract state π, by entering the abstract variable binding at the point P, $\pi(P)$, in the program at the point P. For increased clarity, we only annotate a few prominent program points in this way. As initial state π_p we then obtain:

$$[i \mapsto ?, j \mapsto ?, k \mapsto ?]$$
$$i := 5; j := 0; k := 0;$$
$$[i \mapsto \bot, j \mapsto \bot, k \mapsto \bot]$$
$$\textbf{while } j \leq i \textbf{ do}$$
$$[i \mapsto \bot, j \mapsto \bot, k \mapsto \bot]$$
$$k := k + j; j := j + 1$$
$$[i \mapsto \bot, j \mapsto \bot, k \mapsto \bot]$$
$$\textbf{od}$$
$$[i \mapsto \bot, j \mapsto \bot, k \mapsto \bot]$$

Large parts of our annotated program remain unchanged during several computational steps of our abstract machine. Again to increase clarity, we replace unaltered parts which are irrelevant to the example at that time by '$\cdots$'. After a number of transitions, the abstract machine reaches a state which we can visualize as follows, using the above conventions:

$$[i \mapsto ?, j \mapsto ?, k \mapsto ?]$$
$$i := 5; j := 0; k := 0;$$
$$[i \mapsto 5, j \mapsto 0, k \mapsto 0]$$
$$\textbf{while } j \leq i \textbf{ do}$$
$$\cdots$$

The abstract machine has executed the three assignments and is now just before the **while** loop. The program points downstream of the loop have not yet been visited and still have their initial binding $[i \mapsto \bot, j \mapsto \bot, k \mapsto \bot]$. The next transition propagates the variable binding into the loop:

$$\cdots$$
$$[i \mapsto 5, j \mapsto 0, k \mapsto 0]$$
$$\textbf{while } j \leq i \textbf{ do}$$
$$[i \mapsto 5, j \mapsto 0, k \mapsto 0]$$

$$k := k + j; j := j + 1$$
$$[i \mapsto \bot, j \mapsto \bot, k \mapsto \bot]$$
od
$$[i \mapsto \bot, j \mapsto \bot, k \mapsto \bot]$$

The abstract execution of the loop body leads to:

$$\ldots$$
$$[i \mapsto 5, j \mapsto 0, k \mapsto 0]$$
while $j \leq i$ **do**
$$[i \mapsto 5, j \mapsto 0, k \mapsto 0]$$
$$k := k + j; j := j + 1$$
$$[i \mapsto 5, j \mapsto 1, k \mapsto 0]$$
od
$$[i \mapsto \bot, j \mapsto \bot, k \mapsto \bot]$$

The variable binding at the end of the loop body is then propagated again to the beginning of the loop. There, the union of the variable binding which is already there and the newly propagated binding is formed. After the union has been formed, sharp information about the value of j is no longer available because the values '0' and '1' are inconsistent.

$$\ldots$$
$$[i \mapsto 5, j \mapsto ?, k \mapsto 0]$$
while $j \leq i$ **do**
$$[i \mapsto 5, j \mapsto 0, k \mapsto 0]$$
$$\ldots$$

Up to here, our abstract machine operated deterministically; in every state there was precisely one possibility for continuing the computation. Now, for the first time, we have a choice of two possible transitions; we can again propagate the variable binding before the loop through the loop body or we can propagate it after the loop. It is clearly more favourable to stabilize the information within the loop first and then propagate the stabilized information once after the loop. The formation of the union at the beginning of the loop body and the further propagation to the end of the loop body lead to:

$$\ldots$$
$$[i \mapsto 5, j \mapsto ?, k \mapsto 0]$$
while $j \leq i$ **do**
$$[i \mapsto 5, j \mapsto ?, k \mapsto 0]$$
$$k := k + j; j := j + 1$$
$$[i \mapsto 5, j \mapsto ?, k \mapsto ?]$$

od

$$[i \mapsto \bot, j \mapsto \bot, k \mapsto \bot]$$

Since we have no information about the value of j at the beginning of the loop body, at the end of the body we no longer have any information about the value of k. The propagation of this variable binding before the loop leads to:

$$\cdots$$
$$[i \mapsto 5, j \mapsto ?, k \mapsto ?]$$
while $j \leq i$ **do**
$$\cdots$$

We can propagate the variable binding before the loop through the loop body once again:

$$\cdots$$
$$[i \mapsto 5, j \mapsto ?, k \mapsto ?]$$
while $j \leq i$ **do**
$$[i \mapsto 5, j \mapsto ?, k \mapsto ?]$$
$$k := k + j; j := j + 1$$
$$[i \mapsto 5, j \mapsto ?, k \mapsto ?]$$
od
$$[i \mapsto \bot, j \mapsto \bot, k \mapsto \bot]$$

A further propagation within the loop does not lead to a new abstract state. Thus, the next transition is again uniquely determined, with the variable binding before the loop propagated beyond the loop.

$$[i \mapsto ?, j \mapsto ?, k \mapsto ?]$$
$$i := 5; j := 0; k := 0;$$
while $j \leq i$ **do**
$$[i \mapsto 5, j \mapsto ?, k \mapsto ?]$$
$$k := k + j; j := j + 1$$
$$[i \mapsto 5, j \mapsto ?, k \mapsto ?]$$
od
$$[i \mapsto 5, j \mapsto ?, k \mapsto ?]$$

The abstract machine terminates in this state. It is the result of our abstract interpretation. We can interpret it as follows: at the start of the program we know nothing about the values of i, j and k; at all other points of the program i is guaranteed to have value 5, while the abstract interpretation cannot determine fixed values for j and k.

Dataflow analysis

In the above example, we met an important form of abstract interpretation, which has been used for a long time, namely *dataflow analysis*. Dataflow analysis is distinguished by the fact that it assigns information about the incoming data at each program point to that program point. Unlike in the introduction to this section, where the relationship between dataflow analysis and operational semantics is in the foreground, in the literature, dataflow analysis is usually viewed as a dataflow problem on the control flow graph of the program; see, for example, Hecht (1977). The program to be analysed is translated into an edge-labelled directed graph. Its nodes correspond to the program points; its edges correspond to possible control transitions from one program point to the next. The edges are labelled by functions which transform an abstract description of the data at the initial node into an increment to weaken the abstract data at the destination node. The edges and their labels are in direct correspondence with the transitions of our transition relation $\Rightarrow$. The abstract data at the destination node is weakened as in our definition of $\overrightarrow{\Rightarrow}$ by the formation of the union of the information present at the destination node with the increment. Initially, the dataflow analysis supplies all program points with the sharpest possible information and then feeds in abstract data at the entry point of the graph, which corresponds to our choice of initial state for the abstract interpretation. The dataflow analysis then propagates the data through the control flow graph until the information content can no longer be changed; in our representation, this process corresponds to a calculation of the abstract machine up to its termination.

Dataflow analysis is not solely used for the above example of *constant propagation*. In fact, it can be algorithmically executed whenever the abstract data is described by a partial order with the formation of unions and the ascending chain condition. In the next section, we shall discuss a number of important examples of dataflow problems.

Although Algorithm 10.1 always terminates (when the conditions for the use of dataflow analysis are satisfied), the number of steps required depends largely on how $\bar{z}_{n+1}$ with $\bar{z}_n \overrightarrow{\Rightarrow} \bar{z}_{n+1}$ is chosen. Properties of the graph and the dataflow picture can guide this choice. In a cycle-free graph it is clearly favourable to sort the nodes topologically and visit the nodes correspondingly. In a graph with cycles the same holds for its strongly connected components. An algorithm based on worklists can be used to propagate the information within cycles. The worklist is initialized with the entry node in the cycle. In each step the first element of the worklist is withdrawn and information is forwarded to all direct successors. If the information at a successor changes it is taken into the worklist. The procedure terminates when the worklist is empty.

Implementation aspects

For clarity, in our previous example, we did not annotate all program points with variable bindings, but only some prominent ones. In a practical implementation of dataflow analysis one would do the same to save space. Practical implementations divide the program to be analysed into so-called *basic blocks* and only store the abstract data at the entry point to the basic block. A basic block is defined in such a way that the abstract information can be propagated in a simple manner from the entry point to all other points. Frequently, the basic blocks are taken to be the paths of maximal length with the property that all nodes except the first have precisely one input and all except the last have precisely one output edge. This means that the path can only be entered from its first node and left via its last node. Applied to our example language, this means that sequences of assignments form the basic blocks.

10.3.4   Use of auxiliary semantics

In our study of abstract interpretation based on a denotational semantics, we have seen that the permissibility of transformations is often easier to prove based on an extended auxiliary semantics than based on the standard semantics itself. The same also holds for many types of transformations for languages with operational semantics definitions. This class of transformations includes, in particular, those that are not based on the set of *states* which occur at a program point but on the set of *computations* leading to such a point or beginning there. One example of this is the transformation which removes the *dead* variables and assignments to them.

The trace semantics

It is intuitively easy to understand that the value of a variable v does not have to be stored or computed at a program point P if *every* computation $z_0 \rightarrow \cdots$ starting immediately after P *defines* v before it uses it; in other words, if the value of v is read in the transition $z_n \rightarrow z_{n+1}$ (v is used in the transition $z_n \rightarrow z_{n+1}$), then there exists $i < n$ such that v is assigned a value in the transition $z_i \rightarrow z_{i+1}$ (v is defined in the transition $z_i \rightarrow z_{i+1}$). In this case, we say that *the variable v is dead at the point P*, otherwise, it is said to be *live at the point P*.

Transformations whose permissibility is connected with possible sets of sequences of computations rather than with states can be usefully handled using a semantics extended from the standard semantics, a so-called trace semantics. A mathematical machine $M = (Z, \rightarrow, I, F)$ essentially has two tracing machines, one for the forwards analysis and one for the backwards analysis. The states of these machines are subcomputations of the original machine. The transitions correspond to those of the original machine, but the source state is not 'forgotten' but encoded in the destination state.

The forwards trace machine $fTr(M)$ is given by $(Z^+, \rightarrow_{Tr}, I, \{s \rightarrow f \in Z^+ \mid f \in F\})$. Its set of states consists of the non-empty sequences of states of M, its initial states are inherited from M, and its final states are the sequences of states that end in a terminal state. The transition relation is defined to be the smallest relation with the following property:

$$z \rightarrow z' \implies s \rightarrow z \rightarrow_{Tr} s \rightarrow z \rightarrow z'$$

Here, $s \rightarrow z$ stands for a sequence with initial part s and last element z, while

$s \rightarrow z \rightarrow z' = (s \rightarrow z) \rightarrow z'$ appends z' to this sequence. Thus, if M contains the transition $z \rightarrow z'$, then $fTr(M)$ allows one to continue a computation $s \rightarrow z$ leading to z via the transition to z' to the computation $s \rightarrow z \rightarrow z'$. Thus, the forwards trace machine encodes the initial pieces of M computations in its states.

Analogously, the backwards trace machine $bTr(M)$ is given by $(Z^+, \leftarrow_{Tr}, F, \{\})$. Its initial states are the final states of M, its set of final states is empty; the transition relation is the smallest relation with

$$z \rightarrow z' \Longrightarrow z' \rightarrow s \leftarrow_{Tr} z \rightarrow z' \rightarrow s$$

In other words, $bTr(M)$ encodes the end pieces of M computations in its states. We note that the backwards trace machine for $M = (Z, \rightarrow, I, F)$ is the same as the forwards trace machine for $M_{\leftarrow} = (Z, \leftarrow, F, \{\})$.

Example: live variables

We shall now illustrate the procedure using the example of dataflow analysis of 'live variables'. This analysis is a backwards analysis, that is, we base the abstract interpretation on a backwards trace machine. The example language of Section 10.3.1 is used.

The abstract interpretation represents an end piece of a computation $\sigma = z_n \rightarrow \cdots \rightarrow z_0$ by a pair consisting of a program point P and a set of variables L. The representation is correct, $\sigma \ \delta \ (P, L)$, if z_n has the form (P, vb) and L is a superset of the set of the live variables of σ. Here, the variable v is said to be *live* for σ if it is referenced by reading in a $z_i \rightarrow z_{i-1}$ and v is not defined in $z_j \rightarrow z_{j-1}$ for any $n \geq j > i$.

We shall define the associated abstract machine below. For this we use a non-standard interpretation $[\![\cdot]\!]^{\mathcal{N}}$ for expressions, which interprets an expression by the set of variables occurring in it. This is a safe approximation to the set of the variables which are referenced by reading during the evaluation of the expression. The states of our machine are pairs consisting of a program point and a finite set of variables. Initial states are of the form $(P[\text{result } E \uparrow], \emptyset)$; the set of final states is empty. The abstraction relation between the states of the backwards trace machine and the abstract machine is the relation δ defined above. The transition relation $\Leftarrow$ contains the following transitions:

Assignment

$$(P[v := E \uparrow], L) \Leftarrow (P[\downarrow v := E], (L - \{v\}) \cup [\![E]\!]^{\mathcal{N}})$$

Result statement

$$(P[\text{result } E \uparrow], L) \Leftarrow (P[\downarrow \text{ result } E], L \cup [\![E]\!]^{\mathcal{N}})$$

Conditional statement

$$(P[\text{ if } E \text{ then } \downarrow Q_1 \text{ else } Q_2 \text{ fi}], L)$$
$$\Leftarrow (P[\downarrow \text{ if } E \text{ then } Q_1 \text{ else } Q_2 \text{ fi}], L \cup [\![E]\!]^{\mathcal{N}})$$
$$(P[\text{if } E \text{ then } Q_1 \text{ else } \downarrow Q_2 \text{ fi}], L)$$
$$\Leftarrow (P[\downarrow \text{ if } E \text{ then } Q_1 \text{ else } Q_2 \text{ fi}], L \cup [\![E]\!]^{\mathcal{N}})$$

$(P[\text{if } E \text{ then } Q_1 \text{ else } Q_2 \text{ fi } \uparrow], L)$
$\quad \Leftarrow (P\text{if } E \text{ then } Q_1 \uparrow \text{ else } Q_2 \text{ fi}], L)$
$(P[\text{if } E \text{ then } Q_1 \text{ else } Q_2 \text{ fi } \uparrow], L)$
$\quad \Leftarrow (P[\text{if } E \text{ then } Q_1 \text{ else } Q_2 \text{ fi } \uparrow], L)$

While loop

$(P[\text{while } E \text{ do } \downarrow Q \text{ od}], L)$
$\quad \Leftarrow (P[\downarrow \text{ while } E \text{ do } Q \text{ od}], L \cup \llbracket E \rrbracket^{\mathcal{N}})$
$(P[\text{while } E \text{ do } Q \text{ od } \uparrow], L)$
$\quad \Leftarrow (P[\downarrow \text{ while } E \text{ do } Q \text{ od}], L \cup \llbracket E \rrbracket^{\mathcal{N}})$
$(P[\downarrow \text{ while } E \text{ do } Q \text{ od}], L)$
$\quad \Leftarrow (P[\text{while } E \text{ do } Q \uparrow \text{ od}], L)$

Empty statement sequence

$(P[\varepsilon \uparrow], L) \Leftarrow (P[\downarrow \varepsilon], L)$

Non-trivial statement sequence]

$(P[; (\downarrow S, Q)], L) \Leftarrow (P[\downarrow; (S, Q)], L)$
$(P[; (S, \downarrow Q)], L) \Leftarrow (P[; (S \uparrow, Q)], L)$
$(P[; (S, Q) \uparrow], L) \Leftarrow (P[; (S, Q \uparrow)], L)$

We illustrate the building principle for the above definition using the example of the assignment $v := E$. The concrete machine in the state $(P[\downarrow v := E], vb)$ first evaluates E in the variable binding vb, where all variables occurring in E, that is, $\llbracket E \rrbracket^{\mathcal{N}}$, may be read, and then assigns this value to v. The assignment to v lets v die directly before the assignment; on the other hand, all the variables which were read during the evaluation of E are subsequently live. If L describes the set of live variables at the point $P[v := E \uparrow]$, then $L - \{v\}$ describes the set of live variables immediately before the assignment to v but after evaluation of E, and $(L - \{v\}) \cup \llbracket E \rrbracket^{\mathcal{N}}$ describes the live variables at the point $P[\downarrow v := E]$.

It should be clear to readers that the abstract machine with the given abstraction relation defined above is actually an abstract interpretation of the backwards trace machine. They should also note that, as illustrated by the above example of assignment, the transition relation for the abstract machine can be derived in a quite natural and systematic way from the standard semantics.

Using the standard procedure of the last section, we can transform this machine into a dataflow problem. Since, in the analysis of a program, the live variables that occur belong to the finite set of program variables, the lattice used in the dataflow problem is finite (subsets of the program variables) and thus satisfies the ascending chain condition. The algorithm outlined in the previous section can therefore be used to solve the dataflow problem.

We now demonstrate the procedure using a small example. When the program:

$i := 0;$

while $i < n$ **do**

$$a[i] := b[i];$$
$$i := i + 1$$
od

is compiled, it is typically first translated to a three-address program:

$i := 0;$
while $i < n$ **do**
 $t_1 := i * \mathrm{csize}(b);$
 $t_2 := \mathrm{addr}(b) + t_1;$
 $t_3 := i * \mathrm{csize}(a);$
 $t_4 := \mathrm{addr}(a) + t_3;$
 $\mathrm{mem}(t_4) := \mathrm{mem}(t_2)$
od

The component sizes 'csize(b)' and 'csize(a)' are known to the compiler and equal. The optimization called 'elimination of common subexpressions' leads to the following program:

$i := 0;$
while $i < n$ **do**
 $t_1 := i * \mathrm{csize}(b);$
 $t_2 := \mathrm{addr}(b) + t_1;$
 $t_3 := t_1;$
 $t_4 := \mathrm{addr}(a) + t_1;$
 $\mathrm{mem}(t_4) := \mathrm{mem}(t_2)$
od

We shall now carry out the dataflow analysis of 'live variables' for the temporary variables t_1 to t_4 for this program fragment. The compiler knows (without a special analysis) that these variables are not used outside this program fragment, that is, they are dead at the end of the program fragment. Thus, the initial state for the dataflow analysis is:

$i := 0;$
$\{\}$
while $i < n$ **do**
 $\{\}$
 $t_1 := i * \mathrm{csize}(b);$
 $\{\}$
 $t_2 := \mathrm{addr}(b) + t_1;$
 $\{\}$

$$t_3 := t_1;$$
$$\{\,\}$$
$$t_4 := \mathrm{addr}(a) + t_1;$$
$$\{\,\}$$
$$\mathrm{mem}(t_4) := \mathrm{mem}(t_2)$$
$$\{\,\}$$
od
$$\{\,\}$$

The abstract data is now propagated against the normal control flow. After two steps, we have:

$$\ldots$$
$$\{t_2, t_1\}$$
$$t_4 := \mathrm{addr}(a) + t_1;$$
$$\{t_4, t_2\}$$
$$\mathrm{mem}(t_4) := \mathrm{mem}(t_2)$$
$$\{\,\}$$
od
$$\{\,\}$$

After two more steps, the abstract computation ends in the state:

$$i := 0;$$
$$\{\,\}$$
while $i < n$ **do**
$$\{\,\}$$
$$t_1 := i * \mathrm{csize}(b);$$
$$\{t_1\}$$
$$t_2 := \mathrm{addr}(b) + t_1;$$
$$\{t_2, t_1\}$$
$$t_3 := t_1;$$
$$\{t_2, t_1\}$$
$$t_4 := \mathrm{addr}(a) + t_1;$$
$$\{t_4, t_2\}$$
$$\mathrm{mem}(t_4) := \mathrm{mem}(t_2)$$
$$\{\,\}$$
od
$$\{\,\}$$

We see that following its assignment, t_3 is not alive. Thus, the assignment can be eliminated.

Finally, we include a brief discussion of three dataflow problems which are frequently mentioned in the literature: reaching definitions, available expressions and busy expressions. Each of these problems relates to computations, that is, they relate to a trace semantics. The first two problems are forwards problems, the third problem is a backwards problem.

Example: reaching definitions

A *definition of a variable* v is a program point at which v obtains a value. A definition d of a variable v *reaches a program point* P if there exists a computation $\sigma = z_0 \to \cdots \to z_i = (d, vb_i) \to \cdots \to (P, vb)$ where $z_i \to z_{i+1}$ is the last computation of v, that is, the value of v in the state (P, vb) was assigned at the point d. The information about reaching definitions can be applied to detect indications of program errors, such as the use of uninitialized variables, or to facilitate testing. An abstract interpretation to determine (a superset) of the definitions reaching a program point represents initial fragments of computations by pairs (P, D), where P is a program point and D is a set of definitions. The abstraction relation $\sigma \; \delta \; (P, D)$ is the smallest relation with the property: if $\sigma = z_0 \to \cdots \to (P, vb)$ is a computation and d is the last definition of a variable v in σ, then d in D. The abstract machine is obtained directly from the standard machine. It can be transformed directly into a dataflow problem.

Union and intersection problems

The 'live variables' and 'reaching definitions' problems are so-called *union problems*. The weakening of the information at a program point as a result of newly propagated information involves the formation of a union of the set at the program point and the new set. The larger the set is, the weaker the information represented is. In contrast, the two remaining problems are so-called *intersection problems*. The larger the set is, the sharper the information is. Consequently, the weakening of the information at a program point involves the formation of the intersection of the set at the program point and the newly propagated set.

Example: available expressions

An expression E is said to be *available at a program point* P if *every* computation $\sigma = z_0 \to \cdots \to z_n = (P, vb)$ with $z_0 \in I$ contains a transition $z_i \to z_{i+1}$ in which E is evaluated and subsequently, no further assignments are made to variables on which E depends (in this case we say that E is computed from σ). The associated abstract interpretation represents σ by a pair (P, M), where M is a set of expressions. $\sigma = z_0 \to \cdots \to (P, vb) \; \delta \; (P, M)$ if and only if M is a *subset* of the expressions computed from σ. The definition of the abstract machine can again be derived directly from the trace semantics. When we move to the dataflow problem (from $\Rightarrow$ to $\Rrightarrow$; see page 488) we must remember that in the transition from π to π' the set-theoretic intersection rather than the set-theoretic union is now used. When specifying our initial state for the abstract interpretation, we must also bear in mind that the sharpest possible information is the set of all expressions in the program and not the empty set as in the union problems.

The use of the term 'every computation' characterizes a problem as an intersection problem, while the use of the term 'there exists a computation' characterizes a union problem.

Example: busy expressions

An expression E is said to be *busy* at a program point P, if E is computed by *every* computation end piece $\sigma = (P, vb) \rightarrow \cdots \rightarrow z$ with $z \in F$, before a variable on which E depends is assigned a new value (we say that E is used by σ). The actual values of busy expressions are still required in the remainder of each computation. It can be advantageous to bring its computation forwards or store its value in interim storage or registers, if these are available at the time. The problem is a backwards intersection problem. The abstract interpretation represents end pieces of computations by pairs (P, M), where the M are sets of expressions. $\sigma = (P, vb) \rightarrow \cdots \; \delta \; (P, M)$ is satisfied if and only if M is a *subset* of the expressions used by σ.

Summary

We have presented a general approach which can be used in compilers to obtain algorithmic information about a program: the abstract interpretation. Using this, programs are abstractly interpreted/executed, with abstract data and abstract operations instead of the concrete data/operations. The techniques outlined in this chapter and illustrated by examples can be used to derive appropriate abstract interpretations for numerous optimization transformations in a natural manner.

10.4 Exercises

1:

  (a) Use the nine test to show that the following calculations contain errors:

      (a) $123473 + 22367 + 728493 + 9421 + 72345 = 957199$,

      (b) $24364 * 35111 * 17473 * 42387 = 633566121673376606$.

  (b) The following computation also has an error; the error cannot be detected using the nine test: $81 * 324 = 27216$.

2: Use the interpretation of signs to determine the sign of the following expressions:

  (a) $24493 + (-12(22 + 47))(-24 - 18) + 48\,96$,

  (b) $342 + 247 - 28(32 + 48) + 18$.

3: Formulate the interpretation of signs of Section 10.1.3 as an abstract interpretation of the expression grammar with its standard semantics.

4: In our previous examples, the abstract data domains and semantic functions were always simpler than the data domains and functions of the standard semantics. In this exercise, we meet the opposite case: the interpretation of expressions over intervals. Using the abstract interpretation based on this, the so-called *interval analysis*, compilers attempt to obtain information about the range of values of array indices. Under certain circumstances, this information can be used to avoid runtime checks for violations of array boundaries. The interval interpretation uses intervals in the integers, including the empty set and **Z**, as abstract data domains for expressions. An interval represents an integer z if z lies in the interval.

Formulate an abstract interpretation of the arithmetic expressions with their standard semantics based on this abstraction.

5: Execute the following program with the abstract interpretation of Table 10.4 and check whether the values assigned to r, s and t can be determined at compile time.

$$i := 1; \ j := i + k; \ k := 5; \ r := k * j; \ s := i + k; \ t := r * (s - 6).$$

6: Show that the function $fr: T \to T \to T$ is strict in both arguments:

$$fr = Y(\lambda f.\lambda n_1.\lambda n_2. \text{ if } n_1 = 0 \text{ then } n_2 \text{ else } f \ (n_1 - 1) \ (n_1 * n_2))$$

7:

(a) Show that for types τ_1, the function tr_{τ_1} of the type $\tau := (\tau_1 \to T \to \tau_1) \to \tau_1 \to T \to \tau_1$ defined by:

$$tr_{\tau_1} := Y_\tau(\lambda F.\lambda f.\lambda s.\lambda n. \text{ if } n = 0 \text{ then } s \text{ else } F \ f \ (f \ s \ n) \ (n - 1))$$

is strict in the third argument. Hint: $Y_\tau F = F \ (Y_\tau F)$.

(b) Show that for a function $f : T \to T \to T$ with an abstraction $\overline{f}$ which is strict in the first argument, the function $tr_T \ f$ is strict in the first argument.

(c) Show that for a function $f : \tau_1 \to T \to \tau_1$ with an abstraction $\overline{f}$ which is strict in the first argument, the function $tr_{\tau_1} \ f$ is strict in the first argument. Hint: according to Theorem 10.5 it suffices to prove that $\overline{tr}_{\tau_1} \ \overline{f}$ is strict in the first argument. For this, it is in turn sufficient to prove the following:

$$\overline{tr}_{\tau_1} \ \overline{f} \perp_{\tau_1} \top = \perp_{\tau_1}$$

We have:

$$\overline{tr}_{\tau_1} =: \overline{Y}_\tau \overline{\mathcal{F}} = \bigvee_{n \in \mathbb{N}} \overline{\mathcal{F}}^n \perp_\tau$$

Show that for all n:

$$\overline{\mathcal{F}^n} \, \overline{\mathbb{I}_\tau} \, \overline{f} \, \overline{\mathbb{I}_{\tau_1}} \, \overline{\top} = \overline{\mathbb{I}_{\tau_1}}$$

8:   Carry out the 'constant propagation' dataflow analysis for the program

$$p1 := 20;$$
$$i := 4 * p1; \, j := 0;$$
if $i < 0$ **then** $i := 0;$
$$k := 0;$$
while $k < 2 * i$ **do**
$$\qquad j := j + k;$$
$$\qquad k := k + 1;$$
od;

9:   In Exercise 4 we met the interval interpretation of integers. An abstract interpretation of an imperative language based on this can prove, for many array accesses, that the index lies within the array bounds, whence runtime checking that the array bounds are not infringed becomes superfluous.

(a)   Define an abstract interpretation of the operational semantics of page 486 based on interval interpretation.

(b)   The interval lattice does not satisfy the ascending chain condition. If we use the abstract interpretation to check that static array bounds (that is, those known to the compiler) are not infringed, we do not need to consider any interval with finite bounds outside the maximal array bounds which occur in the given program. The lattice of the remaining intervals is finite and therefore satisfies the ascending chain condition.
Describe this lattice formally. What changes in the abstract interpretation of (a) when you move to this lattice?

(c)   Formulate the interval interpretation as dataflow analysis.

(d)   Analyse the program

$$k := 0;$$
while $k < 10$ **do**
$$\qquad \textbf{if } k < 0 \, \vee \, k > 9 \textbf{ then error};$$
$$\qquad k := k + 1;$$
$$\textbf{od};$$
$$k := 10000;$$

> **while** $k > 0$ **do**
> > **if** $k < 1 \lor k > 10000$ **then error**;
> > $k := k - 1$;
> **od**;

(e)   Formulate an abstract interval interpretation for constructs of the form 'while $v < E$ do' and 'while $v > E$ do', such that in the above example the loops are only passed through once during the abstract execution.

10:

(a)   Carry out the 'live variables' dataflow analysis for the following program:

> $t_0 := 0; i := 0$;
> **while** $i < 10$ **do**
> > $\mathrm{mem}(a + t_0) := \mathrm{mem}(b + t_0)$;
> > $t_0 := t_0 + 4$;
> > $t_1 := t_1 + 4$;
> > $i := i + 4$;
> **od**

(b)   The dataflow analysis of (a) recognizes all variables as live. However, precise consideration of the example shows that the assignment $t_1 := t_1 + 4$ can be eliminated without changing the meaning of the program (if we assume that the t-variables are only used within the given section of the program). To take account of this, we need to move to a sharper concept than that of 'live variables'.

We define the term 'important variable for a computation σ' inductively over σ:

Empty computation. No variable is important for a computation consisting solely of a final state.

Assignment. A variable v is important for a computation

$$(P[\downarrow v' := E], vb) \to (P[v' := E \uparrow], vb)\,\sigma$$

if v is important for σ and $v \neq v'$, or if v' is important for σ and v occurs in E.

Other statements. If $z_1 \to z_2\,\sigma$ is a computation and $z_1 \to z_2$ is not an assignment, then v is important for this computation if v is important for σ

or v is read in the computation step $z_1 \rightarrow z_2$.

The definition was chosen so that assignments to unimportant variables can be eliminated from a computation without altering the result of the computation.

Formulate an abstract interpretation which interprets computation end pieces by the set of their important variables.

(c)   Formulate the dataflow analysis for the abstract interpretation of part (b) and use it to analyse the above program example.

11:   Formulate the dataflow analysis for the abstract interpretations 'available expressions' and 'busy expressions'.

10.5   Literature

Even in early Fortran compilers efficiency-increasing program transformations were executed which required a prior global analysis of the program. Vyssotsky and Wegner (1963) describe such an analyser, which already used an iterative solution for solving dataflow problems. Kildall (1973) discovered the lattice-theoretic foundations of dataflow analysis.

Patrick and Rhadia Cousot represented the well-known dataflow analysis frameworks as an approximation to a standard semantics (1977) and showed how dataflow frameworks and abstract interpretations can be systematically derived (1979).

In addition to the iterative algorithms, which are essentially based on the propagation of information over a fixed graph, a second class of algorithms for solving dataflow problems was developed: the so-called graph algorithms. Graph algorithms are essentially based on a (successive) transformation (simplification) of the graph, the solution of the dataflow problem for the transformed graph and a backwards transformation of the solution for the initial graph. We have not discussed this class of algorithm in further detail here. Those readers who are interested can find further information, for example, in Heckmann (1986) and Muchnick and Jones (1981).

The theory of strictness analysis was developed by Alan Mycroft (1980) for functional programs of the first order. Here, 'first order' means that the arguments of the functions cannot be functions themselves, but must be non-functional data. Mycroft's analysis is an abstract interpretation *par excellence*. In the meantime there are a number of extensions. In Burn *et al.* (1985) the approach is extended to programs of higher order (that is, functions can also be arguments), Maurer (1987) generalizes it to untyped programs, Wadler and Hughes (1987) improve the results for programs (of first order) with data structures. Strictness analysis for typed λ-expressions with unstructured data is due to Burn, Harrin and Abramsky (1985).

The works of Neil Jones, for example Jones (1981, 1987), contain applications of the abstract interpretation of programs with recursive data structures.

The book by Abramsky and Hankin (1987) contains a number of contributions on the abstract interpretation of functional and logic languages.

11

Trees: pattern matching and parsing[†]

- Program transformations

- Code selection

- The pattern-matching problem

- The tree-parsing problem

- Finite tree automata

- Generation of pattern matchers

- Generation of tree parsers

- Tree automata with costs

- Implementation

- Exercises

- Literature

[†] This chapter was written jointly with Christian Ferdinand and Helmut Seidl

In this chapter we discuss a number of problems which are solved using very closely related methods. These all have something to do with the analysis of trees. In the same way that the syntax analysis for words was handled by appropriate word automata in Chapter 7, these methods will now be generalized to trees. The type of automaton used for this is the finite tree automaton.

We have already seen in Chapter 9 that finite tree automata can be used in the strategic phase of attribute evaluation. We presented one tree automaton which computes the lower characteristic dependency graphs and a second which computes the upper characteristic graphs. Another automaton was used to determine the ordered partitions on attribute occurrences. These computations are necessary when one implements powerful classes of grammars such as that of absolutely non-circular grammars.

This chapter has the following structure. First we describe the areas in which pattern matching in trees and tree parsing are applied, namely the implementation of program transformations and code selection. Then we describe how these tasks can be formalized and solved using tree automata.

11.1 Program transformations

We use the term program transformations to refer to the compilation or transformation of intermediate representations of programs. Programs are represented here as trees, which are usually decorated with semantic information.

A program transformation is described by a set of tree transformation rules. In the simplest case, each such rule consists of two **patterns** (p, e), that is, terms with variables at the leaves. Such a rule is usually written as $p \Longrightarrow e$. p is called the **input pattern** and e the **output pattern** or the **expression** of the rule. What it means for a pattern to **match** a (sub)tree t is formally described in Section 11.3. Intuitively, this means that the non-variable parts of the pattern must agree with the tree in terms of the labelling of the nodes, the number of children and the ordering of the subtrees. Here, the variables in the pattern are bound to the subtrees of T corresponding to their position in the pattern. The pattern of Figure 11.1(a) with the variables T_1, T_2 and T_3 matches the tree in Figure 11.1(b). The binding for T_1, T_2 and T_3 is shown in Figure 1.11(c).

Thus, the input pattern p describes the (syntactic) condition for the rule to be applicable. The output pattern e indicates how the matched subtree should be rebuilt. Here, the subtree matched by t is cut out and e inserted, where the variables in e are replaced according to their binding.

Example 11.1 The rule of Figure 11.2(a) applied to the tree of Figure 11.1(b) produces the tree in Figure 11.2(b). □

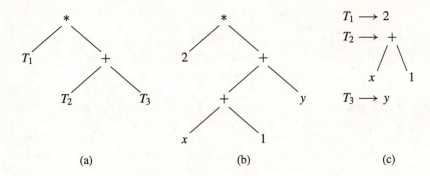

Figure 11.1 (a) A pattern, (b) a tree matched by this pattern and (c) the binding for the pattern variables produced by the match.

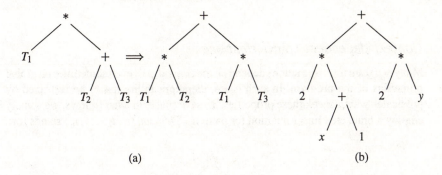

Figure 11.2 (a) A transformation rule and (b) a transformed tree.

11.1.1 Efficiency-increasing program transformations

Many compilers transform the programs they compile to generate more efficient target programs. Since these transformations are applied to the representation of the program as a tree they are called tree transformations.

Algebraic transformations

Algebraic transformations can be formulated as tree transformations. They can be used to simplify arithmetic expressions, such as those that often occur in the sequence of automatic transformations. Figure 11.3 illustrates several rules for algebraic transformation.

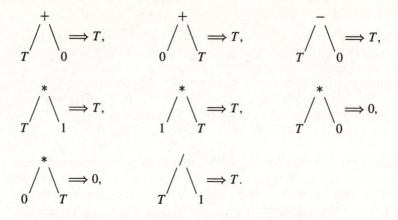

Figure 11.3 Algebraic transformation.

Context-dependent transformations

Many program transformations depend on the context, and even sometimes on global properties of the program. In such cases, the applicability has to be restricted by predicates which check these properties. To save space, in what follows, we usually employ a bracketed linear notation for patterns. Thus, $op\,(t_1, t_2, \ldots, t_n)$ stands for:

Elimination of useless assignments

$assign\,(X, E)$ **where** $notlive\,(X) \Longrightarrow skip$

This transformation eliminates assignments to variables which are not live. It requires information about the uses of the variable X on paths leading from this assignment.

Abstract interpretation is used to compute this information. Assuming powerful generators are used, this can be implemented by attribute grammars. Then the required information is available locally in attributes. A successful transformation must be followed by a new analysis of the transformed program, since the information previously computed may no longer be valid. This is carried out by efficient, incrementally operating attribute evaluators which generate a new consistent state by a minimal recalculation of the attribute instances involved.

We now describe a number of other traditional program transformations.

Movement of loop-invariant computations

If an expression E in a loop only contains variables which are not altered in the loop and its evaluation has no side effects, then the expression can be taken out of the loop and placed before it. An assignment statement $t := E$ is inserted, where t is a new auxiliary variable. In the loop this occurrence of E is replaced by t.

$$S_1.[while\,(B,\,S_3.[assign\,(X,\,E)].S_4)].S_2 \; \textbf{where}\; is\_invar\,(E)$$
$$\Longrightarrow S_1.[assign\,(t,\,E),\; while\,(B,\,S_3.[assign\,(X,\,t)].S_4)].S_2$$

This rule is an example of the complex patterns which may be used in various special transformation languages. It should be read as follows: look for a *while* loop in a statement list, whose body contains an assignment statement with an invariant right side. Introduce a new assignment of this invariant right side E to a new auxiliary variable t before the loop and replace this occurrence of E within the loop by t. Here [...] denotes lists and '.' stands for list concatenation. Let p be a pattern. $S_1.[p].S_2$ 'matches' lists containing an element which is matched by p. Here, S_1 is a variable which is bound to the sublist up to this element and S_2 is a variable which is bound to the sublist from this element.

Folding of constants

In Chapter 10, 'Abstract Interpretation', we described the so-called propagation of constants. For each statement, this computes the variables that have the same statically known value for every execution. If this analysis determines these values for variables in an expression, it may be possible to 'fold' subexpressions, that is, calculate them at compile time. In what follows, conditions may also be folded away.

$$var\,(X)\; \textbf{where}\; isconst\,(X) \Longrightarrow value\,(X)$$
$$\mathrm{plus}(C_1,\,C_2) \Longrightarrow C_1 + C_2 \quad (\text{sum evaluated at compile time}),\; \text{etc.}$$
$$\mathrm{if}\,(true,\,S_1,\,S_2) \Longrightarrow S_1$$
$$\mathrm{if}\,(false,\,S_1,\,S_2) \Longrightarrow S_2$$
$$\mathrm{while}\,(true,\,S) \Longrightarrow \mathrm{forever}\,(S)$$
$$\mathrm{while}\,(false,\,S) \Longrightarrow \mathrm{skip}$$

11.1.2   Standardizing transformations

Some compiler tasks can be made easier if the program representation is brought to a 'standard form'. By this we mean:

- the transformation of different representations of a construct into a selected form and

- the replacement of ambiguous (syntactic) terms by unique representations using context information.

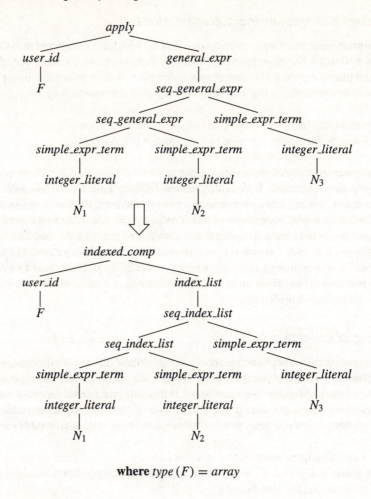

where *type* (*F*) = *array*

Figure 11.4   A standardizing transformation for Ada.

One example of the first standardization is the replacement of all **where** terms by **let** terms in functional programs. An example of the second type of standardization is shown in Figure 11.4. This transformation stems from the description of an Ada front end. A term $F(E_1, \ldots, E_n)$ in an Ada program may have very many different meanings; for example, it may be a procedure call, a function call, an indexed variable and so on. This front end represents such constructs in the abstract syntax as *apply* terms. The rule in Figure 11.4 uses the context information that '*F*' in '$F(1, 2, 3)$' is the name of a three-dimensional array to generate a term for an indexed variable from it.

11.1.3   The underlying problem

The preceding examples have each exhibited a set of rules for certain, efficiency-increasing or standardizing program transformations. If one wishes to apply these transformations to a given program one first has to determine which rules are applicable at which nodes. This is the problem of **pattern matching on trees**.

Similar problems arise when an interactive system supports the programmer in programming work. A set of semantics-preserving transformation rules can lead the programmer from a specification of the program to a more efficient version of it. A pattern matcher will determine which transformation rules are applicable to the program parts worked on by the programmer.

Finite tree automata can usefully be employed for pattern matching on trees. Here, we assume that a finite set of patterns can be preprocessed, that is, before the trees to which they will be applied are available. The preprocessing generates a finite automaton from the patterns, which can localize occurrences of patterns efficiently. Since it is assumed that the same set of patterns is used frequently, an amortization of the necessary preprocessing time over many applications can be expected.

11.2   Code selection

In code generation, we begin with an intermediate representation IR of the program to be compiled, which is constructed in a compiler from the compilation phases preceding code generation. This intermediate representation can be viewed as code for an **abstract machine**. Code generation has the task of converting the intermediate representation into an as efficient as possible instruction sequence for the target machine.

Code selection, that is, the choice of the instructions, together with register allocation and instruction scheduling (for processors with pipeline architectures), is one of the important subtasks of code generation. It plays a special role for the so-called CISC (Complex Instruction Set Computer) machines, in which there are usually several sensible ways of generating code for a program fragment.

Example 11.2
Let us consider the simplest representative of the Motorola 680x0 series, the 68000. This processor has 8 data registers, 8 address registers and a large number of different types of addressing, such as:

- D_n **Data register direct:** accesses the contents of a data register.

- A_n **Address register direct:** accesses the contents of an address register.

- (A_n) **Address register indirect:** accesses a storage location whose address is stored in an address register.

- $d(A_n)$ **Address register indirect with address distance value:** accesses a storage location whose address is given by the sum of the contents of the address register A_n and the 16-bit constant d.

- $d(A_n, I_x)$ **Address register indirect with index and address distance value:** accesses a storage location whose address is given as follows. The contents of the index register I_x is added to the contents of the address register A_n (also called the base register). The result is increased by the 8-bit distance value d.
  Both data registers and address registers may be used as index registers.

- x **Absolute short:** accesses a storage location whose address is given by the 16-bit constant x.

- x **Absolute long:** accesses a storage location whose address is given by the 32-bit constant x.

- #x **Direct:** stands for the constant x.

The MC68000 is a so-called two-address machine, in other words at most two addresses are used in any one instruction. For example, the instruction

ADD D1, D2

adds the contents of the data registers D1 and D2 and stores the result in the data register D2.

Most MC68000 instructions can be applied to bytes, words (two bytes) and double words (four bytes). This is described in the assembler notation here by appending .B, .W and .L, where .W may be omitted.

The execution time for any instruction is given (except for a few exceptions such as the so-called quick instructions) by the sum of the execution time for the operation described by the instruction and the execution time for addressing the operands, that is, the computation of the so-called effective address.

The instruction

MOVE.B 8(A1, D1.W), D5

loads one byte into the lower quarter of the data register D5. The address of the operand is obtained as follows: the lower half of the contents of D1 and the constant 8 are added to the contents of the base register A1. The execution time for this instruction is obtained from the time to carry out the operation itself (4) and the times for the addressing (10). If the cost of an instruction is measured in terms of execution time, that is, the number of processor cycles, then the cost of this instruction is 14.

An alternative code sequence without index addressing and address distance values would be:

Table 11.1 Execution times for computation of the effective address (machine cycles).

	Type of addressing	Byte, Word	Double word
D_n	Data register direct	0	0
A_n	Address register direct	0	0
(A_n)	Address register indirect	4	8
$d(A_n)$	Address register indirect with address distance value	8	12
$d(A_n, I_x)$	Address register indirect with index and address distance value	10	14
x	Absolute short	8	12
x	Absolute long	12	16
$\#x$	Direct	4	8

```
ADDA     #8, A1      Cost: 16
ADDA     D1.W, A1    Cost: 8
MOVE.B   (A1), D5    Cost: 8
         with total cost 32
```

Another alternative is:

```
ADDA     D1.W, A1    Cost: 8
MOVE.B   8(A1), D5   Cost: 12
         with total cost 20
```

These two alternative code sequences only behave equivalently on the memory and on the result register D5. The final states differ in the condition code and the register A1. Thus, the code selector must ensure that the context allows the particular code sequence chosen.

Let us consider the compilation of the Pascal statement

```
b := 2 + a[i]
```

where b and i are integer variables and a is an array [0 .. 1] of integer. The variable b can be accessed via a frame pointer A5 with relative address 4, a can be accessed with 8 and i can be accessed with 6.

One possible code sequence would be:

MOVE	6(A5), D1	Cost 12
ADD	D1, D1	Cost 4
MOVE	8(A5,D1), D2	Cost 14
ADDQ	#2, D2	Cost 4
MOVE	D2, 4(A5)	Cost 12
	with total cost 46	

An alternative code sequence which does not use complicated forms of addressing would be:

MOVE.L	A5, A1	Cost 4
ADDA.L	#6, A1	Cost 12
MOVE	(A1), D1	Cost 8
MULU	#2, D1	Cost 44
MOVE.L	A5, A2	Cost 4
ADDA.L	#8, A2	Cost 12
ADDA.L	D1, A2	Cost 8
MOVE	(A2), D2	Cost 8
ADDQ	#2, D2	Cost 4
MOVE.L	A5, A3	Cost 4
ADDA.L	#4, A3	Cost 12
MOVE	D2, (A3)	Cost 8
	with total cost 128	

Here, the address expressions are considered as arithmetic expressions and compiled into sequences of arithmetic instructions. The two code sequences only behave equivalently with respect to the memory.

These examples show the need for careful code selection for CISC architectures. □

The use of code-selector generators can significantly reduce the cost of producing a code generator for a new machine.

Code-selector generators require a machine description as input. One possibility is to describe machine instructions by the rules of a regular tree grammar. Here, the right side of a rule describes the 'meaning' of an instruction (see Figure 11.5). The terminal symbols, that is, the node labels written in lower case, stand for (sub)operations which the instruction executes. Nonterminals designate locations or classes of resources, such as the different register types. The nonterminal on the left side of a rule indicates where (or in which class of resources) the result of the instruction will be stored. Thus, the terminals are node labels of the intermediate program representation, while the nonterminals denote resources of the target machine.

IR trees for expressions can be derived from such a *machine grammar*.

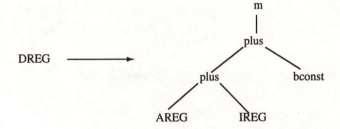

$$DREG \rightarrow m(plus(plus(AREG, IREG), bconst))$$

Figure 11.5   Instruction MOVE $d(A_n, I_x), D_m$.

The derivation tree for an IR tree describes a possible way of generating code for the associated expression. Thus, the choice of instructions reduces to the problem of analysing IR trees according to a machine grammar. As a rule, the machine grammar is ambiguous. In this case, there may be several derivation trees for the same expression, which represent different sequences of instructions. To choose a particularly advantageous sequence of instructions, we associate the rules with **costs**, which might, for example, indicate the number of machine cycles for an instruction. Thus, a derivation tree (or a sequence of instructions) with the lowest cost can be chosen. However, for some processors (for example, Motorola 68020) the number of machine cycles required cannot be precisely predicted beforehand because it depends on the execution context. Here, one has to work with approximations.

For common CISC processors the number of combinations of instructions, addressing modes and word lengths is usually very large. To avoid having to supply rules with costs for all possible combinations, new nonterminals and rules, provided with their own costs, are frequently introduced for a combination of addressing modes and operand and result lengths. These new nonterminals can then be used in the description of the instructions.

To extend the usage of code selection beyond expression trees, branching and assignment operators may also be permitted root nodes of trees. Branches and assignments do not provide a 'result' in the sense described above, so that a *dummy* nonterminal is used on the left side of rules describing these instructions. This nonterminal does not appear on the right side of any rule and represents, so to speak, a starting nonterminal for branches and assignments.

11.3   The pattern-matching problem

Here and in the following sections we shall present fundamental principles underlying a description of the pattern-matching problem and the tree-parsing

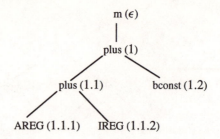

Figure 11.6   Tree with node addresses.

problem. First we formally define what we mean by a tree and what it means for a
pattern to match a tree. Then we introduce the concepts of regular tree grammars
and finite tree automata.

Definition 11.1 (homogeneous tree language)
An **alphabet with an arity function** is a finite set of operators Σ (also called
constructors in functional languages) together with a function $\rho : \Sigma \to \mathbb{N}_0$, the
arity function. We write Σ_k for $\{a \in \Sigma \mid \rho(a) = k\}$. The **homogeneous tree
language** over Σ is the following inductively defined set $B(\Sigma)$:

- $a \in B(\Sigma)$ for all $a \in \Sigma_0$;
- If $b_1, \ldots, b_k$ in $B(\Sigma)$ and $f \in \Sigma_k$, then $f(b_1, \ldots, b_k) \in B(\Sigma)$.

When we name nodes in trees we use the so-called Dewey notation. Thus, nodes are
words over $\mathbb{N}$. The root is ϵ, the empty word over $\mathbb{N}$; if the node n has k children,
these are the nodes $n.1, n.2, \ldots, n.k$ (see Figure 11.6). The **subtree** t/n of t at the
node n is defined by $t/\epsilon = t$ and $t/n = t_j/n'$ if $t = a(t_1, \ldots, t_k)$ and $n = j.n'$. The
label of the node n in the tree t is the operator at the root of t/n.   □

The tree languages thus defined are said to be homogeneous since, apart
from respect for the arity function, they impose no other restrictions on the structure
of trees. Any subtree of $B(\Sigma)$ can be used at any argument position of an operator.

Definition 11.2 (pattern)
Suppose we are also given an infinite set of variables V. We assign them arity 0. An
element of $B(\Sigma \cup V)$ is called a **pattern** over Σ. A pattern is said to be **linear**, if
no variable occurs in it more than once.   □

Example 11.3
Suppose $\Sigma = \{a, cons, nil\}$ with $\rho(a) = \rho(nil) = 0$, $\rho(cons) = 2$. The following
are trees over Σ, that is, elements of the tree language over Σ: a, $cons(nil, nil)$,

$cons(cons(a, nil), nil)$.

      Let $V = \{X\}$. Then X, $cons(nil, X)$ and $cons(X, nil)$ are patterns over Σ.

                                                                         □

Definition 11.3 (substitution)

A **substitution** Θ is a mapping, which assigns variables to patterns, $\Theta : V \rightarrow B(\Sigma \cup V)$. Θ is extended to a mapping $\Theta : B(\Sigma \cup V) \rightarrow B(\Sigma \cup V)$, which replaces variables in patterns, by defining $t\Theta = x\Theta$, if $t = x \in V$ and $t\Theta = a(t_1\Theta, \ldots, t_k\Theta)$ if $t = a(t_1, \ldots, t_k)$ (traditionally the application of a substitution Θ to a pattern t is written as $t\Theta$). We also write $t\Theta = t\{x_1/t_1, \ldots, x_k/t_k\}$, if the variables occurring in t are a subset of $\{x_1, \ldots, x_k\}$ and $x_j\Theta = t_j$ for all j.   □

Example 11.4

The substitution $\{X/a, Y/cons(nil, a)\}$, applied to the pattern $cons(X, Y)$, gives the tree $cons(a, cons(nil, a))$.   □

Definition 11.4 (pattern matches)

A pattern $\tau \in B(\Sigma \cup V)$ with variables $x_1, \ldots, x_k$ **matches** a tree t, if there exist trees $t_1, \ldots, t_k$ in $B(\Sigma)$ such that $t = \tau\{x_1/t_1, \ldots, x_k/t_k\}$. We also say that τ **matches** t **with the substitution** $\{x_1/t_1, \ldots, x_k/t_k\}$.   □

Example 11.5

The pattern $cons(X, nil)$ matches the tree $cons(cons(a, nil), nil)$ with the substitution $\{X/cons(a, nil)\}$ at the root and with the substitution $\{X/a\}$ at node 1.   □

Definition 11.5 (pattern-matching problem)

An instance of the **pattern-matching problem** consists of a finite set of patterns $T = \{\tau_1, \ldots, \tau_k\} \subseteq B(\Sigma \cup V)$ and an input tree $t \in B(\Sigma)$. The **solution** of the pattern-matching problem for this instance is the set of all pairs (n, τ_i), such that the pattern τ_i matches the subtree t/n. We define a **tree pattern matcher** for T to be a mechanism which given as input a tree $t \in B(\Sigma)$ supplies the solution of the pattern-matching problem for (T, t). A **pattern-matching generator** then constructs a pattern matcher for every set of patterns T.   □

Example 11.6

Suppose we are given the patterns $\tau_1 = cons(X, nil)$ and $\tau_2 = cons(a, X)$ and the input tree $t = cons(cons(a, nil), nil)$. Then the solution of the instance of the pattern-matching problem $(\{\tau_1, \tau_2\}, t)$ is the set $\{(\varepsilon, \tau_1), (1, \tau_1), (1, \tau_2)\}$.   □

The algorithms for generating pattern matchers described here are limited to the processing of patterns which do not contain any repeated occurrences of a variable, so-called **linear** patterns. The pattern-matching problem for patterns with multiple occurrences of variables requires tests to determine whether the subtrees matched by the different occurrences of variables are the same. There are two ways of solving the pattern-matching problem for such non-linear patterns. First, if necessary, a test for equality of subtrees can be used. However, this can be very expensive, since the same subtrees may have to be visited several times. The second way involves, as it were, executing all possible tests for equality beforehand. For this, the input tree is represented as a directed acyclic graph containing precisely one node for each possible subtree. For a finite alphabet, this so-called **subtree graph** can be computed in linear time.

11.4 The tree-parsing problem

In Chapter 7, 'Lexical Analysis', and Chapter 8, 'Syntax Analysis', we used regular expressions and context-free grammars to describe languages of character strings. Here, we use regular tree grammars to describe tree languages.

Definition 11.6 (regular tree grammars)
A **regular tree grammar** G is a quadruple (N, Σ, P, S). Here,

- N is a finite set of **nonterminals**,
- Σ is an alphabet (with arity function) of **terminals** (the term terminal was chosen because of the analogy with the context-free case; above, the terminals were called operators),
- P is a finite set of **rules** of the form $X \to s$ with $X \in N$ and $s \in B(\Sigma \cup N)$,
- $S \in N$ is the start symbol.

Let $p : X \to s$ be a rule in P. p is called a **chain rule**, if $s \in N$; otherwise p is called a **non-chain rule**. p is of **type** $(X_1, \ldots, X_k) \to X$, if the jth occurrence of a nonterminal in s counted from the left is the nonterminal X_j. We define the pattern $\tilde{s}$ to be the pattern in $B(\Sigma \cup \{x_1, \ldots, x_k\})$ obtained from s by replacing the nonterminal X_j everywhere by the variable x_j. □

A derivation tree for a tree t describes how t can be produced or derived from the tree grammar G (see Figure 11.7). Every node of a derivation tree stands for an 'application' of a rule. Derivation trees largely correspond to syntax trees for word grammars in Chapter 8.

Definition 11.7 (derivation tree)
An X-**derivation tree** for a tree $t \in B(\Sigma \cup N)$ is a tree $\psi \in B(P \cup N)$ which satisfies the following conditions:

- If $\psi \in N$ then $\psi = X = t$.
- If $\psi \notin N$ then $\psi = p(\psi_1, \ldots, \psi_k)$ for a rule $p : X \to s \in P$ of the type $(X_1, \ldots, X_k) \to X$, such that $t = \tilde{s}\{x_1/t_1, \ldots, x_k/t_k\}$ and ψ_j are the X_j derivation trees for the trees t_j. □

We define the **language** generated according to $G = (N, \Sigma, P, S)$ to be $L(G) = \{t \in B(\Sigma) \mid \exists \psi \in B(P \cup N) : \psi \text{ is an } S\text{-derivation tree for } t\}$.

Example 11.7

Suppose G_1 is the regular tree grammar (N_1, Σ, P_1, L); $\Sigma = \{a, cons, nil\}$ with $\rho(a) = \rho(nil) = 0$, $\rho(cons) = 2$, $N_1 = \{E, L\}$ and

$$P_1 = \{ \begin{array}{lll} L & \to & nil, \\ L & \to & cons(E, L), \\ E & \to & a\} \end{array}$$

$L(G_1)$ is equal to the set of the linear lists of a's including the empty list, that is, $L(G_1) = \{nil, cons(a, nil), cons(a, cons(a, nil)), \ldots\}$.   □

Example 11.8

Suppose G_m is the regular tree grammar (N_m, Σ, P_m, REG); $\Sigma = \{const, m, plus, REG\}$ with $\rho(const) = 0$; $\rho(m) = 1$, $\rho(plus) = 2$, $N_m = \{REG\}$ and

$$P_m = \{ \begin{array}{llll} addmc: & REG & \to & plus(m(const), REG), \\ addm: & REG & \to & plus(m(REG), REG), \\ add: & REG & \to & plus(REG, REG), \\ ldmc: & REG & \to & m(const), \\ ldc: & REG & \to & const, \\ ld: & REG & \to & REG\} \end{array}$$

P_m describes a section of an instruction set for a simple processor, where the rules are labelled with the names of the instructions described. The first three rules stand for addition instructions, which add

- the contents of a storage location whose address is given by a constant,
- the contents of a storage location whose address is in the register, or
- the contents of a register, respectively,

to the contents of a register and store the result in a register.

The last three rules describe load instructions which load

- the contents of a storage location whose address is given by a constant,
- a constant, or
- the contents of a register, respectively,

into a register.

Figure 11.7 shows a tree of $L(G_m)$ and two possible derivation trees.   □

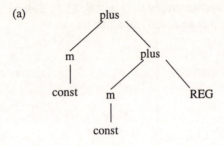

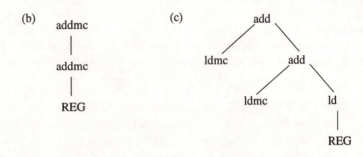

Figure 11.7   (a) A tree for the grammar of Example 11.8 and (b, c) two possible derivation trees.

Definition 11.8 (tree-parsing problem)
An instance of the **tree-parsing problem** consists of a regular tree grammar G and a tree t. The solution of this instance of the tree-parsing problem is the set of all derivation trees of G for t (or a representation thereof). We define a **tree parser** for G to be a mechanism which provides the solution for the instance (G, t) of the tree-parsing problem for every tree $t \in B(\Sigma)$. Finally, a **tree-parser generator** constructs a tree parser for every regular tree grammar G.   □

The languages for regular tree grammars are said to be regular, because they are closely related to regular languages of words. Thus, the sequences of symbols along paths form regular (word) languages. Like regular word languages, regular tree languages, that is, the languages generated by regular tree grammars, are closed under intersection, union and the taking of complements. Since emptiness is decidable, it also follows that the problem of whether a regular tree language is contained in another is decidable.

We shall now reduce the problem of the generation of pattern matchers and tree parsers to the construction of finite tree automata.

11.5   Finite tree automata

We met finite automata in Chapter 7, where they were used for lexical analysis. A finite automaton begins in a starting state and reads the input word from left to right, making a transition for every character according to the transition relation.

In contrast, a finite tree automaton reads trees. For trees, there is no specific a priori order in which the nodes should be visited. The transition relation δ describes the relationship between the state at a node, the label of this node and the states at the children. Thus, a transition for a k-ary symbol a has the form $(q, a, q_1 \ldots q_k)$, where q is the state at the node labelled by a and $q_1 \ldots q_k$ is the sequence of states at the children.

There are two strategies for traversing an input tree:

- **Bottom-up:** For every node a state is chosen in accordance with a transition from the transition relation δ, which matches the states already calculated at the children of the node. There are no children at the leaves; consequently, we can choose a state directly in accordance with δ here.

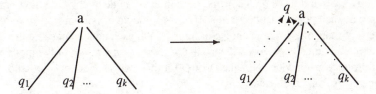

- **Top-down:** A transition from δ matching the state for a node is chosen in order to determine the states for the children. Since the root has no predecessors, we can start with an 'appropriate' state here.

The bottom-up strategy can be implemented using a post-order depth-first traversal through the input tree, the top-down strategy with a pre-order depth-first traversal.

Our definition of a finite tree automaton takes no account of any predefined traversal strategy. This is because all strategies are equivalent (at least for non-deterministic automata). We use deterministic bottom-up automata to solve our pattern-matching and tree-parsing problems and that of their implementation.

Definition 11.9 (finite tree automaton)
A **finite tree automaton** A is a 4-tuple $A = (Q, \Sigma, \delta, Q_F)$. Here

- Q is a finite set of states,
- $Q_F \subseteq Q$ is the set of the final states,
- Σ is the input alphabet (with arity function) and
- $\delta \subseteq \bigcup_{j \geq 0} Q \times \Sigma_j \times Q^j$ is the set of the transitions.

The automaton A is said to be **top-down deterministic** if there is precisely one final state and for every $a \in \Sigma_k$ and every state q there is at most one transition $(q, a, q_1 \ldots q_k) \in \delta$. The automaton A is said to be **bottom-up deterministic** if for every $a \in \Sigma_k$ and every sequence of states $q_1, \ldots, q_k$ there is at most one transition $(q, a, q_1 \ldots q_k) \in \delta$. In this case, δ can also be written as a partial function:

- $\delta : \bigcup_{j \geq 0} \Sigma_j \times Q^j \to Q$ □

During the processing of an input tree t, A traverses the tree (for example, in a depth-first traversal) and takes on a specific state in every node of t, where the transition chosen at each node must be from δ. If A is top-down or bottom-up deterministic, there is at most one possible choice of transition in each node, otherwise there may be more. Technically, we describe such a process as *annotation* of the input tree t. We introduce an extended alphabet $\Sigma \times Q$ for this, whose operators consist of *pairs* of operators from Σ and states from Q.

Definition 11.10 (computation)
Let $\Sigma \times Q$ be the alphabet $\{\langle a, q \rangle \mid a \in \Sigma, \ q \in Q\}$, where $\langle a, q \rangle$ has the same arity as a. We define a q-**computation** ϕ of the finite automaton A on an input tree $t = a(t_1, \ldots, t_m)$ inductively over the structure of t as a tree $\langle a, q \rangle (\phi_1, \ldots, \phi_m) \in B(\Sigma \times Q)$, where the ϕ_j are q_j-computations for the subtrees t_j, $j = 1, \ldots, m$ and $(q, a, q_1 \ldots q_m)$ is a transition from δ. If $q \in Q_F$, then ϕ is said to be **accepting**. The language $L(A)$ of the trees accepted by A consists of all trees for which there exists an accepting computation. A state (transition) is said to be **redundant** if it does not occur in any accepting computation of A.   □

Redundant states and transitions can be omitted without affecting the 'behaviour' of the automaton.

Example 11.9
Let $A_b = (Q_b, \Sigma_b, \delta_b, Q_{F,b})$ be the following bottom-up deterministic finite tree automaton with the states $Q_b = \{q_g, q_u\}$, the alphabet $\Sigma_{b,0} = \{c\}$ and $\Sigma_{b,2} = \{a\}$, the final states $Q_{F,b} = \{q_g\}$ and the transitions:

$$\delta_b = \{ \quad (q_u, c)$$
$$(q_g, a, q_u, q_u)$$

$$(q_u, a, q_g, q_u)$$
$$(q_u, a, q_u, q_g)$$
$$(q_g, a, q_g, q_g)\}$$

A_b accepts those trees of the homogeneous tree language over Σ_b, which contain an even number of occurrences of c.

The following figure shows (a) a tree and (b) the associated computation of A_b.

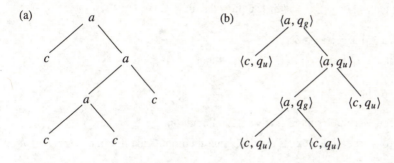

(a)   (b)

$\square$

For both bottom-up and top-down deterministic automata there is at most one computation for each tree, whence there is at most one state at each node.

In the theory of tree automata distinction is sometimes made not only between deterministic but also between non-deterministic bottom-up and top-down tree automata. In fact, such a non-deterministic bottom-up tree automaton can be converted directly into an 'equivalent' non-deterministic top-down tree automaton, and conversely. Thus, the above distinction does not arise in our representation. Moreover, as we shall see in what follows, for every non-deterministic tree automaton it is possible to construct a bottom-up deterministic tree automaton. But it is interesting that not every bottom-up deterministic tree automaton has an equivalent top-down deterministic tree automaton. For example, the language of the automaton of Example 11.9 cannot be recognized in a deterministic top-down manner.

In what follows, we shall refer to bottom-up deterministic tree automata as **deterministic** tree automata, for short. For deterministic tree automata we extend the partial function δ to a partial function $\delta : B(\Sigma) \to Q$ by $\delta(t) = \delta(a, \delta(t_1) \dots \delta(t_k))$, if $t = a(t_1, \dots, t_k)$. It can be shown by induction over the structure of t that $\delta(t) = q$ if and only if there exists a q computation for t.

11.6 Generation of pattern matchers

Suppose τ is a linear pattern in $B(\Sigma \cup V)$. We would like to construct a (possibly non-deterministic) finite tree automaton A_τ, which recognizes whether the pattern

τ matches a given input tree. Intuitively, A_τ works as follows. If a pattern matches a subtree then there is a region 'near' the root of the subtree where the pattern 'covers' the subtree precisely, that is, a region where the operators of the subtree correspond precisely to the operators of the pattern. Outside this region, A_τ takes on an unspecific state $\perp$; within this region the state should denote exactly the subpattern which matches the present node. Since (here), we are not concerned with the precise numbering of the variables, we replace all the variables in τ by $\perp$ ('a variable matches everything'). Therefore, we suppose that $\tau \in B(\Sigma \cup \{\perp\})$.

Then we define $A_\tau = (Q_\tau, \Sigma, \delta_\tau, Q_{\tau,F})$, where $Q_\tau = \{s \mid s \text{ subtree of } \tau\} \cup \{\perp\}$, $Q_{\tau,F} = \{\tau\}$ and δ_τ is defined as follows:

- $(\perp, a, \perp \ldots \perp) \in \delta_\tau$;
- if $s \in Q_\tau$ and $s = a(s_1, \ldots, s_k)$, then $(s, a, s_1 \ldots s_k) \in \delta_\tau$.

Clearly, we have:

(1) for every tree t there exists a $\perp$-computation;

(2) for a tree t there exists precisely one τ-computation if τ matches t.

The example can be easily generalized to the case of a set of linear patterns $T = \{\tau_1, \ldots, \tau_n\}$, for which we again assume without loss of generality that all variables that occur are replaced by the symbol $\perp$. As the set of the states for our automaton A_T we choose $Q_T = \bigcup_{j=1}^{n} Q_{\tau_j}$ with $Q_{T,F} = T$, while the text of the definition of δ_τ is unchanged (although the resulting set of the transitions does of course change).

Example 11.10

Suppose $\Sigma_2 = \{a\}$, $\Sigma_0 = \{b, c\}$ and $T = \{\tau_1, \tau_2\}$ with $\tau_1 = a(a(X_1, X_2), b)$ and $\tau_2 = a(b, X_3)$. Then $A_T = (Q_T, \Sigma, \delta_T, Q_{T,F})$ with $Q_T = \{p_1, p_2, p_3, p_4, p_5\}$ where

$$p_1 = a(a(\perp, \perp), b) \qquad p_2 = a(b, \perp)$$
$$p_3 = a(\perp, \perp) \qquad p_4 = b$$
$$p_5 = \perp$$
$$Q_{T,F} = \{p_1, p_2\}$$

$\delta_T = \{($	$\perp,$	$a,$	$\perp \ \perp$	$),$
$($	$\perp,$	$b,$	ϵ	$),$
$($	$\perp,$	$c,$	ϵ	$),$
$($	$a(a(\perp, \perp), b),$	$a,$	$a(\perp, \perp) \ b$	$),$
$($	$a(b, \perp),$	$a,$	$b \ \perp$	$),$
$($	$a(\perp, \perp),$	$a,$	$\perp \ \perp$	$),$
$($	$b,$	$b,$	ϵ	$)\}$

□

If we wish to find out which patterns match an input tree t at the root, we have to generate an overview of all possible computations of A_T on t. This is done using the **subset construction** for tree automata. The subset construction constructs an equivalent deterministic tree automaton from a non-deterministic tree automaton, which, so to speak, simulates all possible computations of the non-deterministic tree automaton in parallel. The construction corresponds to a simplified version of the NFA $\rightarrow$ DFA algorithm for word automata of Chapter 7.

Definition 11.11 (subset construction I)
Let $A = (Q, \Sigma, \delta, Q_F)$ be a finite tree automaton. The associated subset automaton is the deterministic finite tree automaton $P(A) = (Q_1, \Sigma, \delta_1, Q_{1,F})$ such that

- $Q_1 := 2^Q$ is the power set of Q;
- $Q_{1,F} := \{B \subseteq Q \mid B \cap Q_F \neq \emptyset\}$;
- δ_1 is the function with $\delta_1(a, B_1 \ldots B_k) = \{q \in Q \mid \exists q_1 \in B_1, \ldots, q_k \in B_k : (q, a, q_1 \ldots q_k) \in \delta\}$. $\qquad\square$

The following lemma is proved by induction over the size of the input tree.

Lemma 11.1
Suppose $t \in B(\Sigma)$. Then $\delta_1(t)$ is the set of all states $q \in Q$, for which there exists a q-computation on t. In particular, $L(A) = L(P(A))$. $\qquad\square$

The subset construction allows us to generate tree pattern matchers. For a set of patterns t we construct the deterministic tree automaton $P(A_T) = (Q, \Sigma, \delta, Q_F)$. Then the set $\delta(t) \cap T$ contains precisely the patterns of T which match the input tree t.

To our horror, we find that our construction I is hopelessly inefficient in most practical cases: 2^n states are generated for n states of the original automaton. Even for the above small example, this amounts to $2^5 = 32$ states. Often, however, a large proportion of the new states introduced by construction I are redundant. For instance, in our example, the set $\{a(a(\perp, \perp), b), a(b, \perp)\}$, which contains contradictory patterns that cannot even match the same tree, was generated. Thus, we give a more economical construction II which only generates states that may actually occur in computations.

Beginning with the empty set of states the subset construction II iteratively computes new sets of states of the deterministic tree automaton. In the first iteration the set of states that could possibly be assumed at the leaves of input trees is computed. In subsequent calculations a new set of states is computed for all combinations of operators and states which have already been computed. This is repeated until the set of states does not change. This construction corresponds exactly to the NFA $\rightarrow$ DFA algorithm for word automata of Chapter 7.

Definition 11.12 (subset construction II)
Suppose $A = (Q, \Sigma, \delta, Q_F)$ is a finite tree automaton. The associated (reduced) subset automaton is the deterministic finite tree automaton $P_r(A) = (Q_r, \Sigma, \delta_r, Q_{r,F})$ with $Q_{r,F} = \{B \in Q_r \mid B \cap Q_F \neq \emptyset\}$, whose sets of states and transitions are computed iteratively by $Q_r = \bigcup_{n \geq 0} Q_r^{(n)}$ and $\delta_r = \bigcup_{n \geq 0} \delta_r^{(n)}$, where:

- $Q_r^{(0)} = \emptyset$;
- suppose $n > 0$. For $a \in \Sigma_k$ and $B_1, \ldots, B_k \in Q_r^{(n-1)}$ let $B = \{q \in Q \mid \exists q_1 \in B_1, \ldots, q_k \in B_k : (q, a, q_1 \ldots q_k) \in \delta\}$. If $B \neq \emptyset$, then $B \in Q_r^{(n)}$ and $(B, a, B_1 \ldots B_k) \in \delta_r^{(n)}$. $\qquad\square$

Since for all n we have $Q_r^{(n)} \subseteq Q_r^{(n+1)}$ and $\delta_r^{(n)} \subseteq \delta_r^{(n+1)}$, we can break off the iteration as soon as no new states are generated, that is, $Q_r = Q_r^{(n)}$ and $\delta_r = \delta_r^{(n)}$ for the first n with $Q_r^{(n)} = Q_r^{(n+1)}$. Consequently, the procedure ends after at most $2^{|Q|}$ iterations.

Example 11.11 (continuation of Example 11.10)
For the above example:

$$Q_T^{(0)} = \{\}$$
$$Q_T^{(1)} = \{p_1^{(1)}, p_2^{(1)}\} \text{ with}$$
$$p_1^{(1)} = \{\bot\}$$
$$p_2^{(1)} = \{b, \bot\}$$
$$Q_T^{(2)} = \{p_1^{(2)}, p_2^{(2)}, p_3^{(2)}, p_4^{(2)}\} \text{ with}$$
$$p_1^{(2)} = \{\bot\}$$
$$p_2^{(2)} = \{b, \bot\}$$
$$p_3^{(2)} = \{a(b, \bot), a(\bot, \bot), \bot\}$$
$$p_4^{(2)} = \{a(\bot, \bot), \bot\}$$
$$Q_T^{(3)} = \{p_1^{(3)}, p_2^{(3)}, p_3^{(3)}, p_4^{(3)}, p_5^{(3)}\} \text{ with}$$
$$p_1^{(3)} = \{\bot\}$$
$$p_2^{(3)} = \{b, \bot\}$$
$$p_3^{(3)} = \{a(b, \bot), a(\bot, \bot), \bot\}$$
$$p_4^{(3)} = \{a(\bot, \bot), \bot\}$$
$$p_5^{(3)} = \{a(a(\bot, \bot), b), a(\bot, \bot), \bot\}$$
$$Q_T^{(4)} = Q_T^{(3)}$$
$$Q_{T,F}^{(4)} = \{p_1^{(3)}, p_2^{(3)}\}$$

$\qquad\square$

The following lemma follows by induction over the size of the input tree.

Lemma 11.2

(1)   For every $t \in B(\Sigma)$:

- *If $\delta_r(t)$ is defined, then $\delta_r(t)$ is the set of all states q, for which there exists a q-computation of A on t.*

- *If $\delta_r(t)$ is not defined, then there does not exist a q-computation of A for t for any $q \in Q$.*

(2) $L(A) = L(P_r(A))$.

(3)   For every state $B \in Q_r$ there exists a tree t, such that $\delta_r(t) = B$.   □

Let us consider the automaton A_T. Then we find that not *all* sets of subpatterns are now generated as states, but only those which are **maximally compatible**. Here, a set of patterns $S \subseteq T$ is said to be **compatible**, if there exists a tree t that every pattern in S matches. S is said to be **maximally** compatible, if there exists a tree that is matched by all patterns in S but by no patterns in $T \backslash S$.

The set of states Q_r of the reduced subset automaton for A_T consists of precisely the maximally compatible sets of subpatterns. The reduced subset automaton for A_T has only five states; this represents a considerable saving in comparison with the 32 states of construction I.

11.7   Generation of tree parsers

Suppose $G = (N, \Sigma, P, S)$ is a regular tree grammar. In order to compute all possible S-derivation trees for given trees, we proceed in a similar way as before in the case of the pattern matching problem. First we construct a non-deterministic automaton A_G, whose computations correspond to the derivation trees for G. In a second step, we apply the subset construction to A_G. The resulting subset automaton is the basis for our tree parser.

Intuitively, the automaton A_G acts on an input tree $t \notin N$ as follows. Beginning at the leaves, the non-deterministic automaton guesses the matching right sides of grammatical rules and checks that the right sides actually match. Here, the input tree t is covered by the right sides of the grammar rules, like in a jigsaw puzzle. The automaton operates as in the pattern matching. In addition, the automaton has to check that the grammar rules applied side by side fit together.

Thus, we formally define $A_G = (Q_G, \Sigma, \delta_G, \{S\})$, where $Q_G = N \cup \{s' \mid \exists(X \rightarrow s) \in P$, with s' a proper subpattern of $s\}$. The transition relation δ_G contains transitions of the form $(s, a, s_1 \ldots s_k)$ such that $s = a(s_1, \ldots, s_k) \in Q_G$ and $(X, a, s_1 \ldots s_k)$ such that $\exists(X \rightarrow s) \in P$ and $s = a(s_1, \ldots, s_k)$.

Here, there is a certain 'blurring' resulting from the fact that chain rules of the form $X_1 \rightarrow X_2$ with $X_1, X_2 \in N$ are allowed in the grammar. However, the automaton can only simulate 'true' derivation steps, that is, those in which at least one terminal symbol is generated. Therefore, the effects of all possible applications of chain rules are precomputed and encoded in the transition relation. We define:

$$\delta_G := \quad \{(s, a, s_1 \ldots s_k) \mid s = a(s_1, \ldots, s_k) \in Q_G\} \quad \cup$$
$$\{(X, a, s_1 \ldots s_k) \mid \exists (X' \to s) \in P : \exists X\text{-derivation tree for } X'$$
$$\text{and } s = a(s_1, \ldots, s_k)\}$$

Lemma 11.3
Suppose G is a regular tree grammar and t an input tree.

- *There exists an X-derivation tree for t with respect to G if and only if there exists an X-computation of G for t. In particular: $L(G) = L(A_G)$.*

- *Suppose $A = (Q, \Sigma, \delta, Q_F)$ is the (reduced) subset automaton for A_G. Then $\delta(t) \cap N = \{X \in N \mid \exists X\text{-derivation tree for } t\}$.* $\quad\square$

Example 11.12 Suppose G_m is the regular tree grammar of Example 11.8. The non-deterministic automaton $A_{G_m} = (Q_{G_m}, \Sigma_{G_m}, \delta_{G_m}, Q_{F,G_m})$ for G_m has the set of states

$$Q_{G_m} = \{const, REG, m(const), m(REG)\}$$

and the transitions:

$$\delta_{G_m} = \{ \quad (const, const, \epsilon)$$
$$(REG, const, \epsilon)$$
$$(REG, REG, \epsilon)$$
$$(m(const), m, const)$$
$$(REG, m, const)$$
$$(m(REG), m, REG)$$
$$(REG, plus, m(const) \; REG)$$
$$(REG, plus, m(REG) \; REG)$$
$$(REG, plus, REG \; REG)\}$$

The reduced subset automaton $A_{G_m,r} = (Q_{G_m,r}, \Sigma_{G_m}, \delta_{G_m,r}, Q_{F,G_m,r})$ for A_{G_m} has the set of states $Q_{G_m,r} = \{q_1, q_2, q_3, q_4\}$ with

$$q_1 = \{REG\}$$
$$q_2 = \{const, REG\}$$
$$q_3 = \{m(REG)\}$$
$$q_4 = \{m(const), REG, m(REG)\}$$

$\quad\square$

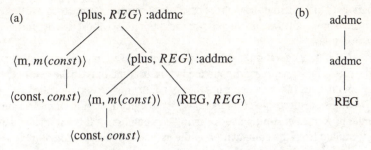

Figure 11.8   (a) A computation for A_{G_m} from Example 11.12 with annotations and (b) the corresponding derivation tree.

The X-derivation trees for an input tree t are easily reconstructed from the X-computations of the non-deterministic automaton A_G for t (note that the number of X-computations for t is always finite, even though the number of X-derivation trees for t may be *infinite*; this corresponds to the fact that chain rules may be applied infinitely often). For all transitions $(X, a, s_1 \ldots s_k)$ of δ_G for a rule $(X' \to a(s_1, \ldots, s_k)) \in P$ X-derivation trees for $a(s_1, \ldots, s_k)$ are tabulated. When A_G runs, these tabulations are used to annotate the computation. In order to construct an X-derivation tree from the annotated computation, it only remains to assemble the annotations according to the tree structure of the computation (see Figure 11.8).

Thus, we can reduce the tree-parsing problem to the problem of reconstructing all accepting computations of the underlying non-deterministic automaton from the computation of a (reduced) subset automaton for t.

Let $A = (Q, \Sigma, \delta, Q_F)$ be a non-deterministic automaton and $A_r = (Q_r, \Sigma, \delta_r, Q_{r,F})$ the reduced subset automaton for A. We present a simple algorithm which, given the input of a B-computation of A_r for a tree t and $q \in B$, can construct the set of the q-computations for t.

For a transition $\tau = (B, a, B_1 \ldots B_k) \in \delta_r$ and $q \in B$ let $\Theta(\tau)_q = \{(q, a, q_1 \ldots q_k) \in \delta \mid q_1 \in B_1, \ldots, q_k \in B_k\}$ be the set of transitions of the non-deterministic automaton A which belong to τ and have q as successor state.

Let $\phi = \langle a, B \rangle(\phi_1, \ldots, \phi_k)$ be the B-computation of A_r. The algorithm traverses the tree ϕ in pre-order. Let τ be the transition at the root of ϕ. The algorithm selects a transition $(q, a, q_1 \ldots q_k) \in \Theta(\tau)_q$. Then q_j-computations ψ_j, $j = 1, \ldots, k$, for the computations ϕ_j are recursively determined. $\langle a, q \rangle(\psi_1, \ldots, \psi_k)$ is issued as a result. Different choices of a transition correspond to different computations of A. Thus, this algorithm can be used to list all computations.

11.8   Tree automata with costs

We would like to use our method for generating tree parsers, among other things, to generate code selectors. Grammars for describing real machines are usually ambiguous. This confronts us with the problem of selecting an inexpensive derivation tree from among the wealth of possibilities. For this we use a cost measure for derivation trees.

As in the generation of a tree parser, we proceed in three steps. We assume that the rules of the grammar are annotated with cost functions. In the case of the code selection, this cost function describes the cost of the instruction modelled by a given rule. We translate these into cost functions for the transitions of the non-deterministic automaton. A most cost-effective accepting computation of this automaton can then be determined from the computation of the associated subset automaton.

Thus, suppose each rule p of the type $(X_1, \ldots, X_k) \to X$ is assigned a k-ary function $C(p) : \mathbb{N}^k \to \mathbb{N}$.

A cost measure C can be extended to a function which assigns a cost $C(\psi) \in \mathbb{N}$ to every derivation tree ψ. If $\psi = X \in N$, then $C(\psi) = 0$. If $\psi = p(\psi_1, \ldots, \psi_k)$, then $C(\psi) = C(p)(C(\psi_1), \ldots, C(\psi_k))$, that is, we apply the function $C(p)$ to the values $C(\psi_1), \ldots, C(\psi_k)$ which have already been computed recursively.

The cost measure C is said to be **monotonic** or **additive** if $C(p)$ is monotonic or of the form $C(p) = c_p + x_1 + \cdots + x_k, c_p \in \mathbb{N}$, for all $p \in P$.

The cost measures used in practice are generally monotonic. Standard cost measures include, for example, the processor cycles needed for execution, the number of storage locations referenced and the number of operands of an instruction. One example of a non-additive cost measure is C_R which determines the number of registers needed to compute an expression. Additive cost measures are frequently used (even when they only approximate the 'reality' very coarsely for very complicated processor architectures), since they are easy to manage. One simple measure is $C_\sharp$, which assigns the cost $C_\sharp(p) = 1 + x_1 + \cdots + x_k$ to each rule $p : (X_1, \ldots, X_k) \to X$. The value $C_\sharp(\psi)$ then gives the number of rules in ψ.

We translate the cost annotation C of the grammar G into a cost annotation C^* of the associated automaton A_G. The procedure described here assumes an additive cost measure. In this case, the cost of each rule can be described by a constant, that is, we view C as a function $P \to \mathbb{N}_0$. We then define C^* for the transitions of A_G as follows.

- If $\tau = (s, a, s_1 \ldots s_k)$ with $s = a(s_1, \ldots, s_k)$, then $C^*(\tau) = 0$.
- If $\tau = (X, a, s_1 \ldots s_k)$, then $C^*(\tau)$ corresponds to the minimal cost of an X-derivation tree for $a(s_1, \ldots, s_k)$.

By analogy with derivation trees, we can extend the cost functions for non-deterministic automata to computation costs. The cost $C^*(\phi)$ of an X-computation ϕ is precisely the minimal cost of an X-derivation tree represented by ϕ.

Let $A = (Q, \Sigma, \delta, Q_F)$ be a finite tree automaton and $C : \delta \to \mathbb{N}_0$ an additive cost function for the transitions of A. Let $A_r = (Q_r, \Sigma, \delta_r, Q_{r,F})$ be the (reduced) subset automaton associated with A.

We give a modification of the algorithm described above for constructing computations of A from a computation of A_r, such that an inexpensive computation results. Instead of computing the costs of all the different computations of A (the number of these may increase exponentially) we take a bottom-up approach and prevent the frequent recomputation of the cost of subcomputations by tabulating the results.

For each node $\langle a, B \rangle$ of a computation ϕ of the subset automaton A_r we tabulate the costs c_q and the transitions d_q for all $q \in B$. Let t be the corresponding subtree of the input tree for a node of ϕ. Then c_q are the costs of a cheapest q-computation of t and d_q is the transition of A chosen for this. This takes place during a post-order pass through ϕ. The values of c_q at the root of ϕ are precisely the costs of a cheapest q-computation of A.

The algorithm to construct a cheapest q-computation scans the annotated computation ϕ in pre-order. Suppose $\phi = \langle a, B \rangle(\phi_1, \ldots, \phi_k)$ is the B-computation of A_r. Suppose $d_q = (q, a, q_1 \ldots q_k)$ is the tabulated transition at the root of ϕ. Then cheapest q_j-computations ψ_j, $j = 1, \ldots, k$, for the computations ϕ_j are determined recursively. $\langle a, q \rangle(\psi_1, \ldots, \psi_k)$ is issued as a result.

Example 11.13 (continuation of Example 11.8)
Let G_m be the grammar of Example 11.8 with the following cost annotations:

$addmc$:	REG	$\rightarrow$	$plus(m(const), REG)$	Cost 3
$addm$:	REG	$\rightarrow$	$plus(m(REG), REG)$	Cost 3
add :	REG	$\rightarrow$	$plus(REG, REG)$	Cost 2
$ldmc$:	REG	$\rightarrow$	$m(const)$	Cost 2
ldc :	REG	$\rightarrow$	$const$	Cost 1
ld :	REG	$\rightarrow$	REG	Cost 1

The non-deterministic automaton $A = (Q, \Sigma, \delta, Q_F)$ for G_m has the states $Q = \{const, REG, m(const), m(REG)\}$ and the transitions (with costs):

$$\delta = \{ \quad (const, const, \epsilon) \qquad\qquad \text{Cost } 0,$$
$$(REG, const, \epsilon) \qquad\qquad \text{Cost } 1,$$
$$(REG, REG, \epsilon) \qquad\qquad \text{Cost } 0,$$
$$(m(const), m, const) \qquad\quad \text{Cost } 0,$$
$$(REG, m, const) \qquad\qquad \text{Cost } 2,$$
$$(m(REG), m, REG) \qquad\quad \text{Cost } 0,$$
$$(REG, plus, m(const)\ REG) \quad \text{Cost } 3,$$
$$(REG, plus, m(REG)\ REG) \quad \text{Cost } 3,$$
$$(REG, plus, REG\ REG) \qquad \text{Cost } 2\}$$

□

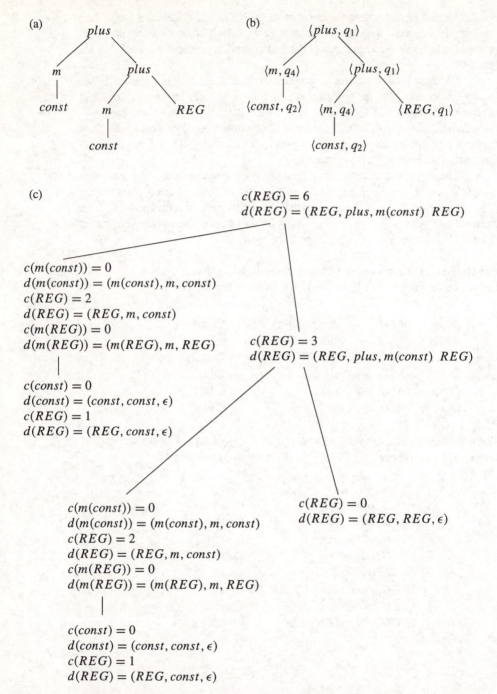

Figure 11.9   (a) A tree for the grammar of Example 11.8, (b) the computation of the subset automaton A_r and (c) the values of c and d.

The management of the cost vector can be very expensive. Thus, one may endeavour to integrate the cost computation as far as possible into the state transitions of the subset automaton itself. For the standard machine grammars $G_m = (N_m, \Sigma, P_m, S)$ the differences in the costs of X-derivation trees with minimal costs for the different $X \in N_m$ are usually bounded by a constant. This is explained by the fact that machine grammars usually have a central nonterminal, which describes 'registers' in the machine, from which (almost) all other nonterminals can be derived by applying chain rules. This means that when choosing a cheapest computation of the non-deterministic automaton $A = (Q, \Sigma, \delta, Q_F)$ from the computation of the corresponding subset automaton one can work, without reservations, with bounded cost differences instead of the real costs.

The finitely many cost differences can be integrated directly into the states of the subset automaton $A_c = (Q_c, \Sigma, \delta_c, Q_{c,F})$ in the subset construction. For this, in each state B of A_c we assign a cost difference d to each reachable state $q \in Q$ of the non-deterministic automaton, that is, $B \subseteq \{\langle q, d\rangle \mid q \in Q \text{ and } d \in \mathbb{N}_0\}$. For $\langle q, d\rangle \in B$ d describes the cost difference between a q-computation of A and a cheapest computation.

Definition 11.13 (subset construction III)
Suppose $A = (Q, \Sigma, \delta, Q_F)$ is a finite tree automaton and $C : \delta \rightarrow \mathbb{N}_0$ a cost function, which assigns a cost in $\mathbb{N}_0$ to every transition of δ. The associated **(reduced) subset automaton with integrated costs** is the deterministic finite tree automaton $P_c(A) = (Q_c, \Sigma, \delta_c, Q_{c,F})$ with $Q_{c,F} = \{B \in Q_c \mid \langle q, d\rangle \in B \text{ and } q \in Q_F\}$, whose set of states and transitions are computed iteratively by $Q_c = \bigcup_{n \geq 0} Q_c^{(n)}$ and $\delta_c = \bigcup_{n \geq 0} \delta_c^{(n)}$, where:

- $Q_c^{(0)} = \emptyset$;
- let $n > 0$. For $a \in \Sigma_k$ and $B_1, \ldots, B_k \in Q_c^{(n-1)}$ let
  $B = \{\langle q, d\rangle \mid \exists \langle q_1, d_1\rangle \in B_1, \ldots, \langle q_k, d_k\rangle \in B_k \text{ and } \tau = (q, a, q_1 \ldots q_k) \in \delta \text{ such that } d = C(\tau) + d_1 + \ldots + d_k \text{ is minimal }\}$.
  If $B \neq \emptyset$, then $norm(B) \in Q_c^{(n)}$ and $(norm(B), a, B_1 \ldots B_k) \in \delta_c^{(n)}$ with $norm(B) = \{\langle q, (d - \epsilon)\rangle \mid \langle q, d\rangle \in B\}$ with $\epsilon = min\{d \mid \langle q, d\rangle \in B\}$. $\square$

The subset construction III is analogous to the subset construction II up to the computation of the finite cost differences. In the various iterations a new set B is computed for all combinations of operators and all states already computed. The cost differences can then be determined from the constant parts in these sets B using the function *norm*.

Example 11.14 (continuation of Example 11.8)
Let $A = (Q, \Sigma, \delta, Q_F)$ be the non-deterministic automaton with costs of Example 11.13. Subset construction III gives the following sets of states:

$$Q_c^{(0)} = \{\}$$
$$Q_c^{(1)} = \{p_1^{(1)}, p_2^{(1)}\} \quad \text{with}$$

$$p_1^{(1)} = \{\langle REG, 0\rangle\}$$
$$p_2^{(1)} = \{\langle const, 0\rangle, \langle REG, 1\rangle\}$$

$$Q_c^{(2)} = \{p_1^{(2)}, p_2^{(2)}, p_3^{(2)}, p_4^{(2)}\} \quad \text{with}$$

$$p_1^{(2)} = \{\langle REG, 0\rangle\}$$
$$p_2^{(2)} = \{\langle const, 0\rangle, \langle REG, 1\rangle\}$$
$$p_3^{(2)} = \{\langle m(REG), 0\rangle\}$$
$$p_4^{(2)} = \{\langle m(const), 0\rangle, \langle REG, 2\rangle, \langle m(REG), 1\rangle\}$$

$$Q_c^{(3)} = Q_c^{(2)}$$

□

The algorithm to construct a q-computation of a non-deterministic tree automaton from the computation of the associated (reduced) subset automaton can be carried over almost unchanged to the construction of a most cost-effective q-computation of the non-deterministic tree automaton from a computation of a (reduced) subset automaton with integrated costs. Let $A = (Q, \Sigma, \delta, Q_F)$ be a non-deterministic tree automaton, $C : \delta \to \mathbb{N}_0$ a cost function and $A_c = (Q_c, \Sigma, \delta_c, Q_{c,F})$ the associated (reduced) subset automaton with integrated costs. For a transition $\tau = (B, a, B_1 \ldots B_k) \in \delta_c$ and $\langle q, d\rangle \in B$ let $\Theta_c(\tau)_q = \{\eta = (q, a, q_1 \ldots q_k) \in \delta \mid \langle q_1, d_1\rangle \in B_1, \ldots, \langle q_k, d_k\rangle \in B_k$, such that $C(\eta) + d_1 + \ldots + d_k$ is minimal $\}$ be the set of cheapest transitions of the non-deterministic automaton A, which belong to τ and have q as successor state.

Let $\phi = \langle a, B\rangle(\phi_1, \ldots, \phi_k)$ be the B-computation of A_c. Analogously to the above, the algorithm traverses the tree ϕ in pre-order. Let τ be the transition at the root of ϕ. The algorithm selects a transition $(q, a, q_1 \ldots q_k) \in \Theta_c(\tau)_q$. Then q_j-computations ψ_j, $j = 1, \ldots, k$, for the computations ϕ_j are determined recursively. As a result $\langle a, q\rangle(\psi_1, \ldots, \psi_k)$ is issued. All possible results are cheapest q-computations of A.

The subset automata of construction III are usually larger than the corresponding automata of construction II without integrated costs. Furthermore, construction III is only possible for tree automata for which the cost differences from cheapest computations for trees t are bounded by a constant. The advantage of subset automata with integrated costs is that they permit a considerably faster construction of a cheapest computation of the associated non-deterministic tree automaton.

11.9   Implementation

In this section we are concerned with skilful implementations of deterministic tree automata. In the simplest case, the set δ_a of transitions for an operator a with k

arguments is represented by a k-dimensional matrix M_a. Here $M_a[q_1, \ldots, q_k] = \delta(a, q_1 \ldots q_k)$, if δ is defined for these arguments, otherwise $\perp$, a special error symbol.

Let us suppose that the input tree t is given as an ordered rooted tree with labelled nodes. The state at a node n of t with label $a \in \Sigma_k$ is $M_a[q_1, \ldots, q_k]$, where $q_1, \ldots, q_k$ are the states at the children of the node n. This computation is implemented, for example, by a post-order traversal of the tree t. The costs of one 'run' of a tree automaton over t consist of the cost of the post-order traversal, which can be carried out in a time proportional to the size of the tree, together with an indexed matrix/array access for each node of t.

On most real computers, the time for an array access $M[i_i, \ldots, i_n]$ is linearly dependent on the number of indices n. Since each subtree of a tree contributes only once to an indexing, the total run time is linear in the number of nodes of t (independently of the arities involved).

Example 11.15 (continuation of Example 11.12)
The transition function δ_r of the reduced subset automaton A_r is described in table form by:

$$\delta_{r,const} = q_2$$
$$\delta_{r,REG} = q_1$$

Child

$$\delta_{r,m} = \begin{array}{|c|c|c|c|} q_1 & q_2 & q_3 & q_4 \\ \hline q_3 & q_4 & \perp & q_3 \end{array}$$

Right child

$$\delta_{r,plus} = \quad \text{Left} \atop \text{child} \begin{array}{c|c||c|c|c|c|} & & q_1 & q_2 & q_3 & q_4 \\ \hline & q_1 & q_1 & q_1 & \perp & q_1 \\ & q_2 & q_1 & q_1 & \perp & q_1 \\ & q_3 & q_1 & q_1 & \perp & q_1 \\ & q_4 & q_1 & q_1 & \perp & q_1 \end{array}$$

The representation of δ as a set of matrices is usually very storage intensive, particularly as the size of a matrix M_a for an operator $a \in \Sigma_k$ is proportional to $|Q|^k$, that is, exponential in the arity of a independently of how many (how few) defined transitions the automaton A has for a. Using standard table compression methods, the space requirement for storing the matrices can be considerably reduced in most cases that arise in practice.

11.10 Exercises

1: The following transformation rules describe the conversion of a Boolean expression into its distributive normal form:

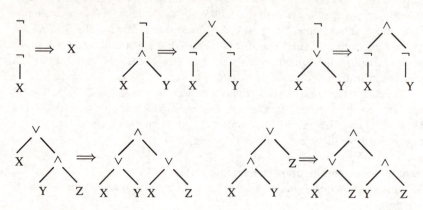

Develop a deterministic tree automaton that recognizes the left sides of the transformation rules.

2: Define a tree automaton to compute the upper characteristic graphs for the attribute grammar of Example 9.9.

3: Suppose p_1 and p_2 are two patterns. p_1 and p_2 are said to be **independent**, if there exist trees t_1, t_2 and t_3, such that:

- t_1 is matched by p_1 but not by p_2,
- t_2 is matched by p_2 but not by p_1,
- t_3 is matched by p_1 and p_2.

Let P be a set of patterns and PF the set of subpatterns of P. Show that if PF contains no independent patterns then a deterministic automaton which recognizes P has $|PF| + 1$ states.

4: Give a class of patterns for which the number of states of the reduced deterministic automaton that recognizes the patterns increases exponentially with the size of the set of input patterns. Here, the size of a set of patterns P is defined to be the number of subpatterns of P.

5: Let us suppose that G_m denotes a tree grammar (N_m, Σ, P_m, REG) where $\Sigma = \{const, m, plus, REG\,AREG\}$ with $\rho(const) = 0$, $\rho(m) = 1$, $\rho(plus) = 2$, $N_m = \{REG, AREG\}$ and

$$
\begin{aligned}
P_m = \{ \ addm2: & \quad REG & \rightarrow & \quad plus(m(plus(AREG, AREG)), REG) & \text{Cost 6,} \\
addm: & \quad REG & \rightarrow & \quad plus(m(AREG), REG) & \text{Cost 5,} \\
add: & \quad REG & \rightarrow & \quad plus(REG, REG) & \text{Cost 1,} \\
adda: & \quad AREG & \rightarrow & \quad plus(REG, REG) & \text{Cost 1,} \\
ldmc: & \quad REG & \rightarrow & \quad m(const) & \text{Cost 3,} \\
ldma: & \quad REG & \rightarrow & \quad m(AREG) & \text{Cost 4,} \\
ldc: & \quad REG & \rightarrow & \quad const & \text{Cost 1,} \\
ld: & \quad REG & \rightarrow & \quad REG & \text{Cost 1,} \\
lda: & \quad AREG & \rightarrow & \quad REG & \text{Cost 1} \}
\end{aligned}
$$

Construct the reduced subset automaton with cost differences for G_m according to subset construction III.

6: Give a tree grammar with costs for which the cost differences can be arbitrarily large, that is, a tree grammar for which the subset construction III does not terminate.

11.11 Literature

Efficient pattern matching on trees (Kron, 1975; Hoffmann and O'Donnell, 1982; Chase, 1987; Möncke 1985) is employed in various systems for the program transformations (Möncke *et al.*, 1986; Heckmann and Sander, 1992). The transformation of page 516 is oriented towards the functional transformation language TrafoLa (Heckmann and Sander, 1992). The Ada standardization transformation of Figure 11.4 comes from Keller and Maas (1990).

The computation of the subtree graph in linear time for the implementation of the recognition of non-linear patterns is described in Downey *et al.* (1980).

Ripken (1977) was the first to propose a machine description language for realistic machines, from which to generate the code generator. Since the tree-parsing methods needed for this were not then known, Glanville and Graham (Glanville, 1977; Glanville and Graham, 1978) proposed a linearization of the intermediate language and code selection by a modified LALR parser. This approach was followed right up to the application by Henry (1984).

Other approaches combine efficient pattern-matching algorithms with dynamic programming to determine locally optimal instruction sequences (Aho and Ganapathi, 1985; Henry and Damron, 1989a; Weisgerber and Wilhelm, 1989) or extend the pattern matcher to the direct selection of locally optimal instruction sequences (Pelegri-Llopart, 1988; Henry and Damron, 1989b).

In a series of publications Giegerich and Schmal (Giegerich and Schmal, 1988; Giegerich, 1990) endeavour to treat the different approaches to pattern matching and tree parsing in a formal framework. The problem of code selection is reduced to the inversion of a 'derivor', that is, a tree homomorphism.

Pelegri-Llopart (1988) and Emmelmann (1992) describe machines by means of term rewriting systems which they use to derive 'automata' that permit an efficient code selection.

The integration of the cost computation into the state transitions of the subset automaton using finite cost differences was described by Pelegri-Llopart in (Pelegri-Llopart, 1988; Pelegri-Llopart and Graham, 1988).

A good survey of the classical results of the theory of tree automata can be found, for example, in Gecseg and Steinby (1984). Without discussing code selection explicitly, Kron (1975) anticipated a number of current techniques for tree pattern matching.

Various methods for compressing tree-automata tables are described in Börstler *et al.* (1991). Another method of representing the transition function δ_a for an operator a involves the use of decision trees. This idea was first proposed for pattern matchers by Kron (1975). Chase (1987) uses the idea of the division into equivalence classes, to generate compressed tables for pattern matching directly.

Ferdinand *et al.* (1994) systematically develop the underlying theory, which is applied in code selection, and make the relationship with tree automata clear, at the same time giving general methods for the implementation of tree automata. In particular they generalize Kron's approach and Chase's compression to arbitrary tree automata. This makes it possible to derive efficient generators of efficient code selectors.

12

Code generation

- Abstract and real machines

- Classification of architectures

- Program representations

- Code generation, integrated methods

- Register allocation by graph colouring

- Instruction scheduling

- Exercises

- Literature

12.1 Abstract and real machines

In Chapters 2–5, we have already given more or less complete specifications of code generation for imperative, functional, logic and object-oriented programming languages. However, in those chapters the target machines are all **abstract** machines, which are defined to make compilation as simple as possible. Let us summarize the characteristics of the four abstract machines described.

12.1.1 Language-specific abstract machines

Memory organization

The four machines have a memory organization appropriate to the lifetimes of the various classes of object. There are one or more stacks for objects whose lifetime corresponds to nested intervals and a heap for objects whose lifetime is not governed by such rules. The stacks are subdivided into frames whose structure can be determined statically. As far as memory organization is concerned, they each use a set of registers, such as stack pointer, heap pointer and frame pointer.

Instruction set

The abstract machines contain complex instructions, which implement the source-language constructs in full or in part.

Example 12.1
The P-machine instruction **mst** creates a stack frame for a called procedure; **retp** and **retf** delete this stack frame.

The MaMa instruction **mark** creates a stack frame for a function application; the **return** instruction deletes the stack frame and tests for over-supply.

The **enter** instruction in the Prolog machine creates a stack frame in the stack, and **popenv** and **restore** release this stack frame. □

Evaluation of expressions

The four abstract machines described have one more thing in common, namely that the evaluation of expressions (or unification in logic programs) involves the use of a 'small' stack. Operands and results always lie in this stack..

12.1.2 Universal real machines

Let us now suppose that we have to implement Pascal, LaMa and Prolog and possibly other languages on just **one** of the four abstract machines. It would be extremely difficult to implement Prolog, for example, on the P-machine. On the other hand, if we wished to implement Pascal on the Prolog machine we could not use most of its instructions. A simple assignment to an array component would be very difficult to realize with the existing instructions. In short, the memory structures and instruction sets oriented towards a class of languages are more of a hindrance than a help when implementing languages of other classes. Real machines should be universal in the sense that they should make it easy to implement the memory organization of an abstract machine and permit efficient simulation of every corresponding instruction set.

Let us now try to list the common characteristics of popular real computers.

Memory hierarchy

Real machines have a memory hierarchy which is determined by the access speed and the length of time the contents remain there. One commonly used hierarchy comprises processor registers, cache, main memory and background memory. The latter can be further subdivided, but is of no further interest as far as code generation is concerned. Neither shall we consider the cache memory further in what follows. Thus, the hierarchy in question reduces to the two levels of processor registers and main memory. The registers are usually on the processor chip. Thus, there is no need to leave the chip when accessing values in registers. An access to main memory (however, some processors have a memory of a few kbytes on the processor chip) usually takes place over the system bus between processor and memory using a memory selection logic, which selects the memory locations addressed. The current memory chips have a longer access time than the processor registers. All this results in a considerable difference in access speed. Therefore, one task of code generation is to hold objects in registers as skilfully as possible to increase the speed of execution.

The main memory is generally a linear store holding the generated code and the stack and heap, where implemented. One important characteristic of main memory is the set of addressable storage units and, in particular, the smallest storage unit that is directly addressable. In today's 32-bit processors the smallest directly addressable units are frequently bytes, followed by words, consisting of two bytes, and double or long words of four bytes.

Processor registers

Real processors generally have different classes of register. The classes are determined by the objects that can be stored in them and the operations that can be executed on them. Common classes include the following:

- **Universal registers**. Arithmetic and logical operations, and also address operations, can be performed in these registers. For the arithmetic operations, often only integer operations are possible.

- In addition, there are **floating-point registers** for operations on floating-point numbers. The floating-point arithmetic is usually simulated or executed by an arithmetic coprocessor, which in turn also has floating-point registers.

- Sometimes, separate **data** and **address registers** are supplied instead of universal registers. For example, the MC 68000 has eight data registers and eight address registers. Address calculations usually involve the full address length, while faster operations for subvalues are also possible in the data registers.

- Occasionally, there are also **base registers**, which are used to address memory segments, for example stack frames, and **index registers**, whose contents can be combined with other addresses for indexing in arrays. In more modern processors universal registers or address registers are used as base registers and index registers.

Then we have processor registers which are used implicitly in operations:

- The **program counter** (PC) points to the next instruction to be executed. It is implicitly used when loading instructions and altered in branches, procedure calls and in the main cycle of the computer.

- Some processors store the result of comparisons, often implicit comparisons with 0, in a **condition code** (CC). This usually contains carry bits (C), overflow bits (V), bits for a test for 0 (Z) and bits for a sign test (positive or negative) (N).

Instruction set

The instruction set of a (universal) real processor should support many language classes and applications. In Section 12.2 'Classification of architectures', we shall see that instruction sets may have very different appearances; the number of instructions may range from approximately 30 to over 1000. The instructions of an instruction set may all be very simple or some may be very complex. They fall into the following categories:

- Computation instructions, that is arithmetic and Boolean instuctions and comparisons, which are frequently distinguished according to the length of the operands.

- Transport instructions to load objects from the memory into registers, store objects from registers in memory and transport objects between registers or storage locations.

- Branches and instructions for subroutine organization.

- Instructions for communication with the operating system and the peripheral devices, for example for input and output.

In some processors, the addressing of operands involves complex forms of addressing, in others, operands must always be present in registers.

The size of a processor's instruction set essentially depends on the product of the number of operations (with their variants for operands of different types and lengths) and the number of permissible forms of operand addressing.

Evaluation of expressions

Most real machines of relevance today are register machines rather than stack machines. The operands and the results of operations lie in registers or in main memory. One of the tasks of code generation is to specify where intermediate results from the evaluation of expressions should be stored. Storage in an available register shortens the subsequent accesses.

A notation for machine instructions

Commercial assembler languages are neither easy to read nor uniform. Thus, in what follows, we shall present machine instructions in a readable assembler notation. Here, an instruction for a binary operation *op* will be written as:

$$< Result > := < Operand_1 > op < Operand_2 >$$

$< Operand >$	$\rightarrow R_i$	Content of register R_i
	$\mid M[< Addr >]$	Content of the storage location addressed
	$\mid c$	Value of the constant c
$< Result >$	$\rightarrow R_i$	Destination register for the operation
	$\mid M[< Addr >]$	Storage location for the result

An arithmetic operation usually sets the condition code at the same time. Thus, the sign of the result and any overflow or other condition are indicated. This means that an instruction actually has several results and thus should be written as $(R_i, cc) := \ldots$. However, we shall only do this when required by the context.

For most processors, the possible forms of addressing form a subset of the following languages:

$< Addr > \rightarrow c$		Value of the constant
	$\mid R_i$	Content of register R_i
	$\mid ++R_i$	Content of R_i after preceding increment
	$\mid --R_i$	Content of register R_i after preceding decrement
	$\mid R_i ++$	Content of register R_i; side effect: following increment
	$\mid R_i --$	Content of register R_i; side effect: following decrement
	$\mid M[< Addr >]$	Content of storage location addressed

	$< Addr > + < Addr >$	Sum of the addresses
	$< Addr > * c$	Product of address and constant c
	$< Addr > . < Size >$	Restriction to parts of a register

$$< Size > \rightarrow \text{L|W|B} \qquad \text{Long word, word, byte}$$

Here, the recursion over the nonterminal $< Addr >$ allowed in concrete machine languages is never very deep, and the number of registers allowed in an address is usually limited to two.

12.1.3 Code generation for abstract and real machines

Our efforts in Chapters 2–5 were not in vain. We can use most of the specifications for code generators given there for code generation for real machines. In what follows, we shall give an exact description of the similarities of and differences between code generation for abstract and real machines.

Control structures

Both the P-machine and the MaMa have a minimal set of conditional and unconditional branches; in contrast, real machines often have a wealth of conditional branches for special situations and even different branches for short and long distances (the choice of short or long branches is not difficult and therefore will not be considered here). Control structures in Pascal and conditional expressions in LaMa are compiled for real machines in essentially the same way as for the given abstract machines. One exception is the short-circuit evaluation of Boolean expressions mentioned in Chapter 9.

Management of recursion

Pascal and LaMa both have a runtime stack to support recursive procedures and functions. The management of (recursive) clauses in Prolog is even more expensive because of the possibility of backtracking. The stack organization, the generation and deletion of stack frames and the management of continuation addresses is implemented in a similar way but using the instructions of the real machine. A number of universal registers or address registers may be dedicated to support the stack organization.

Addressing of variables and parameters

Of course, in implementations on real machines variables and parameters are also provided with static relative addresses, as far as possible. One difference from the representation in Chapters 2–5 is that there objects of all types are stored in one machine word. In fact objects of some types, for example, Boolean values and characters, require less than a word, and several of these can be packed into one word to save space. Floating-point values, in particular those of higher precision, generally require several words. Character strings often have a dynamic length and must be stored in a storage area organized as a heap. On the other hand, dynamic arrays can be handled on real computers as described in Chapter 2. On real computers, the access to global variables is implemented as described in Chapters 2, 3 and 5.

Exploitable capabilities of modern real processors

Abstract machines were designed to simplify the construction of compilers. New real processors should always have an advantage over existing ones. This is usually a performance-related advantage, such as a lower cycle time, a price advantage, or the integration of additional logic such as virtual memory management. Thus, the main difference between code generation for abstract and real machines amounts to the best possible exploitation of the capabilities of real processors. As we shall see, this involves:

- using the registers in the best possible way to store variable values and intermediate results, to compute storage addresses, to deliver actual parameters to procedures and to return function values (register allocation),
- selecting machine instruction sequences for intermediate language constructs and thereby preferring more efficient instructions for special cases (code selection), and
- exploiting the possibilities for parallel execution of operations offered by a real target processor, by skilful scheduling of independent instructions (instruction scheduling).

The relevance and the difficulty of these subtasks depend on the characteristics of the target processor.

Subtasks of code generation

In the last section, we mentioned the three most interesting subtasks of the code generation for the first time.

- Register allocation:
  Source- and intermediate-language programs contain certain objects whose task is to store values, for example variables or procedure parameters, and other objects that must be stored, such as intermediate results of the evaluation of expressions or addresses. Thus, the former have to be mapped onto storage resources of the target machine for all or part of their lifetime. The latter must also be assigned to storage resources where they will be retained. Since, as previously mentioned, access to processor registers is often an order of magnitude faster than access to main memory locations, the generator should make good use of the registers of the target machine (of

which there are usually only a few). This is the task of register allocation.

- Code selection:
Problems of code selection and the methods used to solve these problems are handled in detail in Chapter 11. The task of code selection is to generate a semantically equivalent target-machine program for an intermediate-language program. There are always several possibilities for such target programs. If their costs are very different, we would expect a good code selector to select the most cost-effective instruction sequences. Of course, there may be two different correct compilations for a program fragment, one giving the target program p_1 and the other the target program p_2. According to the measure of costs used, p_1 is cheaper than p_2 but uses more registers. More precisely, p_2 manages with the available registers, but p_1 does not. If code selection is carried out without register allocation, intermediate-storage and load operations must now be introduced, which may make the resulting program more expensive than p_2. Conversely, after a previous allocation of registers the code selector may be unable to choose one of the cheapest instruction sequences, because it has insufficient registers. To get round the problem of the interdependence of code selection and register allocation, code selection is usually done first under the assumption that the target machine has arbitrarily many processor registers.

- Instruction scheduling:
For target machines with parallel-processing capabilities an instruction sequence selected by the code selector must be scheduled so that correct execution on the target machine is guaranteed and the parallel-processing capabilities are exploited in the best possible way.

12.2 Classification of architectures

In this section, we classify current processor architectures, essentially according to how they affect the subtasks of code generation.

12.2.1 CISC (Complex Instruction Set Computer)

CISCs are similar to the abstract machines of Chapters 2–5. They are intended to close the 'semantic gaps' between high-level programming languages and target machines. Thus, they provide complex instructions to support access to data structures and procedure organization. They are characterized by:

- a large number of complex forms of addressing to support efficient access to **data structures** such as arrays, records, lists and stack frames,

- manifold versions of operations for operands of different length and combinations of different sorts of operands and results,

- different execution times for instructions, and
- few processor registers.

These instruction sets necessitate large hardware costs or large microprograms. Previously, the CPU was often realized by a chip set. Even with the increase in integration density, the storage requirement for the complex instruction logic remains considerable. Thus, there is usually little space left for processor registers.

Thus, successor processors to CISCs are largely characterized by extension of the instruction set, the forms of addressing and the (on-chip) cache and optimization of the microcode, rather than by an increase in the number of registers. Prominent representatives of the CISC family include the processors of the VAX series, the Intel 80x86, the Motorola 680x0 and the NSC 32xxx.

Typically, the number of permissible combinations of operation codes, forms of addressing and operand and result size is around 1000.

Because of the small number of registers available, good register allocation is important for CISC computers, but difficult to achieve.

Since for a source- or intermediate-language program CISC processors generally offer a large number of possible correct instruction sequences, possibly with very different costs, a good code selection based on cost measures is important.

12.2.2   RISC (Reduced Instruction Set Computer)

The introduction of the RISC principle was based on the idea of increasing the speed of execution of the individual instructions by simplifying them. The characteristic features of RISC architectures are the following:

- One machine instruction is executed per machine cycle. Since some instructions such as access to main memory last longer than one cycle, pipelining is used.
- Computation operations only take place on register operands and the result is also stored in registers (load/store architecture).
- To simplify the control logic, there are only a few forms of addressing.
- The control is not microprogrammed but hard-wired.

Thus, processors of this class have:

- only a few, very simple instructions,
- a lot of space on the processor chip for registers, functional units operating in parallel and/or communication logic, as a result of the low outlay on CPU logic.

RISC processors frequently have more than 100 processor registers, which are sometimes only accessible via register windows. This organization supports the implementation of procedures and functions. A window of registers is available to a called procedure. This window is divided into three parts: one for the actual parameters, one for its local variables and one for the actual parameters of procedures it calls. In a procedure call, the register window can be quickly changed in such a way that the area with the actual parameters remains in the register window, that is, register windows of called and calling procedures overlap. In this way, an explicit intermediate storage of registers can often be avoided.

The nature of the register organization has a crucial influence on the register allocation algorithm. The code selection problem becomes less important because of the very simple instruction set.

12.2.3   Intraprocessor parallelism

RISC processors require only small chip surfaces for the instruction logic. The available surface can also be used to implement functional units operating in parallel, an instruction pipeline or a data pipeline, as in so-called vector computers.

Long instruction words

Let us suppose that a processor has several functional units operating in parallel, which are each linked to a large set of registers by two input ports and one output port, see Figure 12.1. Suppose the bandwidth of the set of registers is large enough to permit simultaneous loading of operands by the functional units.

The computer only has one instruction stream, one program counter and one control unit. Each individual instruction word is sufficiently long that it contains one subinstruction for each functional unit. Thus, the individual functional units are controlled independently of each other by subwords of the instruction word. The execution times of the individual instructions are statically predictable and short.

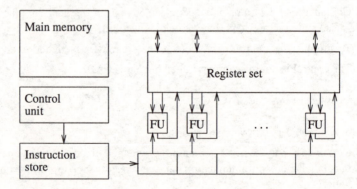

Figure 12.1   Block diagram of a computer with several functional units operating in parallel.

A compiler has the task of packing the instruction sequence generated for a source program into as short as possible a sequence of long or very long instruction words (**VLIW**) without destroying the semantics by this arrangement.

Since the functional units are generally RISCs, code selection is easy. On the other hand, the arrangement of the instruction sequence generated in long instruction words is difficult, particularly if one includes in the arrangement instructions occurring beyond branches. To enable us to determine whether various instructions can be executed in parallel or even in transposed order without altering the semantics of the program, a data-dependency analysis must first be carried out.

Instruction pipeline

At any given time an **instruction pipeline** may contain several consecutive instructions at different stages of execution. One possible division into four phases is the following:

(1) instruction fetch and decode,

(2) operand fetch,

(3) instruction execution,

(4) write result in target register.

One step in the pipeline is responsible for each phase. Every step requires one cycle for execution. This division into phases reduces the cycle time. Figure 12.2 shows the overlapping execution of the instruction sequence $B_1, B_2, \ldots$ for an ideally 'fed' pipeline.

We see that the execution of the instructions should be divided into phases in such a way that all phases have lengths as equal as possible. After an initial three cycles, the ideal filling of the pipeline shown in Figure 12.2 results in the execution of one instruction per cycle. However, it is only possible if consecutive instructions do not require the same hardware resources simultaneously (collision) and if an

		\multicolumn{7}{c}{Cycle}						
		1	2	3	4	5	6	7
Pipe-	1	B_1	B_2	B_3	B_4			
line	2		B_1	B_2	B_3	B_4		
step	3			B_1	B_2	B_3	B_4	
	4				B_1	B_2	B_3	B_4

Figure 12.2   Processing in an instruction pipeline.

instruction does not require a result of a previous instruction that has not yet become available.

An instruction whose operands are in memory accesses the memory several times during its execution. Thus, a collision with subsequent instructions is very likely. Therefore, in such an architecture no instruction should use a hardware resource (for example, a memory bus) more than once. Load/store architectures largely avoid such instructions.

If an instruction attempts to access an operand which a previous instruction has not yet produced, this will be discovered by some processors (as a pipeline hazard) and the feeding of new instructions into the pipeline will be delayed (pipeline interlock) until the required value is available. Since the corresponding logic is expensive and slows the execution of the instruction, it is omitted in some processors. In this case, the code generator is responsible for avoiding such situations. For this, it has to reorder the instructions so that sufficient independent instructions separate two dependent instructions. The pipeline may also have to be padded with 'No Operation' instructions (NOP). Such situations arise, in particular, after load instructions, since the access to the main memory often lasts an order of magnitude longer than the processor cycle time (delayed load).

Another problem arises when a branch, particularly a conditional branch, is executed. Since for an unconditional branch it is unclear which is the next instruction, the pipeline must run empty for a couple of cycles. Some processors allow delayed branches, that is, branches that are first executed after the execution of the following instruction has ended. Then the code generator can move an instruction that precedes the branch instruction and does not affect the branching condition to directly after the branch.

12.3 Program representations

In Chapter 6, the starting point for code generation was chosen to be the representation of programs as decorated syntax trees. However, for code generation, as for abstract interpretation, for code selection and for the reordering of instruction sequences, other representations which we shall now describe are used.

These tasks require a representation of the control flow in a program. A procedure's control flow graph indicates which statements can be executed consecutively. Whether this actually happens during the execution of the program may depend on conditions that in general cannot be evaluated at compile time. The (procedure) call graph describes possible call relationships between procedures.

Definition 12.1 (control flow graph)
The **control flow graph** of a procedure is a node-labelled, edge-ordered, directed graph (N, E, s) with entry node s. Here, for every primitive statement p of the procedure, there exists a node $n_p \in N$, which is labelled by this statement. Composite statements result in the corresponding subgraph as shown in Figure 12.3.

cfg (**while** B **do** S **od**) $=$

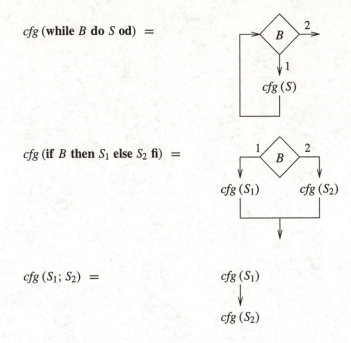

cfg (**if** B **then** S_1 **else** S_2 **fi**) $=$

cfg $(S_1; S_2)$ $=$

cfg (S_1)

cfg (S_2)

Figure 12.3   Control flow graph for composite statements. A subgraph $cfg = (N', E', s')$ is inserted as follows: all ingoing edges lead to s', all outgoing edges lead to the successor node uniquely determined by the context.

Edges belonging to explicit branches lead from the node of the branch to the branch destination. s is the unique entry node of the procedure's control flow graph; it belongs to the first statement of the procedure to be executed. The control flow graph serves, for example, as a basis for the execution of dataflow analyses. The program items used in Chapter 10 correspond to the entry and exit edges of nodes of the control flow graph.   □

Nodes with more than one predecessor are called **joins**; nodes with more than one successor are called **forks**.

The control flow graph is usually assumed to be connected, since a subgraph which is not reachable from entry nodes is 'dead code', that is, redundant.

Sequences of primitive statements are frequently combined and processed together.

Definition 12.2 (basic block)
A **basic block** in a control flow graph is a path of maximal length, which has no joins except possibly at the beginning and no forks except possibly at the end.   □

```
read a;
read b;
while a ≠ b do
    if a < b
    then t := a; a := b; b := t
    else a := a − b
    fi
od
```

S : read a
     read b
     ⟨a ≠ b⟩ →2
     ↓1
     1 ⟨a < b⟩ 2
     t := a   a := a − b
     a := b
     b := t

Figure 12.4   A program with its control flow graph.

For every basic block in a sequential imperative programming language the following holds: if its first statement is executed then the other statements are executed sequentially, if no runtime errors or exceptions occur.

Definition 12.3 (basic block graph)
The **basic block graph** (BBG) G' of a control flow graph G is formed from G, by combining each basic block into a node. Edges in G leading to the first node of a basic block lead into the node of a basic block in G'. Edges in G leaving the last node of a basic block lead out of the node of a basic block in G'.   □

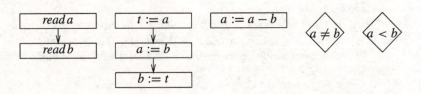

Figure 12.5   The basic blocks of the control flow graph of Figure 12.4.

Different variants of the control flow and basic block graphs, differing essentially in the representation of the primitive statements and conditions, are used in different compilation steps.

One possibility is to label nodes of the control flow graph by the primitive statements and the conditions of the source program, namely in the form of (abstract decorated) syntax trees. A basic block is then a sequence of trees. This form is well suited to code selection. This latter task is restricted to the compilation of basic blocks; the control structure and the procedure organization are compiled, for example, as in Chapter 2. The result of the code selection can again be represented as a control flow graph or a basic block graph, except that the nodes are now machine- or assembler-code sequences.

In Chapter 10, for abstract interpretation, we chose a representation of the control flow graph as an edge-labelled graph. This gives a nicer representation of the theory. The edge labels are approximations to a standard semantics for the statements. Abstract interpretation can be applied at various levels of program representation. For example, one can analyse whether program variables are live at the source-language level or whether machine resources are live at the machine-language level.

The call graph represents the relationship between procedures.

Definition 12.4 (call graph)
There is one node for the main program (this is also the entry node) and one node for each procedure declared in the program. The nodes are labelled by the procedure names. There is an edge from the node for procedure p to the node for procedure q, if p contains a call of q. □

It is easy to see from the call graph whether a procedure is directly recursive or simultaneously recursive with other procedures. The call graph is used for the **interprocedural** analysis of programs. Here, one is interested in certain effects of a procedure call, for example the set of program variables which it may alter or use. Or, one wishes to trace how so-called alias relationships can be constructed, possibly transitively over a chain of calls, using reference parameters. An **alias relationship** exists between a set of variables (also pointers or indexed variables), if they (can) all denote the same storage location.

12.4   Code generation, integrated methods

The following methods for code generation for expression trees integrate register allocation and instruction selection for a simple machine model. For instruction selection they take account of the register requirements and generate the necessary intermediate storage if the requirements exceed the number of available registers. The two methods are only applicable to the given types of target machine.

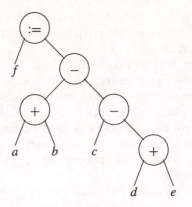

Figure 12.6 A tree for the assignment statement $f := (a + b) - (c - (d + e))$.

12.4.1 Optimal evaluation order

We consider the problem of generating the best possible (for example, the shortest possible) code. This method can be easily extended to assignment statements or whole basic blocks. As an example, we consider the tree of Figure 12.6 for the assignment statement $f := (a + b) - (c - (d + e))$.

The machine model considered is very simple. Because of the direct correspondence between operations in the expression tree and the instructions, code selection is trivial. The target machine has r general registers $R_0, \ldots, R_{r-1}$. The instructions are two-address instructions with the following formats:

R_i	:=	$M[V]$	Load
$M[V]$	:=	R_i	Store
R_i	:=	R_i op $M[V]$	Compute
R_i	:=	R_i op R_j	

where V represents a variable or its address.

Example 12.2

Let us suppose that our target machine has two universal registers R_0 and R_1. One possible instruction sequence for the tree of Figure 12.6 would then be that shown in Figure 12.7.

Intermediate storage is required, since no registers are available for the subtraction $c - (d + e)$. The instruction sequence in Figure 12.8 gets away without intermediate storage and thus saves two instructions. The reason for this is that the subtree for $c - (d + e)$, which requires two registers, is evaluated before the subtree for $a + b$ which only needs one register. □

$$
\begin{aligned}
R_0 &:= M[a] \\
R_0 &:= R_0 + M[b] \\
R_1 &:= M[d] \\
R_1 &:= R_1 + M[e] \\
M[t_1] &:= R_1 \\
R_1 &:= M[c] \\
R_1 &:= R_1 - M[t_1] \\
R_0 &:= R_0 - R_1 \\
M[f] &:= R_0
\end{aligned}
$$

Figure 12.7   An instruction sequence for the tree of Figure 12.6.

$$
\begin{aligned}
R_0 &:= M[c] \\
R_1 &:= M[d] \\
R_1 &:= R_1 + M[e] \\
R_0 &:= R_0 - R_1 \\
R_1 &:= M[a] \\
R_1 &:= R_1 + M[b] \\
R_1 &:= R_1 - R_0 \\
M[f] &:= R_1
\end{aligned}
$$

Figure 12.8   A shorter instruction sequence for the tree of Figure 12.6.

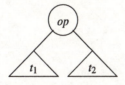

Figure 12.9   A tree for $e_1 \, op \, e_2$.

This is the principle of the following algorithm. Suppose we are given a tree t for an expression $e_1 op \, e_2$ as in Figure 12.9. Suppose the subtrees t_1 and t_2 are the trees for e_1 and e_2, respectively.

Let t_1 require r_1 registers for its evaluation and t_2 require r_2 registers. Suppose the number of available registers is $r \geq r_1 > r_2$. After the evaluation of t_1 all the registers needed for its evaluation become free, except for that holding the result. Thus, enough registers are available for the evaluation of t_2. Therefore, the whole tree can be evaluated with r_1 registers. If t_1 and t_2 both require the same number of registers r_1 then a total of $r_1 + 1$ registers will be needed to evaluate t, if the result of one subtree has to be held in a register while the other subtree is evaluated.

If a tree requires more than r registers, one or more intermediate results for subtrees must be stored in storage locations.

The procedure described requires two phases, a labelling phase to determine the storage needs of the subtrees and a generation phase in which the code is generated (possibly with intermediate storage), the code generation being controlled by the computed register requirements.

Labelling phase

In the first phase, the nodes of the tree are labelled by their register requirements. Here, the fact that only finitely many registers are available is ignored. A bottom-up pass is used for this, that is, this is an S-attribution. 'Left leaves', that is, leaves which are the left children of binary operators, are labelled by 1, since they will have to be loaded into a register. 'Right leaves', on the other hand, will be used as operands and thus have register requirement 0. According to the above argument, the register requirements for the internal nodes are found to be:

$$regreq\,(op(t_1, t_2)) = \begin{cases} \max(r_1, r_2), & \text{if } r_1 \neq r_2 \\ r_1 + 1, & \text{if } r_1 = r_2 \end{cases}$$

where $r_1 = regreq\,(t_1)$ and $r_2 = regreq\,(t_2)$.

Thus, for the tree of Figure 12.6 we obtain the labelling of Figure 12.10.

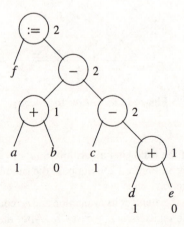

Figure 12.10   A tree labelled by register requirements.

Generation phase

In this phase, optimal code for the original tree is generated. This is done in one pass through the tree. The instruction **Op** for the operation op at the root of the tree $op(t_1, t_2)$ is generated after the code for t_1 and t_2. The order in which the two subtrees t_1 and t_2 are processed is determined by their register requirements. For the instruction generated for op the assertion holds that it finds the value of t_1 in a register. This register is then an operand in the instruction for op. Intermediate results for subtrees whose register requirements are too high are stored in intermediate storage and loaded later.

The available registers are managed in a stack *RSTACK*. This stack is initialized with the full set of available registers. It never becomes empty. The topmost register at the beginning of the processing of a subtree t is the result register for t. After the processing of a subtree all the registers are again available in *RSTACK*. But the topmost register is the result register for t.

Addresses of available intermediate storage cells are managed in the second stack *TSTACK*. The operations *push*, *pop*, *top* and *exchange* are possible in both stacks. *exchange* exchanges the top two elements in the stack.

Algorithm Gen_Opt_Code
Input: Expression tree t.
Output: Optimal code for t.
Method: Recursive pass through t using the procedure *Gen_Code*. The different cases (left leaf, right leaf or internal node) are described by patterns. Here, trees with *regreq* labelling occur among the patterns, written as pairs (t, r). The right column shows which registers are at the top of the stack *RSTACK* and which register is the result register for a given code sequence. Each call of *Gen_Code* begins and ends with two registers, say R' and R'', at the top of the stack; R' is the result register for the code generated. The (recursive) algorithm is described in Figure 12.11. It is called with *Gen_Code(t)* for an expression tree t, after which *RSTACK* is initialized with the set of available registers and *TSTACK* is initialized with the set of intermediate storage locations.

The code generated by these two phases is optimal in terms of the number of instructions generated if the original expression has no multiple occurrences of subexpressions. Such common subexpressions are evaluated several times by the code generated. The fact that the code generated for expressions without common subexpressions is optimal can be seen as follows:

• Precisely one instruction is generated for each internal node.

• Precisely one instruction is generated for each left leaf, which loads these operands into a register.

• Intermediate storage is only generated for those internal nodes whose two children require more than r registers each.

Algorithm	RSTACK – contents and result register
var *RSTACK*: **stack of register**; *TSTACK*: **stack of address**;	
proc *Gen_Code* (*t* : **tree**);	$(R', R'', \ldots)$
var *R*: **register**, *T*: **address**;	
case *t* **of**	
(*leaf a*, 1) : (*left leaf*)	
emit(*top*(*RSTACK*) := *a*);	result in R'
op((*t₁, r₁*), (*leaf a*, 0)) : (*right leaf*)	
Gen_Code(*t₁*);	
emit(*top*(*RSTACK*) := *top*(*RSTACK*) **Op** *a*);	result in R'
op((*t₁, r₁*), (*t₂, r₂*)) :	
cases	
r₁ < *min*(*r₂, r*):	
begin	
exchange(*RSTACK*);	$(R'', R', \ldots)$
Gen_Code(*t₂*);	result in R''
R := *pop*(*RSTACK*);	$(R', \ldots)$
Gen_Code(*t₁*);	result in R'
emit(*top*(*RSTACK*) := *top*(*RSTACK*) **Op** *R*);	result in R'
push(*RSTACK, R*);	$(R'', R', \ldots)$
exchange(*RSTACK*);	$(R', R'', \ldots)$
end;	
r₁ ≥ *r₂* ∧ *r₂* < *r*:	
begin	
Gen_Code(*t₁*);	result in R'
R := *pop*(*RSTACK*);	$(R'', \ldots)$
Gen_Code(*t₂*);	result in R''
emit(*R* := *R* **Op** *top*(*RSTACK*));	result in R'
push(*RSTACK, R*);	$(R', R'', \ldots)$
end;	
r₁ ≥ *r* ∧ *r₂* ≥ *r*:	
begin	
Gen_Code(*t₂*);	result in R'
T := *pop*(*TSTACK*);	
emit(*M*[*T*] := *top*(*RSTACK*));	result in $M[T]$
Gen_Code(*t₁*);	result in R'
emit(*top*(*RSTACK*) := *top*(*RSTACK*) **Op** *M*[*T*]);	result in R'
push(*TSTACK, T*);	
end;	
endcases	
endcase	
endproc	

Figure 12.11   **Gen_Opt_Code** algorithm (the function *emit* issues the machine instructions).

12.4.2   Dynamic programming

We now describe another method for integrated code generation, which can also be applied for architectures with more complex instructions. This method combines non-trivial code selection with an optimal register allocation. Suppose we have a target machine with r available universal registers $R_0, \ldots, R_{r-1}$. Suppose the instruction formats are as follows:

$$
\begin{array}{lll}
R_i & := & e & \text{Compute} \\
R_i & := & M[V] & \text{Load} \\
M[V] & := & R_i & \text{Store}
\end{array}
$$

where V represents a variable or its address.

Here, e is a term whose operands may be registers or storage locations. If e has registers as operands, we assume that the result register R_i is among these to simplify the register allocation. Every instruction has a fixed cost. This may be determined, for example, by the space requirement or the execution time of the instruction. The problem is to generate a cheapest instruction sequence using not more than r registers for every given tree.

Because of the more complex instruction set, we return to the solution of the code selection problem in Chapter 11 and extend it by a cost computation scheme which takes account of the limited set of registers.

The grammar G for the above instruction set has two nonterminal symbols, namely REG and M. REG stands for a register and M for a storage location with a fixed address. Corresponding to the instructions $R_i := M[V]$ and $M[V] := R_i$, the grammar has the two rules $REG \rightarrow M$ and $M \rightarrow REG$. Whence, a state of the subset automaton A generated for G contains the nonterminal REG if and only if it contains the nonterminal M. An occurrence of this nonterminal means that an instruction whose result can be held in a register or temporarily stored matches here. We note that the computation of a subexpression whose result is stored temporarily can be placed earlier. This has the advantage that the whole register set is available both before and after the computation.

Let t be the expression tree for which we wish to generate code, and I an instruction whose associated rule $REG \rightarrow e$ may be at the root of a derivation tree for t. To extend I to a complete instruction sequence for t one has to choose code sequences for the remaining subtrees of t which are not covered by e. For this, one first has to determine the subtrees for which the results have to be stored temporarily. One then has to determine the order in which the results for the remaining trees should be calculated. r registers are then available for the first of these subtrees, $r - 1$ for the second, and so on. To choose an optimal code sequence one has to determine the costs for all matching instructions, for all subsets of intermediate results to be stored temporarily and for all possible schedules of the remaining computations. Recursive application of this procedure leads to an exponential algorithm, since one has to recompute for each subtree and each setting for its siblings what the cheapest computation is using $r, r - 1, \ldots$ registers or leaving the result in temporary storage. Thus, the method of dynamic programming is used as a more efficient procedure.

Dynamic programming involves a bottom-up tree traversal which avoids the exponentially frequent recomputation of costs for subtrees by tabulating the results. A simple version of this method was described in Chapter 11 for the choice of a cheapest computation for a tree automaton with costs. For the integrated procedure considered here we use another cost vector.

Let us consider a computation ϕ of the subset automaton A for the input tree t. Every node n whose state contains REG and M is assigned a cost vector $K[0..r]$. $K[0]$ contains the minimal cost of a code sequence for the subtree t/n, which stores the result for the subtree temporarily. $K[j], j = 1, .., r$ contain the minimal cost of a code sequence for t/n using j registers, where the result is stored in a register. If the cost vectors are computed in a bottom-up manner, the required costs of optimal code sequences for all the possible subtrees are already determined. The step in which this cost vector is computed at node n is as follows. We assume that k different instructions $R_i := e_1, \ldots, R_i := e_k$ match at t/n. The cost vectors at the operand nodes for the e_l are already determined. To compute $K[j]$ for $1 \leq j \leq r$ we consider all combinations of one of the e_l and the cheapest computations of the corresponding subtrees using no more than j registers. $K[j]$ is assigned the minimum of those combined costs. The subcomputations, which are combined to compute $K[0]$, may use all r registers.

This procedure appears expensive, but it is linear in the size of the input tree. In the tabulation, analogously to the code selection procedure of Chapter 11, it is advisable to record the information needed to construct a cheapest code sequence. Here, this consists of the present instruction to be chosen together with the order in which the remaining subtrees are to be evaluated and the number of registers needed for this.

The cheapest code sequence is constructed in a separate pass.

12.5   Register allocation by graph colouring

The methods described so far only allowed a skilful register allocation for expression trees. The register-allocation method which we shall now describe assigns the registers of the target machine globally for all computations within a procedure. The input is an intermediate representation of the program in which every operation and every modified variable is assigned a **symbolic register**. To the, in principle, unlimited number of symbolic registers have to be assigned the limited number of registers of the real machine. Here, a real register can never be assigned two different symbolic registers if these are both 'live' at the same time and it is not certain that they contain the same value.

Definition 12.5 (live, life range)

A symbolic register r is **live** at a program point p, if r is defined on a program path from the entry node of the procedure to p and there exists a path from p to a use of r on which r is not defined. The **life range** of a symbolic register r is the set of the program points at which r is live.   □

Thus, a register is live at a program point if its contents there may still be required. The register interference graph shows the constraints on the assignment of real registers to symbolic registers.

Definition 12.6 (interference, register interference graph)

Two life ranges of symbolic registers **interfere with one another**, if one of them is defined during the life range of the other. The **register interference graph** is an undirected graph. Its nodes are life ranges of symbolic registers, and there is an edge between every two interfering life ranges.   □

The register allocation problem translates into the problem of colouring the register interference graph with k colours, where k is the number of real registers. Thus, the colours correspond to real registers. In the graph colouring, no directly connected nodes should be assigned the same colour.

For $k > 2$, the problem of deciding whether an arbitrary graph can be coloured by k colours is NP complete. However, in the case of graph colouring for register allocation there exist a number of heuristic methods which have been well tried and tested in practice.

The basic idea behind the graph colouring algorithm is the following. If the graph G contains a node n with a degree less than k, then there is certainly a colour left for n, independently of the colours of all its neighbours. We remove n from G and obtain a new graph G' containing one node and several edges fewer. Thus, we have reduced the problem recursively to a smaller problem. If this leads us to the empty graph, the original graph was k-colourable: if we go through the sequence of removals in reverse order and colour the nodes we have finished.

If at some time there are no nodes with degree less than k the algorithm for the remaining graph will not be able to find a k-colouring (that is, in our application no allocation of real registers to life ranges), although the graph may be k-colourable, see Figure 12.12. It then chooses a node heuristically, removes it and all its edges from the graph and attempts to colour the graph obtained with k colours. This removal of the node corresponds to an intermediate storage of the associated symbolic register. Thus, in the program, we have to introduce store operations where this register is defined and load operations where it is used during its life range.

Tried and tested heuristics for choosing the node to be stored temporarily take account of the following:

- The degree of the node. The removal of a node with the highest possible degree increases the chance that the new graph is k-colourable.

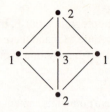

Figure 12.12 Graph colourable in three colours for which the given algorithm does not detect that it can be coloured in three colours.

- The cost of the intermediate storage. Of course, the contribution to the program run time of the instructions introduced cannot be determined exactly, since the instructions may be in (nested) loops, whose number of executions is determined dynamically. Thus, we assume a fixed, but not too low number of executions, so that a preference for intermediate storage outside loops is introduced.

Merging and splitting of life ranges

There are two mutually inverse operations on the set of life ranges which may improve the results of the algorithm. If the program contains assignments of the form $x := y$, and the life ranges of x and y do not interfere with one another, then they are **merged**. All uses of y are renamed to x. The assignment is removed since x and y are assigned the same real register here. The merging of life spans reduces the number of nodes in the register interference graph, which has to be modified accordingly.

It is often a disadvantage that the same real register is assigned to a very long life range, although this register will not be accessed during large parts of the life range. In this case, splitting a life range into several may increase the chance that the graph is k-colourable. The structure of the program may be taken into account when choosing points for splitting. The following heuristics are good for this. One should look for loops (possibly also strongly connected components) in the program that have a large register requirement. Then one should split all life ranges extending from before until after the loops. For this, a code sequence to store and load the register must be inserted for every split life range. In addition, the register interference graph also has to be rebuilt.

12.6 Instruction scheduling

For VLIW processors and processors with instruction pipelines the instruction sequence generated for a program is rearranged to make good use of the functional units operating in parallel and/or the pipeline. Initially, we shall only consider the instruction sequences for basic blocks.

The semantics of the program must not be changed by the reordering. In general, it is altered when the order of instructions is exchanged or instructions are executed in parallel, if the computations are interdependent. The semantic dependencies are expressed by a dependency graph. Other constraints on the scheduling of the instructions may also apply, depending on the target architecture.

12.6.1   Dependency graphs for basic blocks

The instruction sequence for a basic block has a linear order. It is executed in full and in the given sequence when the control passes to its first instruction. Subject to certain constraints, the instructions may be reordered without changing the overall effect of the instruction sequence. These constraints are determined by the dependencies between the instructions. Dependencies exist in the sequence of read and/or write accesses to certain components of the machine state, such as register contents or contents of storage locations. We call these modifications **definitions** (write accesses) and **uses** (read accesses). Definitions of a component X are written as $X :=$, uses are written as $:= X$. We note that an instruction may use several resources and define several resources.

Example 12.3
The instruction

D1 := ADD M[A1+D1.W], D5

uses the registers A1, D1 and D5 and the memory; it writes the result of the addition in register D1 and sets implicitly the N-, Z-, V- and C-bits in the condition code. □

The sequence of definitions and uses in Figure 12.13 shows how dependencies can restrict the reordering of instructions.

Transposing the instructions a and b would generally allow the use of c with another value of X, as would transposing b and c or transposing c and d.

The possible **definitions** in machine programs include:

- Modification of register contents by load instructions, by the storage of results after operations and by automatic incrementing or decrementing of address registers,

$$
\begin{array}{lll}
a: & X & := \\
b: & X & := \\
c: & & := X \\
d: & X & :=
\end{array}
$$

Figure 12.13   A sequence of definitions ($X =:$) and uses ($:= X$) of X.

- Setting of overflow, underflow or carry bits and results of comparisons in the condition code,

- Storage of values in storage locations, and

- Modification of a stack pointer by pushing or popping values and by instructions for procedure organization.

Corresponding **uses** are:

- Use of register contents in operations or for addressing,

- Storage of registers,

- Loading of the contents of storage locations, and

- Testing parts of the condition code in conditional branches.

Thus, the following types of dependency, requiring a sequential scheduling, exist between instructions.

- **Output dependence (definition–definition).** In Figure 12.13 such a dependency exists between the instructions a and b. In this example the instruction b seems to overwrite the effect of a and thus make a redundant. However, we note that b may involve a use of X.

- **True dependence (definition–use).** In Figure 12.13 this dependency exists between the instructions b and c.

- **Antidependence (use–definition).** d depends on c in this way.

How exactly can we extract these dependencies from an instruction sequence? There is no problem for registers; they are named explicitly and with their absolute indices in instructions. However, storage locations may be addressed using dynamic values such as the contents of base or index registers. Thus, a so-called **alias problem** arises here. Two forms of addressing with dynamic components in two different instructions may describe an access to the same location and thus be viewed as **alias names** for the location. Thus, (in the simplest case) as far as the definition or use of storage locations is concerned the whole memory is viewed as one object.

In what follows, we consider a **machine resource** to be either an individual register, the whole of main memory or the bits of the condition code. The dependency graph we now describe only contains edges for direct dependencies between 'neighbouring' definitions and uses. All the dependencies present then result through the transitive closure.

Definition 12.7 (dependency graph of a basic block)
Suppose we are given a basic block of a machine program. Its **dependency graph** is the following labelled, directed acyclic graph. Its nodes are labelled by the instructions of the basic block. An edge runs from the node of an instruction a to the node of another instruction b if a has to be executed before b, that is, if a

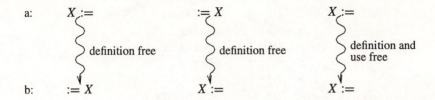

a:

definition free

definition free

definition and
use free

b:

Figure 12.14   Dependencies between *a* and *b*.

comes before *b* in the instruction sequence and if

- *a* defines a resource, *b* uses it and the path from *a* to *b* is definition free, or
- *a* uses a resource, *b* defines it and the path from *a* to *b* is definition free, or
- *a* and *b* define the same resource and the path from *a* to *b* is definition and use free, see Figure 12.14.   □

As a first simple example, we present the full dependency graph of Figure 12.15. In addition, we label the edges according to the form of the dependency, $d - d$ (definition–definition) for output dependence, $d - u$ (definition–use) for true dependence and $u - d$ (use–definition) for antidependence.

We see that, because of the $d - d$ dependencies on the condition code, this dependency graph does not even permit the clear possibility of reordering instructions 1 and 2. Moreover, it is clear that, in fact, no $u - d$ dependency exists

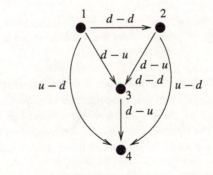

1 :   (CC, D1)   := M[A1 + 4].W
2 :   (CC, D2)   := M[A1 + 6].W
3 :   (CC, D1)   := D1 + D2
4 :   M[A1 + 4]   := D1.W

Figure 12.15   An instruction sequence with its dependency graph. The edges are labelled with the type of the dependence.

```
1:  D1       := M[A1+4];
2:  D2       := M[A1+6];
3:  A1       := A1+2;
4:  D1       := D1+A1;
5:  M[A1]    := A1;
6:  D2       := D2+1;
7:  D3       := M[A1+12];
8:  D3       := D3+D1;
9:  M[A1+6]  := D3
```

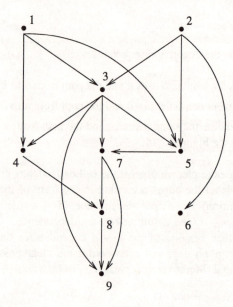

Figure 12.16 The instruction sequence of a basic block and the associated dependency graph (without edges that would arise due to parts of the condition code).

between 2 and 4, since 2 uses a different storage location from that used in 4. We shall return to these problems shortly.

Figure 12.16 shows a basic block and the associated dependency graph. The figure only shows the dependencies on the resources registers and memory; the dependencies on the condition code would make the graph too unclear.

The construction of the dependency graph

The dependency graph of a basic block is built in a backwards pass of the **BBA-Graph** algorithm (Figure 12.17) over the basic block. The set *lastDefins* holds the

Algorithm BBA-Graph
Input: Basic block.
Output: Dependency graph of the basic block.
Method:
var *lastDefins, exposedUses*:
       set of pair (*resource, instructionOccurrence*);
    actInstr: *instruction*;

function *conflict*(*resource,instruction$_1$,instruction$_2$*) :*conflictType*;
    determines whether there is a conflict between *instruction$_1$*
    and *instruction$_2$* on the resource *resource* and if so the nature of the conflict.

procedure *drawEdge*(*a* → *b*)
    draws an edge between the arguments, if one does not already exist.

begin
    actInstr := last instruction of the basic block;
    createnode(*actInstr*);
    lastDefins := {(*r, actInstr*)| *r* ∈ *definitions*(*actInstr*)};
    exposedUses := {(*r, actInstr*)| *r* ∈ *uses*(*actInstr*)};
    while *predecessor*(*actInstr*) *defined* **do**
        actInstr := *predecessor*(*actInstr*);
        createnode(*actInstr*);
        foreach resource *r*, defined or used in *actInstr* **do**
            foreach (*r, b*) ∈ *lastDefins* ∪ *exposedUses* **do**
                case *conflict*(*r, actInstr, b*) **of**
                definition–definition:
                    if there are no pairs (*r, α*) in *exposedUses* **then**
                        drawEdge(*actInstr* → *b*);
                  fi;
                definition–use:
                  drawEdge(*actInstr* → *b*);
                use–definition:
                  drawEdge(*actInstr* → *b*);
                end case;
            od
        od;
        foreach resource *r′*, defined in *actInstr*, **do**
            lastDefins := *lastDefins* −
                {*s* ∈ *lastDefins*|∃*α* : *s* = (*r′, α*)} ∪ {(*r′, actInstr*)};
            exposedUses := *exposedUses* −
                {*b* ∈ *exposedUses*|∃*β* : *b* = (*r′, β*)};
        od;
        foreach resource *r′*, used in *actInstr*, **do**
            exposedUses := *exposedUses* ∪{(*r′, actInstr*)};
        od;
    od
end

Figure 12.17   BBA-Graph algorithm.

last definitions of the machine resources processed; the set *exposedUses* contains the uses which have already been processed and which have not subsequently been overwritten by definitions and thus are upwards exposed. Definitions and uses are represented in the form (resource, occurrence of an instruction). An occurrence of an instruction may be multiple and simultaneous in the two sets. The definitions and uses of the actual instruction are checked for dependency between them and the instructions in *lastDefins* and *exposedUses*.

It is easy to see that because of the **foreach** (r, b) statement this algorithm is of quadratic complexity.

Reduction in size of the dependency graphs

The dependency graph represents the possible degrees of freedom for scheduling the instruction sequences, that is, different valid schedules can be obtained by topological sorting. As we shall see, some of the algorithms for instruction scheduling are variants of the topological sorting algorithms controlled by some heuristics. Depending on the target architecture there are additional constraints on the schedules, for example minimal distances (delays) v between interdependent instructions a and b. This means that a and b must be arranged so that there are at least v machine cycles between the executions of a and b.

A dependency graph with few edges offers more possibilities for scheduling than one with many edges. Thus, the dependency graph should be as small as possible. There are various ways of reducing its size.

Alias analysis   Until now we have viewed the whole memory as **a single** machine resource. Writing to one storage location and then reading from another (possibly different) location led to a dependency in the graph. If alias analysis shows that the effective addresses of these two locations are different whenever the instruction is executed, this edge is omitted. Even individual storage locations may occur as machine resources if they are addressed absolutely. An alias analysis often produces good information, if all storage locations are addressed via the same register. Addresses of different locations occurring in a basic block only differ in their constant components. Thus, they can be distinguished from each other.

Figure 12.18 shows the graph of Figure 12.16, after a preceding alias analysis discovered that the dependencies on the resource memory are in fact non-existent.

Liveness analysis   In Chapter 10, we described an analysis which computes the variables that are live at each program point. In what follows this procedure will be extended to liveness of machine resources.

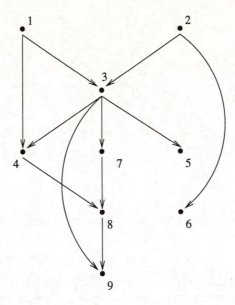

Figure 12.18   The dependency graph of the basic block of Figure 12.16, without the edges dropped as a result of an alias analysis of memory accesses.

Definition 12.8 (live machine resources)
A machine resource is **live** at a point in a basic block if the resource is used after this point without an intervening definition.   □

A liveness analysis begins with information about which resources are still in use in subsequent basic blocks. These are said to be **live on leaving the basic block**. The BBA-Graph algorithm can be modified so that it performs the liveness analysis at the same time (see Exercise 7).

The number of edges in the dependency graph can generally be greatly reduced using liveness-analysis information. In fact, if two instructions a and b define the same resource X, and X is dead at both points, then no edge $a \rightarrow b$ is drawn. This case occurs often for the parts of the condition code. They are set very frequently, but seldom used.

Figure 12.19 shows the dependency graph obtained from the graph of Figure 12.15 by an alias and liveness analysis. The $d - d$ dependency between 1 and 2 disappears, since the condition code is dead at these points. The $d - d$ dependency between 2 and 3 cannot be eliminated if we assume that this instruction sequence is followed by a conditional branch with a test of the condition code. In this case, the condition code would be live at 3. The $u - d$ edge between 2 and 4 is dropped because the alias analysis discovers that different storage locations are addressed in 2 and 4.

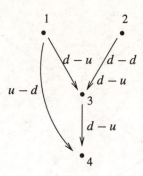

Figure 12.19 The dependency graph of Figure 12.15 made smaller by an alias analysis and a liveness analysis.

The dependency graph of Figure 12.18 can be viewed as the result of the **BBA-Graph** algorithm with liveness analysis and subsequent alias analysis. The condition code is dead everywhere, except at the exit from the basic block, if this is followed by a conditional branch.

12.6.2 Instruction pipeline

The target machine is now a processor with a k-step instruction pipeline. The pipeline discovers no collisions (hazards). We make a simplifying assumption. Whenever an instruction b depends on an instruction a, b can be executed after a delay of one cycle (whence, at the earliest two cycles after a).

Our initial goal is to reorder the instruction sequences within the basic blocks into the shortest possible instruction sequences, taking into account the dependencies and pipeline constraints. All possible schedules contain the same original instructions, possibly in a different order and with a different number of NOPs inserted. The starting point for each basic block is the dependency graph generated according to the **BBA-Graph** algorithm and reduced by liveness and alias analyses. By reducing a scheduling problem to this optimization problem it can be shown to be NP complete. Thus, it is again a matter of finding good heuristics. The procedure described is based on the topological sorting of the acyclic dependency graph.

We recall that topological sorting transforms a partial order R on a set X into a total order T on X, which is compatible with R, that is, $R \subseteq T$. One possible version of the topological sorting computes T, starting with the minimal elements of R. It uses a set of candidates K, containing all elements that may be scheduled next. K is initialized with the set of the minimal elements of R. If an element x of K is chosen to be scheduled next it is removed from K and X. The removal of x means that new elements may lose their last predecessor. These are added to K.

Algorithm FB-Scheduling
Input: Basic block with reduced dependency graph,
  Set of schedules of the predecessor basic blocks.
Output: (Possibly) reordered instruction sequence for the basic block,
  with possibly introduction of NOPs.
Method: Topological sorting taking account of the pipeline
  constraints and the heuristics.

var *Candidates, realCandidates, potCollisions*:
  set of *instructionOccurrence*;

function *colliding*(*cand, potcoll*) : **set of** *instructionOccurrence*;
  computes the set of instructions in *cand*, which collide with those in
  potcoll.

begin
  Candidates := Set of min. elements of the dependency graph;
  potCollisions := Set of the last instructions in the schedules of the
    predecessor basic blocks;
  repeat
    realCandidates:=*Candidates*−*colliding*(*candidates,potCollisions*);
    if *realCandidates* ≠ ∅ **then**
      evaluate real candidates according to the heuristics;
      choose a best candidate *b*;
      schedule it;
      remove *b* from *Candidates*;
      remove *b* and all outgoing edges
        from the dependency graph;
      add nodes, which now no longer have a predecessor,
        to *Candidates*;
      potCollisions := {*b*}
    else append NOP;
      potCollisions := ∅
    fi
  until *Candidates* = ∅
end

Figure 12.20   FB-Scheduling algorithm.

The standard topological-sorting algorithm chooses the next element to be
scheduled non-deterministically from K. The heuristics influence this choice. They
only admit candidates which do not collide with the last instruction scheduled. If
there are no such candidates a NOP instruction is introduced. If there exist candidates
which do not collide, one of them is chosen according to the following criteria, in
order of priority:

- An instruction that can generate collisions with a large number of subsequent instructions. In general, these are the instructions that have the most successors in the dependency graph. Their scheduling hopefully leaves more freedom for the remaining instructions.

- An instruction that lies on a longest path to the leaves of the dependency graph. This provides for uniform processing of all paths in the graph.

This leads to the **FB-Scheduling** algorithm (Figure 12.20).

The instruction sequence generated by the **FB-Scheduling** algorithm for the basic block of Figure 12.16 and its dependency graph of Figure 12.18 is shown in Figure 12.21.

Scheduling for realistic instruction pipelines is more complicated. For example, an individual delay may be needed between two instructions a and b. In this case, the dependency graph must include the least delay as an additional edge label. Then, the **FB-Scheduling** algorithm contains a new data structure instead of the set *potCollision* (see Exercise 6).

A further complication arises if values in the pipeline turn out to be 'hot spots'. These are values which must be consumed exactly a cycle after they were produced, since otherwise they are overwritten. This leads to another constraint on the instruction scheduling with a corresponding increase in expense.

2:	D2	:= M[A1+6];
1:	D1	:= M[A1+4];
6:	D2	:= D2+1;
3:	A1	:= A1+2;
	NOP	
7:	D3	:= M[A1+12];
4:	D1	:= D1+A1;
8:	D3	:= D3+D1;
5:	M[A1]	:= A1;
9:	M[A1+6]	:= D3

Figure 12.21   A possible scheduling of the instruction sequence of Figure 12.16.

12.6.3   Long instruction words

We now consider the problem of generating code for a processor with long instruction words and n functional units operating in parallel. In simple terms, this involves reordering an instruction sequence into n instruction sequences or into one new n-instruction-wide sequence of instruction words.

The possible parallelism within basic blocks is usually very limited (various statistics give a potential degree of parallelism for numerical programs of 2–3;

for non-numerical programs the potential parallelism is usually less). Thus, the many (often more than 10) functional units of a VLIW machine are not exploited. Therefore, we must consider the scheduling of instructions across and beyond the boundaries of basic blocks. One method for this is the so-called trace scheduling, in which whole procedure bodies are considered at once.

The basic idea of trace scheduling is to schedule the instructions from consecutive basic blocks jointly in order to increase the possible parallelism. Here, if possible, those blocks which are frequently executed directly after one another during program execution should be treated jointly. For this, the code generator requires information about how often the basic blocks in a procedure are executed. It can obtain this from measurements or from heuristic estimates. For numerical programs, the frequencies obtained from measurements on test runs with sample data approximate quite well to reality. Moreover, the differences in the frequency distribution for different subpaths are usually very marked. This is not usually the case for non-numerical programs. Thus, the procedure described can be expected to give a larger increase in efficiency for numerical programs.

The procedure decomposes the control flow graph of a procedure into disjoint subpaths. It first considers the basic block which is executed most frequently. Then it decides whether a previous or a subsequent basic block should be jointly scheduled with this, and if so, which. A strategy should specify a relative frequency up to which a possible predecessor (successor) of a basic block should be included in a subpath. The target architecture and the nature of the program to be compiled determine which strategies are advantageous. For example, it is sensible to choose those neighbouring basic blocks which will be executed with a similar frequency. However, the resulting subpath is never extended beyond loop boundaries.

The subpath (**trace**) obtained is now scheduled as skilfully as possible. Instructions in the original basic blocks may even be moved beyond forks or joins. This means that compensation code is needed in basic blocks that lead into or out of this trace. Compensation code guarantees the effect of instructions moved somewhere else, as will be seen soon. From the as yet unscheduled basic blocks we now again choose that which is most frequently executed and repeat the procedure until all basic blocks of the procedure have been scheduled. Figure 12.22 shows the control flow graph of a procedure with a division into traces which are numbered in the order of decreasing frequency.

We now consider the question of how to construct sequences of long instruction words for traces and the corresponding compensation code required.

A trace can be viewed as an extended basic block with forks leading out and joins leading into it. The instructions of the trace now have to be packed into as short a sequence of long instruction words as possible, in such a way that the semantic constraints determined by the dependencies and the control flow are not violated.

Let us suppose that there are an unlimited number of functional units and arbitrarily long instruction words. Then, the shortest possible sequence of long instruction words is as long as the longest (critical) path of the dependency graph. One possible algorithm with optimal result can be derived from topological sorting. Whenever a new instruction word is to be filled there exists a set of candidates,

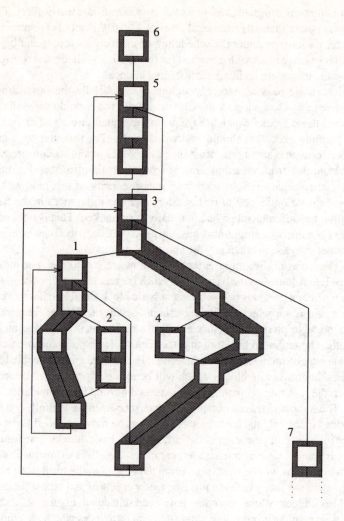

Figure 12.22 Traces in a control flow graph, numbered in decreasing order of the frequency with which they are executed.

that is, instructions, which no longer have a predecessor. These are all inserted into this instruction word. If this involves drawing an instruction past a fork, this can be done using special semantic-preserving transformations which ensure that the necessary compensation code is generated. Conditional forks can also be packed into the current word. The precise number of conditional forks that may be held in a long instruction word, and how these should be treated, depends on the specific hardware. They may be packed from left to right into the instruction word in the order in which they occur, if when processing such an instruction word the machine executes the leftmost branch whose condition is satisfied.

The semantics-preserving transformations mentioned above are based on the **generalized dependency graph**.

Let us consider conditional statements and loops. There are two possible paths for a conditional statement s_0; **if** b **then** s_1 **else** s_2 **fi**; s_3 in the context s_0 and s_3, namely s_0; b; s_1; s_3 and s_0; b; s_2; s_3. The generalized dependency graph contains all dependencies between uses and definitions on these two paths. The algorithm **BBA-Graph** is modified as follows to achieve this. Both paths for the conditional statement are executed from the beginning with the same values of *lastDefins* and *exposedUses*. When both branches have been executed, the union of the actual values of *lastDefins* and *exposedUses* is formed; then the condition is processed.

For a loop s_0; **while** b **do** s_1 **od**; s_2 in the context s_0 and s_2 there are potentially infinitely many paths s_0; b; $(s_1; b)^*$; s_2. To compute the dependencies between definitions and uses in s_0, b, s_1 and s_2, it is sufficient to consider the paths s_0; b; s_2 and s_0; b; s_1; b; s_1; b; s_2. The **BBA-Graph** algorithm is altered as follows to process **while** loops. Each loop is executed twice, first with the values of *lastDefins* and *exposedUses* valid before it, and then with the new values obtained after the processing of the loop is completed, that is, after the loop condition.

Transformations that result in the movement of instructions over conditional forks and joins of the control flow, such as those that occur in conditional statements and loops, can be shown to preserve the semantics using the generalized dependency graph. Suppose the program is represented as a control flow graph (with the additional edges of the extended dependency graph).

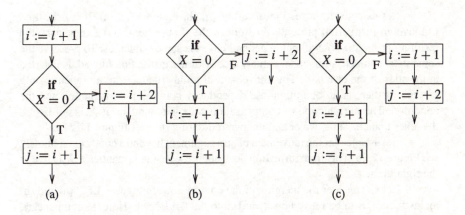

Figure 12.23   Reordering of code with introduction of compensation code.

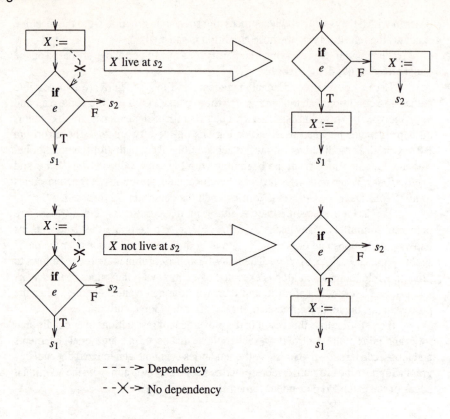

Figure 12.24   Movement of assignments beyond forks.

Let us consider a section of a flow graph, Figure 12.23(a). If it is desired to move an instruction presently in front of the **if** statement to the **then** part, the resulting program, (b), will not in general have the same semantics. To preserve the semantics, compensation code, namely a copy of the instruction moved, is inserted at the start of the **else** part. This movement of an instruction into a branch is only possible if there is no definition–use dependency between the instruction and the condition. The introduction of compensation code is redundant, if X is not live in the other branch. Thus, we obtain the two reordering rules of Figure 12.24.

Let us consider the movement of an assignment beyond a conditional branch, see Figure 12.25. This transformation does not preserve the semantics if X is live in the right branch.

Let us consider the merging of the control flow. In Figures 12.26(a) and (b) an instruction is to be moved backwards into the left branch. Here, to compensate, a copy of the instruction must be introduced at the end of the right path. This leads to the rule of Figure 12.26(c).

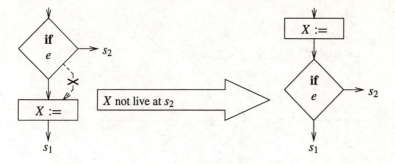

Figure 12.25   Moving an assignment out.

Forks may also be interchanged with forks or with joins. In Figure 12.27, the program fragment in (a) can be transformed to that in (b). The general rule for this is shown in Figure 12.28, in which the box contains a basic block. The second condition must not depend on any of its instructions. The correctness of the transformation of

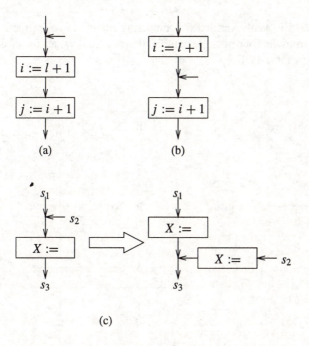

Figure 12.26   Exchange of an assignment and a branch.

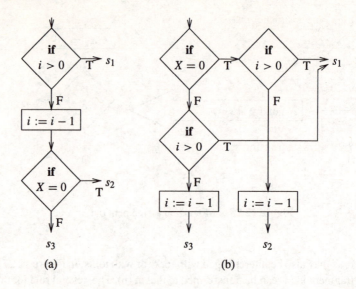

Figure 12.27 Movement of a fork.

Figure 12.28 is easily verified by comparing the executed instruction sequences obtained from the four possible combinations of truth values for e_1 and e_2. These are listed in Table 12.1.

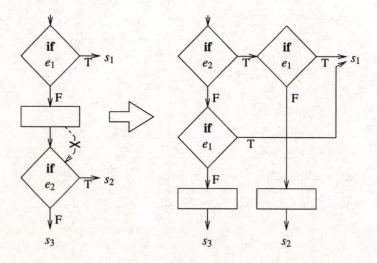

Figure 12.28 Exchange of forks.

Table 12.1   The instruction sequences before (left) and after the transformation of Figure 12.28.

$e_1^{e_2}$	T		F	
T	$e_1; s_1$	$e_2; e_1; s_1$	$e_1; s_1$	$e_2; e_1; s_1$
F	$e_1; \square; e_2; s_2$	$e_2; e_1; \square; s_2$	$e_1; \square; e_2; s_3$	$e_2; e_1; \square; s_3$

Figure 12.29 shows a transformation that moves a fork in front of a join.

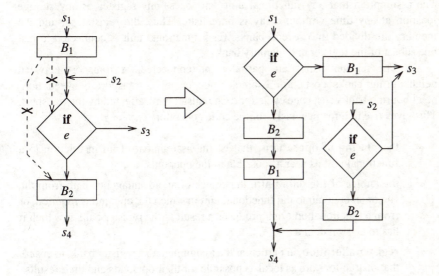

Figure 12.29   Forks and joins.

12.6.4   Realistic VLIW computers

We shall now renounce the unrealistic assumptions about the VLIW machine step by step and describe the additional problems the code generator consequently has to solve.

Finite number of functional units

Let us again consider the instruction sequencing problem as that of scheduling the generalized dependency graph using the given transformations into as few levels as possible. Now, the levels have only a finite width, given by the number of functional units. According to one sensible heuristic, it is advantageous to first schedule the instructions on the longest path if there are more candidates than functional units.

Different execution times of instructions

In real machines a multiplication and a load from memory take longer than an addition. Thus, we label every edge of the dependency graph with the necessary delay. Whence, a path through the dependency graph is critical if the sum of its delays is maximal. The heuristics might say that instructions on the longest path should be preferred in the scheduling.

Limited bandwidth of the register set and the memory

The assumption that any functional unit can access any register or any storage location at any time without delay is unrealistic. Thus, the register set and the memory are divided into several banks. Each functional unit is connected to just one subset of the register and memory banks.

The register banks are partially interconnected. A transport between neighbouring banks costs, for example, one cycle; a transport between non-neighbouring banks costs one cycle for each register bank affected by the transport. This gives rise to three new tasks for the code generator:

- the **placing of operations**, that is, the assignment of an instruction to a functional unit as near as possible to the operands,

- the **choice of the data path**, the choice of an advantageous path from the site of an operand to the functional unit in which the operand is required, or from a functional unit that produces a result to the register bank in which it has to be stored, and

- **register allocation**, in particular the assignment to a register bank, to ensure that instructions are as local as possible for their operands and their results.

A detailed treatment of this problem is beyond the scope of this book.

12.7 Exercises

1: Describe the control flow graph for a **for** loop **for** $I := E_1$ **step** E_2 **until** E_3 **do** S **od** with the following two semantics:

(a) E_2 and E_3 are re-evaluated before each entry into the loop body, and the test $(value(I) - value(E_3)) * sign(value(E_2)) > 0$ is performed.

(b) E_1, E_2 and E_3 are only evaluated once before the loop is entered.

2:

(a) Construct the control flow graph for the following program fragment.

$$
\begin{aligned}
&\textbf{while} \quad d > 0 \textbf{ do}\\
&\qquad a := b + c;\\
&\qquad d := d - b;\\
&\qquad e := a + f;\\
&\qquad \textbf{if } e \neq 0\\
&\qquad\quad \textbf{then} \quad f := a - d;\\
&\qquad\quad \textbf{else} \quad b := d + f;\\
&\qquad\qquad\qquad e := a - c;\\
&\qquad \textbf{fi};\\
&\qquad b := a + c;\\
&\textbf{od}
\end{aligned}
$$

(b) Compute the set of live variables on entry to each statement, assuming that b, c, d, e and f are live on exiting the loop.

3: Use the method of Section 12.4.1 to generate code for the following expressions. The target machine is assumed to be the two-address machine considered, with three universal registers.

(a) $d := a + b * c$

(b) $g := a * (b + c) + d * (e - f)$

4: Complete the method of Section 12.4.2 so that an optimal instruction sequence is produced for expression trees decorated with the corresponding additional information.

5:

(a) Compute the register interference graph for the program of Exercise 2.

(b) Colour the register interference graph of (a) using three colours.

6: Modify the **FB-Scheduling algorithm** so that it schedules dependency graphs whose edges are labelled with minimal delays.

7: Alter the **BBA-Graph** algorithm so that it executes a liveness analysis of the machine resources in parallel and only records definition–definition dependencies if the resource defined is live at least at one of the two definitions.

12.8 Literature

Register allocation

The idea of viewing register allocation as a graph colouring problem first appeared in work by Lavrov (1962). The use of this technique in the ALPHA programming system is described in Ershov (1962). The technique has become famous through the implementation of the heuristic procedure described in Section 12.5 in a PL.8 compiler (Chaitin, 1982, Chaitin *et al.*, 1982). Chow and Hennessy (1990) proposed the splitting and merging of life ranges, to obtain better colouring.

Code selection integrated with register allocation

Some early works considered the code generation problem for expression trees and very simple target machines. Ershov (1958) proposed the well-known labelling algorithm, which calculates the register requirements for subtrees and treats the operands with the greatest register requirements first for every operator. Sethi and Ullman (1970) showed that labelling algorithms of this type generate optimal code for expression trees. For directed acyclic expression graphs, that is, expressions with common subexpressions, the problem of optimal code generation has been shown to be NP complete under simple assumptions (Sethi, 1975; Bruno and Sethi, 1976; Aho *et al.*, 1977). Aho and Johnson (1976) proposed pursuing the various ways of generating code for an expression in parallel, tabulating the corresponding costs for subtrees and thus choosing the cheapest solution in linear time.

Instruction scheduling

The problem of compact scheduling of an instruction sequence first arose in the generation of microcode. Like programs for VLIW machines, microprograms are packed into long instruction words. But the individual instructions, the parts of a 'horizontal' microinstruction word, control not whole functional units but data paths and circuits such as adders or shifters. Fisher (1979) describes the compression of microcode and the basis for scheduling traces. The TRACE VLIW architecture and the code generation for it are described in detail in the dissertation of Ellis (1986). A short description of the code generation techniques can be found in Fisher *et al.* (1984).

Early machines with instruction pipelines, such as the IBM 360/91 and the Control Data 6600, had hardware that dynamically checked the next instructions for collisions and loaded them into the pipeline when no collisions were detected. Important papers on the static scheduling of instruction sequences to avoid collisions include those by Gross and Hennessy (Gross, 1983; Hennessy and Gross, 1983) and Gibbons and Muchnick (1986). The procedure described in Section 12.6.2 follows the latter.

Bibliography

Abramsky S. and Hankin C. (1987). *Abstract Interpretation of Declarative Languages*. Chichester: Ellis Horwood

Aho A.V. and Ganapathi M. (1985). Efficient tree pattern matching: an aid to code generation. In *Proc. 12th ACM Symp. on Principles of Programming Languages*, New Orleans, pp. 334–40. ACM Press

Aho A.V. and Johnson S.C. (1976). Optimal code generation for expression trees. *Journal of the ACM*, **23**(3), 488–501

Aho A.V., Johnson S.C. and Ullman J.D. (1977). Code generation for expressions with common subexpressions. *Journal of the ACM*, **24**(1), 146–60

Aho A.V. and Ullman J.D. (1972). *The Theory of Parsing, Translation and Compiling. Vol.1: Parsing*. Englewood Cliffs, N.J.: Prentice-Hall

Aho A.V. and Ullman J.D. (1973). *The Theory of Parsing, Translation and Compiling. Vol.2: Compiling*. Englewood Cliffs, N.J.: Prentice-Hall

Aït-Kaci H. (1991). *Warren's Abstract Machine – A Tutorial Reconstruction*. Cambridge MA: MIT Press

Alblas H. (1991). Attribute evaluation methods. In (Alblas H. and Melichar B., eds) *Attribute Grammars, Applications and Systems. International Summer School SAGA*, Prague, June, LNCS 545. Berlin, Heidelberg, New York: Springer

Ammann U. (1978). Error Recovery in Recursive Descent Parsers and Run-time Storage Organization. *Rep. No. 25*, Inst. für Informatik der ETH Zürich

Ammann U. (1981). Code generation of a Pascal compiler, In *Pascal – The Language and its Implementation* (Barron D.W., ed.). Chichester: Wiley

ANSI (1990). *The Annotated C++ Reference Manual*. ANSI base document

Apt K.R. (1990). *Logic Programming, Handbook of Theoretical Computer Science*. Amsterdam: Elsevier

Barron D.W. (1981). *Pascal – The Language and its Implementation*. Chichester: Wiley

Bezem M. (1988). Logic programming and PROLOG. *CWI Quarterly*, **1**(3), 15–29. Amsterdam: Centre for Mathematics and Computer Science

Bobrow D.G. and Stefik M.J. (1982). *LOOPS: an Object-Oriented Programming System for Interlisp*

Börstler J., Möncke U. and Wilhelm R. (1991). Table compression for tree automata. *ACM Transactions on Programming Languages and Systems*, **13**(3), 295–314

Bratko I. (1990). *Prolog Programming for Artificial Intelligence*, 2nd edn. Wokingham: Addison-Wesley

Bruno J. and Sethi R. (1976). Code generation for a one-register machine. *Journal of the ACM*, **23**(3), 502–10

Burn G.L. (1987). Abstract interpretation and the parallel evaluation of functional languages. *PhD Thesis*, Department of Computing, Imperial College of Science and Technology, University of London

Burn G.L., Hankin C.L. and Abramsky S. (1985). The theory and practice of strictness analysis for higher order functions. In *Programs as Data Objects* (Jones N.D., ed.), LNCS 217, pp. 42–62. Berlin, Heidelberg, New York: Springer

Burton W., Maurer D., Oberhauser H.-G. and Wilhelm R. (1987). A space-efficient optimization of call-by-need. *IEEE Transactions on Software Engineering*, **13**(6), 636–42

Cannon H.I. (1980). Flavors. *Technical report*, MIT Artificial Intelligence Laboratory

Chaitin G.J. (1982). Register allocation and spilling via graph coloring. In *Proc. SIGPLAN'82 Symp. on Compiler Construction*, Boston, MA, June, SIGPLAN Notices, **17**(6), 201–7

Chaitin G.J., Auslander M.A., Chandra A.K, Cocke J., Hopkins M.E. and Markstein P.W. (1981). Register allocation via coloring. *Computer Languages*, **6**, 47–57

Chase D.R. (1987). An improvement to bottom-up tree pattern matching. In *Proc. 14th ACM Symposium on Principles of Programming Languages* (POPL-14), Munich, pp. 168–77. ACM Press

Chow F. and Hennessy J. (1990). The priority-based coloring approach to register allocation. *ACM Transactions on Programming Languages and Systems*, **12**(4)

Clocksin W.F. and Mellish C.S. (1984). *Programming in Prolog* 3rd edn. Berlin, Heidelberg, New York: Springer

Cohen J. and Hickey T.J. (1987). Parsing and compiling using Prolog. *ACM Transactions on Programming Languages and Systems*, **9**(2)

Courcelle B. (1984). Attribute grammars: definitions, analysis of dependencies. In *Methods and Tools for Compiler Construction* (Lorho B., ed.). Cambridge UK: Cambridge University Press

Courcelle B. (1986). Equivalences and transformations of regular systems. Applications to program schemes and grammars. *Theor. Comp. Sci.*, **42**, 1–122

Cousot P. and Cousot R. (1977). Abstract interpretation: a unified lattice model for static analysis of programs by construction of approximation of fixpoints. In *Proc. 4th ACM Symposium on Principles of Programming Languages*, Los Angeles, January, pp. 238–58

Cousot P. and Cousot R. (1987). Systematic design of data flow analysis frameworks. In *Proc. 6th ACM Symposium on Principles of Programming Languages*, San Antonio, January

Cox B.J. (1986). *Object-Oriented Programming: An Evolutionary Approach*. Reading, MA: Addison-Wesley

Dahl O.-J., Myrhaug B. and Nygaard K. (1984). (Simula 67) Common Base Language. *Technical Report S-22*, Norsk Regnesentral, Oslo, 1970, revised 1984

Damas L. and Milner R. (1982). Principal type schemes for functional programs. In *Proc. 9th ACM Symp. on Principles of Programming Languages*, Albuquerque, January, pp. 207–12

Dencker P., Dürre K. and Henft J. (1984). Optimization of parser tables for portable compilers. *ACM Transactions on Programming Languages and Systems*, **6**(4), 546–72

Deransart P., Jourdan M. and Lorho B. (1988). *Attribute Grammars, Definitions, Systems and Bibliography*, LNCS 323. Berlin, Heidelberg, New York: Springer

DeRemer F.L. (1969). Practical translators for LR(k) languages. *PhD Thesis*, MIT

DeRemer F.L. (1971). Simple LR(k) grammars. *Communications of the ACM*, **14**, 453–60

DeRemer F.L. (1974). Lexical analysis. In *Compiler Construction, An Advanced Course* (Bauer F.L. and Eickel J., eds.), LNCS 21. Berlin, Heidelberg, New York: Springer

DeRemer F.L. and Penello T. (1982). Efficient computation of LALR(1) look-ahead sets. *ACM Transactions on Programming Languages and Systems*, **4**(4), 615–49

Dershowitz N. and Jouannaud J.-P. (1990). Rewrite systems. In *Handbook of Theoretical Computer Science* (Leeuwen J.v., ed.), Chapter 6. Amsterdam: Elsevier

Downey P.J., Sethi R. and Tarjan R.E. (1980). Variations on the common subexpression problem. *Journal of the ACM*, **27**, 758–71

Ellis J.R. (1986). *Bulldog: A Computer for VLIW Architectures*. Cambridge MA: MIT Press

Emmelmann H. (1992). Code selection by regularly controlled term rewriting. In *Proc. Workshop: CODE'91* in Dagstuhl. Berlin, Heidelberg, New York: Springer Workshop

Engelfriet J. (1984). Attribute grammars: attribute evaluation methods. In *Methods and Tools for Compiler Construction* (Lorho B., ed.). Cambridge UK: Cambridge University Press

Engelfriet J. and Filé G. (1982). Simple multi-visit attribute grammars. *Journal of Computer and System Sciences*, **24**, 283–314

Ershov A.P. (1958). On programming of arithmetic operations. *Communications of the ACM*, **1**(8), 3–6 and **1**(9), 16

Ershov A.P. (1962). Reducing the problem of memory allocation when compiling programs to one of coloring the vertices of graphs. *Doklady Akademii Nauk S.S.S.R.*, **124**(4). English translation in *Soviet Math*, **3**

Eulenstein M. (1988). *Generierung portabler Compiler*. IFB 164. Berlin, Heidelberg, New York: Springer

Fairbairn J. and Wray S.C. (1986). Code generation techniques for functional languages. In *Proc. 1986 ACM Conference on LISP and Functional Programming*, Cambridge MA, August, pp. 94–104. ACM Press

Fairbairn J. and Wray S.C. (1987). TIM. A simple, lazy abstract machine to execute supercombinators. In *Functional Programming Languages and Computer Architecture* (Kahn G., ed.), LNCS 274, pp. 34–45. Berlin, Heidelberg, New York: Springer

Ferdinand C, Seidl H. and Wilhelm R. (1994). Tree automata for code selection. *Acta Informatica*, **31**(8), 741–60

Fisher J.A. (1979). The Optimization of Horizontal Microcode within and beyond Basic Blocks: An Application of Processor Scheduling with Resources. *Department of Energy Report C00-3077-161*, Courant Mathematics and Computing Laboratory, New York University

Fisher J.A., Ellis J.R., Ruttenberg J.C. and Nicolau A. (1984). Parallel processing: a smart compiler and a dumb machine. In *Proc. ACM SIGPLAN'84 Symp. on Compiler Construction*, Montreal, June, SIGPLAN Notices, **19**(6), 37–44

Ganzinger H. and Wilhelm R. (1975). Verschränkung von Compilermoduln. In *ESOP '88, 2nd European Symposium on Programming*, Nancy, LNCS 34, pp. 654–65. Berlin, Heidelberg, New York: Springer

Gecseg F. and Steinby M. (1984). *Tree Automata*. Akademiai Kiado, Budapest

Gibbons P.B. and Muchnick S.S. (1986). Efficient instruction scheduling for a pipeline architecture. *SIGPLAN Notices*, **21**(9), 172–84

Giegerich R. (1990). Code selection by inversion of order-sorted derivors. *Theoretical Computer Science*, **73**, 177–211

Giegerich R. and Schmal K. (1988). Code selection techniques: pattern matching, tree parsing, and inversion of derivors. In *Proc. ESOP 88* (Ganzinger H., ed.), Nancy, March, LNCS 300, pp. 247–68. Berlin, Heidelberg, New York: Springer

Giegerich R. and Wilhelm R. (1978). Counter-one-pass features in one-pass compilation: a formalization using attribute grammars. *Information Processing Letters*, **7**(6), 279–84

Glanville R.S. (1977). A machine independent algorithm for code generation and its use in retargetable compilers. *PhD Thesis*, University of California, Berkeley

Glanville R.S. and Graham S.L. (1978). A new method for compiler code generation. In. *Proc. 5th ACM Symp. on Principles of Programming Languages*, Tucson, January, pp. 231–40

Goldberg A. and Robson D. (1983). *Smalltalk-80: the Language and its Implementation*. Reading, MA: Addison-Wesley

Goldberg B. and Hudak P. (1985). Serial combinators, optimal grains of parallelism. In *LNCS 201*, pp. 382–99. Berlin, Heidelberg, New York: Springer

Graham S.L. and Wegman M. (1976). A fast and usualy linear algorithm for global data flow analysis. *Journal of the ACM*, **23**(1), 172–202

Gross T.R. (1983). Code Optimization of Pipeline Constraints. *Technical Report 83-255*, Computer Systems Laboratory, Stanford University

Harrison M.A. (1983). *Introduction to Formal Language Theory*. Reading, MA: Addison Wesley

Hecht M.S. (1977). *Flow Analysis of Computer Programs*. Amsterdam: Elsevier

Heckmann R. (1986). An efficient ELL(1)-parser generator. *Acta Informatica*, **23**, 127–48

Heckmann R. and Sander G. (1993). TrafoLa-H reference manual. In *Program Development by Specification and Transformation; The PROSPECTRA Methodology, Language Family, and System*, LNCS 680. Berlin, Heidelberg, New York: Springer

Henderson P. (1980). *Functional Programming, Application and Implementation*. Englewood Cliffs, N.J.: Prentice-Hall

Hennessy J.L. and Gross T.R. (1983). Postpass code optimization of pipeline constraints. *ACM Transactions on Programming Languages and Systems*, **5**(3), 422–48

Henry R.R. (1984). Graham–Glanville code generators. *PhD Thesis*, University of California, Berkeley

Henry R.R. and Damron P.C. (1989a). Algorithms for Table-Driven Code Generators Using Tree-Pattern Matching. *Technical Report # 89-02-03*, University of Washington, Seattle

Henry R.R. and Damron P.C. (1989b). Encoding Optimal Pattern Selection in a Table-Driven Bottom-Up Tree-Pattern Matcher. *Technical Report # 89-02-04*, University of Washington, Seattle

Hindley R. (1969). The principal type scheme of an object in combinatory logic. *Transactions of the AMS*, **146**, 29–60

Hoffmann C.M. and O'Donnell M.J. (1982). Pattern matching in trees. *Journal of the ACM*, **29**(1), 68–95

Hopcroft J. and Ullman J.D. (1979). *Introduction to Automata Theory, Languages and Computation*. Reading, MA: Addison-Wesley

Hullot J.-M. (1984). Cexy, Version 15:I – une Initiation. *Technical Report 44*, INRIA

Jazayeri M., Ogden W. and Rounds W. (1975). The intrinsically exponential complexity of the circularity problem for attribute grammars. *Communications of the ACM*, **18**, 697–706

Johnson W.L., Porter J.H., Achley S.I. and Ross D.T. (1968). Automatic generation of efficient lexical analyzers using finite state techniques. *Communications of the ACM*, **11**(12), 805–113

Johnsson T. (1984). Efficient compilation of lazy evaluation. In *Proc. ACM SIGPLAN 84 Symposium on Compiler Construction*, Montreal, June, SIGPLAN Notices, **19**(6), 58–69

Jones N.D. (1981). Flow analysis of lambda expressions. In *Symposium on Functional Languages and Computer Architecture*, Aspenaes, Sweden, June, pp. 376–407

Jones N. (1987). Flow analysis of lazy higher-order functional programs. In *Abstract Interpretation of Declarative Langages* (Abramsky S. and Hankin C., eds), pp. 103–22

Kastens U. (1980). Ordered attribute grammars. *Acta Informatica*, **13**(3), 229–56

Keller P. and Maas T. (1990). An OPTRAN-generated frontend for ADA. In *Attribute Grammars and their Applications, Proc. International Conference WAGA*, Paris, September, LNCS 461, pp. 268–83. Berlin, Heidelberg, New York: Springer

Kennedy K. and Warren S.K. (1976). Automatic generation of efficient evaluators for attribute grammars. In *Proc. 3rd ACM Symp. on Principles of Programming Languages*, Atlanta GA, January, pp. 32–49

Kildall G. (1973). A unified approch to global program optimization. In *Proc. ACM Symp. on Principles of Programming Languages*, Boston MA, October, pp. 194–206

Knuth D.E. (1965). On the translation of languages from left to right. *Information and Control*, **8**, 607–39

Knuth D.E. (1968). Semantics of context-free languages. *Math. Systems Theory*, **2**, 127-45

Knuth D.E. (1971). Semantics of context-free languages. Correction in *Math. Systems Theory*, **5**, 95–6

Krieg B.H. (1971). Formal definition of the block concept and some implementation models. *MS Thesis*, Cornell University

Kron H. (1975). Tree templates and subtree transformational grammars. *PhD Thesis*, University of California, Santa Cruz

Landin P.J. (1964). The mechanical evaluation of expressions. *Computer Journal*, **6**(4)

Lavrov S.S. (1961). Store economy in closed operator schemes. *Journal of Computational Mathematics and Mathematical Physics*, **1**(4), 687–701. English translation in *U.S.S.R. Computational Mathematics and Mathematical Physics*, **3**, 1962

Lesk M. (1975). LEX – a Lexical Analyzer Generator. *CSTR 39*, Bell Laboratories, Murray Hill, N.J.

Lewi J., DeVlaminck K., Huens J. and Steegmans E. (1982). *A Programming Methodology in Compiler Construction, part 2*. Amsterdam: North Holland

Lewis II P.M. and Stearns R.E. (1966). Syntax directed transduction. In *IEEE 7th Annual Symposium on Switching and Automata Theory*, Berkeley CA, October, pp. 21–35

Lewis II P.M. and Stearns R.E. (1968). Syntax directed transduction. *Journal of the ACM*, **15**, 464–88

Lipps P., Olk M., Möncke U. and Wilhelm R. (1988). Attribute (re)evaluation in the OPTRAN system. *Acta Informatica*, **26**, 213–39

Lloyd J.W. (1987). *Foundations of Logic Programming* 2nd edn. Berlin, Heidelberg, New York: Springer

Lorho B., ed. (1984). *Methods and Tools for Compiler Construction*. Cambridge UK: Cambridge University Press

Maier D. and Warren D.S. (1988). *Computing with Logic, Logic Programming with Prolog*. Benjamin/Cummings

Mathis N. (1990). Weiterentwicklung eines Codeselektorgenerators und Anwendung auf den NSC32000. *Diploma Thesis*, Universität des Saarlandes

Maurer D. (1987). Relevanzanalyse – eine Kombination von Striktheits- und Datenflussanalyse zur effizienten Auswertung funktionaler Programme. *Dissertation*, Universität des Saarlandes, IFB. Berlin, Heidelberg, New York: Springer

McKeeman W.M. (1974). Compiler construction. In *Compiler Construction, an Advanced Course* (Bauer F.L. and Eickel J., eds) LNCS 21, pp. 1–36. Berlin, Heidelberg, New York: Springer

McKeeman W.M. and DeRemer F.L. (1974). Feedback-free modularization of compilers. 3. GI-Fachtagung über Programmiersprachen, Kiel

Mehlhorn K. (1986). *Datenstrukturen und Algorithmen*. Stuttgart: Teubner

Meyer B. (1991). *Eiffel: The Language*. Englewood Cliffs, N.J.: Prentice-Hall

Meyer B. (1993). *Object-oriented Software Construction*. Englewood Cliffs, N.J.: Prentice-Hall

Milner R. (1978). A theory of type polymorphism in programming. *Journal of Computer and System Sciences*, **17**, 348–75

Möncke U. (1985). Generierung von Systemen zur Transformation attributierter Operatorbäume; Komponenten des Systems und Mechanismen der Generierung. *Dissertation*, Universität des Saarlandes

Möncke U. (1987). Simulating Automata for Weighted Tree Reductions. *Technical Report No. A10/87*, Universität des Saarlandes

Möncke U. and Wilhelm R. (1982). Iterative algorithms on grammar graphs. In *Proc. 8th Conference on Graph Theoretic Concepts in Computer Science*, pp. 177–94. Hanser

Möncke U. and Wilhelm R. (1991). Grammar flow analysis. In *Attribute Grammars, Applications and Systems* (Alblas H. and Melichar B., eds), LNCS 545. Berlin, Heidelberg, New York: Springer

Möncke U., Weisberger B. and Wilhelm R. (1986). Generative support for transformational programming *ESPRIT: Status Report of Continuing Work*. Amsterdam: Elsevier

Muchnick S.S. and Jones N.D. (1981). *Program Flow Analysis, Theory and Applications*. Englewood Cliffs, N.J.: Prentice-Hall

Mycroft A. (1980). The theory and practice of transforming call-by-need into call-by-value. In *Proc. 4th Int. Symp. on Programming*, LNCS 83, pp. 269–81. Berlin, Heidelberg, New York: Springer

Mycroft A. and Nielson F. (1983). Strong abstract interpretation using power domains. In *Proc. ICALP 83. Automata, Languages and Programming: 10th Colloquium* (Diaz J., ed.), Barcelona, July, LNCS 154. Berlin, Heidelberg, New York: Springer

Nielson F. (1986a). Abstract interpretation of denotational definitions. In *Proc. STACS 86. 3rd Annual Symposium on Theoretical Aspects of Computer Science* (Monien B. and Vidal-Naquet, eds), Osay, January, LNCS 210. Berlin, Heidelberg, New York: Springer

Nielson F. (1986b). Expected forms of data flow analysis. In *Proc. DIKU Workshop on Programs as Data Objects*, LNCS 217. Berlin, Heidelberg, New York: Springer

Nielson H. (Riis) (1983). Computation sequences: a way to characterize classes of attribute grammars. *Acta Informatica*, **19**, 255–68

Nijholt A. (1983). *Deterministic Top-Down and Bottom-Up Parsing, Historical Notes and Bibliographies*. Mathematical Centre Amsterdam

Olender K.M. and Osterweil L.J. (1992). Interprocedural static analysis of sequencing constraints. *ACM Transactions on Software Engineering and Methodology*, **1**(1), 21–53

Pelegri-Llopart E. (1988). Rewrite systems, pattern matching, and code selection. *PhD Thesis*, University of California, Berkeley

Pelegri-Llopart E. and Graham S.L. (1988). Optimal code generation for expression trees: an application of BURS theory. In *Proc. 15th ACM Symposium on Principles of Programming Languages* (POPL-15), San Diego, pp. 294–308

Pemberton S. and Daniels M. (1982). *Pascal Implementation, The P4 Compiler*. Chichester: Ellis Horwood

Penello T.J. and DeRemer F.L. (1978). A forward move for LR error recovery. *Proc. 5th ACM Symp. on Principles of Programming Languages*, Tucson, January, pp. 241–54

Penello T.J., DeRemer F.L. and Myers R. (1980). A simplified operator identification scheme for Ada. *ACM SIGPLAN Notices*, **15**(7, 8), 82–7

Peyton Jones S.L. (1987). *The Implementation of Functional Programming Languages*. Englewood Cliffs, N.J.: Prentice-Hall

Randell B. and Russel L.J. (1964). *Algol 60 Implementation*. New York: Academic Press

Ripken K. (1977). Formale Beschreibungen von Maschinen, Implementierungen und optimierender Maschinencode–Erzeugung aus attributierten Programmgraphen. *Dissertation*, TU Munich

Sethi R. (1975). Complete register allocation problems. *SIAM Journal of Computing*, **4**(3), 226–48

Sethi R. and Ullman J.D. (1970). The generation of optimal code for arithmetic expressions. *Journal of the ACM*, **17**(4), 715–28

Sippu S. and Soisalon-Soininen E. (1990a). *Parsing Theory. Vol.1: Languages and Parsing*. Berlin, Heidelberg, New York: Springer

Sippu S. and Soisalon-Soininen E. (1990b). *Parsing Theory. Vol.2: LR(k) and LL(k) Parsing*. Berlin, Heidelberg, New York: Springer

Steel T.B. (1961). A first version of UNCOL. In *Extending Man's Intellect. Proc. Western Joint Computer Conference*, Los Angeles, May, NJCC Conferences 19, pp. 371–8

Sterling L. and Shapiro E. (1986). *The Art of Prolog, Advanced Programming Techniques*. Cambridge MA: MIT Press. 2nd edn.1994.

Stroustrup B. (1990). *The C++ Programming Language*, 2nd edn. Reading, MA: Addison-Wesley

Svensk Standard SS 636114 (1987). *SIS, Data Processing Programming Languages – SIMULA*

Tarjan R.E. and Yao A. (1979). Storing a sparse table. *Communications of the ACM*, **22**(11)

Ullman J.D. (1973). Fast algorithms for the elimination of common subexpressions. *Acta Informatica*, **2**, 191–213

Vyssotsky V. and Wegner P. (1963). A graph theoretical Fortran source language analyser. *Manuscript*. AT&T Bell Labs, Murray Hill, N.J.

Wadler P. and Hughes J. (1987). Projections for strictness analysis. In *Proc. Functional Programming Languages and Computer Architecture*, LNCS 274, pp. 385–407. Berlin, Heidelberg, New York: Springer

Warren D.H.D. (1977). Applied logic – its use and implementation as a programming language tool. *PhD Thesis*, University of Edinburgh

Warren D.H.D. (1983). An abstract PROLOG instruction set. *Technical Note 309*, SRI International

Watt D.A. (1977). The parsing problem for affix grammars. *Acta Informatica* **8**, 1–20

Watt D.A. (1984). Contextual constraints. In *Methods and Tools for Compiler Construction* (Lorho B., ed.). Cambridge UK: Cambridge University Press.

Weisgerber B. and Wilhelm R. (1989). Two Tree Pattern Matchers for Code Selection (Including Targeting). *Technischer Report A 09/86*, Fachbereich Informatik, Universität des Saarlandes. In *Compiler Compilers and High Speed Compilation* (Hammer D., ed.), LNCS 371, pp. 215–29. Berlin, Heidelberg, New York: Springer

Wirth N. (1978). *Algorithms + Data Structures = Programs*, Chapter 5. Englewood Cliffs, N.J.: Prentice-Hall

Index

ε successor state   244, 245
λ-abstraction   64

abstract class   175
  interpretation   386, 464, 491
  machine   5, 487
    MaMa   83
    P   9
    WiM   138
    syntax   389
abstraction relation   464
accumulation property   493
action table   360
Ada   391, 395, 398, 545
address
  assignment   229
  environment   43, 45
    MaMa   88
    WiM   140
  register   550
addressing
  forms   519, 550
Algol   19, 34, 53, 387, 391, 395, 398
alias
  analysis   576
  name   572
  problem   572
  relationship   561
alphabet   236
  with arity function   524
alternatives
  (for nonterminals)   271
  (for predicates)   116
analysis
  lexical   223, 236, 271
  phase   222
  semantic   226, 386
  syntax   225, 266
answer
  computed   125
  correct   124
argument register   161
arity function   524

array
  descriptor   25, 45, 51–2
  dimension   21
  dynamic   24
  range   21
  static   19
ascending chain condition   495
assignment   10
associative array   213
ATOM   139
attribute   173, 406
  dependence   418
  evaluation   417, 433, 437
    parser-driven   447
    visit-oriented   437
  grammar   405
    l-ordered   434, 442
    non-circular   420, 428
      absolutely   444
    ordered   444
    production-local dependence   418
    well-formed   409, 421
  instance   405, 408
  occurrence   405, 406
    applied   406
    defining   406

background memory   549
backtrack   153
backtrack frame   161
backtrack point   135, 151, 154
backtracking   151
backwards analysis   501
backwards problem   490
backwards trace machine   501
base
  class   175, 197
BASIC   86
basic
  block   559
    graph   560
  value   72
BBA-Graph   575, 583

bind   117
binding   81
   dynamic   35
      LaMa   74–5
      Pascal   35
   pointer
      MaMa   89
      Prolog   121
   static   35
      LaMa   74–5, 77
      Pascal   35
branch   559
   indexed   16
breadth-first search   130
BTP (WiM)   151

C   28, 34, 391
cache   549, 555
call
   graph   558, 561
   Pascal   46
   Prolog   114
call-by-name   74
call-by-need   74, 81, 84–7
call-by-value   74
case statement   16
character   271
   class   249, 251
characteristic finite automaton   343
characteristic graph
   lower   421, 428
   upper   422, 429
CISC   519, 554
clause   118, 150
   body   119
   definite   119
   deterministic   152, 161
   empty   119
   head   119
   Horn   119
   indexing   165
   non-deterministic   161
   notation   119
   query   119, 120
   unit   119
closed formula   118
CLOSURE   86
closure   75, 79, 80, 86, 93, 94, 99–102,
      103
   existential   119
   universal   119
code   155

code_A   142
code_P   155
code_PR   155
code_Q   155, 156
code_U   145
code generation   547, 552, 558, 561
code optimization   228
code selection   227, 519, 554, 557, 561
combination function   288
compensation code   581
compile time   4, 18
compiler generation   233
composition of substitutions   122
computation   484, 530
   accepting   530
   redundant   530
   rule   127, 131
concatenation
   k-   295
concrete
   machine   487
   syntax   389
condition code   550
conditional statement   13
configuration   240, 279
   error   366
   final   240, 279
   initial   240, 279
conflict   359
   shift–reduce   351, 359
   reduce–reduce   359
context   80, 485
   condition   386, 392
   lower   466
   upper   466
context-free grammar (cfg)   270, 271
continuation address
   MaMa   89
   negative (WiM)   152
   positive (WiM)   141
control flow   8
   graph   558
cost measure   538
current state   279
currying   67

D frame   162
data area   38
data memory   9
data register   550
data type
   user-defined   67

dataflow analysis   386, 499
declaration   388
definition
    reaching   505
    Prolog   119
        variable   505
delayed branches   558
delayed load   558
denotational   462
    semantics   462
dependence
    anti-   572
    functional   405
    global   426
    graph   419
        generalized   583
        individual   420
    output   572
    true   572
depth-first search   131
dereferencing   30
derivable   272
derivability   120
derivation   125, 272
    computed   125
    direct   125
    leftmost   276
    regular   317
    rightmost   276
    successful   125
    tree   526
    unsuccessful   125
derive   120
derived class   175
deterministic pushdown automaton
    280
DFLR algorithm   133
dynamic   18, 39, 89, 386, 434
    binding   177
    link (DL)   38, 46
    programming   567

environment   75, 81–3, 136
evaluation
    applicative order   74
    lazy   74
    normal order   74
    order   424, 433
    partial   3
expansion transition   281
expression   8
    available   505

expression continued
    Boolean   415
    busy   505, 506
    evaluation   548, 554
    let   404
    Prolog   121
external rule   407
extreme stack pointer   29

fact   116, 119
FB-scheduling   579
features   173
final state   240, 279
finite automaton
    characteristic   343
    deterministic   243, 244
    non-deterministic   239, 241
FIRST   295
FIRST$_1$ 319
folding of constants   517
FOLLOW   295
FOLLOW$_1$ 319, 364
forks   559
formula   118
    atomic   118
    closed   118
Fortran   391, 398
forwards problem   490
forwards trace machine   500
FP (WiM)   139
frame pointer   85
    MaMa   88
function
    anonymous   64
    appplication   87, 89
    definition   64
        LaMa   79, 80, 92, 94
    higher-order   65, 76
    symbol   118
functional abstraction   72
functional result   86
FUNVAL   86
    object   79–80, 86, 95–9

garbage collection   29
generic   404
    class   209
    data type   209
genericity   178, 207
goal   116, 125, 142, 144
    list   125
    selected   125

grammar
  ambiguous   273
  attribute   405
  LALR(1)   364
  L-attributed   447
  LL-attributed   448
  LL(1) (simple)   305
  LL(*k*)   304, 305
    strong   309
  reduced 273
  S-attributed   448
  underlying   405
grammar flow analysis (GFA)   286, 425
  problem   288
    I/O graphs   431
    lower characteristic graphs   428
    upper characteristic graphs   429
graph colouring   568
greatest lower bound   492
ground
  instance   121
  substitution   121
  term   118

H (WiM)   139
handle   345
head of a rule   116
head term   144
heap
  MaMa   83–6
    memory management   83
  P-machine 29
  WiM   139
Herbrand universe   120
Horn clause   119
hot spots   580
HP (WiM)   139

implication   120
inactive   132
incarnation   8, 33
  live   33
  path   33
  Prolog   137
incomplete strategy   131
index register   550
indexed branch   16
inheritance   175
initial call list   116
initial state   240, 279
input alphabet   239, 279
input pattern   514

instance   121
instantiation   178, 209
instruction
  decode   557
  execution   557
  fetch   557
  pipeline   557, 578
  reordering   554, 557, 571
  scheduling   554, 557, 570
  set   548, 550, 551
interpretation
  abstract   386, 464, 491
  non-standard   501
interpreters   3
intersection   492
  problem   505
item
  complete   280
  context-free   280
  history   280
  pushdown automaton   280, 281, 304, 343
  rrpg   318
  valid   346
iterative statement   13, 14

joins   559

k-colourable   569
keyword   256

L value   10, 49
LALR(1) grammar   362, 364
language   272, 279
  accepted   240, 241
  defined   272
LAST symbol   328
lattice
  complete   290
least upper bound   492
left recursive   310
left value   10
letrec expression   102–3
lexical analysis   223, 236 271
life range   569
LISP   35
lists   104–8
literal   119
LL(*k*) grammar   304
logic program   114
logical consequence   114
lower characteristic graph   421, 428

LR-DFA   347
LR(k)   352
  parser   356

machine
  abstract   487
  concrete   487
  description   522
  grammar   522
  mathematical   484
  resource   572, 577
    live   577
main cycle
  MaMa   83, 84
  P-machine   10
MaMa   83, 84
mathematical machine   484
memory
  allocation
    dynamic   28
  hierarchy   548, 549, 554
  main   549, 554
  organization   548, 553
  release (MaMa)   84
meta-character   238
mode   139
model   120
module   222
Motorola 680x0   519

name
  bound   34
  free   34
  global   34
  local   34
ND frame   162
nesting depth   39
new
  MaMa   84
nine test   460
non-circular   433
  absolutely   433, 444
non-ground term   118
nonterminal   271
  productive   287, 291
  reachable   287, 292
  unproductive   273
  unreachable   273
normal form   406

object   173
  methods   173

object continued
  program   4
  proper   177
occur check   122
occurrence
  bound   76, 77
  free   76, 77
one-pass compiler   232
operand fetch 557
ordered partition   438
organizational cells
  MaMa   84, 89
  P-machine   38
output pattern   514
overloading   212, 397
over-supplied   87, 88
over-supply   98

P-machine   9
  data memory   9
  heap   29
  main cycle   10
  program memory   10
  runtime stack   37
parameter
  actual   46, 49
  formal   49, 53
  passing   46, 49
    LaMa   74
parse tree   273
parser   226, 271
  left   285
  right   285
Pascal   9, 270, 391, 395, 521
pass   232
passing of arguments
  WiM   142
pattern   524
  input   514
  linear   524
  matches 525
  output   514
PC (WiM)   139
peephole optimizer   230
pipeline   557, 570, 578
  hazard   558
  interlock   558
PL/I   34, 391
pointer   28
polymorphism   66, 177, 401
precomputation   3

predecessor
dynamic 38
static 36, 38
symbol 337
predicate 114
symbol 118
prefix
k- 295
viable 345
private 178
procedure
body 32
call 32, 46
declaration 32, 48
descriptor 54, 55
exiting 46
formal 53, 55
function 48
Pascal 32
Prolog 114
processor register 549, 555–8
produced 272
directly 272
production rule 271
program
Prolog 119
program clause 119
program counter 10, 550, 556
program expression (LaMa) 77, 78, 90, 291
program item 485
program memory
P-machine 10
WiM 139
program point 466
program transformations 514
algebraic 515
context-dependent 515
efficiency-increasing 228, 515
standardizing 517
Prolog 132, 302
computation 132
proof tree 134
propagation of constants 499
PS (WiM) 139
public 178
pushdown automaton 278, 279, 281
configuration 279
deterministic 280
item- 280, 304, 343
with output 284

quantifier 118
query 116, 119
query clause 119, 120

R value 10
record 27
recursive
directly 310
equation 64
left 310
right 310
reduction transition 282
REF 139
referential transparency 75
refutation 125
register
allocation 227, 553
base 550
collision 558
data 550
floating-point 549
index 550
interference graph 569
requirements 564
symbolic 568
window 556
regular
expression 238
language 238
subexpression 318
relative address 12, 18, 27
MaMa 88, 89, 95
P-machine 39
renaming 136
substitution 121
residue modulo four 459
resolution 125
resolvent 125
return address 38
return jump 48
right value 10
RISC 555
RLL(1) parser 321
recursive descent 322
row-major ordering 19
rule 115, 119
body 116
head 116
run time 4, 18
runtime type 177

scanner   223, 271, 372
  generation   251
scope   34, 70, 118, 390
scoping rules   386
screener   225
search
  breadth-first   130
  depth-first   131
  rule   131
  tree   130
segment   135
semantic analysis   226
  dynamic   226
  static   226
semantics
  auxiliary   500
  denotational   462, 500
  dynamic   226
  standard 500
  static   222, 226
sentence   272
  ambiguous   273
sentential form   272
  left   276
  right   276
set of states   279
shift transition   282
sign rule   460
SL   38
SLD resolution   125
SLR(1) grammar   362
source language   4
SP (WiM)   139
ST (WiM)   139
stack
  frame
    MaMa   84, 88, 95
    P-machine   37
    Prolog   136, 137
    WiM   141
  MaMa   84–5
  P-machine   9
  WiM   139
standardizing transformations   517
start address
  adjusted   25
start node   241
start symbol   271, 334
state
  current   279
  final   240, 279
  inadequate   351

state continued
  initial   240, 279
statement   8
  conditional   13
  iterative   13, 14
  static   18, 28, 39, 82, 88–90, 386, 418, 434
    binding   177
step relation   240
STRUCT   140
structure   121
subset automaton with integrated costs   541
subset construction   533, 534, 541
substitution   117, 121, 122
  composition   122
subtree   524
subtree graph   526
successful path   130
suffix   237
  proper   237
symbol   223, 236, 271
  class   236, 257
  LAST   328
  start   334
  table   393, 395
syntax
  abstract   389
  concrete   389
  error   267
    LL(k)   326
syntax analysis 225, 271
  bottom-up   267, 339
  top-down   267, 300
syntax tree   273
synthesis phase   222

tag   86
tail recursion   111, 165
target program   227
term   118
terminal   271
total step function   290
TP (WiM)   139
TR (WiM)   139
trace   581
  scheduling   581
  semantics   500
trail   154
  WiM   139
transfer function   288

transition 279
  diagram 241, 242
  expansion 281
  reduction 282
  relation 240, 279
  shift 282
tree automata
  deterministic 531
  finite 529
    bottom-up deterministic 530
    top-down deterministic 530
  implementation 542
  with costs 537
tree grammar
  regular 526
tree language
  homogeneous 524
  regular 528
tree-parser generation 535
tree parsing 526
  problem 528
tree of static predecessors 36
tree transformation rules 514
type 387
  calculation 411
  consistency 395
  inference 66, 401
  synonym 70
  tightening 217
  weakening 217

under-supplied 87
under-supply 86, 97
underlying grammar 405
unification 117, 144, 145
  code 139
unifier 122
  most general 122
unify 122
union 492
  problem 505
unit clause 119
universal closure 119
universal register 549

unsuccessful path 130
upper characteristic graph 422, 429

variable 8, 53
  bound (LaMa) 76, 77
  dead 490, 500
  free
    LaMa 73, 75–77, 79, 80
    Prolog 118
  global 34
  LaMa 93
  lifetime 34
  live 500, 501, 502
  permanent 164 11
  Prolog 118 11
  reaches 505
  temporary 164
variant 121
VECTOR 86
view 182
visibility 34, 391
  rules 386
visit 438
VLIW 557, 570, 587

Warren abstract machine (WAM) 139
WiM 139
  FP 139
  H 139
  heap 139, 140
  HP 139
  PC 139
  program store 139
  PS 139
  SP 139
  ST 139
  stack 139
  stack frame 140
  TP 139, 152
  TR 139
  trail 139
word 236, 237
  accepted 279
  subword 237
write mode 145